PENGUIN REFERENCE BOOKS

The Penguin Dictionary of
TWENTIETH-CENTURY H

D0625289

Alan Palmer was born in 1926 and educated at Bancroft's School in Essex and Oriel College, Oxford. For sixteen years he was senior history master at Highgate School, London. He has written biographies of Metternich, George IV, Tsar Alexander I, Frederick the Great, Bismarck, Kaiser William II, Kemal Atatürk, Marshal Bernadotte and the Emperor Francis Joseph. Among Alan Palmer's other books are: *The Gardeners of Salonika*, on the Macedonian campaign of 1915–18; *Napoleon in Russia*; *The Lands Between*, a history of eastern and central Europe, 1800–1968; *An Encyclopaedia of Napoleon's Europe*; *The Chancelleries of Europe*, international relations 1814–1918; *The Decline and Fall of the Ottoman Empire*; and histories of the Crimean War and life in London's East End over four centuries. His *Victory 1918* marked the 80th anniversary of the four armistices ending the First World War. He is also the co-author (with the late C. A. Macartney) of *Independent Eastern Europe*. Alan Palmer and his late wife, Veronica, jointly compiled: *Quotations in History*; *Who's Who in Shakespeare's England*; *Royal England; A Historical Gazetteer*; and *The Pimlico Chronology of British History*. In 1980 Alan Palmer was elected a Fellow of the Royal Society of Literature. His main recreational interests are travel and watching cricket. He lives in Woodstock, Oxfordshire.

The Penguin Dictionary of
TWENTIETH–CENTURY HISTORY

Alan Palmer

FIFTH EDITION

PENGUIN BOOKS

PENGUIN BOOKS

Published by the Penguin Group
Penguin Books Ltd, 80 Strand, London WC2R 0RL, England
Penguin Putnam Inc., 375 Hudson Street, New York, New York 10014, USA
Penguin Books Australia Ltd, Ringwood, Victoria, Australia
Penguin Books Canada Ltd, 10 Alcorn Avenue, Toronto, Ontario, Canada M4V 3B2
Penguin Books India (P) Ltd, 11 Community Centre, Panchsheel Park, New Delhi – 110 017, India
Penguin Books (NZ) Ltd, Cnr Rosedale and Airborne Roads, Albany, Auckland, New Zealand
Penguin Books (South Africa) (Pty) Ltd, 24 Sturdee Avenue, Rosebank 2196 South Africa

Penguin Books Ltd, Registered Offices: 80 Strand, London WC2R 0RL, England

www.penguin.com

First published 1979
Published simultaneously by Allen Lane
Reprinted with revisions 1981
Second edition 1983
Third edition 1990
Fourth edition 1992
Fifth edition 1999

3

Set in 9/10.5pt Monotype Bembo
Typeset by Rowland Phototypesetting Ltd,
Bury St Edmunds, Suffolk
Printed in England by Clays Ltd, St Ives plc

To Emma and Frances
with love

PREFACE

When the first edition of this *Dictionary of Twentieth-Century History* was completed in April 1979 Britain was engaged in the election campaign which brought Margaret Thatcher to Downing Street and John Major for the first time to Westminster. The statesmanship of President Carter was then in the ascendant: he was sponsor in Washington of a peace treaty between Israel and Egypt and co-signatory with the Soviet President, Brezhnev, in the old Habsburg palace at Vienna of a SALT arms limitation agreement. Rhodesia (not yet Zimbabwe) had its first black Prime Minister; Idi Amin of Uganda was a fugitive; so, too, was Pol Pot of Kampuchea/Cambodia. Ayatollah Khomeini's Islamic Puritanism enveloped Iran in a cloud of uncertainty; but in Ireland expectations were high for a visit from a Pope who was to beg young people 'to turn away from violence'. After three decades locked in superpower confrontation, there was no doubt, in this spring of 1979, that the world was fast changing, perhaps for the better. As I completed the last entries I wondered if events would outdate my typescript before the book was published.

That fear remains, four editions and nineteen years later – and is, indeed, felt more acutely. For so rapid has been the pace of transformation since the fourth edition was finished in July 1991 that I have had to revise over 235 entries and add 73 new ones. The fifth edition is therefore substantially longer than its predecessors. The most extensive changes since 1991 have been in the former Soviet Union and Yugoslavia, in southern and central Africa, in Palestine, in the growth of the European Union, in the relationship between NATO and its potential ex-enemies in the Warsaw Pact, and in the revival of Islamic militancy. Less dramatic have been a growing public awareness of environmental issues, concern in the southern hemisphere for the lost land rights of indigenous peoples, and attempts to bring clarity and cohesion to the post-imperial Commonwealth. New place names slip uneasily from the tongue: Chechnya; Nagorny-Karabakh; Rwanda; Myanmar. Albania and Katanga again make the headlines. Sadly some problems, first noted in 1979, are unresolved; there is violence still in the Middle East, in the Basque provinces of Spain and in Northern Ireland. In Cambodia, tanks rolled once more through the streets of Phnom Penh, and the fugitive Pol Pot was at last confirmed dead.

The principles of compilation remain unchanged from earlier editions of this dictionary. It contains entries on political, diplomatic, military, economic, social and religious affairs but not on the arts, music, sport, literature, pure science or abstract thought. No attempt has been made to summarize the histories of the United Kingdom or the United States in single entries: for these lands the reader will find detailed cross-references (shown by ➤) under the entries on prominent personalities and political parties. Personal and place names are given in the form commonly used in Britain, but the original version is retained if there is no anglicized equivalent. Pinyin phonetic spelling was adopted by China in January 1979, but most Chinese names appear in this dictionary in the traditional form, with the Pinyin version in brackets. For names that did not become familiar in the West until after 1979, however, the Pinyin form is given (thus, Deng Xiaoping rather than Teng Hsiao-Ping, but Chiang Kai-shek rather than Jiang Jieshih). Dates follow the Gregorian calendar (unless otherwise stated) since this reckoning was in general use by 1900 and adopted by China in 1912 and by Russia and Turkey in 1918. There is, of course, no correlation between the length of an entry and its apparent historical importance. Events, and biographical details, are updated to 22 July 1998.

In preparing each edition I have received helpful suggestions and corrections from friends in this country and overseas to whom I remain grateful. For errors, opinions and assessments I alone am responsible. This book is now dedicated to my goddaughter, Emma Darby, and her sister, Frances, neither of whom were born when the first edition appeared. The dedication carries with it a hope that their generation will find in the twenty-first century a spirit of peace and tolerance and that breadth of human understanding and respect for nature's resources which has continued to elude all of us throughout the twentieth century.

Alan Palmer
Woodstock, Oxford
22 July 1998

A

Aaland Islands. ►Åland Islands.

Abd-el-Krim (1882–1963), Moroccan nationalist leader. Born at Ajdir and accepted by the Arabs of the Rif mountains as the chief organizer of resistance to Spanish and French colonial policies in Morocco. He gained a remarkable victory against a Spanish army at Anual (21 July 1921) in which the Spanish sustained more than 12,000 casualties. Chronic warfare culminated in further pitched battles in 1924 and 1925 but in May 1926 Abd-el-Krim was forced to surrender to a massive Franco-Spanish army, commanded by Marshal Pétain. For more than twenty years Abd-el-Krim was kept under detention on the island of Réunion but, in 1947, he was given permission to live in France. Before reaching Europe, however, he was able to escape to Cairo where he was accorded privileged treatment for the remainder of his life as a founding father of the North African revolution and was held up as an inspiration to young Arabs in their struggle against imperialism.

Abdication Crisis (December 1936). On 16 November 1936 King ►Edward VIII informed his Prime Minister, Stanley Baldwin, that he wished to marry Mrs Wallis Simpson, an American citizen whose second marriage had been ended by the award of a decree nisi at Ipswich Assizes three weeks previously. Rumours of the King's romance had been current in government circles and in London society for some months but the British Press remained silent, although speculation was widespread in American newspapers. Baldwin believed marriage to a divorcee was inconsistent with the King's titular position as 'Supreme Governor' of the Church of England. The cabinet, the leaders of the Labour and Liberal parties, the Prime Ministers of the Overseas dominions and many senior political figures agreed with Baldwin. A morganatic marriage (a private Act denying the King's wife the status of Queen) was considered, but rejected after consultation with the dominion governments. When the British newspapers broke their self-imposed censorship on 3 December, there was widespread popular support for the King but little in the House of Commons, except from Churchill. Edward VIII, faced with the alternative of giving up 'the woman I love' or the throne, chose to abdicate on 10 December. After broadcasting to the people on the following evening, he went into voluntary exile in France, being created Duke of Windsor by his successor, George VI. The Duke of Windsor married Mrs Simpson at the Château de Candé on 3 June 1937.

Abdul Hamid II (1842–1918; reigned 1876–1909), Sultan of Turkey. Son of Sultan Abdul Majid, succeeded his insane brother Murad V during the great Eastern Crisis which culminated in the Treaties of San Stefano and Berlin, 1878. Abdul Hamid's grant of a parliamentary constitution to Turkey in December 1876 was rescinded in May 1877 and he thereafter ruled despotically for more than thirty years. Administrative reforms in certain provinces (notably Syria and Palestine) improved the efficiency of government but the Sultan's ministers remained, for the most part, reactionary clericalists and he became notorious throughout Europe for his inability to restrain the Kurdish irregular troops who were largely responsible for a series of Armenian massacres in 1895–6. These atrocities alienated most of the Great Powers which had earlier protected Turkey from Russian encroachment, although Kaiser William II of Germany maintained friendly relations with the Sultan. Abdul Hamid was forced to summon a parliament in 1908 by the ➤Young Turks. When he attempted a counter-revolution in April 1909 he was deposed and exiled to Salonika (then still within the Ottoman Empire).

Abdullah Ibn Hussein (1882–1951), King of Jordan. Second son of Emir Hussein, King of the Hijaz 1916–24, and brother of King ➤Feisal I of Iraq. Abdullah, a vice-president of the Turkish Parliament in 1914, was one of the leaders of the Arab Revolt against Turkey, generally associated with T.E. ➤Lawrence. He was largely responsible for guerrilla raids on the southern sector of the Hejaz railway, near its terminus at Medina, where he kept the Turkish garrison isolated. In 1921 Abdullah was recognized by the British as Emir of Transjordan, a section of eastern Palestine which had passed under British mandate on the fall of the Ottoman Empire. Abdullah remained on good terms with the British, receiving a knighthood from George V in 1927 and being made an air commodore in the RAF. When the British mandate expired, Transjordan was created a kingdom under Abdullah's rule (May 1946). In December 1948 he was proclaimed King of Palestine by a Pan-Arab congress meeting in Jerusalem but this action did not receive international recognition and in June 1949 he accepted, instead, the sovereignty of the Hashemite Kingdom of Jordan, which included territory west of the Jordan river which had been reckoned as within Palestine during the mandate. Abdullah's primacy among the Arab leaders aroused resentment in Cairo and he was assassinated in Jerusalem on 20 July 1951, in the presence of his grandson, ➤Hussein, who succeeded to the Jordanian throne a year later.

Abdullah, Muhammed, Sheik (1905–82), leader of the Muslims of ➤Kashmir against both the British and the ruling Hindu Maharajah between 1931 and 1947. Although recognized by the government of the Indian Republic as Chief Minister of Kashmir in 1947, he was imprisoned from 1953 to 1968 for alleged treason. Indira ➤Gandhi gave a measure of autonomy to Kashmir and for the last seven years of his life Sheikh Abdullah again served as Chief Minister. For his Islamic compatriots he remains a national hero, the 'Lion of Kashmir'.

Abu Dhabi. ➤United Arab Emirates.

Abyssinia. ➤Ethiopia.

Abyssinian War (1935–6). Had its origin in the desire of Mussolini to establish an East African Italian Empire (Eritrea, Ethiopia and Somalia) and to avenge the Italian defeat by the Ethiopian Emperor, Menelek, at Adowa in March 1896. The immediate cause of the war was a clash at the oasis of Walwal (5 December 1934) in which 100 Ethiopians were killed while an Italian colonial expeditionary force, which had penetrated fifty miles beyond the frontier of Italian Somaliland, suffered some fifty casualties. Attempts by the ➤League of Nations to settle the dispute were rejected by Mussolini, whose troops invaded Ethiopia, without a declaration of war, on 2 October 1935. The primitive equipment of the Ethiopians was of little use against aircraft, tanks and poison gas. The Italians were undeterred by a declaration by the League of Nations condemning Mussolini's act of aggression and imposing limited ➤sanctions on Italy. The Ethiopian Army was defeated at a pitched battle near Marchew early in April 1936 and the capture of Addis Ababa by Marshal Badoglio on 5 May 1936 marked the virtual end of Ethiopian resistance. The historical importance of the Abyssinian War lies in the failure of the League of Nations to deter aggression and make sanctions effective.

Acheson, Dean Gooderham (1893–1971), US Secretary of State. Born in Connecticut: educated at Yale and Harvard Law School, practising law in New York before becoming Assistant Secretary of State to the ailing Cordell Hull in 1941. From 1945 to 1947 Dean Acheson served as Under-Secretary of State. He was largely responsible for the Acheson–Lilienthal Plan of March 1946, which proposed the establishment of an International Atomic Authority to control fissionable material and check the spread of nuclear weapons. In February 1947 he outlined the ➤Truman Doctrine to check communist seizures of power and on 8 May 1947 he made the first major American speech advocating an aid programme to Europe (➤Marshall Plan). He was Secretary of State from 7 January 1949 until the establishment of Eisenhower's Republican Administration four years later but was under constant attack in Congress both for his alleged liberalism and for failing to forestall communist aggression by emphasizing American determination to defend the Republic of ➤Korea.

Action Française. French right-wing political movement, active from 1899 to 1944 and founded by the poet and political journalist Charles Maurras (1868–1952). The movement rallied the defeated opponents of Dreyfus: it was royalist, anti-Semitic and nationalistic, attacking the democratic institutions of the Third French Republic as corrupt and decadent. From 1908 onwards it attracted support through its newspaper (of the same name) which Maurras edited jointly with the gifted pamphleteer and essayist, Léon Daudet (1867–1942). Although Maurras was a free-thinker, he regarded the French Catholic tradition as a valuable antidote to the republicanism which he deplored. Some members of the hierarchy in France welcomed the activities of the Action Française but, from 1926 onwards, Pope Pius XI cold-shouldered the movement, which became increasingly indistinguishable from fascism. From 1940 to 1944 the movement and its newspaper warmly supported the Vichy Government (►Vichy France). The Action Française was broken up when France was liberated, and Maurras was sentenced to penal servitude for life as a collaborator, but the basic teachings of the movement continued to appeal to those who favoured a conservative paternalism rather than the uncertain changes of the Fourth Republic.

Adams, Gerald (Gerry) (1948–), Irish nationalist. Born in Belfast, he spent his childhood in the Falls Road district. He joined ►Sinn Féin, and was interned as a suspect member of the ►IRA, 1972–6 and 1978–83. While being held in Long Kesh he was named Vice-President of Sinn Féin, becoming President on his release and winning election to both the Northern Ireland assembly and to parliament. In accordance with Sinn Féin practice he declined to take his seat at Stormont or Westminster, and in 1993 was banned from entry into Britain by the Prevention of Terrorism Act. A year later, however, he actively supported the peace initiative which brought an IRA ceasefire on 31 August 1994. Adams was feted and respected in the United States, but his influence over IRA policy was in doubt when the bombing in England suddenly resumed in February 1996. Adams, who was defeated in Belfast West in 1992, was again returned to Westminster in the 1997 General Election but, as he continued to refuse to take the oath of allegiance to the Queen, could not speak or vote or maintain an office in the Commons. At Stormont, on 13 October 1997, he became the first Sinn Féin leader in 76 years to hold direct talks with a British prime minister. He subsequently took a prominent part in persuading Sinn Féin to accept the ►Good Friday Accord and took his seat in the Northern Ireland Assembly after the election of 25 June 1998.

Addams, Jane (1860–1935), American social reformer. Born at Cedarville, Illinois; established Hull House, Chicago, in 1889 as a prototype for social settlements in America, helping immigrants and coloured workers, in particular. Jane Addams sponsored educational projects for foreign-born adults, child-labour laws and separate juvenile courts. In 1909 she became one of the founders of the NAACP (National Association for the Advancement of Colored People). She was politically a progressive Republican and an ardent Christian pacifist. Her vigorous leadership of the 'Women's International League for Peace and Freedom' won her a Nobel Peace Prize in 1931, sharing the award with another American worker for peace, the sociologist N.M. Butler (1862–1947). Jane Addams was the first woman recipient of a Nobel Peace Prize.

Aden. A volcanic peninsula in Arabia at the southern entrance to the Red Sea, annexed by the British in 1839 and administered by the British Government in India until 1 April 1937, when Aden became a crown colony, together with the islands of Perim and Kamaran in the Red Sea and Sokotra in the Indian Ocean.

The British also assumed a protectorate over more than 100,000 square miles of the Arabian hinterland. The port of Aden was valuable to the British as a coaling station on the route to India and an oil refinery was developed there, but the importance of Aden declined with the lessening of British seaborne trade in the Indian Ocean during the 1950s. At the same time Aden responded to a growth in Arab nationalist sentiment. In 1959 the British set up a South Arabian Federation of Arab Emirates for the hinterland protectorate, to which Aden colony acceded in January 1963, with a suggestion that the Federation might achieve independence within the British Commonwealth in 1968. The establishment of this Federation coincided, however, with the triumph in the neighbouring ►Yemen of a republican movement, backed by Nasser's Egypt, and from September 1965 onwards there was a state of civil war in the port of Aden and its vicinity. In two years of unrest 129 British servicemen were killed. The British gave up sponsorship of the Federation and withdrew from Aden in November 1967. The former colony and protectorate was then established as the independent People's Republic of South Yemen. On 30 November 1970 the name was changed to the People's Democratic Republic of the Yemen. Discussions continued intermittently throughout the 1980s for union of the Democratic Republic with the Arab Republic of Yemen to the north. These talks were interrupted in January 1986 by violence in Aden itself against the influence of several thousand Soviet 'advisers', who were hurriedly withdrawn. Yemeni unification was at last proclaimed on 22 May 1990. The union was thrown into jeopardy in 1993 when representatives of Aden on the presidential council in the Yemeni capital, Sana'a, returned home in protest at the treatment of the south by the north. Civil war erupted in May 1994; Aden was occupied by northern Yemeni troops on 7 July. An uneasy peace followed, in both city and port, with promises of constitutional amendments to satisfy the southern Yemenis.

Adenauer, Konrad (1876–1967), West German Chancellor. Born in Cologne; studied at the universities of Freiburg, Munich and Bonn, practised law in Cologne and was Chief Burgomaster of the city from 1917 to 1933. Under the Weimar Republic he was a prominent member of the ►Centre Party and presided over the Prussian State Council (1920–33). He was dismissed from office by the Nazis in 1933, briefly imprisoned in 1934 and again in 1944, but reinstated as Burgomaster in 1945, until sacked by the British military administration for alleged inefficiency. Adenauer accepted the division of Germany into East and West and sought to build up a Christian Democrat Party, wider in scope than the discredited Centre Party and appealing to the former western allies as a barrier against communism. He was elected first Federal Chancellor in September 1949 and re-elected in 1957, also serving as Foreign Minister from 1951 to 1955. His old-fashioned dexterity in political manoeuvres enabled him to offer the British and the Americans a stable and prosperous western Germany provided they complied with his demands that Germany should be treated as a partner rather than as a former enemy. Federal Germany became a member of NATO and was integrated on a position of equality within a European union long before Adenauer's final retirement in October 1963. He was less committed to the idea of a 'cold war' with the Russians than were some of his domestic critics: he visited Moscow in 1955 in order to establish diplomatic links with the Soviet Union and he showed restraint during the crisis over the Berlin Wall of 1961–2. Above all, he created a sense of Franco-German friendship, rare in modern history.

Afghanistan. Historically for more than a century Afghanistan served as a buffer state between the British Indian Empire and Russia and on three occasions (1838–42, 1878–9 and 1879–80) there were wars between the British and the Afghans. The independence of Afghanistan was confirmed by the British in 1919 after further fighting along the north-west frontier of India. The British intervened in 1929 to establish General Nadir Shah on the throne after brigands had seized control of Kabul. Nadir's reforms alienated the Moslem clergy and he was assassinated in 1933. Nadir's son, Mohammed Zahir, reigned from 1933 until the monarchy was abolished after a *coup* by the King's cousin, General Mohammad Daoud, on 17 July 1973. Daoud's republican regime was itself overthrown, on 27 April 1978, by a left-wing 'Armed Forces Revolutionary Council'. Nationalistic unrest and religious fervour threatened anarchy from September 1979 onwards and, in the closing week of the year, Soviet troops occupied the country. This action was condemned by most Western countries as well as by Pakistan and Iran. Soviet aggression led both President Carter and Mrs Thatcher to call for a boycott of the ►Olympic Games in Moscow and curbed economic and cultural contacts between East and West. Moslem guerrillas resisted the Soviet occupation vigorously throughout 1980–81, succoured from camps in Pakistan. By the spring of 1982 Ahmed Shah Massoud, leader of the insurgent Mujaheddin ('holy warriors'), had established a base in the Panshir valley, some forty miles north-east of Kabul. Over the following eighteen months guerrilla warfare spread to every Afghan province. Despite assaults on their Panshir stronghold each spring by Soviet and Afghan troops, the Mujaheddin sustained their resistance until in May 1988 Soviet forces began the phased withdrawal, completed in February 1989. Although the guerrillas bombarded Kabul with missiles intermittently from October to December 1989, the Mujaheddin could not gain a political victory. The gradual implementation of the revised 1987 Constitution won increasing support for the former communist security chief, General Najibullah (1947–96) who, as President from October 1986, made ultimately unsuccessful attempts to end the chronic civil war. In April 1992 the Mujaheddin at last seized Kabul and set up an Islamic republic, but discord soon split the Muslim factions and internecine fighting between eight armed groups resumed in December 1992. For two years Afghanistan was thrown into even deeper political confusion. By late 1994 a new movement of militant Islamic fundamentalist students, the Taliban, was in the ascendancy, using the northern citadel of Herat as a base for an offensive against the capital, 400 miles to the south-east. Kabul suffered daily rocket attacks from January to May 1996. Taliban troops entered Kabul on 27 September, once again imposing strict Islamic law. Fighting continued in outlying provinces with resistance to Taliban organized by rival warlords. On 27 April 1998 peace talks opened in Islamabad under UN auspices. There were severe earthquakes in March and June 1998 in the northern regions of Afghanistan.

African National Congress. Formed at Bloemfontein in 1912 as the principal body protecting the interests of the coloured peoples in South Africa. The Congress grew out of a Native Education Association established in Cape Colony in 1882. In 1926 the Congress established a joint Front with representatives of the Indian community in South Africa at a conference in Kimberley, and thereafter sought the creation of a unified and racially integrated democratic southern Africa. The Congress inclined towards the non-violent tactics of passive resistance, originally practised by ►Gandhi in India, especially under the leadership of the Natal chieftain, Albert ►Luthuli, from 1952 until his death in 1967. Although many younger Africans left the ANC because it seemed to them insufficiently militant, it was condemned as dangerously revolutionary by the South African Government and declared illegal in 1961. In that year an avowedly militant wing was formed, the Umkhonto We Sizwe. It has been held responsible for a number of acts of sabotage, especially from 1986 onwards. The South African ban on the ANC was lifted on 2 February 1990. Talks between the Government and ANC leaders in August 1990 provided for the eventual repatriation of 40,000 political exiles but failed to make progress in discussing constitutional reform. At the same time there was grave fighting in the Johannesburg townships between ANC supporters and the Zulu ►Inkatha movement. The ANC, now able to be led openly by Nelson ►Mandela, played a prominent role in the Convention on a Democratic South Africa (Johannesburg, 1991–2). In the country's first multi-racial election (April 1994) the ANC won 252 seats in a parliament of 400 and received two thirds of the cabinet posts in President Mandela's first government.

Agadir. A small port on the Atlantic coast of Morocco and the centre of the second Moroccan Crisis (July–November 1911). A German gunboat, the *Panther*, was sent to Agadir on 1 July, allegedly to protect German commercial interests threatened by French expansion in Morocco. Kiderlen-Wächter (1852–1912), the German Foreign Minister, maintained that France had ignored the Moroccan agreement reached at ►Algeciras in 1906 and that a show of strength would gain Germany compensation either in Morocco or in central Africa. The '*Panther*'s leap' alarmed the British rather than the French, since the British Government was already concerned over German naval activity and thought Germany wished to establish a naval base at Agadir, close to Gibraltar and vital British trade routes. On 21 July the Chancellor of the Exchequer, Lloyd George, gave a strong warning to Germany in a speech at the Mansion House, London. The Germans denied any desire to annex Moroccan territory and, for some months, negotiated directly with the French. These negotiations nearly broke down in September and war seemed probable, but Germany gave way and, by agreements signed on 3–4 November, recognized French rights in Morocco in return for the cession of territory in the French Congo. The Agadir Crisis confirmed British suspicions of Germany, and prompted for the first time close cooperation between the Admiralty and the War Office in facing a possible war. On 29 February 1960 Agadir was devastated by the worst earthquake recorded on the African continent.

AIDS (Acquired Immune Deficiency Syndrome). World-wide medical problem of the late twentieth century. The prevalence of an HIV virus that destroys natural immunities and causes the AIDS condition first aroused major concern in America and western Europe in the summer of 1985. AIDS symptoms had, however, been identified six years earlier. The worst affected countries have been Rwanda, Zambia and Zaire in Africa, and by the end of 1986 it was estimated that 1.5 million people in the USA were suffering from AIDS and there was growing alarm in Europe and Australasia, too. While research on a vaccine continued in several countries (and especially in France) fear of the spread of the condition through sexual promiscuity influenced social behaviour, curbing the permissive conduct widely accepted during the previous twenty years. In February 1988 an international conference in London, attended by delegates from 150 countries, called for more enlightened sex-education to combat the spread of AIDS and pressed for government encouragement of 'a spirit of social tolerance' towards men and women suffering from the condition. By 1994 the incidence of the disease had become especially grave in ►Uganda, where one in ten of the population was believed to be infected.

Airlines. The rapid development of aeronautics in the early twentieth century enabled civil aircraft to revolutionize world transport much as had railways and steamships in the nineteenth. The first airline using aeroplanes rather than ►Zeppelins was a British company, Aircraft Transport and Travel Limited, founded in 1916 and operating a London–Paris service by 1919. ATT assisted the newly founded KLM (Royal Dutch Airlines) to set up a London-to-Amsterdam route in the winter of 1919–20. In 1924 ATT merged with four smaller companies to establish Imperial Airways, which developed routes to Egypt and the Persian Gulf in 1927, India (1929), Cape Town (1932), Singapore (1933) and Brisbane (1935), as well as routes to six European capitals. In 1932–3 Imperial Airways opened up an airmail route to Australia, in collaboration with Qantas Empire Airways and in fierce competition with KLM, who opened their regular and fast service to Java in 1930. Imperial Airways was always government-subsidized since it was held to be a valuable link within the Empire. In 1935 several small British companies combined to establish British Airways, which offered better European services than Imperial Airways; and in 1936 British Airways, too, received a state subsidy. Such administrative anomalies led the government to establish the state-owned British Overseas Airways Corporation (BOAC) on the eve of the Second World

War, the Corporation assuming responsibility for the aircraft of both Imperial and British Airways on 1 April 1940. In 1946 the European network of BOAC was assigned to British European Airways: BOAC and BEA were reunited under the familiar name 'British Airways' in 1972. Most European nations developed state-subsidized or completely nationalized companies during the 1920s or early 1930s, among them Belgian Sabena (1923), German Lufthansa (1926) and Air France (1933). The Soviet Aeroflot was established in 1932 but did not expand internationally until the late 1940s. The largest American company, United Air Lines, was set up in 1933: it remained a domestic service. Pan American Airways (1927) began by flights from Florida to Cuba, opening South American routes in 1928 and a prestigious 'Clipper' service of flying-boats across the Pacific in 1935. In June 1939 Pan American inaugurated regular passenger flying-boat services from New York to Southampton and to Marseilles: Imperial Airways opened their weekly transatlantic service on 5 August 1939. Wartime necessities made transatlantic passenger flights commoner and safer: as early as January 1942 the British Prime Minister flew from Washington to Plymouth by way of Bermuda in a Boeing flying-boat. Regular commercial services between Europe and North America were resumed early in 1946, jets being used by BOAC and by Pan American for the first time in 1958. BOAC established a weekly service to Australia, with Qantas collaboration, on 31 May 1945: by the end of the year there were three flights a week to Australia and BOAC claimed that, by flying 12,000 miles in 63 hours, they were operating 'the longest and fastest service in the world'.

Before 1939 airline travel had been expensive, and few people took advantage of it. It was only in the 1950s and 1960s that the aeroplane became accepted as the commonest form of international passenger transport. Technical improvements to airliners increased the speed of flight and cut distances by making it possible for aircraft to fly considerably longer 'hops' without refuelling. Passenger capacity, too, increased rapidly: in 1947 the Boeing 377 Stratocruiser (the first post-war transatlantic airliner) carried fifty passengers in comfort or 100 if the seating was densely packed: but the Boeing 747 Jumbo Jet, operated by many airlines from 1969 onwards, carried 350 to 500 passengers as a normal load. This increased capacity, together with the speed and frequency of flights, enabled the airlines to put most of the great ocean liners out of business by 1972. Within the USA airline competition virtually destroyed long-distance railway passenger services between 1950 and 1970, and the railway express services of Europe and Australia were almost as badly hit. In 1976–7 the introduction by British Airways and Air France of the supersonic ►Concorde offered yet another challenge to rival airlines in the constant search for speedier and more comfortable passenger transport. From 1968 onwards, however, airliners and airports have been targets for terrorist activity, particularly ►hijacking. At least two Boeing 747s have been destroyed in the air by explosives: an Air India flight off Ireland in January 1985 and a Pan-Am flight over Lockerbie, Scotland, on 21 December 1988. The worst airline disaster was a collision on the runway at Tenerife in March 1977, when 583 people were killed.

Alamein. El Alamein, a small Egyptian town sixty miles west of Alexandria, formed the central feature of a defensive position, thirty-five miles long, established by General Sir Claude ►Auchinleck in midsummer 1942 to check the advance of the combined German and Italian armies of Marshal Erwin ►Rommel. In the first battle of El Alamein (30 June to 25 July 1942) Auchinleck prevented a breakthrough to Cairo, Alexandria and the Nile delta and prepared the Eighth Army for the allied counter-offensive which began, under the direction of General ►Montgomery, with the second battle of El Alamein (23 October to 4 November 1942). This formed the prelude to an advance of over 1,400 miles which in six months ejected German and Italian forces from northern Africa.

Åland Islands (Ahvenanmaa). An archipelago at the entrance of the Gulf of Bothnia, midway between Sweden and Finland. The islands were Swedish until 1809 when (together with Finland) they passed under Russian rule. On the fall of the Tsarist Empire in 1917 the Swedes sought to recover the islands but Swedish troops were ejected by German units which supported the Finnish independence movement. After the Peace Settlement of 1919, the future of the islands was referred to the League of Nations which, in 1921, declared that the islands should remain under Finnish sovereignty but should be demilitarized and granted a semi-autonomous status. A ten-nation convention put the League's decision into practice. The islands' assembly voted for union with Sweden in September 1945, but no action was taken although it was confirmed that Swedish was the official language. The terms of the 1921 convention remain valid today.

Alaska. The first settlements in the vast Alaskan peninsula were Russian, but the territory was formally purchased from Tsar Alexander II by the US Secretary of State, W.H. Seward, in 1867 and was organized as an American judicial district in 1884. The Klondike Gold Rush of 1896 began to open up the territory but its strategic importance was not appreciated until 1942 when the international 'Alaska Highway', a route of 1,500 miles, was constructed (in nine months) in order to allow men and material to be transported rapidly to America's northern bases. In 1959 Alaska became the forty-ninth US state, being both the largest in area and the smallest in population. The most severe earthquake ever recorded occurred in southern Alaska on 28 March 1964 but, as the area was sparsely populated, only 300 lives were lost. In 1969 a valuable oil strike was discovered and a trans-Alaskan pipeline was constructed to the ice-free port of Valdez on the Gulf of Alaska. On 24 March 1989 the shores of the state were afflicted by the largest man-made environmental disaster when the tanker *Exxon Valdez* struck a reef, releasing more than 11 million tons of crude oil into Prince William Sound.

Albania. Remained under Turkish suzerainty until after the Balkan wars of 1912–13 when it was constituted as an independent Moslem principality. Political conditions remained anarchic throughout the First World War, with six regimes each claiming to be the legitimate government, and Albania's future was finally settled in November 1921 after a long dispute between Italy, Greece and Yugoslavia. A regency council ruled the country until 1924. In 1925 a republic was proclaimed following a rebellion by the large landowner, Ahmed Bey Zogu (1895–1961), who became President, assuming the title King Zog I in September 1928. Zog's Albania was economically dependent on Italy, with the 'National Bank of Albania' operating from Rome. On Good Friday 1939 Mussolini formally occupied Albania, chasing Zog into exile, and the King of Italy assumed the Albanian crown. Mussolini used Albania as a stepping-stone to the Italian dominance which he sought in south-eastern Europe. The Italian attack on Greece from Albania in 1940 failed disastrously but, with the German occupation of the Balkans in 1941, the Axis Powers were able to maintain a hold on the country until 1944. Vigorous guerrilla resistance was led by the communist Enver ➤Hoxha, who established a republican government recognized by the British, Americans and Russians on 10 November 1945. Hoxha had difficulty in asserting Albania's independence from Yugoslavia until the split between ➤Tito and Stalin in 1948. From 1948 until 1955 the Albanians were favoured clients of the Russians but Hoxha declined to accept the denunciation of Stalinism made by ➤Khrushchev at the Twentieth Party Congress of February 1956 and was subsequently condemned by the Russians as a deviationist. Albania was excluded from Comecon and the ➤Warsaw Pact in 1961 but continued a close economic and ideological association with China until 1978. After the death of Hoxha in 1985, relations with Yugoslavia became strained through the activities of the Albanian minority in the ➤Kosovo region of ➤Serbia. In February 1988 the Albanian foreign minister ended his country's self-imposed isolation by travelling to Belgrade for a Balkan conference (➤Balkan Pact) and in October 1990 delegates from five other Balkan states came to Tirana for a further conference, marked by strong Greek criticism of Albania's slow progress towards democracy. Political reforms introduced in January 1990 failed to satisfy the younger generation. After violent student protests, in December 1990 an opposition 'Democratic Party' was founded. Multi-party elections, held on 31 March 1991, confirmed the communist party in power, largely through the vote of the peasantry. The communists adopted a reformist approach, changed the name of their movement to Socialist Party but lost heavily in the elections of March 1992 to the Democratic Party (DPSh), whose leader, Dr Sali Berisha (1943–), became the first non-communist president since Zogu. But outside the capital the pace of economic change towards privatization remained slow. Allegations of corruption and intimidation against the DPSh were followed by a new election in June 1996, which the main opposition boycotted, giving the DPSh an unrepresentative majority. The collapse of government-backed pyramid investment schemes in February 1997 precipitated a rising in the southern port of Vlora. Anarchy spread across the country, thousands seeking refuge in Italy. Berisha refused to resign and imposed a state of emergency. General lawlessness prevailed, most Albanians arming themselves with looted weapons. Under external pressure Berisha accepted the arrival both of an Italian-led multinational force of 6,000 troops and of European observers to monitor a general election. Ex-king

Zog's son, Leka (1939–), a businessman with interests in South Africa, returned to the country from which he was carried into exile as a baby fifty-eight years before; a referendum showed some support for a monarchy. Sufficient order was restored to allow elections on 29 June and 6 July 1997; they were won by the Socialist Party, led by Fatos Nano; the more moderate Rexhef Medjanj was elected President by the legislature. In the early summer of 1998 fighting between Serbs and ethnic Albanians in Kosovo caused tension along the frontier.

Albert I (1875–1934; reigned 1909–34). King of the Belgians. Succeeded his uncle, Leopold II, at a time when the Belgian royal house was discredited by scandals arising from Leopold's methods of acquiring a fortune in his enterprises in the Congo. Albert restored the prestige and dignity of the monarchy both by his courageous leadership during the First World War and by his willingness to modernize the electoral system. He accepted the need for recognizing the status of the Flemish language, while in international questions he favoured close collaboration with France, especially over military matters. He was killed in a mountaineering accident in the Ardennes, and was succeeded by his son, Leopold III (1901–83).

Alexander (1888–1934; reigned 1921–34), King of Yugoslavia. Born in Cetinje, the son of Prince Peter Karadjordjević (1844–1921) who became King of Serbia in June 1903. Alexander was educated in Switzerland and at St Petersburg. He commanded an army in the Balkan Wars and in July 1914 became Prince Regent owing to his father's ill-health. He was titular commander-in-chief of the Serbian Army throughout the First World War, participating in its retreat over the Albanian mountains in 1915 and in the victorious advance from Salonika to Belgrade in 1918. He ruled the newly unified kingdom of Serbs, Croats and Slovenes as Regent from 1 December 1918, succeeding as King in August 1921. Bitter disputes between Serbs and Croats, culminating in a shooting affray in parliament, led Alexander to establish a royal dictatorship (6 January 1929). In foreign affairs he warmly supported the ➤Little Entente and, at the end of his life, was improving relations between the Balkan states. But, although he changed the name of the kingdom to 'Yugoslavia' in the interests of greater unity, he tended to favour the Serbs at the expense of his other nationalities. A terrorist in the pay of the extreme Croatian ➤Ustaše movement assassinated Alexander in Marseilles on 9 October 1934 at the start of a state visit to France. He was succeeded by his eleven-year-old son, Peter II (1923–70), for whom Alexander's cousin, Prince Paul (1893–1976), acted as chief Regent until March 1941.

Alexander, Harold Robert Leofric George (1891–1969, created viscount 1946 and Earl Alexander of Tunis, 1952). The third son of the fourth Earl of Caledon, born in the family home in County Tyrone. He was educated at Harrow and Sandhurst and commissioned in the Irish Guards, serving with distinction as a battalion commander in France in 1915. Between the wars he saw active service as a brigadier-general on the north-west frontier of India. He commanded the First Division of the BEF in 1939–40 and was the last officer evacuated from the Dunkirk beaches. In 1942 he was flown hurriedly to Burma to command the final withdrawal from Rangoon to Assam in the face of overwhelmingly superior Japanese air power. Churchill appointed him commander-in-chief Middle East in August 1942 and he was responsible for directing the advance to Tunis across North Africa. He commanded the allied armies which landed in Sicily and Calabria, but thereafter suffered from loss of men and material diverted to other fronts. Although the ►Anzio landing was not the success for which he had hoped, his forces penetrated to Rome by the first week of June 1944 and he maintained a vigorous offensive from the Po valley northwards until the end of the war in Europe. He was appointed field-marshal in December 1944. From 1946 to 1952 Alexander served as Governor-General of Canada, returning to London as Minister of Defence in Churchill's cabinet (1952–4). Earl Alexander was a military commander with little taste for panache but distinguished by imperturbable confidence. He possessed remarkable gifts for utilizing and reconciling opposing points of view.

Alfonso XIII (1886–1941; reigned 1902–31), King of Spain, a posthumous son of Alfonso XII. Until his sixteenth birthday the royal prerogative was exercised through the regency of his mother, Queen Maria Christina of Habsburg (1858–1929) and she remained a powerful influence on the early years of his reign. Anarchist outrages occurred frequently, and in May 1906 several onlookers were killed by a bomb thrown at the nuptial coach when Alfonso and his bride, Eugenia (Ena) of Battenberg (1887–1969), were returning from their wedding in Madrid. A bitter labour dispute in Barcelona led to a general strike and anti-clerical rioting. In this *Semana Tragica* ('Tragic Week', 26 July to 1 August 1909) over a hundred civilians perished and fifty religious buildings were destroyed. The subsequent wave of repression discredited Alfonso's standing abroad while, at home, he became distrusted by the parliamentary leaders because of his alleged liking for intrigue. He survived, in all, five assassination attempts. The prestige of the monarchy declined rapidly in the early 1920s, partly because of the King's failure to make concessions to Catalan regional feeling, but even more because of the defeat of his army by ►Abd-el-Krim in Morocco. Alfonso's attempt to bolster his authority through the establishment of a right-wing dictatorship under ►Primo de Rivera proved a failure. Primo's resignation in January 1930 encouraged the political leaders to blame the King for having attempted to impose 'a Mussolini' on the nation. When republicans gained overwhelming successes in the municipal elections of 1931, Alfonso left the country (14 April 1931) and settled in Rome, where he died ten years later. No king ruled in Spain between the flight of Alfonso and the accession of his grandson, ►Juan Carlos, in November 1975.

Algeciras, Conference of. An international Conference of the Great Powers to settle the first ►Moroccan Crisis was held at Algeciras, southern Spain, from January to April 1906. German diplomats had hoped the Conference would condemn the forward policy of the French and destroy the growing friendship between Britain and France, but the British delegate, Sir Arthur Nicolson, succeeded in isolating and outvoting the Germans, who regarded the Conference as a major diplomatic defeat. The 'Act of Algeciras' pledged France and Spain to respect the Sultan of Morocco's independence but authorized the two countries to police Morocco jointly, under a Swiss Inspector-General. The terms of the actual settlement are historically of less importance than the evidence of close Anglo-French collaboration. By strengthening the ►Entente Cordiale, Algeciras emphasized to France's ally, Russia, the advantages to be gained from a similar understanding with the British.

Algeria. Colonized by French soldiery, for the most part, between 1830 and 1860. In 1882 the three chief departments (Algiers, Oran and Constantine) were 'attached' to metropolitan France, but there remained administrative anomalies and at the start of the twentieth century the Arab population had virtually no political rights. In 1919 especially privileged Arabs were naturalized as French citizens and given the vote, provided they abandoned their Muslim traditions. In November 1942 allied troops landed in French North Africa and on 3 June 1943 a 'Committee of National Liberation' was set up in Algiers under de Gaulle's auspices to free France from ►Vichy control. In 1947 the Algerians were promised a full share in the political and social life of the country, which would gradually pass under Moslem control. But throughout the ►Fourth Republic the intransigently right-wing attitude of the French military authorities prevented fulfilment of the 1947 promises and aggravated a growing sense of Arab nationalism. The country was devastated by armed rebellion from 1954 to 1962 (►Algerian War). Algeria's independence was proclaimed on 3 July 1962: ►Ben Bella was President until June 1965 when he was deposed by his Defence Minister, Colonel Houari ►Boumédienne, who established a left-wing government in which he was himself 'President of the Council of Revolution'. Boumédienne's international socialism at times threatened his neighbours, Tunisia, Morocco and Mauritania; there was heavy fighting between Moroccan and Algerian troops around the fort of Amgala in the former Spanish Sahara during February 1976. Boumédienne's long illness throughout 1978 paved the way for the peaceful succession of Bendjedid Chadli as President in the last days of the year. He eased the repressive character of the Boumédienne regime, established closer relations with France and improved the international standing of Algeria, notably as an intermediary in securing the release of the American hostages in ►Iran, in January 1981. Chadli was re-elected president in 1984, but four years later the fall in oil prices led him to take unpopular austerity measures and there were serious riots in Algiers and Oran in October 1988, fomented by Islamic fundamentalists. More than 150 people died in the riots which forced Chadli to pledge social and political reform. A revised constitution in 1989 transferred power away from the presidency, permitting the legalization of opposition parties. The ruling FLN was weakened by the spread of Islamic fundamentalism which erupted in armed rebellion during 1992 and over the following six years caused the deaths of more than 44,000 Algerians and foreign residents.

Algerian War (1954–62). A guerrilla war was waged by the Algerian FLN (Front de la Libération Nationale) against the French military and administrative authorities in Algeria from 1 November 1954 until the conclusion of the ➤Évian Agreements of March 1962. The FLN was at first heavily outnumbered: 800 Arabs against a French army in 1954 of 20,000 veterans. Isolated terrorism met a violent French response, which increased rapidly the strength of the FLN and the unity of the Arab resistance. FLN atrocities against Europeans in the Constantine area of eastern Algeria on 20 August 1955 provoked cruelties from the army which the Governor-General, Soustelle, could not control. Fighting was concentrated in eastern Algeria for the first two years of the war but spread to the city of Algiers in the winter of 1956–7. General Massu and the 10th Parachute Division were given police powers in Algiers early in 1957, which they used savagely against alleged terrorists and strikers. As the French generals gained the military advantage in Algeria, they turned against the French Government at home, suspecting it would negotiate with the FLN. By insisting on keeping Algeria French ('*Algérie Française*') the settlers and the army helped overthrow the Fourth Republic of France in May 1958. Their subsequent discovery that General ➤de Gaulle favoured a settlement with the Arabs led to two more acts of military insubordination in Algiers (January 1960 and 22 April 1961) and abortive plots by General ➤Salan and his ➤OAS. Militarily the French army remained in control of Algeria throughout the 'Algerian War', but the conflict convulsed France in a moral and intellectual crisis. To de Gaulle it seemed as if the only way to solve the crisis was to offer the Algerians a free choice of complete integration, complete independence or self government in association with France. The bitterness aroused by the methods of the army ensured that, in the plebiscite proposed for Algeria by de Gaulle, 99 per cent voted for independence.

Allenby, Edmund Henry Hynman (1861–1936; created viscount 1919), British general. Educated at Haileybury and Sandhurst, commissioned in Inniskilling Dragoons and served in South Africa. Commanded cavalry division BEF in 1914 and Third Army in the battle of Arras, 1917. In June 1917 he was appointed commander in Palestine and began a methodically prepared advance against the Turks in October, through Gaza and Jaffa, capturing Jerusalem on 9 December. Although many of his units were withdrawn to France, he was able to mount another major offensive on 18 September 1918, and, by skilful use of cavalry, rolled the Turks back through Syria before they signed an armistice at Mudros (30 October 1918). He served as High Commissioner in Egypt, 1919–25. Allenby was a scholarly field commander of great drive and vitality.

Allende, Salvador (1908–73), President of Chile. Born in Valparaiso, practised medicine and helped found the Chilean Socialist Party, a Marxist organization independent of the orthodox Communist Party. He was a Socialist Deputy from 1937 to 1945, serving briefly as Minister of Health, and a Socialist senator from 1945 to 1970. After unsuccessfully contesting three Presidential elections, he became in September 1970 the first Marxist to attain the Presidency by free democratic election. He sought to build a socialist society in Chile while maintaining parliamentary government, but he was faced with mounting opposition from business interests, supported by the ►CIA. Widespread industrial unrest in 1972 and 1973 led to violence, culminating in a crippling strike, summoned by the National Confederation of Lorry Owners. Allende was overthrown by a military junta, led by General Pinochet, on 11 September 1973 and perished in the fighting at the Presidential palace in Santiago.

Alliance for Progress (1961). A conference attended by representatives of all the American States except Cuba was held at Punta del Este, Uruguay, in August 1961 to give form to a plan for economic and social development in the Americas proposed by President Kennedy in March 1961. The conference produced a formal alliance ('charter') which pledged the members to help each other by coordinating the economies of Latin America and by resisting the spread of communism. Funds were received from the US Agency for International Development from 1962 onwards. The Alliance for Progress, which was seen in Washington as a powerful diplomatic weapon against Fidel ►Castro, was at its strongest under the Presidencies of Kennedy and Johnson.

Alsace–Lorraine. Provinces of northern France, linked in name only after annexation by Germany in 1871. Most of Alsace was French from 1648 onwards, while Lorraine was formally added to the French Kingdom in 1766. Except for a small area of Lorraine around Belfort, the provinces were ceded to Germany by the Treaty of Frankfurt (May 1871) after the defeat of the French in the Franco-Prussian War. The provinces were constituted an 'imperial territory' (*Reichsland*) in June 1871, and not accorded any degree of autonomy until 1911. The industrial output of the provinces increased dramatically between 1878 and 1900 as a result of the Gilchrist–Thomas process of making steel, and this new wealth intensified the German desire to assimilate the provinces. Several incidents showed Alsatian resentment; the most serious of these were the riots which occurred at Zabern (Saverne) in November 1913 after a German lieutenant insulted some young Alsatians. Within France, indignation at the loss to Germany of Alsace–Lorraine effectively prevented any diplomatic collaboration between the two countries: in Paris, the statue representing the city of Strasbourg was permanently veiled from 1871 to 1918. The Treaty of Versailles (1919) restored Alsace–Lorraine to France, although between the two world wars disputes over religious questions led to occasional demands for autonomy from within the provinces. In 1940 Alsace–Lorraine was declared an integral part of Hitler's Germany, but was liberated once more in 1945.

Alto Adige. Italian name for the region of the ►South Tirol ceded to Italy by the Peace of St Germain in 1919 so as to give the Italians a frontier on the Brenner Pass but creating a German-speaking minority of 200,000 Austrians within Italy. Agreements in 1939 and 1946 failed to safeguard the interests of the Austrian community, but a new settlement providing for considerable autonomy was approved by the Italian Senate in June 1971 and embodied in an Austro-Italian Treaty signed a month later and backed by the International Court of Justice at The Hague.

Amethyst **Incident**. On 20 April 1949, during the last phase of the Chinese revolution, the frigate HMS *Amethyst* was fired on by communist guns on the Yangtze-Kiang while sailing up river with supplies for the British community in Nanking. Seventeen officers and ratings were killed and thirty wounded. Attempts to rescue the frigate by three other naval vessels failed, with over seventy further casualties. *Amethyst* remained off an island in the river, with her crew suffering considerable privations, for more than fourteen weeks of extremely hot weather. Eventually, on the night of 30–31 July, the *Amethyst*, commanded by Lt.-Cdr J.S. Kerans (1915–85), successfully sailed 140 miles down river to the sea, maintaining a speed of over 22 knots so as to avoid the gunfire from the five lines of forts along the river. The escape of HMS *Amethyst* was greeted with much jubilation in Britain. Although it was not clear why the vessel was attacked and detained by the communists, people assumed the incident was intended as an assertion of exclusively Chinese sovereignty over an international waterway. The courageous escape of the frigate came as a welcome fillip to falling national pride.

Amin, Idi (1926–), Ugandan President. On 25 January 1971 the Ugandan army and police, headed by the commander-in-chief Major-General Idi Amin, seized control of Kampala while President Obote was out of the country. Amin, a former sergeant in the King's African Rifles, proclaimed himself head of state next day and on 2 February dissolved parliament and formed a Defence Council under his own chairmanship. His rule favoured the Moslems of northern Uganda (among whom he had originated) at the expense of other tribes and national groups. Most Ugandan Asians were expelled in the autumn of 1972 and many British nationals were also required to leave. Relations between Britain and Uganda were strained on several occasions: in the summer of 1975, over a threat of execution against Mr Denis Hills, the British author of an unpublished book which criticized the President; in July 1976, over the disappearance of Mrs Dora Bloch, an elderly hostage of British and Israeli nationality who was in a Ugandan hospital during the raid on ►Entebbe; and early in 1977 over the sudden death of the Archbishop of Uganda. Amin's relations with his African neighbours were frequently tense and there were armed clashes between Ugandan troops and soldiers from both Kenya and Tanzania, even though Amin served as Chairman of the ►Organization of African Unity in 1975–6. No other political figure in modern Africa so blatantly championed the interests of a small section of his people against the rest. In April 1979 he escaped to Libya after the overthrow of his government.

Amritsar. A town in the Punjab, a Sikh religious shrine. On 10 April 1919 rioting broke out in Amritsar at a time of great agitation for Indian self-government. The local British commander, General Dyer, called out his troops and, without adequate warning, ordered them to fire on an angry but unarmed mob: 379 Indians were killed and 1,200 wounded. Subsequently a government commission of inquiry severely censured Dyer and he was required to resign his commission. The shooting left a bitter legacy in Anglo-Indian relations. Sixty years later Amritsar became a centre for Sikh extremists demanding autonomy for the Punjab within the Indian Republic. So grave was the threat of civil war that on 5 June 1984 Mrs Indira ►Gandhi ordered the army to occupy the Golden Temple at Amritsar and 37 other shrines. The Sikhs resisted and there were over 300 deaths. The assault on the Temple intensified Sikh hostility towards Mrs Gandhi, who was killed by a Sikh member of her bodyguard on 31 October 1984. A further attack, to flush out alleged fanatics from the Golden Temple complex, was ordered by her son and successor, Rajiv Gandhi, in May 1988.

Anarchists. As a political movement anarchism dates from the middle of the nineteenth century. Originally, in theory and practice, it was idealistic and pacifist: 'Government, like the wearing of clothes, is a sign of lost innocence' was a traditional adage. The most famous of the idealists were the Russians, Leo Tolstoy (1828–1910) and Prince Peter Kropotkin (1842–1921), and the archetypal anarchist, believing in the nihilistic virtue of destruction, was Mikhail Bakunin (1814–76), also a Russian but of greatest influence in Spain. The American, Emma ►Goldman, and the Italian, Enrico ►Malatesta, originally shared the idealistic rejection of violence, preached by Tolstoy and influencing many writers and artists. In the 1890s and 1900s, however, anarchism became associated with violence and assassination. Anarchists were responsible for the deaths of twenty members of a fashionable audience in a Barcelona theatre (November 1893), and for the assassinations of the French President Sadi-Carnot (June 1894), the Austrian Empress Elizabeth (September 1898), the Italian King Umberto I (July 1900), the American President McKinley (September 1901) and the killing of many prominent Russians during the ►Revolution of 1905. In France and Spain, and to a lesser extent in Italy, the anarchist movement was organized as a loosely knit political party from 1913 onwards: in Spain the anarchists abandoned their principles to such an extent that they even participated in the government from November 1936 until May 1937. Anarchist influence was also powerful on the development of ►syndicalism. There remained, however, individual anarchists who were determined on acts of terrorism, such as the murder of the Archbishop of Saragossa in 1923 and the attempt on the life of Alfonso XIII in Paris a year later. All forms of anarchism declined with the conflict between communists and anarchists within the republican ranks during the ►Spanish Civil War and with the mounting prestige of Soviet communism from 1941 to 1948. Anarchist sentiment revived in the 1960s when student revulsion at the accepted social code of a westernized affluent society coincided with disillusionment at Soviet external policy. Terrorism was particularly prevalent in the new anarchist movement of West Germany, notably the ►Baader–Meinhof Group.

Andreotti, Giulio (1919–), Italian Prime Minister. Born in Rome, he studied law and was a founding delegate at the Italian republic's constituent assembly in 1946–7, subsequently sitting in parliament as a Christian Democrat from 1948 until 1994. He served in every government from February 1954 until May 1992, becoming Prime Minister of the first of seven coalitions in 1972. Andreotti dominated Italian political life in the 1970s and 1980s. In March 1993 he was among several leading Italian political figures investigated for links with the ►Mafia and other crime syndicates. Allegations were made that he had concealed information damaging to himself after the murder of his colleague Aldo ►Moro. In July 1994 he was formally charged with membership of the Mafia and 'protecting' the organization 'from at least 1978', while holding the highest political offices. He was put on trial in Palermo in September 1995, the case being adjourned to Rome, where a new hearing began in April 1996.

Andropov, Yuri (1914–84), Soviet leader. Born near Stavropol, in the northern Caucasus, he became a Communist Party official in shipyards on the lower Volga in the early 1930s. From 1940 to 1945 he was in Karelia, organizing the Soviet system in territory annexed from Finland and leading guerrilla resistance during the war. At the age of forty he became Soviet ambassador in Budapest and played a sinister role in suppressing the ►Hungarian National Rising of 1956. In 1957 he began a quarter of a century of service to the Soviet secret police (KGB), of which he was head from 1967 to 1982. He succeeded ►Brezhnev as General Secretary of the Communist Party in November 1982 and checked mounting corruption and inefficiency. His chief spokesman and political protégé was ►Gorbachev, who came from the same region of Russia. But Andropov was in power for only fifteen months, dying from kidney disease in February 1984.

Anglo-French Entente. On 8 April 1904 a convention was concluded between France and Britain which settled outstanding colonial differences and established the Anglo-French Entente, or 'Entente Cordiale'. The agreement resolved old disputes in West Africa, Siam, Madagascar, the New Hebrides, over Newfoundland fishing rights and, above all, in Egypt and Morocco: the British were allowed a free hand to develop Egypt in return for giving France a free hand in Morocco, although it was accepted that no fortifications should be erected which threatened Gibraltar and that Spanish historic rights should be respected. The agreement ended a long period of Anglo-French friction. Negotiations to settle old disputes began in August 1903, the main participants being ►Lansdowne, ►Cromer, ►Delcassé and Paul ►Cambon. The popular belief that Edward VII 'made the Entente' has no foundation in fact, although his tactful behaviour on a visit to Paris in 1903 stilled latent anti-British sentiment. The Entente was not intentionally anti-German although German policy in the ➤Moroccan Crisis strengthened collaboration between the British and French and led to the first ➤Military Conversations. An 'entente' is, by definition, an understanding and not specifically an alliance; and no treaty of alliance was signed between Britain and France until after the outbreak of the First World War in 1914

Anglo-Russian Entente. On 31 August 1907 a convention was concluded in St Petersburg between the British and the Russians which defined spheres of influence in Persia and the attitudes of the two countries to Tibet and Afghanistan. This understanding, which was similar in character to the Anglo-French Entente, was the culmination of long negotiations, beginning with abortive proposals by Lord Salisbury in 1898. The talks had been resumed in earnest by ➤Grey after the Algeciras Conference of 1906 had shown the close collaboration between Britain and France, Russia's ally. The agreement was anti-German only in the sense that it sought to check German penetration of the Middle East and to end German attempts to exacerbate Anglo-Russian relations. There was no mention in the agreement of European affairs, although the Russians were told that in future Britain would no longer oppose Russian ambitions to control the Bosphorus and the Dardanelles, provided other powers agreed. The Anglo-Russian Entente was never so close as the 'Entente Cordiale', partly because of continued Russian intrigues in Persia and partly because of criticism in Britain of Tsarist Russia's internal policy and, especially, treatment of the Jews. Nevertheless, the Entente opened the London money market to Russia and thereby assisted her to recover from her military defeat at the hands of Japan (1904–5) and from the revolutionary chaos of 1905.

Angola. A 'People's Republic' on the west coast of southern Africa, established in 1975, after 320 years of Portuguese paramountcy with Portuguese trading settlements going back to the beginning of the sixteenth century. From 1655 to 1951 Angola had colonial status, and was a source of slaves for more than 200 years. Between 1951 and 1955 Angola enjoyed special status as a 'Portuguese Overseas Territory'. From 1955 until 1975 it was reckoned a province of metropolitan Portugal, although receiving a limited autonomy in December 1970. The reluctance of the Portuguese authorities to decolonize their African possessions led to the formation of Angolan independence movements, operating originally from within the Congo, and Portuguese military reinforcements were sent out from Lisbon to face an incipient rebellion in June 1960. Civil war broke out in February 1961, with the MPLA (People's Movement for the Liberation of Angola) receiving support from the socialist and communist states, the UNITA (National Union for the Total Independence of Angola) receiving support from the western states and the FNLA (National Front for the Liberation of Angola) receiving support from the 'non-Left' power groups in southern Africa. Portugal announced

Angola's independence on 10 November 1975. There followed three months of confused fighting with MPLA forces, backed militarily by Cubans with Russian-built tanks, advancing from the colonial capital of Luanda on districts which supported the two rival movements. Foreign mercenaries sought to bolster FNLA resistance and South African units crossed Angola's southern frontier. Intervention of this character increased the moral authority of the MPLA which by February 1976 claimed victory and was widely recognized as the government of the Angolan People's Republic. The Angolans then put on trial thirteen mercenaries, the proceedings being televised; three British mercenaries and one American were executed on 10 July 1976, despite world-wide appeals for clemency. The use of Angolan bases by SWAPO guerrillas operating in ▸Namibia led the South African Government to send punitive motorized columns of troops deep into Angolan territory on several occasions. An agreement for South African withdrawal, signed at Lusaka in February 1984, proved abortive, and the Pretoria government continued to back UNITA whose leader, Jonas Savimbi (1934–), established his headquarters at Jamba, in southern Angola. In 1985 many right-wing Americans, alarmed at the heavy Cuban presence in Angola, began to refer to Savimbi's followers as 'freedom fighters'. American arms, supplied to UNITA through Zaire, enabled Savimbi to establish a northern base near Quimbele in 1987. By then more than 50,000 Cuban troops were allegedly in Angola. A UN sponsored agreement, signed in New York in December 1988, provided for an end to South African support for UNITA and the return home of all Cuban forces before April 1989. UNAVEM (United Nations Angola Verification Mission) began supervising the Cuban withdrawal in January 1989. Renewed fighting in January 1990 delayed the Cuban withdrawal. A peace plan was agreed by UNITA and MPLA twelve months later. But when the MPLA candidates won the elections of September 1992, UNITA resumed the civil war. It continued until November 1994, when UN mediators secured a peace of exhaustion. Savimbi became one of two vice-presidents, under the former MPLA leader and elected President, Jose Dos Santos (1942–). The recovery of Angola from more than thirty years of warfare was hampered by the presence of unmapped landmines over large areas of the country.

Anschluss. The union of Austria and Germany. With the collapse of the Habsburg monarchy in 1918, the majority of its German-speaking remnant wished to unite with the new German Republic. This was forbidden by the terms of the Treaties of Versailles and St Germain. Agitation for an Anschluss continued throughout the 1920s, especially in the Tirol and Salzburg. In 1931 a projected customs union between Germany and Austria was abandoned because France and her ▸'Little Entente' allies complained that this would have been the first step towards Anschluss. Demands for union increased after Hitler became German Chancellor in January 1933. A Nazi *coup* in Vienna in July 1934 failed but the reconciliation of Italy and Germany in 1936 left the Austrian Government isolated in the face of Nazi agitation. In February 1938 Hitler invited the Austrian Chancellor, Kurt von Schuschnigg

(1897–1977), to meet him at Berchtesgaden and demanded concessions for the Austrian Nazi Party, including cooperation in the government. When Schuschnigg tried to forestall Hitler by a plebiscite on the question of Austrian independence, the Germans submitted an ultimatum demanding his resignation (11 March 1938). Schuschnigg was replaced by the Austrian Nazi, Seyss-Inquart, who invited the German Army to occupy Austria and proclaimed union with Germany on 13 March. On 10 April a Nazi-controlled plebiscite returned a vote of 99.75 per cent in favour of the Anschluss. The ban on an Anschluss was reiterated when the second Austrian Republic was recognized by the Western Powers in January 1946.

Antarctica. The Antarctic continent was first extensively charted on Captain James Cook's second voyage in 1773–4, although he never came nearer than 1,130 miles to the South Pole. British, American, French, Russian and Norwegian expeditions discovered and claimed territories in the course of the nineteenth century, but a German expedition, headed by Professor Drygalski, made the first explorations by sledge across the Antarctic ice in 1901–3. The intensive period of overland exploration was between 1903 and 1917, with famous expeditions led by Captain R.F. ➤Scott, Sir Ernest Shackleton and the Norwegian, Roald Amundsen, who reached the pole on 14 December 1911. So too, on 17 January 1912, did Scott and four companions, but they perished in a blizzard on the Ross Barrier at the end of March. The Ross Dependency was placed under New Zealand's jurisdiction by an Order in Council of 30 July 1923, and a similar Order established the Australian Antarctic Territory on 7 February 1933, a huge area, little smaller than Australia itself, between longitudes 45° and 160° East. The Norwegians declared Queen Maud Land and other adjacent islands to be Norwegian territory in January 1939, giving Norway about one-fifth of Antarctica. Other lands were claimed by Britain, France, Chile and Argentina. The two South American republics refused British proposals in 1954 and 1956 to refer disputed claims to the International Court of Justice but joined the six principal Antarctic claimants which (together with Japan, Belgium, South Africa and the Soviet Union) concluded the Antarctic Treaty of December 1959. The Treaty, valid from June 1961 until December 1989, accepted a status quo in matters of territorial claims to all Antarctica south of latitude 60° South, reserving the area for peaceful development and pledging international scientific cooperation. Nuclear explosions were thus prohibited within the area. Concern over contraction of the ice cap because of global warming was expressed at conferences at Vina del Mar (Chile) in 1989 and Madrid in April 1991.

Anti-Clericalism. Hostility to the political power of the Church, identified in modern times with attempts to subordinate its non-spiritual functions to the state. It originated in revolutionary France and continued to be one of the characteristics of the ➤radicals in France under the Third Republic. A similar conflict arose in Spain (notably in 1873, 1909–13 and 1931–6) and in parts of Latin America. German anti-clericalism was limited to the *Kulturkampf* of 1871–87 and to Nazi attempts to restrain individual church leaders (Catholic and Lutheran) during the years 1937–45. Italian anti-clericalism, limited during the monarchical period to resentment at the Pope's territorial claims, became primarily concerned with the Church's attitude to marriage under the Italian Republic, and there has been special concern over proposed divorce legislation since 1971. There has been some anti-clericalism in Moslem countries (notably the ➤Turkish Republic) and in recent times it has flourished in communist states, largely because of the government's identification of the upper clergy with former quasi-fascist regimes (➤Mindszenty and ➤Stepinac).

Anti-Comintern Pact (25 November 1936). An agreement between Nazi Germany and Japan declaring the hostility of the two countries to international communism (the ➤'Comintern'). The Pact was a triumph for ➤Ribbentrop who, although not appointed Foreign Minister until February 1938, was seeking acceptance of an ideological foreign policy based on opposition to communism. Italy adhered to the Pact a year later. The Japanese demanded, and secured, recognition of their puppet regime in ➤Manchuria as a price for signing the Pact.

Anti-Semitism. There have been periods of hostility towards Jewish minorities in most European countries: insistence on religious conformity often concealed envy at Jewish commercial successes. Specifically racialist prejudice dates from the early 1870s when a group of German writers, using the Frenchman Renan's concept of the linguistic distinctions 'Semitic' and 'Aryan' as racial terms, began to attack Jews as members of a distinct and inferior alien race. Anti-Semitic political parties were active in Germany from 1881 and in Austria–Hungary from 1885. There was strong anti-Semitic feeling in France at the turn of the century because of the Dreyfus case, a reaction against the agitation from 1897 to 1906 to clear the name of a French Jewish officer court-martialled in 1894 for allegedly selling military secrets to Germany. Anti-Jewish violence on a large scale was practised in Tsarist Russia (particularly Lithuania, Poland and the Ukraine) from 1905 to 1909 when outrages were organized by the terrorist 'Black Hundreds'; it is estimated there were 50,000 Jewish victims. Jewish minorities also suffered considerably in Romania and, between the wars, in Poland and Hungary. Hitler's anti-Semitism had its origins in pre-war Vienna, where the Jews formed a tenth of the city's population and where Karl Lueger (Burgomaster 1897–1910) encouraged educational segregation and permitted anti-Jewish demonstrations. From 1920 to 1933 Hitler preached anti-Semitism in Germany, especially in Munich, representing the Jew as a scapegoat for every misfortune that had befallen Germany. Hitler developed the theory of an 'Aryan' master-race popularized in the 1900s by H.S. ➤Chamberlain. In the Nuremberg Laws of September 1935 the Nazis sought to codify their racial myth. Jews were denied German citizenship and forbidden to marry 'Aryan' Germans. A further law in November 1938 confiscated Jewish property. Persecution of Jews increased with the coming of war and was extended to all lands through which Hitler's armies advanced. Between 1939 and 1945 the Nazis caused the deaths of more than one-third of the total Jewish population in the world: over 5 million Jews perished in ➤concentration camps. Since the Second World War anti-Semitism has flourished mainly in reaction against the state of ➤Israel and ➤Zionism. Vocal anti-Semitism, hardly distinguishable from the prejudice of Tsarist Russia, re-emerged in the Soviet Union in 1953 and there was serious violence shown towards Jewish communities in 1958–9, notably in Moscow, Minsk and Odessa. Reports of the execution of Jews for 'economic crimes' in 1962–3 aroused protests in the USA and western Europe. Further protests were made between 1968 and 1976 over the imprisonment of Soviet Jews seeking to emigrate to Israel, although during these years over 120,000 Jews were allowed to leave Russia. Jewish dissident members of the Helsinki Human Rights Group (➤Helsinki Conference) were put on trial, and given heavy sentences in the summer of 1978. Soviet anti-Semitism, although tragically inhumane and at variance with socialist principles, did, however, never achieve the systematic barbarity of Nazi Germany.

Antonescu, Ion (1882–1946), Romanian dictator. Born in Pitesti, served as a colonel in the First World War and subsequently as military attaché in Rome and London, identifying himself closely with the Romanian fascist movement. After serving briefly as Chief of the General Staff in 1937, General Antonescu was arrested and imprisoned by ➤Carol II in 1938 for plotting against the pro-French government in Bucharest. The changing balance of power in Europe led to Antonescu's release and his appointment, first, as Minister of War and, later, as head of a right-wing government. In the autumn of 1940 Antonescu forced Carol into exile and ruled the country in the name of the young King Michael (born 1921) for the next four years. Antonescu allied Romania with the Axis Powers and had himself proclaimed *Conducator*, thus emulating the claims of Hitler and Mussolini to be *Führer* and *Duce* of their respective countries. Romania entered the war against Russia in June 1941, Antonescu sending thirty divisions to the front line. In October 1941 these divisions, with German support, captured the port of Odessa which was renamed 'Antonescu' in honour of the dictator, who had been created a marshal two months previously. Subsequently the Romanians suffered heavy losses in the advance to the Volga and in the battle of ➤Stalingrad. These sufferings undermined Antonescu's position and on 23 August 1944 he was arrested in a palace revolution staged by King Michael as a preliminary to Romania's change of sides in the war. He was put on trial for alleged war crimes in May 1946, condemned to death, and shot.

Anzac. A word derived from the initials of the Australian and New Zealand Army Corps, which landed at a cove (subsequently named after them) on the ➤Gallipoli peninsula on 25 April 1915, and which held out for eight months despite persistent Turkish counter-attacks. Subsequently Anzacs fought at Arras and Messines in 1917, in Palestine under ➤Allenby, and helped to stem the German advance on the western front in March 1918.

Anzio Landing. During the advance of the joint Anglo-American Fifth Army up the west coast of the Italian peninsula General ➤Alexander sought to speed the capture of Rome by landing 50,000 troops in the rear of the German defensive position. The area around Anzio was chosen for the landings since it was over sixty miles behind the enemy front and only thirty-five miles from Rome. The landings took place on 22–23 January 1944 and were, at first, a complete success, taking the defenders by surprise. While the allied force was consolidating its bridgeheads, the Germans rushed reinforcements to contain them and thereby prevented the break-out towards Rome for which Alexander had hoped. Anzio withstood German counter-attacks until the last week of May, when the Germans withdrew and the allied force was able to make contact with the main body of the Fifth Army, which reached the suburbs of Rome on 4 June. Although the Anzio landing failed to bring a quick and decisive victory, the presence of American and British troops threatening his rear made it impossible for Kesselring, the German commander, to establish a permanent defensive line through the mountains south of Italy's capital.

ANZUS Pact. A tripartite security treaty concluded between Australia, New Zealand and the United States at San Francisco on 1 September 1951 providing for collaboration should any of the three countries be the victim of 'an armed attack on the Pacific area'. For Australia and New Zealand the Pact marked a new independence in foreign affairs, away from Britain and towards closer collaboration with the USA. In American policy, the Pact was part of a general clarification of policy in the Far East, coming two days after the signing of a mutual defence pact with the Philippines and a week before the formal conclusion of a treaty of peace with Japan and the signing of a similar security pact between Japan and the USA.

Apartheid. A slogan used by the Afrikaner National Party in the South African general election of May 1948 to imply the need for a condition of 'separation' between whites and non-whites. The victory of the National Party under Dr Daniel ➤Malan led to the adoption of a policy of apartheid, a system under which the racial segregation practised in South Africa since the first days of colonization was intensified and the apparatus already guaranteeing white Afrikaner supremacy in the Transvaal was extended to other provinces in the Union. Under the successive premierships of Malan, ➤Strijdom, ➤Verwoerd and ➤Vorster, the apartheid policy dominated the legislative programme of the South African parliament despite the hostility it aroused abroad, notably from 1952 onwards at the United Nations General Assembly. The apartheid laws included the partial disenfranchisement of the Cape Coloured voters (1956), the prohibition of strikes by African workers (1953–7), deportation of Africans collectively or individually from specified districts (1952), segregated supervision of all education for African children (1953), a prohibition of mixed marriages and the tightening of an earlier Immorality Act, intended to forbid sexual relations between whites and non-whites. Opposition and criticism of the apartheid policy was countered within South Africa by a

'Suppression of Communism Act' (1950), which forced men and women accused of holding communist beliefs to prove their innocence rather than leaving the onus of proof on the authorities. The positive side of apartheid was represented by the Bantu Self-Government Act of 1959 which provided for the eventual establishment of seven native African areas, with non-white chief ministers. The first of these Bantustans was created by the ►Transkei Constitution Act of 1963. Anti-apartheid riots at ►Sharpeville in March 1960 led to the deaths of sixty-seven Africans, and to widespread revulsion in Great Britain, the Commonwealth and the United Nations Assembly. A state of emergency was proclaimed in South Africa (March to August 1960) and there were widespread arrests. When apartheid was condemned at the conference of Commonwealth Prime Ministers in March 1961, Verwoerd announced that South Africa would leave the Commonwealth rather than modify the existing policy, and South Africa became an independent republic on 31 May 1961. Throughout the succeeding fifteen years international protests continued at the practice of apartheid. In many countries South African goods and produce were boycotted: South African teams were excluded from the Olympic Games and other sporting events so long as rigid racial separation was applied to social life. Unrest caused by resentment at particular aspects of apartheid intensified in 1976–7: rioting in ►Soweto in June 1976 led to ten days of grave disturbances in which at least 176 people were killed; and the death in detention of the moderate black leader Steve Biko (12 September 1977) prompted renewed denunciation of the security policy by many world figures. The threat of economic sanctions eroded business confidence and there was some relaxation of controls; the constitutional reforms of 1983–4 (►South Africa) made concessions to non-whites. These changes intensified the campaign against apartheid, especially in the segregated black townships. From July 1985 to March 1986 the apartheid laws were rigidly enforced under special 'state of emergency' powers in 36 districts: nearly 8,000 opponents of apartheid were detained and 750 died; and in August 1985 President P.W. ►Botha publicly reaffirmed the National Party's commitment to apartheid. Selective economic sanctions were imposed by President Reagan in September 1985. On 12 June 1986 an even stricter 'state of emergency' was imposed on the whole country: the names of detainees imprisoned without trial were withheld by the security forces. Eight days later a conference of 120 nations, organized under UN auspices in Paris, called for tough economic sanctions against South Africa so long as apartheid was practised. Mrs Thatcher, who had opposed sanctions at the 1985 ►Commonwealth Conference in Nassau, did not agree. By 1988 right-wing Conservatives in South Africa and Eugene Terreblanche's Afrikaner Resistance Movement were campaigning vigorously for the full implementation of apartheid. After talks with ANC leaders in 1990, President ►de Klerk told Parliament on 1 February 1991 that he intended to end apartheid. Over the next five months the basic apartheid laws were repealed.

Apollo Missions. In May 1961 President Kennedy urged the USA to set itself the task of landing a man on the moon and returning him to earth before 1970. This proposal formed the basis of the 'Apollo' project for manned space flight: Congress assigned $24,000 million to space exploration, for purposes of national prestige and the improvement of scientific knowledge. The Apollo missions reached their final form in October 1968 when Apollo 7, a three-man moon-ship, was launched in orbit round the earth. Two months later Apollo 8 went into a close orbit around the moon and safely returned to the Pacific Ocean. Apollo 9 (March 1969) successfully tested a lunar module in earth orbit, while Apollo 10 (May 1969) provided for a module to descend to less than six miles above the moon's surface. The Apollo 11 moonship (with Neil ➤Armstrong, Edwin Aldrin and Michael Collins aboard) was launched from a Saturn rocket at Cape Kennedy on 16 July 1969; it landed on the moon on 20 July, allowing Armstrong and Aldrin to walk on the moon's surface on 21 July, before returning safely to earth on 24 July. The Apollo missions continued for another six years, partly in order to fulfil the terms of a Soviet–American agreement of 1972 for a 'space link-up'. This was achieved on 17 July 1975 when the American Apollo 16 spaceship successfully docked in space beside the Soviet Soyuz 19 spaceship, the two craft remaining locked together for almost 48 hours during which the Russian and American crews exchanged visits. The Apollo 16 mission was said to have cost $500 million: and the mounting expense of manned space flights finally put an end to the Apollo project.

Appeasement. A foreign policy which seeks to propitiate an aggrieved rival by making concessions over matters otherwise likely to lead to war. The term has been particularly applied, generally in a pejorative sense, to the attempts of the British and French Governments to satisfy Hitler's demands between 1936 and 1939 by reaching direct agreements with both Germany and Italy. It is associated especially with the premiership of Neville ➤Chamberlain. The policy of appeasement permitted Hitler to send German troops to the demilitarized ➤Rhineland, achieve an ➤Anschluss with Austria and acquire the Sudeten areas of Czechoslovakia in the ➤Munich Agreement of September 1938. It is generally accepted that the policy ended when Hitler, in defiance of his assurances at Munich, occupied the rest of the Czech lands in March 1939. Appeasement was then replaced by a policy of 'guarantees', by which the British and French pledged themselves to aid Romania, Greece and Poland should any of these countries be attacked. The German invasion of Poland on 1 September 1939 led to the implementation of this guarantee by Britain and France in their declaration of war on Germany two days later.

Aquino, Cory (née Maria Curazon Cojuangco, 1933–) President of the Philippines. A sugar merchant's daughter, educated at a Manila convent school and at universities in America and the Philippines. In 1954 she married Benigno Aquino (1932–83), a liberal politician who became a senator and led the opposition to the martial law established by President ➤Marcos in 1972. When he was sentenced to death for subversion in 1977 there were such widespread protests that his life was spared, and in 1980 he was allowed to leave for America, as a sick man in need of heart surgery; Cory Aquino accompanied him. On his return to Manila on 21 August 1983 Benigno Aquino was assassinated at the airport by a military guard. This crime united opposition to the Marcos regime and, with full backing from the Roman Catholic Church, his widow stood against Marcos in the presidential election of 7 February 1986. When the official result of the poll gave victory to Marcos, Cory Aquino accused his supporters of ballot-rigging and encouraged a non-violent civil disobedience campaign which on 25 February forced the Marcos family to flee the country. Cory Aquino took the presidential oath the same day. She introduced a new, democratic constitution, effective from July 1987; but her reforms were hampered by communist insurgency in the mountains of northern Luzon and Mindanao, and by the delaying tactics of wealthy landowners. She faced, too, a series of seven attempted military *coups* before retiring from political life in June 1992.

Arab League. In September 1944 representatives of the Arab governments in Egypt, Iraq, Lebanon, Saudi Arabia, Syria, Transjordan and the Yemen, together with a spokesman for the Arabs in Palestine, met in conference at Alexandria and resolved to establish an Arab League to promote inter-Arab cultural, technical and economic links and minimize conflicts between the Arab peoples. The pact of the League, signed on 22 March 1945, set up a council in Cairo but the League remained an essentially loose association of states and never acquired a strong central authority. The League was joined by Libya (1951), Sudan (1956), Tunisia and Morocco (1958), Kuwait (1961), Algeria (1962), South Yemen (➤Aden) (1968), Bahrain, Qatar, Oman and the Trucial States (1971). Until 1967 the League was primarily concerned with organizing opposition to Israel and with curbing French influence in north Africa and the Lebanon. During Nasser's lifetime the League was dominated by Egypt, but it lost political influence to the ➤Palestine Liberation Organization and in the Sadat era cut its links with Cairo, establishing new headquarters in Tunis. Intensification of the ➤Intifada in Palestine led to an Arab League summit meeting in Casablanca (May 1989), which showed deep rifts between member states. A further conference at Baghdad in May 1990 was boycotted by Syria, Algeria, Lebanon and Oman. Twelve of the twenty Arab League members approved the sending of troops to support the UN in the Second ➤Gulf War.

Arafat, Yasir (Muhammed Abed Ar'ou Arafat, 1929–), President of the Palestinian National Authority. Born in Cairo, he was orphaned at the age of four and spent his boyhood in Jerusalem, gun-running for Arab guerrillas when he was sixteen. After studying engineering at Cairo he found employment in Kuwait where, in September 1957, he was co-founder of Al-Fatah. In 1964 it merged with other Arab resistance groups to form the ➤Palestine Liberation Organization; Arafat became chairman in 1969. The civil war in ➤Jordan in 1970 forced Arafat to build up the PLO in neighbouring Syria and Lebanon. After the PLO received UN recognition in 1974, Arafat became an international spokesman for the Palestinian cause, readily identifiable by the traditional *keffiyeh* covering his head when he was in khaki uniform. Israeli intervention forced him out of Lebanon in 1983. He established headquarters near Tunis, where he remained for almost eleven years, seeking to curb extremists while reaching a compromise settlement with the Israelis. In September 1993 he signed an agreement with the Israeli Prime Minister, Yitzhak ►Rabin, acknowledging the existence of a Jewish state in return for grants of Arab autonomy in certain regions of ►Palestine. Arafat – who shared the Nobel Peace Prize of 1994 with Rabin and the Israeli Foreign Minister, Shimon Peres – then became President of the 'national authority' in ►Gaza. The electoral victory of the right-wing Likud Party in ►Israel in May 1996 placed a severe strain on his efforts to hold in check his more radical Arab supporters.

Arcos Raid. An episode in Anglo-Soviet relations. In the last week of May 1927 Baldwin's Conservative Government ordered Scotland Yard to search the headquarters of the Soviet trading company (Arcos) in Moorgate Street, London, since it had been told that the company was a front for communist subversion. Two hundred police spent six hours ransacking the offices but no evidence was ever produced to show Arcos was interfering in British affairs. The government asserted, however, that as the Soviet authorities were intriguing against British imperial interests the Anglo-Russian trade agreement concluded three years earlier would be annulled, and diplomatic relations were broken off and not resumed until October 1929. The incident marked the peak of 'anti-Red' suspicion following the General Strike.

Ardennes Offensive (1944). A final German attempt in the Second World War to prevent British and American forces from invading Germany, by breaking the allied front in the West, capturing Antwerp and cutting off supplies. Field Marshal von Rundstedt (1875–1953) launched a surprise attack on the centre of the allied positions through northern Luxembourg and the Belgian Ardennes on 16 December 1944 and inflicted heavy losses on the Twelfth American Army Group. ►Montgomery was then (19 December) given command of the front north of the salient and ►Bradley south of the salient. Combined operations plugged the gap. An American unit, encircled at Bastogne on 22 December, successfully resisted all attacks until relieved on 26 December. Despite heavy snow, the allies launched a counter-offensive on the Ardennes salient on 3 January 1945, clearing the whole region by 16 January, with a loss to Germany of 120,000 men.

Argentina. The largest Spanish-speaking republic in South America; finally achieved independence from Spain in July 1816. Throughout much of the nineteenth century the country was racked by civil war, firm government coming only from tyrannical dictators, with the US-style federal constitution of 1853 remaining largely inoperative. The first relatively free presidential election was held in 1916 and led to the triumph of the Radical Party under Hipólito Irigoyen, who was President 1916–22 and 1928–30. The comforts of office inclined Irigoyen to forget his earlier advocacy of progressive reform. He was overthrown by a bloodless revolution in September 1930, which followed the brutal repression of a strike movement. Reactionary conservative government by landowners, backed by army officers, and opposed to the interests of the urban communities, continued until February 1946 when Juan ►Perón, an admirer of the Spanish form of fascism, was elected President. Perón's regime was based on the expansion and organization of the urban working class at the expense of agriculture. The idolization of Perón's wife, Eva, offset the natural discontent of the Argentinians with a cumbersome system of repression. Her death in July 1952 left the President out of touch with public feeling: he failed to understand the patriotic resentment aroused by his decision to allow an American oil company to prospect within Argentina, nor did he anticipate the opposition caused by his conflict with the Church over the legalizing of divorce and prostitution. In September 1955, officers acting 'in defence of Catholic Christianity' overthrew Perón and Argentina reverted to rule by a military junta from the traditional governing caste. From 1957 to 1966 attempts were made to follow the principles of the 1853 constitution but, since each election raised the Peronista political following, repeated intervention by army commanders led to rule by Presidential decree from 1966 to 1971. After a further bloodless *coup* in March 1971 fresh pledges were given of free elections, which two years later led to an outright victory of the Peronista party. Juan Perón returned after eighteen years of exile and was sworn in as President in October 1973, with his second wife, Maria Estela Perón, as Vice-President. When Juan Perón died nine months later, she succeeded him as President. Economic crises, intensified by the activities of the left-wing guerrillas (*Monteneros*), led in March 1976 to her overthrow by a bloodless army *coup d'état* – the seventh in twenty-one years. Once again the republic accepted government by a military triumvirate, but the repeated failure of the urban reformist movement to achieve drastic political changes left many town-dwellers disillusioned, frustrated and receptive to ideas of social revolution. For five years, 1976–81, the junta was headed by General Jorge Videla and Argentina's persistent violation of human rights led the Carter Administration to impose a ban on all aid to the republic. Videla was succeeded in March 1981 by General Viola, under whom inflation soared within eight months to 131 per cent. Viola's apparent incompetence led the commander-in-chief of the army, General Leopoldo Galtieri (born 1924), to oust him from the Presidency on 11 December 1981. Galtieri, a fiery nationalist and ruthless opponent of the Monteneros, was at first encouraged by the Reagan Administration to put Argentina at the head of Latin American resistance to communist infiltration. A harsh economic policy, fashionably monetarist in principle, provoked street violence in Buenos Aires in the second and fourth weeks of March 1982. As a diversion from internal grievances, Galtieri authorized the sending of an invasion force to realize the long cherished Argentinian ambition of seizing the 'Malvinas Islands' (►Falklands Conflict). The consequent diplomatic crisis destroyed the improvised Argentine–American entente while the British military victory in the Falklands led to Galtieri's downfall on 17–18 June 1982 and to demands for a return to civilian rule and a more democratic administration. Galtieri's successor, General Reynaldo Bignoni, began his Presidency with a pledge of liberal political reforms. Elections held on 30 October 1983 were won by the Radical Party, led by Raoul Alfonsin. Six weeks later he was sworn in as President, ending Argentina's eight years of military rule. Galtieri and other leaders of the junta were subsequently put on trial and in May 1986 were sentenced to imprisonment for their conduct of the Falklands war. In April 1987 and twice in 1988 the Alfonsin government survived attempted military coups, the chief challenge coming from supporters of Lt-Colonel Aldo Rico. Hyperinflation contributed to the defeat of Alfonsin's Radical Party by the neo-Peronist Justicialist Party candidate, Carlos Menem, in the presidential election of May 1989. Menem introduced economic reforms which cut inflation, though leaving a high level of unemployment. He secured amendments to the constitution in order to strengthen presidential executive powers. Menem and the Justicialists also won the 1995 elections.

Aristide, Jean-Bertrand (1953–), Haitian President. Born at Port Salut, he trained for the priesthood and was ordained in 1962. As a parish priest in Port-au-Prince he courageously championed human rights and, against the wishes of his religious superiors, stood for the presidency of ►Haiti. He was duly elected in December 1990, but was forced into exile for seven months by a military *coup*. Although in 1994 he returned to Haiti, with the backing of the UN and American troops, he had only fifteen months of his term of office in which to pursue his anti-corruption campaign. Constitutionally he was barred from a second successive term and accordingly withdrew from active politics in January 1996.

Armenia. Inland republic in the extreme south of the Caucasus, capital Erevan. There was a unified Armenian state as early as 95 BC and in AD 301 it adopted Christianity as an official religion. By the end of the fourth century the Armenian lands were divided between the Byzantine and Persian empires: they were never again united. Western Armenia was under Ottoman rule from the sixteenth century until 1920 when it was confirmed as part of the Turkish republic by the Soviet-Turkish treaty of Kars (March 1921) after its peoples had suffered grievously (►Armenian Massacres). Eastern Armenia (including the present republic) was under Persian sovereignty from 1639 until 1828, when the Persians ceded it to Tsar Nicholas I. With the fall of the Russian monarchy ex-tsarist Armenia proclaimed its independence on 28 May 1918 but was occupied by the Bolsheviks and became a Soviet Socialist Republic on 29 November 1920. A brief nationalist revolt in 1921 left ►Stalin strongly prejudiced against the Christian Armenians, preferring to support their nominally Muslim neighbours, the Azeris. Accordingly when, in 1922, Armenia was absorbed in a new trans-Caucasian Federal Soviet Socialist Republic, the most eastern Armenian communities, in ►Nagorny-Karabakh, were grouped administratively in an autonomous region within ►Azerbaijan. This division seemed perpetuated when both Armenia and Azerbaijan became constituent republics of the ►Soviet Union under the 1936 Constitution. Hostility to communist rule in Armenia grew rapidly between 1987 and 1990 for four main reasons: contempt for Party corruption; anger at an inefficient government response to the 1988 earthquake; fear of industrial pollution, ignored by the authorities; and nationalistic feelings of sympathy for kinsfolk in Nagorny-Karabakh who were seeking self-determination. Armenian independence, proclaimed on 21 September 1991, was therefore followed in May 1992 by open warfare with Azerbaijan over Nagorny-Karabakh, which continued for two years, delaying vital economic reforms until 1994–5. The Pan-Armenian National Movement, which came to power in 1990, consolidated its hold on the republic at elections in July 1995. Robert Kolharyan, a former leader of the Armenians in Nagorny-Karabakh, became Prime Minister in March 1997 and defeated the ex-Communist Party boss, Karel Demirchyan, in the presidential election of 30 March 1998.

Armenian Massacres. In the last quarter of the nineteenth century the Armenian racial minority in the Ottoman Empire was encouraged to assert its nationhood by exiled groups, operating from the USA, from Geneva and from Tbilisi. Repression by Ottoman irregulars – mainly ►Kurds – led to the slaughter of some 30,000 Armenians in eastern Anatolia in 1894–96; several thousand more were also slaughtered in Constantinople in August 1896, after Armenian extremists seized the Ottoman Bank to draw world attention to their plight. Threat of intervention by the Great Powers halted the killings, but the genocide was resumed, even more systematically, in May 1915 when Ottoman army commanders began mass deportation of Armenians from eastern Turkey, where it was thought they might help the Russian invaders. Thousands were forcibly marched from the Anatolian frontier provinces towards Syria; it is estimated that 1.3 million Armenians perished in this first instance during the century of 'ethnic cleansing'. Some 150,000 Armenians still live in northern Syria, in and around Aleppo.

Armistice. The suspension of fighting pending a definite peace settlement. 'The Armistice' is a term applied to the document signed in a railway coach at Compiègne by representatives of Germany and of the allied and associated Powers on 11 November 1918, ending the First World War at 'the eleventh hour of the eleventh day of the eleventh month'. Earlier armistices had been signed with Bulgaria (Salonika, 29 September 1918), Turkey (Mudros, 30 October 1918) and Austria-Hungary (Padua, 3 November 1918). On 22 June 1940 Hitler required French representatives to sign an armistice with victorious Germany in the same railway coach at the same spot as in November 1918. An armistice between representatives of the King of Italy and the allies was signed near Syracuse on 3 September 1943, although not announced until 8 September. Attempts by the Hungarian Regent, ►Horthy, to secure a similar armistice on 15 October 1944 were frustrated by German countermoves, although the Russians signed armistices with the Romanians and Finns in September 1944 and eventually with a provisional Hungarian Government on 20 January 1945. No formal armistice was concluded with

Germany or with Japan in 1945: individual fighting fronts surrendered, and there was no provision for a mere suspension of hostilities. The Korean War of 1950–53 was ended by an armistice signed at Panmunjom, 27 July 1953.

Armstrong, Neil (1930–), American astronaut. Born Wapakoneta, Ohio, and served as a fighter pilot in the Korean War before beginning to train as an astronaut in 1962. He commanded the Gemini 8 space flight in 1966 and in 1969 took part in the successful Apollo 11 mission to the moon, becoming the first man to set foot on the surface of the moon (21 July 1969).

Arnhem, Battle of (17–26 September 1944). Part of 'Operation Market Garden', an Anglo-American plan to outflank the German defences along the Rhine by a massive turning movement through Holland into northern Germany. The British 1st Airborne Division (including a brigade of Polish parachutists) sought to capture the steel road-bridge over the Lower Rhine at Arnhem while American airborne units seized bridges at Nijmegen and Grave. The British Second Army would then advance fifty miles to link up with the airborne forces, taking advantage of the bridges they had seized The Airborne Division encountered unexpectedly strong German resistance, organized by Field Marshal Model, who was by chance in Arnhem, with German armoured troops regrouping after the ►Normandy landings. The Second Army were unable to break through before the German defenders had recovered from the surprise descent and prevented the British from securing the bridge. This failure at Arnhem destroyed allied hopes of early victory in the West, but it was a bold strategic gamble which had come close to success.

Asad, Hafez al- (1928–), Syrian President. Born in the village of Qardaha, near Latakia in northern Syria, he is a member of the Alawi, a warrior sect of Shiites considered heretical by many Muslims. Asad joined the ►Ba'ath Party while a junior officer and rose rapidly to command the air force by the age of thirty-five. He became Minister of Defence in February 1966 and led a *coup* in November 1970, amending the constitution so as to become an executive President in March 1971, subsequently being re-elected every seven years. He sought recovery of the Golan Heights, lost to ►Israel in the ►Six-Day War, and by the ►October War of 1973 did at least recover the town of Queneitra. Two years later he authorized Syrian military intervention in ►Lebanon. Internally he was long dependent on Soviet aid. The promotion of Alawis in the army officer corps aroused resentment, especially from the Muslim Brotherhood, the most active extremists among Sunni believers. The Brotherhood killed sixty Alawi military cadets in Aleppo in 1979 and in 1982 Asad, fearing a general rebellion, ordered his army to take control of Hama, the city on the Orontes which was the centre of Brotherhood activities. This action caused heavy loss of life and the destruction of much of historic Hama, including the Great Mosque. Thereafter Asad's primacy in Syrian politics went unchallenged; although remaining hostile to Israel, he also mistrusted the ambitions of Saddam ►Hussein in ►Iraq, backing ►Iran throughout the First Gulf War (1980–

88) and sending Syrian troops to fight alongside the Egyptians against Iraq in the Second Gulf War.

Asquith, Herbert Henry (1852–1928, created Earl of Oxford and Asquith 1925). Born in Yorkshire; educated at City of London School and Balliol College, Oxford, barrister 1876, Liberal MP for East Fife 1886–1918. He was Home Secretary 1892–5 but incurred the displeasure of many Liberals by supporting the anti-Boer 'imperialists' during the South African War, 1899–1902. Nevertheless he became Chancellor of the Exchequer in 1905 and his intellectual gifts and parliamentary skill made him a natural successor as Prime Minister when ➤Campbell-Bannerman resigned in April 1908. The first years of Asquith's administration saw the completion of numerous social reforms but were dominated by the dispute with the House of Lords over the 'People's Budget' of 1909, which precipitated the ➤Parliament Act of 1911. Asquith was also faced with the problem of the militant ➤suffragettes, industrial strife encouraged by the ➤syndicalists, the threat of civil war in Ireland over the Home Rule proposals of 1913–14, and the international crises which led to the First World War. As wartime Prime Minister Asquith sought the maximum amount of political solidarity and in May 1915 formed a coalition government which he headed until December 1916, when he was ousted by a combination of the supporters of ➤Lloyd George and the Conservatives, who thought Asquith was indiscreet and lacked vigour. From 1916 to 1925 a feud between Asquith and Lloyd George so weakened the Liberal Party that it ceased to be the normal 'alternative party' to the Conservatives. Asquith lost his seat at East Fife in the 1918 Election but was MP for Paisley 1920–24 and was recognized as leader of the Liberal Party again from 1923 to October 1926. However, the traditional liberalism which he upheld could not attract voters who had become more concerned with economic planning than political principles.

Atatürk, Mustapha Kemal (1881–1938). Born in Salonika, where he was known as 'Mustapha', receiving the complimentary name 'Kemal' as a cadet. He served in the Turkish cavalry against the Italians in Libya (1911) and against the Bulgars in the Balkan Wars (1912–13). As a divisional commander at ➤Gallipoli, he successfully held the vital Sari Bair ridge against the Anzac forces. Subsequently he fought in the Caucasus and Syria. In May 1919 he began a nationalist revolution at Samsun (Anatolia), organizing resistance to the post-war dismemberment of Turkey and, in particular, to Greek attempts to seize ➤Smyrna and its hinterland. Victory over the Greeks in September 1922 enabled Kemal to secure revision of the Turkish peace settlement by the Treaty of ➤Lausanne and to gain control of Constantinople after the ➤Chanak crisis – Kemal had set up a provisional government in Ankara on 23 April 1920 and this regime formally abolished the Sultanate in November 1922. Eleven months later a Turkish Republic was proclaimed, with Kemal as President. The abolition of the traditional religious institution, the Caliphate, in March 1924 enabled Kemal to secularize Turkey, which he governed as a ruthless dictator until his death. He encouraged western modes of dress, emancipated women, introduced a Latin alphabet, developed industry, and substituted a narrowly Turkish national pride for the older Islamic loyalties. In 1935 he assumed the patronymic 'Atatürk' ('Father of the Turks'), at a time when he wished all Turkish families to adopt surnames in the accepted western fashion. Kemal Atatürk's imposed social and political revolution within Turkey established a model followed, with local variations, by other national leaders in the Middle East, notably by ➤Nasser.

Atlantic, Battle of the. A phrase invented by Churchill in a directive dated 6 March 1941 to describe the struggle for control of the vital supply routes to the British Isles in the Second World War. The 'battle', which was waged continuously from the first to the last day of war in Europe, involved on the German side surface raiders, long-range bombers and minelaying operations as well as the U-boats (*Unterseebooten*, i.e. submarines) with which it is chiefly associated in retrospect. The admiral commanding U-boats, ➤Doenitz, intensified the threat to Britain in the second winter of war by developing tactics which enabled his vessels to hunt allied convoys in packs, attacking at night and on the surface, thus countering the British underwater detection device, Asdic. The first 'wolfpack' attacks were made on two eastbound convoys on 18–19 October 1940, sinking 32 ships. Improved air cover checked this initial assault but after ➤Pearl Harbor the rapid construction of long-range U-boats, supplied by submarine tankers, carried the battle to the American coast, where the German commanders had great success. Over 1942 as a whole the allies lost an average of 96 ships a month, sunk by U-boats. The institution of escorted convoys off the American continent in midsummer 1942 checked the U-boat menace in these waters but there remained a gap in mid-Atlantic where it was impossible to give land-based air cover until the establishment of a squadron of 'Liberators' in Iceland (in spring 1943). As late as March 1943 the U-boats were able to sink 108 merchant ships for the loss of only one vessel. Two months later British and American countermeasures proved effective. The arrival of special escort aircraft carriers and a wider use of radar, supported by new and powerful groups of destroyers, enabled the allies to inflict a severe defeat on the U-boats in May 1943, a month in which Doenitz lost 41 of his submarines. Although Germany developed new technical devices (radar decoys, acoustic torpedoes and the 'Schnorkel' breathing tube for staying submerged for prolonged periods) the U-boats never again inflicted the heavy losses of 1942. The average monthly figure of allied merchantmen sunk was cut to 12 vessels over the last year and a quarter of the battle.

Atlantic Charter. A statement of fundamental principles for the post-war world issued to the Press after the first of the Churchill–Roosevelt meetings in Placentia Bay, Newfoundland, 9–12 August 1941. The two leaders exchanged visits between their respective warships: the British battleship, *Prince of Wales*, and the American cruiser, *Augusta*. The statement emphasized British and American opposition to further territorial aggrandisement and to any territorial changes contrary to the wishes of the people immediately concerned. It asserted the need of peoples to choose their own forms of government and to live free from fear and want. It favoured post-war economic collaboration and proposed that the aggressor nations be disarmed pending the establishment of a general security system. A British draft statement which would have committed the USA (still technically at peace) to join some form of international organization in the post-war period was amended out of all recognition by the American delegation. Although a month later it was announced that the Atlantic Charter had been endorsed by the Soviet Union and the fourteen other countries at war with Germany and Italy, little reference was made to the declaration at any subsequent conference. Principally the Charter was of value as a propaganda exercise: a demonstration to the Axis Powers of the growing collaboration between Britain and the USA and of the decline in American isolationist sentiment. But it was also a first exercise in drafting war aims, a restatement of democratic ideals to answer the Nazi claim of introducing a 'New Order' into world affairs.

Atomic Bomb. The possibility of developing a weapon of mass destruction by nuclear fission was known to scientists in Europe and America during the interwar period: ➤Rutherford split the atom at Cambridge in 1932; and the Italian scientist, Enrico Fermi (1901–54), discovered atomic chain reaction in Rome, 1934. Nazi Germany was slow to realize the destructive potentiality of nuclear energy, which was developed in the USA by a team of American, British, Canadian and refugee scientists, including Fermi. The so-called ➤'Manhattan Project' perfected an experimental bomb exploded in the deserts of New Mexico on 17 July 1945. An American aircraft dropped an atomic bomb on the Japanese city of Hiroshima three weeks later (6 August), killing 78,000 people and gravely wounding another 90,000. A second bomb was dropped on Nagasaki on 9 August, and the Japanese surrendered on 14 August. The Soviet Union, whose scientists had been secretly working on a nuclear weapon since 1943, exploded an atomic bomb in 1949, the British in 1952, the French in 1960, the Chinese in 1964. The development of the ➤hydrogen bomb intensified the condemnation of all forms of nuclear warfare (➤Test-Ban Treaty).

Attlee, Clement Richard (1883–1967, created Earl Attlee, 1955). Born at Putney, Surrey; educated at Haileybury and University College, Oxford; barrister 1906, tutor at Ruskin College and the London School of Economics, living in the East End of London and concerning himself with social problems. He was commissioned in the South Lancashire Regiment in 1914 and served in Gallipoli, Mesopotamia and France, finishing the war as a major. In 1919–20 he was Mayor of Stepney and entered the House of Commons as Labour MP for Limehouse in 1922, retaining the seat until the constituency was abolished in 1950, when he became MP for West Walthamstow. Attlee served as a junior minister in the Labour Government (➤MacDonald, James Ramsay) in 1930–31 but (unlike his later colleagues, H. ➤Morrison and A.V. Alexander) was not a member of MacDonald's cabinet. In 1931 he supported ➤Lansbury in refusing to join the National Government. Attlee's mastery of parliamentary detail and his cautiously reliable judgement made him a prominent member of the Labour Front Bench, even though his speeches always lacked the fire of radical oratory. When Lansbury retired in 1935, Attlee was elected Labour leader on the second ballot, narrowly defeating Morrison. He consolidated his position over the next five years by steering a middle course between liberals and communists and by gaining first-hand knowledge of European affairs. During the ➤Spanish Civil War he vigorously supported the British volunteers fighting against Franco and visited the International Brigade on the Guadalquivir front in December 1937. His authority within the party was unchallenged in 1940 when he entered Churchill's coalition war cabinet as Lord Privy Seal and, in effect, Deputy Prime Minister, a post formally accorded him in February 1942 when he also became Dominions Secretary. During the war Attlee acted as a brake on the wilder schemes of both the Prime Minister and some of his own party. At the same time he showed his skill as a chairman responsible for expediting political business. This quality marked his period as Prime Minister of the first Labour Government to possess a clear majority (1945–51). He was responsible for achieving domestic reforms long advocated by the Labour Party including nationalization of the railways, coal, electricity, gas and steel and the introduction of a ➤National Health Service. Attlee was personally concerned with the growth of the Commonwealth and, in particular, with the transfer of power in India and Pakistan. He continued to keep the Labour movement well-disciplined until 1950, despite growing rifts between Left and Right within the party. His business-like approach to politics did not make him a popular idol, and the general election of May 1950 cut his majority to five. Ill-health weakened his management of affairs over the next twelve months and the Labour Party was narrowly defeated in October 1951. He remained Leader of the Opposition for another four years, seeking to balance the opposing views on major issues within the party so as to hold it together. When he retired in December 1955 he was succeeded as leader by Hugh ➤Gaitskell, an exemplar of the moderate democratic socialist tradition which Attlee consistently upheld.

Auchinleck, Sir Claude John Eyre (1884–1981). Educated Wellington College, joined the Indian Army in 1904 and served in Egypt, Palestine and Mesopotamia in the First World War. Commanded British force at Narvik in 1940, but was sent out to India as commander-in-chief early in 1941, exchanging commands with ➤Wavell, the commander-in-chief, Middle East, in July 1941. 'The Auk' prepared a major offensive in the desert, launched on 18 November 1941. He suffered from shortage of armour and anti-tank guns and from a series of misfortunes to his senior commanders in the field, but his troops reached Benghazi and controlled all Cyrenaica by the end of the year. A counter-offensive by ➤Rommel in the first half of 1942 recovered all the land gained by Auchinleck's offensive. On 25 June 1942 Auchinleck assumed personal command of the Eighth Army, established a defensive position and won the first battle of ►Alamein. Churchill undervalued Auchinleck's qualities and replaced him by General ►Alexander in August 1942, but Auchinleck's gifts of organization and his far-sightedness are now widely recognized. In 1943 he became commander-in-chief in India and was promoted field-marshal, 1946. He served as supreme commander in India and Pakistan during the difficult period up to independence, 1947.

Aung San Suu Kyi (1945–), Burmese politician, born in Rangoon. Her father, General Aung San (1915–47), was the outstanding Burmese nationalist in the Second World War. At the time of her birth he was leading the Anti-Fascist People's League against the Japanese invaders, with whom he had earlier cooperated. The General was assassinated at a cabinet meeting in Rangoon on 19 July 1947, while preparing for his country's independence. Suu Kyi was educated at English schools in Burma and India and at St Hugh's College, Oxford, subsequently marrying a fellow undergraduate, Michael Aris. She did not return to her homeland until 1988, having by then worked for the UN, taught at universities in Japan and India, and written a life of her father. In Burma she soon became the focus of passive resistance to General Saw Maung's military dictatorship in the country he renamed ►Myanmar. She organized the National League for Democracy (NLD) which won multi-party elections in May 1990, even though Aung San Suu Kyi had been placed under house arrest ten months earlier. The Myanmar government ignored the verdict of the electors and held her (and more than 2,000 civil rights campaigners) in detention despite international protests. Aung San Suu Kyi received the Nobel Peace Prize in 1991 but was not freed from house arrest until July 1995 and, with other members of the NLD, remained still subject to restraints.

Australia, Commonwealth of. Australian political history in the first years of the Commonwealth's existence (►Australian Commonwealth Act) was dominated by three issues: immigration; the growth of a labour movement; and the need to develop a federal, as opposed to a local, loyalty. All parties believed in controlling immigration (►Immigration Restriction Acts) so as to maintain a 'White Australia'. The Immigration Restriction Act of July 1902 accordingly imposed a linguistic ability test and was accompanied by measures intended to counter the near-slavery practised in some districts: thus the Solomon Islands Kanakas, who had worked on the sugar plantations in Queensland since 1864, were repatriated between 1902 and 1906. The Australian ►Labour Party was the best-organized political group in the Commonwealth and formed minority governments in 1904 and 1908 but did not gain a clear electoral victory until September 1914, largely through an anti-union bias on the part of women voters enfranchised in 1902. Under W.M. ►Hughes, Prime Minister in October 1915, the Labour movement became increasingly federalist in outlook, a development matched by the conscious Australian patriotism evoked in the war of 1914–18. More than 300,000 Australian volunteers fought in the Middle East and on the western front, of whom nearly a fifth were killed. Hughes's patriotic sentiments made him, in 1916, advocate conscription for overseas service, but this proposal led to his expulsion from the Labour Party and was twice rejected by a popular referendum (October 1916 and December 1917). Hughes organized a 'National War Government' in February 1917 and remained Prime Minister until February 1923, reckoning himself a 'Nationalist' rather than a representative of Labour.

The First World War completed the emergence of Australia as a world power, marked subsequently by membership of the League of Nations and by mandates for the former German colonies in New Guinea and the Solomon Islands. The necessity to raise additional defence revenue led to an increase in federal authority; with the return of peace, there was friction over taxation between the Commonwealth Government and the state governments. Resentment at the incidence of federal taxation was intensified in the agricultural regions by the ►Depression, and in April 1933 Western Australia voted to secede, petitioning the King and Privy Council for the right to enjoy separate dominion status. In 1934 it was ruled that a state could only secede if a majority of the Australian people as a whole approved the act of secession in a referendum. The rise in wool prices in the mid thirties and the need for federal defensive measures against the Japanese silenced all talk of breaking up the Australian Commonwealth. The government of R.G. ►Menzies entered the Second World War on the same day as Britain and France. The Australians fought magnificently in Libya and Greece in 1941 and in Malaya after ►Pearl Harbor, before concentrating on defence of the Australian continent. Japanese aircraft raided Darwin on fourteen occasions between February and April 1942, as well as bombing the Western Australian towns of Wyndham, Broome and Derby and the railhead of Katherine in the Northern Territories. On 31 May 1942 Japanese submarines sought unsuccessfully to penetrate Sydney Harbour. The chief battle zone was in the 'islands' (►Australian New Guinea), with Australian troops bearing the main burden of land fighting in the south-west Pacific.

The Second World War emphasized the strategic links between Australia and the USA as Pacific Ocean powers; it also stimulated the growth of industry. Both of these trends were reflected in the post-war period: the ►ANZUS Pact in 1951 led logically to the (unpopular) decision of the second Menzies Government in 1965 to send troops to Vietnam: and the need for more factory workers led to encouragement of 'white' immigration, especially from the war-devastated countries of Europe. Major industrial enterprises were developed, notably in Queensland, while the federal Snowy River Project in New South Wales brought electrical power and water to an area as large as Devon and Cornwall. By 1975 trade with Japan and the USA was increasing sufficiently to offset the steady decline in trade with Britain, which began in the early 1960s and was intensified by Britain's entry into the Common Market (1972). Australian sentiment towards the former 'mother country' has always tempered nostalgic affection with a healthy contempt for anything socially inegalitarian. In this spirit there has occasionally been criticism of the constitutional position of the Governor-General as representative of a distant sovereign. This point was emphasized during the long crisis caused by the dismissal of the Labour Prime Minister Gough ➤Whitlam, by Sir John Kerr in November 1975. Doubts over the wisdom of Sir John's action eventually led to his resignation as Governor-General (14 July 1977). Whitlam was succeeded by Malcolm ➤Fraser, whose coalition of the ➤Liberal and ➤Country parties won the elections of 1975, 1977 and 1980 but lost to Labour under Bob Hawke (1929–) in the elections of 1983, 1984, 1987 and March 1990. Hawke handed over the Labour Party leadership to his Finance Minister, Paul Keating (1944–), in December 1990. Keating, who was of Irish Catholic descent, was less sympathetic to the British connection than his predecessors, and during 1993 developed plans for Australia to become a republic at the millennium. Keating was, however, defeated in the General Election of 2 March 1996; a Liberal and Country coalition under John Howard (1952–) took office. In February 1998 a Constitutional Convention recommended the ending of monarchical links, but agreed to a referendum on the issue in late 1999.

The aborigine peoples in Australia (barely a quarter of a million in a population of over 18 million) only became full citizens in 1967. A land rights campaign achieved partial success in the Northern Territory (where the aborigines form a fifth of the inhabitants) in 1984 but it was not until December 1993 that the federal Native Title Act gave protection to native lands throughout Australia. White resentment over recognition of aboriginal rights encouraged the growth in 1997–8 of Pauline Hanson's right-wing One Nation Party, which was also hostile to Australians of Asian origin.

Australian Commonwealth Act. This measure, accepted by the British parliament on 9 July 1900, achieved the union of the six Australian colonies under a federal government. Demands for federation first arose in 1891, partly through disquiet at the colonial activities of the French, Germans and Americans in the Pacific and the East Indies. A federal convention at Hobart prepared a provisional constitution in 1897 but it aroused opposition in New South Wales and was amended by conferences of Prime Ministers from the Australian colonies, meeting in Sydney and Melbourne in 1898. Discussions with the British Government (and in particular with the Colonial Secretary, Joseph ➤Chamberlain) continued for over a year: Queen Victoria disliked the word 'Commonwealth', because of its Cromwellian associations, but was reconciled to the project on learning of the loyalty shown by the Australians during the Boer War. The Commonwealth of Australia came into being on 1 January 1901, although it was not until 1909 that agreement was reached on the site of a capital, in territory ceded by New South Wales at Canberra. The federal government functioned in Melbourne until May 1927 when the Duke of York (later King ➤George VI) opened the new Parliament House in Canberra.

Australian New Guinea. The eastern half of the island of New Guinea, comprising Papua and the former German imperial protectorates of Kaiser Wilhelm's Land and the offshore settlements of Neu Pommern (New Britain), Bougainville and Buka, territories administered by Germany from 1884 to 1914. Papua was transferred from British to Australian administration in 1906 and the Australians assumed responsibility for the ex-German colonies under a League of Nations mandate in 1920. The enlightened administration of J.H. ►Murray prepared the islands for self-government despite Australian concern to retain the region as a defensive outpost against Japan. In February 1942 the Japanese landed on New Britain and established a base at Rabaul, crossing to north-eastern New Guinea at Lae early in March. While Japanese seaborne invasions were checked in the battle of the ►Coral Sea their overland thrust on the vital base of Port Moresby was repulsed by the Australians in difficult mountain terrain less than fifty miles from the town. A gruelling campaign continued in the islands throughout 1943-5, with the Japanese not surrendering until 8 September 1945. The removal of the Japanese threat encouraged the Australians to extend the system of local administration, under United Nations trusteeship. In 1968 the name of the territories was changed to ►'Papua New Guinea', a preliminary to the full independence achieved in September 1975.

Austria–Hungary. By the Compromise (*'Ausgleich'*) of 1867 the former Austrian Empire was transformed into the Dual Monarchy of Austria–Hungary, a political unit which dominated central Europe until 1918. The Compromise divided territories of the Emperor ►Francis Joseph into what was generally called 'Austria' (technically, 'the lands represented in the Imperial Parliament') and the Kingdom of Hungary. These two states had a common monarch, joint control of foreign policy, the army and the navy, and a common finance ministry. Each state had a prime minister and a parliament, but sixty members from each parliament ('the Delegations') were summoned annually by the Emperor-King to meet alternately at Vienna or Budapest and discuss, independently of each other, matters relating to Austria–Hungary as a whole. Tension was caused between the Austrians and Hungarians by disputes over their respective financial contributions and, especially after the turn of the century, by Hungarian efforts to secure greater independence for Hungarian regiments in the 'Imperial and Royal Army'. The most serious conflicts in Austria–Hungary were, however, between the two master peoples and the subject nationalities. The Hungarians met strong opposition from the Croats and Serbs living within the borders of the Hungarian Kingdom, and to a lesser extent from Slovak and Romanian minorities. The Czechs of Bohemia-Moravia (assigned to the 'Austrian' half of the Monarchy) deeply resented the privileged position of the Hungarians and found a powerful spokesman in Tómaš ►Masaryk. Francis Joseph died in 1916 and his successor, ►Charles, held out a promise of constitutional reform for the Dual Monarchy, but the support given by the allies to the aspirations for independence of Masaryk and other exiles made the disintegration of Austria–Hungary inevitable. The treaties of ►St Germain and ►Trianon in 1919-20 formally recognized the break-up of the Dual Monarchy.

Austrian Republic. The first Austrian Republic was proclaimed on 12 November 1918 on the withdrawal of Emperor ►Charles. A constituent assembly (with the socialist, Karl Renner, 1870–1951, as Chancellor) voted Austria an integral part of Germany in March 1919, but the peace treaties forbade any Austro-German union, and a new constitution created an Austrian federation on the Swiss model (October 1920). There remained, however, little specifically 'Austrian' feeling in the republic: political affiliations were regionally patriotic, Pan-German, or nostalgically Habsburg. A quarter of the republic's population lived in Vienna and suffered privations through the dismemberment of the old empire. Vienna became socialist, while the provinces were predominantly clericalist: there were frequent clashes between rival 'private armies', the Heimwehr (fascist) and the Schutzbund (socialist), culminating in serious riots in the capital in July 1927. All Austria suffered from the economic Depression of 1931–2, which was intensified by the failure of a leading bank, the Credit Anstalt (May 1931). The chancellorship of ►Dollfuss was marred by a brief civil war which led to the defeat of the socialists (February 1934) and the promulgation of a new, virtually fascist, constitution. Dollfuss was murdered five months later in an abortive Nazi putsch. The authority of his successor, Kurt von Schuschnigg (1897–1977), was weakened by increasing Nazi pressure, culminating in the ►Anschluss of March 1938. Austria existed as a province of Greater Germany from 1938 to 1945. Under the experienced guidance of Karl Renner a second Austrian Republic was established in December 1945. The second Republic proved more stable than its predecessor and benefited from a greater sense of Austrian national patriotism. The withdrawal of the armies of occupation in 1955 (►Austrian State Treaty) was followed by a period of rapid industrialization which reached a peak in the years 1970–73. Politically the republic was dominated until 1983 by moderate socialists who tended to emphasize the neutral status of Austria, enabling Vienna, in particular, to develop as an international conference centre rivalling Geneva. Only between 1966 and 1970 were socialists not in the government. Bruno Kreisky (1911–), Chancellor from 1970 to 1983, headed Social Democrat administrations which lifted the general standard of living for the workers. His fellow socialist, Franz Vranitzky (1937–), Chancellor from June 1986 to January 1997, led a coalition with the centre-right People's Party; Austria joined the ►European Union in 1995. Vranitzky's successor, Viktor Klima (1950–), formed a similar coalition, with mounting opposition from the right-wing Freedom Party, led by Jorg Haider.

Austrian State Treaty. A settlement concluded in the Belvedere Palace, Vienna, on 15 May 1955 by the Foreign Ministers of the Soviet Union, the USA, Britain and France, providing for the withdrawal of occupying troops from Austria and the restoration of Austria's independence within the frontiers of 1937. The Treaty represented a sudden shift in policy by the Soviet Union, which had for nine years opposed attempts by the Western Powers to conclude an Austrian settlement. The Treaty reaffirmed the ban made after the First World War on any ►*Anschluss* linking Germany and Austria, or on any restoration of the Habsburg dynasty. It also required passage by the Austrian parliament of a constitutional law pledging

Austria to permanent neutrality. The occupation forces withdrew from Austria within five months of the signing of the treaty. Hopes in the West that the Treaty signified Russia's willingness to disengage troops holding the line of the ►'Iron Curtain' were premature: the Treaty followed, by one day, conclusion of the ►Warsaw Pact which ensured the continued presence of the Red Army in central Europe.

Avon, Earl of. ►Eden, Anthony.

Axis, Rome–Berlin. The name given to the collaboration of Nazi Germany and fascist Italy between 1936 and 1945. The metaphor was first used by Mussolini, speaking at Milan on 1 November 1936: 'This Berlin–Rome Line is not a diaphragm but rather an axis.' A loose understanding between the two countries (the 'October Protocols') had been reached in Berlin a week previously. A formal alliance, the 'Pact of Steel', followed on 22 May 1939. Cooperation with Japan began with the German–Japanese Anti-Comintern Pact of 25 November 1936, to which Italy acceded a year later, consolidated by the ►Tripartite Pact of September 1940. The term 'Axis Powers' was applied during the Second World War to Germany, Italy, Japan and their allies, Hungary, Slovakia, Romania and Bulgaria.

Ayub, Mohammed Khan (1907–74), President of Pakistan. Born in Abbottabad, on the north-west frontier, the son of an NCO in the British Army, educated at Aligarh University and the Royal Military College, Sandhurst, commissioned in the British Indian Army in 1928, served with distinction in the Burma Campaign 1942–5. He held high rank in the Pakistani Army from 1948 onwards, becoming the first commander-in-chief of the army when the post was created in January 1951, with the rank of full general, helping impose severe repressive measures as Minister of Defence from October 1954 until August 1955. In October 1958 martial law was proclaimed in Pakistan and Ayub Khan assumed the powers of head of the government, ruling through the army for over ten years, and winning Presidential elections in 1960 and 1965. Field-Marshal Ayub Khan (as he had now become) believed in what he called 'Basic Democracies', a form of devolved responsibility from himself down to local level. He carried through limited land reforms but became unpopular (especially with the Bengalis) because of the militaristic and repressive form of his government. Lack of success in the fighting with India over the Rann of Kutch area and ►Kashmir in 1965 lost him prestige and his settlement of the disputes with ►Shastri at Tashkent provoked widespread criticism. Imprisonment of the opposition led to serious student riots in 1968 and the Field-Marshal was induced to resign on 24 March 1969, handing over the Presidency to General ►Yahya Khan.

Azaña, Manuel (1880–1940). Spanish President. Born in Alcalá de Henares, studied law in Madrid and Paris, entered the civil service, winning respect as an intellectual journalist. In 1924 Azaña founded a Republican Party, which was soon suppressed, and he was briefly imprisoned. When ►Alfonso XIII fled in April

1931 he became Minister of War, succeeding to the Presidency six months later. Azaña followed a middle-of-the-road line, favouring democratic social reforms, but his changes were too rapid and drastic for many Spaniards and he was forced to resign in September 1933. He was again imprisoned briefly in October 1934 for supporting Catalan autonomy during an insurrection in Barcelona. This episode made him appear a hero-statesman to the embryonic ►Popular Front and it was with the Front's backing that he returned to the Presidency in May 1936, only ten weeks before the outbreak of the ►Spanish Civil War. Throughout the civil war he remained head of state seeking to keep the republican camp unified. In the closing months of 1938 he tried unsuccessfully to secure peace in Spain by outside mediation. Azaña fled to France early in February 1939, refusing the pleas of fanatical supporters that he should prolong a war he knew Franco had won. He died in Montauban a year later.

Azerbaijan. Republic in the southern Caucasus, on the Caspian Sea, capital, Baku. The Azeri people, kinsfolk to the Turks and converted to Islam by the Arab caliphates in the seventh century, came under Russian rule in 1828. The region experienced an oil boom between about 1902 and 1905. Brief independence from May 1918 to April 1920 was followed in 1922 by incorporation in the Trans-Caucasian Soviet Federal Socialist Republic. Azerbaijan achieved statehood within the ►Soviet Union in 1936, including the mainly Armenian autonomous region of ►Nagorny-Karabakh. An oil pipeline linked Baku with Batum, on the Black Sea. Independence was proclaimed in August 1991. The secession of Nagorny-Karabakh led to open warfare with Armenia and to an influx of refugees. On 18 June 1993 a military uprising brought the ex-communist Heidar Alliyev to power. He crushed three attempted *coups*, secured a ceasefire, brought Azerbaijan into the ►CIS and in September 1994 authorized a twelve-company consortium to open up huge reserves of oil, on land and underwater. Difficulties arose from outdated Soviet drilling rigs and over how to export oil through neighbouring regions wracked by war and political instability – ►Chechnya, ►Georgia, ►Armenia, ►Iran, ►Turkey.

Azikiwe, Nnamdi (1904–), Nigerian President. Born at Zungeri, northern Nigeria, educated at Lincoln and Pennsylvania Universities in the United States. From 1937 onwards he took a prominent part in the Nigerian nationalist movement, serving as a banker and purchasing a newspaper chain. He was recognized as a father-figure in the movement for liberation before he was forty. His powerful personality and sense of presence won him acceptance even though his tribe, the Ibo, was less widely respected than the Hausa of the north, from whom Azikiwe's rival, Abubakar ►Balewa, emerged. In 1957 an attempt was made to discredit Azikiwe by suggestions that he had benefited improperly from government contacts with the African Continental Bank, of which he was the principal director. A judicial tribunal did not entirely clear his name but when Nigeria gained independence in 1960 he was a natural first choice as Governor-General, becoming at the same time a Privy

Councillor. He succeeded to the Presidency on the proclamation of the Nigerian Republic in October 1963. Tribal divisions weakened the central authority of Nigeria, and a military *coup* – led mainly by Ibo – deposed Azikiwe and ousted the civilian government in 1966. Although Balewa was murdered, 'Zik's' prestige ensured his own safety. From the relative sanctuary of private life he denounced the mounting anarchy within the country and vainly urged the Ibos not to secede and plunge the country into civil war (►Biafra).

B

Baader–Meinhof Group. The name given by the German Press to the anarchistic Rote Armee Faktion ('Red Army Faction') of urban guerrillas, who claimed responsibility for terrorist outrages in the German Federal Republic from 1968 onwards. They were led by Andreas Baader (1943–77) and Ulrike Meinhof (1934–76). Baader was arrested in 1968 but forcibly released on 14 May 1970 in an operation principally conducted by Meinhof, a former television journalist. The group saw itself as a spearhead of resistance to capitalist society in West Germany and, in particular, to the presence of US forces in Europe. It claimed to provide a link between the traditional ➤anarchism of the nineteenth century and the abortive student protest movement of 1968. The group was held by the authorities to be responsible for at least six murders, more than fifty attempted murders, and for bombings, bank raids and the taking of hostages. The leaders were arrested in June 1972. On 9 May 1976 Ulrike Meinhof was found dead in her cell at Stuttgart, where she (with others of the group) had been on trial for eleven months. An official inquiry reported Meinhof had committed suicide; but her death led to mass protests by extreme radical students, to whom she seemed a left-wing martyr. In April 1977 Baader and two associates were sentenced to life imprisonment. Six months later an attempt to secure their release failed when police commandos freed hostages at ➤Mogadishu; and on 18 October it was announced that the three terrorists had killed themselves in Stammheim Gaol.

Ba'ath Socialist Party. A Pan-Arab movement based upon the union in 1952 of two Syrian political parties, the Ba'ath ('resurrection') Party of Michel Aflaq (1912–89), founded in 1947, and the Socialist Party of Akram al-Hawrani (1911–87). The ideological basis of the movement was the Ba'ath philosophy, evolved by Aflaq in the years 1944–6, of 'Freedom, Unity, and Socialism' in 'One Arab nation with an eternal mission'. The Ba'athists, although primarily Syrian, transcended national frontiers and were powerful in Iraq, Lebanon, Jordan and the Persian Gulf states as well as providing an alternative to the pragmatic national socialism of ➤Nasser in Egypt. The peak of Ba'ath influence was between 1956 and 1959, and was marked by the union of Syria and Egypt in the United Arab Republic. The Ba'athists were disillusioned by the authoritarian character of Nasser's rule and by the excessive influence of military leaders on the Pan-Arab movement. Failure to realize the original, democratic ideals of the Ba'ath Party encouraged a trend towards one-party rule, especially in Syria from 1963 onwards. A one-party Ba'ath movement emerged in Iraq in 1963 and a Ba'athist military regime dominated the republic from July 1968, culminating in severe repression under Saddam ➤Hussein. But the influence of the Ba'ath, with its belief in socialism as an instrument of Arab renaissance, was far greater on the Arab peoples than its divisive periods of political office might suggest.

Badoglio, Pietro (1871–1956), Italian soldier and political leader. Born at Grassano Monferrato in Piedmont, commissioned in the artillery, fought against the Ethiopians in the disastrous Adowa campaign of 1896, against the Turks in Libya in 1911 and, as a general in 1917, helped stabilize the front after the rout at ➤Caporetto. Badoglio was created a field-marshal and served Mussolini as Governor of Libya, 1929–33, before being sent to complete the conquest of Ethiopia, entering Addis Ababa in May 1936. He was Chief of the General Staff in 1940 and opposed Italy's entry into the war. After the failure of the Greek campaign he resigned (December 1940). King ➤Victor Emmanuel III appointed him Prime Minister on the fall of Mussolini in July 1943. Badoglio concluded an armistice with the allied powers in September 1943 and, a month later, took Italy into the war on the allied side against Germany. When the allies liberated Rome in June 1944 the anti-fascist Resistance leaders refused to serve under Badoglio and he retired from public life.

Bahrain. An independent state, rich in oil and petroleum, comprising a group of islands in the Persian Gulf. The islands were under British protection from 1861 to August 1971, when Bahrain's ruler, Sheikh Isa ibn Sulman (1932–), declared the islands' independence, at the same time ending federal links with the neighbouring Arab Emirates, which the British had encouraged in 1968. Iranian claims to the islands, dating from the late eighteenth century, were rejected by a United Nations commission in 1970. Commercial production in the oilfields dates from 1934.

Balance of Power. A type of diplomatic policy aimed at ensuring peace, especially in Europe, by preventing any single country, or group of countries, from exercising so great a military strength that the independence and liberty of other countries is endangered. Traditionally the policy was followed by the British, opposing France for many centuries but supporting the ➤Anglo-French Entente when German naval and military power appeared predominant, 1904–14. During the early 1920s the British favoured a rapid recovery of Germany as a counterweight to the supremacy shown by the French in the crisis over the ➤Ruhr in 1923. After 1945 no attempt was made by the British to follow a balance-of-power policy, largely because of the emergence of two 'superpowers' engaged in a nuclear arms race. The so-called 'balance of terror', in which potential rivals keep the peace for fear that their own nuclear attack would be countered by a devastating retaliatory nuclear strike, has none of the freedom of action permitted by the old 'balance of power', of which it is sometimes claimed to be the successor.

Baldwin, Stanley (1867–1947, created Earl Baldwin of Bewdley 1937). Born in Worcestershire; educated at Harrow School and Trinity College, Cambridge;

Conservative MP for Bewdley (his birthplace) from 1908 to 1937, succeeding his father in the seat. He held minor office in the coalition of 1916–22, entering the cabinet as President of the Board of Trade in 1921. On 19 October 1922 he played a prominent part in the famous Carlton Club meeting at which the Conservatives decided to leave the coalition. Under Bonar ►Law he served for six months as Chancellor of the Exchequer (1922–3) and succeeded Law as Prime Minister in May 1923, being preferred to ►Curzon. On failing to get a clear majority in the 1923 election, Baldwin resigned, but returned as Prime Minister from 1924 to 1929, the period being marked by the ►General Strike and rising unemployment. He was Lord President of the Council in MacDonald's 'National Government' of 1931, becoming Prime Minister again in June 1935. His handling of the crisis which culminated in ►Edward VIII's abdication was much praised. He retired in June 1937, and took no further part in public life. His apparent political myopia in the face of resurgent German nationalism from 1935 until 1937 was long criticized. The opening of archives, however, made it clear that Baldwin was more conscious of the need to build up Britain's defences than his successor Neville ►Chamberlain, whose policy of 'appeasement' at Munich was not to Baldwin's liking.

Balewa, Alhaji Abubakar Tafawa (1912–66), Nigerian political leader. Born in Bauchi, the son of a butcher and member of the Hausa tribe. He was a founder-member of the best-organized political party in Nigeria, the Northern People's Congress, entered the Legislative Council in 1947 and, while Nigeria was still a British colony, served as Minister of Works (1952), of Transport (1953) and Prime Minister (1957), guiding the country towards independence. British regard for his statesmanship was shown by the conferment on him of a knighthood on the eve of Nigeria's independence (October 1960), but he was distrusted by many of his compatriots, especially the Yoruba people of western Nigeria, two of whose leaders (Chief Awolowo and Chief Enahoro) were arrested on Balewa's orders in 1962. Tribal divisions hampered the efficiency of Balewa's administration and in January 1966 he was assassinated in a military *coup* led by officers who were predominantly Ibos from eastern Nigeria, traditional enemies of the Hausa tribe. The fate of Tafawa Balewa emphasized the difficulty of constructing a federal democratic system in an African state in which the tribes were jealously protective of their interests and resentful of centralized authority.

Balfour, Arthur James (1848–1930, created Earl of Balfour 1922). Born at Whittingehame, East Lothian; educated at Eton and Trinity College, Cambridge, Conservative MP for Hertford 1874–85, for East Manchester 1885–1905 and for the City of London 1906–22. Balfour attended the Congress of Berlin in 1878 as secretary to his uncle, Lord ►Salisbury. He achieved political distinction by his firmness as Chief Secretary for Ireland, 1887–91, and had the unique constitutional experience of serving as First Lord of the Treasury in 1891–2 and 1895–1902 while not holding the premiership. In July 1902 he succeeded his uncle as Prime

Minister but despite successes in educational reform and foreign affairs soon found his government split by the ➤Tariff Reform proposals of Joseph ➤Chamberlain and suffered a major defeat in the 1906 election. He remained leader of the Conservatives during the disputes over the 'People's Budget' and House of Lords reform, but by 1911 his habitual unhurried casualness had lost him the support of the party and he resigned in favour of Bonar Law. His interest in philosophy led him to write two considerable books on the need for intellectual liberty and to deliver the Gifford Lectures on 'Theism and Humanism' in 1914 and on 'Theism and Thought' in 1922–3. No other British Prime Minister was so respected as an intellectual, but his metaphysical dabbling puzzled and confused many members of his party. During the wartime coalitions he was First Lord of the Admiralty, 1915, and Foreign Secretary, 1916–19. He headed a political mission to the USA in 1917, played a prominent part in shaping the new Europe, and was second plenipotentiary at the Paris Peace Conference as well as chief British representative at the League of Nations in 1920 and the Washington Conference, 1921–2. From 1925 to 1929 he was Lord President of the Council, the 'elder statesman' of Baldwin's cabinet. Towards the end of his life he maintained that the most worthwhile act of his political career was the ➤Balfour Declaration.

Balfour Declaration. A communication made on 2 November 1917 by Balfour, the British Foreign Secretary, to Lord Rothschild, a leader of ➤Zionism, declaring British support for the establishment of a Jewish national home in Palestine provided that safeguards could be reached for the 'rights of non-Jewish communities in Palestine' and that the Jewish political status in any other country should not thereby be endangered. The Declaration was confirmed by all the allied governments and formed a basis for the League of Nations mandate for ➤Palestine assigned to the British at the San Remo conference of 1920.

Balkan League (1912). ➤Balkan Wars.

Balkan Pact. On two occasions in this century attempts have been made to bind together the countries of south-eastern Europe by a system of non-aggression treaties and guarantees of Balkan frontiers. The first attempt, sponsored by King ➤Alexander of Yugoslavia in 1933, sought an agreement linking Yugoslavia, Romania, Greece, Turkey and Bulgaria. But when the Balkan Pact was concluded in February 1934 the Bulgarians stayed out of it, because they were not prepared to accept the existing division of ➤Macedonia. Subsequently the Balkan Pact countries formed a Balkan Entente, a regional grouping with a permanent council and with provision for regular conferences between the member states. This arrangement, however, did not survive the tensions of 1940 when the various Balkan nations sought separate ways of placating Hitler's Germany. A second Balkan Pact, between Yugoslavia, Greece and Turkey, was concluded at Bled in August 1954 and provided for common military assistance should one of the three countries be the victim of aggression. Although this Pact was nominally operative for twenty years, it ceased to be effective within a few months because of mounting Greek and Turkish tension over ➤Cyprus. A further attempt at Balkan collaboration was made in February 1988 when the foreign ministers of Albania, Bulgaria, Greece, Romania, Turkey and Yugoslavia met in Belgrade, but on this occasion no formal pact was concluded.

Balkan Wars. In March 1912 the rival Balkan states Bulgaria and Serbia were induced by Russian diplomats to sign an alliance providing for the future partition of ➤Macedonia, then still a province of the Turkish Empire. Greece and Montenegro associated themselves with this alliance, known subsequently as the Balkan League. In October 1912 the four members of the Balkan League attacked Turkey and won swift victories. The Great Powers, meeting in an ambassadorial conference in London, tried to end the war. In May 1913 they secured a preliminary peace, under which the Turks surrendered most of their European territory on the understanding that the Powers would create a new, independent state of Albania – an arrangement unwelcome to Serbia and Montenegro, who wished to acquire the Albanian coastline. Subsequently friction arose between the Serbs and Greeks on the one hand and the Bulgarians on the other. The Bulgarians, who had suffered three-quarters of the casualties in the first Balkan War, rightly believed that Serbia and Greece were planning to divide Macedonia, giving only formal compensation to Bulgaria. On 29 June 1913 the Bulgarians began the 'Second Balkan War' by launching a surprise attack on the Serbs and Greeks but found themselves invaded by the Romanians and the Turks (with whom Serbia and Greece were still technically at war). Inevitably, the Bulgarians were rapidly defeated. The subsequent Treaty of Bucharest (August 1913) divided most of the lands claimed by Bulgaria in Macedonia and Thrace between Serbia and Greece, and also made Bulgaria cede southern ➤Dobrudja to Romania. The general effect of the Balkan Wars was: (1) to limit Turkey's European possessions to the area around Constantinople and Adrianople; (2) to create the ill-defined state of ➤Albania; (3) to double the size of Serbia and Montenegro, giving these two southern Slav states a common frontier; (4) to make Greece the most important power on the Aegean Sea, possessing the key port of Salonika; (5) to leave Bulgaria bitterly resentful. This settlement was to determine the behaviour of the Balkan states during the First World War, when those which had lost most by the Bucharest Treaty (Turkey and Bulgaria) entered the war on the German side, while Serbia, Montenegro, Greece and Romania fought on the Entente side.

Baltic Republics. The collective name given to ➤Lithuania, ➤Latvia and ➤Estonia, part of the Russian Empire until 1917, independent from 1918 to 1940, and subsequently Soviet Socialist Republics within the USSR. A strong movement in favour of autonomy developed in the three republics in October 1988. Full independence was restored in September 1991.

Banda, Hastings Kamuzu (c.1902–97), President of Malawi. Born in Nyasaland, worked as a child in the Rand gold-mines, allowed to receive education in the United States (Ohio, University of Chicago, and a medical school in Nashville, Tennessee), subsequently qualifying as a doctor of medicine at Edinburgh and serving as a general practitioner in London for more than ten years. He returned to Nyasaland in 1958 and led the Malawi National Congress in resisting white Rhodesian dominance of his homeland through the Central African Federation (►Rhodesia). Banda was arrested in March 1959 and imprisoned, but he was released a year later and appointed Prime Minister of Nyasaland when the British introduced self-government in February 1963. In July 1964 Nyasaland became independent, within the Commonwealth, changing its name to Malawi. Banda was elected first President of the Malawi Republic in July 1966, becoming President for life five years later. Although Banda pursued a moderate and cautious policy towards South Africa, avoiding provocative clashes, he established a ruthless one-party state in Malawi, retaining for himself the powers of Prime Minister, Foreign Minister and Minister of Justice and accepting responsibility for public-works projects and agricultural expansion. Foreign financial pressure imposed reforms in 1992–3 and in May 1994 Banda was defeated in a presidential election by the United Democratic Front, under Bakili Maluzi. In December 1995 a jury cleared Banda of having ordered the murder in 1983 of political rivals. He died from pneumonia in Johannesburg in November 1997. Despite the harsh record of his later years in office he was accorded a state funeral in Lilongwe.

Bandaranaike, Solomon West Ridgeway Dias (1899–1959), founder-leader of the Sri Lanka Freedom Party. Born at Colombo, educated at St Thomas's College, Colombo and Christ Church, Oxford; a barrister in 1925, presided over the Ceylon National Congress movement in the early 1930s and championed the Sinhalese against the Indian Tamils in Ceylon's political controversies on the eve of independence in 1948. He was Minister of Health from 1948 to 1951, effectively stamping out malaria. In 1951 he organized a specifically Sinhalese socialist movement, the Sri Lanka Freedom Party, which returned him to power as Prime Minister of a 'People's United Front' in April 1956. He closed all British naval and military bases in Ceylon but caused serious riots by his nationalization policies and his attempts to make Sinhalese the sole official language. Indian rioting led to his assassination in September 1959, apparently by a Buddhist monk.

Bandaranaike, Mrs Sirimavo (1916–). Born in Ratnapura, the daughter of a Sinhalese landowner and local dignitary. In 1940 she married Solomon ►Bandaranaike whom she succeeded as head of the Sri Lanka Freedom Party. In July 1960 her party won an overwhelming majority of seats in the Ceylonese general election and she became the first woman Prime Minister anywhere in the world. Her persistence in trying to impose Sinhalese as the sole language, and a conflict with powerful interests which resented her policy of nationalizing basic industrial ventures, led to the constant threat of a right-wing military *coup*. She survived this danger but was defeated in the election of 1965, returning to power with an increased majority in May 1970. Although in 1971 Mrs Bandaranaike was forced to crush an insurrection by left-wing Sinhalese militants, her second government was marked by 'an advance to socialist democracy' and by the adoption in 1972 of a new constitution which established ►Ceylon as the Republic of ►Sri Lanka. Her government was defeated in the turbulent general election of July 1977. Allegations of unconstitutional practices led the Sri Lanka parliament to disenfranchise Mrs Bandaranaike in October 1980 and deprive her of the right to sit in the assembly for seven years. She was forced to vacate the parliamentary seat of Attanagalla, which members of the Bandaranaike family had held for fifty years. In 1988 she stood unsuccessfully as a candidate in the Sri Lankan presidential election. She returned as Prime Minister of a People's Alliance coalition in November 1994 after her daughter, Mrs Chandrika Bandaranaike Kumaratunga, was elected President. In an attempt to satisfy the Tamils, Sirimavo Bandaranaike drew up plans for a new federal structure for Sri Lanka.

Bandung Conference (17–24 April 1955). The first international political conference of states from the African and Asian continents. President ►Sukarno of Indonesia was host to twenty-nine Asian and African countries, together with observers representing the Greek Cypriots, American Negroes and the ►African National Congress. Sukarno wished the conference to adopt a 'non-aligned and neutral' attitude towards the so-called 'cold war' confrontation between the Sino-Soviet bloc and the West, although he also championed a 'united front' against colonial oppression. The Indians warmly supported these attempts to set up an Afro-Asian 'area of peace' and, at the conference, the chief Chinese delegate, ►Chou En-lai, was conciliatory. But the rapidly intensifying rivalry of India and China within Asia, together with the separate objectives of anti-colonialism in Africa and Asia, weakened the subsequent effectiveness of the conference. An attempt to hold a second Afro-Asian Conference in Algeria in June 1965 was abandoned, partly because of conflicting intrigues between the representatives of Soviet and Chinese interests, and partly because of the overthrow of the Algerian government of ►Ben Bella. Conferences of 'non-aligned nations' were held in Belgrade (1961) and Cairo (1964) but were not specifically Afro-Asian in composition.

Bangladesh. A 'people's republic' on the bay of Bengal, established in 1971. Until 1947 this region constituted the East Bengal province (and part of Assam province) in British India. Since it was inhabited by a Muslim majority, the region then became part of ►Pakistan even though 1,000 miles separated West and East Pakistan. The Bengali Pakistanis believed themselves economically exploited by the authorities in Karachi, who imposed on them a foreign policy which was concerned with the Middle East and of little importance to the people of the Ganges delta. From 1954 onwards the Awami League (led by Mujibur ►Rahman) sought autonomy, eventually winning an overwhelming electoral victory in December 1970. The failure of talks aimed at establishing a new constitutional structure led to the establishment of a Bangladesh Government-in-Exile in Calcutta (April 1971). This act of secession precipitated a civil war and the flight of nearly 10 million refugees from East Pakistan into India. The breakdown of all government in the Ganges delta, together with the threat of famine and the spread of cholera, led India to intervene and there was a brief war between India and Pakistan (3–16 December 1971) before the Pakistani forces in East Pakistan surrendered unconditionally. Bangladesh was recognized by most of the world powers in the early months of 1972. Mujibur Rahman, as Prime Minister, sought to establish a parliamentary democracy, which would be fundamentally socialist in character. The problem of carrying through a social revolution in the most densely populated region in Asia at a time of famine was, however, beyond the ability of the Awami League leaders. In January 1975 Mujibur Rahman, as an emergency measure, introduced a form of one-party government which allowed him dictatorial powers, but seven months later he was overthrown and murdered in a military *coup*. The leader of the army dissidents, Brigadier Khaled Mosharraf, was himself assassinated in further violence during November 1975. A non-political administration, headed for two years by a former chief justice, sought to restore calm and confidence in the republic, but there was much illegal emigration to Assam. Major-General Zia Rahman became President on 21 April 1977, cautiously leading the country back towards democracy. In June 1978 he won a Presidential election by a four to one majority, founded the Bangladesh Nationalist Party and prepared for parliamentary elections, which his party won easily on 19 February 1979. Unrest, however, mounted during 1980 with complaints of corruption in the ruling party and with an embryonic guerrilla revolt seeking autonomy for the tribesmen in the Chittagong hills. A rebellion in the south-east of Bangladesh was suppressed on 30–31 May 1981, but only after mutinous troops had assassinated President Zia Rahman at Chittagong. General Ershad became President in March 1982, dependent for survival on massive foreign aid. A cycle of floods and famine took the lives of over five million Bangladeshis in the period 1971–88, 10,000 dying in the cyclone of May 1985. Ershad was deposed in December 1990. Seventy political parties contested the first democratic elections in twelve years (February 1991), won by the Bangladesh National Party, led by Begum Khaleda Zia, widow of the assassinated President. Despite widespread strikes, the Begum remained Prime Minister until the Awami League won elections in June 1996, when she was succeeded by Sheikh Hasina, who filed corruption charges against the Begum and former ministers two years later.

'Barbarossa'. Code-name selected by the German Supreme Command for the invasion of the Soviet Union in 1941. Plans were drafted in November 1940 and approved by Hitler in Directive no. 21, dated 18 December 1940 and headed 'Operation Barbarossa'. It was proposed to complete arrangements for the invasion by 15 May 1941; the Germans were to advance to a line running from Archangel to the Volga by the autumn. The German need to intervene in the Balkans against

➤Greece and ➤Yugoslavia postponed the invasion by seven weeks. Ultimately, on 22 June 1941, seventy-nine German divisions, supported by Romanian and Finnish forces, crossed the frontier. There were three main army groups: Army Group North (Field-Marshal von Leeb) was to advance from East Prussia to Leningrad in a month; Army Group Centre (Field-Marshal von Bock) was to launch a two-pronged thrust through Minsk and Smolensk on Moscow; Army Group South (Field-Marshal von Rundstedt) was to capture Kiev, the Ukraine, the Don Basin and the Black Sea coast. This largest military operation in history failed for two main reasons: Russian reserves and resilience were greater than Hitler had anticipated; and Hitler himself intervened, ordering a concentration against Moscow when Leningrad had already been encircled, while at the same time moving tank forces from the central thrust southwards and thus giving the defenders of Moscow a respite. By the time winter came, only Army Group South had fulfilled the original orders in the directive.

Barton, Sir Edmund (1849–1920), first Australian Prime Minister. A barrister born and educated in Sydney, from 1887 to 1897 he campaigned vigorously for the federal union of all the Australasian colonies, including New Zealand. The New Zealanders confirmed their independence at a convention in 1891. Six years later Barton's first draft of a constitution was rejected by his home state. He successfully continued negotiations in Melbourne, Sydney and London, and in January 1901 was a natural choice as first Prime Minister of the federated Commonwealth of ➤Australia. He held office for two years, concentrating on defence and immigration restraints, so as to exclude non-whites. For the last seventeen years of his life Barton was a High Court Judge, specializing in states' rights.

Baruch, Bernard Mannes (1870–1965), US financier and special adviser to successive Presidents. Born of Jewish parentage in South Carolina, received elementary education in New York, making a fortune through shrewd speculation on Wall Street before the turn of the century. Baruch was chosen by President Wilson to advise on problems of manpower and raw materials during the First World War, heading the War Industries Board, 1917–19. In this capacity he exercised economic powers without precedent in American life, fixing prices, mobilizing national resources and allocating raw materials. He served as economic adviser to the Peace Commission in 1919 and as a member of the Presidential commission on agriculture established by President Harding in 1922. He again acted as adviser on manpower problems for Roosevelt in the Second World War and in 1946 was appointed American representative on the United Nations Atomic Energy Commission. In this capacity he put forward the Baruch Plan for an international authority to control fissionable material (➤Acheson) and to inspect atomic developments in any country. Although on 30 December 1946 the Energy Commission approved the plan, it aroused Russian suspicions and little was done to implement Baruch's proposals. Baruch was a close friend of Winston Churchill, who frequently sought his advice between 1929 and 1952.

Basques. A race of some 600,000 people settled since earliest times around the western Pyrenees. About 100,000 Basques are French citizens but the remainder live in the four Spanish provinces of Álava, Guipúzcoa, Navarra and Vizcaya (the 'Provincias Vascongadas'). The Basques, traditionally intensely religious, have retained a distinctive language, markedly different from their neighbours. In the early Middle Ages they evolved a communal political system based on biannual assemblies meeting under an oak tree in the city of Guernica. Basque rights were respected by the rulers of Castile from the fourteenth century until 1839, when they were abrogated by the Cortes in Madrid as a punishment for Basque support to the Carlist claimant in the dynastic civil wars endemic to mid-nineteenth-century Spain. Basque national feeling intensified with the coming of industrialism to the port of Bilbao at the beginning of the twentieth century, but it was not until 1931 that the Basques found an astute political leader, in José Antonio Aguirre y Lecube (1904–60). Aguirre induced the Basques to support the Spanish Republicans, despite Basque disapproval of the government's anti-clericalism, and the Basques were promised autonomy within Spain, an undertaking honoured three months after the outbreak of the ►Spanish Civil War. Aguirre was elected President of the Basque Republic (known as 'Euzkadi') at a ceremony in Guernica on 7 October 1936, but had no opportunity to organize his state as five months later the Franco nationalists, with German and Italian support, launched an offensive in north-western Spain. Guernica was virtually destroyed by bombs dropped by Heinkel 111 and Junkers 52 bombers on 27 April 1937. With the fall of Bilbao on 18 June the Euzkadi Republic ceased to exist, although Aguirre maintained a government-in-exile in Barcelona, Gerona and, after Franco's final victory, in France. Franco consistently ignored Basque national sentiment, which became a powerful (though clandestine) political force again in the early 1970s. The refusal of the Spanish authorities to release political prisoners led in 1974 to terrorist outrages and, at the end of the year, to a strike movement throughout the Basque provinces. The relaxation of tension after the accession of King Juan Carlos In November 1975 permitted open championship of 'Euzkadi' claims although the Basque extremist organization (ETA) continued to seek independence through a campaign of terrorism. On 31 December 1977 the Spanish Government promised the Basques a condition of 'pre-autonomy', pending the promulgation of a new constitution. The establishment of a Basque parliament, elected on 9 March 1980, failed to satisfy militants who demanded self-determination and the incorporation of neighbouring Navarre in the Basque region. Outrages continued in the Bilbao–San Sebastian area, in Madrid in April 1986, and as distant as Seville in June 1986 and Barcelona a year later. Anti-terrorist campaigns by Spanish security forces (with French cooperation) led to the capture and imprisonment of most separatist leaders during 1991–2, but occasional outrages continued: a car bomb in Madrid killed six people in December 1995; a judge was assassinated two months later; and at midsummer 1996 fire bombs threatened the Spanish tourist industry. By January 1998 more than 750 people had died in twenty-four years of intermittent terrorism.

Batistá, Fulgencio (1901–73), Cuban right-wing dictator. Born in Oriente province, Cuba, joined the army rising to the rank of sergeant before participating in a military *coup* against President Machado, which allowed Batistá to promote himself colonel and to establish a fascist-inspired corporative state in Cuba. But Batistá remained unpredictable. In 1937 he permitted the foundation of rival political parties and held reasonably free elections in 1939, when he was elected President. He remained in power until 1944, when he decided not to perpetuate his term of office and went voluntarily into exile in the Dominican Republic. In 1952 General Batistá returned to power by means of another military *coup d'état*, suspended the constitution and established a one-party dictatorship. From December 1956 onwards Batistá was faced by a left-wing partisan movement, led by Fidel ➤Castro in the mountains. The corrupt and oppressive character of the Batistá regime lost him all support in the army and on 31 December 1958 he was forced to flee to the Dominican Republic, totally discredited.

Battle of Britain. ➤Britain, Battle of.

Battle of the Atlantic. ➤Atlantic, Battle of the.

Bay of Pigs Incident. On 17 April 1961 a force of 1,500 Cuban exiles, led by José Cardona, landed at Cochinos Bay ('the Bay of Pigs') in southern Cuba in an attempt to overthrow the government of Fidel ➤Castro. The project was planned by the American ➤CIA during the last months of the Eisenhower Administration. Originally it was intended to give the landing force American air support, but this proposal was vetoed by President Kennedy when he heard of the planned invasion shortly after his inauguration. The exiles assured the CIA that the Cubans would rise against Castro. No rising took place and the whole operation was a fiasco. By 20 April the invaders had been killed or captured. Castro's prestige and popularity rose rapidly because of his victory against the invaders. At the same time the incident made him turn naturally to Soviet Russia. Kennedy, though accepting responsibility for the failure of the Cuban raid, emphasized to his aides the need for strict presidential control of the CIA and its activity overseas.

BBC. Until 1922 ➤broadcasting in Britain, as elsewhere, was largely experimental, with three companies (Marconi, Metropolitan-Vickers and Western Electric) competing for novel ways of presenting music and the spoken word. To avoid conflict and confusion a 'British Broadcasting Company' (BBC) was formed in October 1922, under the auspices of the Postmaster-General and the management of John Reith, who remained as director-general of the BBC until June 1938. His ideal of unobtrusive public service, turning a novelty into a responsible institution, was acknowledged by the royal charter which transformed the 'Company' into the 'Corporation' on 1 January 1927. During his sixteen years of office Reith stamped his personality on the character of British radio: nothing disturbingly controversial; much to bring comfort and courage into the home; a raising of public standards in music and drama; the encouragement of a uniform Christian

morality; dignity with brightness, except on the Sabbath. Reith was largely responsible for moving the BBC from commercial studios on Savoy Hill to the architec-
turally imposing Broadcasting House in Portland Place: the first broadcast from
this *templum artium et musarum* (as it is called in an entrance-hall inscription) took
place on 15 March 1932 – Henry Hall conducting the BBC Dance Orchestra.
Throughout the 1930s and 1940s, the BBC had a social influence unique among
the media of the democratic states, seeking to standardize English pronunciation
as well as to fulfil a moral and cultural mission. An 'Empire Service' for Australasia,
India and Canada began transmission from a new station at Daventry in December
1932: Arabic, Spanish, German, Italian and French broadcasts were, however, not
begun until 1938, partly because the BBC continued to see itself as a source of
information rather than as an instrument for ➤propaganda. Respect for the BBC's
high standards of responsible broadcasting increased its effectiveness as the wartime
'voice of Britain'. With the return of peace, the role of the BBC rapidly changed.
Regular programmes of ➤television had been relayed from Alexandra Palace from
November 1936 to September 1939 and were resumed on 7 June 1946, with some
12,000 viewers. By 1960 nearly 10 million people held television licences while
fewer than 5 million held sound-broadcasting-only licences. In attempting to satisfy
visual, as well as aural, needs, the BBC gradually freed itself from a didactic legacy
which was no longer generally acceptable to the public's taste. The formation of
an Independent Television Authority in 1954 and the subsequent competition
from commercial channels (September 1955 onwards) helped to mellow the
institutional character of the BBC. Highbrow and lowbrow programmes were
segregated to a greater extent than in Reith's time, and controversy and confrontation encouraged rather than eschewed. Yet the basic assumption that the BBC
was concerned with a 'public' and not with a 'market' remained valid.

Beaverbrook, Lord (William Maxwell Aitken, 1879–1964; knighted 1911, created
a baron 1917). Newspaper magnate and political champion of the British Empire.
Max Aitken was born in Maple, Ontario, the son of a Scottish Presbyterian minister.
By the age of thirty he had made a fortune by purchasing and amalgamating
Canadian cement-mills. He emigrated to England in September 1910, establishing
a close friendship with the Conservative leader Bonar ➤Law, who like himself was
born in a New Brunswick manse. Within three months of settling in England.
Aitken was elected Conservative MP for Ashton-under-Lyne, receiving his knighthood in the coronation honours the following summer. In 1915–16 Aitken served
as Canadian representative on the western front, returning to Westminster where
he used his energy to help overthrow the Asquith coalition and bring Lloyd George
to power as Prime Minister in December 1916. Aitken was raised to the peerage
(against the wishes of King George V) a month later and became Chancellor of
the Duchy of Lancaster and Minister of Information in 1918. At the end of the
war Beaverbrook left public office and rapidly built up a newspaper empire, based
on the *Daily Express* which he had purchased early in 1917. He continued to

support Bonar Law, helping him bring down the coalition in October 1922, but did not accept political office again until he entered Churchill's war cabinet in August 1940. Beaverbrook had a missionary zeal in imperial politics, vigorously campaigning in his newspapers for 'Empire Free Trade', and strong prejudices. He consistently regarded Baldwin as a political enemy and in the ➤abdication crisis supported Edward VIII, favouring a morganatic marriage. His relentless dynamism was ably harnessed by Churchill whom he served as Minister of Aircraft Production (1940–41), Minister of Supply (1941–2) and Lord Privy Seal (1943–5) as well as heading the first top-level Anglo-American mission to Moscow in 1941 and serving as British Lend-Lease administrator in the USA in 1942. For much of the war Beaverbrook was Churchill's closest friend, but he distrusted the ideas and personality of ➤Bevin and ➤Cripps, later turning against any public figures concerned with the establishment of an independent India and Pakistan. Beaverbrook was also a gifted, but hardly dispassionate, historian of the contemporary political scene.

Begin, Menachem (1913–92). Israeli Prime Minister. Born in Brest-Litovsk and educated at Warsaw University before being held for several months in a Siberian concentration camp after the Russians occupied eastern Poland in 1939. He succeeded in emigrating in the winter or 1941–2 and reached Palestine where he became a leader of ➤Irgun Zvai Leumi, the extremists who blew up Jerusalem's King David Hotel in July 1946. Begin was a member of the Knesset from 1948 and minister without portfolio in the Levi Eshkol Government from 1967 to 1970. From 1973 onwards he led the right-wing *Likud* (Unity) Party which won the elections of May 1977. Begin became Prime Minister on 21 June 1977. His premiership was marked by a constant struggle against the ➤Palestine Liberation Organization in southern ➤Lebanon, by an assertion of Israeli control over the predominantly Arab towns on the west bank of the Jordan, by high inflation, and by the relaxation of tension with Egypt, following the ➤Sadat Initiative of November 1977. Begin – the one-time Irgun terrorist – accepted the Nobel Peace Prize for 1978, awarded jointly to himself and President Sadat for their work for an Israeli–Egyptian peace settlement. In July 1981 Begin gained a narrow victory in a general election. He retired into private life in September 1983 and was succeeded by his Likud colleague, Yitzhak Shamir.

Belarus. A sovereign republic within the ➤Commonwealth of Independent States, capital Minsk. From the thirteenth century until 1772 the region formed part of Lithuania–Poland. It was then integrated in the tsarist empire, as 'White Russia', but developed a separate national consciousness at the start of the twentieth century and sought recognition as the Byelorussian National Republic in March 1918. But the Red Army occupied Minsk in January 1919 and the region formed the Byelorussian Soviet Socialist Republic until the collapse of the Soviet Union. Belarus asserted a sovereign status on 27 July 1990; formal independence came a year later. The economy was, however, so dependent on its ex-Soviet neighbours that Belarus always needed support within the Commonwealth of Independent

States. The election of Alexander Lukashenko as President in July 1994 was followed in May 1995 by a referendum which backed economic union with Russia and enabled the President to appoint ministers and exercise virtual dictatorial authority. Meetings between Lukashenko and ➤Yeltsin in April 1996 tightened the political and economic links between Minsk and Moscow.

Belgian Congo. In 1885 a conference of the great European Powers at Berlin recognized the area south of the Congo River in equatorial Africa as the 'Congo Free State', a huge territory in the personal possession of King Leopold II of the Belgians (reigned 1865–1909), who had been the principal shareholder of a Belgian company which established trading stations on the Lower Congo between 1879 and 1884. An agitation in Britain and the USA in 1903–4, complaining of the ill-treatment of the natives in the Congo, forced Leopold to hand over his 'Free State' to the Belgian Government which, from November 1908 to June 1960, administered the territory (which was eighty times as large as Belgium) as a colony. The Belgians continued to deny the native population political rights until 1956 when a small group of Africans were given the vote. The Belgian Congo remained backward despite the rich mineral resources of ➤Katanga. Riots in the capital, Léopoldville, in January 1959 marked the belated spread to the colony of African national feeling. The threat of further disorders led the Belgians to summon a round-table conference in Brussels at the end of January 1960 which decided on independence within six months. This precipitate act left the native politicians dependent upon tribal rather than national support. When the Congo Republic was established (30 June 1960) there was chaos, and the ➤'Congo Problem' remained a matter of deep concern for the United Nations until 1964. In October 1971 the native word ➤'Zaire' replaced the unpopular 'Congo' as the name both of the republic and its principal river.

Belgium. An independent kingdom since 1831. The Treaty of London of 1839 affirmed that Belgium was 'an independent and perpetually neutral state' under the collective guarantee of Britain, France, Prussia, Russia and Austria. The entry of German troops into Belgium in August 1914 led King ➤Albert to appeal for help from the other signatories of this treaty. He received support from the British and French; throughout the First World War a small segment of the country remained in Belgian hands. The rapid development of industry made Belgium between the wars the most densely populated country in Europe. On 10 May 1940 Germany again invaded Belgium: after eighteen days of resistance Leopold III (1901–83, reigned 1934–51) ordered his army to capitulate. While Leopold remained a prisoner of war, his government went into exile and continued to fight with the allies. Leopold's conduct weakened the prestige of the monarchy and in July 1951 the King abdicated in favour of his son Baudouin (1930–93). Internally Belgium has suffered from the communal strife between the French-speaking minority, the Walloons (45 per cent of the population), and the Flemish majority, whose language was only recognized legally and administratively in 1920. In July

1971 constitutional amendments were passed by the Belgian parliament in an effort to safeguard the cultural and political rights of the two linguistic communities. Subsequently these safeguards were extended to the small German-speaking minority around ➤Eupen-Malmédy. This movement towards a federalist kingdom has, since 1948, run parallel with increasing international cooperation, marked originally by ➤Benelux and later by the establishment in Brussels of the European Commission, the European Council of Ministers and (since March 1967) the headquarters of the ➤North Atlantic Treaty Organization.

Belize. An independent republic within the British Commonwealth. The earliest British settlers came to Belize in Charles I's reign and established a tenuous foothold in Central America despite Spanish incursions. Spain recognized the British occupation in 1798, the settlement becoming the colony of 'British Honduras' in 1862 although remaining administratively subordinate to Jamaica until 1884. In 1946 the Attlee Government offered to refer the territorial claims of Belize's western neighbour, Guatemala, to the International Court of Justice but the Guatemalans rejected the proposal. In 1964 a new constitution gave the colony self-government, the name being changed from British Honduras to Belize in 1973. A constitutional conference in London in April 1981 completed the process of decolonization and Belize became formally independent on 21 September 1981. Guatemala cut off consular relations with Britain in protest at the creation of the republic; a British force of 1,800 men, with naval and air support, remained in Belize to safeguard independence.

Ben Bella, Mohammed Ahmed (1916–), leader of the Algerian national revolution. Born at Maghnia, on the Algerian frontier with Morocco; served in the French Army during the Second World War. In 1947 he became leader of the extremist Algerian national movement, the 'Special Organization'. He was arrested and imprisoned by the French in 1950 but escaped to Cairo in March 1952 where he founded and directed the FLN (National Liberation Front) which began the ➤Algerian War with France two years later. During the ➤Suez Crisis of October 1956 the French authorities persuaded a Moroccan airliner, on which Ben Bella was travelling from Cairo to Tunis, to fly on to Algiers, where Ben Bella was arrested and imprisoned in France until March 1962. He was released in order to conclude the ➤Évian Agreements with the French. On his return to Algeria he became Prime Minister of the provisional government in September 1962, defeating his rivals and being elected the first President of the Algerian Republic in April 1963. He established a personal government, similar in character to Nasser's system in Egypt, but was less Pan-Arab in sentiment than some of his supporters and remained reluctant to establish close ties with the Soviet Union. On 19 June 1965 he was overthrown in a military *coup d'état* led by his Minister of Defence, Colonel Houari ➤Boumédienne and was kept under house arrest until July 1979 when he was exiled to France. He resumed political activity in Algeria in 1990 as leader of the MDA ('Movement for a Democratic Algeria').

Benelux. A form of collaboration between Belgium, the Netherlands and Luxembourg, which became effective with the establishment of a customs union on 1 January 1948. In the late 1950s the three governments agreed on joint commercial relations with other countries and for the free movement of capital, goods and people between their respective states. This agreement was embodied in an Economic Union which came into force on 1 November 1960, supporting collaboration already achieved within the Common Market (►European Economic Community).

Beneš, Eduard (1884–1948), Czechoslovak President. Born into a peasant family at Kozlany, Bohemia, educated at the Universities of Prague, Dijon and Paris (where he gained a doctorate in sociology). He escaped from Austria–Hungary in 1915 and returned to Paris where he joined T.G. ►Masaryk in the movement for Czechoslovak independence. By his considerable powers of persuasion he enlisted the support of several eminent French politicians for the Czech cause. From 1918 to 1935 he was Foreign Minister of Czechoslovakia, building up the ►Little Entente and developing close ties with France and the Soviet Union. He also worked ardently for the League of Nations, and he served briefly as Czechoslovak Prime Minister in 1921–2. When President Masaryk retired in December 1935 Beneš succeeded him as Czechoslovakia's head of state but the ►Munich Agreement of 1938 seemed to him so grave a betrayal by the West that he resigned office and went into voluntary exile. In 1940 he became head of a Czechoslovak provisional government in London, although his administration did not receive full recognition by the British authorities until 18 July 1941. He visited Moscow in 1943, trying to act as an arbiter and interpreter of East to West; but for this independent role he was treated with some suspicion both in London and Washington. In March 1945 he again flew from London to Moscow and accompanied the Russian-sponsored Czechoslovak Corps of General ►Svoboda back through Slovakia to Brno and Prague. He remained President for three years, scrupulously observing the letter of the constitution despite the spread throughout the administration of a communist influence alien to him. In February 1948 Klement ►Gottwald established a government in which the key posts were held by communists. Beneš sought at first to keep the Presidency neutral but he finally resigned on 6 June 1948 when it was clear Gottwald wished to introduce a Russian-style political system. He died, a broken man, three months later.

Ben-Gurion, David (1886–1973), first Prime Minister of Israel. Born David Green, in Plonsk, Russian Poland, emigrated to Palestine in 1906, working in farming settlements and becoming an enthusiastic supporter of ►Zionism. He strongly favoured the acceptance of Hebrew as the Jewish national language, changing his name to Ben-Gurion in 1910. After working on the editorial staff of a Zionist periodical he studied law at the Universities of Salonika and Constantinople. He was exiled from Turkey for his Zionist activities and subsequently served in a Jewish battalion of the British Army fighting against the Turks in Palestine.

From 1921 to 1933 he was secretary-general of the Jewish Labour Federation in Palestine and in 1930 he became leader of the Mapai Party, the principal socialist group among the Palestine Zionists. In 1935 he became chairman of the ►Jewish Agency, a post he held for thirteen years, thereby gaining the administrative experience which made him a natural choice as Prime Minister when the state of ►Israel was proclaimed on 14 May 1948. His two terms (1948–53 and 1955–63) were overshadowed by the Arab–Israeli conflicts, but he was able to achieve much of the industrial and agricultural programme of reform he had proposed before independence. Although retiring in 1963, he returned to active politics in 1965 to lead a breakaway group of old Mapai Party members (the Rafi), critical of Golda ►Meir but including General ►Dayan among its spokesmen.

Bennett, Richard Bedford (1870–1947, created Viscount Bennett 1941), Canadian statesman. Born in New Brunswick, made a fortune as a lawyer and businessman in western and central Canada, became leader of the Canadian Conservative Party in 1927, winning a clear majority in the election of July 1930 and remaining Prime Minister until October 1935. Bennett's strength and weakness lay in his masterful personality: to an electorate alarmed by the world economic recession he gave a reassuring impression of firm confidence in Canada's imperial connection; but he had scant regard for the views of others, whether they were cabinet colleagues or provincial premiers chafing under his centralism. His vigorous advocacy of 'Empire Free Trade' (►imperial preference) led in the summer of 1932 to the ►Ottawa Conference over which he presided. Although the Conference gained for Canada a privileged market in the United Kingdom, Bennett's success was offset by resentment at the way in which he was building up and extending the powers of the civil service within the Canadian federation. In January 1935 Bennett announced drastic reforms which seemed to the Canadians reminiscent of Roosevelt's ►'New Deal'. That autumn the voters turned against federalized social and economic legislation, decisively defeating Bennett and ensuring that the ►Liberal Party dominated Canadian politics for the next twenty-two years.

Beria, Lavrenti Pavlovich (1899–1953), Soviet commissar. Born in Merkheuli, Georgia. When the Russian Revolution began Beria was at college in Baku, where he organized a Bolshevik group. From 1921 to 1931 he directed secret police activity in Georgia, eventually becoming first secretary of the Georgian Communist Party. His fellow Georgian, Stalin, appointed Beria Commissar for Internal Affairs in December 1938, and he was in charge of the NKVD, the Soviet security service, until after Stalin's death in March 1953. Beria was feared by the other leading Soviet Communists (especially ►Molotov and ►Khrushchev) who believed he was planning to succeed Stalin and that he had deliberately hastened Stalin's death. The exact fate of Beria is not clear: it was announced on 10 July 1953 that he had been dismissed from office and at the end of the year that he had been tried and shot as a traitor, but it is possible he was executed, without the formality of a trial, as early as June.

Berlin. Capital of the Prussian kingdom since 1701 and of a unified Germany since 1871. Berlin was entered by the Red Army on 21 April 1945, the whole city being in Russian hands by 1 May. Subsequently, in accordance with agreements made at ➤Yalta, the three western allies were given zones of occupation in the city and allowed access along specific corridors from Western Germany. In 1946–7 tension mounted between the western allies and the Soviet authorities, originally over elections in Berlin but subsequently over the introduction of a new currency in West Germany, which the Russians declined to accept in Berlin. The Russians maintained that these developments did not accord with the wartime agreements and, to emphasize their control of Berlin, imposed restrictions on rail traffic coming to the city from the west on 30 March 1948. Three months later they followed up this move by halting all road traffic from the west, thereby effectively blockading Berlin. The Americans and British responded by organizing an airlift which flew in food and fuel as well as men and mail. The fortitude of the Berliners in the winter of 1948–9 and the courageous initiative of the American and British air crews convinced the Russians that they could not unilaterally determine the future of Berlin without risking a general war. In February 1949 the Russians and the western allies began secret talks over the Berlin crisis and the blockade was lifted in May, although the airlift continued until September in case the Russians suddenly re-imposed restrictions. The Berlin blockade has a double historical significance: it showed the determination of the Americans to keep their advance-posts deep in Europe; and it marked the virtual division of Berlin, and ultimately of Germany, into two administrative units. For twelve years after the lifting of the blockade inter-allied tension was less apparent in Berlin. The West sought to build up the British, American and French sectors as showplaces of capitalism while the Soviet Union encouraged the East Germans to regard the Soviet sector as part of the ➤German Democratic Republic, establishing the government offices of the GDR in Pankow, a district of north Berlin only five miles from the centre of the historic capital. The contrast in living standards between the eastern and western sectors led to strikes and rioting in East Berlin in June 1953 and to a constant stream of refugees, fleeing to the West. This drain on the GDR's economic resources led ➤Krushchev in November 1958 to demand the withdrawal of all occupation forces from Berlin, a move seen in the West as a preliminary to incorporation of the whole of the city in the GDR. No positive action was taken until the summer of 1961, when the Russians proposed to hand over all Berlin's access routes to East German control. On 13 August 1961 the East German security forces suddenly sealed off sixty-eight of the eighty crossing points in Berlin, erecting overnight a barrier of barbed wire and, in places, of concrete across the city and restricting all interzonal movements. The British and the Americans protested at the erection of this 'Berlin Wall' and a powerful American tank division was moved to Berlin as a sign of the determination in the West to maintain a military presence in the city. Freer access to West Berlin was conceded by the East Germans early in November

1989; sections of the Berlin Wall were breached. The first unified Berlin city assembly met on 11 January 1991.

Berlin–Baghdad Railway. In 1899 a German company, with government encouragement, received a concession from the Turks to construct a railway from the Bosphorus to the Persian Gulf. This project was given the grandiose title 'Berlin–Baghdad Railway' since German interests already dominated the railways of south-eastern Europe and had been active in Asia Minor for six years. The Russians (who themselves had plans for Persian railways) were angered by the project, but it met with a divided reception in Britain, some seeing a potential menace to India in a German-dominated port on the Gulf but others favouring it as a means of entangling Germany and Russia. Opinion in London hardened against the project with the conclusion of the ►Anglo-Russian Entente and with further Turkish concessions to Germany. Russo-German differences were settled by an agreement in 1911, and a further agreement, early in 1914, satisfied the main objections of the British and French. Although the railway increased Turkey's dependence on Germany and thereby helped determine the Sultan's reaction to the coming of war in 1914, the project was, on the whole, a comparatively minor irritant in Anglo-German relations. Two important sections of the line had not been constructed by the outbreak of war.

Berlusconi, Silvio (1936–), Italian Prime Minister. Born in Milan, by the age of thirty he was a property magnate. He later gained control of a chain of retail stores and extensive media interests, including 90 per cent of Italian commercial television. In October 1993 Berlusconi founded a political movement, *Forza Italia* (FI), which joined other right-wing parties in a 'Freedom Alliance'. Berlusconi's influence as a media tycoon enabled the Freedom Alliance to win 322 out of 630 seats in the parliamentary election of March 1994, and on 20 May Berlusconi became Prime Minister, promising tax reform, the creation of a million new jobs, and the recovery of national pride. He could not, however, provide employment on such a scale, and became unpopular because he sought to advance his own nominees in state television and the Bank of Italy, as well as allegedly seeking to restrict the power of magistrates investigating corruption. His government fell on 21 December 1994. Although veteran politicians continued to smear Berlusconi's name, a national referendum backed his right to retain control of three commercial television channels. In December 1997 he was sentenced to sixteen months' imprisonment for false accounting and in July 1998 to another twenty-eight months for illegal party financing. The start of a long appeals process kept him out of prison and, despite these convictions and the prospect of five further trials, he remained the leader of the FI.

Bernadotte, Count Folke (1895–1948), nephew of King Gustavus V of Sweden and great-great-grandson of Marshal Jean-Baptiste Bernadotte, the French soldier who ruled as Charles XIV of Sweden from 1818 to 1844. Folke Bernadotte entered the Swedish Army but in his early twenties became interested in the work of the Red Cross movement and helped in exchanges of war prisoners during the closing phases of the First World War. Between the wars Count Bernadotte continued his close association with the Red Cross and encouraged the spread of the Boy Scout movement. During the Second World War he arranged exchanges of sick and disabled prisoners of war at Gothenburg in October 1943 and September 1944. In February 1945 ►Himmler used Bernadotte as an intermediary to seek the surrender of German forces to the British and Americans, while continuing to resist the Russians. This proposal was rejected in London and Washington. As President of the Swedish Red Cross, Count Bernadotte was in May 1948 invited by his friend Trygve ►Lie, the UN Secretary-General, to serve as United Nations Mediator in Palestine, seeking to enforce a truce between Arabs and Jews. On 17 September 1948 Bernadotte was assassinated in Palestine by Jewish terrorists.

Bernstein, Eduard (1850–1932), German socialist. Born in Berlin but lived for many years in Switzerland and in England where he met Marx and Engels and was influenced by the ►Fabian Society. Bernstein gained intellectual prominence in 1896–8 through articles which criticized the rigidity of Marxist theory. He thought that the collapse of capitalism was more distant than Marx had maintained, and he developed the theory of ►'revisionism', arguing that German workers had a duty to seek reform within the existing system rather than to precipitate revolution. His views were condemned at the German Social Democrat Party's congresses at Hanover in 1899 and Dresden in 1903 and were attacked by both Lenin and Stalin as early as 1901. Bernstein's outstanding opponent on the German Left before the First World War was ►Kautsky, but the two men later collaborated as anti-militarist independent socialists. Bernstein more than any other theorist was responsible for ensuring that revolutionary Marxism had an evolutionary social democratic alternative in the German-speaking lands.

Bessarabia. Historically, a disputed province lying between the rivers Pruth and Dniester, rich agriculturally and with a mixed population of Romanian and Ukrainian origin. Turks and Russian Tartars disputed the region until 1812, when the province was added to the Russian Empire. Southern Bessarabia was ceded to the future Romanian kingdom after Russia's defeat in the Crimean War (1856) but recovered by Russia in 1878. Bessarabia renounced Russian rule in February 1918 and two months later a local council at Kishinev proclaimed union of the province with Romania, a decision confirmed by the Paris Peace Conference in 1919 but never recognized by Soviet Russia (nor, indeed, by the USA). At the end of June 1940 the Russians sent an ultimatum to Romania demanding the cession of Bessarabia and the Romanians, isolated in eastern Europe by the overthrow of their former French ally, complied. Bessarabia was once again administered by the Romanians from July 1941 to March 1944 but was thereafter incorporated in the Moldavian Soviet Socialist Republic. Resentment at the loss of southern Bessarabia occasionally strained Soviet–Romanian relations in the post-Stalin era, notably in 1964–6, but there was never any prospect of further frontier revision in the area. The Moldavian SSR became the independent republic of ►Moldova in 1991.

Bethmann Hollweg, Theobald von (1856–1921), German Chancellor. Born at Hohenfinow, Brandenburg, studied law and became a civil servant. He was Prussian Minister of the Interior (1905–7), accepting similar responsibilities in Germany as a whole from 1907 to July 1909 when he succeeded ►Bülow as fifth Chancellor of the Reich. By training and temperament Bethmann was a doctrinaire bureaucrat, personally loyal to Kaiser ►William II but inexperienced in foreign affairs and under pressure from both Admiral ►Tirpitz and the army leaders. Bethmann wished to modernize the constitution but believed he could only carry through reforms if he could count on the Kaiser's support, for which a success in foreign affairs was essential. From 1909 to 1913 he sought an understanding with the British. When this policy failed (mainly through naval rivalry) Bethmann chose the dangerous alternative of seeking victory in a short, localized war. He argued that sooner or later war would anyhow be forced on Germany by her neighbours and he believed, in 1914, that he could still count on British neutrality. When he realized a general continental war (not a localized conflict) was imminent, he tried vainly to reverse his policy. During the war Bethmann succeeded in delaying an unrestricted U-boat campaign for two and a half years, rightly fearing it would bring America into the conflict. In July 1917 Bethmann was forced out of office by threats of resignation from ►Hindenburg and ►Ludendorff, who then established a virtual military dictatorship. Subsequently most historians have regarded Bethmann as a weak politician who stumbled into war through sheer incapacity; but in 1961 a Hamburg professor, Fritz Fischer (born 1908), published a book, *Grif nach der Weltmacht*, in which he argued that Bethmann sought consciously to achieve German domination of Europe through war. Fischer cited in particular a memorandum by Bethmann on war aims, dated 9 September 1914. Many younger historians accepted this interpretation, but throughout the 1960s an acrimonious and unresolved academic debate continued in the German universities and Press.

Bevan, Aneurin (1897–1960). Born in Tredegar, Monmouthshire, the son of a miner, left school at thirteen and worked on the coal-face, rapidly advancing in trade-union politics until by 1926 he was spokesman for the miners of South Wales in the General Strike. From 1929 until his death he was MP for Ebbw Vale, first as a member of the Independent Labour Party, but within the Labour Party from 1931. He was a skilful orator, in the radical tradition, trenchant in debate. During the Second World War he was the most constructive of Churchill's critics in the House of Commons. As Minister of Health from 1945 to 1951 Bevan introduced and pioneered the ►National Health Service. He became Minister of Labour in January 1951 but on 21 April resigned from the cabinet (together with Harold ►Wilson) in protest at the imposition of health-service charges to meet defence costs. The 'Bevanite' Left, which he led from 1951 to 1956–7, criticized high defence expenditure (particularly on nuclear arms) and opposed the reformist wing in the Labour Party, represented by ➤Gaitskell who defeated Bevan in the contest for Labour leadership in December 1955. In the following year Bevan became chief Labour spokesman on foreign affairs, speaking brilliantly in the debates on the ➤Suez Crisis and at the Labour Party Conference of 1957, when he opposed demands by the former Bevanites for unilateral renunciation by the British of the hydrogen bomb. He became deputy leader of the Labour Party in 1959, but was already a sick man and died the following summer.

Beveridge Report. A *Report on Social Insurance and Allied Services*, written by the Master of University College, Oxford, Sir William Beveridge (1879–1963) and published on 1 December 1942. The Report proposed a comprehensive scheme of social insurance 'from the cradle to the grave' in order to check the old evils of capitalist society – poverty and mass unemployment. Beveridge personally was a Liberal but the Report aroused great enthusiasm in the Labour Party. When the Report was debated in the House of Commons on 18 February 1943 Labour members considered the Churchill coalition was treating it with indifference. Against the orders of their leaders, they criticized the government, the biggest parliamentary 'revolt' between 1940 and 1945. Subsequently the principles of the Beveridge Report formed a basis for the social legislation of the Labour Government, 1945–50, notably the ➤National Health Service.

Bevin, Ernest (1881–1951). Born on the Somerset–Devon border. After serving as a farm labourer Bevin moved to Bristol, where he became a carter, working in close touch with the dockers. In 1911 he became assistant secretary of the Dockers' Union, building up its power in the difficult period of syndicalist disturbances. Ten years later he had achieved such respect that he was able to unite nearly fifty unions into the largest in the world, the Transport and General Workers' Union. Bevin became famous in the first instance by his able presentation of the dockers' case before wage tribunals but he subsequently won respect for his gifts of conciliation and compromise within the trade-union movement, and by his international outlook. From 1925 to 1940 he was prominent in the TUC General Council, of which he was chairman in 1937. He undertook a tour of the Commonwealth in 1938–9, helping to improve labour relations with the overseas dominions. In May 1940, although not then an MP, he was appointed Minister of Labour in Churchill's coalition, with the responsibility for the organization of the British working effort throughout the war. In July 1945 he became Foreign Secretary in Attlee's Labour Government and held the post until March 1951, five weeks before his death. As Foreign Secretary he was responsible for the prompt acceptance of the ➤Marshall Plan, for the Brussels Treaty of 1948 and for supporting the creation of NATO in April 1949. On his own initiative he summoned a conference of Commonwealth Foreign Ministers in February 1950 from which emerged the ➤Colombo Plan. Bevin's sense of Commonwealth unity made him oppose schemes for the integration of the European states. Within his own party he was criticized for suspicion of the communist Left in Europe and hostility to Israeli claims in disputes over ➤Palestine.

Bhutto, Benazir (1955–), Pakistani Prime Minister. Born in Karachi, the daughter of Z.A. ➤Bhutto. She completed her education in Oxford, at Lady Margaret Hall, and remained in Europe after her father's execution. She returned to Pakistan in April 1986 as an avowed, and popular, leader of the opposition to President ➤Zia, re-establishing her father's political movement, the Pakistan People's Party (PPP), which won elections held in November 1988, three months after Zia's death. Benazir Bhutto (who married Asif Ali Zardar in 1987) took office as Prime Minister on 2 December 1988: she brought Pakistan back into the Commonwealth in October 1989; became the first Prime Minister to give birth to a child; and encouraged a westernized approach to government and social problems. These policies lost her support in traditionalist rural areas. The PPP was defeated in the elections of November 1990. Benazir Bhutto returned to office after success in a further election in October 1993, but her hold on the outlying provinces, where Islamic fundamentalism was strong, remained tenuous. Allegations of PPP corruption and attempts to influence the judiciary led President Farooq Leghari to dismiss the government on 5 November 1996. A subsequent General Election on 3 February 1997 was won by the Muslim League. Relatively few electors bothered to vote; it was clear that Benazir Bhutto had lost the popular appeal she enjoyed ten years earlier.

Bhutto, Zulfiqar Ali (1928–79). Member of an aristocratic Rajput family, educated in California and at Christ Church, Oxford, briefly teaching international law at Southampton University before returning to Pakistan to practise as a barrister. Served in a number of internal ministries under President ➤Ayub Khan between 1958 and 1963, when he became Foreign Minister. He improved Sino-Pakistani relations and took a strong line towards India over the ➤Kashmir problem but resigned in 1966 because he did not approve of the Indo-Pakistan truce agreed at Tashkent. In 1967 he established a People's Party, pledged to a form of Muslim socialism and strongly anti-Indian in character. The People's Party won a majority of seats in the Pakistan Assembly in December 1970, and when Pakistan was defeated a year later in the war with India over ➤Bangladesh, Bhutto became President, the first non-soldier to hold the post since the creation of Pakistan. When Britain, Australia and New Zealand recognized the independence of Bangladesh, Bhutto took Pakistan out of the Commonwealth (30 January 1972). At home he carried through basic reforms, including nationalization of major industries, and in the summer of 1973 he introduced a new constitution which made the Prime Minister, rather than the President, effective chief executive. He resigned the Presidency in August 1973, taking office as Prime Minister and minister responsible for defence, foreign affairs and atomic energy. Accusations of ballot-rigging in the election of March 1977 led to hostile demonstrations and riots during the following spring and summer, and he was overthrown by a military *coup d'état* on 5 July

1977. Two months later he was arrested on a charge of conspiracy to murder and was sentenced to death (18 March 1978). He was hanged on 4 April 1979. His daughter Benazir ►Bhutto formed her first government nine and a half years after her father's execution.

Biafra. The inter-tribal conflict in the Federation of ►Nigeria led on 30 May 1967 to the secession of the predominantly Ibo eastern region, which was proclaimed the independent republic of Biafra by the former military governor of the area, Colonel Odumegwa Ojukwu (1933–). The Nigerian President, General Gowon, sent troops into Biafra in July. Earlier Biafran military successes were countered by a Nigerian thrust which captured the Biafran capital of Enugu in September and the important base of Port Harcourt on 19 May 1968. The civil war (in which the British sent supplies to the federal forces while the French supported Biafra) dragged on for another twenty months since the Nigerians had difficulty in occupying and policing the captured towns and main roads. Eventually Biafran resistance collapsed in January 1970, with the flight of Colonel Ojukwu to the Ivory Coast. The area was divided into three states, under military administration.

Bidault, Georges (1899–1976). Born at Moulins, served as General de Gaulle's chief political leader with the Resistance and was present in Paris when the city rose against the German occupation forces on 19 August 1944. Bidault helped found the MRP (Mouvement Républicain Populaire), a moderate socialist party, and served twice as Prime Minister under the Fourth Republic as well as holding office as Foreign Minister. The ►Algerian War induced him to take a firm stand with the French colonial settlers and to move politically to the Right. He favoured the return to power of de Gaulle in 1958, but later bitterly opposed his attempts to settle the Algerian problem. In April 1961 he identified himself with the OAS (►Organisation de l'Armée Secrète), which brought terrorist extremism into French political life. Under threat of arrest for treason, Bidault escaped to Brazil in April 1963 and did not return to France until the summer of 1968, when the warrant was withdrawn.

Björkö, Treaty of (24 July 1905). An abortive Treaty signed by Kaiser William II and Tsar Nicholas II when they exchanged courtesy visits to each other's yachts moored off Björkö in southern Finland. The Treaty, an exercise in personal diplomacy on the part of the Kaiser, provided for a Russo-German defensive alliance against attack by any other power in Europe. The agreement was opposed by the Russian foreign office, because it appeared to them unacceptable to Russia's ally, France. It was also opposed by the German Chancellor, ►Bülow, largely because he resented the Kaiser's initiative in diplomatic questions. Since Russia was dependent on financial aid from France, the subsequent Franco-German tension over the first ►Moroccan crisis removed any desire on the part of the Russians for a treaty of this nature.

Black and Tans. The name given to the special additional members of the Royal Irish Constabulary recruited by the British authorities in 1920. The recruits wore dark green caps, almost black, with khaki tunics and trousers, and it was from this dress that they received their name (which was also the name of a familiar breed of Irish hounds). The Black and Tans were active in suppressing Irish national unrest between March 1920 and January 1922. They were provoked into excessively ill-disciplined reprisals by terrorist activity. The most serious action was at Balbriggan, near Dublin, in September 1920 when homes, public houses and a factory were wrecked and two Irishmen killed. Three months later they set fire to one of the main streets in Cork, destroying the County Hall and Library. These wild acts aroused a considerable outcry in Britain, especially in the Liberal Press, and in the USA.

Black Hand. The name generally given to a Serbian secret society, 'Unity or Death' (*Ujedinjenje ili Smrt*), formed in Belgrade in May 1911 to seek the union of the Serb minorities within Austria–Hungary and Turkey with their kinsfolk living in independent Serbia. Most members of the society were young army officers and they exerted great influence on Serbian policy in the Balkan Wars. In 1913–14 the Black Hand clashed with the Serbian Government over the method of administering the lands newly liberated from Turkey. The leader of the Black Hand, Colonel Dragutin Dimitrijević ('Apis'), authorized the training of a group of young Bosnians in terrorist activity and sent them back into Bosnia to assassinate the heir to the Austrian throne at ►Sarajevo on 28 June 1914, a crime assumed at the time to have been committed with the connivance of the Serbian Government. The Black Hand and the Serbian authorities continued in conflict after the outbreak of war. In December 1916 Dimitrijević and his chief associates were arrested by the Serbian authorities in exile at Salonika and accused of plotting the murder of the Serbian Prince Regent. After a highly irregular trial (June 1917) 'Apis' and two other Black Handers were shot and the society was broken up. An attempt was made to rehabilitate the reputation of the Black Hand in 1953 and the 1917 verdict was formally quashed by the Supreme Court in communist Serbia.

Black Power Movement. A radical offshoot of the ►Civil-Rights Movement in the USA, active from the mid-1960s until the late 1970s. The earliest effective militant activist in the movement was Malcolm X (1925–65), who drew his strength from a Black Muslim movement, founded in 1930 but led from 1934 until his death in 1975 by Elijah Muhammad. Black Power had no sympathy with the non-violence advocated by Martin Luther ►King, although it encouraged the registration of black voters and their participation in democratic elections. There were Black Power riots in Los Angeles, Detroit, Newark and Chicago during the years 1965–8. In the early 1970s the movement merged with other militant protest groups against the ►Vietnam War.

Blair, Tony (Anthony Charles Lynton) (1953–), British Prime Minister. Born in

Edinburgh, educated at Fettes School and St John's College, Oxford, becoming a barrister in 1976 and entering the Commons as Labour MP for Sedgefield in 1983. After serving as Opposition spokesman on energy and on employment he became shadow Home Secretary in 1992, under the party leadership of John Smith (1938– 94). Blair's popularity with the constituencies led to his election as leader of the ►Labour Party on 21 July 1994. Over the following two years he campaigned vigorously to create a 'New Labour' image, less subject to trade union influence and no longer committed to public ownership of the means of production, distribution and exchange, as proposed in Clause 4 of Labour's 1918 Constitution. New Labour won widespread popularity in the winter of 1996–7 and made 148 gains in the General Election of 1 May 1997. This landslide victory warmly endorsed Blair's slightly left of centre policies. He formed a government next day, with a majority of 177 in a House of Commons of 659 members. Much attention in his first year of office was given to Northern Ireland, with the ►Good Friday Accord of April 1998 holding some promise of peaceful constitutional progress.

Blériot, Louis (1872–1936), French pioneer airman. On 25 July 1909 Blériot became the first person to fly the English Channel, crossing from Calais to Dover in 37 minutes. The significance of the flight, as a challenge to Britain's traditional insularity, was readily apparent to the public, the War Office and the military staffs of the leading continental armies. Blériot's flight gave a fillip to aircraft development which was out of all proportion to the actual distance covered – twenty-six miles.

Blitzkrieg ('lightning war'). A German term originally applied to the rapid penetration in depth by armoured columns of tanks and tracked vehicles, a technique perfected by General ►Guderian in France in 1940. British newspaper usage distorted the meaning of the term, applying it to massive attacks from the air, notably the assault on London and other British cities at night from 7 September 1940 until 10 May 1941. 'The Blitz' of everyday speech in wartime Britain thus came to mean a sustained bombing offensive rather than the lightning campaign of Germany's military commentators.

Bloody Sunday. The term 'Bloody Sunday' was first used in radical literature to describe a clash between police and socialist demonstrators in Trafalgar Square, London, on 13 November 1887: Life Guards were summoned to clear the square and two of the crowd died from injuries. In Russian history, the term describes the incident in St Petersburg on 22 January 1905 when a procession of workers and their families, led by a priest, Father George Gapon, was fired on by troops guarding the Winter Palace as it was carrying a petition to the Tsar (who was not, in fact, in residence) asking for a political amnesty, the summoning of a Constituent Assembly, and an eight-hour working day: more than a hundred people were killed and several hundred wounded. The massacre led to strikes in many towns, thereby beginning the ►Revolution of 1905. The term 'Bloody Sunday' has also been applied to the events of 30 January 1972 when thirteen civilians were killed by troops in Londonderry during a demonstration in favour of a unified Ireland.

Blum, Léon (1872–1950), French statesman. Born in Paris, of Alsatian Jewish parentage, was respected in his twenties as an intellectual journalist, already distinguished as a dramatic critic (his younger brother, René, became an outstanding ballet impresario but was killed in Auschwitz concentration camp in 1942). Léon Blum joined the socialist group led by ➤Jaurès in 1899 but did not become a Deputy until 1919. In 1925 he was accepted as leader of the SFIO, the French Socialist Party. When he became head of the ➤'Popular Front' Government in June 1936 he was France's first socialist Prime Minister. He remained in office for twelve months, introducing social reforms which included the much-disputed '40-hour' week. Despite his determination to keep France's military potential up to Germany's level, he found the French industrialists uncooperative and was rapidly ousted when he returned for a few weeks of office in 1938. The ➤Vichy authorities imprisoned him in October 1940, putting him on trial at Riom in 1942 as one of the scapegoats for France's military unpreparedness, but he successfully turned the tables on his accusers. When the Germans occupied Vichy France he was sent to the concentration camps of Buchenwald and Dachau, remaining in custody until May 1945. He headed an economic mission to the United States in 1946, returning to serve briefly as Prime Minister (1946–7) and to ensure that the moderate, reformist ideas of the French socialists were reflected in the constitutional safeguards of the ➤Fourth Republic. Blum was also the author of several studies of literature, aesthetics and the problems of an intellectual in society, which are marked by incisive judgement and a natural elegance of style.

Boer War. The name given to the South African War of 1899–1902, fought between the British and the Boer descendants of Dutch settlers in southern Africa. The war was caused by the resentment of the Boers, under the leadership of ➤Kruger, at the colonial policy of Joseph ➤Chamberlain, which they feared would deprive the ➤Transvaal of its independence. Kruger hoped for sympathetic support in Europe, especially from Germany, but he failed to distinguish between encouragement and armed intervention (which never came). There were three main phases in the war: (1) October 1899 to January 1900, a series of Boer successes on the borders of Cape Colony and Natal, with British garrisons besieged in Ladysmith, Mafeking and Kimberley; (2) February–August 1900, British counter-offensives under Lord Roberts leading to the relief of the garrisons and the occupation of the Boer capital, Pretoria, on 5 June; (3) September 1900 to May 1902, a period of guerrilla warfare, with Kitchener trying to prevent Boer commandos from raiding isolated British units by erecting blockhouses and moving civilian sympathizers with the Boers into ➤concentration camps. The war was ended by the Treaty of ➤Vereeniging, May 1902.

Bokassa, Jean Bedel (1921–96), former ruler of the Central African Republic. Born at Bagandou in the Lobaye district of Ubanghi Shari, French Equatorial

Africa, and educated at missionary schools. He served in the French colonial army from 1939 to 1960, reaching the rank of Captain and being awarded the Legion of Honour and the Croix de Guerre. When Ubanghi Shari became the independent Central African Republic in August 1960, Bokassa transferred to the new army of the republic's first President, David Dacko. Colonel Bokassa overthrew the Dacko Government on 1 January 1966 and ruled the CAR as a capricious tyrant for thirteen years. In foreign affairs he saw himself as a Francophile, his professed friendship with ►Giscard d'Estaing later proving an embarrassment to the French President. Bokassa monopolized the offices of state, proclaimed himself a Marshal in 1974 and Emperor Bokassa I in December 1976, crowning himself a year later in a ceremony modelled on the Napoleonic coronations. His personal greed and repressive policies provoked unrest in his capital, Bangui, in the early months of 1979. School children were imprisoned for demonstrating against compulsory uniforms made in a factory which Bokassa himself owned. Reports reaching Paris that forty of these children had been killed in Bokassa's presence led President Giscard to order French troops to occupy Bangui on 21 September 1979 while Bokassa was in Libya. The French restored Dacko as President while Bokassa found sanctuary on the Ivory Coast. Bokassa was tried in absentia in December 1980 and sentenced to death on charges of murder, cannibalism, fraud and having intelligence contacts with Libya. He remained on the Ivory Coast, his claim that he was still a French citizen being firmly rejected in France's courts of law. In September 1986 he unexpectedly returned to Bangui and was arraigned in person. After a further trial the death sentence was commuted to life imprisonment.

Bolivia. Land-locked republic in central South America, rich in tin and other mineral deposits but with the majority of the Indian inhabitants (two-thirds of the population) living in abysmal poverty. The republic, named after the 'Liberator', Simón Bolívar (1783–1830), gained independence in 1825. Frontier disputes led to frequent wars in the nineteenth century. In the most serious conflict, the War of the Pacific (1879–84), the Bolivians were defeated by Chile, who then deprived Bolivia of her strip of Pacific sea-coast. Despite a treaty with Chile in 1904 giving railway access to the Pacific port of Arica, the Bolivians turned eastwards, hoping to improve communications down the Paraná river to the South Atlantic. This switch of policy led to disputes with Paraguay over the ►Chaco region and to a war (1932–5) in which the Paraguayans inflicted humiliating defeats on Bolivia. A sense of thwarted national pride induced junior army officers in May 1936 to establish a dictatorship, which they claimed to be socialist although its ideology was fundamentally fascist. The brutal suppression by the army of a tinminers' strike at Catavi in 1942 led the political opposition to coalesce into a 'National Revolutionary Movement' (MNR), headed by Dr Paz Estenssoro, an admirer of ►Perón in Argentina. The MNR supported a military *coup* by General Villaroel in December 1943, and for two and a half years Paz as chief minister under Villaroel was able to introduce some social reforms. With the assassination of Villaroel in

July 1946, the old conservatives and the military were able to keep the MNR out of office until they were swept to power on a wave of enthusiasm in 1952, after electoral victories the previous year had been ignored by the army. As President (1952–6 and 1960–64), Dr Paz nationalized the mines and divided some of the great estates. He was deposed by his right-wing Vice-President, General Barrientos, in 1964 and the former landlords were in many cases allowed to reclaim dispossessed property. The Barrientos dictatorship had no difficulty in suppressing the embryonic guerrilla movement of Ché ➤Guevara in October 1967. After Barrientos's death in a helicopter crash (27 April 1969) there were four military *coups* in Bolivia in twenty-eight months. The dictatorship of Colonel Banzer (President, 1971–8) was overthrown by General Asbun on 21 July 1978 after a court ruling that elections, held a fortnight previously, were fraudulent. Political instability became even more pronounced, the iteration of military *coups* broken by the novelty of a woman president, Lidia Gueiler, from November 1979 to July 1980. General Meza, who overthrew President Gueiler, established a vigorously anti-trade union military government which he claimed he would lead for twenty years, but he was ousted within thirteen months. Inconclusive elections in July 1985 brought back Paz Estenssoro for a third term. In May 1989 he was succeeded by President Jaime Zamora of the right-wing Democratic Nationalist Alliance. Zamora's government pursued a vigorous anti-drug-trafficking campaign. Elections in 1993 were won by the centrist National Revolutionary Movement, but in 1997 there was a political swing to the right, and the Democratic Nationalists returned to power, led by the military dictator of the 1970s, President Banzer.

Bolsheviks. The revolutionary wing of the Russian Social Democratic Party. The name originated at the Second Party Congress, in exile in London (August 1903), when a vote was taken on the composition of the editorial board of *Iskra*, the party newspaper. The vote gave a majority to Lenin's group, who thereupon assumed the name 'Bolsheviki' ('members of the majority') although over many other questions the Leninists were outvoted. Their opponents, the more moderate Social Democrats, were known as ➤'Mensheviks'. The Bolsheviks remained a radical group within the Russian Social Democratic Party until 1912, when Lenin established a separate Central Committee. After the ➤Russian Revolution Lenin's party adopted the name 'All-Russian Communist Party (Bolsheviks)' in 1918. The word Bolshevik was retained in the official name of the Soviet Communist Party until the Nineteenth Party Congress of October 1952.

Borden, Robert Laird (1854–1937, knighted 1914), Canadian statesman. Born in Grand Pré, Nova Scotia, practised as a barrister and became leader of the Conservative Opposition in the Canadian parliament in 1901. For ten years he had a difficult parliamentary task in seeking to defeat the Liberals, who enjoyed a considerable majority under ➤Laurier. But the Canadian voters turned against the Liberals in 1911 over a trade agreement with the USA and Borden became Prime Minister on 10 October 1911. He was head of an exclusively Conservative government for six years, and then presided over a coalition from October 1917 until July 1920. In home affairs he had difficulty in securing the passage of legislation through a Senate in which the Liberals still held a majority, although the coalition in March 1918 secured the passage of a franchise bill giving the vote to women over the age of twenty-one. His two outstanding achievements were the organization of Canada for war, sending an army of almost half a million volunteers overseas, and his successful fight to have the dominions recognized as equal partners with the United Kingdom in international affairs. Borden was the first Dominion Prime Minister to attend a British cabinet meeting (14 July 1915), as well as representing Canada on the Imperial War Cabinet in 1917–18. As a Canadian plenipotentiary to the Paris Peace Conference in 1919–20 he gained acceptance of the principle that representatives of self-governing dominions might sign the peace treaties and, in due course, be elected to the council of the ►League of Nations. Sir Robert Borden was himself Canada's representative on the League Council in 1930.

Boris III (1894–1943; reigned 1918–43), King of Bulgaria. Eldest son of ►Ferdinand I. As a Crown Prince he commanded an army on the Macedonian front in the First World War and was respected by his troops, who supported him against a republican movement when he came to the throne on his father's abdication (3 October 1918). Boris was intelligent, astute and devious: to safeguard his person and throne he gave an impression of boredom with politics, delighting in the mechanics of clocks and railway engines. In reality, he was a ruthless political manipulator. He benefited from the murder of the radical peasant leader ►Stamboliisky in 1923, even if he may not have planned it; and in November 1935 he freed himself from dominance by a League of Officers, appointing a friend (Georgi Kiosseivanov) as nominal prime minister. From March 1936 until his death Boris was dictator of Bulgaria in everything but name. Although he did not risk defying Hitler openly, the King limited the degree of Bulgarian participation in Hitler's 'New Order', acquiring territory from Yugoslavia and Greece as Germany's ally in 1941 but declining to collaborate with Germany in the Russian campaign or to fight actively against the British and Americans (with both of whom Bulgaria was technically at war). Hitler's exasperation with Boris caused him to summon the King to his headquarters in East Prussia in August 1943, but Boris would not change his policy. Three days after flying back from East Prussia, Boris suddenly died. Inevitably rumour said he had been poisoned, although there is no evidence that he did not die from natural causes. He was succeeded by his six-year-old son King Simeon, for whom Boris's brother, Prince Cyril (1895–1945), acted as chief Regent.

Borneo. An island in the South China Sea, three times as large as Britain. At the beginning of the century the island, much of which is thick jungle, was politically divided between the Dutch and the British. Dutch Borneo (nearly three-quarters of the island) was regarded by the Netherlands Government as an 'outpost' of the Dutch East Indies and there was frequent skirmishing between colonial troops and the native population from 1903 to 1908. The colony of British North Borneo and the two protectorates of Brunei and Sarawak were less backward. The whole of Borneo was occupied by the Japanese between January and March 1942. In 1945 Dutch Borneo – Kalimantan – associated itself with the struggle for independence of ►Indonesia and was recognized as part of the Republic of Indonesia in December 1949. British North Borneo (Sabah) and Sarawak acceded to the Federation of ►Malaysia when it was established in September 1963. Indonesia, claiming all of Borneo, resented the union of Sabah and Sarawak with the former Malayan states and sent troops to fight in Borneo. This policy of 'confrontation' necessitated the dispatch to the island of British and Gurkha troops, and fighting continued intermittently until the change in Indonesian policy which followed the fall of ►Sukarno in 1967–8. Brunei declined to join Malaysia and remains a sultanate, under British protection.

Bose, Subhas Chandra (1895–1945), Indian nationalist. Born in Calcutta, where he received his early education, before going to Cambridge to study law. On his return home he became an active supporter of independence, at first working closely with ►Nehru. While still in his twenties Bose was deported to Mandalay, where he was held in detention for three years as a dangerous subversive. His book, *The Indian Struggle* (1935), raised his status in the Congress Party; he served as its President in 1938. Bose was imprisoned for supporting the Axis cause in July 1940 but he escaped, crossing Afghanistan and the Soviet Union, and was given asylum in Berlin, from where he broadcast appeals to his compatriots to sabotage the war effort. He made a submarine voyage to Japan in 1942 and was appointed *Netaji* (leader) of the Indian National Army (INA), largely recruited from Indian prisoners of war after the fall of Singapore. By the closing months of 1943 he commanded a force of 20,000 men, established in battle headquarters at Rangoon. The INA supported the Japanese thrust across the Burmese frontier and into Assam, but the troops soon began to desert on a massive scale, seeking to rejoin families at home. Bose perished in an air crash in Taiwan during the last weeks of the war. Many Indians continue to regard him as a patriot hero in the struggle for independence.

Bosnia-Herzegovina. A region in Yugoslavia, under Turkish rule from the fifteenth century until 1908. From 1878 to 1908 the provinces were occupied by Austro-Hungarian troops and developed as though they were Austrian colonies, Turkish authority being reduced to a mere formality. The ►Young Turk movement made the Austrians fear that their control would be challenged and in consequence they formally annexed the provinces in October 1908. This action was particularly resented by Serbia (since most of the people in the provinces were Serbs) and by Russia, which wanted compensation for increased Austrian power in eastern Europe by concessions over the Bosphorus and Dardanelles (►Eastern Question). This Bosnian Crisis was resolved by threats from Austria's ally, Germany, which forced Russia to recognize the annexation without compensation in March 1909.

The crisis left much international bitterness. The Serbs within Bosnia began an anti-Austrian terrorist agitation which culminated in the 1914 assassinations at ►Sarajevo and so led to general war. Between 1918 and 1941 Bosnia-Herzegovina formed part of the Yugoslav kingdom. The woods and ravines of the provinces provided cover for bitter guerrilla warfare during the Second World War. In May 1943 a considerable battle was fought along the river Neretva, the main artery from Bosnia to the Adriatic, by the partisans of ►Tito against German and Italian troops. Bosnia-Herzegovina became one of the federated republics within Yugoslavia by the communist constitution of January 1946.

Census returns in 1991 showed the population of Bosnia-Herzegovina as 4.4 million, of whom 44 per cent were Muslims, 31 per cent Serbs and 17 per cent Croats. The collapse of the federal system in ►Yugoslavia during 1991 was followed by a declaration of independence in the Bosnian capital, Sarajevo, on 1 March 1992 by the leader of the (Muslim) Democratic Action Party, Alija Izetbegović (1925–), who sought acceptance as President of a multi-faith and multi-ethnic republic, which received recognition by the European Community and America and was admitted to the United Nations in May 1992. Izetbegović was opposed by the Bosnian Serbs under Radovan Karadžić (1945–), who set up a Republika Srpska at Pale, outside Sarajevo, and received modern weapons, tanks and 'volunteers' from Belgrade. In the ensuing civil war of 1992–5 Muslim enclaves in eastern Bosnia were overrun by Bosnian Serbs, who perpetrated atrocities, such as 'ethnic cleansing', on the helpless villagers. Sarajevo was besieged and shelled. At the same time Bosnian Croats challenged Muslim control of Mostar, the administrative capital of Herzegovina, where the historic old city was virtually destroyed. Attempts by the UN to distribute humanitarian aid and deploy peacekeeping troops were frustrated by the Bosnian Serbs; joint initiatives by UN and EU representatives to impose a peace plan ran into opposition both from Karadžić and from the President of rump Yugoslavia, ►Milošević, in Belgrade. Only in Mostar was it possible in February 1994 to end the fighting and set up a fragile UN-supervised Muslim–Croat Federation for Herzegovina. Despite NATO intervention and air strikes against the Bosnian Serbs in the spring of 1994, it proved impossible to protect Muslims who had found shelter in UN 'safe areas' around Goražde or, in 1995, around Žepa and Srebrenica. Only a full-scale invasion from Croatia, together with intensification of NATO air strikes in August and September 1995 led the warring parties to accept a US-sponsored peace accord: an eventual agreement reached at ►Dayton in Ohio in late November 1995. By then the war had reduced the population to an estimated 2.9 million: at least one in three Muslims was dead or 'missing'.

The difficult task of maintaining Bosnia-Herzegovina as a single state, territorially divided into a Bosnian and Croat Federation and a Bosnian Serbian Republic was entrusted in December 1995 to IFOR, a 60,000-strong multinational peace Implementation Force which in December 1996 was succeeded by SFOR, a peace Stabilization Force (including – controversially – 3,000 German troops). A

Reconstruction Conference in Brussels, meeting in April 1996, pledged some £800 million to restore basic necessities in this most devastated region of Europe during the second half of the century.

Botha, Louis (1862–1919), South African statesman and soldier. Spent his youth farming in the Transvaal, fought for the Boers at Colenso and Spion Kop in 1899 and, as a general, organized guerrilla resistance in the final phase of the ►Boer War. Subsequently he worked for reconciliation: he was Prime Minister of the Transvaal (1907–10) and was so respected both by the Boers and by his former enemies that in 1910 he became the first Prime Minister of the Union of South Africa, a post he held until his death. During the First World War he suppressed a pro-German Boer revolt with firmness and clemency and conducted a successful campaign in German South-West Africa, which surrendered to him in July 1915. He participated in the Paris Peace Conference of 1919 and signed the Treaty of ►Versailles, although he urged the allied Powers to show less rancour towards defeated Germany rather than risk encouraging a mood of vengeance.

Botha, Pieter Willem (1916–), South African President. Born a farmer's son at Paul Roux in the Orange Free State, he worked for the National Party executive in Cape Province 1936–48 when he entered the Pretoria parliament as member for George, a constituency midway between Cape Town and Port Elizabeth. In 1966 he became Minister of Defence under ►Vorster, whom he succeeded as prime minister in September 1978. He appeared more flexible over ►apartheid than his predecessors and in 1983 introduced constitutional changes that restored some political rights to non-whites (►South Africa). In June 1984 he held talks with Mrs Thatcher at Chequers, the first South African prime minister received in Britain since the Republic left the Commonwealth. Three months later (14 September 1984) Botha was elected State President, the new constitution having replaced the premiership by an executive presidency. On 18 January 1989 he suffered a stroke; he resigned as leader of the National Party a fortnight later and was succeeded as President by F.W. ►de Klerk in October. His refusal to co-operate with investigations into his past record led to a charge of contempt of the Truth and Reconciliation Commission (January 1998).

Boumédienne, Houari (1925–78), Algerian President. Born at Guelma in eastern Algeria under the name Mohammed Bou Kharrouba and educated mainly in Cairo and Paris, serving briefly in the French Army before becoming a schoolmaster. In the winter of 1954–5 he joined the Algerian National Liberation Front (FLN) and for seven years fought against France in the ►Algerian War, at first in operations around Oran and from 1960 onwards as the FLN's Chief of Staff, with headquarters within Tunisia. ►Ben Bella made him Minister of National Defence in September 1962, with the rank of colonel. Gradually Boumédienne's ascetic Islamic socialist beliefs were offended by Ben Bella's more doctrinaire and westernized approach to the problems of Algeria's future. On 19 June 1965 he overthrew Ben Bella and for the following eleven years governed Algeria as President of the Council of Revolution, only accepting election as President of the republic in December 1976. Boumédienne was largely responsible for the Four Year Plan of 1969–73 which developed industry and reformed agriculture, nationalizing French oil interests in 1971. From 1973 to 1975 he played a considerable part in deciding Pan-Arab policy, breaking with President ►Sadat much as he had earlier turned against Ben Bella. Boumédienne's ideal of a North African Socialist Federation of Arab states remained unrealized when his health gave way in the autumn of 1978. Despite the attention of more than sixty specialists, he died in the last week of the year, being succeeded by President Chadli.

Bourguiba, Habib ibn Ali (1903–), Tunisian President. Born in the Tunisian coastal town of Monastir, studied at the Sorbonne in Paris, returning to Tunis in 1921 and campaigning for the moderate Tunisian Constitutional Party (Destour). In 1934 he led a more radical and nationalistic wing of 'Neo-Destours' and was imprisoned by the French authorities from 1934 to 1936 and from 1938 to 1942. He refused to cooperate with the Italians during the war but the French colonists continued to treat him with suspicion and in 1945 he took refuge in Cairo. By now he was a firm believer in the total independence of Tunisia. He returned home in 1949 but was again arrested by the French (1952) and served a further two-year prison sentence. The ►Mendès-France Government of 1954–5 saw the wisdom of placating moderate Arab sentiment and encouraged Bourguiba to consolidate his position as natural leader of the Tunisian national movement. He became Prime Minister when Tunisia gained independence in the spring of 1956. When the Tunisian Constituent Assembly abolished the monarchical powers of the traditional ruler, the Bey, in July 1957, Bourguiba was elected the first President of the Tunisian Republic. He was re-elected in 1959, 1964, 1969 and 1974 and in March 1975 was proclaimed President for life by the National Assembly. Although Bourguiba took a firm stand against the French use of Tunisian naval and air bases (1959–62) he favoured close trade relations with the former imperial power. His moderate form of Arab socialism was criticized as too cautious by his neighbours, Boumédienne in ►Algeria and Gaddafi in ►Libya. Islamic fundamentalist riots threatened his authority in 1983–4. On 7 November 1987 he was deposed by his prime minister, General Ben Ali (born 1926), who claimed that Bourguiba was too senile to remain in office.

Boxer Rising. An outbreak of anti-foreign violence in northern China. Rapid development of European commerce and the acquisition by Germany, Russia and Britain of bases on the Gulf of Pechili (1897–8) aroused resentment in the Chinese Empire. With the connivance of the Chinese authorities and the active support of the Dowager-Empress Tzu Hsi (1834–1908), young Chinese enrolled in a secret organization, 'The Society of Harmonious Fists', popularly termed 'Boxers'. Attacks on converts to Christianity, on missionaries and on workers employed by foreign-controlled railways induced the European Powers to safeguard their nationals.

When British reinforcements sought to reach the Chinese capital they were fired on by the forts at Taku. A Boxer outbreak at once occurred in Peking itself: on 19 June 1900 the German Minister was assassinated and the foreign legations besieged. A six-nation expeditionary force relieved the legations on 14 August, some units then looting Peking. A German punitive expedition, commanded by Field-Marshal Count von Waldersee (1832–1904), arrived later in the year and took strong measures to avenge the diplomat's murder. Boxer disturbances also occurred in Shensi Province and Manchuria, which the Russians occupied, ostensibly to protect their railway interests. The methods used by the Western Powers to break up the Boxers intensified anti-imperialist feeling among the younger Chinese, many of whom joined the national and republican movement which looked for inspiration to ►Sun Yat-sen. The Peking Protocol of 1901 imposed an annual monetary indemnity to be paid by the Chinese to the Great Powers as recompense for Boxer crimes; it also permitted the Powers to station troops in China and to control the diplomatic quarter of Peking if the central authority seemed powerless. The Protocol was not abrogated until January 1943.

Bradley, Omar Nelson (1893–1981), American soldier. Born in Clark, Missouri, graduated from the US Military Academy in 1915 and fought in France, 1918. He was commandant of an infantry school in 1941 but was rapidly promoted, taking command of the American Second Corps in Tunisia in 1943, capturing Bizerta (7 May) and, after crossing to Sicily, entering Messina (16 August). In 1944 Bradley commanded the American landings in Normandy on ►D-Day, advancing to Cherbourg and then driving through the Avranches Gap into the heart of France. As commander of the US Twelfth Army Group from 1 August 1944 until the end of the war, Bradley had under his orders more than 1¼ million men, the largest American army ever entrusted to a single general. The Twelfth Army Group was engaged in the ►Ardennes, crossed the Rhine at Remagen and linked up with the Russians on the Elbe on 25 April 1945. Bradley served as chairman of the US Joint Chiefs of Staff from 1948 to 1953, being promoted in 1950 to the highest American rank, General of the Army. He was largely responsible for building up NATO and for assessing the significance of the ►Korean War in America's global strategy. Mistrust of ►MacArthur led Bradley to tell a Senate committee in May 1951 that the proposal to carry the Korean conflict into China was to fight 'the wrong war, at the wrong place, at the wrong time, and with the wrong enemy'.

Brandt, Willy 1913–92), West German Chancellor. Born Karl Herbert Frahm in Lübeck where from 1930 to 1933 he was active as an anti-Nazi socialist worker. He fled to Norway in 1933, changing his name to Brandt, assumed Norwegian citizenship and graduated from Oslo University before becoming a journalist. In 1940 he escaped from Norway to Sweden and served as a link between the Norwegian and German Resistance movements. He returned to Berlin in 1945, recovered his German citizenship in 1948 and built up democratic socialism in the western sectors of the former capital, entering the West German assembly, the Bundestag, in 1949. He achieved international renown as mayor of West Berlin from 1957 to 1966 because of his determined opposition to Russian and East German threats and blandishments. Brandt became chairman of the German Social Democrats (SPD) in 1964 and Foreign Minister from 1966 to 1969 in Kiesinger's Grand Coalition Government. SPD successes in the elections of September 1969 enabled him to become Chancellor, in coalition with the FDP 'Liberals'. He was again successful in the election of November 1972 but was forced to resign on 6 May 1974 over criticism that he had unwittingly employed an East German spy as a personal aide. Both as Foreign Minister and Chancellor he worked for reconciliation with the Eastern bloc. His *Ostpolitik* was marked by treaties with Poland and the Soviet Union in 1972 which accepted the ➤Oder–Neisse line and indirectly acknowledged the *de facto* authority of the ➤German Democratic Republic. These conciliatory gestures made him many political enemies (especially in the West German Press) and they readily exploited the security lapse which caused his downfall. Outside Germany, Willy Brandt was recognized as the outstanding pragmatic social democrat on the Continent. He was the first German Chancellor since ➤Stresemann to be awarded the Nobel Peace Prize (1971).

Braun, Wernher von (1912–77), pioneer rocket scientist. Born in Wirsitz, studied engineering at the Universities of Berlin and Zürich, appointed technical director of the rocket research station at Peenemünde in 1936, within two years producing a prototype rocket capable of carrying a warhead for eleven miles. Interdepartmental rivalry prevented Braun from perfecting this weapon until in 1943 he was given personal backing from Hitler, with instructions to develop the rocket known as the V-2 (*Vergeltungswaffe* – 'reprisal weapon' – 2). One thousand and fifty of these V-2 rockets, capable of carrying a ton of explosives for almost 200 miles, landed in England between 8 September 1944 and 27 March 1945. In May 1945 Braun surrendered to the Americans, who took him to the USA. He became an American citizen, was appointed director of the US Ballistic Missile Agency in Alabama, and developed the rocket which launched America's earth satellite from Cape Canaveral on 31 January 1958. He was also responsible for the Saturn rockets used in the ➤Apollo Missions, most notably on the successful moon flight of July 1969.

Brazil. A Portuguese possession from 1500 to 1822 and then an empire under a branch of the Portuguese royal dynasty until 1889 when a republic was established which adopted a federal constitution as the United States of Brazil two years later. The main economic and social problems for Brazil were the price of coffee and rubber and the rise in population (1850, 8 million; 1920, 30 million; 1950, 57 million; 1975, 107 million). Social unrest in the 1920s led to a major revolt in 1930 and the establishment of a right-wing authoritarian government under Getúlio Vargas (1883–1954) who met the challenge of the world depression by proclaiming a 'New State' (*Estado Novo*) philosophy, similar to the Portuguese variant of fascism. From 1937 to 1945 President Vargas was a dictator, but nevertheless took Brazil into the Second World War in 1942 against Germany and Italy. When Brazil sent an expeditionary force to Italy in 1944 she became the first South American republic ever to dispatch fighting troops to another continent. In 1945 Vargas resigned the presidency but returned in 1951 when Brazil was faced by another economic depression. The second Vargas presidency (1951–4) was, however, a disaster: corruption was rampant, and the army feared the growth of an urban proletariat. After Vargas's suicide, Brazil experienced five years of economic boom, marked by the presidency of the extravagant Dr Kubitschek, who was responsible for founding the new city of Brasilia (officially Brazil's capital from April 1960). From 1961 to 1964 President Goulart tried to revive the social doctrines of the *Estado Novo* but was considered too left-wing for the army and the industrialists. A military *coup* in April 1964 placed the army firmly in control. This was cautiously relaxed when President Figuereido took office in March 1979 and promised 'a democracy without qualifications'. A grave financial crisis, a prolonged drought and a failure to initiate land reform led to serious rioting at São Paulo in April 1983. After a bad fall from his horse in June 1984, Figuereido accepted a constitutional amendment for an indirect presidential election which in January 1985 was won by a social democrat, Tancredo Neves. On inauguration day, however, Neves was rushed to hospital with peritonitis and he died soon afterwards. Vice-President Jose Sarnay (born 1930) then took office (22 April 1985) and, with the annual inflation rate running at 220 per cent, introduced radical currency reforms in February 1986, backed by major loans from the World Bank. A three-year plan for economic growth and land reform followed five months later, but successive governments in Brasilia have been criticized for neglecting the human rights of the Amazonian peoples in encouraging forest burning for road and rail construction and industrialization. Constitutional revision intended to strengthen the presidency in 1988 was followed in December 1989 by a presidential election won by Fernando Color de Mello. He was succeeded in January 1995 by Fernando Cardoso, a Social Democrat.

Brazzaville Declaration. In January 1944 General de Gaulle presided over a meeting of representatives of his Free French movement and of France's African colonies at Brazzaville in the French Congo to discuss the post-war relationship between the French Republic and her overseas territories. The final declaration affirmed the indivisibility of the French colonial empire but recommended the participation of the overseas territories in elections for a French parliament. It also proposed the setting up of territorial assemblies in each colony, the advancement of the native population in the public services and a number of economic reforms. The Brazzaville Declaration formed the basic statement on colonial policy for the Fourth Republic. From June 1946 all peoples in the 'French Union' were guaranteed equal rights as citizens of the republic. By denying rights of autonomy and rejecting the possibility of independence the Brazzaville Declaration failed to satisfy even the moderate nationalists in North Africa. Conversely, the settlers – especially in Algeria – regarded the principle of assimilation as too radical and effectively delayed its application.

Brest-Litovsk, Treaty of (3 March 1918). The peace Treaty between Bolshevik Russia and the Central Powers. A conference between a Russian delegation, headed by ►Trotsky, and German and Austrian representatives began at Brest-Litovsk on 3 December 1917 in order to end Russian participation in the First World War. By skilled delaying tactics Trotsky deferred signature of a Treaty, hoping that socialist revolutions would spread through Germany and Austria–Hungary. After nine weeks of prevarication the German army resumed its advance eastwards, penetrating so deeply and rapidly towards Petrograd that Lenin ordered his delegates to accept the German terms immediately. By the Treaty the Russians surrendered the Ukraine, Finland, the Baltic provinces, the Caucasus, White Russia and Poland. The German Armistice in the West (November 1918) formally invalidated the Treaty.

Bretton Woods Conference. An international monetary and financial conference summoned on the initiative of President Franklin D. Roosevelt at Bretton Woods, New Hampshire, in July 1944. Twenty-eight nations participated and agreed to establish an international Monetary Fund and a World Bank. The Fund was designed to operate a system of cash reserves on which member countries can draw in order to meet deficits in balance of payments. The World Bank was intended to advance loans for viable projects of major importance to a country's general development. It was assumed that international monetary cooperation would prevent the financial crashes which had harmed world trade in the 1920s and early 1930s.

Brezhnev, Leonid Ilyich (1906–82), Soviet leader. Studied engineering at his birthplace, Dneprodzerzhinsk in the Ukraine, and worked on land conservation and in a metallurgical factory before becoming a Communist Party official in 1938. From 1941 to 1945 he was a political commissar, serving as a colonel on the Ukrainian front. His career was advanced by his compatriot, ►Khrushchev, and he was elected to the Supreme Soviet by the Dnepropetrovsk district in 1950. Four months before Stalin's death, Brezhnev was appointed to the Party Central Committee and joined the Politburo in 1957. Three years later he became head of the Soviet state, serving in this largely honorific capacity as President of the Presidium of the Supreme Soviet from May 1960 to July 1964 when, as Khrushchev's deputy, he gained control of the party machine. On 15 October 1964 he succeeded Khrushchev as First Secretary of the Soviet Communist Party. Although ►Kosygin was titular Prime Minister, Brezhnev used his post much as Stalin had done in the 1930s and emerged as the principal ruler in a nominal collective leadership. Brezhnev was largely responsible for the decision to intervene in ►Czechoslovakia in 1968, maintaining the doctrine that a socialist state has an obligation to intervene in another socialist state if the continuance of socialism is threatened. Revision of the Soviet Constitution in 1977 allowed Brezhnev again to become President while still shaping policy. On his death (10 November 1982), he was succeeded by Yuri Andropov (1914–84).

Briand, Aristide (1862–1932), French statesman. Born at Nantes. Briand was a socialist colleague of ➤Jaurès from 1894 to 1906, when he was expelled from the Socialist Party for accepting office in a predominantly Radical coalition. As Minister of Public Instruction and Worship (1906–9) he completed the separation of Church and State in France. Between 1909 and 1929 Briand was Prime Minister on eleven occasions, yet the instability of politics was so great in the Third French Republic that his total period as head of a government was a mere fifty-eight months. During his first ministry (July 1909 to November 1910) he alienated his former socialist colleagues when he broke a railway strike by calling up for military service all strikers who were army reservists. His wartime ministry (October 1915 to March 1917) showed a lack of vigour in combating the defeatism of ➤Caillaux but during the 1920s Briand's was the dominant voice in French foreign policy. He strongly supported the League of Nations, advocated international arbitration and championed Franco-German reconciliation. He shared the Nobel Peace Prize of 1926 with ➤Stresemann and took the initiative the following year in proposing the ➤Kellogg Pact on the renunciation of war as an instrument of national policy.

Brinkmanship. A word used to describe the policy advocated as Secretary of State by John Foster ➤Dulles. He claimed, in an interview in *Life Magazine* on 11 January 1956, that 'the necessary art' for a statesman is 'the ability to get to the verge of war without getting into war' adding that 'if you are scared to go to the brink, you are lost'.

Britain, Battle of. The contest between the British and German air forces fought over southern England between 10 July and 31 October 1940. The Germans, with an initial force of nearly 1,400 bombers and 1,020 fighters, launched a series of attacks, first against shipping, then against airfields and finally against the towns, the whole operation being a prelude to invasion. The main air defence rested with nearly 700 'Hurricane' and 'Spitfire' fighters (with 100 planes a month arriving from the factories). The highest German losses were sustained on 15 August, when the RAF shot down 75 German planes, losing 34 fighters themselves. Changed tactics swung the balance of the battle in Germany's favour in the first week of September, but in two actions on 15 September the British inflicted such heavy casualties on the bomber force that the Germans gave up their invasion project and switched to the indiscriminate night bombing of the larger cities, especially London. Confused reports led to an original British claim of 185 planes destroyed on 15 September whereas the actual figure was 56; but the day was already commemorated as 'Battle of Britain Day' during the later war years and has remained so since then. During the twelve-week battle 1,733 German aircraft were destroyed for the loss of 915 British fighters (and the lives of 449 fighter-pilots).

British Commonwealth. The term British Commonwealth was occasionally used in the nineteenth century as an alternative for 'British Empire'. An Imperial War Conference of dominion prime ministers, which met in March–April 1917, used the phrase 'Imperial Commonwealth'. A report on the nature of the imperial relationship, drawn up by Earl ►Balfour in 1926, preferred the concept of a British Commonwealth of Nations. This title was widely accepted until 1949, when the appellation 'British' dropped from formal usage. The first official document to refer to a British sovereign as 'Head of the Commonwealth' was the Accession Proclamation of Queen Elizabeth II in February 1952. In 1949 the ►Commonwealth comprised the United Kingdom and its colonies, six dominions (Australia, Canada, Ceylon, New Zealand, South Africa, Pakistan) and the independent republic of India. By 1998 there were fifty-four member states of the Commonwealth, including one – Mozambique – which never owed allegiance to the British crown.

Broadcasting. The invention of wireless telegraphy by ►Marconi in 1895 was originally developed by the mercantile marine and by the armed services of most countries. During the First World War wireless operators were trained in large numbers and technical equipment acquired a longer range. With the return of peace businessmen in America and Britain advocated the application of wireless technique to the instantaneous communication of news and entertainment to a mass audience. The Marconi Company developed an experimental public broadcasting station at Writtle, Essex, between 1920 and 1922, while in Pennsylvania the Westinghouse Company transmitted the Presidential election results in November 1920. Local radio stations proliferated in the USA in 1922–3, but in Britain the Post Office (as the licensing authority for radio stations) insisted on centralization and on 18 October 1922 the British Broadcasting Company (►BBC) was established in Marconi House, The Strand, London ('2LO'). Most other countries allowed governmental radio stations and commercial stations to develop in competition with each other. The peak of broadcasting influence was reached in the mid 1930s, both in Europe and America, where President Roosevelt early discovered the power of a 'fireside chat' carried into millions of homes. The first use of wireless for political propaganda came in February 1918 when the Bolshevik authorities in Petrograd transmitted messages inciting German troops to mutiny and rebellion. Broadcasting (and the ►cinema) offered the right-wing dictatorships new forms of mass indoctrination, fully exploited in Germany by ►Goebbels. During the Second World War attempts to mould the opinions of enemy listeners were made by both allied and Axis propagandists, a technique continued during the so-called 'cold war'. From 1936 onwards radio broadcasting was challenged by ►television. Because of the Second World War, the full social impact of television in Europe and America was delayed until the 1950s.

Bruce, Stanley Melbourne (1883–1967, created Viscount Bruce of Melbourne, 1947), Australian political leader. Born and educated in Melbourne, read law at

Trinity Hall, Cambridge, practised at the English bar, and served from 1914 to 1917 in English regiments, being wounded at Gallipoli and on the Western Front. Bruce returned to Victoria in 1918 and entered politics as a supporter of ►Hughes. He was, however, a stronger believer in free enterprise than Hughes and early in 1923 led a section of Hughes's Nationalist Party into coalition with the ►Country Party. Bruce was Prime Minister of this coalition from February 1923 until defeated by Labour in the election of October 1929. His government was markedly conservative, passing in 1925 a supplementary ►immigration act and relaxing federal controls originally developed by Hughes in wartime. Bruce's 'English' style of Conservatism alienated many voters – he was derided for wearing spats in Parliament House – and in 1929 he surrendered the party leadership to J.A. ►Lyons. In 1932, Bruce was sent as principal Australian delegate to the Ottawa Conference and was speedily accepted as Australia's foremost spokesman overseas. From 1933 to 1945 he was High Commissioner in London, and represented Australia at meetings of Churchill's war cabinet, 1942–5. He encouraged schemes for training pilots in the overseas dominions and favoured a more lenient post-war policy towards the ex-enemy states than Churchill envisaged. Viscount Bruce settled in England for the closing twenty years of his life.

Brüning, Heinrich (1885–1970), German Chancellor. Born at Münster, of middle-class Catholic parentage; educated at Bonn (gaining a doctorate in economics), commissioned in the Machine-Gun Corps, 1914, winning the Iron Cross (First Class) in 1918, and entered the Reichstag as a Centre Party deputy from Silesia in 1924. His knowledge of economics ensured him rapid advancement and on 28 March 1930 President ►Hindenburg appointed him Chancellor, hoping he would stabilize the economy and stem the rising popularity of Hitler's movement. Brüning, however, never possessed a Reichstag majority and could govern only through Presidential decrees. He was thus dependent on Hindenburg's goodwill and the support of the army leaders. Abroad Brüning tried to counter the Depression, in central Europe, by proposing an Austro-German customs union (March 1931) but met strong opposition from France and the ►Little Entente. Ultimately he lost Hindenburg's confidence by seeking to split bankrupt Junker estates in East Prussia into smallholdings. On 30 May 1932 he was ousted from the chancellorship in favour of Franz von Papen. Brüning escaped from Germany into Holland in 1934, eventually settling in the USA and lecturing at Harvard, although he returned to Westphalia in 1947 and taught at Cologne University. He was the last resolute opponent of Nazism in the ►Weimar Republic Yet in governing by decree he helped undermine the democratic system and thus facilitated the Nazi revolution which he abhorred.

Brusilov, Alexei Alexeivich (1853–1926), Russian general. Served as a cavalry officer in the Russo-Turkish War of 1877 and the Russo-Japanese War of 1904–5, commanded the Russian Eighth Army during the successful invasion of Galicia in 1914 and during the retreat of 1915, appointed commander of the south-west

Russian front in late March 1916. A fortnight later he was authorized by the Tsar to prepare an offensive in depth for the summer. Brusilov launched his attack, primarily against the Austrians between the Pripet Marshes and the Carpathians, on 4 June 1916, breaking through the lines at Lutsk and capturing a quarter of a million men. Within a month Brusilov had cleared a corridor 200 miles wide and, in places, more than 60 miles deep. This meticulously planned offensive finally encouraged ➤Romania to enter the war on the allied side. The offensive came to a halt in mid August through failure of munition supplies. Brusilov held supreme command from May to July 1917 under the Provisional Government. He was appointed by the Soviet authorities as an adviser to the Red Army in the Russo-Polish campaign of 1920, serving as inspector of cavalry, 1923–4, and establishing the new cavalry stud farm outside Moscow, 1924–6.

Brussels, Treaty of (17 March 1948). An alliance, valid for fifty years, pledging Belgium, France, Great Britain, Luxembourg and the Netherlands to render to each other 'all military and other aid and assistance' if any one of the five nations should suffer an armed attack in Europe. The Treaty also provided for quarterly conferences of the Foreign Ministers and established a Permanent Military Committee and several economic and social subcommittees to further the ideas of a Western European Union. Italy and the German Federal Republic formally associated themselves with the organizations established by the Brussels Treaty in May 1955.

Bryan, William Jennings (1860–1925), American political leader and orator. Born in Salem, Illinois, practised law in Nebraska 1887–91, served in Congress from 1891 to 1895, and became nationally famous through his denunciation of the gold standard at the Democratic Party's convention at Chicago on 8 July 1896: 'You shall not press down upon the brow of labor this crown of thorns, you shall not crucify mankind upon a cross of gold'. This speech won him the Democratic Presidential nomination in 1896, but he failed to carry the electors with him that year or on the two other occasions when he was nominated, 1900 and 1908. Bryan, an anti-imperialist and passionate reformer, was distrusted by the party bosses but his influence was decisive in securing the nomination of Woodrow ➤Wilson in 1912 and Bryan was appointed Secretary of State when Wilson won the election. Wilson and Bryan worked in partnership over Latin American affairs, but Bryan distrusted European affairs and refused to support the President's protests at the sinking of the *Lusitania* in 1915. Bryan left the administration in June 1915 and spent his later years crusading for fundamentalist religious beliefs. In July 1925 he was state prosecutor in the famous trial at Dayton, Tennessee, of John T. Scopes, who was found guilty of teaching Darwinian biological theories which conflicted with the account of the Creation in the book of Genesis, an offence under Tennessee state law. The bitter clashes in court left Bryan exhausted: he died in Dayton five days after the trial ended.

Bucharest, Treaty of (10 August 1913). Peace settlement after the ➤Balkan

Wars concluded between Greece, Serbia, Montenegro, Romania and Bulgaria. Subsequently the frontier between Bulgaria and Turkey was defined by the Treaty of Constantinople of 29 September 1913, but its provisions are normally regarded as part of the general Bucharest Settlement.

Buganda. A kingdom within Uganda, traditionally ruled by a Kabaka, principal town Kampala. From 1953 to 1955 there was a major constitutional dispute over the position of Kabaka Sir Edward Mutesa II, who claimed the right of his kingdom to secede from the Ugandan protectorate. This right was denied by the Ugandan High Court and a conference at Namirembe insisted that the interests and security of Buganda required continued union with the remaining regions of Uganda. In October 1963 Kabaka Mutesa II was elected first President of Uganda (a post then principally honorific) but in April 1966 he was ousted by his Prime Minister, Dr Milton Obote, and exiled to England where he died in 1969. Obote's constitutional reforms denied Buganda any special status, a centralizing tendency carried even further under Obote's successor, ►Amin.

Bukharin, Nicolai Ivanovich (1888–1938), Russian revolutionary. Born in Moscow, sent to Siberia as a student, he escaped to America in 1911. By the autumn of 1912 he was back in Europe, meeting ►Lenin for the first time at Cracow. Lenin respected Bukharin as an economic theorist and he became editor of *Pravda* in 1918. Bukharin supported Stalin against ►Trotsky and he was a member of the Politburo until 1929 when he fell into disgrace for 'right-wing deviationism'. He edited *Izvestia* 1934–7, but was liquidated in the Stalinist purge of old Bolsheviks in 1938. In July 1988 he was formally rehabilitated, his reputation vindicated.

Bukovina. A small, heavily wooded, region of south-eastern Europe, inhabited for the most part by Ruthenes (Ukrainians) and until 1918 forming a province of Austria–Hungary, with its administrative centre at Czernowitz (Cernăuţi, Chernovtsy). By the Treaty of ►St Germain of 1919 the Bukovina was incorporated in Romania but, under German political pressure, the Romanians were forced to cede the region (together with ►Bessarabia) to the Soviet Union in June 1940. The Bukovina now forms the trans-Carpathian region of the ►Ukraine.

Bulganin, Nikolai (1895–1975), Soviet Prime Minister. Born in Nizhni-Novgorod (Gorki), fought in the ranks in the First World War, joining the Communist Party at the Revolution and serving in the secret police from 1918 to 1922. From 1931 to 1937 he was chairman of the Moscow Soviet ('Mayor of Moscow'), responsible for ambitious town-planning projects, grandiose but aesthetically drab. He helped organize the defence of Moscow in 1941, with the rank of lieutenant-general, and was created a Marshal of the Soviet Union in 1945, succeeding Stalin as Minister of Defence in 1946. When Stalin died, Bulganin served ►Malenkov as Vice-Premier until February 1955 when he became Prime Minister. In this capacity he appeared to share authority with the secretary of the party, ►Khrushchev, whom he accompanied on visits to Yugoslavia (May 1955) and Britain (April 1956). By the autumn of 1956 it was clear Bulganin was primarily a mouthpiece for Khrushchev, who felt so sure of his position that he ousted Bulganin from the Premiership on 27 March 1958. Five months later Bulganin was dropped from the Party Presidium, becoming chairman of the Soviet State Bank.

Bulgaria. Although there had been a powerful Bulgarian Empire in the tenth century, modern Bulgarian national feeling dates from the 1870s when the Russians encouraged the Bulgars – as a Slav people – to revolt against the Turks, who had ruled them for 500 years. The Treaty of San Stefano of March 1878 created, under Russian auspices, a Bulgaria as extensive as in the Middle Ages, but a few months later the Treaty of Berlin considerably reduced the size of the Bulgarian principality. The San Stefano 'Greater Bulgaria' remained the ideal of nationalist politicians in Sofia throughout the reigns of King ►Ferdinand and his son, ►Boris. Bulgaria followed a tortuous policy of balance between the rival Great Powers at the beginning of the century. Disappointed in the ►Balkan Wars, Bulgaria sided with the Germans in 1915 but was defeated on the Salonika front in 1918. After a period of peasant dominance under ►Stambolisky Bulgaria became virtually a dictatorship under royal nominees, political life being dangerously enlivened by the terrorists known as ►IMRO. King Boris joined the Germans in occupying Yugoslavia in 1941, but astutely kept out of the Russian campaign. The Red Army, however, invaded Bulgaria in September 1944 and set up a predominantly Communist regime under ►Dimitrov, proclaiming a republic in September 1946. After Dimitrov's death in June 1949, there was a complex power struggle in Sofia from which Dimitrov's brother-in-law, Vulko Chervenkov, emerged as leader of the country. Chervenkov (1900–1980) slavishly copied Stalin until April 1956 when, at the height of the Khrushchev ascendancy, he was replaced by Anton Yugov, a Macedonian. The real power in Bulgarian political life from 1956 to 1989 lay with the secretary of the Bulgarian Communist Party, Todor Zhivkov (1911–98), and under his direction Bulgaria remained the loyalest supporter of Soviet policy in the Warsaw Pact. Zhivkov became Prime Minister in November 1962 and President (Chairman of the Council of State) in July 1971, being re-elected in 1976, 1981 and 1986. Zhivkov effectively built up Bulgaria's engineering industry, but his general policy aroused mounting opposition. In July 1987 Zhivkov put forward a series of reforms, including more self-management in industry. In January 1988 he claimed that his *preustroistvo* policy was 'restructuring' the state, like ►*perestroika* in the Soviet Union. In 1985–6 the Turkish ethnic minority (about 10 per cent of the population) began to complain of enforced Bulgarization. Demands for liberalization forced Zhivkov's resignation on 10 November 1989. The one-party political system was abolished a month later. Free elections held in June 1990 were won by the Bulgarian Socialist Party (the Communist Party re-named). A further election in October 1991 brought to power a democratic coalition which encouraged privatization but failed to check inflation or corruption. A non-party government of alleged technocrats in 1993–4 fared no better, and the Bulgarian Socialists formed a new coalition, which they dominated, in December 1994. Privatization made slow progress, and one in five of the labour force was unemployed a year later; there is a rare freedom of speech and expression, even for the Turkish minority. In May 1996 ex-King Simeon II (1937–, acceded 1943) was allowed to visit Bulgaria after half a century in exile. After six months of mounting political tension, a general election was held in April 1997 in which the Union of Democratic Forces defeated the ruling Socialist Party.

Bülow, Bernhard von (1849–1929, created a Prince, 1905), German Chancellor. Born at Flottbek-on-the-Elbe: the son of a diplomat, originally in the service of Holstein-Lauenburg but later State Secretary for Foreign Affairs under Bismarck (1877–9). The younger Bülow fought in the Franco-Prussian War, entered the diplomatic service in 1873–4 and eventually became ambassador to Italy in 1894. He was much favoured at first by Kaiser ➤William II and was a protégé of the Kaiser's principal friend, Philip ➤Eulenburg. Bülow was appointed State Secretary for Foreign Affairs in June 1897 and Chancellor on 17 October 1900, the Kaiser hoping he would 'be my Bismarck'. Although Bülow was an adroit diplomat, he lacked passionate convictions and was widely distrusted in Europe. He had few ideas on domestic policy and, even in foreign affairs, was dominated by others, notably Baron Holstein (the influential Counsellor of the Foreign Ministry). Relations between Bülow and the Kaiser deteriorated because the Chancellor's vanity was piqued by his sovereign's initiatives in foreign affairs (notably at ➤Björkö). In November 1908 he deeply disappointed the Kaiser by giving him little support in the Reichstag debate on the controversial 'interview' with William which the *Daily Telegraph* had printed in the previous month. A dispute with the Reichstag over budget proposals in July 1909 gave the Kaiser the opportunity to dismiss Bülow. From December 1914 until the spring of 1915 Bülow again served as ambassador in Rome, vainly seeking to prevent Italy from joining Germany's enemies. The Kaiser resisted pressure at court to reappoint Bülow Chancellor in 1917.

Burgenland. The most eastern province of the Austrian Republic. From 1867 until 1918 this region – an area of some 1,500 square miles – was part of the Kingdom of Hungary. In racial composition, however, it was predominantly German. Accordingly, in 1920 Hungary was obliged by the Treaty of ➤Trianon to cede the region to Austria, the only instance at the Paris Peace Conference of a transference of territory from one 'ex-enemy' state to another. In December 1921 the inhabitants of the town of Sopron were allowed to hold a plebiscite which rejected incorporation in Austria, and the city has remained Hungarian.

Burma. On three occasions in the nineteenth century the Kingdom of Burma appeared to threaten British dominance of Bengal and Assam. Punitive expeditions were mounted against the Burmese in 1826, 1852 and 1885, ending with the deportation by the British of the allegedly Francophile King Thibaw in December 1885 and the establishment of Upper Burma as a province of the British Indian Empire a month later. Anti-British riots in the 1930s led to concessions in the Government of India Act (1935), by which in April 1937 Burma was constituted a British crown colony with some measure of self-government. When the Japanese invaded Burma and captured Rangoon (►Burma Campaign) they were welcomed by some Burmese as liberators. They established a puppet government, of which the most important members were Aung San and U Nu. Both subsequently assisted the British and the Indians to eject the Japanese in the spring of 1945. Aung San was invited by ►Attlee to London in 1946, where the British agreed to give Burma independence. On 19 July 1947, shortly after his return to Rangoon, Aung San was assassinated by gunmen in the pay of a rival, and it was U Nu who completed the negotiations which led to Burma's independence on 4 January 1948. Civil war weakened the new republic and, within a year, the Karen tribesmen of the Irrawaddy delta established a firm hold on the country's main food supplies. Resistance to the Karens, and their communist guerrilla allies, was led by General Ne Win (1911–89). He successfully divided the opposition, favouring a unified and socialist Burma, in which the various ethnic groups could keep their identity and enjoy a limited autonomy. U Nu, a devout Buddhist, was Prime Minister from 1948 until 1962 (except for the period 1958–60). In March 1962 the army took control of Burma and Ne Win abolished the parliamentary system, setting up a 'Socialist Republic of the Union of Burma'. Despite the continued resistance of the Karens along the Thai border and of the outlawed Burma Communist Party in the north-east, Ne Win remained in effective control of the Republic until August 1988, when a General Strike and student demands for the restoration of democracy forced him out of office. On 18 September 1988 General Saw Maung seized power; his military régime, the 'State Law and Order Restoration Council', officially changed the name of Burma to Myanmar. Long-promised elections were held in May 1990. Despite ruthless intimidation they were won by the Opposition movement, the National League for Democracy, led by ►Aung San Suu Kyi, daughter of the political leader assassinated in 1947. General Saw Maung refused to relinquish power and placed Aung San Suu Kyi and forty-four elected deputies under arrest. Despite UN condemnation the Myanmar military dictatorship persisted in denying the country democratic rights although when, in April 1992, Saw Maung was replaced by General Than Shwe as head of the government, a constitutional convention was summoned and during 1995–6 more than 2,000 political detainees were released. A sentence of twenty-five years' imprisonment on a leading NLD spokesman, Daw San San, in April 1998 reaffirmed the repressive character of the military regime.

Burma Campaign. Lasted from 20 January 1942, when the Japanese crossed the Burma–Siam frontier, until 25 July 1945, when the British Fourteenth Army captured the railhead of Taunggyi in the Shan State of eastern Burma. Most of the land fighting on the allied side was undertaken by British, Gurkha and Indian units under the command of Sir William ➤Slim, although US and Chinese troops under General Joseph Stilwell put pressure on the Japanese from the north. The Burma Campaign falls into four main phases: (1) the Japanese advance against ill-prepared positions, which gave them all Burma by the end of May 1942; (2) an abortive allied offensive in the Arakan jungle (October 1942 to March 1943) which failed primarily because of the difficulty of maintaining links with bases in India; (3) the decisive battle of Imphal (March to June 1944) when Japanese attempts to besiege isolated garrisons were frustrated by use of air power until the besiegers themselves were forced to surrender – the worst defeat ever sustained by the Japanese on land; (4) the recovery of the Irrawaddy basin and Rangoon (February to May 1945), a victory made possible by the army's response to the decision of the Supreme Allied Commander in south-east Asia, Lord ➤Mountbatten, that fighting should continue through the five months of monsoon. Improvisation and unorthodox tactics – brilliantly exemplified by Major-General ➤Wingate and his 'Chindits' – destroyed the myth of Japanese invincibility in jungle fighting.

Burns, John (1858–1943), pioneer British socialist. Born in Vauxhall, London, of Scottish descent, apprenticed to engineering. Burns learned his socialism from a veteran of the Paris Commune, exiled since 1871, and acquired his gift of oratory from temperance meetings, before becoming a trade unionist. He played a prominent part in organizing the first London Dock strike (1889). In 1892 he was elected MP for Battersea as an independent socialist, remaining in parliament as a 'Lib-Lab' until 1918 and holding office in the Liberal governments (President of the Local Government Board, December 1905 to February 1914, and President of the Board of Trade, February–August 1914). Burns was the first working-man to sit in a British cabinet and become a Privy Councillor. In 1914 his pacifism made him resign from Asquith's government, whereafter he virtually withdrew from public life.

Burundi. Former Belgian trusteeship in central Africa, north-east of Lake Tanganyika, covering an area only slightly smaller than Belgium itself. The first Europeans to control the region were the Germans, who annexed the territory to German East Africa in 1890. Burundi, with neighbouring ➤Rwanda, passed into Belgian hands as a League of Nations mandate in 1919; it became an independent constitutional monarchy in July 1962 and a republic in November 1966. Political power was exercised by the Tutsi, a traditionally warrior people, but a small minority in a republic where 83 per cent of the population was Hutu. The Tutsi savagely repressed political demonstrations by Hutu in 1965, 1969, 1972 and 1988 but, under foreign pressure, an attempt was made in 1992–3 to set up a coalition government, with ministers from both peoples. The Tutsi-led army refused to accept the new government and in October 1993 plunged the republic into civil war, especially bitter around the capital, Bujumbura. Half a million Hutu refugees fled to neighbouring Rwanda, Tanzania and Zaire. Despite attempts to form other coalitions the fighting between the Tutsi army and the Hutu militia intensified. By July 1996 the massacres were so widespread that six leading African nations imposed economic sanctions on the military regime in Burundi in the hopes of ending the bloodshed.

Bush, George Herbert Walker (1924–), forty-first President of the USA. Born in Milton, Massachusetts, served in the US Navy, and studied economics at Yale, he became an active Republican campaigner in 1962 after making a fortune in Texan oil. He stood unsuccessfully for the Senate (1964 and 1970), was a Congressman 1966–70. Under ►Nixon he represented America at the UN but, as chairman of the Republican National Committee when the ►Watergate Affair became a scandal in 1974, put pressure on the President to resign. He was briefly ambassador in Peking and, later, headed the CIA. After failing to gain nomination himself in 1980, Bush became Reagan's running-mate and was Vice-President 1981–9. In the presidential election of 1988 he easily defeated the Democrat candidate, Michael Dukakis, only losing seven states. No sitting Vice-President had won a presidential election this century. His administration followed a vigorous foreign policy in the Middle East, especially after the Iraqi seizure of ►Kuwait. At home his Republican-ism was more centrist than Reagan's. Lack of a cohesive domestic policy aroused state self-assertiveness. In November 1992 a bored electorate preferred ►Clinton and the Democrats. Bush retired to Texas.

Bustamente, (William) Alexander (1884–1977, knighted 1955), Jamaican political leader. Born the son of an Irish planter, near Kingston; spent an adventurous youth in Spain, Morocco, Cuba, New York and Panama, before returning to Jamaica in 1932 and becoming an active militant trade unionist. Although interned under emergency powers in 1940, he was able to found the Jamaican Labour Party in 1943 and secure a majority of seats in the 1944 elections of the House of Representatives. From 1949 he was recognized as the chief political spokesman of the Jamaicans but was strongly opposed to any West Indian Federation. When Jamaica gained dominion status in August 1962 Bustamente became the island's first Prime Minister, retiring through ill-health in 1965. His demagogic gifts stirred politically apathetic people into action.

Butler, Richard Austen (1902–82, created a life peer, Lord Butler of Saffron Walden, 1965), British Conservative politician. Born in India, educated at Marl-borough and Pembroke College, Cambridge, elected MP for Saffron Walden in 1929, holding the seat until elevated to the peerage. He held minor posts in the MacDonald, Baldwin and Chamberlain governments from 1932 to 1940. As Under-Secretary for Foreign Affairs in 1938 he was a convinced supporter of ►'Munich'. Churchill appointed him President of the Board of Education in 1941 and he was responsible for the English Education Act of 1944, which established the three types of free secondary education – grammar, technical and modern: the

Butler Act, dependent on an 'eleven plus' examination, set the pattern of state education in England and Wales for the next twenty years. Butler entered the cabinet as Minister of Labour in May 1945, but had less than two months of office before Attlee's electoral victory threw the Conservatives into opposition. Between 1945 and 1951 he encouraged the Conservative Party to accept the principles of a welfare state: subsequently he was always regarded as slightly to the left of centre by members of the party machine. He was Chancellor of the Exchequer (1951–5), Home Secretary (1957–62), Foreign Secretary (1963–5) and deputy Prime Minister from 1962 to 1965. Twice he was a contender for the premiership: in January 1957 when the Conservative elder statesmen advised the Queen to appoint ➤Macmillan rather than Butler as Eden's successor; and in October 1963 when Sir Alec ➤Douglas-Home succeeded Macmillan. Although Butler loyally supported six successive Conservative leaders and worked unstintingly to modernize the party, he never warmed the hearts of the electorate as a whole. On retiring from politics in 1965 he accepted the Mastership of Trinity College, Cambridge.

Byrnes, James Francis (1879–1972), US Secretary of State. Born in Charleston, South Carolina, became a lawyer and sat as a 'Southern Democrat' Congressman from 1911 to 1925. In 1930 he was elected a Senator for his native state, serving ten years in office. Although uneasy at the more radical aspects of the ➤New Deal, Byrnes played a major role in securing Roosevelt's nomination for a third term in 1940. He was then successively a Justice of the Supreme Court (1941–2), director of economic stabilization (1942–3) and director of war mobilization (1943–5) before being appointed Secretary of State by President Truman on 1 July 1945. Byrnes favoured a policy of action through the United Nations rather than any direct confrontation with Russia but he also encouraged Germany's economic revival, under American auspices. He was the first Secretary of State to travel widely abroad while in office (prompting a Republican critic to comment, 'Truman fiddles while Byrnes roams'). In January 1947 he was succeeded by General ➤Marshall. From 1951 to 1955 Byrnes was Governor of South Carolina, showing himself a traditionalist over civil rights and race relations.

C

Caillaux, Joseph (1863–1944), French politician. Born at Le Mans, served as a tax inspector before being elected a Deputy in 1898. Within a year of entering the French Chamber he was appointed Minister of Finance in Waldeck-Rousseau's Radical-Socialist Government. Caillaux was Minister of Finance under seven different Premiers, holding the office 1899–1902, 1906–9, 1911–14, 1925, 1926 and 1935. In the Clemenceau Ministry of 1906 he proposed an income tax, a rare and unpopular source of revenue in France. From June 1911 to January 1912 Caillaux was Prime Minister of a predominantly Radical Government. He was suspected of favouring reconciliation with Germany, and his alleged pro-German sympathies led to his arrest and imprisonment by the Clemenceau Government in 1918. His political fortunes were not helped by the mistaken loyalty of his second wife who on 16 March 1914 assassinated the editor of *Figaro*, at a time when the newspaper was making a series of accusations against her husband as Minister of Finance. Although Caillaux lost his seat in the Chamber of Deputies in 1919, he was elected a Senator for Sarthe (his home department) in 1925 and remained in the Senate until his death. He played a considerable part in overthrowing the ►Popular Front Government in the Senate in 1937.

Cairo Conference (22–26 November 1943). A summit conference between Churchill and Roosevelt, preliminary to the ►Teheran Conference. The Cairo meeting was especially concerned with the Far East, and was unique in being attended by the Chinese generalissimo, ►Chiang Kai shek. The conference approved war aims for the Far East, which included the unconditional surrender of Japan and her deprivation of all conquests made since 1894.

Callaghan, (Leonard) James (1912–), British Prime Minister. The son of a naval chief petty officer, he was educated at Portsmouth and became an official of the Inland Revenue before serving in the navy throughout the Second World War. In 1945 he was elected Labour MP for South Cardiff, the constituency being changed to Cardiff South-East in 1950. He held minor government offices from 1947 to 1951 and in 1963 stood unsuccessfully against Harold Wilson and George Brown for leadership of the Labour Party. Callaghan was Chancellor of the Exchequer (1964–7), Home Secretary (1967–70) and Foreign Secretary (1974–6). When Harold Wilson announced his pending resignation on 16 March 1976, Callaghan again stood for the Labour leadership, winning 176 votes on the third ballot against 137 for Michael Foot. He became Prime Minister on 5 April 1976, holding office until defeated in the general election of May 1979. He resigned the

Labour Party leadership on 15 October 1980 but remained an MP until June 1987, when he received a life peerage.

Calwell, Arthur (1896–1973), Australian politician. Born in Melbourne and became a civil servant. Prominent in the Australian ►Labour Party, as a progressive Roman Catholic, from 1940 onwards. He was Minister of Information in 1943 but became best known as Minister of Immigration in the government of ►Chifley from 1945 to 1949. Calwell determined the form of post-war immigration, adhering strictly to the principle of a 'white Australia' but admitting more southern and eastern European workers than did earlier governments. Calwell was deputy leader of his party in opposition from 1951 and leader from 1960 until 1967.

Cambodia. The centre of a powerful empire in south-east Asia between about 1010 and 1280, became a French protectorate in 1863 and from 1884 onwards was treated as part of ►Indo-China though allowed to retain its dynasty. In 1947 the reigning sovereign Prince Sihanouk (1922–) issued a constitution promising parliamentary government. This was followed by independence within the French Union (1949), total independence in November 1953 and the establishment of a constitutional monarchy free from all foreign links in January 1955. Inevitably Cambodia was influenced by the contest between Communists and non-Communists in neighbouring ►Vietnam. Prince Sihanouk's neutralist policy was interpreted by US observers as favouring the North Vietnamese and in March 1970 his rule was overthrown by a militarist revolt, headed by Marshal Lon Nol (1913–85), who proclaimed a republic (officially, the 'Khmer Republic'). For three years the USA built up the forces of Lon Nol, who was forced to wage a civil war against the communist 'Khmer Rouge' movement (backed by Prince Sihanouk from exile in Peking). The Communists rapidly gained control of the countryside, leaving Lon Nol powerful in the capital, Phnom Penh, until the city fell to the Khmer Rouge in April 1975. A full-scale Marxist revolution was thereupon carried out in 'Democratic Cambodia', with the population of the capital being forced to work in the fields as part of the political re-education. Prince Sihanouk resumed his position as head of state in September 1975 but resigned seven months later. Effective control was thereafter exercised by the bloodthirsty regime of the nominal Prime Minister Pol Pot (1928–98). Frontier disputes east of the Mekong River led to open warfare between Cambodia and Vietnam in December 1977. With Soviet backing, the Vietnamese shifted their support from Pol Pot to the 'Kampuchean National United Front for National Salvation', led by Heng Samrin. A combined Vietnamese and Kampuchean army invaded the country in December 1978, captured Phnom Penh on 7 January 1979 and established the 'People's Republic of Kampuchea'. Khmer Rouge forces of Pol Pot received political patronage from both China and the United States, continuing to resist on the borders of the country. By the end of 1979 it was calculated that more than three-and-a-half million Kampucheans (half the estimated population of the country) had perished in the fighting, famine and political killings of the previous five years. International relief organizations helped the Kampuchean economy to recover during 1980–81. Prince Sihanouk and the Khmer Rouge formed a coalition government in territory held by Khmer Rouge soldiers along the Thai border in June 1982, threatening a resumption of the strife which has weakened Cambodia/Kampuchea intermittently for a quarter of a century. Sihanouk's government represented Cambodia at the UN, and by March 1986 controlled the important town of Battambang. Meanwhile, bolstered by the presence of 120,000 Vietnamese troops, Heng Samrin's 'People's Revolutionary Council' (PRK) in Phnom Penh revived rice production and basic industries in a region devastated by the atrocities of the Pol Pot regime. The Vietnamese withdrew their High Command in June 1988. Talks between neighbouring governments continued for the remainder of the year in the hopes of establishing an administration in Kampuchea which, while keeping out Pol Pot, would also curb PRK's political influence. In April 1989 the name Kampuchea was formally dropped, the country being once more officially called Cambodia. Fighting between the PRK government forces, the Khmer Rouge rebels and Sihanouk's American-backed 'non-communist' troops continued throughout most of the following two years. Under a new constitution in September 1993 Cambodia became a parliamentary monarchy, with Sihanouk formally elected King. The Khmer Rouge set up a provisional government along the frontier with Thailand but over the following two years there were massive defections and by June 1997 the power of the communists seemed broken. But on 6 July there was an upsurge of fighting in the capital, when the Second Prime Minister, Hub Sen, attempted to oust the First Prime Minister, Prince Ranariddh. Phnom Penh was looted and sacked in several days of anarchy. The Khmer Rouge was too weak and discredited to take advantage of the chaos; the death of Pol Pot was confirmed by neutral doctors in April 1998. He had been held in detention by his former followers, but died from a heart attack.

Cambon, Jules (1845–1935), French diplomat, brother of Paul Cambon (see below). Born in Paris; was Governor-General of Algeria, 1891–7; ambassador in Washington, 1897–1903; ambassador in Madrid, 1903–7; ambassador in Berlin, 1907–14; and a delegate to the Paris Peace Conference of 1919–20.

Cambon, Paul (1843–1924), French diplomat, brother of Jules Cambon (see above). Born in Paris; ambassador in Madrid, 1886–91; ambassador in Constantinople, 1891–8; and ambassador in London, 1898–1920. Although he arrived in London during a period of great tension caused by imperial rivalry in Africa, Paul Cambon worked throughout his mission for Anglo-French cooperation, achieving the ►Entente Cordiale of 1904 and the military alliance of the First World War. The Cambon brothers were masters of diplomatic statecraft, unmatched as ambassadors in their generation.

Cameroons. The Cameroons, lying on the west coast of central Africa, were acquired as a German Protectorate in 1884 and occupied by Anglo-Nigerian and French forces in 1915–16. Under the Treaty of Versailles of 1919 the Cameroons were partitioned, the larger area becoming a French mandate and the smaller area a British mandate, linked administratively with neighbouring Nigeria. The French granted independence to their section of the Cameroons in January 1960. A United Nations plebiscite in the British Cameroons led to an overwhelming vote for union with its independent neighbour, which was achieved on a federal basis in October 1961. Eleven years of peaceful development were followed in July 1972 by a constitutional amendment which created the United Republic of Cameroon. In November 1995 the Cameroon Republic joined the ►Commonwealth.

Camp David Talks (5–17 September 1978). Conversations between the Israeli Prime Minister Menachem Begin and President Sadat of Egypt were held at Camp David, Maryland, under the chairmanship of President Carter to promote a Middle East peace settlement, following the ►Sadat initiative of November 1977. Agreement was reached on the signature of an Israeli–Egyptian peace treaty within three months, providing for normal diplomatic and economic relations between the two states. Provision was also made for demilitarized security zones on the frontier, for gradual Israeli withdrawal from Sinai, and for a five-year transitional period on the West Bank of the Jordan which would permit the development of some Palestinian autonomous authority. Ambiguity of expression left uncertainty over some aspects of the agreements, which prompted the resignation of the Egyptian Foreign Minister. Despite condemnation by the ►Palestine Liberation Organization the talks were generally recognized as holding out the prospect of a settlement. A peace treaty was finally signed at Washington on 26 March 1979. Israel at last handed back Sinai to Egypt on 25 April 1982 after fifteen years of occupation, but opposition from Israeli right-wing zealots made achievement of the other Camp David objectives a remote possibility.

Campaign for Nuclear Disarmament (CND). A movement launched on 17 February 1958 by Bertrand ►Russell and Canon L. John Collins for the abandonment of nuclear weapons and for a substantial reduction in British defence spending. The movement developed from protests made originally at Easter 1956 outside the Atomic Weapons Research Establishment at Aldermaston, Berkshire. The Easter 'Aldermaston March', culminating in a major protest in Trafalgar Square, attracted wide support from 1958 to 1964. CND demonstrations in Trafalgar Square during the crisis caused by the building of the Berlin Wall in September 1961 led to over 1,300 arrests. Unilateral disarmament resolutions triumphed at the Labour Conference of 1960 but subsequently lost their appeal to the party (►Bevan). The more militant wing of CND, 'the Committee of One Hundred', broke away from the movement in 1962, which thereafter seemed to lose its momentum. At its peak in 1960–61 CND had more active supporters than any mass movement in Britain since the Anti-Corn Law League of the 1840s. Similar protest movements developed outside Britain, notably in the USA, France and Australasia. CND began to revive in June 1980 with the probability that Cruise missiles would be deployed in Western Europe. Some 50,000 people attended a CND rally in London on 26 October 1980. There were further demonstrations against nuclear missiles in Britain and in other European countries (including Romania) in the winter of 1981–2 and there was a powerful protest in New York in June 1982. In Britain both the TUC and the Labour Party voted in favour of unilateral nuclear disarmament at the annual conferences held in September 1981, a change of mood attributed largely to the fresh impetus from CND.

Campbell-Bannerman, Henry (1836–1908), British Prime Minister. Born Henry Campbell, the son of a Lord Provost of Glasgow. (The additional surname Banner-man was added in 1871, on inheriting property from an uncle.) 'C-B' was educated at Glasgow High School and Trinity College, Cambridge, becoming Liberal MP for Stirling in 1868 and holding the seat for forty years. He was Gladstone's Chief Secretary for Ireland, 1884–5, but did not enter the cabinet until he became War Secretary in 1886, an office he held again with particular distinction, 1892–5. Although never a good parliamentary speaker, he became Liberal leader in the Commons in 1898 and increasingly identified himself with the progressive wing of the party: thus, he opposed the Boer War and began to demand radical social reforms. In December 1905 he was asked to form a government – becoming the first man ever to hold the official title 'Prime Minister'. His government introduced land reforms and trade-union legislation; above all, it paved the way for a reconcili-ation with South Africa, culminating in the grant of self-government to the defeated Boer states. 'C-B' was an extremely popular party leader, but he was dogged by ill-health, which forced him to resign on 3 April 1908. He died – at 10 Downing Street – less than three weeks later.

Canada. By the British North America Act of 1867 the four existing provinces of Canada – Quebec, Ontario, Nova Scotia and New Brunswick – were united in one dominion. They were joined by British Columbia (1871) and Prince Edward Island (1873), while Manitoba was constituted a province in 1870. By the start of the twentieth century Canada was therefore accustomed to a dual system of government through provincial legislatures and a bicameral federal parliament in Ottawa. But Canada's sense of unity was impaired by the narrowly regional loyalties of the French-speaking Canadians who, though concentrated in Quebec Province, formed more than a quarter of the population. From 1896 to 1911 the ►Liberal Party was in office under a French Canadian, ►Laurier. At first he successfully combated the separatist tendencies of his compatriots. Religious sentiment was, however, stirred by the creation of two new provinces, Alberta and Saskatchewan (1905), where there were disputes over the future of church and state (secular) schools. The Liberals suffered principally from accusations that Laurier was further-ing 'the Americanization of Canada', a charge made originally in 1907 but reiterated in 1911 when a reciprocity agreement with the United States seemed to favour American trading interests. The ►Conservative Party was in power from 1911 until December 1921, led for nine years by Sir Robert ►Borden.

Nearly half a million Canadian soldiers fought in Europe during the First World War, one in eight of whom were killed. The international status won by Canada was offset by increasing isolationist separatism in Quebec. The federal structure of Canada was at its weakest in the 1920s, not only because of this friction between English- and French-speaking Canadians, but through suspicion that urban communities were exploiting rural areas and that the eastern provinces ignored the interests of the western. For most of the period 1921–30 the Liberals were in office under Mackenzie ►King, but never with a sufficiently large representation in parliament to give strong government. The impact of economic depression in 1930 gave an electoral victory to the Conservatives under Richard ►Bennett, who imposed heavy tariffs against American goods and appeared to strengthen Canadian trade at the imperial economic conference of 1932 in ►Ottawa. Subsequent Conservative attempts to introduce a centralized 'New Deal' policy aroused resentment in every province and the 1935 election gave King's Liberals a landslide victory.

The Liberals remained in power for twenty-two years: from 1935 to 1948 under King; from 1948 to 1957 under Louis ►St Laurent. These years saw a double (and complementary) change in Canada's relationship to the outside world: she became a major industrial nation, harnessing vast natural resources; and she began to pursue an increasingly independent foreign policy, collaborating closely with the United States from 1940 onwards for defence of North America, and subsequently joining NATO as a founder member. This policy of world commitment (also marked by vigorous participation in United Nations enterprises and by support for the ►Colombo Plan) was in contrast to the isolationism of interwar years. Uneasiness at the increasing economic dependence of the dominion on the USA contributed to the Conservative return to power under John ►Diefenbaker in 1957. Diefenbaker strengthened Commonwealth links, but could not reduce the interdependence of the American and Canadian economies. The Liberals, under Lester ►Pearson, won the election of 1963. Pearson's five-year premiership saw an increase in Canadian support for the United Nations (Canada sent soldiers and airmen on fifteen UN peacekeeping missions) and a refusal to become involved in Vietnam. At the same time French Canadian separatism began to assert itself dramatically, with a demand for ►'Québec libre', a policy encouraged by an irresponsible speech from President de Gaulle of France during a visit in July 1967. These problems intensified under the Liberal Governments of Pearson's successor, Pierre ►Trudeau, April 1968 to May 1979. The short-lived Conservative Government of Joe Clark (May 1979 to February 1980) was followed by a third Trudeau ministry which was particularly concerned with 'patriation' of the constitution (i.e. abolishing the links with Britain surviving from the 1867 British North America Act). Fear of excessive centralization at Ottawa made the proposal suspect to Trudeau's critics. Security officers were summoned to the chamber because of the violent scenes in parliament when patriation was debated in October 1980. Nevertheless Canada formally asked Britain for patriation of the constitution in December 1981. Queen Elizabeth II travelled to Ottawa to acknowledge Canada's complete national sovereignty on 17 April 1982 (►Newfoundland.) Trudeau resigned office on 30 June 1984. An election three months later was won by the Progressive Conservatives, led by Brian Mulroney (1939–) who formed a government of Thatcherite inclinations on 17 September. He gained another victory in the snap election of November 1988, by which he won support for a US–Canadian trade agreement. But Mulroney's attempts at constitutional reform, designed to satisfy Quebec, were rejected in a national referendum in October 1992. Eight months later he handed over the premiership to Kim Campbell; she was herself defeated by the Liberals under Jean Chrétien (1934–) in the general election of October 1993. The Liberals were confirmed in power in June 1997 by a further electoral victory.

Canterbury, Archbishop of. Primate of All England, and therefore recognized as leader of the Anglican communion of churches throughout the world. At the start of the twentieth century the primacy was held by Frederick Temple (1821–1902), primate from 1896 until his death, and the ninety-fifth Archbishop of Canterbury since the foundation of the see by St Augustine in 597. Temple was succeeded by Randall Davidson (1848–1930), primate 1903 to 1928, who was the first Archbishop to resign on the grounds of age. Cosmo Gordon Lang (1864–1945), formerly Bishop of Stepney and Archbishop of York, held the primacy from 1928 to 1942 and played a prominent role in the ►Abdication crisis of 1936. Lang's successor was William Temple (1881–1944), son of the ninety-fifth Archbishop. As Bishop of Manchester from 1921 to 1929 and then as Archbishop of York until 1942, William Temple was respected for his Christian Socialist beliefs, which made him sympathetic to the aspirations of the working masses. He championed cooperation between the churches, working out with the leaders of other denominations a joint statement of principles for the post-war world. He died suddenly in October 1944, only two and a half years after becoming primate, and was succeeded by the Bishop of London, Geoffrey Fisher (1887–1972), Archbishop from 1945 to 1961. In November–December 1960 Fisher became the first Archbishop of Canterbury to visit the Ecumenical Patriarch of Constantinople (Istanbul) and the Pope in Rome. Collaboration between the Christian churches was also emphasized by Fisher's successor, Michael Ramsey (1904–88), Archbishop of Canterbury from 1961 to 1974, who paid an official visit to Pope ►Paul in March 1966 and encouraged a movement for unity between the Anglican and Methodist churches. Ecumenicism continued during the primacy of Donald Coggan (1909–), 1974–80. His successor, Robert Runcie (1921–), was enthroned on 25 March 1980 and on 29 May 1982 welcomed Pope ►John Paul II to Canterbury for an impressive ecumenical service in the cathedral. In July 1988 he presided, at Canterbury, over the largest Lambeth Conference of archbishops and bishops of the Anglican communion. Dr George Carey (1935–), Bishop of Bath and Wells, was enthroned as Dr Runcie's successor in April 1991.

Caporetto, Battle of (24 October to 4 November 1917). Caporetto (Karfreit) is a small town on the river Isonzo, ten miles inside the Austrian frontier of 1915. This distance represented the limit of Italian advances in eleven battles fought on the Isonzo during the first two and a half years of Italy's War. On 24 October 1917 an Austro-German counter-offensive broke the Italian line at Caporetto, forcing the Italians back over the pre-war frontier. Italian attempts to hold defensive positions on the river Tagliamento on 31 October were frustrated by the momentum of the offensive. The front was only stabilized along the river Piave at the end of the first week in November by the hurried arrival of British and French reinforcements and by the inability of the Austrian supply services to keep up with their troops. Nearly 300,000 Italians were taken prisoner: even more deserted. Shame at this humiliating rout had important consequences in later years, Mussolini's fascist movement being anxious to 'wipe away the stain of Caporetto' by fostering military virtues in the Italian people.

Carol II (1893–1953; reigned 1930–40). King of Romania. Eldest son of King Ferdinand (reigned 1914–27) and Queen Marie; married Princess Hélène of Greece, 1921. Carol's playboy behaviour as Crown Prince led Ferdinand to disinherit him in 1925, and Carol settled in France with his mistress, Magda Lupescu, the red-headed daughter of a Jewish chemist. On Ferdinand's death Carol's six-year-old son, Michael, came to the throne, under a council of regency. Carol was in exile until June 1930 when, with the support of the Romanian Prime Minister (Juliu Maniu), he flew suddenly to Bucharest and was proclaimed King. For seven years Romania remained nominally a parliamentary democracy but in 1937 Carol's admiration for Mussolini led him to establish a disguised royal dictatorship, openly assuming all essential powers of government in February 1938, when he suppressed the Romanian political parties. Carol, who paid state visits to London and Paris in the following autumn, believed he could play off the Western Powers against Hitler, using Romania's wealth in oil and wheat as bargaining counters. But Carol miscalculated: he made economic concessions to Hitler in the winter of 1939–40 only to find the Germans unwilling to support Romania when she was faced with demands for frontier revision from the Soviet Union, Bulgaria and Hungary. Between June and August 1940 Carol was forced to cede ►Bessarabia, northern ►Bukovina, southern ►Dobrudja and half of ►Transylvania. The Romanians, finding it difficult to reconcile these losses with his bombastically patriotic speeches, turned against him. He abdicated on 6 September 1940 in favour of his son, Michael, and went into exile again, accompanied by Magda Lupescu (1896–1977), whom he married shortly before his death.

Cars ►Motor Vehicles.

Carson, Edward Henry (1854–1935, knighted 1900, created a baron 1921). Born and educated in Dublin, was Unionist MP for Dublin University from 1892 to 1918 and for a Belfast constituency from 1918 to 1921. He became a formidable barrister. From 1900 to 1906 he was Solicitor-General under Salisbury and Balfour. In 1910 he organized British Protestant resistance to Irish Home Rule, setting up an Ulster Unionist Council in 1911. A year later he established the Ulster Volunteers, a private army of 80,000 men pledged to resist Home Rule. In May 1915 he became Attorney-General in the Asquith wartime coalition, but left the government five months later and became a leader of dissident Tories. In December 1916 he assisted Bonar Law and Lloyd George to secure the resignation of Asquith and became First Lord of the Admiralty (December 1916 to July 1917), subsequently serving for six months as a Minister without Portfolio in the War Cabinet. After the war Carson tried to find a compromise solution to the Irish problem. From 1921 to 1929 he was a Lord of Appeal.

Carter, Jimmy (James Earl) (1924–), thirty-ninth President of the USA. Born at Archery, Georgia, educated at South Western College, Georgia, and the US Naval Academy, commissioned in the navy 1947, serving in battleships and submarines until 1953 when he returned to Georgia and engaged in peanut farming. From 1962 to 1966 he was a State Senator (Democrat) and was elected Governor of Georgia in 1971. He gained the Democratic Party nomination for the Presidency at the party's New York convention on 14 July 1976, choosing Senator Walter Mondale of Minnesota as his Vice-Presidential running mate. At the subsequent election on 3 November Carter won 51 per cent of the popular vote against Gerald Ford's 48 per cent, and he duly took office in January 1977. Inexperience of Washington politics marred Carter's relations with Congress, while the contraction of world oil supplies in 1979 posed an energy crisis he never really solved. The ►Camp David Talks and a further round of ►SALT talks brought some success in international affairs. These gains were offset by the deterioration of American– Soviet relations over ►Afghanistan and by the collapse of the Shah's government in ►Iran. The seizure of American hostages at the American embassy in Teheran on 4 November 1979 and the failure of a rescue mission by helicopters authorized by the President (24–25 April 1980) destroyed Carter's standing with the American public. In the Presidential election of November 1980 he was decisively defeated by the Republican candidate, Ronald ►Reagan. The Iranians handed over the hostages on the day Carter left office (20 January 1981).

Casablanca Conference (14–24 January 1943). A meeting in French Morocco between Churchill and Roosevelt. Plans were agreed for the invasion of Sicily, for an increase in American bombing of German territory, and for the eventual transference of British military resources to the Far East after the defeat of Italy and Germany. Roosevelt issued a statement, agreed with Churchill, insisting on the 'unconditional surrender' of the Axis powers rather than a negotiated settlement. Attempts to lessen friction between Roosevelt and the 'Free French' were only partially successful: General de Gaulle (who met the US President for the first time at Casablanca) resented being invited to an allied conference held on French territory without his prior knowledge.

Casement, Roger David (1864–1916, knighted 1911). Born in Kingstown (Dun Laoghaire), near Dublin, and entered the British consular service in 1892, gaining distinction by his reports of 1903 and 1910 on atrocities in the rubber plantations of the Congo and Brazil. He retired from the consular service shortly after his knighthood and became a fervent Irish nationalist. At the outbreak of the First World War he travelled from the United States to Berlin in order to secure German aid for Irish independence. For eighteen months he vainly sought to recruit Irish prisoners of war for the German army. On the eve of the ➤Easter Rising of 1916 he was landed from a German U-boat near Tralee but was arrested within a few hours. He was brought to London, tried for high treason at the Old Bailey, and hanged. His so-called 'Black Diaries', containing homosexual passages, were circulated by British agents to discredit him and discourage any movement for a reprieve. To the Irish he remains a patriot martyr.

Cassino. A small town in the mountains of south-eastern Latium, dominated by the monastery of Monte Cassino founded by St Benedict in the early sixth century. In November 1943 Field-Marshal Kesselring ordered the construction of extensive fortifications around Cassino as part of the German 'Gustav Line' against the allied armies who had already advanced 300 miles up the Italian peninsula. Cassino effectively barred entry into the Liri Valley and the route to Rome. In February and March 1944 the Germans withstood a series of attacks by British, Canadian, American, Indian and New Zealand troops. General ➤Alexander wrongly believing there were German troops in the monastery, reluctantly ordered it to be destroyed by bombing on 15 February 1944 as it was a vantage point for the defenders; but it was not until 18 May 1944 that Monte Cassino was taken by Polish and British troops, opening the way to Rome which fell seventeen days later.

Castro, Fidel (1927–). The son of a sugar-planter, with land near Santiago de Cuba. Castro studied law at the University of Havana in the late 1940s, later practising law as a defender of the poor in Havana. On 26 July 1953 he led an armed revolt against the Moncada barracks, close to his birthplace. The revolt failed but helped create a myth: Castro subsequently called his band of revolutionaries the '26 July Movement'. After serving two years in prison, Castro was freed as part of a general amnesty and went into exile, mainly in Mexico, where he prepared a guerrilla campaign against the regime of ➤Batistá. On 2 December 1956 he returned secretly to east Cuba in the yacht *Gramma*, accompanied by some eighty followers who included his younger brother, Raul, and Che ➤Guevara. For eighteen months Castro conducted guerrilla operations from a base in the Sierra Maestra, winning for himself a legendary reputation as a latter-day Garibaldi, a mysterious and romantic nationalistic liberal revolutionary. In March 1958 Castro issued a manifesto calling on the Cubans to make 'total war' against Batistá. The insurrection was so successful that he entered Havana in triumph on 8 January 1959, becoming Prime Minister of Cuba a month later. The Americans, who originally patronized Castro, turned against him in 1960 when he strengthened contacts with Russia and China. The ➤Bay of Pigs incident of April 1961 encouraged him to look for help in Moscow and he celebrated the fifth anniversary of his return to Cuba by a speech in which he claimed to have been a Marxist-Leninist since his days as a student. The ➤Cuban Missiles Crisis of 1962 convinced the Americans he was a threat to US security, although he was in that year involved in conflict with the principal doctrinaire Cuban communist, Anibale Escalante, whom he exiled. His concern to promote revolution in Latin America and to encourage liberation movements in Africa made him an increasingly difficult partner for his Russian allies. Basically his movement remained dependent on his personality, leadership and sense of destiny. His 'Marxist-Leninism' had an arbitrary and individualistic quality inappropriate to any other region in the world. Castro's absence from national celebrations in the summer of 1997 led to reports that he was gravely ill, but he was able to deliver a seven-hour speech to the Communist Party Congress in October 1997 and received Pope ➤John Paul II on his visit to Cuba three months later.

'Cat and Mouse Act' (1913). Term generally applied to the 'Prisoners, Temporary Discharge for Health, Act'. This measure was introduced by the Liberal Government of Asquith to provide for the release on licence of ➤suffragettes who refused to take food while in prison for violent offences. The licence would be revoked if the released prisoner committed a further offence. Although the Act reduced the need to resort to forcible feeding, it was criticized on humanitarian grounds by many prominent figures and was not successful as a deterrent.

Cavell, Edith (1865–1915), English nursing sister. Born at Swardeston, Norfolk, and appointed matron of the first Belgian teaching hospital in Brussels, 1907. She remained in Brussels after the German occupation of 1914 and helped British, French and Belgian wounded soldiers to escape to neutral Holland. most of them eventually reached England. In August 1915 she was arrested by the Germans and court-martialled. She admitted having assisted about 200 men of military age to reach the border. On 12 October 1915 she was executed by firing squad in Brussels. Her death aroused widespread indignation in Britain and was exploited for propaganda purposes. Responsibility for her death rested solely with the occupation authorities in Brussels: neither the Kaiser nor the High Command were informed that she had been sentenced to death. The Kaiser deplored her execution, which he considered a political mistake.

Ceauşescu, Nicolae (1918–89), President of the Romanian Socialist Republic. Born eighty miles north-west of Bucharest, near Piteşti; entered the underground Communist Party in 1936, assuming responsibility for building up the Union of Communist Youth, both before and after the entry of Soviet troops into Romania in August 1944. Ceauşescu's career was advanced by Gheorghe ➤Gheorghiu-Dej,

General Secretary of the Romanian party from 1954 onwards. Ceauşescu was appointed to the party secretariat in April 1954, and from 1957 until Dej's death in 1965 he was, in effect, deputy leader of the country. In March 1965 he became General Secretary of the party and, after overcoming a threat to his position from the pro-Soviet chief of the security services, he was elected head of state in December 1967, a post to which he was re-elected when the constitution was modified in March 1974. Ceauşescu frequently criticized Soviet policy, emphasizing the national sovereignty of each Communist state. He denounced the Soviet occupation of Prague in 1968 but made no attempt to take Romania out of the ➤Warsaw Pact or ➤Comecon. In reviving the Romanian sense of national pride, he tolerated increasing abuse of the guarantees assured to national minorities by the 1952 Constitution, especially in his treatment of Magyar communities in ➤Transylvania. In 1978 he made a State Visit to London and was fêted as an independent communist but in his later years the harsh character of his repressive policies intensified. He promoted his own family and embarked on eccentric and grandiose public works projects. He was overthrown in ten days of violent revolution in December 1989. After a summary trial Ceauşescu and his wife were executed by a firing squad on Christmas Day.

Central Intelligence Agency (CIA). Established by Congressional authority in 1947 to coordinate and analyse foreign intelligence reports for the US President (to whom the Agency was solely responsible) and his policy-makers. The chairman of the National Security Council was also director of the CIA: the principal directors were Allen Dulles (who held office 1953–61), John McCone (1961–5) and Richard Helms (1966–73). Under Allen Dulles the original purpose of the CIA – intelligence analysis – was changed into the planning of 'covert operations', intended to remove foreign governments whose policies ran counter to US interests. Early successes in Guatemala and Iran (1953–4) were invalidated in April 1961 by the fiasco of the ➤Bay of Pigs which induced President Kennedy and John McCone to curb the operational planning role of the CIA and improve its intelligence reporting. This change of emphasis enabled the CIA to provide accurate information on the events leading to the ➤Cuban Missiles Crisis of 1962. At the same time CIA activities were occasionally continued without reference to McCone, notably plans to assassinate Castro and to increase US influence in south-east Asia. The presidencies of Johnson and Nixon saw a revival of 'covert operations' (culminating in the overthrow of the Allende Government in ➤Chile) and a decline in effective intelligence reporting, strikingly illustrated by the failure to predict the ➤Yom Kippur War of 1973 or the crisis in ➤Cyprus nine months later. The ➤Watergate Scandal revealed a proliferation of agencies which often infringed civil liberties and raised doubts in Washington over the role of the CIA. Committees of the House of Representatives and of the Senate were established to study 'governmental operations with respect to intelligence activities'. The report of the Senate committee, under the chairmanship of Senator Church, was published on 26 April 1976: it called for stricter control of the intelligence services and greater accountability of the system to the American public through Congress.

Central Powers. Before 1914 the phrase was used to describe the combination of Germany, Austria–Hungary and Italy, which had been formally linked as allies since Bismarck concluded the Triple Alliance of 1882. When Italy remained neutral on the outbreak of war in 1914, the phrase was loosely used to distinguish Germany and Austria–Hungary (together with their ally, Turkey, and later Bulgaria) from the 'Entente' Allies (France, Russia and Britain).

Centre Party. The principal political organization for Roman Catholic voters in Germany between 1871 and 1933. Originally the Centre Party sought to defend Catholic interests against the predominantly Prussian Protestant policy of Bismarck, but it later became an effective conservative force against the expanding socialist groups. From 1893 to 1907 the Centre Party had the dominating voice in the coalitions supporting the Chancellors in parliament, but it subsequently lost influence to more nationalistic and Pan-German groups. The Centre Party leader Mathias Erzberger (1875–1921) carried a parliamentary Peace Resolution in July 1917, favouring a negotiated peace, free from annexations. Erzberger ensured that the Centre Party remained influential under the Weimar Republic. Among the leaders of the party were ➤Brüning and Papen. With other German democratic parties it was dissolved on Hitler's orders on 5 July 1933. ➤Adenauer, a member of the Centre Party for more than thirty years, preferred to create a Christian Democrat Union after the Second World War rather than revive an outdated political body.

Ceylon. An island in the Indian Ocean, developed by the Portuguese in the sixteenth century and the Dutch in the seventeenth; passed under British rule in the Napoleonic wars and remained a British colony from 1815 to 1947, with its economy mainly dependent on tea and rubber. There were two predominant racial and religious groups in Ceylon: the Sinhalese, traditionally Buddhist, formed three quarters of the population; the remainder of the people were mainly Hindu Tamils. Universal suffrage, introduced in 1931, provided for an elected legislature and an executive council on which people born in Ceylon shared authority with the British. The Ceylon Independence Act of 1947 gave the island dominion status within the Commonwealth, and a government was established by the United National Party, headed by Don Senanayake and, after his death in 1952, by his son, Dudley Senanayake. The socialist 'Sri Lanka Freedom Party' (associated with the ➤Bandaranaike family) provided a more radical alternative, while at the same time appealing to narrowly Sinhalese loyalties. The SLFP were in power from 1956 to 1965, their attempts to establish Sinhalese rather than English as the official language leading to rioting. A further electoral victory for Mrs Bandaranaike in 1970 was followed in May 1972 by a new constitution which established the island as the Republic of ➤Sri Lanka.

Chaco Dispute. The Chaco Boreal, a plain at the foot of the Andes, was disputed intermittently by ➤Bolivia and ➤Paraguay from 1879 onwards. Rumours of oil deposits led to serious clashes in 1927, which were referred to the League of Nations. An arbitration convention, drawn up in August 1929, was rejected by both sides. The Paraguayans withdrew from negotiations in Washington in 1931, and open war broke out in the Chaco (July 1932). The Paraguayans occupied the whole region and inflicted a series of defeats on Bolivia before a truce was concluded in June 1935. Peace negotiations were held at Buenos Aires and provided for a territorial settlement to be decided by six Latin American Presidents. Their decision, announced on 10 October 1938, awarded the greater part of the Chaco Boreal to Paraguay although guaranteeing that Bolivia should have a trade route to the South Atlantic by way of the Paraguay river. It is believed the war cost the lives of 100,000 men.

Chad. A land-locked republic in north-central Africa, covering an area twice as large as France. Chad was formerly the northernmost territory of French Equatorial Africa. It was organized as a French colony in March 1920 although the capital, Fort Lamy (now N'Djamena), was controlled by the Governor-General of Equatorial Africa in Brazzaville, on the lower Congo, 1,100 miles to the south. In August 1940 Chad was the first French territory to respond to General de Gaulle's call to the ➤Free French to continue the fight against the Axis Powers. Chad became a self-governing state within the French Community in 1958, independence following in August 1960. It was, however, weakened by a chronic political conflict between the nomadic Arabs of the North, who looked across the border to ➤Libya, and the black African Christians of the South. The first President, Francois Tombalbaye, was assassinated in a military *coup* in May 1975, his death beginning a period of unrest marked by Libyan backing of the Chad northerner, Goukouni Oueddei. Goukouni's tenure of the Presidency was safeguarded by the presence of Libyan troops from January to November 1981. A peacekeeping force of Nigerian, Senegalese and Zairean troops from the ➤Organization of African Unity failed to prevent civil war engulfing Chad from 19 November 1981 until 7 June 1982 when the rebel army, FAN ('Armed Forces of the North'), entered the capital and ousted President Goukouni in favour of the forty-two-year-old national-ist leader, Hissene Habré. Goukouni, and his Libyan backers, controlled Chad north of the 16th parallel. French troops and aircraft were sent to N'Djamena in 1984 and 1986 when it seemed as if civil war would again erupt, but in May 1988 Libya formally recognized the Habré government. President Habré began a further seven-year term of office in December 1989.

Chamberlain, (Joseph) Austen (1863–1937, created a Knight of the Garter, 1925). Born in Birmingham, the eldest son of Joseph ➤Chamberlain and half-brother of Neville ➤Chamberlain. He was elected Conservative MP for East Worcestershire in 1892 and remained in the House of Commons until his death. He served as Chancellor of the Exchequer under Balfour, 1903–5, but failed to win the

Conservative leadership in 1911. During the coalition governments he was Secretary of State for India, 1915–17, Minister without Portfolio, 1918–19, Chancellor of the Exchequer, 1919–21, Lord Privy Seal, 1921–2. His most constructive work was as Foreign Secretary in Baldwin's government, 1924–9, when he played a prominent role in the discussions leading to the ►Locarno Treaties of 1925, for which he received a Nobel Peace Prize.

Chamberlain, Houston Stewart (1855–1927), racialist writer. Born in Kent, the son of an admiral in the Royal Navy, and educated at Cheltenham. Admiration for the music of Richard Wagner (whose daughter he married) encouraged Chamberlain to settle in Germany, where he decided that 'the moral and spiritual salvation of mankind depends on German qualities' (as he told Kaiser William II). From this assumption he developed theories of German racial purity which he expressed in his book, *The Foundations of the Nineteenth Century* written in German and published in 1899. This work popularized the myth of Aryan superiority within Germany, a philosophy basically imperialistic, anti-liberal and anti-Semitic. Chamberlain became a naturalized German in 1914. As early as October 1923 he greeted Hitler as the saviour destined to purge and restore Germany; and Hitler paid tribute to the 'wisdom of his civic principles' when he wrote *Mein Kampf*.

Chamberlain, Joseph (1836–1914). Born in London, the son of a shopkeeper and educated at University College School, but made his fortune as a manufacturer in Birmingham. His pioneering slum-clearance schemes as a radical Lord Mayor of Birmingham won him national recognition in 1875. Two years later he entered the House of Commons for a Birmingham constituency: the people of the city remained politically loyal to him for the remainder of his life, even though he moved from radical liberalism to imperialism. He was Gladstone's President of the Board of Trade, 1880–85, but his opposition to Irish Home Rule in 1886 split the Liberals and brought down the government. From 1895 to 1903 he was Colonial Secretary in the Conservative-Unionist governments of Salisbury and Balfour, working especially for expansion in Africa and for imperial federation. His influence within the cabinet was second only to that of the Prime Minister and he frequently intervened in matters of foreign policy, notably in 1898 and 1899 when he sought an Anglo-German alliance. From 1903 to 1905 he campaigned for ►Tariff Reform, a cause which led to splits in the Conservative Party almost as divisive as those which had earlier rent the Liberal Party. He was struck down by paralysis in 1906 and took no further part in politics.

Chamberlain, (Arthur) Neville (1869–1940). Born in Edgbaston, the son of Joseph Chamberlain and half-brother of Austen, educated at Rugby, spent seven years in the Bahamas vainly trying to make profits from a sisal plantation purchased by his father. After returning to Birmingham in 1897, he went into the copper-brass business and entered local politics, becoming Lord Mayor in 1915. For seven months in 1916–17 he was director-general of National Service but was abruptly dismissed by Lloyd George, who did not understand Chamberlain's methodical and detailed conduct of affairs. From 1918 to 1929 he was Conservative MP for the Ladywood division of Birmingham and from 1929 until his death he represented Edgbaston. His municipal experience made him a successful Minister of Health in the Baldwin Government of 1924–9. From November 1931 to May 1937 he was an orthodox Chancellor of the Exchequer. When Chamberlain became Prime Minister (28 May 1937) he knew little of foreign affairs but was faced by a succession of European crises. His stubbornness inclined him to prefer the reports of his personal adviser, the senior civil servant, Sir Horace Wilson (1882–1972), to information from the Foreign Office. Chamberlain's policy of ►appeasement rested on the belief that if Germany had legitimate grievances, these could be settled in man-to-man talks between Hitler and himself. During the Czechoslovak crisis of September 1938 Chamberlain flew to Berchtesgaden and to Bad Godesberg in the hope of securing agreement with Hitler, believing that at ►Munich he had ensured 'peace for our time'. Chamberlain, who overrated Germany's strength and unity of purpose, abandoned appeasement after Hitler's occupation of Prague in March 1939 and offered Poland (which seemed threatened by Germany) military support. Attempts to secure an Anglo-Russian alliance were half-hearted and abortive, but in September 1939 Chamberlain's government honoured the pledge to Poland and went to war with Germany. During the first winter of war Chamberlain's hesitancy and bad handling of personal relations aroused criticism in parliament and the Press. He resigned on 10 May 1940, after the German surprise occupation of Denmark and Norway. Chamberlain was already a sick man but he served as Lord President of the Council in Churchill's coalition until his death six months later.

Chanak Crisis (September–October 1922). A crisis in Anglo-Turkish relations arising from the victory of Mustapha Kemal (►Atatürk) over the Greeks at ►Smyrna and his intention of carrying the war into the European territories assigned to Greece by the abortive Treaty of ►Sèvres. In London, it was feared that Kemal would also attack the allied army of occupation guarding the approaches to Constantinople. The Prime Minister, Lloyd George, favoured the reinforcement of British detachments serving at Chanak, on the Asiatic shore of the Dardanelles. The crisis eased with the conclusion of a convention at Mudania (11 October 1922) between the British commander, General Harrington, and the Turkish representative, General Ismet (►Inönü). This agreement pledged the return to Turkey of eastern Thrace and Adrianople, provided the Turks accepted the neutralization of the Dardanelles and Bosphorus, and the convention formed a basis for the Treaty of ►Lausanne in July 1923. The Chanak Crisis had the incidental effect of precipitating the break-up of the Lloyd George coalition, since the Conservative leaders were alarmed by his apparent irresponsibility in bringing the country to the brink of a war with Turkey. Lloyd George was out of office within a fortnight of the Mudania convention.

Channel Tunnel. A treaty was signed by the British and French foreign ministers at Canterbury on 12 February 1986 providing for government cooperation in the construction by a private consortium of a twin-tunnel rail-link between Cheriton (Kent) and Fréthun (Pas-de-Calais). The first Channel Tunnel Company was set up in 1881 and the project was given serious study by the Suez Canal Company in 1957; both governments approved the project in 1964 and two years later gave an estimated completion date of 1975. Slow progress was made until 1973 when the Heath Government tackled the project with vigour. Rising costs led to the abandonment of this scheme by the Labour Government in 1975, interest returning only when the heads of the EEC governments met at Bonn in May 1985. When the Canterbury treaty was ratified in July 1987 hopes were expressed that the tunnel would be in use by 1993. Pilot tunnels, constructed from either coast, met on 1 December 1990 to give a land link between Britain and the Continent; but the first passenger rail service did not begin until 14 November 1994.

Charles (1887–1922, reigned 1916–18), Emperor of Austria and King of Hungary. Became heir to the Habsburg throne on the murder of his uncle, ➤Francis Ferdinand, at Sarajevo in 1914. He succeeded his great-uncle, ➤Francis Joseph, on 21 November 1916. Charles was anxious to take Austria–Hungary out of the First World War through a negotiated peace, wishing then to introduce reforms in the constitutional structure of his realm. Through Prince Sixte of Bourbon-Parma – brother of his wife, the Empress Zita (1892–1989) – Charles secretly contacted the British and French: preliminary talks were held before the Germans discovered about the peace feelers and tightened control over their ally. His reform proposals came too late to prevent disintegration of the Empire in November 1918. Charles refused to abdicate, withdrawing into private life in Switzerland. Twice in 1921 he secretly returned to Hungary and attempted to recover his throne, but he was forced to leave the country through the hostility both of the ➤Little Entente and of the Hungarian Regent, Admiral ➤Horthy. Charles died from pneumonia in exile in Madeira on 1 April 1922: his eldest son, Archduke Otto (1912–), became claimant to his titles.

Chechnya. The Chechens are a historic people, long settled in the north-eastern Caucasus. They attacked Russian settlements so often in the early nineteenth century that in 1818 Tsar Alexander I ordered the construction of a heavily fortified town, Grozny, to serve as a military base for subduing Chechnya. Even so, the Chechens withstood Russian attempts to incorporate them in the tsarist empire from 1826 to 1860, and again rebelled in 1877–8. The Soviet Union administered the Chechen lands as the autonomous republic of Chechen-Ingush within the Russian Soviet Federal Socialist Republic: Grozny became the capital and expanded rapidly as a major centre of the petroleum industry. German troops penetrated Chechnya to within sight of Grozny's oil refinery in September 1942, the furthest advance eastwards of Hitler's armies. In November 1991 Chechnya seceded from

Yeltsin's new ➤Russia and sought to establish an independent republic. Civil war began in February 1994, although it was not until the following December that Yeltsin ordered the bombing of Grozny and a military invasion of Chechnya. The Russians occupied Grozny early in February 1995 but the Chechens continued to resist, instigating terrorist acts and guerrilla raids within Russia. Attempts at a compromise settlement, agreed in July 1995 and followed by an offer of autonomy in December, failed to satisfy the Chechens, who mounted an attack on Grozny in March 1996. War-weariness in Russia brought a ceasefire which lasted from May to July 1996, when the Chechens again entered ruined Grozny. A definitive ceasefire was concluded by General Alexander Lebed and the Chechen leader, Aslan Maskhadov, on 27 August 1996: the conflict ended, but a decision on Chechnya's political status was postponed until 2001. A meeting between Yeltsin and Maskhadov in Moscow in May 1997 re-affirmed the mutual peace pledge and left open the question of Chechen independence. The European Union immediately pledged more than £1 million in aid to Chechnya.

Chernobyl, site of Soviet nuclear power station in the Ukraine, 80 miles north of Kiev. On 26 April 1986 unauthorized experiments with inadequate safety measures culminated in the destruction of one of the plant's four graphite-moderated reactors, releasing large quantities of radiation. During the following fortnight twenty other countries were affected by the atmospheric pollution, especially Sweden, Finland, Poland and Czechoslovakia. Sheep and cows in parts of Scotland, Cumbria and Wales were also found suffering from high levels of radiation. More than thirty people died in the initial explosion; it was calculated that for the remainder of the century there would be several thousand cancer deaths associated with this nuclear disaster. In July 1987 the former senior executives at Chernobyl were found guilty of criminal negligence and sentenced to imprisonment with hard labour.

Chetniks. The original Chetniks were Serbian guerrillas seeking to liberate their homeland from the Turks. Chetnik bands were especially active in Macedonia between 1907 and the outbreak of the ➤Balkan Wars. During the First World War the Chetniks raided German supply lines through the occupied regions of the Balkans. An embryonic Chetnik organization was retained in interwar Yugoslavia and in 1941 was placed under the command of General ➤Mihailović. Although the Chetniks at first offered resistance to the German occupation forces, their ideology was narrowly Serbian rather than Yugoslav in sentiment and they were strongly opposed to communism. The Chetniks received British support until the beginning of 1944: they aided allied airmen who had been shot down; and as late as October 1943 they blew up an important bridge over the river Lim in Bosnia. Yet there was no doubt that several Chetnik commanders collaborated with the Germans and Italians against the ➤partisans of Tito, notably on the river Neretva in March 1943. Mihailović advised the Chetnik commanders to avoid active resistance to the occupation forces until the arrival of an Anglo-American army of liberation. But it was the Russians, rather than the British and Americans, who entered the Balkans; and the Chetniks could therefore expect no mercy. Although rigorously suppressed in Tito's communist Yugoslavia, the Chetnik insignia and right-wing Serbian chauvinist ideology reappeared in 1990–91, to fuel fresh hatred of Croats and Bosnian Muslims as Yugoslavia disintegrated.

Chiang Kai-shek (Jiang Jieshih, 1887–1975), Chinese nationalist general and President. Born in Fenghwa, Chekiang province, the son of a village merchant, received military training at the Imperial Military Academy and a Japanese staff college, serving in the Japanese Army for several years. He was an early supporter of Sun Yat-sen and on the establishment of the Chinese Republic in 1911, he returned home in order to assist Sun build up a republican army. Chiang spent six months in Moscow in 1923, studying the Red Army, and subsequently set up the Whampoa Military Academy at Canton, tending in later years to favour officers whom he had trained there. When Sun died in March 1925 there was a struggle for succession among the leaders of his party, the ►Kuomintang (Guomindang). Chiang Kai-shek had two advantages over his rivals at this time; a disciplined and ready army; and a politically central position. In 1926 Chiang consolidated his authority by a brisk and effective campaign against the warlords. By June 1928 he was in firm control of Nanking, Peking and Canton as well as holding the posts of chairman of the Kuomintang and commander-in-chief. Four months later an Organic Law formalized Chiang's presidential dictatorship over the republic. His hold on the country was, however, never secure. Intermittent conflicts with the communists absorbed his attention from 1927 to 1931; he was faced by major army rebellions in 1930, 1933 and 1936; and the Japanese occupation of ►Manchuria in 1931 limited his freedom of action in northern China. Chiang's critics maintained that he was too concerned with preserving his monopolistic dictatorship to resist the Japanese; but they recognized his international prestige, which he had acquired both as legitimate head of the Chinese state and through the influence of his American-educated second wife, Soong Mei-ling (Suoeng Meiling) (a sister-in-law of Sun Yat-sen). Chiang himself accepted Christian beliefs, counting himself a Methodist from 1930 onwards.

Early in December 1936 Chiang was kidnapped by dissident officers in Sian. The officers were in contact with the Chinese communists and Chiang was only released after thirteen days through the intervention of ►Chou En-lai (Zhou Enlai), who travelled to Sian and secured from Chiang an assurance he would call off his campaign against the communists and accept their aid in resisting Japanese encroachments. The prospect of a united front in China encouraged the Japanese to act speedily. In July 1937 they launched a full-scale war against Chiang's strongholds and by the end of the year had forced Chiang to establish his capital in Chungking, Szechwan province. He remained there, organizing resistance to Japan until the end of the Second World War. American respect for Chiang's capabilities won him acceptance as one of the 'Big Four' allied war leaders. In

1943 he attended the ➤Cairo Conference and met Roosevelt and Churchill, his only direct contact with western statesmen. By 1945 it was clear his allies had exaggerated his power. Despite talks between Chiang and the communist leader, ➤Mao Tse-tung (Mao Zedong), in the autumn of 1945, Kuomintang and communist army brigades fought each other on the Yangtze and in Manchuria. When civil war spread in 1947 Chiang was unable to control the corruption within the Kuomintang, and was soon faced by massive military defections. He expected American intervention which did not materialize, largely because President Truman's advisers had no confidence in his army's will to resist. When Peking fell to the communists in January 1949, Chiang resigned as President of China, but he returned as chairman of the Kuomintang seven months later in order to supervise the departure of his remaining followers for ➤Formosa. There, on 1 March 1950, he formally resumed the Presidency, hoping he would eventually return with US military backing to the mainland. He remained President in Formosa (Taiwan) for the last twenty-five years of his life, unable to gain a footing on the mainland, but seeing Taiwan enjoy boom prosperity through its close economic links with Japan and the USA.

Chifley, (Joseph) Benedict (1885–1951), Australian Prime Minister. Born in Bathurst, New South Wales, the son of a blacksmith, of Irish Catholic origin. He became a railway worker and was, for a time, an engine driver, being a prominent member of the railway union from 1917 onwards. He sat as a Labour member of the federal parliament from 1928 to 1931 and was a controversial Minister of Defence, 1929–31. He remained out of parliament from 1931 to 1940, but became Finance Minister (Treasurer) under ➤Curtin in October 1941, subsequently also assuming responsibility for post-war planning. He prepared a comprehensive social-insurance scheme for Australia. When Curtin suddenly died on 5 July 1945, Ben Chifley was his natural successor as head of a Labour administration. Chifley – a man of humour, strong moral convictions, homespun principles and considerable experience – was a legendary figure, idolized by Labour voters as none of his predecessors had been. His proposed nationalization of the banks was, however, unpopular outside Labour ranks and his authority was weakened in 1949 by a seven-week coal strike, inspired by communists and settled only after the mines had been manned by army units. In the general election of December 1949 a Liberal-Country Party coalition, under ➤Menzies, decisively defeated Chifley's government, largely through fears of the growing communist influence in key unions.

Chile. Achieved independence from Spain in 1818. During the nineteenth century the republic became the dominant power in western Latin America, a position marked from 1861 onwards by sound and basically democratic government and consolidated by military victory against Bolivia and Peru in the 'War of the Pacific' (1879–83). The export of nitrate in the First World War created a boom which was followed by a disastrous economic slump in the 1920s. Radical liberal governments under Arturo Alessandri in 1920–24, 1925 and 1932–8 introduced social reforms, but were opposed by the army, by fascist groups and by an active communist movement (which received greater freedom of expression in Chile than elsewhere in South America). Marxists collaborated in Popular Front governments under Aguirre Cedra in 1938 and under Gabriel Videla in 1946, but a right-wing reaction in 1947 led to communist-led strikes and in September 1948 the Chilean Communist Party was proscribed. A left-wing coalition party reappeared in the elections of 1958 and 1964, which were, however, won by Christian Democrats. In failing to check inflation or to redistribute wealth, the Christian Democrats paved the way for an electoral success of the Left; and in September 1970 Dr ►Allende became the first democratically elected Marxist head of state. Allende's attempts to 'open the road towards socialism' included the nationalization of copper-mines owned by US subsidiaries. The CIA regarded Allende as a pro-Castro communist and encouraged opposition to his reforms. On 11 September 1973 leaders of the armed forces attacked the Presidential palace in Santiago, overthrew the Allende government and established a military junta, headed by General Augusto Pinochet (1915–). President Allende was killed during the putsch (or, as the new government claimed, committed suicide): all political parties were dissolved, and a regime of severe repression instituted against socialists and liberals. Even when Pope John Paul II visited Chile in April 1987, police opened fire on a crowd of 600,000 people in Santiago where he was celebrating an open-air Mass of Reconciliation. A new constitution, drafted in 1980–81, confirmed General Pinochet as President, with provision for a plebiscite in seven years' time to decide if his Junta should continue in office until 1997. On 5 October 1988 56 per cent of the electorate voted against Pinochet. The constitution gave him the right to remain in office for another eighteen months; he finally handed over to President Azocar on 11 March 1990. Although Pinochet remained titular commander-in-chief of the armed forces until 1997, the republic completed a transition to democratic rule under Azocar and his elected successor, Eduardo Frei, who took up office in March 1994.

China. On 10 October 1911 a revolt organized by the ►Kuomintang (Guomindang) under ►Sun Yat-sen overthrew the Manchu dynasty, which had ruled China since 1644. Although Sun was made President of a provisional republican government his authority was disputed by local war-lords and from 1917 until his death in 1925 his power was limited to the area around Canton. There followed a struggle for succession, won by General ►Chiang Kai-shek (Jiang Jieshih), who established a national government, with Nanking as its capital, in 1928. His rule was, from the outset, challenged by the communists, under ►Mao Tse-tung (Mao Zedong), and a Chinese Soviet Republic was proclaimed in Kiangsi province in 1931. Nationalist military campaigns against the Kiangsi Soviet forced Mao and his communists to leave southern China: in October 1934 they set out on an epic twelve-month ►'Long March' to establish a new base in northern China, around Yenan in Shensi province. Meanwhile Japan took advantage of China's weakness to occupy

➤Manchuria in 1931 and begin a full-scale invasion of northern China in July 1937, following an 'incident' on the Marco Polo bridge outside Peking. Although Chiang's army and Mao's communists at first collaborated to resist the Japanese, the whole of the eastern seaboard was in Japanese hands by October 1938. From his wartime capital in Chungking, Chiang Kai-shek was able to keep in touch with the British and Americans, who until 1942 sent him supplies from Burma. The communists controlled much of north-western China from Yenan: a puppet Japanese regime was established in Nanking, until Japan's surrender in August 1945. The allies had hoped Chiang's Kuomintang dictatorship would be transformed into a broad coalition which, with American help, would give a lead to China's post-war economic recovery. But both the communists and the Kuomintang sought control of Manchuria, where civil war broke out before the end of 1945. For twelve months the US envoy, General ➤Marshall, tried to reconcile a nationalist spokesman and Mao's representative, ➤Chou En-lai, but the task was beyond him and the USA formally gave up all attempts to mediate in China on 29 January 1947.

Foreign observers at first assumed that Chiang, with his superior equipment, would defeat the communists in the civil war. The communists concentrated on the countryside, abandoning cities and evading major battles until the Kuomintang overstretched their supply lines and resources. By the end of 1947 the communists had isolated Kuomintang strongholds in Manchuria and were threatening central China, going over from guerrilla warfare to major set battles in the spring of 1948. The decisive military action of the revolutionary civil war was fought between November 1948 and early January 1949 around the walled towns of Suchow and Yungcheng: it is known in China as the 'battle of ➤Huai-Hai'. The Kuomintang lost more than half a million men in this battle: Tientsin and Peking were occupied by the communists in January 1949, Nanking in April, Shanghai in May, Canton in October. The Chinese People's Republic was formally proclaimed in Peking on 1 October 1949. Only ➤Formosa and some offshore islands remained under the authority of Chiang Kai-shek.

From 1949 to 1953 the Chinese communists concentrated, in home affairs, on achieving strongly centralized control from Peking while carrying through basic land reforms. Foreign policy was dominated by the ➤Korean War, fulfilment of a Soviet–Chinese Alliance Treaty (February 1950) and the establishment of a Chinese presence in Tibet. Soviet aid helped industrial undertakings within the first Five-Year Plan of 1953–7. After encouraging criticism in 1957, a more repressive regime was introduced in 1958, together with the radical innovations known as the ➤'Great Leap Forward'. This attempt to speed up the creation of a communistic society by the institution of large rural communes proved a failure. Setbacks in production were intensified by mounting ideological friction between ➤Khrushchev and Mao which led in August 1960 to the withdrawal of Soviet technical assistance. Economic hardship was countered by a vociferously aggressive foreign policy (which led to border warfare with India in 1961–2) and by a cult of the personality of Mao Tse-tung, including throughout the 1960s the intensive study of his 'thoughts'.

From August 1966 until the early months of 1969 a ►'cultural revolution' sought to impose Maoist principles on the people, largely by use of student rallies. The 'cultural revolution' purged the administration, but disrupted both industry and formal education. Chou En-lai, Prime Minister since the establishment of the People's Republic, survived the 'cultural revolution' – the one experienced veteran, apart from the rapidly ageing Mao. Under Chou's guidance the republic improved diplomatic relations with the western world, gaining admission to the ►United Nations in October 1971. The explosion of an atom bomb in October 1964 and of a hydrogen bomb in June 1967 emphasized China's independent status as a 'superpower'. Improvements in China's internal economy were accompanied by increasing intervention in African affairs, challenging the Soviet role as principal patron of international Marxism.

The death of Chou in January 1976, followed within eight months by the deaths of ►Chu Teh (Zhu De) and Mao Tse-tung, left considerable political uncertainty in China. On 12 October 1976 ►Hua Kuo-feng (Hua Guofeng) was named as the new Chairman of the Chinese Communist Party. It was also announced that six radical politicians had been arrested, including Mao's widow, Chiang Ching (Jiang Qing), who had played prominent parts in the 'cultural revolution'. Ten counter-revolutionaries were eventually put on trial in Peking on 20 November 1980. Mao's widow was found guilty of sedition and conspiracy and a suspended death sentence passed upon her (25 January 1981).

Hua's authority remained considerable until 1978, but he was thereafter over-shadowed by the influential veteran ►Deng Xiaoping, a 'pragmatic modernizer'. Two of Deng's associates, Zhao Ziyang (1918–) and Hu Yaobang (1916–89), edged Hua out of office. When relations with Britain improved over ►Hong Kong, Zhao Ziyang came to London (June 1985) and Queen Elizabeth II visited China in October 1986. Amid mounting student unrest the reformist Hu Yaobang lost his hold on the Politburo. The Party Congress of November 1987 saw the apparent triumph of Zhao: he became General Secretary of the Party while the traditionalist authoritarian Li Peng (1929–) became Prime Minister. A gradual thaw in Sino-Soviet relations healed a rift of 32 years: Qian Qichen, as Foreign Minister, was received in Moscow in December 1988; ►Gorbachev visited China in May 1989. By then, however, the death of Hu Yaobang in April had sparked off student demands for democratic reform and brought thousands of demonstrators into Tiananmen Square, Peking. After seven weeks of peaceful protests aimed at discrediting the ailing Deng and the unpopular Li Peng, tanks and armoured personnel carriers were sent into Tiananmen Square on 4 June 1989, massacring more than 3,000 protesters. Zhao was replaced as party boss by Qian Qichen. There was martial law in Peking until January 1990. Trials of dissidents continued through eighteen months of repression.

Deng's influence ensured that the 14th Party Congress in 1992 backed a 'socialist market economy' and radical economic changes, but the effective head of the ruling State Council, Li Peng, showed greater caution; he imposed austerity restraints throughout 1993–5 in the hopes of checking inflation. Deng's death, early in 1997, a few months before the retrocession of Hong Kong, left plans for economic liberalization unfulfilled. Li Cheng was succeeded in March 1998 by Zhu Rongji (1937–), a former Mayor of Shanghai with a reputation for carrying through progressive reforms.

Chou En-lai (Zhou Enlai, 1898–1976). Chinese communist Prime Minister. Born in Shauhsing, Chekiang province; educated at a missionary school in Tientsin. In 1920–21 he was in Paris, where he worked briefly in the Renault car factory as well as continuing his studies: he was impressed by the anti-imperialism and communist beliefs of fellow students from Indo-China and met the thirty-year-old ➤Ho Chi Minh. By 1924 Chou was back in China, organizing communist cells in Shanghai and (in 1927) an abortive rising in Nanchang. From 1931 onwards he was Mao Tse-tung's (Mao Zedong) principal adviser on urban revolutionary affairs. His knowledge of the outside world made him a natural envoy: he negotiated terms for the release of ➤Chiang Kai-shek after the Sian kidnapping episode of 1936; and throughout most of the period 1941–5 Chou served as a liaison officer at Chiang Kai-shek's wartime capital, Chungking. From December 1945 until January 1947 Chou represented the communists in talks with the US mission seeking to mediate in China's civil war. When the People's Republic was established in 1949 Chou En-lai became Prime Minister, holding the office until his death in January 1976. Until 1958 he was also Foreign Minister, showing diplomatic skill at the ➤Geneva Conference of 1954 and a year later at ➤Bandung. He remained throughout the sixties and early seventies the principal international spokesman for China; he had insisted on maintaining contact with the Americans (who refused to recognize Communist China) through ambassadors in Warsaw, and he led the *détente* with the United States during the Nixon–Kissinger period, especially in 1972–3. In home affairs Chou reluctantly accepted the ➤'cultural revolution' as a means of purging the party machine, but he ended it as speedily as possible in order to develop China's economy. By 1973, when he presided over the Tenth Party Congress, Chou seemed Mao's natural successor but he was, by then, already suffering from cancer and predeceased Mao by eight months.

Chu Teh (Zhu De, 1886–1976), creator and commander-in-chief of the Chinese Red Army. Born in Szechwan province, the son of a wealthy landowner, commissioned in the Chinese Imperial Army but supported ➤Sun Yat-sen in 1911. Although Chu Teh was a brigade commander by the age of thirty, he was also a drug addict, dependent on the smoking of opium until nearly forty. He visited Germany and Paris in the early 1920s, became interested in communism and, on his return to China in 1925, presented his considerable fortune to the Communist Party. He joined ➤Mao Tse-tung (Mao Zedong) in 1928 and set up the earliest Guard units of the Kiangsi Soviet in 1931, beginning a period of twenty-three years in which he was commander-in-chief of the Chinese communist armies. He organized the breakout of the Red Army from Kiangsi in 1934 and the subsequent

➤Long March to Shensi, during which he evaded encirclement and pursuit by Chinese nationalist forces deployed by the former commander of the German Reichswehr, General von ➤Seeckt. Chu Teh commanded the Eighteenth Route Army against Japan, 1937–45, and then evolved the double policy of guerrilla operations followed by set battles which defeated the Kuomintang (Guomindang) in the civil war of 1947–9. He was created a marshal in 1955 and until 1959 seemed the only possible alternative leader to Mao (seven years his junior). In 1965 Chu Teh was widely criticized as an old-fashioned reactionary by the young Red Guards of the 'cultural revolution', but he was formally reinstated in 1967.

Churchill, Winston Leonard Spencer (1874–1965; knighted 1953). Born in Blenheim Palace, Woodstock, the son of Lord Randolph Churchill (who had married an American, Jennie Jerome) and grandson of the 7th Duke of Marlborough. Educated at Harrow and Sandhurst, commissioned in the Fourth Hussars, observed fighting between Spanish and Cuban rebels (1895), saw action on the Indian north-west frontier, took part in the charge of 21st Lancers in the battle of Omdurman (1898). He was a war correspondent in the Boer War (1899–1900), was taken prisoner, escaped and served in the force which relieved Ladysmith. Although elected Conservative MP for Oldham in 1900, his Free Trade principles made him join the Liberals in 1904, and he became Liberal MP for North-west Manchester (1906–8) and for Dundee (1908–22). He became a cabinet minister under Asquith as President of the Board of Trade (1908–10), carrying through important social legislation, including the establishment of employment exchanges. He served as Home Secretary in 1910, and was criticized for using troops to maintain order during a Welsh miners' strike (➤Tonypandy Riots) and for deploying a detachment of Scots Guards to cover an East London house from which two armed anarchists were firing on the police ('Siege of Sidney Street', 3 January 1911). From October 1911 to May 1915 he was First Lord of the Admiralty, supporting modernization of the navy, encouraging aviation, and making certain the fleet was ready for war six days before the British ultimatum to Germany in 1914. He was made a scapegoat for failure at the ➤Dardanelles in 1915 and after six months as Chancellor of the Duchy of Lancaster, he rejoined the army, commanding a battalion of the Royal Scots Fusiliers on the Western Front until May 1916. He served as Minister of Munitions (1917–18), Minister for War and Air (1919–20), and Colonial Secretary (1921–2), visiting Cairo and Jerusalem in order to settle Middle East problems, with T.E. ➤Lawrence as his adviser on Arab affairs. Defeated in the election of 1922, he left the Liberals, was elected as a 'constitutional anti-socialist' MP for Epping (October 1924), becoming Chancellor of the Exchequer (1924–9) under Baldwin six days later, rejoining the Conservative Party early in 1925. He remained MP for Epping until 1945, when the constituency was divided: he then represented the southern half of the old constituency, Woodford and Wanstead, until retiring in 1964. His dislike of concessions to India and his attempts to alert Britain to the new German menace excluded him from office between 1929 and 1939, but he returned to the Admiralty as First Lord on 3 September 1939 under Neville ➤Chamberlain. On 10 May 1940 he became Prime Minister of a coalition government, thus leading the British people in 'their finest hour', sustaining them until the collapse of Germany in May 1945. His popularity during the war enabled him to survive criticism caused by the loss of ➤Singapore and an unsuccessful censure motion in the House of Commons occasioned by reversals in Libya (July 1942). Churchill met ➤Roosevelt on nine occasions between August 1941 (➤'Atlantic Charter') and February 1945 (➤Yalta); and he had five meetings with Stalin between August 1942 and July 1945 (➤Potsdam). With the defeat of the Conservatives in the 1945 general election, Churchill became Leader of the Opposition, visiting America in March 1946 and making his ➤'Iron Curtain' speech at Fulton, Missouri. He suffered the first of several strokes in August 1949, but the news was kept from the general public and he became Prime Minister again, with a small majority, in October 1951. Although still prepared for a ➤summit conference and willing to fly to Washington and the Caribbean for talks with Presidents Truman and Eisenhower, Churchill was too out of touch to offer creative statesmanship. He was made a Knight of the Garter in April 1953, two years before he reluctantly resigned office. For his historical writings he received the Nobel Prize for Literature in October 1953: ten years later he enjoyed the unique distinction of the conferment of honorary US citizenship by Congress. His death on 24 January 1965 was followed by a state funeral for which he had himself worked out the precise details; and he was buried at Bladon, Oxfordshire, less than a mile from his birth-place.

CIA. ➤Central Intelligence Agency.

Ciano, Galeazzo, Count (1903–44), Italian fascist. Born in Leghorn (Livorno), the son of an admiral, became a journalist and entered the diplomatic corps. In April 1930 he married Mussolini's daughter, Edda (1911–95). After serving for two years as Italy's envoy in China, he returned to Rome in charge of the Press before serving briefly as a bomber-pilot in the ➤Abyssinian War. From January 1936 to February 1943 he was Italian Foreign Minister, negotiating the ➤Axis agreements with Germany and favouring Italian expansion into the Balkans. Although to many he seemed irresponsible and excessively imitative of his father-in-law, his diaries show him as an intelligent critic of Nazi pretensions. The Germans distrusted him, suspecting that, as Italian ambassador to the Vatican from February to July 1943, he would seek a separate peace. After voting for Mussolini's overthrow at the Fascist Grand Council of 25 July 1943, he was tricked by agents of ➤Ribbentrop into travelling through Munich, where he was arrested by the Gestapo. Hitler blamed Ciano for Mussolini's downfall. On Germany's insistence he was tried by a neo-fascist court on a charge of treason, and executed at a fort outside Verona on 11 January 1944.

Cinema. Dominant mass entertainment for the first half of the twentieth century.

Silent motion pictures as an art form using professional actors were perfected in Paris by George Méliès (1861–1938) in 1896 and by 1903, when Edwin Porter (1869–1938) completed his *Great Train Robbery*, continuity was provided within a story. American dominance of the art emerged with the technical skills as a director of D.W. Griffith (1878–1948), whose *Birth of a Nation* (1915) first fully used the visual effects which distinguished cinema from theatre. At the same time there was world-wide acceptance of the comedy-pathos perfected by the English-born Charles Chaplin (1889–1977). A 'star' system, developed in the USA from 1907 onwards, projected the personalities of silent actors such as Rudolph Valentino (1895–1926) and Mary Pickford: the low price of admission to cinemas and the simple emotional content of films appealed to mass audiences. US commercial resourcefulness speedily converted entertainment into big business, building up the Los Angeles suburb of Hollywood until it was recognized by 1925 as world centre of the film industry. Hollywood maintained a lead in technical development, popularizing sound films with Al Jolson in *The Jazz Singer* (1927) while colour films were gradually perfected between 1928 and 1935. Competition from television forced Hollywood to develop unusual effects – stereophonic and, at times, crudely spectacular – from 1950 onwards. While American directors were moved principally by commercial considerations, good cinema was exploited in both Nazi Germany and Soviet Russia as an instrument of propaganda: Lenin claimed that the simplicity of contrasted visual images made the cinema the most important of art forms for revolutionary socialism. The Soviet film director, Sergei Eisenstein (1898–1948), was concerned with the impressionistic effects of a crowd rather than any 'star' cult, an aesthetic approach which influenced the great French directors, René Clair and Jean Renoir, as well as British documentary films. After the Second World War the appeal of the cinema declined, despite successful ventures in Italy, Sweden and Japan. By 1968 the mass audience in almost every highly developed country preferred the domestic intrusiveness of television to the communal shared visual experience of cinema.

CIS ▸Commonwealth of Independent States.

Civil-Rights Movement. The series of attempts in the USA to implement the Fourteenth and Fifteenth Amendments to the constitution (1868 and 1870), which established Negro citizenship and right to vote. Segregation, through such devices as a poll tax and literacy tests, was long protected in the South by Supreme Court rulings in 1883 and 1896 which upheld state rights, as opposed to federal rights, in separating one racial group from another. These rulings were reversed by a unanimous Supreme Court decision in the case of Brown *v.* Board of Education of Topeka (May 1954) which asserted that segregation deprived Negro citizens of the equal protection guaranteed by the fourteenth amendment. Federal enforcement of this decision, and of other rulings by the Supreme Court, required the dispatch to Little Rock, Arkansas, of US troops (September 1957). At the same time the Eisenhower Administration passed two Civil-Rights Acts (1957 and 1960) which established a federal agency of six commissioners to investigate complaints that citizens were being denied equal protection of the laws. The violence of white reaction in the South to these measures (together with complaints from Negroes that progress in desegregation was slow) led in 1960 to 'sit-ins' and other forms of direct action. Martin Luther ►King was recognized as leader of this phase of the movement, which culminated in the 'March on Washington' of 28 August 1963 when nearly a quarter of a million Negroes demonstrated peacefully in support of their rights. Under President ►Johnson the Civil Rights Act of July 1964 and the Voting Rights Act of August 1965 formally outlawed racial discrimination over employment, voting, education and public accommodation. Subsequently black militancy, with violent outbursts in Harlem (July 1964) and the Watts district of Los Angeles (11 August 1965), suggested the existence of a more radical movement, for whose followers the Johnson reforms were an unacceptable palliative. Splits in the Negro movement, and the murder of Martin Luther King in April 1968, led to a weakening of federal resolve on civil-rights issues in the Nixon Administration.

Clemenceau, Georges (1841–1929), French Radical Prime Minister. Born at Mouilleron-en-Pareds in La Vendée of an atheistic, republican family; studied medicine, settled in Montmartre where he was mayor in 1870, narrowly escaping death in the Paris Commune. He was a Radical member of the Chamber of Deputies from 1876 to 1893 and Senator for Var from 1902 to 1920. His caustic tongue, sharpened in debate, made him more enemies than friends: he was known as 'the Toppler of Ministers', later as 'The Tiger'. An unhappy marriage to an American ended in separation and intensified his misanthropy. He never held office until March 1906 when he was appointed Minister of Home Affairs, becoming Prime Minister seven months later. His government lasted for two and three-quarter years, the second longest in the Third Republic: it was marked by violent attacks on the socialists and attempts to check the spread of strikes. From 1914 to 1917 Clemenceau was an outspoken critic of military incompetence and defeatism. In November 1917 he became Prime Minister of a government of nonentities, whom he himself called 'the geese that saved the Capitol'. His indomitable courage kept France together under the severe blows of March 1918, enabling him to lead the nation to victory in the following November. Policy was for him determined by temperament rather than doctrinaire principles: he was a patriot and a fighter, not a constructive statesman. His realistic scepticism at the Paris Peace Conference of 1919 infuriated the idealistic Woodrow ►Wilson, but it was felt in France that he had been too lenient towards Germany: this criticism, coupled with resentment by politicians at his exercise of authority, led to his eclipse in January 1920. In retirement he feared a resurgent Germany, even predicting that 1940 would be the year of gravest danger: the title of his memoirs, *The Grandeur and Misery of Victory*, well illustrates his disillusionment.

Clinton, William Jefferson Blythe (1946–), forty-second President of the United States. Born in Arkansas, educated at Georgetown University and University

College, Oxford (as a Rhodes scholar) before completing law studies at Yale. In his home state he was Attorney General in 1977 and Governor, 1979–81 and 1985–92. He was nominated as presidential candidate by the Democrats in 1992 and won the election, with Senator Albert Gore as his running-mate. Bill Clinton became President on 20 January 1993. His first term was hampered by widespread media attacks on alleged property deals while he was state Governor, and the midterm elections of 1994 returned Republican majorities in both houses of Congress. He travelled widely, successfully promoting peace in the Middle East and securing a compromise settlement in Bosnia by the ➤Dayton Accord; he also gave encouragement to the peace process in Ireland by visits to London, Belfast and Dublin shortly before Christmas in 1995. His worldwide prestige, and shrewd political campaigning, gained him a second term in the elections of November 1996 but left him facing a hostile Congress. During 1997 he became exposed to allegations of sexual harassment in earlier years, a charge given wide publicity by political enemies at home. He visited Europe in May 1997 to conclude the NATO agreement with Russia, and in London became the first foreign visitor to address the British cabinet.

Cod War. The name given in the British Press to the period of sustained tension between Great Britain and Iceland (September 1972 to June 1976) originally caused by Iceland's unilateral extension of fishing limits from twelve to fifty miles. The 'cod war' was marked by incidents between Icelandic gunboats and British trawlers, Royal Navy frigates being sent on several occasions to protect vessels fishing in Icelandic waters. A compromise agreement on 1 June 1976 permitted up to twenty-four British trawlers to fish within a 200-mile zone claimed by Iceland.

Coggan, (Frederick) Donald (1909–). ➤Canterbury, Archbishop of.

Cold War. The political and diplomatic conflict between the Western Powers, under US leadership, and the Eastern European bloc. The term originated in a speech of Bernard ➤Baruch in Columbia, South Carolina, on 16 April 1947 at a time when the United States Congress was discussing the ➤'Truman Doctrine', which sought to check further Soviet penetration in Europe by giving American economic and military aid to governments threatened by communist subversion. The ➤Marshall Plan followed within three months. The initial Soviet response was the foundation of the ➤Cominform. The communist take-over in ➤Czechoslovakia and the blockade of ➤Berlin intensified the conflict, while the division of Europe was completed by the formation of the ➤North Atlantic Treaty Organization in 1949–50 and the Soviet-dominated ➤'Warsaw Pact' of May 1955. Moments when tension eased – for example at the ➤Geneva Summit Conference of July 1955 – were followed by new crises: ➤Hungary and ➤Suez in 1956; the ➤Berlin Wall in 1961; ➤Cuban Missiles in 1962. The abortive Rapacki Plan of October 1957 and the *Ostpolitik* of the West German Chancellor, Willy ➤Brandt, from 1970 to 1972 held out prospects of reconciliation. Technically there is no point at which the 'Cold War' ended. Tension relaxed during the early years of the Gorbachev era. After the reunification of Germany in 1990 and the growth of democracy in Hungary and Czechoslovakia, President Bush celebrated the end of the Cold War in his State of the Union message of January 1991.

Collins, Michael (1890–1922), Irish Prime Minister. Born in Cork, the son of a farmer, worked in London as a postal clerk and a bank cashier before returning to Ireland as an extreme nationalist, assisting in organizing the ➤Easter Rising of 1916. His militant views led to short terms of imprisonment in 1916 and 1918. As a member of the first Dáil Éireann he was sent as a delegate to the London Conference on Ireland in October 1921 which gave southern Ireland dominion status as the 'Irish Free State'. Collins became the first Prime Minister of the Free State in January 1922. He was faced, however, by a new wave of terrorism, organized by the Irish Republican Society, and it was one of their extremist groups which assassinated him in August 1922 while he was inspecting troops of the new Irish Army.

Colombia. Fourth largest state in South America, was colonized by Spain in the early sixteenth century and achieved independence in 1819 but did not become a unitary republic until 1886. A series of civil wars (basically between groups sympathetic to, or hostile to, the USA) reached a climax in the War of the Thousand Days (1899–1902) in which two extremely bloody battles were fought (1901). A separatist group, financed by Americans interested in constructing a ➤Panama Canal, secured the independence of the department of Panama in 1903. Thereafter, despite frequent eruptions of urban violence, Conservative administrations elected on a limited franchise held on to government in the capital, Bogotá, until 1930 when for eighteen years they gave way to nominally Liberal governments. From 1948 to 1957 – an era known as *La Violencia* – these two opposing groups resorted to open warfare in which one in twenty-five of the population perished. From 1957 to 1974 a system of alternating power and office between Conservatives and Liberals was allowed to function, until the republic was thrown into further civil war by a neo-fascist military group (FARC) and by the emergence of four left-wing guerrilla factions. During the 1980s the chronic insurgency was intensified by an alliance of neo-fascists and drug barons with power bases in the second and third largest towns, Medellin and Cali, which were said to control four-fifths of the world's illicit cocaine 'industry'. A new democratic constitution introduced in 1991 soon saw the re-emergence of the two traditional rival parties. The presidential victory of the reformist Ernesto Samper in 1994 promised an end to corruption but chronic guerrilla war continued, with Samper's credibility destroyed by allegations that £3 million for his election campaign came from drug barons. The frequent planting of bombs by the left-wing ELN movement along the trans-Andean oil pipeline crippled Colombia's legitimate economy. Hopes of peace returned when Andres Pastrana was elected President on 21 June 1998 and at once met leaders of the main guerrilla groups. It was agreed to summon a national convention within three months in order to promote reforms and a lasting ceasefire. Independent paramilitary leaders also gave assurances of peace once the guerrillas laid down their weapons.

Colombo Plan. A meeting of Commonwealth Foreign Ministers was held at Colombo, Ceylon, in January 1950 to discuss ways in which the richer nations (Australia, Canada, New Zealand and the United Kingdom) could assist the economic development of the poorer lands in southern and south-eastern Asia. Details of the Plan were worked out at a meeting of the Commonwealth Consultative Committee, also held in Colombo, in February 1951. Originally the Plan proposed the provision of money, advice and technical training primarily for India, Pakistan, Ceylon, Burma, Malaya and other territories closely associated with the United Kingdom. But the Australian Government, headed by ►Menzies, wished the Plan to have American backing, believing it might check the spread of communism in Asia, much as had the ►Marshall Plan in Europe. The USA therefore participated in the scheme, contributing eventually more funds than the older Commonwealth governments. At the same time the scope of the Plan was enlarged so that the Philippines, South Korea, the non-communist successor states in Indo-China, Thailand, Indonesia, Afghanistan and Nepal might also benefit from the capital aid and training programmes.

COMECON (Council for Mutual Economic Assistance). An organization established in Moscow (January 1949) for improving trade between the Soviet Union and other Eastern European states. The original members were Albania, Bulgaria, Czechoslovakia, Hungary, Poland, Romania and Russia. East Germany joined in 1950, Mongolia in 1962, Cuba in 1972 and Vietnam in 1978; Albania was expelled in 1961. Stalin, in founding Comecon, regarded it as primarily an institution for enforcing an economic boycott on dissident ►Yugoslavia. Gradually, however, it was used by Mikoyan and ►Khrushchev as a Soviet response to the growing interdependence of the western European economies. Between 1955 and 1960 the Russians sought a common economic policy and pattern of trade: other members of the council were reluctant to follow their lead. Basic statutes and principles of cooperation were agreed in 1960, but in September 1962 there was fierce opposition from Romanian and Bulgarian ministers to Khrushchev's proposals for supranational economic planning in eastern Europe: Romania and Bulgaria were declared agricultural lands, while Czechoslovakia and East Germany were to be predominantly industrial. After twelve months of intensive Romanian hostility, led by ►Ceauşescu, the Soviet proposals were substantially modified. The decisions of the Comecon committees remained, however, more divisive within the Eastern bloc than any issues raised by the ►Warsaw Pact. The establishment of closer links between member states and the ►European Community in 1990 was followed in January 1991 by a meeting in Moscow at which it was decided to disband Comecon by midsummer.

COMINFORM (Communist Information Bureau). Established in October 1947 after a conference in Warsaw of Communist Party leaders from the Soviet Union, France, Italy, Bulgaria, Czechoslovakia, Hungary, Poland, Romania and Yugoslavia. The Bureau, with headquarters in Belgrade, was to coordinate party activities throughout Europe. Ironically the first important decision of the Cominform (agreed at a special meeting in Bucharest, June 1948) was the expulsion of Yugoslavia and the condemnation of ➤Tito. The Bureau was formally dissolved on 17 April 1956, as a gesture of reassurance from Khrushchev both to the Western Powers and to Tito, with whom he sought reconciliation.

Comintern (Komintern). Abbreviated title of the ➤Third International, established March 1919, formally dissolved 22 May 1943.

Common Market. ➤European Economic Community.

Commonwealth. The name normally used for the Commonwealth of Nations which, with the accession of Queen ➤Elizabeth II in 1952, emerged from the ➤'British Commonwealth', itself a successor to the British Empire. It includes a quarter of the world's population. Although at first a loosely structured and informal association, an attempt was made in 1965 to achieve administrative cohesion by setting up a non-executive Commonwealth Secretariat with headquarters at Marlborough House, London. To counter possible anglocentricity the Commonwealth secretary generals have been successively a Canadian, a Guyanan of Indian origin and a Nigerian. The Secretariat encourages economic, scientific, medical and cultural cooperation, notably by a Commonwealth Fund for Technical Cooperation, set up in 1971, and since 1982 by a Commonwealth Science Council. The bi-annual ➤Commonwealth Conferences bring together heads of government for informal discussions. Attempts to reach agreement on common principles for the Commonwealth led to the Singapore Declaration of 1971, which stressed the importance of peace initiatives and condemned racial prejudice and discrimination, and the Harare Declaration of 1991 which emphasized the need to promote democratic government, advance the status of women and safeguard human rights. Collectively the Commonwealth leaders have worked for racial harmony in southern Africa. No member has been expelled from the Commonwealth, although in 1995 ➤Nigeria was threatened with expulsion unless democratic rule was restored within two years, and both Sierra Leone and Gambia were warned of the need to follow more closely the Harare principles. As the Commonwealth is a voluntary association, member states have a right to resign: ➤South Africa left in 1961 and was re-admitted in 1994; ➤Pakistan resigned in 1972 but returned in 1989. The Republic of ➤Ireland formally left the Commonwealth in 1949. ➤Fiji left in 1987 but was re-admitted in October 1997. All members acknowledge Queen Elizabeth II as Head of the Commonwealth: seventeen states accept her direct sovereignty; thirty are republics. By January 1998 there were fifty-four independent members of the Commonwealth. Apart from the 'special case' of ►Mozambique and part of ►Cameroon all these territories were formerly within the British Empire.

Commonwealth Conferences. Periodic meetings of heads of government within the ►Commonwealth, an extension of the system of ►Imperial Conferences in George V's reign. The first Conference to accept the British King as head of a Commonwealth which included a republic (India) met in London in April 1949. Further Conferences gathered in London in 1951, 1953, 1955, 1956, 1957, 1960, 1961, 1962, 1964, 1965, September 1966, 1969 and 1977. Commonwealth Conferences were also held at Lagos in January 1966, Singapore in January 1971, Ottawa in 1973, Kingston, Jamaica, in April 1975, Lusaka in June 1979, Melbourne in September 1981, New Delhi and Goa in 1983 and Nassau in October 1985 (where Mrs Thatcher stood alone in opposing sanctions against South Africa). Conferences followed at Vancouver (1987), Kuala Lumpur (1989), Harare (1991), in Cyprus (1993), Auckland (1995) and Edinburgh in October 1997. Conferences have emphasized the multi-racial character of the Commonwealth, the most serious divisions arising over ►Rhodesia and over apartheid in South Africa. It was after attacks on its racial policy at the 1961 Conference that South Africa left the Commonwealth; and at the Singapore Conference a proposal by the newly elected Conservative Prime Minister, Edward ►Heath, that Britain would resume the sale of arms to South Africa, threatened Commonwealth unity. On that occasion only the skilful chairmanship of Lee Kuan Yew prevented the disintegration of the Conference. In general the Conferences have sought to avoid the open wrangling which has received such publicity in the United Nations Assembly. Commonwealth leaders emphasize the value of informal sessions and private discussion.

Commonwealth of Independent States (CIS). Formed on 8 December 1991 as a successor body to the ►Soviet Union, with ►Russia, ►Ukraine and ►Belarus as founder sovereign state members. They were subsequently joined by the former central-Asian Soviet republics: Kazakhstan, Kyrgyzstan, Tajikistan, Turkmenistan. ►Armenia was too heavily engaged in the conflict over ►Nagorny-Karabakh to become an effective member of CIS. Azerbaijan, ►Moldova and ►Georgia did not complete the process of joining this hasty improvisation until 1993 when a formal CIS Charter sought to create a genuine union, with an executive secretariat based in Minsk (Belarus). The chief function of CIS was to coordinate economic plans in response to assistance from Western Europe, the USA and international organizations. It also had to settle military questions, notably over joint command of nuclear weapons air defence. None of these problems could be resolved without controversy and suspicion, as all the republics except Belarus were showing a deep mistrust of Yeltsin's Russia. By April 1996, when Yeltsin and the President of Belarus signed a treaty to establish a Commonwealth of Sovereign States, the future of CIS and of all further collaboration between the successor republics remained very much in doubt. A heads of state meeting in Moscow in April achieved nothing.

Communist Parties. Although the word 'communism' was used as early as 1840, specifically communist parties did not come into being until after 1918, when extreme Marxists broke away from the ▶Social Democrats in emulation of the Russian ▶Bolsheviks. Moscow's dominance of world communism caused Soviet disputes to find echoes in other national parties. The most important conflicts have been: (1) the rivalry of ▶Stalin and ▶Trotsky; (2) the Stalinist purge known as the ▶Yezhovshchina; (3) anti-revisionism, as a reaction to the independence of ▶Tito; (4) denunciation of the 'personality cult' by Khrushchev at the Soviet party's ▶Twentieth Congress in February 1956. Soviet ideological dominance was thereafter challenged by ▶China. Most European parties dropped the name 'Communist' during the 1989–91 period of liberalization.

English-speaking countries. Communist parties have not been powerful in Britain, the USA or the white Commonwealth nations. The British Communist Party, established in June 1920, unsuccessfully sought affiliation with the Labour Party in 1921, 1922 and 1936. It never gained complete control of a trade union nor was it ever represented at Westminster by more than two MPs at a time: the most effective was the Clydeside workers' leader, William Gallacher (1881–1965), MP for West Fife 1935–50. The British party changed its name to 'Democratic Left' in March 1991. The US Communist Party, founded in 1919, was led by William Foster from 1919 to 1934 and 1945 to 1948 and by Earl Browder from 1934 to 1945: both were Presidential candidates, Foster gaining 102,000 votes in the 1932 election. The American party suffered heavily from the anti-Red hysteria of ▶McCarthyism, 1950–53, as also, by geographical proximity, did the small Canadian party, which had won some votes in the Quebec provincial elections of 1944. The Australian Communist Party, founded in Sydney in 1920, consistently offended Moscow by individualistic factionalism, but had some influence on the dockers and, as a wartime expediency, was banned from May 1940 to December 1942. An attempt by ▶Menzies to proscribe the party in April 1950 was successfully resisted in the courts, with the distinguished statesman, Herbert ▶Evatt, as chief counsel for the defence. In New Zealand the Communist Party, founded 1921, has had little impact on events.

Western Europe. In France the left wing of the Socialist Party seceded at the party conference at Tours in 1920 to form the French Communist Party, which was dominated by Maurice Thorez (1900–1964) as secretary-general from 1930 until his final illness. Thorez's dogmatic Stalinism was relaxed by his successor, Waldeck Rochet (Secretary-General 1964–8), and totally rejected by Georges Marchais (1920–), who as Secretary-General in 1968–94 favoured electoral combinations with other parties of the Left. Significantly the twenty-second French Party Congress (February 1976) repudiated the Marxist-Leninist doctrine of a dictatorship of the proletariat. The Party joined the socialist coalition government of 1981–4 and the Left coalition formed by Lionel Joslin after the elections of June 1997. The Italian Communist Party was founded in 1921 by the Sardinian Antonio ▶Gramsci (1891–1937), but was forced underground by Mussolini, who imprisoned

Gramsci for the last eleven years of his life. The Italian communists re-emerged as partisans in 1945 and within three years became the second strongest party in the republic. From 1956 to 1964 their leader, Pietro Togliatti (1892–1964), championed the important principle of 'polycentrism', claiming that Communist Parties should work out independent strategies rather than accept Moscow's lead. Under Enrico Berlinguer (1922–84), secretary-general of the Italian party from 1972 onwards, the communists – with nearly 2 million party members – made rapid electoral gains, receiving more than one third of the votes in the 1976 election as well as securing control of Rome, Naples, Florence and Bologna. The Italian Party lost ground in 1988–9 and at the Bologna Party Congress of March 1990 resolved to change its name. In February 1991 a majority of members formed the Democratic Party of the Left (PDS), which gained more than 20 per cent of the national vote in the March 1994 election: a minority of members formed the more traditionally Marxist Party of Refounded Communists (PRC), which in 1994 gained 6 per cent of national votes. By contrast, the Spanish Communist Party, formed in 1923, has remained small in numbers, having been proscribed between 1939 and April 1977. The tradition of communist resistance to Franco in the ➤Spanish Civil War was maintained in exile in Moscow by 'La Pasionaria', Dolores ➤Ibarruri, but from 1960 to 1982 the party was led by Santiago Carrillo (1915–), who sought to mould its form on the pattern established by Berlinguer in Italy. The communists received 9 per cent of the vote in Spain's 1977 election and won twenty-three parliamentary seats two years later but fared disastrously in 1982, and in 1986 became the main party of a United Left Front (IU). The IU has never effectively challenged the left-centre Spanish Socialist Workers Party (PSOE).

Eastern and Central Europe. The German Communist Party was founded on 30 December 1918, but suffered a severe setback within a fortnight when German irregular troops murdered its leaders, Rosa ➤Luxemburg and Karl Liebknecht. The party remained numerically strong until the advent of Hitler, but made the tactical error of not resisting Hitler's appointment as Chancellor, in the belief that Nazism would soon collapse, heralding a German communist revolution. In 1945 the party was reorganized in East Germany by a surviving founder-member, Walther ➤Ulbricht, as the Socialist Unity Party (SED). After German reunification in 1989–90 the SED became the PDS, Party of Democratic Socialism; the communist PDS won little support in western Germany but still attracted more than 11 per cent of voters in the east. The Hungarian Communist Party had a brief spell of office in 1919 under Bela ➤Kun, before being outlawed until the arrival of the Soviet Army in 1944–5, when it achieved power under ➤Rákosi as the Hungarian Socialist Workers Party; the word 'socialist' being dropped with the coming of a multi-party system in October 1989. The Hungarian Party re-formed as a social democratic party in October 1989. Soviet 'liberation' also assisted the rise of ➤Gomulka in Poland and ➤Gheorghiu-Dej in Romania, even though both men were 'home-grown' communists, not Moscow-indoctrinated party members: the Polish and Romanian parties date from 1920, but were severely repressed from

1924 onwards. The Polish Party held a final congress in January 1990, splitting into a Marxist Social Democratic Party and a more liberal Social Democratic Union. On the fall of ➤Ceauşescu in December 1989 the Romanian communists abandoned Marxism to become the Front of National Salvation (FSN); communist parties were officially banned, but a Socialist Labour Party (PSM), pledged to revive socialism, won thirteen seats in the 1992 elections. The Bulgarian Communist Party, founded early in 1919, staged a major revolt in September 1923 which was brutally suppressed: the Bulgarian party leader, ➤Dimitrov, was a key figure in the Third International until his triumphant return to Sofia in November 1945. The Communist Party (BKP) dominated Bulgaria's coalitions of the Left until 1989 and was re-launched as the Bulgarian Socialist Party in 1990. Between the wars there was an influential Czechoslovak Communist Party (founded, as in France, by a secession of socialists in 1921). It gained nearly 1 million votes as early as 1925 and emerged as the largest single party in the (scrupulously fair) parliamentary elections of May 1946; its leader, ➤Gottwald, came to power by less democratic methods in February 1948. With the end of forty years of dictatorship in 1989 the party broke up but was refounded within the Czech Republic as the Communist Party of Bohemia and Moravia in 1990, a reformist splinter group seceding in 1993. In ➤Slovakia the Communist Party became the Democratic Left Party in 1991 but gained less than 15 per cent of the vote in the first multi-party elections. A Yugoslav party was established in April 1919, became the strongest party in municipal elections in Belgrade, Zagreb and Niš (1919–20) but was outlawed in the summer of 1921 after the assassination of the Minister of the Interior. Communism continued to appeal to the Yugoslav intelligentsia (➤Djilas), many of whom joined the ➤partisans in 1941 but remained critical of Moscow after Tito came to power in 1945. The party became the League of Yugoslav Communists in 1952, surviving until the disintegration of the Yugoslav federation. The League's communist successors are the Socialist Party of Serbia, led by ➤Milošević, and the Democratic Socialist Party of Montenegro. In Albania the Party of Labour founded and shaped by ➤Hoxha was the country's sole political movement from 1944 until 1990, surviving from 1991 onwards as the reformist Socialist Party of Albania. The Greek Communist Party, founded in 1920, returned ten deputies to parliament in 1926 and fifteen in 1936, but its attempt to call a general strike on 5 August 1936 led to the establishment of a right-wing dictatorship which broke up its organization. The Greek Communist Party was reconstituted as part of the resistance movement to the German occupation, calling itself 'National Liberation Front' (EAM), with a military arm, 'National People's Liberation Army' (ELAS): this organization formed the insurgent force in the ➤Greek Civil War. In October 1990 the Greek Communist Party was renamed Democratic Party of the Left (PDS).

Other regions. Communist parties were powerful in ➤Mexico, ➤Cuba and ➤Chile. Although the orthodox, Moscow-trained leaders of the original Cuban party were treated with scant respect by ➤Castro, his 'Party of Socialist Revolution' was renamed 'Communist Party of Cuba' in October 1965. In many parts of Africa and Asia, the Communist Parties became the first form of organized Marxism in the area (the exceptions being India and Indonesia, where Communist Parties were developed by secessionists from Marxist trade-union groups). The most important organized movement outside the USSR was the Chinese Communist Party, established in July 1921 by two Peking university professors, Chen Tu-hsui (Chen Duxiu) and Li Ta-chao (Li Dazao). The party suffered heavy losses in conflict with the ►Kuomintang (Guomindang) in 1926-7 and a new party was developed under the leadership of ►Mao Tse-tung (Mao Zedong), who had attended the founding congress in 1921. Mao's political lieutenant, ►Chou En-lai (Zhou Enlai), had established contact in Paris with the pioneer Annamese Marxist leader, ►Ho Chi Minh, who as a delegate to the Tours conference of 1920 was a founder-member of the French Communist Party.

Concentration Camps. The term 'concentration camp' was originally applied to the internment centres for Boer civilians established by Kitchener in 1900: poor administration and bad hygiene made these camps notorious. In Germany the Nazis established camps at Dachau and Oranienburg in 1933, detaining political and racial 'enemies' in them. By 1939 there were six such camps in Greater Germany, holding some 21,000 prisoners. During the Second World War the system was expanded: new camps were converted from places of 'preventive detention' to 'extermination centres' for Jews, in which sadistic medical experiments were authorized. Some camps provided slave labour for the German armaments industry. The most notorious camps were Belsen, Buchenwald (239,000 prisoners between 1937 and 1945) and Ravensbruck in Germany, Mauthausen in Austria, Theresienstadt in Czechoslovakia, Vught in Holland, and Auschwitz, Treblinka and Sobibor in Poland. Germany's allies also had concentration camps, notably in Hungary and Romania. A camp was set up in the German-occupied Channel island of Alderney in 1942. Corrective labour camps – known by the acronym GULAG – were established in the Soviet Arctic in 1932 and imposed a harsh system of slave labour until after Stalin's death; hundreds of thousands of detainees perished.

Concordat. A treaty between the Papacy and a temporal power concerning ecclesiastical affairs, the most famous being the Napoleonic Concordat of 1801 which has been accepted by successive French regimes, except for a period of intense ►anti-clericalism from 1905 to 1914. Twentieth-century Concordats have included: the ►Lateran Treaty of 1929 with Mussolini's Italy; a German Concordat of July 1933 which protected German Catholic property and educational institutions on condition that the priests abstained from politics; and a formal convention between the Vatican and the Hungarian communist authorities in September 1964 recognizing freedom of worship.

Concorde. The name given to a supersonic airliner deriving from a joint Franco-British project agreed in November 1962 and receiving full support from both governments. A French-assembled prototype flew on 2 March 1969, with the maiden flight of its British-built counterpart coming five weeks later (the Soviet Tupolev-144 supersonic airliner had made a trial flight ten weeks ahead of the French-built Concorde). The mounting expense of constructing the Concorde, together with criticism of its alleged noisiness, made the project highly controversial. Inaugural commercial flights, operated by Air France and by British Airways, took place on 21 January 1976.

Congo Problem (1960–65). The precipitate decision of the government in Brussels to grant the ►Belgian Congo independence on 30 June 1960 created a series of crises. Originally the new republic was to be a unitary state governed from Léopoldville (Kinshasa) by President Kasavubu (1917–69), and his Prime Minister, the radical Patrice ►Lumumba. Native Congolese troops defied their Belgian officers in a series of mutinies in early July 1960, and on 11 July the federalist political leader, ►Tshombe, declared the rich mining province of ►Katanga to have seceded, under his leadership. The UN Security Council agreed to send troops to help restore order and protect lives in the Congo, but the situation remained confused. Friction between Kasavubu and Lumumba led the Congolese Army commander, Colonel ►Mobutu, to establish a new government in September 1960 which excluded Lumumba but retained Kasavubu. Fragmentation of the republic continued with the setting-up of a radical regime, favourable to Lumumba, at Stanleyville (Kisangani). Lumumba himself fell into Katangese hands and was murdered in January 1961 with the connivance of Tshombe and his white mercenary army, which in the following August attacked the UN forces. While seeking talks with Tshombe, the UN Secretary-General ►Hammarskjöld, was killed in an air crash on 17 September, near what was then the Congolese–Northern Rhodesian frontier. Intermittent fighting between UN troops and the Katangese continued until Tshombe fled to Europe in 1963. Technically Katanga was reunited with the Léopoldville government on 14 January 1963, although UN troops remained in the Congo for another year. Suspicion of Chinese communist influence in Stanley-ville led American (and Belgian commercial) interests to put pressure on the Léopoldville authorities. Tshombe returned from exile to Léopoldville in July 1964, was appointed Prime Minister by Kasavubu, and used mercenaries and Belgian troops in November 1964 to gain control of the remaining rebellious areas. Disturbances broke out once more in May 1965, when it appeared that Tshombe had rigged elections in several provinces, and he was dismissed by Kasavubu in August. On 25 November 1965 the Congolese Army again intervened: Mobutu staged a second *coup d'état*, declaring himself head of state. An election in 1970 gave backing to his Presidential regime; and on 27 October 1971 he declared the name of the state changed to Republic of ►Zaire. In May 1997 Laurent Kabila (1941–) marked his victory in Zaire's civil war by restoring the name Congo to his 'free, democratic republic'.

Congress Party. The government party in India from independence in 1947 until the defeat of Mrs Indira ➤Gandhi in the 1977 general election. The Indian National Congress was formed in December 1885 primarily as an educational association, to train Indians in government, and was supported by the viceroys until the arrival of ➤Curzon in 1898. His decision to split Bengal into two provinces in 1905 threw Congress into violent political opposition under the leadership of the Hindu extremist Bal Gangadhar Tilak, who was succeeded as leader in 1915 by the more moderate, but spiritually inspiring, Mohandas Karamchand ➤Gandhi. Throughout the 1920s and 1930s his doctrine of non-violent civil disobedience dominated the Congress Party, which took office in six provinces after the 1937 elections (➤India Act, 1935). The Congress leaders refused to support the viceregal authorities over entry into the Second World War, because Indian opinion was not consulted. Congress leaders were interned from August 1942 until 1945 but were released for consultations over the supersession of British rule. Under ➤Nehru, Prime Minister of India from 1947 until his death in 1964, Congress became a comprehensive political movement including nationalists of all opinions except the extreme Left and Right. This umbrella character was retained for the two-year government of Nehru's successor, Lal ➤Shastri, but Congress began to break up after the party (under Mrs Gandhi's leadership) lost seats in the 1967 elections. The process of disintegration was speeded up by growing signs of corruption and anti-democratic practices in the 1970s. Electoral defeat in 1977 gave Congress a chance to reorganize, and the party returned to power again in January 1980 with an absolute majority in the Indian parliament. Congress remained precariously in power for the following nine years. The party was out of office from November 1989 until June 1991 when a narrow electoral victory enabled Narasinha Rao to establish a government assured of a majority only with backing from independents. This weak administration survived until Rao resigned after electoral defeat in May 1996. Within a month Congress recovered parliamentary influence as chief support of a United Front coalition government. Sonia Gandhi became the party leader in March 1998.

conscription. Compulsory enlistment for military service, dating in modern times from the French Revolutionary *levée en masse* of August 1793. Most continental armies introduced conscription during the nineteenth century. A dispute over the need for conscription arose in Britain in the winter of 1915–16, with strong opposition from the Labour Party, but the National Service Act became effective in February 1916 and conscription was retained in the United Kingdom until April 1920. The reintroduction of conscription by Nazi Germany in March 1935 led to demands in Britain for peacetime military training, and a new National Service Act in April 1939 permitted the conscription of men aged twenty to twenty-one. Five months later the age limit was amended to nineteen to forty-one and in December 1941 it was extended to single women aged twenty to thirty, while the call-up for men was lowered to eighteen and a half. With the return of peace conscription was abolished for women and limited to eighteen months for men extended to two years in September 1950 because of the ➤Korean War but ended in the autumn of 1960. A form of conscription ('Selective Service') was introduced in the United States, May 1917, but ended in 1919. The Selective Service and Training Act of 1940 introduced peacetime conscription for the first time in American history, extending its scope in 1942. The Act expired in 1947 and was replaced by the Universal Military Training Act of 1948, which determined conscription throughout the Korean and Vietnam Wars. Conscription has been an especially controversial political issue in Australasia and Canada. In Australia conscription was advocated in 1916 by W.M. ➤Hughes but twice rejected by popular referenda: in New Zealand, conscription was introduced by parliamentary vote in August 1916, but was resisted so forthrightly by Labour that several leaders were imprisoned, including the future Prime Minister, Peter ➤Fraser; and in Canada the Compulsory Military Service Act of September 1917 produced such severe rioting in Quebec (29 March to 2 April 1918) that four civilians were killed. The Japanese threat in the Second World War led to the imposition of conscription for service in the south-west Pacific both in Australia and New Zealand, but there remained serious opposition in Canada, with disputes in Quebec in both 1942 and 1944.

Conservative Party. The word 'Conservative' appears to have been first used by Canning in 1824, although the modern Conservative Party really dates from Peel's 'Tamworth Manifesto' of 1834. From 1886 to 1922 the party was generally known as the 'Conservative and Unionist Party' because of its opposition to Liberal proposals to end the Union with Ireland by introducing ➤Home Rule in Dublin. More positively, the party was associated with vigorous imperialism and principles of moderate reform, grafted on to older concepts of respect for established institutions. The party was in office under ➤Salisbury and ➤Balfour from 1895 to 1905. Disputes over ➤Tariff Reform – and lack of a social policy – led to the party's eclipse, until it returned to power under Bonar ➤Law in October 1922. Between 1923 and 1955 the party was led successively by ➤Baldwin, Neville ➤Chamberlain and ➤Churchill. The Suez Crisis of 1956 discredited the leadership of ➤Eden but ➤Macmillan rallied the party sufficiently to win the election of 1959. On Macmillan's retirement in October 1963, the succession passed to Lord Home (Sir Alec ➤Douglas-Home), who was narrowly defeated in the general election of 15 October 1964. Criticism of the manner in which Home had been appointed leader of the party led in 1965 to the institution of a system by which the leader was elected by Conservative Members of Parliament. On 28 July 1965 the Conservatives elected Edward ➤Heath as leader and he became Prime Minister after the Conservative victory in the election of June 1970. Conflict with the trade unions led to a Conservative defeat in the election of February 1974. After Heath failed to win the following election (October 1974), demands arose for a change of leadership. On 11 February 1975 the Conservative MPs elected Mrs Margaret ➤Thatcher as leader. She became the first woman Prime Minister when the Conservatives won the election of May 1979. Conservatism thereafter became more right-wing in character. The Party attracted less votes but won many more seats in the election of June 1983, giving it a majority of 144 in the Commons, cut to 101 in the 1987 election. After an indecisive election for the party leadership in November 1990 Mrs Thatcher resigned and was succeeded by John ➤Major. In April 1992 the Conservatives broke all precedent by winning a fourth consecutive electoral victory, though the overall majority was cut to twenty-one. The party suffered from increasingly deep divisions over Europe in the following four years. Major resigned as party leader in June 1995, but received overwhelming endorsement in the subsequent leadership contest. Further wrangling over Europe and press allegations of ministerial misconduct weakened the government over the following year, and in the General Election of 1 May 1997 the Conservatives suffered their greatest defeat of the century, with 178 seats lost and only 165 retained. Major resigned as party leader and, after a further leadership contest among Conservative MPs, was succeeded on 19 June by the Thatcherite Eurosceptic, William Hague (1961–), who defeated the former Chancellor of the Exchequer, Kenneth Clarke (1940–) on the third ballot.

Conservative Party (Canada). ➤Progressive Conservative Party.

Constantine I (1868–1923, reigned 1913–17, 1920–22), King of the Hellenes. Eldest son of George I (1845–1913), married Sophia, the sister of Kaiser William II, in 1889. As Crown Prince, Constantine led the Greek Army to victory in the ➤Balkan Wars, coming to the throne on the assassination of his father in the newly occupied city of Salonika on 18 March 1913. Constantine's subsequent opposition to the pro-allied policy of the Greek statesman, ➤Venizelos, led to British and French military intervention in Athens and in June 1917 Constantine handed over the Greek throne to his second son, Alexander, who reigned until dying from a monkey bite in October 1920. A plebiscite two months later voted overwhelmingly for Constantine's return, but Greece's military failure against the Turks in Anatolia and ➤Smyrna in 1922 was (unjustifiably) blamed on the King. He abdicated on 27 September 1922, dying in exile in Sicily a year later.

Constantine II (1940–, reigned 1964–73), King of the Hellenes. Grandson of Constantine I and son of Paul I (1901–64) and Queen Frederika (1917–81). When Constantine came to the Greek throne on the death of his father from cancer (6 March 1964), he was extremely popular, having won a gold medal for sailing at the Rome Olympics and being about to marry a beautiful princess, Anne-Marie of Denmark. He was confronted with international tension over ➤Cyprus and by distrust, among the army leaders, of the more radical Greek politicians. A *coup* by a junta of ➤Greek Colonels on 21 April 1967 suspended parliamentary government on the eve of elections. Constantine collaborated with the Colonels until 13 December 1967 when he unsuccessfully attempted a counter-*coup*, escaping to voluntary exile in Rome. In the summer of 1973 the Colonels alleged that Constantine was plotting to overthrow them and Greece was proclaimed a republic on 1 June. The fall of the Colonels a year later was followed on 8 December 1974 by a referendum to settle the constitutional position of King Constantine: the Greek people voted by 69·2 to 30·8 per cent against his restoration.

Constantinople Agreements (March–April 1915). Secret assurances given to the Russians by the British and French that, after the war, Constantinople and the hinterland of the Bosphorus and the Dardanelles would be incorporated in the Russian Empire, provided the western allies 'achieved their aims in the Near East and elsewhere'. These agreements, promising the Russians a prize for which they had sought for over a century, reflected a growing fear that Russia would otherwise conclude a separate peace. After the Revolution of 1917, the Bolsheviks repudiated all agreements made by the Tsarist governments. In the spring of 1918, however, the Bolsheviks published the text of the secret treaties, thereby stiffening resistance in Turkey and provoking protests from liberals in Britain and the United States.

Containment, Policy of. A basic assumption made by the formulators of US foreign policy from 1947 onwards that communist influence should be contained within existing territorial limits, either by armed intervention (Korea, Vietnam) or, more often, by economic and technical assistance (➤Marshall Plan, ➤Colombo Plan).

Coolidge (John) Calvin (1872–1933), thirtieth President of the USA. Born in Plymouth, Vermont, the son of a storekeeper. He was educated at Amherst, became a lawyer, and was elected Republican Governor of Massachusetts in 1916, attracting nation-wide attention in September 1919 when he crushed a police strike in Boston by calling out the militia. He was nominated vice-presidential running-mate to ➤Harding in the 1920 election, automatically succeeding to the Presidency on Harding's death on 3 August 1923 and winning the 1924 election. His Administration was marked by the rapid growth of commercial monopolies: 'The business of America is business' he declared. His *laissez-faire* and isolationist conservatism epitomized Republican government between the wars. He declined to stand for re-election in 1928, backing his Secretary of Commerce, ➤Hoover. Although the Republican Party claimed that 'Coolidge prosperity' was 'permanent', much company speculation during the 1923–8 period lacked adequate coverage and, within seven months of Coolidge's retirement, American business was shattered by the ➤Wall Street Crash.

Cooperative Movement. Began with the establishment of the Rochdale Equitable Pioneers in 1844, in an attempt to realize within a capitalist society the ideals of consumers' cooperative associations formulated by Robert Owen (1771–1858). The movement flourished in Britain and in the USA (especially in the Mid-West) towards the end of the nineteenth century. From 1918 onwards Cooperative Movement parliamentary candidates have contested elections in Britain, in alliance with the Labour Party.

Coral Sea, Battle of the (4–8 May 1942). The first of several protracted naval actions between US and Japanese naval forces in the south-west Pacific, fought mainly between aircraft-carriers. A Japanese invasion force was concentrated at Rabaul for a seaborne assault on Port Moresby. Two US carriers and seven cruisers faced three Japanese carriers and six cruisers in the Coral Sea. On 7 May the Americans sunk or immobilized all three Japanese carriers for the loss of the carrier *Lexington*. The American success effectively checked the Japanese naval offensive southwards towards Australia. Tactically it was a prelude to the decisive victory of ►Midway Island four weeks later.

Corfu Incident (August 1923). An Italian general and four members of his staff were shot while engaged in determining the Greek–Albanian frontier on 27 August 1923. The incident was interpreted by ►Mussolini as a national insult. To demonstrate the fascist belief in power politics he sent a strong demand for compensation to Greece and proceeded on 31 August to order a naval bombardment and occupation of the Greek island of Corfu. The Greeks appealed to the League of Nations and, under pressure from Britain and France, Mussolini withdrew his force from Corfu on 27 September. The League referred the dispute to the Council of Ambassadors, which required Greece to accept most of the Italian demands, including payment of a considerable indemnity.

Corfu, Pact of (20 July 1917). A basic charter of unity for ►Yugoslavia. When Serbia was overrun in the First World War, the Serbian government-in-exile was established on the Greek island of Corfu. There an agreement was concluded between the Serbian Prime Minister, ►Pašić, and the leader of the refugee South Slavs from Austria–Hungary, Ante Trumbić (1868–1938). The Pact declared that all the South Slavs – Serbs, Croats, Slovenes and Montenegrins – should form a single Yugoslav kingdom under the Karadjordjević dynasty of Serbia: the kingdom would have a democratic constitution and local autonomy. When, in the 1920s, Serbs began to dominate Yugoslavia the leaders of the other national groups complained that Pašić had tricked Trumbić at Corfu in order to win support at a time of weakness for the Serbian cause.

Country Party (Australian). In 1913 associations of farmers in New South Wales backed conservatively inclined politicians who would represent the interests of the agricultural community against the urban politicians. By January 1920 ten of these rural conservatives were returned to the Federal Parliament where they were organized by the Tasmanian, W.J. McWilliams, into a powerful minority party. In the elections of December 1922 this Country Party, now led by Dr (later Sir) Earle Page, won fourteen seats and held the balance of power between the Nationalists and Labour, who had won the most seats. The new Nationalist leader, ►Bruce, accordingly formed a coalition government with the Country Party, who shared power from 1922 to 1929, 1934 to 1941, 1949 to 1972, and from 1975 onwards under Malcolm ►Fraser. Arthur Fadden, the party's acting leader, was coalition Prime Minister for six weeks in 1941, even though there were only thirteen Country Party members in parliament at that time. The influence of the Country Party, consistently safeguarding the prices of wool and wheat, was greater than the number of its members returned to Canberra. Its history provides a significant example of the value of a small, disciplined and well-organized 'third force' within a traditionally two-party system.

Crete. An island in the eastern Mediterranean, disputed by the Venetian Republic and the Ottoman Empire in the late medieval period and finally occupied by the Turks in 1669. The island remained nominally under Turkish sovereignty until united to Greece in December 1913. In practice, however, Crete was ruled by Egyptians from 1824 to 1840 and, after a series of Greek nationalist revolts in the nineteenth century, Turkish garrisons were withdrawn in November 1898. Crete thereafter enjoyed considerable autonomy, with the Greek King's second son (Prince George) administering the island as High Commissioner, 1898–1906. In December 1916 the Cretan-born Greek statesman, ►Venizelos, established a pro-allied rebel government in the island, which remained a Venizelist political stronghold for the next twenty years. After the fall of Greece in 1941, the Germans launched an attack on Crete, 1,500 parachutists dropped on 20 May being followed by glider landings the next day. Despite naval interception of invasion vessels and fierce resistance by British, Greek, Australian and New Zealand troops, the island was in German hands by 1 June. The battle of Crete was the first successful airborne invasion in military history. Guerrilla resistance continued in the mountains until the liberation of the island in 1945.

Cripps (Richard) Stafford (1889–1952, knighted 1930), British Labour politician and ambassador. Born in London, a nephew of Beatrice Webb (►Fabian Society), educated at Winchester and University College, London, where he read chemistry and law. In the First World War he served with the Red Cross in France and supervised a munitions factory. He was recognized as a brilliant barrister in the 1920s, specializing in company law, and became Solicitor-General in the MacDonald Government of 1930–31. Cripps was regarded throughout the 1930s as a doctrinaire left-wing MP, but was expelled from the Labour Party in 1939 for advocating a ►Popular Front and remained technically an independent MP until readmitted to the Labour Party in 1945. From 1940 to 1942 Cripps was ambassador in Moscow. In February 1942 he was brought back to England where he was respected as spokesman of a Christian Socialist ideal, widely acceptable during the war. He became Lord Privy Seal, Leader of the House of Commons and a member of Churchill's war cabinet in February 1942. In April 1942 he was sent on a special mission to India, in the vain hope that he would win the support of ►Congress for the war by an offer of self-government. From November 1942 until May 1945 he was Minister of Aircraft Production (without a seat in the cabinet). He became President of the Board of Trade in Attlee's government of July 1945 and Chancellor of the Exchequer from 1947 to 1950. The combination of his passion for stern simplicity in life with professional mastery of economic detail won him a moral and intellectual authority attained by no other Chancellor this century: his doctrine of 'austerity', with its strict taxation and a voluntary wage-freeze, kept inflation in check although he was forced to devalue the pound in September 1949. Ill-health caused him to resign from office and parliament in October 1950.

Croatia. Region of ►Yugoslavia, capital Zagreb. Although there was an independent Croatia in the tenth century, the region was incorporated in Hungary from 1102 to 1918, enjoying a measure of autonomy for the last fifty years of this period. From 1905 onwards the leading Croatian politicians favoured some form of South Slav ('Yugoslav') union. In 1917 Croatian exiles signed with the Serbian Government the ►Corfu Pact providing for the establishment of a Yugoslav state after the war. The Croats, however, were Roman Catholic and more westernized than the Serbs (Orthodox in religion) and they complained that they were excluded from office in Yugoslavia until 1939. Croatian fascist fanatics (►Ustaše) resorted to terrorism. With Yugoslavia's defeat in 1941 they proclaimed an independent kingdom of Croatia, with an Italian duke as titular 'King of Croatia', although he never dared visit his realm. The Ustaše regime perpetrated appalling atrocities against Serbs, communists and Jews and thereby provoked bitter reprisals. In 1946 Croatia became a 'People's Republic' within communist Yugoslavia. Exiled Croatian extremists committed terrorist acts against Yugoslav institutions abroad in the 1970s and early 1980s. A secessionist liberal movement emerged within Croatia in 1988-9, the Croatian Democratic Union winning free elections in April 1990, thus threatening the unity of Yugoslavia. A new democratic Croatian Constitution was approved by the National Assembly in Zagreb in December 1990. Serbs living in the Krajina enclave sought to secede from Croatia and set up a Serbian Autonomous Region. Croat police and civilians were killed in clashes with Serbs on 2 May 1991. Croatia (like ►Slovenia) proclaimed independence on 25 June but, faced with military intervention by the Yugoslav Federal Army, on 8 July accepted mediation by the European Community, thereby postponing secession. Fighting nevertheless continued until January 1992 when the Federal Army withdrew but left ethnic Serb forces in control of large areas, including Krajina and much of eastern Slavonia. Franjo ►Tudjman, Croatia's President, deployed a powerful army in 1995 which took western Slavonia in May, the Krajina in August and eastern Slavonia in November enabling Croatia to be reintegrated by the end of the year. Tension remained high in ►Bosnia-Herzegovina with the Croats mistrusted both by the Bosnian Serbs and by the Muslims at Mostar, the chief town in Herzegovina, long coveted by Croatia. In May 1996 the Council of Europe rejected Croatia's application for membership because of its bad human rights record.

Cromer, Earl of (1841–1917; born Evelyn Baring, created an earl in 1892, taking his title from his birthplace), British imperial statesman. A soldier and administrator in India before being appointed Consul-General in Egypt in 1883. In this capacity he virtually ruled Egypt as British 'Agent' until his retirement in 1907, rescuing the country from near-bankruptcy and restoring its agricultural yield by irrigation schemes. To check French intrigues he became a strong supporter of Anglo-French collaboration at the turn of the century and helped conclude the ►Anglo-French Entente in 1904.

Cuba. A Caribbean island under Spanish colonial rule, 1515–1898. The United States, having supported the Cuban struggle for independence, policed the island from 1899 to 1902; and the Cuban constitution of 1901 confirmed the USA's right to intervene militarily in Cuba if the political situation deteriorated. This right (the 'Platt Amendment') was valid until 1934 when it was abrogated in return for a trade agreement: US marines intervened in 1906, 1912–13, 1917 and 1933; and during and after the Second World War the Americans built up a strategic base on land leased at Guantánamo. Disputed Presidential elections and veiled dictatorships threatened anarchy intermittently between 1906 and 1933. The rule of ►Batistá, direct or indirect from 1933 to 1944, was succeeded by two inefficient, corrupt but nominally democratic presidencies under Grau San Martín (1944–8) and Prio Socarras (1948–52). Batistá returned as head of state in March 1952, his administration becoming so tyrannical that in 1957 the US Government cut off supplies of arms to Cuba, and encouraged the resistance movement of Fidel ►Castro. The success of Castro in January 1959 was, however, followed by rapid deterioration in Cuban–American relations caused partly by Cuba's political flirtation with China and the USSR and partly by Castro's nationalization of industrial enterprises and a series of agrarian reforms which placed large plantations under state control. Diplomatic relations between Cuba and the USA were broken off in January 1961. The ►Bay of Pigs fiasco of April 1961 was followed in October 1962 by the major crisis over ►Cuban missiles. From 1965 to 1971 Castro, following the lead of Che ►Guevara, sought to promote revolution in Latin America, a policy pursued largely independently of both China and the Soviet Union. Economic problems forced Cuba in 1972 to join ►Comecon. With Russian support, Cuban revolutionary zeal was transferred from Latin America to southern Africa and particularly to ►Angola, where Cuban troops assisted the MPLA establish a 'People's Republic' in 1975–6. In October 1965 Castro's political party, hitherto known as the 'United Party of the Socialist Revolution', changed its name to 'Communist Party of Cuba' and proceeded to complete the nationalization of commercial enterprises. A party congress in December 1975 approved a socialist constitution which became effective in February 1976. Direct elections were introduced in 1993, but all candidates had to be approved by the Communist Party. President Clinton intensified US sanctions against Cuba in February 1996 after the Cuban air force shot down two light aircraft operated by Cuban exile groups. A visit by Pope John Paul II in January 1998 marked an improvement in church–state relations.

Cuban Missiles Crisis (October 1962). During the spring and summer of

1962 intelligence sources in Washington reported a heightened interest on the part of Russia in Cuban affairs. The Soviet Government admitted on 2 September that it was supplying arms to Cuba, denying a week later that these weapons were for offensive purposes. On 16 October aerial photographs convinced President ►Kennedy that ballistic missiles with atomic warheads were being installed in Cuba. It was calculated that forty-two missiles, capable of reaching any city in the USA, were in Cuba, or on their way to Cuba. On 22 October Kennedy announced that the US Navy would impose a blockade of Cuba: he followed up this initiative with a formal request to ►Khrushchev for the removal of all offensive missiles from the island. On 26 October the Russians offered to withdraw their weapons if all NATO missiles were removed from Turkey, a condition rejected by the Americans. There seemed a grave risk of nuclear war; but on 28 October Khrushchev agreed to order withdrawal of the missiles under United Nations supervision, provided America lifted the naval blockade and gave assurances not to invade Cuba. ►Castro refused to admit the UN observers to Cuba, resenting his exclusion from the Kennedy–Khrushchev exchanges. But by the end of the first week in November the US Defence Department was satisfied that the missiles had been dismantled. The naval blockade ended on 20 November, with a Soviet pledge to withdraw all Russian bombers and rocket personnel from the island within a month. Kennedy's firmness in this crisis enhanced his prestige as a statesman at home and abroad.

Cultural Revolution. The name given to the reassertion of Maoist doctrines in ►China between 1965 and 1968. The movement began with a speech by Marshal Lin Piao (Lin Biao) on 3 September 1965 urging pupils in schools and colleges to return to the basic principles of the revolutionary movement and to criticize liberal and Khrushchevian trends in the party. Criticism, encouraged by 'Red Guards' and voiced in monster parades and through wall-posters, extended to writers, economists and to the nominees of the President, ►Liu Shao-chi (Liu Shaoqi), in the party apparatus. The effect of the 'cultural revolution' was to encourage a cult of ►Mao Tse-tung (Mao Zedong), who was virtually in retirement from 1959 to May 1966, and to impose a largely bloodless purge on the party. The excitement caused by the Red Guards, however, closed schools and colleges and threatened the general economy of the republic. ►Chou En-lai (Zhou Enlai), who had earlier made an uncharacteristic speech to Red Guards in Peking urging every party member to submit to public criticism, was by the late summer of 1966 eager for a return to normal. The dismissal of Liu from all his posts in the party and the republic, announced on 13 October 1968, may be said to mark the end of the 'revolution'.

Curie, Marie (1867–1934), Franco-Polish physicist. Born Marie Sklodowska, in Warsaw, her family being doctors or teachers. She was educated in Warsaw and at the Sorbonne in Paris, where in 1895 she married the distinguished professor of physics, Pierre Curie (1859–1906). She collaborated with him in the researches which led to the discovery of radium, sharing his Nobel Prize for 1903. When he was run over and killed, she succeeded to his chair at the Sorbonne, the first woman to hold such high academic rank. Her further researches into radium gained the unique distinction of a second Nobel Prize in 1911. The prospect that her discoveries might lead to a cure for cancer won her popular fame, accentuated by her apparently disinterested devotion to science and her triumph over the misogynous prejudice of male colleagues. A successful fund-raising tour of the USA helped finance a research institute named in her honour. She became, and remains, the lay saint of an Age of Science, revered both for her discoveries and for vindicating women's rights to higher education. In 1926 her daughter, Irene (1897–1956), married her mother's principal research assistant, Frederick Joliot (1900–1958), the couple taking the surname Joliot-Curie. They shared the 1935 Nobel Prize for Chemistry, as discoverers of artificial radioactivity.

Curragh Incident (March 1914). The threat of Ulster opposition to ➤Irish Home Rule became so acute in the spring of 1914 that the British Government feared it would be necessary to use troops to keep order in northern Ireland. Officers stationed at the Curragh, near Dublin, were told they might resign their commissions if their conscience would not permit them to fire on Ulstermen, in which case they would be dismissed from the army. Fifty-eight of the seventy-one officers in the Third Cavalry Brigade, including their commander, said they would 'prefer to accept dismissal if ordered north'; and some infantry officers supported them. Senior military authorities sympathized with the officers, who received a written assurance that they would not, after all, be required to force Home Rule on Ulster. The threat of resignation was then withdrawn. Technically the incident was not a mutiny, as it has sometimes been called. It was a rare instance of the British officer class putting pressure on the civil government to modify an unpopular policy.

Curtin, John (1885–1945), Australian Prime Minister. Born near Ballarat, Victoria, the son of a policeman in an Irish Roman Catholic family, became a socialist in 1906, remaining in Victoria as secretary of the Timber Workers' Union until 1917. He then crossed to Western Australia, spending eleven years building up the Labour Party around Fremantle, the constituency he represented in Canberra 1928–31 and 1934–45. He became leader of the party in 1935, defeating Arthur Fadden of the ➤Country Party on a budget vote in October 1941 to become Prime Minister. Curtin, an opponent of conscription in his youth, was an able wartime leader, collaborating closely with the USA in the south-west Pacific to resist the Japanese but, from the closing months of 1943 onwards, seeking to build up a British naval presence in Australasian waters as a counter to the mounting power of General ➤MacArthur. He attended the conference of Empire Prime Ministers in London in May 1944, urging some form of institutional link to formulate common policies for the governments of the United Kingdom and the overseas dominions. Ill-health prevented his developing this proposal, which seemed to many colleagues out of date: his able External Affairs Minister, Dr ►Evatt, preferred to champion the new United Nations rather than the old Empire. Curtin died five weeks before the end of the war in Asia, and was succeeded by ►Chifley.

Curzon, George Nathaniel (1859–1925, created Baron Curzon of Kedleston 1898, earl 1911, marquis 1921). Educated at Eton and Balliol College, Oxford, Conservative MP for Southport 1886–98, travelled widely and wrote a scholarly study of Persia; Under-Secretary of State for India 1891–2 and for Foreign Affairs 1895–8, achieving such distinction that he was appointed Viceroy of India while still under forty. His seven-year viceroyalty was marked by administrative reform, irrigation schemes, the development of scientific agriculture, extension of railways, and strengthening of the north-west frontier. It was marred by an arrogant manner which offended Indian susceptibilities, by a decision to partition Bengal, and by major differences with ►Kitchener over control of the Indian Army. From 1905 to 1915 Curzon took little part in public life, although he was from 1907 onwards an extremely active Chancellor of Oxford University. He held minor office in the Asquith Coalition of 1915–16, serving as Lord President of the Council, and he was in Lloyd George's War Cabinet from 1916 to 1919. In January 1919 he became Foreign Secretary, remaining at the Foreign Office for almost five years. During this period he was largely responsible for the settlement at ►Lausanne and for frustrating French encouragement of separatism in the Rhineland. On the resignation of ►Bonar Law in May 1923 Curzon suffered bitter disappointment at being passed over as Prime Minister, a decision taken partly because he would have had to sit in the Lords (a House in which the Labour Opposition was not then represented) and partly because his haughtiness convinced the outgoing Prime Minister he was out of touch with public opinion. Curzon loyally served the new Prime Minister, Baldwin, for eight months as Foreign Secretary, and from November 1924 until his death in March 1925 as Lord President of the Council. He was the last of the aristocratic proconsuls whose style in politics remained dominated by a sense of British imperial responsibility.

Curzon Line. A proposed settlement of the Russo-Polish frontier put to the Poles by Lloyd George on 10 July 1920. Subsequent correspondence was handled by the British Foreign Secretary, ►Curzon, who thus gave his name to the line of demarcation. The line – from Grodno through Brest-Litovsk and Przemysl to the Carpathians – would have excluded from Poland lands predominantly inhabited by Ukrainians, Lithuanians and Russians. The Poles rejected the proposal, subsequently securing territory twice as large as Lloyd George had suggested. In September 1939 the Curzon Line (with minor variations) became the boundary between the German and Russian spheres of occupied Poland; and in 1945 it was accepted as a definitive frontier by the Polish and Soviet Governments.

Cyprus. An island in the eastern Mediterranean, captured by the Turks from the Venetians in 1571 and remaining under Turkish sovereignty until 1914. The

Cyprus Convention of 1878 permitted Britain to station troops in the island, largely to help protect Turkey from Russia. When Turkey entered the First World War as an ally of Germany, the British annexed Cyprus. In 1915 ➤Constantine I of Greece rejected an offer of the island in return for participation in the war on the side of the Entente, and in 1925 Cyprus became a British crown colony. Since Greeks formed four-fifths of the population, demands arose for union with Greece, ➤Enosis. Riots in 1931 led to suspension of the Legislative Council. When the British Labour Government offered a new constitution in 1948 it was rejected by the Greek community because it did not offer institutional links with Athens. Proposals by the Greek Government for a special status which would have given the Cypriots a form of Enosis were firmly rejected by the British Foreign Secretary, ➤Eden, in 1951 and 1953. On 1 April 1955 extremists in the EOKA movement, led by ➤Grivas, made a series of bomb attacks in Cyprus which launched four years of terrorism. The conflict between EOKA and the British occupation forces strained Anglo-Greek relations and led to a risk of conflict between Greece and Turkey, as the Ankara government consistently sought to defend the Turkish minority in Cyprus. In March 1956 the spiritual leader of the Greek community, Archbishop ➤Makarios, was deported to the Seychelles because the Governor suspected he supported EOKA. In April 1957 he was allowed to return to Athens and later to plead the Greek-Cypriot cause at the United Nations. Under the guidance of a new Governor of Cyprus, Sir Hugh Foot, a compromise solution was worked out at talks in Zürich and London (February 1959) by which Cyprus became an independent republic within the Commonwealth on 16 August 1960. Elections the previous December had returned Makarios as President, with the leader of the Turkish Cypriot community, Fazil Kuchuk, as Vice-President. Relations between the two men were as strained as the relations between the two racial communities. A threat of war between Greece and Turkey over disputes in the island led the United Nations to send a peace-keeping force to Cyprus in April 1964. There were also clashes between EOKA veterans and Makarios's supporters, and the President survived several assassination plots. By 1970 the Turkish minority had ceased to recognize the legality of the House of Representatives in Nicosia, electing an unofficial chamber of their own in northern Cyprus. On 15 July 1974 Greek-born EOKA sympathizers officering the Cyprus National Guard launched a *coup d'état* against President Makarios, who narrowly escaped death, going into exile for six months. The *coup* threw Cyprus into near-anarchy, the Turkish authorities in Ankara seizing the opportunity to land an army in northern Cyprus which, by mid-August, had occupied two-fifths of the island. Within this area the Turks established a 'Turkish Federated State', forcing Greek Cypriot families to flee and thereby effectively partitioning the island. Attempts at reconciliation between Makarios and Turkish-Cypriot spokesmen in the winter of 1976–7 were beginning to ease the tension when, on 3 August 1977, the President died from a heart attack. He was succeeded as President by Spyros Kyprianou (1930–) who was succeeded in February 1988 by the left-wing Georgios Vassiliou. The democrat lawyer Glavkos Clerides (1919–) defeated Vassiliou in the election of February 1988 to begin a term of office marked by patient attempts to secure reunification. The Turks maintained an army of 35,000 men in the Federated State, which in November 1983 declared its independence as the 'Turkish Republic of Northern Cyprus'. Only Turkey recognized the republic, of which the veteran Turkish Cypriot spokesman Rauf Denktas (1924–) was elected President. Direct talks between Clerides and Denktas, under UN auspices, in 1994 and in June 1997 kept alive the prospect of reunification. Attempts to encourage confidence and trust between young Cypriots of differing ethnic origin have been made by UN mediators; a pop concert in May 1997 led to violent clashes between Greek and Turkish Cypriots. Tension with the Ankara government increased in the winter of 1997–8, with the chief-designate of the Turkish General Staff commanding large-scale military exercises in northern Cyprus itself. President Clerides strengthened Cypriot links with Russia, visiting Yeltsin in Moscow in July 1998 and purchasing Soviet-designed surface-to-air missiles, expected to reach Cyprus in November 1998.

Czechoslovakia. A republic created in 1918 from the former western Slavonic provinces of Austria-Hungary. A revolutionary National Assembly, meeting in Prague on 14 November 1918, elected Tómas ►Masaryk as President, thus recognizing his role as chief spokesman in exile for a joint Czech and Slovak state. The new republic comprised 7 million Czechs, 2 million Slovaks, 3¼ million Germans in the ►Sudetenland, 700,000 Hungarians and 450,000 Ruthenes. Some of the most developed industrial areas of Austria-Hungary were included in Czechoslovakia. Internal politics between the wars were marred by latent racial conflicts, ill-feeling arising from the predominance of the industrious Czechs over the other nationalities. External policy was marked by fears of a Habsburg restoration and of German expansion. Under the direction of Dr ►Beneš, the Czechoslovaks based their foreign policy on the ►Little Entente system and friendship with France, but failed to improve relations with France's ally, Poland, because of rival claims to ►Teschen. Sudeten German agitation increased between 1935 and 1938, when war was prevented only by the ►Munich settlement which forced Czechoslovakia to cede 10,000 square miles to Germany, another 5,000 square miles to Hungary – the ►Felvidék – and a smaller area to Poland. After Munich, ►Slovakia became autonomous, gaining a tenuous independence under Monsignor ►Tiso when Hitler annexed the Czech provinces of Bohemia and Moravia in March 1939.

A provisional Czechoslovak government-in-exile was established by Beneš in London (July 1940), receiving recognition from Britain and the Soviet Union on 18 July 1941. Czech resistance to Nazi occupation was vigorous, protracted and courageous: 1,300 Czechs were executed in seven weeks during the summer of 1942 and two villages (►Lidice and Lezaky) wiped out. A Czechoslovak Army Corps, commanded by General ►Svoboda, was raised in the Soviet Union and helped liberate Czechoslovakia in 1944–5. At first the pre-1938 frontiers were restored but Ruthenia was ceded to the Soviet Union in June 1945 and a small enclave south of Bratislava was acquired from Hungary by the ►Paris Peace Treaties of 1947. The communists won 114 of the 300 seats in the parliamentary elections of May 1946 and dominated the coalition headed by their leader, ►Gottwald. Popular sentiment hardened against the communists in the following eighteen months, partly because the government, under Soviet pressure, reversed an earlier decision to accept aid from the ►Marshall Plan and partly because the communist Minister of the Interior was known to be packing the police with nominees for senior posts. New elections were due in May 1948. Before they could take place, Gottwald carried through a successful reorganization of his government (21–25 February 1948) which was, in effect, a communist revolution, accomplished with the backing of a workers' militia and the police. (No Soviet troops were at that time in Czechoslovakia.) Gottwald established a Stalinist repressive system directed against non-communists and dissident communists, culminating in the famous trial of Rudolf ►Slansky in 1952. When Gottwald died in March 1953 he was succeeded as effective dictator in Czechoslovakia by ►Novotný, who remained in power until early in 1968.

Resentment at alleged economic exploitation of Czechoslovakia by the Soviet Union was first openly voiced in May 1966 and was soon linked to complaints in Slovakia of over-government from Prague. Criticism of Novotný at a Writers' Union Congress in June 1967 was followed in October by student demonstrations and on 5 January 1968 by the appointment of the Slovak, ►Dubček, to succeed Novotný as First Secretary of the Party. An action programme of reform was adopted on 5 April, and was followed by the presentation to the legislature of proposals for constitutional amendments which would have brought back a measure of political democracy and conceded greater personal freedom. Attempts were made by the Soviet authorities to persuade Dubček to halt this process of liberalization, but he declined, although assuring Brezhnev that Czechoslovakia would remain within the Warsaw Pact. On the night of 20–21 August 1968 Soviet troops, accompanied by token contingents from Poland, Hungary, Bulgaria and East Germany, entered Czechoslovakia, allegedly to forestall a counter-revolution plotted within West Germany. Most of the projected reforms were abandoned, although a federal system dividing the state into separate Czech and Slovak 'socialist republics' was approved in October 1968. Dubček was ousted from office in April 1969, the succession passing to a former victim of Stalinist repression, Gustav Husák (1913–), who in May 1975 became President of the republic while retaining his position as First Secretary of the Party. The failure of the reform movement emphasized the continuing hold of the Soviet armed strength on all the Warsaw Pact states. Although the Czechs were spared the destructive tragedy of the ►Hungarian National Rising of 1956, it remained clear that the heirs of Stalin and Khrushchev were no more willing than their predecessors to tolerate a partially open society in a country which formed, geographically, a strategic corridor 370 miles long between American-garrisoned Bavaria and the Ukraine. Lubomir Strougal (1925–),

Prime Minister 1970–88, gradually introduced cautious reforms in the 1980s, but he lost influence when Husák resigned as First Secretary of the Party in December 1987 and Strougal's rival, Milos Jakeš (1922–), succeeded Husák as Party leader. Soon afterwards Strougal was replaced as Prime Minister by Ladislaw Adamec. Attempts by Jakeš to silence demands for reforms were countered by mass protests in Prague and Brno (19–23 November 1989), with a quarter of a million demonstrators in the streets of the capital. Jakeš and the whole Politburo resigned on 24 November. 'Civic Forum', an opposition movement inspired by the playwright Vaclav Havel (1936–), succeeded in gaining from Adamec recognition that the leading role of the Communist Party must come to an end. Free elections brought Civic Forum to power a month later. Havel became President on 29 December 1989, strengthening the republic's links with the West. Czechoslovakia joined the ➤Council of Europe in January 1991 as a first step towards membership of the European Community. The Czech Republic accepted the secession of Slovakia in January 1993, when federal Czechoslovakia was dissolved.

D

D-Day. Wartime code-name given to the first day of the ►Normandy Landings, 6 June 1944.

Daladier, Édouard (1884–1970), French politician. Born at Carpentras, near Avignon, the son of a baker. Daladier, who was briefly a teacher of modern history, retained close links with his birthplace, becoming mayor of Carpentras in 1912 and serving as a Radical Party Deputy for his native district, the Vaucluse area of Provence, in 1919–40 and 1946–58. He first held ministerial office in 1924 (Colonies) and was Prime Minister for ten months in 1933 and two months in 1934. His principal term as Prime Minister was from 10 April 1938 until 20 March 1940. From December 1932 to January 1934, and from June 1936 to 18 May 1940, he was also in charge of the vitally important Ministry of War and Defence. Although his outwardly forceful personality made him known as 'the bull of Vaucluse', his government favoured ►appeasement and he was a signatory of the ►Munich Pact. After the outbreak of war he showed as much active hostility to the communists as to the Germans. In March 1940 he was replaced as Prime Minister by the more enterprising Reynaud but Daladier's hold on the Radical Party ensured that he remained in the government until the fall of France. He then sought to establish a government in North Africa which would defy ►Vichy but was arrested. With other democratic leaders he was put on trial at Riom in February 1942 accused of taking France into a war for which she was unprepared. His courageous defence made nonsense of the trial, but he remained in prison until 1945, spending the last two years in German custody. His influence on the Radical Party under the ►Fourth Republic was considerable, though he never held ministerial office again.

D'Annunzio, Gabriele (1863–1938), Italian poet, novelist, war-hero and political adventurer. Born of noble family at Pescara, on the Adriatic coast of the Abruzzi. Three sensual and erotic novels at the turn of the century won him a European reputation which was enhanced by the lyricism of his poetic dramas between 1901 and 1904. In 1914 he used his literary gifts to propagate nationalist views, favouring Italy's entry into the war against Austria-Hungary. He served with courage in the Italian Air Force (1915–18), winning the highest award for valour and achieving fame for long-distance raids on Cattaro (Kotor) and Vienna. Dissatisfaction with the Peace Conference induced him to lead an irregular band of Italian troops to ►Fiume on 12 September 1919. He occupied the port and city, declaring Fiume an integral part of Italy, even though it was claimed by Yugoslavia at the Peace

Conference. For sixteen months D'Annunzio administered Fiume, striking flamboyant authoritarian political attitudes later associated with Mussolini's fascism. He was eventually ejected in January 1921 by a naval force sent against him by the Liberal Government of ►Giolitti in Rome, which was pledged to establish Fiume as a Free City. In 1922 D'Annunzio welcomed the fascist ►'March on Rome' and he spent the last sixteen years of his life in retirement at his villa on lake Garda, holding each morning a patriotic flag-ceremony on the fo'c'sle of a veteran warship beached in his gardens. The Roman salute – appropriated by Mussolini, Hitler and Franco – was first revived by D'Annunzio at Fiume.

Danzig (Gdańsk). Port at the mouth of the river Vistula, a Prussian city from 1793 to 1919. The Treaty of Versailles constituted Danzig a Free City so as to give Poland an outlet to the sea. The city was administered by a League of Nations Commissioner, with an elected senate which in 1933 passed under the control of the local Nazi Party. On 1 September 1939 the Nazi Gauleiter for Danzig, Albert Forster, proclaimed the union of the city with Germany, thereby unleashing the Second World War. The Soviet Red Army captured Danzig on 30 March 1945, handing it over to the Poles two months later. The Polish authorities expelled the German population, polonized the city – which was renamed Gdańsk – and linked it for administrative purposes with Gdynia, the neighbouring port constructed in the 1920s in Polish territory. In the 1980s the Gdańsk shipyards became centres for ►Solidarity.

Dardanelles. The channel between the Aegean Sea and the Sea of Marmora, forming the first part of the strategic waterway which, through the Bosphorus, links the Mediterranean and the Black Sea. The narrowest point of the Dardanelles lies some 130 miles south-west of the old Turkish capital, Constantinople (Istanbul), which is on the Bosphorus. On 15 January 1915 the War Council in London accepted proposals from ►Churchill for a naval expedition to force the Dardanelles 'with Constantinople as its objective'. Bombardments of Turkish defences on 19 and 26 February 1915 were followed by the attempted passage up the Straits of an Anglo-French fleet comprising seventeen battleships, a battle-cruiser, destroyer flotillas and minesweepers. A third of the capital ships were sunk or put out of action before the fleet reached the Narrows, and the naval assault was abandoned in favour of a land operation to seize the Turkish forts on ►Gallipoli. The Dardanelles operation was a strategically imaginative plan which, it was hoped, would rally Turkey's traditional Balkan opponents to the allied cause and, at the same time, open up a short warm-water route for supplies to the Russian front, where there was an acute shortage of shells. It failed because of inadequate planning, bad coordination, lack of persistence and loss of the advantage of surprise through preliminary bombardments.

Darlan, Jean Louis Xavier François (1881–1942), French admiral and politician. Born at Nérac in Aquitaine, distinguished himself as a naval commander in the

First World War, and became executive head of the French Navy from 1933 to 1939, when he was appointed commander-in-chief. After the French collapse in 1940 the British fired on French warships at ➤Mers-el-Kébir to ensure that they would not be surrendered to Germany. This action confirmed Darlan's latent mistrust of the British. He served ➤Vichy France as Minister of Marine and acted as chief minister from February 1941 to April 1942. Although he discussed Franco-German military collaboration with Hitler at Berchtesgaden on 11 May 1941, the Germans treated him with suspicion. By chance, he was in Algiers when British and American troops invaded the port (8 November 1942). This action precipitated the occupation of the whole of France by German troops, a move which Darlan interpreted as freeing him from loyalty to Vichy. He therefore agreed to collaborate with the Americans in North Africa, ordering the French forces there not to fire on the allies. His devious policy aroused resentment and on Christmas Eve he was shot dead by a royalist fanatic in Algiers.

Dawes Plan. The American banker, Charles G. Dawes (1865–1951), in April 1924 presented a report on German economic problems to the Allied Reparations Committee. The report proposed a plan for instituting annual payments of ➤reparations on a fixed scale, while at the same time reorganizing the German State Bank so as to stabilize the currency, which would be supported by a foreign loan. The Dawes Plan helped Germany meet her treaty obligations in the period 1924–9.

Dayan, Moshe (1915–1981), Israeli general. Born at Degania, to the south of the Sea of Galilee, studied science at the Hebrew University in Jerusalem, joined ➤Haganah and was imprisoned by the British authorities in Palestine, 1939–41. Subsequently released and commissioned in an auxiliary force supporting the British and Free French army which cleared Syria of Axis supporters in June 1941. During this operation he was wounded, losing his left eye. During the last years of the mandate Dayan became a political protégé of ➤Ben-Gurion. On Israel's independence he assisted General Yigael Yadin, the Israeli chief of operations, mount the counter-offensive of 25 May 1948, which checked the initial Arab incursions into Israeli territory. General Dayan served on the armistice commission in Rhodes which sought a settlement with the Arabs and in 1949–50 he held secret talks at Shuneh with King ➤Abdullah of Jordan, but showed himself a hard negotiator, disinclined to compromise. As Israel's Chief of Staff from 1953 to 1958 Dayan directed the ➤Sinai Campaign of 1956, his troops reaching the Suez Canal and the mouth of the Gulf of Aqaba in less than a week. This skill in conducting lightning operations was shown again in 1967. At a time of mounting tension General Dayan (who had been in opposition for three years) was appointed Minister of Defence on Thursday, 1 June 1967: on Monday, 5 June, Israel launched a surprise attack on her Arab enemies which brought victory by Saturday, 11 June (➤Six-Day War). Dayan, who had already served as Minister of Agriculture from 1959 to 1964, remained Minister of Defence until 1974, a period which included the ➤'October War' of 1973: but he came to disapprove of the policies pursued by the governing ➤Labour Party and moved into opposition. He returned to office as Foreign Minister in the government of ➤Begin after the 1977 election. Dayan became increasingly critical of his Prime Minister, particularly over Begin's attitude to the Arabs on the West Bank of the Jordan, and he resigned as Foreign Minister on 21 October 1979.

Dayton Accord. On 21 November 1995 an agreement over the future of ➤Bosnia-Herzegovina was concluded at Dayton, Ohio, after meetings attended by the Bosnian, Serbian and Croatian presidents. The agreement provided for the preservation of Bosnia-Herzegovina as a single state, territorially divided between a Bosnian–Croat Federation (51 per cent) and the Republika Srpska (49 per cent: Bosnian Serbs). There would be three administrations: a Muslim–Croat federal government in Sarajevo; a Bosnian Serb republican government in neighbouring Pale; and a national government within Sarajevo, with executive authority vested in an elected presidential triumvirate, the members representing each community. The elected parliament would have two thirds of the deputies from the Bosnian–Croat Federation and one third from the Republika Srpska. Indicted war criminals were barred from office. Bosnian Serb troops evacuated five suburbs of Sarajevo in return for frontier adjustments elsewhere, including access to the Adriatic, south of Dubrovnik. An international force from NATO would implement the Accord for one year, under guidance from a High Representative appointed by the European Union. The Dayton Accord formed the basis of a peace treaty signed at Paris on 14 December 1995.

Deakin, Alfred (1856–1919), pioneer Australian Commonwealth statesman. Born and educated in Melbourne, coming from a middle-class family and taking a law degree at Melbourne University. From 1879 to 1900 Deakin was a member of the Victoria state legislature and was responsible in 1896 for the first legislation in the British Empire to protect unskilled labourers in sweated industries – a measure followed by Winston Churchill in his Trade Boards Act of 1909. From 1890 onwards Deakin was a strong advocate of Australian federation. He accepted office as the second Prime Minister of the ➤Australian Commonwealth in September 1903. Although personally a Liberal protectionist, he was dependent for support on Labour, who revolted against his trade-union legislation within six months. He returned to power in July 1905, won respect throughout the Empire for his visionary championship of ➤Imperial Preference and introduced the first old-age and sickness benefits for Australia, succumbing to another Labour revolt in November 1908. A third premiership of ten months in 1909–10 achieved little. 'Affable Alfred's' historical reputation rests both on his ideal of Empire (unity through diversity) and on the value to a new Australian legislature of his understanding of parliamentary conventions.

De Gasperi, Alcide (1881–1954), Italian Prime Minister. Born at Pieve Tesino in the Trentino (then an Austrian province); educated at Vienna University; and elected to the Austrian parliament in 1911. From 1919 to 1925 de Gasperi was a deputy in the Italian parliament, serving as secretary-general of the People's Party until 1925, when non-fascist parties were banned. He was imprisoned by Mussolini in 1926 but from 1929 to 1943 found refuge in the Vatican, working in the papal library but maintaining links with the liberal-clericalist Resistance movement. In 1945 he took the lead in building up the Italian Christian Democrat Party and served as Prime Minister from December 1945 until July 1953, becoming the outstanding political personality in the Italian Republic. He was an early supporter of European integration, carrying his country into NATO, the Council of Europe and the European Coal and Steel Community. His resolute hostility to communism ensured him support from the United States which greatly assisted his reconstruction programme.

De Gaulle, Charles André Joseph Marie (1890–1970), French general and President. Born at Lille into a family of teachers and school administrators, graduated from St Cyr, 1909, choosing to serve in the 33rd Infantry Regiment under Colonel ►Pétain, whom he much admired. He was wounded and taken prisoner at Fort Douaumont, Verdun (February 1916), but saw active service again on the French military mission to Poland (1919–20), acquiring a deep respect for Marshal ►Pilsudski. In 1923 de Gaulle was a lecturer at the Staff College, developing ideas on the use of tanks and aircraft which he published in a book in 1934. After successfully commanding an armoured division in May 1940 and briefly holding junior office in Reynaud's government, he escaped to England, calling on his compatriots to continue resistance to the Nazis under his leadership. His pride, aloofness, sense of mission and reverence for the grandeur of France made him, as leader of the ►'Free French', a difficult ally for Churchill and Roosevelt. De Gaulle never courted popular favour but he was ready to take easy offence (as at ►Casablanca). In June 1943 he became head of the French Committee of National Liberation in Algiers. Almost exactly a year later he returned to France, landing in Normandy a week after D-Day. He triumphantly progressed through Paris on foot on 25 August 1944 while German sharpshooters were still on the roofs. His administration was officially recognized as the government of France by the allies on 23 October 1944, but he was affronted by their refusal to treat France as a Great Power or to invite him to join the 'Big Three' at ►Yalta or ►Potsdam. He was formally elected provisional President on 13 November 1945 but resigned within ten weeks because the constituent assembly ignored his proposals that the new ►Fourth Republic should be given a strong American-style Presidency. In April 1947 he established an anti-communist political movement, the Rassemblement du Peuple Français. Despite its electoral successes he remained principally an observer of politics for the next eleven years, writing his memoirs at Colombey-les-deux-Églises in Haute-Marne department, awaiting the summons to save France which he was sure would come to him from Paris.

In May 1958 the revolt of right-wing extremists in Algiers led to the fall of the

Fourth Republic and to the formation by de Gaulle of a 'government of national safety' in Paris (29 May 1958). Four months later a constitution for the ➤Fifth Republic was submitted by referendum to the French people at home and overseas: it strengthened the executive, giving a President the powers de Gaulle had sought in 1945–6. The constitution was approved, and de Gaulle elected President on 21 December 1958 with 78 per cent of the popular vote. His resolve to end the Algerian War threw the right-wing army officers under General ➤Salan into armed resistance in April 1961 and he was fortunate to survive several assassination plots, the most dangerous being the machine-gunning of his car at Petit Chamart on 22 August 1962 by members of the ➤OAS. As President he conducted a vigorously independent foreign policy, authorizing ➤Pompidou to conclude the ➤Évian Agreements with the Algerians, insisting on developing a specifically French nuclear deterrent, refusing all concessions when the British sought to join the ➤EEC and in 1965 declining to cooperate with France's partners through hostility to the Common Market's agricultural policy. Differences with the Americans led de Gaulle to withdraw French contingents from ➤NATO in July 1966, requiring all NATO installations to be evacuated from France by May 1967. His assertion of independence led him to put great stress on bilateral agreements with West Germany and with the Soviet Union. In successive visits to Moscow, Warsaw and Bucharest (1966–8) he urged the creation of a Europe stretching 'from the Atlantic to the Urals', without any apparent response. Although French trade and industry flourished, there was resentment at high taxation for military needs while health, education and social services were neglected. The ➤student demonstrations in the spring of 1968 forced de Gaulle to make economic concessions. He then drew up a scheme for major changes in regional institutions and in the Senate which he submitted to a referendum on 28 April 1969. When the electorate rejected his proposals, he resigned, retiring once more to Colombey where he died suddenly on 9 November 1970.

De Klerk, Frederik Willem (1936–), South African President: born in the Transvaal and educated at Potchefstroom University before establishing a law practice at Vereeniging, the town he represented in the South African parliament 1972–89. He held ministerial posts under ➤Vorster and P.W. ➤Botha and in 1982 became National Party leader in the Transvaal. Seven years later he succeeded Botha both as party leader in February and as State President in August. He fought and won a general election in September 1989 on the basis of gradual reform of ➤apartheid in order to secure better contacts abroad. In 1990 he ended the ban on the ANC, ordered the release of ➤Mandela and began talks with black leaders on the abandonment of apartheid. On 1 February 1991 he told Parliament he would repeal the apartheid laws, a task accomplished by midsummer. He promoted an interracial convention on a democratic South Africa, which opened on 20 December 1991. Despite opposition from the ➤Inkatha Zulus, and from his own right-wing Afrikaners, de Klerk persisted with the talks and on 22 December

1993 secured parliamentary approval for an interim multiracial constitution. When the multiracial election of April 1994 was won by the ANC, de Klerk stepped down from the Presidency, but on 10 May 1994 he accepted office as second deputy to President Mandela. In 1993 De Klerk and Mandela shared the Nobel Peace Prize.

Delcassé, Théophile (1852–1923), French statesman. Born at Pamiers, in the Ariège department, became a primary-school-teacher before a rich marriage gave him the backing to enter politics, as an admirer of the legendary republican, Léon Gambetta (1838–82). In 1889 Delcassé was elected to the Chamber of Deputies, where he vigorously supported African expansion, serving as Colonial Minister 1893–5. He became Foreign Minister in June 1898, holding the office until June 1905, a longer term than any other Minister in the Third Republic. Since he believed France could not be on bad terms simultaneously with Britain in Africa and with Germany in Europe, he worked for closer Anglo-French understanding, helping achieve the ►Entente Cordiale of 1904. He was forced to resign during the Moroccan Crisis of 1905 by a conspiracy of his colleagues under German pressure. As Navy Minister (1911–13) he continued to strengthen Anglo-French collaboration, especially in the Mediterranean. He was ambassador to Russia for seventeen months, returning as Foreign Minister (August 1914 to October 1915) and helping to negotiate the Treaty of ►London which brought Italy into the war.

Delhi Durbar (12 December 1911). King ►George V and Queen Mary as Emperor and Empress of India held a ceremonial Court (for which the Hindustani word 'Durbar' was used) at Delhi, the ancient seat of the Mogul emperors, during their state visit to India. This magnificent ceremony, in which the Indian princes did obeisance to the King-Emperor, was unique in the history of British India. In his speech on that occasion George V announced the transfer of the Indian capital from Calcutta to Delhi and the restitution of Bengal as a united province after the highly unpopular attempt by ►Curzon in 1905 to divide Bengal for administrative convenience.

Democratic Party. One of the two main political parties in the USA. The party was founded in 1828 and was dominant until 1860, when it became identified with the South, not winning a Presidential election again until the growing political strength of the West helped bring Cleveland to the White House in 1885 and 1893. The party was out of office for the first decade of the century, but opposition to monopolistic trusts contributed to the success in the 1912 Presidential election of Woodrow ►Wilson, who headed the Democratic Administrations from 1913 to 1921. After the economic Depression of 1929 the Democrats emerged as champions of government action to end unemployment and stimulate industry. These proposals were embodied in the ►New Deal of Franklin ►Roosevelt, President from 1933 to 1945. The Democrats won control of the Senate and the House of Representatives in 1932. They lost control of Congress in the mid-term elections of 1946 but recaptured it in the successful Presidential campaign of ►Truman in 1948. Adlai ►Stevenson, the Governor of Illinois, lost the elections of 1952 and 1956 to ►Eisenhower, with the ►Republican Party winning the House of Representatives on the first of these occasions. The Democrats were successful in the 1960 campaign, under the leadership of John ►Kennedy, and in 1964 the incumbent President, Lyndon ►Johnson, won more popular votes than any previous candidate. Although the Democrats lost the Presidential elections of 1968 and 1972, they retained control of Congress, thereby hampering the legislative programmes of the Republican Presidents, ►Nixon and ►Ford. The traditional influence of the southern states reasserted itself in a new character during the 1976 campaign, ensuring the nomination and eventual victory of the former Governor of Georgia, Jimmy ►Carter. Under Wilson, Roosevelt and Truman the Democrats showed a sense of world responsibility, in contrast to Republican isolationism. This distinction between the parties became less marked after 1952. From 1960 onwards the Democrats favoured social welfare, aid to underdeveloped countries, and ►civil rights. During the first ►Clinton administration of 1993–7 the Democrats reasserted their awareness of world responsibility, with peace initiatives in the Middle East, Bosnia and Northern Ireland.

Deng Xiaoping (Teng Hsaio-Ping, 1902–97), Chinese statesman. Born in Szechwan, he received his university education in France, at Lyons. He was active in the Marxist agitation at Shanghai in 1927 and by 1931 was a close colleague of ►Mao Tse-tung (Mao Zedong), whom he supported throughout the party disputes of the 1930s and with whom he shared the hardships of the ►Long March. He joined the central committee of the Chinese Communist Party in 1949 and was General-Secretary 1956–66, when he was denounced as a revisionist during the ►'cultural revolution'. ►Chou En-lai (Zhou Enlai) brought him back to the central committee in 1973 and he was vice premier for the following three years. He also served ►Hua Kuo-feng (Hua Guofeng), as principal deputy and as chief of the general staff 1977–80. Deng was the most influential politician in shaping China's post-Mao era, even though he did not hold the highest offices of state. By 1987 he had brought forward a younger communist politburo, willing to accept modern cultural ideas and technology under the leadership of Deng's political protégé, Zhao Ziyang. Although Deng was in poor health by the beginning of 1989 he was still titular Chairman of the Central Military Commission on 4 June when the army attacked demonstrators in Tiananmen Square, Peking. He finally resigned office on 9 November 1989, but he retained influence until a few months before his death, notably over the 14th Party Congress in 1992, where he encouraged the growth of a 'socialist market economy'.

Denikin, Anton Ivanovich (1872–1947), Russian general. Entered the Tsar's army as a boy of fifteen, served as a major in the Russo-Japanese War, and as a senior staff officer 1914–16. He was appointed deputy chief of staff with the rank of lieutenant-general in February 1917. Denikin, long critical of demoralizing influences at the Tsar's court, served the Provisional Government as commander of Russia's western front in March 1917, moving to the south-western front two months later. After the Bolshevik Revolution he assumed command of a 'White' army, the 'Armed Forces of the South', which from 1918–20 sought to establish a 'United Russia', purged of Bolsheviks. His army received considerable help from the British from January 1919 onwards. He inflicted a severe defeat on the Bolsheviks in the Caucasus in early February 1919 and mounted a major offensive in the Ukraine in August, entering Kiev on 2 September and advancing to within 250 miles of Moscow. A Red Army counter-attack in December led to the loss of Kharkov and to Denikin's eventual withdrawal to the Caucasus, where he held out until the end of March 1920. Denikin's cause suffered from his narrowly Russian sense of patriotism which prevented him from making contact with Ukrainian and Polish anti-Bolshevik forces. He even established a blockade of Georgia and Azerbaijan, fearing that the non-communist nationalists in the Caucasus would set up independent republics. In the spring of 1920 he escaped to Constantinople, settling later in France and dying in the USA.

Denmark. Formed part of a united Scandinavian kingdom until the fifteenth century and remained linked with Norway until 1815. Denmark became a constitutional monarchy in June 1849, the constitution being revised on several occasions, notably in 1866 and 1953 (when Greenland became an integral part of the kingdom). Throughout the First World War Denmark maintained strict neutrality but, at the peace settlement, recovered northern Schleswig, which had been lost to Prussia in 1864. Denmark was occupied by the Germans in April 1940, a strong resistance movement developing by the autumn of 1943. Although Danish foreign policy had been traditionally neutralist, the kingdom joined NATO in 1949 and the ►European Free Trade Association in May 1960, withdrawing to become a member of the European Economic Community in January 1973. Moderate left-wing coalitions, dominated by the Social Democrat Party, formed governments in 1929–40 and 1957–68, gradually building up a welfare state based upon the extensive social-service reforms introduced by the government of Theodor Stauning, 1933–5. The Social Democrats returned to power in September 1971 but after the 1974 elections could only form a minority government. Greenland was accorded internal autonomy in May 1979 and in January 1985 left the EEC. Denmark's Social Democrats went into Opposition in 1982 and the election of September 1987 kept in office a right of centre four-party coalition, headed by Poul Schluter (1929–). A referendum in June 1992 rejected the ►Maastricht Treaty, but a second referendum eleven months later approved a version which allowed the Danes to 'opt-out' from five commitments, including a single currency. The Schluter government fell in January 1993 after criticism of its treatment of a group of Tamil asylum-seekers. The Social Democrat leader Poul Rasmussen (1943–) formed a left-of-centre coalition, his party strengthening its representation after the September 1994 election. The projected completion in June 2000 of a ten-mile motorway tunnel and bridge linking Copenhagen with Malmö in Sweden is expected to lead to major changes in Denmark's economy.

Depression. An economic condition marked by a decline in trade and general prosperity. The Depression of 1929–34 – 'the World Slump' – was more far-reaching than any other recession, before or since. It began with a fall in agricultural prices: first (in 1928) in the value of timber, because of Soviet competition, but most disastrously in 1929 when over-production of wheat in Canada and the USA forced down the price of the basic crop in all agrarian lands, whether European, American or Australasian. The agricultural recession was aggravated by a general financial collapse, especially in the USA, where a fever of speculation led to withdrawal of funds from Europe and subsequently in October 1929 to the panic known as the ➤Wall Street Crash. In May 1931 French bankers withdrew short-term credits to a major Austrian bank, the Credit Anstalt, which failed to meet its obligations. This disaster brought bankruptcy to many institutions in central and eastern Europe: it led German bankers, in self-defence, to repudiate foreign liabilities by a moratorium, which in turn imperilled British bankers who had invested heavily in Germany; and there was throughout the summer of 1931 a run on the pound. Shortage of capital led to a fall in exports and in internal consumption throughout all the industrialized countries: the lack of a market necessitated closures of factories; fewer goods needed less transport, a reduction which harmed both shipping and shipbuilding. In all countries the consequence of the recession was mass unemployment: 13.7 million unemployed in the USA, 5.6 million in Germany, 2.8 million in Britain (maximum 1932 figures). The Depression also had significant consequences in Latin America, cutting off foreign capital and commodity exports in a region almost entirely dominated by bankers and merchant entrepreneurs from the United States and Europe. The general effect of the Depression was to lead to: (1) increased economic planning (➤New Deal); (2) intensified economic nationalism in the form of tariffs; (3) the encouragement of romantic-authoritarian political movements as an alternative to communism (e.g. the German Nazis, the Austrian Fatherland Front, the Romanian Iron Guard etc.). The Depression, more than any other single cause, explains the violent political swing to the Right in continental Europe and Latin America between 1932 and 1938.

De Valéra, Éamonn (1882–1975), Irish President. Born in New York of a Spanish father and Irish mother, educated in Ireland, becoming a lecturer in mathematics at Maynooth. He joined ➤Sinn Féin, distinguished himself as battalion commander of the Irish Volunteers at Boland's Hill, Dublin, in the ➤Easter Rising of 1916. He was captured by the British and sentenced to death but not executed, serving a year's imprisonment at Lewes. On returning to Ireland he was elected President of Sinn Féin, a post he held from 1917 to 1926. Throughout these years he continued to resist the British: he was imprisoned at Lincoln, 1918–19, escaping and eventually travelling to the USA where he spent seventeen months (1919–20) raising more than £1 million for the ►Irish Republican Army. His hostility to those of his compatriots who accepted dominion status for Ireland – men like Michael ►Collins – led him to conduct internal warfare throughout the 'Free State', 1922–3. Eventually in 1926 he decided to change his tactics, accepting the existing parliament (Dáil), for which he built up a new political party, the Fianna Fáil, in opposition 1926–32. The Irish general election of February 1932 enabled him to form a government of Fianna Fáil and Labour supporters. He remained Prime Minister for sixteen years, gradually cutting the links binding Dublin to British rule: a new constitution in June 1937 created the sovereign democratic state of ►Eire. De Valéra made the achievement of a United Ireland the prime object of his policy, using the continuance of partition as the prime reason why he remained neutral throughout the Second World War. By 1948 his government seemed to represent outmoded concepts and he was forced into opposition. He returned as Prime Minister from 1951 to 1954 and from 1957 to 1959, when he stood for President, gaining a majority of 120,000. In 1966 he offered himself for re-election and won the contest, though his majority was down to a mere 10,000. His prestige abroad, especially in the USA (where he became the first Irish leader to address a joint session of Congress, June 1964), was greater than his appeal at home during the last ten years of his active political life. He retired, at the age of ninety, in May 1973, dying twenty-seven months later.

Diana, Princess of Wales (1961–97). Third daughter of Viscount Althorp, later 8th Earl Spencer (1924–92). Lady Diana Spencer spent her earliest years at Park House, Sandringham, as her father was a royal equerry. Her engagement to Charles, Prince of Wales (1948–), was announced in February 1981; marriage followed at St Paul's Cathedral on 29 July, a 'fairytale' royal wedding televised live in seventy-two countries. Their first child, Prince William, was born in June 1982 and Prince Harry in September 1984. Marital strain and disillusionment led to a formal separation in December 1992 and divorce in August 1996. Princess Diana worked tirelessly and with attractive spontaneity for charities, notably for children and the sick, especially sufferers from AIDS and leprosy. From January 1997, when she spent four days in Angola, she campaigned vigorously for a ban on anti-personnel land mines, also visiting Bosnia on 2 August. Intrusive world-wide media coverage of her movements reached a climax on her return from Bosnia when, for the second time that summer, she made holiday trips with Dodi Fayed, only son of the owner of Harrods store and the Ritz Hotel, Paris. In the early hours of 31 August 1997 the Princess died after a car crash in Paris in which Dodi Fayed and their chauffeur were also killed. The funeral service at Westminster Abbey on 6 September followed a week's display of public grief without precedent in Britain; millions of flowers were laid by mourners in front of London's royal palaces. The emotional response to the tragedy punctured the restraints traditional to royal protocol. Princess Diana was buried on an island in the lake at Althorp, Northamptonshire.

Díaz, Porfirio (1830–1915), Mexican dictator, of part Indian descent. Although educated for the Church, Díaz entered politics as a radical revolutionary in the 1850s, eventually seizing power in 1876 and retaining control of the country for nearly thirty-five years. Ruthless but, in general, efficient government was administered by a hand-picked clique of personal supporters. Díaz offered good terms to foreign investors, favoured all schemes of international cooperation sponsored by the USA, and enjoyed a prestige abroad which was in contrast to the unpopularity of his greedy followers with the peasantry at home. In March 1908 he made the error of telling an American journalist that he personally favoured democratic opposition. A millionaire rancher, Francisco Madero, took him at his word, but was imprisoned on the eve of the 1910 election. Popular indignation in the countryside led in the spring of 1911 to mob violence in Mexico City. On 25 May 1911 Díaz resigned and escaped to France. His downfall was followed in ➤Mexico by seven years of revolution and civil war.

Diefenbaker, John George (1895–1979), Canadian Prime Minister. Born at Normanby Township, Ontario; educated at the University of Saskatchewan, becoming a barrister in 1919. He was elected to the federal parliament at Ottawa in March 1940, becoming leader of the ➤Progressive Conservative Party in December 1956. Seven months later an inconclusive election gave him the opportunity of forming a minority government, thus ending twenty-two years of Liberal rule. A second election, on 31 March 1958, gave him a majority of 153 seats. He sought closer ties with the Commonwealth and an increase in Canadian exports to the United Kingdom. Under his auspices a conference at Montreal in 1958 agreed to establish a system of Commonwealth Assistance Loans, but he could not break America's mounting share of Canadian trade. The electorate, which had turned to Diefenbaker in 1958 in a mood of anti-Americanism, was alienated by a dispute over defence policy, in which Diefenbaker appeared subservient to US needs. He resigned on 17 April 1963, leading the opposition to the Liberal Prime Minister, Lester ➤Pearson, until 1967, when he retired from politics.

Diego Garcia. ➤Mauritius.

Diem, Ngo Dinh (1901–63), first President of South Vietnam. Born at Hué into a strongly Roman Catholic family, received some of his education in the United States and entered the French administrative service for Indo-China; was a provincial governor 1929–32 and, for a few months, in charge of internal affairs for the whole of French Indo-China. From 1933 he developed anti-French views and abstained from political action until 1947, being imprisoned by the communists in 1945 for his allegedly reactionary ideas. In 1947 he founded a non-violent anti-communist and anti-French political body, the National Union Front, which was outlawed by the French, prompting him to go into exile in the United States and in Belgium. He returned to Saigon in 1954 under the patronage of both the Americans and the French, in order to head an anti-communist government. In the autumn of 1955 an apparently rigged election chose him as head of state in preference to the former Emperor of Annam, Bao Dai (1913–). Ngo Dinh Diem became President of South Vietnam in October 1955. He cleaned up the night-life of Saigon, improved the trade figures but established a harsh and repressive system, with his brother serving as head of political police and other members of the Ngo family in key positions. Conflict with the Buddhists offended many sections of the people. A military *coup* (which appears to have been encouraged by the US ►Central Intelligence Agency) led to the murder of Ngo Dinh Diem and his brother on 2 November 1963. (►Vietnam.)

Dien Bien Phu. Village in northern Vietnam, 100 miles west of Hanoi and 75 miles south of the Chinese frontier, commanding a valley into Laos, 20 miles farther west. The village was the scene of the decisive engagement in the French war in ►Indo-China, 1946–54. In May 1953 a new French commander-in-chief, General Henri Navarre, argued that the only way to defeat the Viet-Minh guerrillas of ►Ho Chi Minh was to entice their commander, General ►Giap, to fight a set-piece battle against a series of fortified positions in which the superiority of French firepower, equipment and military understanding would scatter Giap's largely peasant army. French airborne troops seized Dien Bien Phu, which was deep in Viet-Minh territory, on 21 November 1953, establishing a fortified camp under the command of Colonel de Castriès. The French consistently under-estimated Giap's skill and were surprised by the resourcefulness which enabled 50,000 coolies to establish siege guns in the hills over the village, making it virtually impossible to fly in supplies to the airstrips. From 13 March to 7 May 1954 Dien Bien Phu was besieged, its defenders (16,500 men) being subjected to eight weeks of constant bombardment, which they sustained with great heroism. The loss of Dien Bien Phu was followed within two months by an armistice which marked the end of French rule in Indo-China. The defeat was a bitter blow to the prestige of the French army and thereby weakened the ►Fourth Republic. Only 3,000 defenders of Dien Bien Phu survived the siege and the subsequent harsh conditions in prison camps.

Dieppe Raid (19 August 1942). The most ambitious seaborne raid on German-occupied Europe. The object of the raid was to establish the possibility of seizing a Channel port in the German defensive position known as the 'Atlantic Wall'. The raid was a failure with extremely heavy casualties. Over 6,000 troops were employed in the raid, 5,000 of them Canadians. Nearly 4,400 men were killed or taken prisoner, the Canadians alone losing 3,379 officers and men. It is said that the information gathered during the raid was of great value in planning the ►Normandy Landings of 1944.

Dimitrov, Georgi (1882–1949), Bulgarian communist leader. Born at Pernik, near Radomir, became a printer and a pioneer trade unionist in Bulgaria, helping to organize a wave of strikes as early as 1905. He secretly directed the Bulgarian communist movement inside the country, 1917–23, thereafter escaping to Russia and becoming a prominent member of the Comintern. In March 1933 he was arrested in Berlin, while on a secret mission, and charged with complicity in starting the ▸Reichstag fire. During his trial at Leipzig his brilliant defence won him widespread sympathy and helped discredit the Nazis, and in particular ▸Goering. Dimitrov was acquitted and deported to the Soviet Union. He returned to the newly liberated Bulgaria in November 1945, becoming Prime Minister almost exactly a year later. Although Dimitrov ruthlessly supervised the 'Sovietization' of the Bulgarian Republic, he showed an increasing independence of Moscow in foreign affairs. He favoured a dual republic of Yugoslavia–Bulgaria and in August 1947 travelled to Bled for conversations with ▸Tito where an agreement was signed for close political, cultural and economic cooperation between the two states. Early in 1948 Dimitrov visited Romania and spoke publicly of an eventual socialist federation for all south-eastern Europe. These plans were unacceptable to Stalin: Dimitrov was summoned to Moscow, and appears to have changed his policy. By now, however, his health was bad and he took little part in the denunciation of revisionists which followed the Soviet–Yugoslav breach of June 1948. He returned to the Soviet Union for medical treatment, dying in Moscow in July 1949.

Disarmament. The Covenant of the League of Nations held out a promise of reduced armaments. Attempts to secure an agreement were made at the ▸Disarmament Conference, Geneva, between 1932 and 1934 but without success. After the Second World War the United Nations established committees on Conventional Armaments and on Atomic Energy, merging these bodies into a Disarmament Commission in 1952. Talks on banning nuclear weapons and on cutting the size of conventional forces were held from 1955 to 1957, the Russians walking out of the Commission in disgust at the lack of progress in November 1957. The Commission continued to function, sponsoring another disarmament conference at Geneva (January to August 1966). Progress towards disarmament was made primarily through conventional diplomatic discussions: a partial ▸Test-Ban Treaty in 1963 was followed by a non-proliferation treaty in 1968 and an agreement outlawing germ warfare in April 1972. ▸'Strategic Arms Limitation Talks' (SALT) were held between the Soviet Union and the United States (November 1969 to May 1972) and resulted in a treaty reducing the total number of nuclear weapons. Further talks on ▸strategic arms reduction (acronym START) were held in Geneva from July 1982, culminating in December 1987 in the Washington agreement on eliminating medium and short range nuclear missiles, concluded by Gorbachev and Reagan at their third summit-meeting. A thirty-five nation conference on disarmament and ways to curb the risk of war in Europe opened at Stockholm in January 1984 and, after ten sessions, produced the ▸Stockholm Accord which provided for advance notice to be given of troop movements and manoeuvres.

Disarmament Conference, Geneva (1932–4). A meeting of sixty nations under League of Nations auspices but including non-members such as the USA and the USSR. The Conference sat for five months in 1932, eight in 1933 and two weeks in 1934. It failed, partly because of French insistence that a scheme of general security should precede disarmament and partly because of the heightened international tension which resulted from the advent to power of Hitler in January 1933. Germany withdrew from the Conference in October 1933, thereby effectively ruling out any agreement.

Djilas, Milovan (1911–95), Yugoslav communist dissident. Born in the small town of Kolašin, Montenegro, became a communist at Belgrade University in 1929, imprisoned for his political views by the Yugoslav royalist government 1933–6, distinguished himself as a partisan commander in Montenegro and Bosnia 1941–4, travelling to Moscow as one of the first representatives of Yugoslav communism, 1944–5. From 1945 to 1953 he was a close friend of ►Tito, in the inner circle of Yugoslav leaders and, for a time, a Vice-President. His intellectual honesty and trenchant style of writing made him a critic of abuses, which he exposed in articles for the leading Belgrade newspaper, *Borba*, and for a literary-political review, *Nova Misao* ('New Thought') of which he was editor. He was expelled from the Communist League in 1954, losing all government posts and receiving a cautionary suspended sentence for 'hostile propaganda' in 1955. He was imprisoned in December 1956 (returning to the same cell at Sremska Mitrovica in which he was detained by King Alexander's government), released in 1961, re-arrested in 1962 for continuing to show dissent and only allowed personal freedom again in 1966. Three years later he was forbidden to travel abroad, a ban not lifted until January 1988. His book *The New Class*, written in 1955 and published in western Europe and the USA in 1956, condemned the way in which communist societies produce a 'party oligarchy' which has usurped and perpetuated the class distinctions of the privileged capitalists of the pre-revolutionary system. Djilas himself remained a fervent believer in the socialist ideal, arguing that the dictatorship of the New Class inevitably carried within it the seeds of its own destruction.

Dobrudja. Coastal region between the Black Sea and the northward loop of the Danube, disputed 1878–1947 by Bulgaria and Romania. The littoral between the important Romanian port of Constanta and the Bulgarian port of Varna, eighty miles to the south, is an ethnic jumble of Bulgars, Romanians, Turks, Greeks and immigrant Caucasian seafarers. Most of the area has been Romanian since the Treaty of Berlin of 1878 and is organized as the Romanian province of Dobrogea. The southern Dobrudja (an area of some 3,000 square miles) was annexed by Romania from Bulgaria in 1913 (Treaty of ►Bucharest), briefly recovered by Bulgaria in May 1918, lost to Romania again by the Treaty of ►Neuilly in November 1919, and retroceded to Bulgaria in September 1940, under Hitler's auspices. In 1947 the ►Paris Peace Treaty upheld Bulgaria's claim, and Romania no longer seeks recovery of the southern Dobrudja.

Dodecanese. A group of twelve islands, racially overwhelmingly Greek, off the coast of Asia Minor. The principal islands are Rhodes, Kos, Leros and Patmos. Until the ►Young Turk Rebellion of 1908 the islands had enjoyed special privileges under Turkish rule for nearly 400 years. The loss of these rights prompted resistance to Turkey which was exploited by the Italians in their war with Turkey over ►Libya in 1911. The Italians occupied the Dodecanese (April–May 1912), assuring a delegation of islanders in October that they recognized their wishes for union with Greece and that their occupation would be only temporary. Italy, however, refused to leave the islands after the First World War. Under Mussolini the ports and airfields were developed as a major base for Italian ambitions in the eastern Mediterranean, and on the collapse of Italy in 1943 were garrisoned by the Germans. Attempts by the British to secure a foothold in Kos or Leros (September–October 1943) met only limited success. The Dodecanese were formally ceded by Italy to Greece in the ►Paris Peace Treaty of 1947. Occasional friction with Turkey led the Greeks, as a goodwill gesture, in 1954 to order the demilitarization of Leros, as the island is less than thirty miles from the Turkish shore; but the Dodecanese continued to impose a strain on Greco-Turkish relations, and there was particular tension during the successive crises over ►Cyprus.

Doenitz, Karl (1891–1980), German admiral. Born in Grünau, Prussia; entered the Imperial German Navy, specializing in submarine warfare from 1916 onwards. He built up Hitler's U-boat fleet in 1936–9. As flag officer U-boats he developed the 'wolf–pack' strategy, which was of great value to Germany in the battle of the ►Atlantic. On 30 January 1943 he succeeded Admiral Raeder (1876–1960) as commander-in-chief of the German fleet, with the rank of Grand Admiral. Shortly before his suicide, Hitler drew up a final testament in which he appointed Doenitz President of the German Reich. Technically Doenitz served as head of state from 1 May until 23 May 1945, when he was interned. He attempted to conclude a separate peace in the West but when there was no response to his approach, he authorized acceptance of an instrument of unconditional surrender (7 May). The Allied Military Tribunal at ►Nuremberg sentenced him in 1946 to ten years' imprisonment for war crimes. He was released from Spandau Prison on 30 September 1956.

Dogger Bank Incident (21 October 1904). During the ►Russo-Japanese War the Russian Baltic Fleet was dispatched to the Far East. While passing through the North Sea the fleet encountered vessels which, from faulty intelligence reports, their commander, Admiral Rozhdestvensky (1848–1909), believed to be Japanese torpedo boats. The Russians opened fire: in reality, they were firing on Hull fishing boats and sank a trawler, killing two crew members. Indignation in Britain was so intense that the two countries were almost plunged into war. French diplomatic intervention induced the Russians to put the responsible officers (although not their admiral) ashore at Vigo to await international arbitration. The rest of the fleet resumed the voyage to the Far East and was annihilated at ►Tsushima.

The Dogger Bank incident represents a nadir in Anglo-Russian relations but the obvious regret in St Petersburg at the naval error, together with Russia's acceptance of claims for compensation, eased tension between the two nations, indirectly facilitating the making of the ➤Anglo-Russian Entente.

Dollfuss, Engelbert (1892–1934), Austrian Chancellor. Born the illegitimate child of a farmer's daughter in Lower Austria, educated at the Hollabrunn Gymnasium, studied theology (briefly) and law at the University of Vienna, served as a machine-gun lieutenant in the Tirolean Rifles (*Kaiserjäger*) winning eight decorations for bravery and the reputation of being the smallest officer in the Imperial and Royal Army (under five feet tall). As a devout Catholic with a good war record he was welcomed in the post-war Christian Social Party, specializing in agrarian reforms and administration of the nationalized railways. In March 1931 he became Minister of Agriculture and Forestry, combating the difficulties of the ➤Depression so effectively that he was appointed Chancellor on 10 May 1932. His fear of socialist revolt led him, in March 1933, to suspend parliamentary government. In February 1934 a demonstration by socialist workers led Dollfuss to order the Austrian Army to attack the huge socialist housing estates in the suburbs of Vienna, and for five days there was a fierce civil war before the socialists were crushed. His foreign policy sought cooperation with the Hungary of ➤Horthy and relied on the friendship of ➤Mussolini. In May 1934 he promulgated a new and fundamentally fascist Austrian constitution, but he was politically an isolated figure, abhorred alike by the Marxists and by National Socialists who wanted union with Germany, an ➤*Anschluss*. On 25 July 1934 he was murdered in his Chancellery by Austrian Nazis trying unsuccessfully to stage a *coup d'état*.

Dominican Republic. The eastern part of the island of Hispaniola, in the Caribbean, the western part forming the Republic of ➤Haiti. Santo Domingo was a Spanish colony from 1511 to 1821. It was then subjugated by Haiti until 1844, when an independent Dominican Republic was established. Anarchy and frequent bloody clashes with Haiti led to American intervention on several occasions. US marines were landed on 26 June 1914 and on 29 November 1916 a formal proclamation of US military occupation was read in the capital. American interests (which dominated the country's industry and agricultural export trade) required a marine presence until the belated establishment of a constitutional government in July 1924 under President Horacio Vasquez. His benevolently inefficient rule was overthrown by Rafael ➤Trujillo in February 1930. Trujillo remained a corrupt and despotic ruler of the republic until his assassination on 30 May 1961. A brief spell of democratic government under President Juan Bosch from December 1962 until September 1963 was succeeded by a military junta. Fear of a communist takeover, as in neighbouring ➤Cuba, led the Americans to intervene again in the civil war which flared up in April 1965, the US peace-keeping mission being subsequently supported by units from Nicaragua, Honduras, Costa Rica and Brazil. Joaquin Balaguer (1907–) was elected President in June 1966 and re-elected in

1970 and 1974. American aid helped him improve the economy but he was defeated in the election of May 1978 by Silvestre Guzman (1911–). The veteran Balaguer returned to office in 1986, defeating a no less resilient Juan Bosch in the presidential contest of 1990. Balaguer won a further election for his Christian Social Reform Party in May 1994, before stepping down through ill-health. After months of political confusion, Balaguer's nominee for the succession was defeated in the election of June 1996 by the progressive Dominican Liberation Party leader, Leonel Fernandez. Tension between the two Hispaniolan republics has remained high since 1967, when all land links between Santo Domingo and Haiti were blocked at the frontier.

Douglas-Home, Alexander Frederick (1903–95; known as Lord Dunglass until 1951, when he became the 14th Earl of Home; created a Knight of the Thistle, 1962; disclaimed his peerage, October 1963; created a life peer, Baron Home of the Hirsel, 1974). Educated at Eton and Christ Church, Oxford, Unionist Member of Parliament for South Lanark, 1931–45, Conservative MP for Lanark 1950–51, and for Kinross and West Perth, 1963–74. From 1937 to 1939 he was parliamentary private secretary to the Prime Minister, Neville ➤Chamberlain. A back injury incapacitated him for two years during the war. He was recommended as Minister of State for Scotland to Churchill in 1951, who remarked 'Never heard of him', but gave him the appointment. Home remained at the Scottish Office until 1955, when Eden brought him into his cabinet as Minister for Commonwealth Relations, an office he held for five years before serving Macmillan as Foreign Secretary 1960–63. When Macmillan resigned in October 1963 his recommendation to the Queen to send for Lord Home caused widespread surprise. Sir Alec (as he became) had shown he could speak plainly and firmly as Foreign Secretary, but he was not a skilled Commons debater. Most of his year in office was concerned with projecting his relatively unknown personality to the electorate. His party lost the election of October 1964 by a narrow margin, Labour emerging with a majority of 5 seats. Sir Alec remained Leader of the Opposition for nine months and was brought back as Foreign Secretary by Heath from June 1970 until February 1974. He is the only Prime Minister to have played first-class cricket, appearing occasionally for Middlesex, 1924–5.

Dreadnoughts. A class of 'all-big-gun' battleship, deriving its name from HMS *Dreadnought*, laid down in October 1905, launched in February 1906 and at sea by October 1906. The *Dreadnought* carried ten 12-inch guns and had a speed of 21 knots: she could outrange and outpace any other vessel and therefore represented a revolution in naval shipbuilding. Since foreign designers were already planning such warships, the *Dreadnought* began a full-scale naval armaments race. Earlier battleships were rendered obsolete, and rival fleets could start the construction of new capital ships on almost level terms. Work began on the German *Nassau* class, similar in character to the *Dreadnought*, in July 1907. By 1914 Britain had nineteen Dreadnoughts (or improved versions of the *Dreadnought*) at sea and thirteen under construction, compared with Germany's thirteen at sea and seven in the shipyards. Other fleets with Dreadnoughts at sea by 1914 were: the US, eight; French, eight; Japanese, four; Austro-Hungarian, two; and Italian, one. Opposing Dreadnoughts were in action on only one occasion: twenty-eight British and sixteen German Dreadnoughts exchanged fire for twenty minutes at the battle of ➤Jutland on the evening of 31 May 1916. The supremacy of these capital ships was challenged by the limitations of the ➤Washington Conference, 1921–2, and by the growth of air power and underwater weapons.

Dubai. ➤United Arab Emirates.

Dubček, Alexander (1921–92), Czechoslovak communist reformer. Born in Uhrovek, ➤Slovakia, his family emigrating to the Soviet Union when he was four years old. He returned to Slovakia in 1938, secretly joined the Communist Party in 1939 and fought with the Slovak Resistance from August 1944. He was appointed a full-time official of the party in 1949 but sent back to Moscow for political education, 1955–8. On his return (with the reputation of being a good Khrushchev supporter) he became principal secretary of the Slovak Communist Party in Bratislava. He did not lead the mounting attacks on First Secretary ➤Novotný but allowed himself to be nominated as Novotný's successor at a meeting of the party's Central Committee on 5 January 1968. Dubček favoured a reduction in the totalitarian character of the Communist Party without the loss of its predominance within ➤Czechoslovakia. In talks with the Soviet leaders at Cierna-nad-Tisou on the Slovakian–Ukrainian frontier (29 July to 1 August 1968) he sought to assure them that his reform programme would not endanger Czechoslovak socialism. He gave further assurances to his Warsaw Pact allies at a meeting in Bratislava on 3 August. Nevertheless the Russians (and token Warsaw Pact forces) invaded Czechoslovakia on 20/21 August. Dubček was arrested but soon released after talks in Moscow. He remained First Secretary until April 1969, when he became Speaker of the Federal Assembly. Although expelled from the party in 1970 and banished to Bratislava, he became politically active again in Prague in November 1989 and became Speaker once more. He was strongly opposed to the Slovak separatist movement. In July 1992 he was gravely injured in a car accident outside Prague and died four months later.

Dulles, John Foster (1888–1959), US Secretary of State. Born in Washington, DC, educated at Princeton and in Paris, established himself as a lawyer in New York, but was selected by Woodrow Wilson to attend the Paris Peace Conference of 1919, becoming chief US spokesman on reparations. His belief in Christian ideals led him between the wars to attend numerous international conferences of churchmen. In 1945 he participated in the ➤San Francisco Conference and helped draft the preamble to the UN Charter, subsequently attending the General Assembly of the United Nations as a US delegate in 1946, 1947 and 1950. His deep and long understanding of international affairs induced Eisenhower to appoint him Secretary of State in January 1953. He visited forty countries in his first year of office, building up NATO and creating ►South East Asia Treaty Organization as part of his belief in opposing Soviet threats with the deterrent of 'massive retaliation', a policy of ►'brinkmanship'. His inability to collaborate with ►Eden led to tension in Anglo-American relations: he wished for a compromise settlement to the ►Suez Canal dispute; and strongly opposed the Anglo-French invasion of Egypt (October–November 1956). His Middle East policy showed greater confusion than his policy within Europe: in particular, his formulation of the ►'Eisenhower Doctrine' of 1957 illustrated his inability to anticipate the reactions of Arab nationalists to outside intervention. During his last year as Secretary of State he was weakened by illness, dying from cancer on 24 May 1959, only five weeks after resigning office.

Duma. The Tsarist Russian parliament instituted by Nicholas II in response to the demands in the ►Revolution of 1905. The first Duma (10 May to 21 July 1905) was elected on a broad suffrage: its meetings were mainly concerned with securing a recognition of rights, especially over finance, and with limiting the Tsar's power to legislate by decree: the session ended in deadlock. The second Duma (5 March to 16 June 1907) seemed to the Tsar so radical that it was dissolved. a new electoral decree increased the representation of the middle classes at the expense of the commonalty. The third Duma, elected on this basis, sat from the end of 1907 until 1912 and passed reforms in the local administration of justice as well as a health-insurance scheme for workers (June 1912). The fourth Duma (October 1912 to 1917) was less effective, because of the international crisis and the war; nevertheless it completed a series of educational reforms, initiated by the third Duma but opposed by the church authorities. Criticism of the regime led the Tsar to suspend the Duma for much of the war, although a session in mid-November 1916 gave clear warning of impending revolution unless there was a fundamental change in the direction of the war and the organization of supplies on the home front. (►Russian Revolution.) The 1993 Constitution of the Russian Federation revived a democratically elected State Duma as the lower house in the new Federal Assembly.

Dumbarton Oaks Conference (August–October 1944). A series of meetings held in Washington, DC, and attended by representatives of Britain, China, the Soviet Union and the United States to discuss the form and structure of the proposed United Nations Organization and in particular the character of the Security Council and its relationship to the discredited ►League of Nations. Problems arose over the use of veto powers, a question referred in the first instance to the summit conference at ►Yalta and finally to the fifty-nation conference at ►San Francisco which drafted the UN Charter.

Dunkirk Evacuation. In the fourth week of May 1940 the capitulation of the Belgian army in the north and the rapid advance of German tank forces to

Amiens and Abbeville in the south cut off the French First Army and the British Expeditionary Force. The commander of the BEF, Lord Gort, anticipated such a disaster as early as 19 May and the British had drawn up plans for 'Operation Dynamo', evacuation of the army from the port of Dunkirk, and its surrounding beaches. Between 27 May and 3 June nearly 200,000 British troops and 140,000 French troops were evacuated in 860 vessels, half of them small craft hurriedly sent across from England. All heavy equipment was abandoned. For reasons which are not clear the German tank thrust south of Dunkirk was halted on 23 May, possibly through fear the advance units were outrunning supplies, perhaps because ➤Goering claimed that his bombers could destroy the army as it was concentrated around Dunkirk. Fighter patrols from the United Kingdom protected the troops whose withdrawal was assisted by calm seas and occasional cloud cover.

Dunkirk, Treaty of (4 March 1947). An Anglo-French treaty of alliance for joint action against any aggressive threat from Germany. The Treaty also pledged the two governments to be in constant consultation over economic matters of joint concern. The importance of the Treaty lies less in what was said than in the fact it acknowledged France to be a major European Power once again. At the same time the two governments hoped to revive the ➤Entente Cordiale, independently of any special relationship with the United States.

Duvalier, François (1907–71). ➤Haiti

E

Earhart, Amelia (1898–1937), pioneer American airwoman. Born in Atchison, Kansas. In June 1928 she became the first woman to fly the Atlantic, as one of a crew of three in a triple-engined seaplane. Four years later (May 1932) she made the first solo Atlantic flight by a woman, gaining in America a prestige to rival the 'star treatment' accorded in Britain to Amy ➤Johnson. In June 1937 her plane was lost without trace in the south-west Pacific as she was completing the last stage of a round-the-world flight.

East Timor. ➤Timor.

Easter Rising (24–29 April 1916). A rebellion in Dublin seeking immediate independence for Ireland. The movement was led by Patrick Pearse of the Irish Republican Brotherhood and James Connolly of ➤Sinn Féin. Pearse proclaimed a provisional government of the Irish Republic from the General Post Office in Sackville Street which served as the rebel headquarters. The rebels also took over the Four Courts, St Stephen's Green, a workhouse in south Dublin and fortified Boland's Flour Mill on the main route from which reinforcements would be marched into the city. Attempts to capture the Castle and the arsenal in Phoenix Park failed. Hopes of German aid were not realized. Pearse, Connolly and twelve other leaders were executed in Kilmainham Gaol. Some prominent rebels were spared, among them the commandant at Boland's Mill, Éamonn ➤de Valéra. All rebel prisoners were released by an amnesty in June 1917. The Rising became a legendary epic in Irish national sentiment.

Eastern Question. A collective term for the problems raised in south-eastern Europe by the weakness of the Ottoman (Turkish) Empire and the rivalry of its successors. The two neighbouring supranational empires (Russia and Austria–Hungary) sought to benefit at Turkey's expense: Tsarist Russia advanced religious claims to seek rights in Constantinople, and racial claims as the protector of the Slav peoples ('Panslavism') to gain domination of the eastern Balkans; Austria–Hungary treated the western Balkans as a natural area of imperialist expansion, commercial and economic, achieving success with the occupation of ➤Bosnia-Herzegovina in 1878, annexing these provinces in 1908, and thereafter being threatened by the nationalistic hostility in the Balkans earlier directed against the Turks and now serving as a contributory cause of war in 1914. Until 1897 the principal upholder of Turkey's territorial integrity was Great Britain, consistently seeking to prevent Russian domination of the Bosphorus and the Dardanelles. The failure of Sultan ➤Abdul Hamid to reform the corrupt Ottoman administration, or to prevent massacres of Armenians and other minorities, alienated British opinion in the last years of the nineteenth century. With the visit of Kaiser William II to Constantinople in 1898, Turkey began to rely increasingly on Germany, rather than Britain, for support and gave the Germans valuable railway and commercial concessions (➤Berlin–Baghdad Railway), receiving in exchange a military mission and becoming Germany's ally in 1914. The Eastern Question was complicated in the twentieth century by the political interplay of the recently independent Balkan national states (especially ➤Bulgaria, ➤Serbia, ➤Romania and ➤Greece), which advanced conflicting claims to such areas as ➤Macedonia and the ➤Dobrudja. The ➤Balkan War of 1912 was the last occasion upon which the nationalities combined against Turkey: it provoked bitter rivalry between Serbia and Bulgaria, the two countries subsequently opposing each other in the First World War. The period 1915–23 marked the end of the traditional Eastern Question, with the repudiation by the Bolsheviks of the ➤Constantinople Agreements, and the success of Mustapha Kemal (➤Atatürk) in saving the nucleus of a Turkish national state after the defeat of 1918, an achievement recognized in the Treaty of ➤Lausanne of July 1923.

Economic and Monetary Union (EMU). Plans for European monetary union (to which the acronym EMU is also often applied) were outlined in 1969 but not given serious attention by the European Commission until the establishment of a European Monetary System in March 1979. A series of intergovernmental conferences led, in 1991, to the inclusion in the treaty of ➤Maastricht of proposals for gradual economic and monetary union, which would be prepared by a European Monetary Institute (EMI), duly set up in January 1994 as a prototype central bank for the ➤European Union. Mistrust of EMU by national parliaments, resentful of 'outside interference' with member states' financial and economic policies, delayed progress, as also did occasional speculation in specific currencies, notably the pound and the lira. At the Madrid heads-of-government conference in December 1995 it was agreed to seek the completion of EMU by 1 January 1999, when a single currency, the Euro, would be introduced. But it was also agreed that founding members of EMU would not be chosen until 1998 and then only if their economic performance in 1997 met the three 'Maastricht criteria': (1) a budget deficit of less than 3 per cent of gross domestic product; (2) a government debt not exceeding 60 per cent of gross domestic product; (3) inflation rates must be not more than 11.5 per cent and interest rates of not more than 2 per cent above the three best performing economies in the European Union. In March 1998 an EU report indicated that every member state except Greece had met the Maastricht rules, though some critics questioned the accuracy of the assessments, especially in the case of Portugal. The single currency would therefore begin in January 1999 for eleven states. But not for Greece, nor for Britain, Sweden and Denmark, who preferred to delay entry until it was clearer if the Euro system was sound and stable.

Ecuador. Republic in equatorial Latin America, spanning the western Andes, capital Quito, and also including the Galapagos Islands, 500 miles offshore in the Pacific. Ecuador achieved independence in 1830 but had little political stability until after the Second World War. During the 1930s the army made and unmade heads of state with unique rapidity: there were eleven presidents in the decade. The most enterprising was José Maria Velasco Ibarra, a lawyer who took office in September 1934 but was arrested by his army chiefs eleven months later, when threatening to break up the great hacienda estates. He returned as President on four later occasions (1944–7, 1952–6, 1960–61, 1968–72), his initiatives regularly curbed by army *coups*. Military junta controlled the republic in 1963–6 and 1972–9. A democratic constitution, enfranchising women as well as men, became effective in August 1979; the first elected President, Roldos Aguilera, was killed in an unexplained air crash within two years. Limited economic reforms, instituted by President Ballen in 1992–3, caused unrest in the cities. In July 1996 a populist Democrat, Abdala Bucaram, began a four-year term as President by appointing as head of government Vargas Pazos, an air force general with the rare distinction of having led, in March 1986, a *coup* which failed. President Bucaram survived an assassination attempt in December 1996. He was removed from office by the legislature three months later, when said to be mentally incapacitated. The presidential election of July 1998 was narrowly won by the centre-left Mayor of Quito, Jamil Mahuad. Ecuador's frontier with Peru is ill-defined and caused brief wars in 1941 and February 1995.

Eden, (Robert) Anthony (1897–1977, Knight of the Garter 1954, created Earl of Avon 1961), British statesman. Born near Durham, educated Eton and Christ Church, Oxford, served on Western Front 1915–18, winning the Military Cross at the battle of the Somme, elected Conservative MP for Warwick and Leamington in 1923, holding the seat until 1957. Eden's main interest was always in foreign affairs: he was parliamentary private secretary to Austen Chamberlain at the Foreign Office 1926–9, Under-Secretary for Foreign Affairs 1931–4, Minister for League of Nations Affairs 1934–5, Foreign Secretary 1935–8, 1940–45 and 1951–5. His only other ministerial posts were as Dominions Secretary (September 1939 to May 1940) and War Secretary (May 1940 to December 1940): in both offices he was principally concerned with external affairs. The assured style of his diplomacy inspired confidence and he was regarded as natural successor to Churchill as Prime Minister, although he personally began to chafe at the long period in which he remained heir-apparent. He only became Prime Minister on 6 April 1955, when his health was failing and he had already undergone three operations. His premiership was marked by a period of prosperity at home but increasing tension in the Middle East. Eden's hostility towards Nasser's Egypt tempted him to support Anglo-French military intervention in the ►Suez Crisis, largely because he insisted on comparing Nasser with Hitler and the dictators of the 1930s, whom he believed the West should have resisted at an early stage. This Suez policy lost Eden the support of most Commonwealth leaders, and aroused the particular ire of the US

Secretary of State, ►Dulles, whom Eden had already found personally antipathetic. Many British people who had admired Eden as a Foreign Secretary were dismayed by Suez. Eden, always highly sensitive to criticism, was unable to ride out the storm: his health collapsed entirely in the last weeks of 1956 and he resigned on 9 January 1957, after a mere twenty-one months as Prime Minister.

Education Acts (English). Although the first grant of public money for educational purposes in Britain was made in 1833, it was not until 1870 that education was recognized as a public service and, by the turn of the century, state responsibility was still limited to the basic task of combating illiteracy. Balfour's Education Act of 1902 placed 'board schools' under local education authorities in boroughs or counties, authorizing them to establish secondary and technical schools as well as develop existing elementary schools. In 1918 the Education Act of the historian, H.A.L. Fisher (1865–1940), provided ancillary services (medical inspection, nursery schools, special centres for defectives etc.) and declared in favour of compulsory part-time education for all young people between the ages of fourteen and eighteen, a project postponed for reasons of economy. The Education Act of 1944 – introduced by R.A. ►Butler – transformed the Board of Education (set up in 1899) into a Ministry, raised the school-leaving age to fifteen, abolished the remaining fees for state grammar schools, and reorganized the system of state-aided education by dividing it into primary, secondary and further educational stages. The basic principle behind the 1944 Act – 'every child must have the education appropriate to his age, aptitude and ability' – was later subjected to critical analysis by educational theorists, who questioned the possibility of assessing ability and aptitude by a written examination at the age of eleven and deplored the socially divisive consequences of assigning pupils to either grammar or secondary-modern schools. Between 1944 and 1976 there were fifteen education Acts, amending the Butler Act and substituting a predominantly comprehensive system. The 1964 Act – introduced by Sir Edward Boyle (1923–81) – offered local authorities greater independence in establishing age limits for differing types of school. The pace of transition to a comprehensive system has depended largely on directives to local education authorities from the Department of Education and Science, beginning with a circular letter in 1965. At the end of 1976 almost three-quarters of state secondary-school pupils were in 'comprehensives'. The Conservatives' Education Acts of 1979 and 1980 repealed the statutory requirement of 1976 which had required secondary schools to 'go comprehensive' and increased parental involvement in all maintained schools; local educational authorities were required to publish information about schools and admission arrangements and were relieved of a commitment to provide pupils with meals and milk. Changes in the examination system – notably the introduction in 1988 of a General Certificate of Secondary Education (GCSE) to replace O-level (1951–87) and CSE (1965–87) – did not require legislation. The 1992 and 1993 Acts widened the school inspection system.

Edward VII (1841–1910, reigned 1901–10), King-Emperor. Eldest son and second child of Queen Victoria, educated briefly at Christ Church, Oxford, and Trinity College, Cambridge, married Alexandra (1844–1925), elder daughter of Christian IX of Denmark. As Victoria thought him indiscreet, she denied him official duties and he was not allowed access to cabinet papers until he was over fifty. His natural liking for ceremonial pomp and circumstance created the illusion that, as King, he enjoyed a power he did not possess; and he was, in consequence, misunderstood by many foreign statesmen. His influence on policy has been especially exaggerated by German writers, who have read into his dislike of his nephew, Kaiser ➤William II, and his delight in European travel some fiendish scheme of 'encirclement'. His role in bringing about the ➤Anglo-French Entente was limited to exercising a felicitous gift of unruffled urbanity on determinedly republican ears during a visit to Paris in 1903 (a year in which he also became the first reigning English King to visit the Pope in Rome for over 600 years). Over home affairs he intervened politically much less than his mother, or indeed his son, George V. His affability, and his enthusiasm for horse-racing, made 'Edward the Peacemaker' the best-loved monarch in England since Charles II.

Edward VIII (1894–1972, reigned 20 January to 11 December 1936), King-Emperor. Eldest son of King ➤George V and Queen Mary, born at White Lodge, Richmond Park, educated at the Royal Naval Colleges of Osborne and Dartmouth and at Magdalen College, Oxford (1912–14), formally invested as Prince of Wales in a newly instituted ceremony at Caernarvon, 13 July 1911. He served with the Grenadier Guards as a staff officer on the Western Front, in Egypt and Italy during the First World War. During the 1920s the Prince of Wales made a series of world tours, representing George V on visits to the Empire and serving as an 'ambassador of goodwill' to the United States and other lands. As he grew older he began to make forthright comments deploring conditions of poverty, especially in South Wales. In 1931 he met Mrs Wallis Simpson, whom he wished to marry, and the whole of his brief reign was overshadowed by his infatuation for this fashionable American woman, although the affair was not made public in England until 3 December 1936, thereby posing the ➤Abdication Crisis. He was created Duke of Windsor on the day after his abdication, marrying Mrs Simpson seven months later, and living most of his remaining days in France, although serving as Governor of the Bahamas from 1940 to 1945. He died in his Paris home on 28 May 1972, ten days after receiving a visit from his niece, Queen Elizabeth II.

EEC ➤European Economic Community.

EFTA ➤European Free Trade Association.

Egypt. Technically part of the Ottoman Empire from 1517 until 1914, although from 1805 onwards a succession of Khedives (Governors) in Cairo left the Turkish Sultan little effective sovereignty. A nationalistic and xenophobic revolt in 1882 led the British to occupy Egypt, largely to protect the ➤Suez Canal and safeguard the revenue of Egypt's European creditors. British troops remained on Egyptian soil continuously until June 1956, and from 1883 to 1907 Lord ➤Cromer, as Agent and Consul-General, was *de facto* ruler of the country. The British declared a Protectorate in 1914 but after the First World War they were faced by nationalistic demonstrations and riots. In 1922 the British recognized Egypt's sovereign independence and a year later accepted Sultan Ahmad Fuad as King ➤Fuad I. Nationalist agitation, fanned by the ➤Wafd Party, continued throughout the inter-war period. In 1936 an Anglo-Egyptian Treaty provided for the gradual withdrawal of British forces, except from the Canal Zone. The British departure was postponed by the Italian invasion of Egypt in 1940 and the subsequent Libyan campaign. After the war a radical nationalism spread rapidly among the younger army officers, stimulated by three grievances: the continued presence of the British in the Canal Zone; the extravagance of Fuad's son, King ➤Farouk; and the failure of Farouk's military leaders in war against the new state of Israel in 1948. A *coup d'état* in July 1952 left effective power in the hands of a military council, headed by General Neguib, who completed the transition from monarchy to republic – proclaimed 18 June 1953 – and was himself President until deposed by Colonel ➤Nasser in November 1954. The withdrawal of the last British units was followed in July 1956 by Nasser's nationalization of the Suez Canal, by renewed war with Israel and by Anglo-French military intervention during the ➤'Suez Crisis'. The hostility of world opinion to the Anglo-French action considerably raised Nasser's popularity and prestige among the Arabs. Egypt remained a powerhouse of Arab nationalism for the next fourteen years, with Nasser receiving Soviet aid, particularly in the construction of the Aswan High Dam, the key to Egypt's economic growth. From February 1958 until September 1961 Egypt and ➤Syria were linked in the ➤United Arab Republic, a name retained by the Egyptian Government for ten years after Syria's secession. (The formal style 'Arab Republic of Egypt' was only assumed in September 1971.) The defeat of Egypt and her Arab allies in the ➤Six-Day War of 1967 weakened, but did not destroy, Nasser's hold on the country and Egypt's dominance of the Middle East; but the sudden death of Nasser in 1970 was followed by drastic changes of policy. His successor, Mohammed Anwar el ➤Sadat, continued a policy of military confrontation with Israel for the first three years of his government, allowing the Egyptian generals to seek revenge on Israel in the ➤'October War' of 1973. But when this venture failed, President Sadat strengthened his contacts with the West, terminated Egypt's military dependence on the Soviet Union, and gave greater attention to North African affairs than to the problems of Palestine. The Suez Canal, blocked since the Six-Day War, was reopened to international shipping on 5 June 1975. New tension, however, developed on Egypt's western frontier, and in July 1977 there were several days of fighting between Egypt and ➤Libya, whose leader, Colonel Gaddafi, remained a fanatical champion of Pan-Arab socialist unity. The ➤Sadat Initiative of November 1977 held out a prospect of peace with Israel, realized at the cost of arousing hostility from most other Arab nations. Mounting Moslem fanaticism led to the assassination of Sadat in October 1981. His successor, President Hosni ➤Mubarak, began his term of office with tentative moves towards a reconciliation with the more moderate Arab rulers. Mubarak sent 36,000 Egyptian troops to serve in the UN force in the Second ➤Gulf War. Terrorist attacks by Islamic fundamentalists (especially by the Muslim Brotherhood) continued intermittently from 1992 to 1997, with tourism, the Coptic Church and government institutions as the chief targets. Some 22,000 militants were arrested by the Egyptian police.

Eichmann, Adolf (1906–62), German Nazi. Born in Bavaria but like Hitler received his secondary schooling at Linz, in Upper Austria. When he joined the Nazi Party in 1932 Eichmann was a travelling salesman for a vacuum-cleaner company. After a period of guard duty at Dachau concentration camp in 1933–4, he was enrolled in the Jewish Department of the German secret service and sent to Palestine on a secret mission. After the ➤Anschluss he was put in charge of Jewish emigration from Vienna, a task he also undertook in Prague when Bohemia was occupied in March 1939. Two years later Eichmann became head of the Gestapo department responsible for Jewish affairs, with the rank of Lieutenant-Colonel in the SS. He assumed responsibility for the extinction of unwanted Jewish internees from January 1942 onwards. Between May and July 1944 Eichmann supervised the deportation of Jews from Hungary, organizing a special detachment (*Sonderkommando*) of slave labourers from among them. Eichmann was interned by American troops in 1945 pending trial for war crimes; he escaped from custody and fled to South America. In May 1960 Israeli agents kidnapped him in Argentina. A year later he was put on trial in Jerusalem, charged with crimes against the Jewish people. Eichmann was hanged on 31 May 1962.

Einstein, Albert (1879–1955), mathematical physicist. Born of Jewish parentage in Ulm, educated at Munich and Zürich, becoming a naturalized Swiss in 1901. In 1905 he formulated his first special theory of relativity, which revolutionized concepts of physics inherited from Newton and Clerk Maxwell. He followed this up with a law of photochemical equivalence in 1912 and by the general theory of relativity (1915–16). After holding professorial chairs in Zürich and Prague (1909–14), he was director of the Kaiser Wilhelm Institute of Physics in Berlin from 1914 to 1933, when Nazi anti-Semitism caused him to settle in the United States. He was much concerned over the possibility that Hitler's scientists might develop a bomb based upon atomic fission. In September 1939 he wrote to President Roosevelt warning him of this danger. Einstein became a US citizen in 1940 and accepted a chair at Princeton, remaining in the United States for the last fifteen years of his life. He urged the United Nations to assume all responsibility for the control of atomic weapons, and in 1953–4 protested at the inquisitorial methods of ➤McCarthyism. Practical experiments in 1919 and again in 1960 confirmed the validity of his general theory. His contribution to the theoretical knowledge of the universe was greater than that of any physicist since Newton in the later seventeenth century.

Eire. Name adopted by the former Irish Free State under the constitution of 1937 and retained so long as the country remained a dominion within the British Commonwealth. The name reflected the enthusiasm of ►De Valéra for the Irish Gaelic language (Eire being Irish for Ireland) and he remained Prime Minister for eleven of the twelve years in which the word was used. His successor, John Costello, was a constitutional lawyer who, finding the relationship between Eire and the British Commonwealth confused, introduced a 'Republic of Ireland Bill' into the Dublin parliament on 17 November 1948 which would sever all links with the British Crown; and on 18 April 1949 – an Easter Monday – the Republic of Ireland was officially proclaimed at the General Post Office in Dublin, a place rich in historical associations with the ►Easter Rising of 1916.

Eisenhower, Dwight David (1890–1969), general and thirty-fourth President of the USA. Born in Denison, Texas, but grew up in Kansas, graduating from West Point in 1915. Roosevelt appointed him general responsible for war plans in the Chief of Staff's office in February 1942, giving him command of the allied invasion of French North Africa in November 1942. His gift for securing inter-allied collaboration led to his selection as supreme allied commander for the invasion of Europe in 1944, and the subsequent choice of a 'broad front' advance into Germany rather than the concentrated thrust favoured by ►Montgomery. Despite a setback in the battle of the ►Ardennes Eisenhower was able to reach the Elbe by the second week in April 1945. He served as Chief of Staff in Washington from December 1945 until accepting the presidency of Columbia University in 1948. In 1951 he returned to Europe as Supreme Commander, NATO. During his absence a powerful lobby in the Republican Party put his name forward as a Presidential candidate even though he had never identified himself with any particular political party or group. He resigned from the army in April 1952 to campaign as Republican nominee. His popularity – 'I like Ike' – enabled him to win the election of November 1952 with more popular votes than any previous candidate; and on 20 January 1953 he became the first soldier-President of the United States since Grant in 1869–77. His eight-year administration was marked at home by new social-security laws, improved interstate highways and firm action in support of ►civil rights. Party matters he left largely to his Vice-President, ►Nixon, but Eisenhower was prepared to intervene drastically when the Committee on Un-American Activities (on which Nixon had previously served) began to assail the army commanders (►McCarthyism). Until 1958 Eisenhower relied in domestic matters on his principal White House aide, Sherman Adams, a former governor of New Hampshire. Similarly, until the spring of 1959 he entrusted foreign policy to ►Dulles, but Eisenhower showed his old skill as an amiable conciliator in meetings with Churchill and Macmillan and at the summit conference in ►Geneva in 1955.

Eisenhower Doctrine. In January 1957 the US Government, which had refused to support Anglo-French action during the ►Suez Crisis the previous October, became alarmed at the growing Soviet influence in the Middle East. In a message to Congress on 5 January President Eisenhower recommended the use of American forces to protect Middle East states against overt aggression from any other nation 'controlled by international Communism'. He also proposed an offer of economic aid and military advice to governments in the area which felt their independence threatened. This new departure in US policy was called the 'Eisenhower Doctrine' (►Truman Doctrine). It was applied in only two instances: in April 1957 to help King Hussein meet a threat from the Left in ►Jordan; and in July 1958 when 10,000 marines were landed at Beirut at the request of the Lebanese President, Camille Chamoun, who faced a Moslem insurrection at home and feared intervention by the new revolutionary government of Brigadier ►Kassem in Iraq. The unpopularity of these American moves in other Middle East countries convinced the State Department that the Eisenhower Doctrine was based upon a hurried and fallacious assessment of Arab nationalism. With the death of Secretary of State ►Dulles in the spring of 1959 the Doctrine was allowed to lapse.

El Salvador. The smallest and most densely populated republic in Central America, covering an area the size of Wales. El Salvador was a Spanish colony from 1526 until 1821 when it joined the Central American Federation. Independence in 1839 was followed by a century of political instability. Social inequalities exposed by the fall in world coffee prices during the Depression of 1931 led to a left-wing insurrection, brutally suppressed by General Hernandez Martinez, who was Presidential dictator from December 1931 until he was overthrown by students and rival generals in 1944. The dominance of the 'Party of National Conciliation' (first organized as a central-right movement by the traditional wealthy oligarchy in 1961) was challenged in 1979-80 by socialist guerrillas, the FMLN (Farabundo Marti Liberation Front). At the same time right-wing 'death squads' hastened the spread of civil war. A para-military unit was responsible for the murder on 24 March 1980 of Archbishop Oscar Romero, a fearless champion of human rights shot in his cathedral at San Salvador while officiating at a Requiem Mass for a demonstrator killed on the streets of the capital. Thirty-nine people were shot when troops again opened fire after the Archbishop's funeral. The murder of three American nuns and a lay social worker led President Carter to suspend economic and military aid to El Salvador for five weeks. The Reagan Administration backed the Christian Democrat José Napoleon Duarte, as an anti-communist, and, after Duarte promised land reforms, encouraged him to call a general election on 28 March 1982. The left declined to participate in the elections, which were won by the extreme right-wing 'ARENA party', led by Major Roberto d'Aubuisson, who had been refused entry to the United States after Archbishop Romero's murder. A banker, Alvaro Magana, succeeded Duarte as President, with fierce fighting continuing in the civil war in the southern province of Usulutan and the north-eastern province of Moazan. In the two years, March 1980 to March 1982, three-quarters of a million Salvadoreans sought refuge in neighbouring states. The

Archdiocese of San Salvador reported that known political murders, which averaged 120 a week throughout the first quarter of 1982, doubled immediately after the election and reached 5,399 for the whole year. Pope John Paul II visited El Salvador on 6 March 1983 and appealed for an end to the civil war; the fighting died down in the following year. Re-elected as President in 1984, Duarte contracted cancer in 1988 and was succeeded by Alfredo Cristiani. Renewed fighting in San Salvador led to over 600 civilian deaths in November 1989. After protracted peace talks, a ceasefire became effective on 1 February 1992. FMLN disarmed under UN supervision and contested elections in 1994 which were won by the right-wing ARENA party; FMLN then became a parliamentary opposition.

Elizabeth II (1926–), Queen and Head of the Commonwealth. Born at 17 Bruton Street, London, the elder daughter of the Duke and Duchess of York and third grandchild of the reigning sovereign, ►George V, becoming heir-presumptive at the accession of her father, ►George VI, in December 1936. Princess Elizabeth was privately educated. She was commissioned in the ATS (Auxiliary Transport Service) in March 1945, and married Lieutenant Philip ►Mountbatten in November 1947. The Princess was in Kenya at her accession (6 February 1952), flying back to London the following day. The first twenty-five years of her reign saw drastic changes in relationship between the Crown and the former overseas empire, the Queen making it her special concern to strengthen the loose constitutional ties within the ►British Commonwealth while not encroaching on individual aspirations for national independence. Rapid air transport enabled the Queen to shed the close identification with the United Kingdom associated with her predecessors: no monarch before her has travelled so many thousands of miles, nor met personally so many subjects from differing races, religions and cultural traditions. The informal 'walkabouts' introduced on the Queen's tour of Australia in 1963, have emphasized the visibly human aspect of contemporary monarchy, a development intensified by discreet use of television. But excessive media attention lowered the mystique of monarchy when, in the early 1990s, intrusive journalism probed the married life of her sons, the Prince of Wales (►Diana, Princess of Wales) and the Duke of York. Criticism of the monarchy also sprang from envy of apparent tax privileges. A 'Memorandum of Understanding', presented to the House of Commons in February 1993, provided for the payment of income tax by the Queen on a voluntary basis. In Australia, New Zealand and Canada republican sentiment intensified, with mounting disapproval of an 'absentee' Head of State.

Encyclical. A circular letter sent by a bishop to all churches within a certain area; normally a letter of major importance from the Pope. The encyclical *Rerum Novarum*, issued by Pope Leo XIII in 1891, formulated the basic modern political and social theory of Catholicism, rejecting socialism but stressing the importance of social justice in the industrial state. *Quadragesimo Anno* (Pius XI, 1931) revised *Rerum Novarum* and emphasized the evils implicit in excessive free competition or centralization. The encyclical *Mater et Magistra* (John XXIII, July 1961) modified

Rerum Novarum still farther, recognizing that in some instances a form of socialism could be for the common good. Two encyclicals of Pius XI in 1937 were concerned with rival authoritarian teachings: *Domini Redemptoris* denounced 'the false doctrines of the Bolshevik atheists'; and *Mit brennender Sorge*, a letter in the German language read from all pulpits in Germany on Palm Sunday, condemned the theoretical basis of Nazism as fundamentally unchristian. Among other encyclicals were: *Humani Generis* (Pius XII, August 1950), condemning existentialist philosophy; *Aeterna Dei* (John XXIII, December 1961), welcoming the prospect of Christian unity; *Pacem in Terris* (John XXIII, April 1963), deploring nuclear weapons and emphasizing the need for peace; *Humanae Vitae* (Paul VI, July 1968) condemning contraception; *Laborem Exercens* (John Paul II, September 1981) on the obligations of employers, workers and unions to each other and *Mulieris Dignitatem* (John Paul II, September 1988), on the dignity and vocation of women, which, while upholding the traditions of a male priesthood, affirmed the right of women to participate fully in church life.

Enosis Movement. A campaign in ►Cyprus for union with Greece. The idea of Enosis dates from the late nineteenth century. Riots supporting Enosis broke out on the island in 1931. The most sustained campaign lasted from 1954 until the arrival of Turkish troops in July–August 1974 effectively partitioned the island. (►Grivas and ►Makarios.)

Entebbe. Principal airport of Uganda. On 27 June 1976 members of the 'Popular Front for the Liberation of Palestine' hijacked an Air France aircraft flying from Tel Aviv to Paris soon after it took off from Athens. They ordered the pilot to fly to Entebbe, demanding the release of fifty-three Arab terrorists from various countries. They freed 100 passengers but detained 100 hostages (mostly Jewish) at Entebbe, with the collaboration of the Ugandan authorities and the support of President ►Amin. On 3 July an Israeli commando unit, transported 2,250 miles in three Hercules aircraft, made a surprise attack on Entebbe. In a half hour battle it rescued the hostages from an airport building, destroyed eleven MIG pursuit planes of the Ugandan air force, and then flew back with the freed hostages to Israel. Twenty Ugandan soldiers, seven hijackers, three hostages and an Israeli officer were killed. The raid – unprecedented in military history – discredited Amin, deterred hijacking by showing that even distant havens from Israel were not immune from retaliation, and boosted Israeli prestige at a time when the Western Powers were beginning to show greater understanding of Palestinian Arab grievances.

Entente Cordiale. A phrase first used in the 1840s for the 'understanding' between the two liberal powers, Britain and France, and revived as a description of their relationship following the ►Anglo-French Entente of 1904. The friendship implied by the phrase was frequently strained, notably by the crisis over the ►Ruhr in

1923, and was virtually destroyed in 1940 by the naval operations at ➤Mers-el-Kébir and ➤Oran. In 1947 the Treaty of ➤Dunkirk sought to revive the friendship.

Entente Powers. The name frequently applied to the collaboration of Britain, France and Russia in the years 1907–17. The ➤Anglo-French and ➤Anglo-Russian Ententes were transformed from diplomatic associations to a military alliance on 3 September 1914; and thereafter 'the Entente Powers' was often used as a synonym for 'the allies', especially by their enemies.

Enver Bey (1881–1922), Turkish general. Born at Apana; commissioned in the Turkish Army, receiving some of his military instruction in Germany. While serving in the Salonika garrison he worked out plans for modernization of the Ottoman Empire, becoming one of the three leaders of the ➤Young Turks when they rebelled in July 1908. Subsequently Enver Pasha (as he was generally known) went to Berlin as a military attaché, 1909–10. At this point Enver was uncertain whether to turn for support to Turkey's old ally, Britain, or to Germany. He met Churchill at German manoeuvres in 1909 and again in London, early in 1910. By 1911, however, Enver had decided to seek German military support, and his influence was all-powerful in Constantinople, Sultan Mehmet V (reigned 1909–18) being virtually his puppet. Enver commanded Turkish forces fighting against Italy in Libya (1911) and in the ➤Balkan Wars. In 1914 he became Minister of War, assuming a field command as general responsible for the Turkish campaign against the Russians in Caucasia, seeking to defend Trebizond and Erzerum. After the Bolshevik Revolution Enver became interested in massive Turkish expansion in the Caucasus, the establishment of a 'Pan-Turania'. Before these hopes could be realized, Turkey was defeated in 1918 and Enver sought refuge in Turkestan, where he was eventually killed, leading an anti-Bolshevik revolt. His remains were brought back to Turkey in March 1997 and interred with much ceremony at Edirne (Adrianople), the city his cavalry had recovered from the Bulgarians in the last phase of the Balkan Wars (June 1913).

EOKA (Ethniki Organosis Kyprion Agoniston). The 'National Organization of Cypriot Fighters,' a secret anti-British guerrilla movement in ➤Cyprus led by ➤Grivas and especially active 1955–9.

Erhard, Ludwig (1897–1977), West German Chancellor. Born at Fürth; made a specialist study of economics during the 1920s, was head of an economic research institute before the Second World War and Professor of Economics at Munich University, 1945–9, serving also as head of Bavaria's industrial reconstruction organization and chairman of the Economic Executive Council for the British and American occupation zones established in 1948. He thus had considerable experience of post-war economic problems before becoming a Christian Democrat member of the West German Bundestag in 1949. He was at once appointed Federal Minister of Economic Affairs by Chancellor ➤Adenauer, holding the post from 1949 to 1963 and thus presiding over the West German 'economic miracle', a transition from wartime devastation to prosperity. Erhard, appointed deputy Chancellor in 1957, succeeded Adenauer in October 1963; he lacked, however, his predecessor's skill in international affairs and there was some tension in Franco-German relations during his chancellorship. Fearing an economic recession Erhard proposed a series of tax increases in 1966 but failed to carry his colleagues with him, resigning office in November 1966 and retiring into private life.

Eritrea. A predominantly Muslim region extending along 670 miles of the southern Red Sea in Africa. The territory was first colonized by Italians in 1882, with a colonial administration formally established in 1890. The colony provided a base for Italian attacks on ►Ethiopia in 1895–6 and 1935–6 but, in the Second World War, was occupied by the British in the spring of 1941 and remained under British administration until September 1952. Ethiopian claims to the ex-colony were disputed by the Eritrean Muslim leaders who maintained that their language (Tigrinya) was totally distinct from the Amharic tongue of Ethiopia, and that their religious and cultural heritage had nothing in common with the Coptic Christianity of their Abyssinian neighbours. In December 1950 the UN General Assembly proposed, however, that Eritrea should be constituted an autonomous federal region within the Ethiopian Empire. This status was observed by the Ethiopians from 1952 to 1962 when Eritrea was absorbed as an integral part of Ethiopia and governed directly from Addis Ababa. A National Liberation Front (ELF) began guerrilla activities in 1963, increasing its activities with the growth of anarchy in Addis Ababa 1974–5. A punitive expedition organized by the Ethiopian Revolutionary Council in June 1976 was halted on the borders of Eritrea at the request of the more radical Arab national leaders who have consistently supported the Eritrean cause. Eritrean guerrilla successes, July–December 1977, were countered by Soviet and Cuban support for the Ethiopians in the opening months of 1978. The ELF, ejected from the mountain stronghold of Keren in November 1978, established new positions at Nafka where they defeated the Ethiopians in December 1979 and March 1984. Sporadic fighting continued, despite the ►famine of 1983–5, with the Ethiopians faced by guerrilla threats in the neighbouring Tigré province. The ELF helped Ethiopian democrats to overthrow the Mengistu regime in 1991 and the new Ethiopian government permitted a referendum on Eritrea's future in April 1993. Independence was proclaimed in Asmara, the capital, on 24 May 1993. In the mainly Coptic Christian region of northern Eritrea, frontier disputes with Ethiopia led to open conflict in May 1998: the Ethiopians bombed Asmara early in June; Eritrean planes attacked Ethiopian towns in Tigré province.

Estonia. The most northerly of the three ►Baltic republics achieving independence from Russia after the Bolshevik Revolution and retaining a separate existence until being constituted Soviet republics in August 1940. The Estonians, under Swedish rule in the sixteenth and seventeenth centuries, were Lutheran by religion and had closer linguistic and racial affinities with the Finns than with their immediate neighbours. Estonia was annexed to Russia by Peter the Great in 1709 and settled

primarily by German-speaking 'Baltic Barons', with big landed estates. During the
1920s agrarian reforms led to the emergence of a prosperous peasant community.
From 1934 to 1939 Estonia was governed by a virtual dictator, Konstantin Paets,
who favoured veterans from armies which had opposed the Bolsheviks in the
►Russian Civil War. Paets's attempts to reach defensive agreements with Germany
were invalidated by the ►Nazi–Soviet Pact of 1939. The Russians demanded naval
bases in September 1939 and occupied the whole of Estonia in June 1940. Persistent
demands for independence were made throughout 1990 and achieved success in
August 1991.

Ethiopia. A nation that has flourished since biblical times, maintaining its independence despite incursions from Portuguese (1528–1633) and Italians (1882–1941).
The Emperor Menelek's decisive defeat of the Italians at the battle of Adowa (1
March 1896) ensured that Ethiopia survived as the one independent kingdom in
Africa after the era of imperial partition. The accession of the Emperor ►Haile
Selassie in 1930 was followed by attempts to give the country the outward
appearance of westernized modernity. Haile Selassie's reform programme was cut
short by renewed threats from the neighbouring Italian colonies in ►Eritrea and
Somalia, leading in 1935–6 to the ►'Abyssinian War'. Italian occupation (1936–
41) improved the road system in a country divided by formidable barriers of ravine
and mountain. In February 1941 Sir Alan Cunningham, as commander of allied
forces in East Africa, led a joint British, South African and Abyssinian Army back
into Ethiopia, enabling Haile Selassie to re-establish his authority in the early
summer of 1941, thereafter concentrating on improving the economy, with both
British and American help. Eritrea came under Ethiopian rule in 1952. During the
1950s Ethiopia emerged as a centre of African 'neutralist' opinion, acquiring an
international status disproportionate to the poverty and backwardness of the
empire's rural regions. Haile Selassie encouraged the emergence of a parliament
from 1955 to 1957 but refused to permit its members real responsibility, continuing
to keep political control in his own hands. Thus he remained Foreign Minister
himself until 1966. This reluctance to devolve authority led to disaster when the
failure of the annual rains in 1973 was followed by famine and unprecedented
social distress. A provisional reform government was set up in February 1974 under
a progressively minded member of the imperial family, the Oxford-educated
Endelkatchew Makonnen (1926–74). Before he could put his liberal principles
into practice, Makonnen's government was swept aside by a radical force of junior
army officers who deposed Haile Selassie on 12 September 1974 and imprisoned
or executed many reformers, including Makonnen. Executive power passed to a
'Provisional Military Administrative Council' under the chairmanship of Brigadier
Teferi Benti, who was himself killed in a *coup* led by Colonel Mengistu in February
1977. The Council was faced by revolutionary unrest in Eritrea, where a National
Liberation Front had been active for ten years, and by threats from a Western
Somali Liberation Front, supported by the Somali Government in Mogadishu. In

the summer of 1977 the Somalis gained control of the Ogaden desert while in September a third 'Liberation Front', representing the Somali Abo region, occupied most of the southern province of Bale. Soviet and Cuban military assistance, with tanks and aircraft, cleared the Ogaden in two offensive thrusts between 21 January and 5 March 1978, and helped contain the guerrilla threat in Eritrea. A secessionist movement in Tigré province gained control of several north-western towns. Mengistu's attempts to impose Soviet-style rule were hampered by chronic ▸famine and by the incessant guerrilla activity, but a draft constitution for the People's Democratic Republic of Ethiopia was at last published in June 1986, consolidating Mengistu's powers in an executive presidency. A peace settlement with Somalia in April 1988 led to the military evacuation of the Ogaden. A month later Mengistu granted an amnesty to the princesses of Haile Selassie's family, held captive for fourteen years. Mengistu's own authority was challenged by an abortive *coup* in May 1989 while he was visiting East Germany. The Tigré rebels, reconstituted as the Ethiopian People's Revolutionary Democratic Front, were involved in ten weeks of heavy fighting at the close of 1989 and into 1990. A sustained offensive in March and April 1991 led to the flight of Mengistu on 21 May, the downfall of his regime, and the entry of Democratic Front forces into Addis Ababa on 28 May 1991. Ethiopia formally became a 'Federal Democratic Republic' on 22 August 1995, after multiparty elections brought to power a Democratic Front government, headed by the principal architect of Mengistu's fall, Meles Zenawi.

Eulenburg, Philip zu E. und Hertefeld (1847–1921, created a prince 1900), German diplomat and court favourite. Born at Königsberg, took a doctorate in jurisprudence, served with a Guards regiment 1866–71, winning the Iron Cross for bravery in 1870, entered the diplomatic corps, finally serving as ambassador in Vienna, 1894–1902. He was author of a satirical novel, composed *Lieder*, and wrote poems, showing specialist knowledge of Nordic ballads. Early in 1886 he met the future Kaiser ▸William II and was his principal friend and confidant for twenty years, influencing his policy and advancing the career of their common friend, ▸Bülow. In 1906 Maximilian Harden, a Jewish journalist alienated by Eulenburg's persistent anti-Semitism, launched Press attacks on Eulenburg, alleging homosexual behaviour and criticizing the morals of friends he entertained at Liebenberg, his country estate (where the Kaiser stayed for some hunting every October). The scandal led the Kaiser to ostracize Eulenburg from April 1907. Charges brought against the Prince were not proven since his health gave way on the two occasions he appeared in court (1908 and 1909) and the trial was abandoned. The Kaiser later declared he was convinced of Eulenburg's innocence: but the scandal threatened the stability of the throne and contributed to a nervous breakdown which William suffered in the closing weeks of 1908.

Eupen-Malmédy. Two small segments of territory on the German–Belgian frontier, whose inhabitants are predominantly German-speaking. The region was part of the Low Countries (Austrian Netherlands) in the eighteenth century but was ceded to Prussia by the Treaty of Vienna in 1815. It was incorporated in Belgium in 1919 (►Treaty of Versailles), partly as compensation for the devastation of Belgian industry during four years of war and occupation. A Cultural Council to protect the linguistic rights of the German minority was set up in 1972.

Euratom. Abbreviation for the European Atomic Energy Community, established by the second of the ►Rome Treaties of March 1957, and forming since 1967 part of the general ►European Community, with similar membership. Euratom has sought the cooperation of member states in the technical development of nuclear research and in the rapid and large-scale production of nuclear energy for peaceful purposes.

Europe, Council of. A European organization – remaining independent of the ►European Community – set up in May 1949 to achieve greater unity between its members, safeguarding their common heritage and maintaining and furthering human rights and basic freedoms. The original ten members were Belgium, Denmark, France, Ireland, Italy, Luxembourg, the Netherlands, Norway, Sweden and the UK. They were joined by Greece, Iceland and Turkey (1949), West Germany (1951), Austria (1956), Cyprus (1961), Switzerland (1963), Malta (1965), Portugal (1976) and Spain (1976). In November 1990 Hungary was the first ex-communist republic to join the Council; Czechoslovakia joined two months later. The Council functions through an executive Committee of Ministers (meeting once or twice a year) and their deputies, who have tended to meet up to ten times a year. The consultative European Assembly is a non-legislative parliamentary institution meeting for three one-week sessions each year in Strasbourg to debate reports on matters of common concern (including an annual meeting with the European Parliament, representing the European Community). In April 1955 the Council established a Commission and Court of Human Rights, to hear complaints brought either by one member state against another or by individuals against their governments. The Council of Europe has been of greatest value as a pioneer institution examining methods for submitting a federal democratic order in place of the discredited national sovereignty of the inter-war period.

European Coal and Steel Community (ECSC). The earliest of the European Communities, functioning from July 1952. The ►Schuman Plan of May 1950, proposing a union of the Franco-German coal, iron and steel industries, was followed by ministerial talks between France, West Germany, Italy and ►Benelux. The six countries concluded a Treaty in Paris (18 April 1951) establishing a single authority which would encourage these industries, eliminate tariffs and other restrictions, and favour a free labour market within the member states. In 1967 the ECSC was merged with the ►EEC and ►Euratom under the administration of a single commission, the 'High Authority' of the ►European Community. When Britain, Denmark and Ireland joined 'the Common Market' on 1 January 1973 they automatically became members of the ECSC. Steel production within the

ECSC steadily increased, 1952–70. The coal industry expanded 1952–4 but contracted rapidly after 1957 with the growth of oil as an energy source. From 1972 to 1976 the oil crisis emphasized the need for an energy policy established by the Community as a whole and assessing the contribution of nuclear and hydroelectric resources as well as of coal. The ECSC accordingly lost some of its independence as a planning force, necessarily accepting greater integration in the Community for which it had been the prototype institution.

European Community. Came into being in July 1967 through a merger of the executive bodies of the three existing Communities, ►ECSC, ►EEC and ►Euratom. The framework of the Community rested on five constituents: a Commission, appointed by member countries; a Council of Ministers; the European Parliament, set up in 1952 as part of the ECSC and expanded by the ►Treaties of Rome to cover EEC and Euratom affairs; the European Court of Justice (also originally an ECSC body); and the European Investment Bank, which was established in 1958 to aid investment in underdeveloped areas of the EEC and to finance projects serving the Community as a whole. A 'European Council' of heads of government was created in December 1974 to meet at least three times each year. Since December 1969 the Community has been committed to a programme of establishing closer economic and political links between member states by a gradual process of integration. In July 1976 it was accepted that the European parliament would change character in the course of 1978 or 1979, 410 elected members replacing the 198 members nominated by the nine national parliaments of the Community. Plans were also discussed in 1976–7 for monetary union and a report on the whole concept of European Union was submitted to the European Council by the Belgian Prime Minister, Leo Tindemans, in December 1975: membership of the European Community must necessarily be identical with membership of the EEC, the 'Common Market'. In January 1986 the foreign ministers of the twelve states concluded the Single European Act, which modified the Treaty of Rome, seeking to speed up decision-making and increase the powers of the European Parliament, while favouring European political cooperation. At the same time efforts were made to achieve the objective agreed at a summit meeting at Milan in June 1985: the completion of a free and unified market, with the removal of technical, physical and fiscal barriers, by December 1992. Mrs ►Thatcher remained critical of many measures more closely associating Britain with the EC, in particular the growth of the European Monetary System. At the Strasbourg summit meeting in December 1989 all European leaders except Mrs Thatcher approved the Community's 'Charter of the Fundamental Social Rights of Workers'. In October 1990 Britain agreed to participate in the European Exchange-Rate Mechanism. The Treaty of ►Maastricht of December 1991 provided for closer integration of the EC and its titular transformation to a ►European Union on 1 November 1993.

European Defence Community (EDC). An abortive project to create a supranational European army, with common institutions. The proposal was made by the French Prime Minister, René Pleven, in October 1950, after a number of European statesmen – including Churchill – had spoken in favour of a continental army earlier in the summer. Pleven proposed that, within the army, there would be no specifically national unit larger than a battalion. He believed this method might reconcile the French people to German rearmament. A Treaty to establish the European Defence Community was signed in Paris on 27 May 1952 by France, West Germany, Italy, Belgium, the Netherlands and Luxembourg, the six countries about to enter the ►European Coal and Steel Community. The British declared their support for the EDC, although declining to join because of their overseas commitments. In fact, however, the member countries of the EDC (especially France and Italy) showed reluctance to establish the international army. On 30 August 1954 the French National Assembly refused to ratify the 1952 Treaty, thereby destroying the EDC before it was ever brought into being. Under strong American and British diplomatic pressure the French, however, accepted the alternative plan of expanding the ►Brussels Treaty relationship into a Western European Union so as to include Germany and Italy (October 1954). Subsequently the French overcame their fears of West Germany sufficiently to admit the German Federal Republic as a member of ►NATO in May 1955.

European Economic Community (EEC). The 'Common Market'. Best-known of the European communities. A meeting of Foreign Ministers of the ►ECSC was held at Messina in June 1955 at which the Belgian statesman Paul-Henri ►Spaak was asked to examine the possibilities of expanding the existing community into an economic association based upon free trade, joint social and financial policies, the abolition of restrictive trading practices and free movement of capital and labour. Spaak's proposals formed the basis of the EEC, formally constituted when Belgium, France, West Germany, Italy, Luxembourg and the Netherlands signed the ►Treaties of Rome on 25 March 1957, bringing the Common Market into being on 1 January 1958. The signatories accepted Spaak's recommendation that, though other peoples of Europe might apply to join the Community, any member state could block new entries. Spaak, a social democrat, believed this right of veto would enable the socialists to keep out ideologically unwelcome applicants such as Franco's Spain and Salazar's Portugal. The veto was, however, primarily used by the French, under the leadership of President ►de Gaulle to block attempts by the British to join the Common Market: an application by the government of Harold ►Macmillan made on 10 August 1961 was vetoed by the French in January 1963 after over a year of negotiations, conducted by Edward ►Heath, and an application by the Labour Government of Harold Wilson in May 1967 suffered a similar fate seven months later. The other five members of the Common Market especially resented de Gaulle's attitude since France was also preventing the further growth of the European institutions and declined to cooperate with her partners in the EEC in 1965. With the resignation of de Gaulle in April 1969, tension within the EEC eased, and in June 1970 the Six invited four applicants (Britain, the Irish Republic, Denmark and Norway) to resume negotiations for membership. The four applicants signed the treaty of accession in Brussels on 22 January 1972, but in September the Norwegians withdrew their application after a referendum had shown a majority of Norwegian voters opposed to membership. Britain, the Irish Republic and Denmark became members of the EEC (and the ►European Community) on 1 January 1973. Criticism from the left wing of the Labour Party led Harold Wilson to propose a referendum on British membership of the Common Market once Labour had returned to power in 1974. The referendum (the first in British history) was held on 5 June 1975: 67.2 per cent of votes favoured membership; 32.8 per cent were opposed. The only areas to show a majority against membership were the Shetlands and the Western Isles of Scotland. Subsequently the Common Market reached agreement with ►EFTA on many trading issues and expanded earlier arrangements with the African states through the ►Lomé Agreement of 1975. Greece entered the EEC in January 1981; Spain and Portugal were admitted in 1985, the year in which Greenland, an autonomous part of a member state (►Denmark), seceded. Meetings at Milan and Luxembourg in 1985 examined ways of creating a genuine common market with no internal barriers by 1992. But progress towards this objective – and towards the Single European Act, agreed in January 1986 (►European Community) – was slow: Britain and Denmark, and the Irish and German Opposition parties, remained critical of the proposed reforms.

European Free Trade Association (EFTA). Established by a convention of seven European states concluded at Stockholm on 20 November 1959 and becoming effective in May 1960. The original seven members were Austria, Denmark, Great Britain, Norway, Portugal, Sweden and Switzerland. All seven members wished to promote economic expansion and trade in the 'area of the Association' but were opposed, for various reasons, to the political implications of the ►European Economic Community, established two years earlier. All non-agricultural tariffs between member states were officially abolished by a process of gradual reduction over a seven-year period, although the British broke the convention in 1966 by imposing import surcharges on certain goods. EFTA suffered in competition with the more highly industrialized rival organization, the EEC ('Common Market'), but the original seven members were joined by Iceland in 1970, having already accepted Finland as an associate member in 1961. Denmark and Great Britain left EFTA on 31 December 1972 to join the EEC, and the remaining members then negotiated a new agreement with the EEC which provided for free trade in industrial products between the members of the two organizations. In April 1984 a joint EFTA–EEC ministerial meeting in Luxembourg celebrated a further reduction in tariff barriers. In 1994 Sweden, Austria and Finland (a full member from 1986) joined the ►European Union. Iceland, Norway, Switzerland and Liechtenstein remained active in EFTA, making separate free trade agreements or provisions for economic cooperation with Israel, the Baltic republics, Slovenia, Albania, Egypt, Morocco and Tunisia.

European Monetary Union. ➤Economic and Monetary Union.

European Union. The Treaty of ➤Maastricht of 1991 provided for the transformation of the ➤European Community into a more integrated European Union, which was established on 1 November 1993. The principal change was the recognition of a common European citizenship and extension of the powers of the European parliament over the joint budget and over decisions of the European Commission and the Council of Ministers (the heads of government, or their nominees, who meet twice a year to shape policy direction). Initially the EU was particularly concerned with the ➤economic and monetary union. The accession of Austria, Finland and Sweden to the EU in January 1995 increased membership to fifteen. A further ten states were, in June 1997, awaiting decisions over applications for membership, the Council of Ministers having turned down Turkey, Cyprus, Malta and Morocco. In ➤Norway a national referendum, held in November 1994, again rejected membership. The Amsterdam Treaty of June 1998 agreed on inter-governmental cooperation over employment, proposed an anti-discriminatory charter of human rights, reaffirmed the Maastricht social chapter on workers' rights, gave the EU a collective identity so as to negotiate as a single entity, and accepted the abolition of border controls (though exempting Ireland, Britain and Denmark from this obligation).

European Parliament. ➤European Community.

Euzkadi. ➤Basques.

Evatt, Herbert Vere (1894–1965), Australian statesman. Born in East Maitland, New South Wales, educated and taught at Sydney University and became well known in the late 1920s as a lawyer who defended the civil liberties of strikers in trade-union cases. From 1931 to 1940 he served as a justice of the High Court in Australia but was returned to the federal parliament in the 1940 election, becoming in October 1941 Attorney-General and Minister of External Affairs in the Labour Government of ➤Curtin. He represented Australia at conferences in London in 1942–3 and played a leading role in asserting the influence of governments from the smaller nations at the ➤San Francisco Conference of 1945. In San Francisco he showed himself a vigorous opponent of the veto accorded to the permanent members of the UN Security Council; and he personally modified the character of the UN Charter more than any other single delegate, successfully carrying through twenty-six amendments designed to strengthen the General Assembly and the Economic and Social Council. Dr Evatt remained Minister of External Affairs under ➤Chifley until December 1949. He successfully opposed in the courts the attempt to proscribe the ➤Australian Communist Party, 1950–51. From 1951 to 1960 he led the Australian Labour Party in opposition to the government of

➤Menzies but he had to spend excessive political time and energy in combating a militantly anti-Communist and strongly Roman Catholic splinter group in the state of Victoria. Dr Evatt retired from politics in 1960, serving as chief justice of New South Wales, 1960–62.

Évian Agreements (March 1962). Talks to end the ➤Algerian War were held at Évian, on the French shore of lake Geneva, during the third week of March 1962. The principal spokesman for the French was Georges ➤Pompidou, who was then Prime Minister under President de Gaulle, and for the Algerians ➤Ben Bella, released from internment to take part in the discussions. It was agreed that there would be an immediate ceasefire in Algeria which would be granted independence, all French forces being withdrawn by the end of 1962. These Évian Agreements were submitted to referenda in France and Algeria (8 April and 1 July 1962) and received overwhelming popular backing, despite terrorist outrages organized by the secret organization of army officers and settlers (➤OAS) under General ➤Salan.

F

Fabian Society. Originally a group of predominantly middle-class intellectuals who, in January 1884, established the society to spread socialist ideas among the educated public and to work out the application of socialist principles to the British system. The name was derived from Quintus Fabius Maximus, general of Rome in the second Punic War, who sought to avoid pitched battles with the Carthaginians, preferring to weaken them by harassing operations. The Fabian Society accordingly rejected revolutionary tactics, believing socialism must eventually triumph as a sequel to universal suffrage although only as the climax to a long period of political evolution. Among prominent twentieth-century Fabians were Bernard Shaw (1856–1950), Beatrice Webb (1858–1943) and Sidney Webb (1859–1947). The Fabian Society was one of the constituent elements which set up the Labour Representation Committee (later the ►Labour Party) in 1900. Subsequently the society has tended to act as a specialized research agency for the Labour Party, although consistently advocating what Sidney Webb called the 'inevitability of gradualness' (in a Labour Party conference speech, 26 June 1923).

Falange. The official Spanish fascist party, founded in 1933 by José Antonio Primo de Rivera (1903–36), the son of the former Spanish dictator, General ►Primo de Rivera. José Antonio sought to emphasize the Spanish national tradition rather than the narrowly fascist ideology, but was seized by the republicans at the start of the civil war and executed in Alicante on 20 November 1936. From 1937 onwards the residual Falange movement was expanded by ►Franco and his political advisers, becoming the 'Traditionalist Spanish Falange', the only party permitted in Franco's Spain. From June 1939 until July 1942 the Grand Council of the Falange served as the principal legislative body in Spain, responsible for the transition to a corporate state headed by the Leader (*el Caudillo*), General Franco. In later years Franco sought to free himself from dependence on the Falange, whose influence declined rapidly and considerably.

Falkland Islands. A British colony in the South Atlantic, comprising East and West Falkland and many smaller islands. East Falkland is some 300 miles east of the Strait of Magellan and the dependency of South Georgia lies a further 800 miles south-east of the Falklands themselves. The islands – the Malvinas, in Spanish – were disputed between Spain and Britain in the late eighteenth century and have been a source of chronic tension between Argentina and Britain since they were occupied by a British naval squadron in 1832–3 at a time when the Argentine provinces were too racked by political anarchy to assert the sovereignty which they claimed as residual legatees of the Spanish American colonial empire. Argentina took the Malvinas dispute to the United Nations in 1946 and over the following thirty years there were several anti-British demonstrations in Buenos Aires and occasional incidents around the islands and their waters. In 1977 the Callaghan Government (Labour) stationed warships in the South Atlantic while holding talks with the Argentinian Government to seek a reduction in tension. The Thatcher Government (Conservative) sent a Foreign Office Minister to the Falklands and to Argentina in 1980 but found that proposals for a negotiated settlement were heavily criticized by Conservative, Labour and Liberal MPs in a debate at Westminster on 2 December 1980. Mounting Argentinian impatience coincided with a reduction in British naval strength in the South Atlantic. When, on 19 March 1982, an Argentinian warship landed a party of 'scrap dealers' on South Georgia, the British had only a detachment of marines on East Falkland and an ice patrol vessel, armed with two 20mm guns, to protect all the Falkland dependencies. Domestic unrest in ►Argentina induced the ruling junta to seek a prestigious victory by sending an invasion force which seized the Falkland Islands on 2 April 1982, precipitating the ten-week ►Falklands Crisis. London responded angrily to this 'naked aggression' against a British community of rather less than two thousand people. After the islands were liberated, a powerful military presence was retained. The right of the islanders to self-determination was affirmed by a constitution (October 1985). In June 1984 a Falkland Islands Development Corporation was set up; in 1993 underwater oil exploration began in 200 miles of sea around the islands. By 1995 an Anglo-Argentinian agreement anticipated joint development of offshore oilfields.

Falkland Islands, Battle of the (8 December 1914). Naval engagement in which the British South American squadron (Admiral Sturdee), consisting of two battle-cruisers, five cruisers and an armed merchant cruiser, destroyed six of the seven vessels in Vice-Admiral von Spee's German Pacific squadron, which had inflicted a defeat on the Royal Navy off Coronel (in Chile) five weeks previously. Admiral Sturdee's victory virtually ended German surface cruiser actions in the outer oceans, enabling the Royal Navy to concentrate in home waters and the Mediterranean for the remainder of the First World War.

Falklands Crisis (1982). The name given to the ten weeks of undeclared war in the South Atlantic between Argentina and Great Britain which followed the Argentinian military occupation of the ►Falkland Islands and their dependencies on 2 April 1982. Attempts at a peaceful settlement through negotiation were made by the US Secretary of State, Alexander ►Haig, by the Secretary-General of the United Nations, and by Peru. They broke down on the unwillingness of the Argentine Junta, under the Presidency of General Galtieri, to withdraw their troops so long as the Thatcher Government in London insisted on maintaining British sovereignty over the Falklands. In a remarkable triumph of logistical improvisation the British assembled a task-force of some thirty warships, with supporting aircraft and auxiliary vessels, and 6,000 fighting troops were conveyed 8,000 miles to recover the islands by force of arms. The dependency of South Georgia was recaptured with little difficulty on 25 April. Air raids on East Falkland and a naval bombardment began on 1 May and were followed by a commando raid on West Falkland on 14 May. A week later troops were landed at San Carlos, in Falkland Sound, to begin a pincer movement on the town of Stanley. A final attack was launched on Port Stanley on 13 June, the Argentinian forces surrendering on the following evening.

Nearly a thousand British and Argentinian servicemen and civilians were killed during the conflict: 368 Argentinian seamen died when the cruiser *General Belgrano* was torpedoed by a British submarine on 2 May; and the British lost more than fifty soldiers and seamen in air attacks on landing ships south of Bluff Cove on 8 June. The conflict emphasized the vulnerability of warships to air attack: the Royal Navy lost two destroyers and two frigates while an Exocet missile sank the chartered Cunard container ship *Atlantic Conveyor* off San Carlos on 25 May. The immediate political consequence of the British victory was the fall of President Galtieri in Argentina.

Famine. During the twentieth century the age-old scourge of famine has spread through communities in which a natural disaster has been compounded by war or political upheaval. Thus China suffered gravely in the closing months of 1920 from the effects of floods, bad harvests and the depredations of war-lords; and there was famine in many regions in 1959–61 when severe droughts and floods coincided with Mao's ➤'Great Leap Forward'. Similarly, Soviet Russia experienced its greatest famine in 1920–21 (➤Nansen) when Lenin was experimenting with war communism, thus forcing him to improvise his ➤New Economic Policy; and the food shortages caused by Stalin's collectivization of agriculture reached grave proportions both in 1928–9 and 1932, when harvests were ruined by the weather. In British India the threat of Japanese invasion and confusion over the responsibilities of the Imperial administration and of the locally elected government in Bengal aggravated the famine of 1943, in which more than three million people died. Alarm at the probability of widespread devastation and food scarcity in the aftermath of war led, in October 1942, to the formation of the Oxford Committee for Famine Relief (Oxfam, from c.1958 onwards) which, with many other charities, sought to convey food supplies and clothing to post-war Europe and eventually to Palestine, Korea, etc., supplementing the work of the UN special agencies. The need for famine relief became world-wide, partly because of the rising birth-rate in the so-called Third World.

By October 1983 a combination of drought, civil wars, short-sighted agricultural policies and neglected roads and railways had left twenty-two of the fifty African nations with critical food shortages, requiring international aid. A year later it was clear that much of north-east Africa, especially Ethiopia, the Sudan, Chad, Somalia and northern Kenya, was faced with the failure of all rain-dependent crops and pastures after an extensive drought. The great African famine forced millions to set out on what often became a fatal migration. Help from governments in other continents, with improvised air services, relieved the disaster's impact by early 1985. Television reports of the famine so moved the Irish singer-songwriter Bob Geldof (1951–) that he composed *Do They Know It's Christmas?*, a song which was recorded by many pop stars together and raised £8 million for African famine relief. A 'Live Aid' concert, organized by Geldof on 13 July 1985 with simultaneous shows beamed by satellite both ways across the Atlantic, raised more than £48 million for further famine relief. In 1988 a new emergency caused by flooding of the upper Nile was made worse by the passage eastwards across northern Africa of a plague of locusts; the civil war in the ➤Sudan heightened the suffering. A further drought in the winter of 1990–91 led to another grave famine throughout north-east Africa.

Farouk (1920–65, reigned 1936–52). King of Egypt. Son of King ➤Fuad, born in Cairo, educated in England, attained his majority in 1938, and duly ousted the ➤Wafd government of Nahas Pasha (who had headed the Regency Council for two years). Farouk tried to launch schemes of land reform and economic advancement but corruption was rife and his earlier popularity rapidly dwindled. He remained uncooperative when Italian troops crossed the Egyptian–Libyan frontier and in February 1941 the British authorities demanded, and secured, the dismissal of Farouk's Italophile Prime Minister in favour of Nahas Pasha and the Wafd. Farouk's resentment at this humiliation, together with Egyptian feeling that the Wafd was by now an old and discredited movement, led the King to appoint a succession of anti-British ministries from October 1944 until 1952. The failure of the army in Palestine in 1948 focused criticism on the corruption and profligacy of the King. Army officers sought a more consistently active policy than Farouk and his nominees were prepared to give to Egypt. On 23 July 1952 General ➤Neguib marched on Cairo and, in a few days of bloodless revolution, secured Farouk's abdication and flight to Italy.

Fascism. The principal political manifestation of romantic authoritarian revolutionary zeal. It was a response of the middle classes to fear and frustration, 1919–36. The name originated in Milan with the foundation on 23 March 1919 of the Fascio di Combattimento, an anti-socialist militia which took symbol and name from the bundle of rods borne before a Roman magistrate. Although the character of Italian fascism owed much to ➤D'Annunzio the final form was established by ➤Mussolini in the period 1922–32. Mussolini's fascism emphasized the need for pride in the nation, radical destruction of the old order, hostility towards Marxism, contempt for the 'putrefying corpse' of parliamentary democracy, admiration of military virtues, and obedience to a leader. Italian fascism was not fundamentally racialist, although in July 1938 Mussolini issued anti-Semitic decrees (the *Manifesto della Razza*) in imitation of his German ally. In 1932 Mussolini declared that fascism was an Italian creed, 'not for export'. Aspects of fascism had, however, already been usurped by the more intensely racialist ►Nazi Party. Subsequently movements closely akin to Italian fascism developed in Spain (►Falange), in ►Austria, in Croatia (►Ustaše), and from 1936 to 1945 in ►Portugal. In ►Romania the Iron Guard movement of Codreanu (1899–1938) was founded in 1923 in close imitation of Mussolini's fascism, emphasis being placed on the Latin traditions linking Romania and Italy; but significantly the Romanian dictator, ►Antonescu, stamped out the Iron Guard in 1941 rather than be bound by its ideology. France's pre-fascist ►Action Française was influenced by fascism but despised its right-wing radicalism. The principal French fascist movement was an ex-servicemen's organization, the Croix de Feu, established in 1927, attaining some influence between 1932 and 1936 under Colonel de la Rocque and providing many later supporters of ►Vichy. The most notorious of the Vichy 'fascists', Jacques Doriot (1898–1945), followed Hitler's example rather than Mussolini's while the 'national revolution' preached by ►Pétain found inspiration in supposedly French traditions outside the twentieth century. The British Union of Fascists under ►Mosley noisily shadow-acted continental politics in 1936 but remained ineffectual. Between 1930 and 1945 in South America, especially ►Argentina and ►Brazil, a fashionably fascist jargon was appropriated by the militaristic regimes endemic to the region: ►Franco rather than Mussolini was their model. 'Pure' fascism did not survive Mussolini. Since 1945 the word 'fascist' has been used principally as a pejorative. Neo-fascist movements, such as the Movimento Sociale Italiano (founded 1956), have asserted their fundamentally democratic image in efforts to prevent repression under laws designed to protect the constitution. No neo-fascist party has found a leader with the stature or demagogic style of a *Duce*. Fascism, like Bonapartism before it, was a phenomenon shaped by, and limited to, a particular age.

Fatima. Small town in central Portugal, eighty miles north-east of Lisbon. On 13 May 1917 three shepherd girls, aged between ten and thirteen, saw a vision of a lady outside the town. The vision reappeared at monthly intervals until 13 October 1917 when the apparition declared herself to be 'Our Lady of the Rosary', expressing a wish for a chapel to be built at Fatima where people of all nations could practise penance for their great sin. Since the visions coincided with the arrival on the Western Front of a Portuguese Expeditionary Force (against the wishes of Portuguese clericalists) it was assumed that the great sin was the war itself. A basilica was duly erected at Fatima and the shrine became a centre of intense religious observance. Two of the shepherd girls died in 1919, the third (Lucia Santos) became a Carmelite nun at Coimbra. The Fatima Madonna is the most publicized instance of visionary mysticism in a predominantly sceptical century. Doubters within the Church were rebuffed – although far from silenced – by the decision of Pope ►Paul VI to make a personal pilgrimage to Fatima in 1967. ►John Paul II, too, visited Fatima in May 1982.

Fawcett, Mrs Henry (1847–1929, born Millicent Garrett), leader of campaigns for women's higher education and for women's suffrage. Born at Aldeburgh,

Suffolk, the younger sister of Mrs Elizabeth Garrett Anderson (1836–1917), a pioneer of women's rights within the medical profession. Mrs Fawcett, herself privately educated, was active in founding Newnham College, Cambridge (1871) and championed the Married Women's Property Act of 1882, but her greatest interest was in extending the electoral franchise to women, a cause with which she identified herself as early as 1867. From 1897 until 1918 she was President of the National Union of Women's Suffrage Societies, urging successive governments to give women the vote but deploring the militant tactics of the suffragettes under Mrs ➤Pankhurst's leadership. Mrs Fawcett's husband (1833–84), though blinded in an accident when a young man, was a distinguished Cambridge economist and Liberal MP; after their marriage in 1867 she habitually used his full name rather than seeking to preserve her own names of birth. In 1925 she was created a Dame of the British Empire.

Feisal I (1885–1933, reigned 1921–33), King of Iraq. Born in Ta'if, third son of Emir Hussein (King of the Hijaz, 1916–24) and brother of ➤Abdullah of Jordan. Feisal lived in Constantinople for much of his childhood. He joined his father in leading the Arab Revolt in June 1916, becoming the principal Arab military commander and entering Damascus with ➤Lawrence on 3 October 1918. After pleading the Arab cause at the Paris Peace Conference in 1919, Feisal proclaimed himself King of Syria and Palestine on 10 March 1920. Within fifteen weeks he was deposed by the French but the British created a new throne for him in Mesopotamia (Iraq). His nomination as King was approved by a referendum in Iraq and he was enthroned in Baghdad on 23 August 1921, preserving until his death twelve years later a sympathetic attitude towards the British which few of his subjects shared.

Feisal II (1935–58, reigned 1939–58), King of Iraq. Grandson of Feisal I and son of King Ghazi (reigned 1933–9), who was killed in a car accident. Until 1953 the royal powers were exercised by Feisal's uncle, Emir Abdul Ilah, as Regent, while the young King was educated at Harrow where he was a close friend of his cousin and coeval, Hussein of Jordan. In February 1958 the royal cousins sought to federate Iraq and Jordan to counterbalance the United Arab Republic of Egypt and Syria, a move warmly supported by the veteran Iraqi statesman ➤Nuri-es-Said. This initiative was violently denounced by Cairo radio, which encouraged a group of army officers, under Brigadier ➤Kassem, to plot a Nasserite revolution in Baghdad. On 14 July 1958 Feisal was murdered in his palace, with other members of the royal family, their mutilated bodies being dragged through the streets. A republic was proclaimed.

Felvidék. The name given by the Hungarian authorities to the areas in southern Slovakia and Ruthenia retroceded from Czechoslovakia to Hungary in November 1938 by the first of the ➤Vienna Awards. The region, which included the towns of Kosiče (Kassa) and Uzhgorod (Ungvar), had been in the Kingdom of Hungary until the Treaty of ►Trianon of 1920. The Felvidék comprised an area of some 5,000 square miles and three-quarters of its population were of Hungarian nationality or Magyar-speaking. In March 1939 Hungary incorporated the remaining districts of Ruthenia in the Felvidék. The Soviet Red Army entered the region in the winter of 1944–5, restoring the pre-1938 frontiers in an armistice concluded with the provisional Hungarian republican government on 21 January 1945. At the end of June 1945 the Ruthene areas were ceded by Czechoslovakia to the Soviet Union and added to the Ukrainian Soviet Socialist Republic under the name of Transcarpathia.

Feminism. ►Women, Emancipation of.

Ferdinand (1861–1948, reigned 1887–1918), King of Bulgaria. Born in Vienna, youngest son of Prince Augustus of Saxe-Coburg (a first cousin of Queen Victoria and the Prince Consort) and Princess Clementine (daughter of ex-King Louis Philippe of France). Ferdinand served in the Austrian Army but his monarchical connections made him a natural candidate for the crown of the principality of Bulgaria, which he accepted in August 1887. His sly political behaviour and diplomatic astuteness won him the nickname of the 'fox of the Balkans'. He secured Bulgaria's total independence from Turkey in October 1908, taking the title of King, a dignity confirmed by his parliament in July 1911, although in Bulgarian usage he was frequently accorded the title of 'Tsar'. Ferdinand's miscalculation during the ►Balkan Wars lost him ►Macedonia, which Bulgaria coveted, and the ►Dobrudja. In October 1915 he allied his country with Germany, Austria–Hungary and Turkey and gained some military successes on the Salonika Front, but when his troops became demoralized and mutinied in September 1918, he abdicated (4 October) in favour of his son, ►Boris.

Fifth Column. Sympathizers within an enemy camp, prepared to wait their time to commit an act of treason. The phrase seems first to have been used by the Spanish nationalist general, Emilio Molo (1887–1937), when at a Press conference shortly before his death he was asked which of his four army columns he expected to capture Madrid. Since he thought the city would fall to disruptive elements already within its defences he replied, '*La quinta columna*'. During the Second World War forces ready to collaborate with the Germans in Norway (►Quisling), Belgium, France and Yugoslavia were referred to as the 'Fifth Column', although generally known later as 'collaborationists'.

Fifth Republic (French). The system of government established in France in 1958, first manifested by the Presidencies of ►de Gaulle, ►Pompidou and ►Giscard d'Estaing. The constitution of the Fifth Republic, promulgated on 6 October 1958, reflected the views of its founding-father, General de Gaulle. Accordingly it differed from the Fourth Republic in creating a strong Presidency, with the power of governing through emergency decree and the right of nominating the Prime Minister and dissolving parliament. Reference to the people was to be through plebiscites and referenda. At the same time the constitution envisaged a

'French Community' of states, more formally linked through common institutions than its British equivalent, the Commonwealth. The strong Presidency has remained, with parliament less influential in France than at any time since the Second Empire (1852–70), but rapid decolonization made the Community institutions unpopular, and the Community came to depend on specific economic, financial or technical agreements between the former French colonies and Paris. The legacy of the ➤Algerian War dominated the politics of the Fifth Republic until the elimination of the army conspirators in the ➤OAS in the spring of 1963. The Fifth Republic consistently emphasized France's independence over economic policy, nuclear deterrence, and in membership of the ➤European Community. The good trading position and monetary advantages which made possible President de Gaulle's show of independence were less marked after a crisis over the value of the franc in October 1968. Significantly there were many more abstentions among the electorate during the referenda of Pompidou than under his predecessor. Socialist, radical and communist critics complained in 1973–5 that the Fifth Republic perpetuated a Gaullist system no longer competent to meet the internal stresses in French society. Nevertheless, in the Presidential elections of May 1981 the socialist, François ➤Mitterrand, triumphed over the right-wing candidate, Giscard. The socialists won a majority in the parliamentary elections of June 1981, lost it in March 1986 but recovered ground in June 1988 and led centre-left coalitions until March 1993. There was then a swing to the neo-Gaullist RPR (*Rassemblement pour la République*) whose candidate, Jacques Chirac (1932–), became the fifth President of the Fifth Republic in May 1995. Resentment at the RPR's austerity programme and mistrust of its support for a single currency led to victory for the Left in the parliamentary elections of June 1997; President Chirac had to accept a socialist-led government formed by Lionel Jospin (1940–) in which the ➤Communist Party held a balance of power.

Fiji, Melanesian archipelago, 1,100 miles north of New Zealand. Fiji became an independent member of the Commonwealth in October 1970, having been a British colony since 1874. Complaints that the government was dominated by Indian immigrant families rather than indigenous Fijians led in May 1987 to a military *coup*, organized by Colonel Sitiveni Rabuka. In October he declared the islands an independent republic. He maintained military rule in Fiji for a further three months, taking Fiji out of the Commonwealth. The 1990 Constitution established a bicameral parliament. Elections held in 1992 and 1994 confirmed Rabuka's hold on the government, as prime minister of a coalition. Fiji rejoined the Commonwealth in October 1997.

Finland. United with Sweden from the early Middle Ages until 1809, thereafter a Russian grand duchy until 1917. Until 1898 the Russians respected Finland's autonomy but there followed seven years of intensive Russification until, after the ➤Russian Revolution of 1905, the Finns were allowed to elect a Diet chosen by universal suffrage of both sexes. A further period of repression from 1910 to 1916 stimulated the growth of national sentiment and the Finns seized the opportunity of revolutionary chaos in Russia to proclaim their independence (6 December 1917). Throughout 1918 there was civil war between Bolsheviks and 'Whites', led by ►Mannerheim. Conservative groups, headed by Pehr Svinhufvud, favoured a German connection in 1917–18 but with the end of the European war this faction disintegrated, and in July 1919 Finland adopted a democratic and republican constitution. Foreign policy was marked by frontier disputes with Sweden (over the ►Åland Islands) and with Russia, where the Finnish border in Karelia was only eighteen miles from Leningrad. In 1930 and 1932 a fascist movement (Lapua) twice attempted *coups d'état* and secured the passage of anti-communist laws. Russian demands for bases and for revision of the frontier in the Karelian isthmus were rejected by the Finns in November 1939, and there followed a fiercely fought fifteen-week war (30 November 1939 to 12 March 1940). Although the Finnish defences in the 'Mannerheim Line' checked the Russian advance, the Finns lost more than one-fifth of their fighting force in three months. By a peace treaty in Moscow Finland surrendered some 16,000 square miles of territory to the Soviet Union. In the hope of recovering these lost lands the Finns again went to war after Hitler's attack on Russia on 22 June 1941. Although they were initially successful, the weight of Russian arms forced the Finns to sue for peace on 25 August 1944. The 1940 frontier was restored and the Finns also ceded the Petsamo region (giving the Soviet Union a common border with Norway) together with fleet facilities at Porkkala, returned by the Russians in 1955. Juho ►Paasikivi established good relations with the Soviet Union and accepted the principle of neutralism. The policy was continued by the predominantly social democratic governments since the war. Finland became associated with Norway, Sweden, Denmark and Iceland in the 'Nordic Union' in 1956 but this body was purely concerned with economic, cultural and legal cooperation and had no military or political significance. In June 1961 Finland became an associate, but not a full member, of the ►European Free Trade Association and on 1 January 1974 accepted free trade in industrial goods with the ►EEC. But these commitments did not modify Finland's neutral status and it was natural for the Finnish President, Dr ►Kekkonen, to be host for the thirty-five-nation summit conference to promote peaceful cooperation in Europe which met at Helsinki, July–August 1975 (►Helsinki Conference). The easing of Cold War tension, followed by the dissolution of the Soviet Union, led to a gradual change in Finland's external policy; Finland was a full member of EFTA from 1986 to 1994, entering the ►European Union in January 1995.

Fisher, Geoffrey (1887–1972). ►Canterbury, Archbishop of.

Fisher, Herbert Albert Laurens (1865–1940). Historian and Liberal Member of Parliament, President of the Board of Education, 1916–22. ►Education Acts.

Fisher, John Arbuthnot (1841–1920, created Baron Fisher of Kilverstone, 1909). British admiral; born in Ceylon, entered navy in 1854, seeing action in China,

1859. Although trained under sail Fisher was always alive to the importance of technical developments and became an early enthusiast for the torpedo. His drive, and capacity for self-publicity, won him rapid promotion. As commander-in-chief Mediterranean, 1899–1902, he revolutionized training and tactics. He served as First Sea Lord from 1903 to January 1910 and was thus responsible for preparing the navy to face the German threat in the North Sea. He also identified his fiery personality with the race to build ➤Dreadnoughts. Although widely recognized as the greatest British admiral since Nelson his bellicose personality made him many enemies and he had a serious dispute with Lord Charles Beresford, the commander-in-chief Channel Fleet, 1907–9. Fisher retired in 1910 but was brought back as First Sea Lord by Churchill in October 1914. The two men were, however, too similar in temperament for collaboration. Fisher resented Churchill's insistence on moving ships to the Mediterranean for the ➤Dardanelles and resigned in a huff in May 1915.

Fiume (Rijeka). Principal Hungarian commercial port in the late nineteenth century, the population being predominantly Croatian and partly Italian. Fiume was claimed by both Yugoslavia and Italy at the Paris Peace Conference of 1919. While the future of the port was under discussion, the Italian nationalist, ➤D'Annunzio, seized the city and harbour, defying the peacemakers until ejected in 1921. A plan to establish a Free City at Fiume was abandoned after Mussolini came to power, and in January 1924 the Yugoslavs recognized the incorporation of the greater part of Fiume in Italy, although Yugoslavia retained the adjoining small harbour of Sušak. Under Italian rule the trade and prosperity of Fiume declined, for Mussolini did not wish it to compete with ➤Trieste and Venice, but from 1927 onwards the Hungarians were accorded special commercial facilities in the port which their entrepreneurs had developed. The Yugoslavs renewed their claim in 1945 and the ➤Paris Peace Treaties of 1947 formally ceded the region to Yugoslavia. In 1991 Rijeka became the chief commercial port of ➤Croatia.

Five-Year Plans. Stalinist system for organizing the Soviet economy. The first Five-Year Plan (1928–32 inclusive) was a gigantic social revolution which developed heavy industry and organized a centralized agricultural economy based on the collective principle and imposing considerable suffering on the ➤kulaks. The second Five-Year Plan (1933–7) enabled more consumer goods to be produced. The third (1938–42) again imposed heavy burdens on the people, as it cut consumer production in order to concentrate on armaments and defence. Typical achievements of the plans were Magnitogorsk, a new steel-city in the Urals, and the hydroelectric plant at Dnepropetrovsk in the Ukraine.

Fleming, Alexander (1881–1955, knighted 1944), British bacteriologist. Born at Loudon, Ayrshire and educated at Kilmarnock, embarking in 1902 on a studentship and subsequent medical career at St Mary's Hospital, Paddington, eventually becoming Professor of Bacteriology at London University (1938). In 1928, largely by chance, he began to investigate the mould, penicillin, which he found to have unrivalled antibiotic powers. With the collaboration of the pathologists Florey and Chain he perfected a method of producing the drug by 1940, and two years later it was in large-scale production, being hailed as the greatest discovery in bacteriology since Ronald Ross's work on the malaria bacillus in 1897. Sir Alexander Fleming, Sir Howard Florey and Sir Ernest Chain shared the Nobel Prize for chemistry in 1945 in recognition of their work on the discovery of penicillin

Foch, Ferdinand (1851–1929, created Marshal of France, 1918). Born at Tarbes in the department of Hautes-Pyrénées, the son of a civil servant; fought in the Franco-Prussian War, 1870–71, became an artillery specialist on the General Staff, commandant of the École de Guerre 1907–11, French observer at the German army manoeuvres of 1913. In September 1914 he led the French Ninth Army at the ➤Marne, subsequently serving in Flanders and as commandant of the French Army group on the Somme in July 1916. After a spell of retirement he returned in May 1917 as chief of staff to the French commander-in-chief, General ➤Pétain. Foch showed more initiative than Pétain and so impressed the allied commanders that during the critical German offensive of April 1918 he was appointed supreme generalissimo of the allied armies on the Western Front. He mounted the counter-offensive along the Marne on 15 July 1918, following this attack with operations in August which led the Germans to seek an armistice in November. After playing a prominent part in the Paris Peace Conference, trying to induce ➤Clemenceau to impose tougher terms on Germany, he retired from public life. His victory in 1918 assured him great popularity and respect in all the allied nations: he is the only French commander to have been made an honorary field-marshal in the British army and commemorated by an equestrian statue in London.

Food and Agriculture Organization (FAO). A specialized agency of the United Nations. The FAO was established on 16 October 1945 to raise standards of nutrition throughout the world by exchange of information and technical assistance undertaken through intergovernmental collaboration and by administering a World Food Programme for underdeveloped countries. Although the ➤League of Nations had encouraged international collaboration on food problems during the inter-war period its resources were too limited to achieve much. The FAO from its inception worked with the ➤World Bank and, from 1948, with the ➤World Health Organization to provide investment and knowledge in agriculture, fisheries and forestry.

Ford, Gerald Rudolph (1913–), thirty-eighth President of the United States. Born in Omaha, Nebraska, educated at University of Michigan and Yale Law School, served in US Navy aboard aircraft-carriers in the Second World War, practised as a lawyer and sat in the House of Representatives as a Republican Congressman from Michigan, 1948–73, serving as House Minority leader, 1965–73. Although there had been a move among Republicans to nominate Ford as a Vice-Presidential candidate in 1960, he was little known outside Congress until President ►Nixon chose him in December 1973 as successor to Vice-President Spiro Agnew, who resigned office because of allegations concerning financial matters when he was Governor of Maryland. Ford was Vice-President during the mounting criticism of Nixon over ►Watergate, and when Nixon resigned the Presidency on 9 August 1974, Ford was immediately sworn in as his successor. He is thus the only man in America's history to have held non-elected office as President and Vice-President. For most of his two and a half years in the White House President Ford was overshadowed by the world prestige of his Secretary of State, ►Kissinger. He successfully gained the Republican nomination for the 1976 Presidential election but was defeated by the Democrat, Jimmy ►Carter.

Ford, Henry (1863–1947), US industrialist. Born and died in Dearborn, Michigan. For five years he served as a machine-shop apprentice in Detroit, building his first car there in 1892–3 but not organizing the Ford Motor Company for another ten years. In 1909 he perfected the assembly-line technique that enabled the company to mass-produce the first cheap and standardized car, thus revolutionizing the motor-car industry which was now able to expand rapidly. Ford was a social pioneer, introducing as early as 1914 an eight-hour day, with a minimum daily wage equivalent to £1 and a profit-sharing scheme for all his employees. In 1915 he sent a much-publicized 'Peace Ship' to Scandinavia, in an effort to secure neutral mediation in the First World War; but once the United States became a belligerent, he mass-produced motor vehicles for the army in France. He was president of the Ford Motor Company in 1903–19 and 1943–7.

Formosa. An island in the China Sea, with a population Chinese in origin. Formosa was part of the Chinese Manchu Empire from 1683 until 1895 when the island was annexed by Japan (Treaty of Shimonoseki). The Japanese established a provincial administration under a governor-general in March 1896 and controlled the island until 1945, modernizing the towns and the communications. In September 1945, Chinese troops loyal to ►Chiang Kai-shek occupied Formosa, which resumed its ancient Chinese name of ►Taiwan.

Fourteen Points. A peace programme outlined by President Woodrow Wilson in his address to the US Congress on 8 January 1918: (1) renunciation of secret diplomacy ('Open covenants openly arrived at'); (2) freedom of the seas; (3) removal, where possible, of economic barriers; (4) reduction in armaments; (5) impartial adjustment of colonial claims; (6) Germans and their allies to evacuate Russian territory; (7) restoration of Belgium; (8) liberation of occupied France, and return to France of Alsace-Lorraine; (9) Italian frontiers readjusted 'along clearly recognizable lines of nationality'; (10) nationalities in Austria–Hungary to have autonomous development; (11) occupation forces to evacuate Romania, Serbia and Montenegro, with Serbia receiving access to the sea; (12) self-development for non-Turkish peoples within Ottoman Empire, and free passage of Dardanelles; (13) creation of an independent Poland, with access to the sea; (14) formation of a general association of nations to guarantee the political independence of all states. It was on the basis of these 'Fourteen Points' that Germany and Austria–Hungary sought ►armistices in 1918, Wilson having made it clear that he wished the tenth point amended to 'complete independence for the people of Austria–Hungary'; and the allied Powers having expressed reservation over the meaning of the second point and having demanded the imposition on their enemies of ►reparations. Subsequently many Germans, Austrians and Hungarians maintained that the ►Paris Peace Conference violated the principle of self-determination implicit in the Fourteen Points, especially in forbidding a German–Austrian ►Anschluss and in seeking to fulfil secret promises to Italy (►Treaty of London) and ►Romania which ran counter to Wilson's principles.

Fourth Republic (French). The system of government operating in France between 24 December 1946 and 5 October 1958, when it was replaced by the ►Fifth Republic. In October 1945 the provisional government established in Paris on the city's liberation in 1944 organized a referendum throughout France in which the voters rejected the constitution of the ►Third Republic, an institution discredited by the collapse of 1940. Discussions over the nature of the new republic lasted for over a year. De Gaulle's desire for a strong Presidency was rejected, and so too was the first draft constitution, submitted to referendum in May 1946 and disliked because it established a single-chamber legislature. The second constitution, setting up a 'National Assembly' and a weak second chamber, 'the Council of the Republic', was submitted to the people and accepted by a small majority, although contemptuous indifference led nearly 8 of the 26 million voters to abstain. Ultimately the political character of the Fourth Republic differed little from the political character of the Third. The two Presidents, Vincent Auriol, 1947–53, and René Coty, 1953–8, were figureheads: there were twenty-three governments in slightly under twelve years, an average length of life almost identical with the inter-war period. Veteran parliamentarians of the Third Republic reappeared in its successor, perpetuating old habits and established procedure. The Radical Socialist, Henri Queille, for example, had sat in nineteen of the thirty-four cabinets between 1924 and 1938 before at last becoming Prime Minister in September 1948 and forming another Fourth Republic government in 1951. While the Fourth Republic achieved more success than its predecessor in European affairs, thanks largely to the achievement of Robert ►Schuman, it lost prestige heavily outside Europe, notably through defeat at ►Dien Bien Phu and the protracted ►Algerian War. The republic defied the anti-parliamentary forces of the ►Communist Party and ►Poujade, successfully building up the French economy from the disasters of war. In ►Mendès-France the republic found a courageous Radical Prime Minister of high calibre but the institutional structure created in 1946 never won popular approval. The combination in 1958 of army defiance in Algeria and political deadlock in Paris threatened France with civil war: the French people preferred the alternative of de Gaulle and a strong Presidential republic.

France. ➤Third Republic; Fourth Republic; Fifth Republic; Vichy; etc.

Franchet d'Esperey, Louis Félix (1856–1942), Marshal of France. Born at Mostaganem in Algeria to a devout Catholic family with royalist traditions, graduated from St Cyr, serving with the cavalry in Algeria, Tunis, Indo-China, Morocco and with the international force which policed Peking after the ➤Boxer Rising. After some years as a staff officer in Paris and an instructor at St Cyr he was appointed commanding general of the Fifth Army in 1914, distinguishing himself on the ➤Marne. In the spring of 1918, as commander of the Ninth Army Group, he failed to check Ludendorff's offensive on the Western Front and was sent by Clemenceau to be commander-in-chief of the allied armies in Macedonia, with headquarters at ➤Salonika. Franchet d'Esperey, who knew the Balkans and central Europe well, galvanized the Macedonian front into action, launching an offensive along the Dobropolje mountains on 15 September 1918 which knocked Bulgaria out of the war within a fortnight. The subsequent advance by the French and the Serbs was the farthest and speediest of the First World War, carrying the allied armies from the Balkans to the plain of Hungary. When the war ended Franchet d'Esperey was preparing to advance from Budapest on Dresden and Berlin. He received his Marshal's baton in 1921, serving for many years in North Africa, where he was seriously injured in a motor-car accident. In the 1930s he had political connections with the extreme Right in Paris, but he refused to assist the only other surviving Marshal of France in the 'national revolution' of ➤Vichy.

Francis Ferdinand (1863–1914), Archduke of Austria. Nephew of Emperor Francis Joseph and from 1889 to 1914 heir to the Austro-Hungarian throne. He was a man of strong character who distrusted the Hungarian influence within ➤Austria–Hungary and favoured political concessions to the Slav minorities, especially the Czechs. In 1900 he married a Czech countess, Sophie Chotek, who was considered too lowly in social status to be consort to a future emperor. Francis Joseph insisted that their marriage should be a morganatic union, and Francis Ferdinand's two sons accordingly had no right of succession to the throne. The insults and affronts to which his wife was exposed by the antiquated conventions of etiquette at the Habsburg Court aroused Francis Ferdinand's hostility to the existing order. Speculation on the extent to which Francis Ferdinand would have reformed the Dual Monarchy is, however, vain: on 28 June 1914 he was assassinated with his wife while on a ceremonial visit to ➤Sarajevo, an event that precipitated the First World War.

Francis Joseph (1830–1916, reigned 1848–1916), Emperor of Austria, King of Hungary. Succeeded to the Austrian throne on the abdication of his uncle Ferdinand in December 1848, crowned King of Hungary in 1867. His political ideas were formed in the autocratic reaction to the revolutions of 1848. He continued throughout his life to distrust all notions of party government, preferring bureaucratic administration under a benevolent dynasty to rigid adherence to constitutional rule. Towards the end of his life he described himself to President Theodore Roosevelt as 'the last monarch of the old school'. He was a conscientious head of state who sought to turn the Habsburg dynasty into an impersonal institution, thereby steeling himself to survive a series of personal tragedies: his brother, Maximilian, was proclaimed Emperor of Mexico but executed by Mexican republicans in 1867; his son Rudolf shot himself in an apparent suicide pact with his mistress, at Mayerling in 1889; his wife, the Empress Elizabeth, was stabbed to death by an anarchist at Geneva in 1898; and his nephew, Francis Ferdinand, was assassinated at Sarajevo in 1914. Francis Joseph reigned in full sovereignty for a longer period than any other European monarch; and on his death in November 1916 was succeeded by his great nephew, Archduke ►Charles.

Franco (y Bahamonde), Francisco (1892–1975), Spanish general and head of state. Born at El Ferrol in Galicia into a naval family, educated at Toledo Infantry Academy (1907–10), served mainly in Morocco from 1910 to 1927, distinguishing himself in operations against ►Abd-el-Krim. In 1927 he became a full general and principal of Saragossa Military Academy. He cautiously stayed outside politics until called to suppress a soviet established by the miners of the Asturias in October 1934, an episode which gained him an enduring reputation for brutality. The confused political situation in the winter of 1935–6 found him Chief of the General Staff. In this capacity he came to London as Spain's representative at the funeral of George V, 28 January 1936. Six months later (18 July) while serving as Governor of the Canary Islands, he led the anti-socialist revolt which began the ►Spanish Civil War. On 1 October 1936 a military junta in Salamanca proclaimed Franco generalissimo of 'Nationalist' Spain and head of state, his government receiving recognition from Hitler and Mussolini a month later. The British and the French recognized his government in February 1939, soon after his capture of Barcelona, and the United States only on 1 April 1939, four days after the surrender of Madrid. During the war years he modelled his corporate state largely on the Italian experience under a single political party, the ►Falange. He met Hitler at Hendaye on 23 October 1940 but declined to enter the war. Despite condemnation of his regime by the Western Powers in 1945–6, his authority was strengthened by a declaration in July 1947 that he should remain head of state (*Caudillo*) for life, pending restoration of a monarchy. His refusal to modernize the institutions or appreciably relax his dictatorship led to mounting opposition, from students, from the Catholic hierarchy and more dangerously from the ►Basques. At the same time, Franco received patronage from several US leaders, notably ►Dulles, who visited him in November 1955. On 22 July 1969 Franco nominated Prince ►Juan Carlos to succeed him, and the Prince assumed sovereign powers 'provisionally' on 30 October 1975, three weeks before Franco's death.

Fraser (John) Malcolm (1930–). Australian Prime Minister. Born in Melbourne and educated at Melbourne Grammar School and Magdalen College, Oxford. He was elected as a Liberal Member of the Federal Parliament for Wannon in 1955 and became Minister for the Army in the Liberal-Country Party coalition of Harold Holt in 1966. Subsequently he served as Minister for Education and Science, 1968–9 and 1971–2, and as Minister of Defence 1969–71. He became leader of his party in March 1975 and eight months later succeeded ▶Whitlam as caretaker Prime Minister pending a general election. Fraser led the Liberal-Country Party coalition to victory (13 December 1975) and increased his majority two years later. He supported a 'new federalism', giving greater initiative to state governments. The chairmanship of an Asia-Pacific area summit meeting at Sydney (February 1978) and a Commonwealth Conference at Melbourne (September 1981) raised his international stature. The general election of October 1980 enabled him to keep control of the House of Representatives but not of the Senate. He was succeeded by Bob Hawke in March 1983.

Fraser, Peter (1884–1950), New Zealand Prime Minister. Born in Ross-shire, Scotland; emigrated to Auckland in 1910 becoming a docker and organizing a successful strike a year later. During the First World War he was imprisoned for sedition, having opposed conscription. His earlier 'Red Federation' radicalism mellowed as he rose in the New Zealand ▶Labour Party until he became deputy leader in 1933, entering the cabinet in 1935 and succeeding Prime Minister ▶Savage, March 1940. As wartime leader he asserted the dominion's control over all New Zealand units but was respected by Churchill for his sentiments of imperial unity. He came to London in 1941, and achieved close collaboration with Roosevelt when he visited Washington a year later. In 1943 he took over responsibility for external affairs, working closely with the Australian External Affairs Minister ▶Evatt. Fraser attended the ▶San Francisco Conference, and chaired the committee which determined the form of United Nations trusteeship. He remained Prime Minister until 1949, organizing a gift of £10 million from New Zealand in 1945 to assist post-war reconstruction in Britain. In home affairs he encouraged state control of industry but was better remembered for his patronage of the arts, 1947–9, a cultural generosity which may have contributed to his narrow defeat in the election of December 1949.

Free French. The name given during the Second World War to the supporters of General ▶de Gaulle when he flew to London in June 1940 and called on his countrymen to reject the armistice and continue resistance. The 'Free French' represented both a rallying-point for French patriots and a political alternative to ▶'Vichy'. Recruitment was at first slow, partly because of British naval action at ▶Oran and ▶Mers-el-Kébir and the Vichy-controlled troops in Dakar refused to support 'Free France' when de Gaulle tried to establish a base there in September 1940. It was only when Vichy's conservatism rejected the principles of the 1789 Revolution that exiles, and administrations in French overseas colonies, began to accept de Gaulle as a champion of the alternative tradition, failing to see that his concept of democracy was Bonapartist rather than parliamentarian. De Gaulle's 'Comité National Français' (24 September 1941), which maintained contact with the French Resistance, was recognized unofficially in London as a 'pre-government'. During the invasion of North Africa (November 1942) the Americans viewed de Gaulle's movement – renamed the 'Fighting French' – with suspicion but by the summer of 1943 they had come to accept it as the authoritative voice of national liberation.

Frelimo. Abbreviated form of Frente de Libertação de Moçambique, the Marxist liberation movement in ➤Mozambique, which waged a guerrilla war against the Portuguese 1964–74, subsequently becoming the dominant political force in the People's Republic of Mozambique.

Freud, Sigmund (1856–1939), founder of psychoanalysis. Born of Jewish parentage in Moravia, studied at the University of Vienna and in Paris. By 1893 he was accepted as a leading Austrian neurologist and paediatrician. His first essays on psychoanalysis appeared in *Studien über Hysterie* (1895) but *The Interpretation of Dreams* (1900) established his fame. Further studies of psychopathology followed in 1901 and 1905. Between 1908 and 1911 Freud made Vienna a centre of psychoanalytical study although two of his foremost colleagues, Alfred Adler (1870–1937) and Carl Gustav Jung (1876–1961), broke away from Freud in, respectively, 1911 and 1913. Other disciples, however, upheld Freud with the intensity of religious believers. Quite apart from their therapeutic value, Freud's theories influenced art, literature and social thought, especially in the United States, Scandinavia, Weimar Germany and Britain, but they were received coldly in France and banned, as of 'decadent Jewish origin', by Hitler. When Austria was united with Germany in 1938 diplomatic intervention was necessary before Freud and his family were allowed to leave Vienna. He died in Hampstead, three weeks after the outbreak of the Second World War. Basically Freud sought to explain human behaviour by placing emphasis on pre-rational sexual appetites and impulses which are restrained by checks (taboos) imposed by the conventions of society. In exploring the unconscious he was formulating theories which could not readily be tested experimentally, and therefore his interpretation was received with much hostility, as Darwin's in another field had been half a century before. Freud's view that all religion is a sublimation of the sex instinct was condemned by church leaders, who preferred Jung's emphasis on the need for dogma and ritual as psychological securities making for integration in human life. Nevertheless Freud's concepts have been absorbed into the commonplace jargon of the twentieth century, misrepresented by many who look facilely for understanding of the irrational.

Friedman, Milton (1912–), American economist. Born in New York, studied at the universities of Chicago and Columbia, he served with the National Resources Committee 1935–41. He developed his theories of 'monetarism' while working for federal economic research departments during World War II and as a professor at Chicago from 1946 onwards. His belief in the freedom of market forces and of the need to check inflation by controlling the money supply made him a powerful critic of ►Keynes and of the economic assumptions implicit both in the New Deal and in Britain's welfare state. As a columnist in *Newsweek* from 1966 onwards Friedman acquired great influence among right-wing policy makers in Britain and the United States. He received the Nobel Prize for the Economic Sciences in 1976. Friedman joined Reagan's Economic Advisory Board in 1981.

Fuad I (1868–1936, reigned 1923–36), King of Egypt. Born Ahmed Fuad, younger son of Khedive Ismail (who had sold the Egyptian Suez Canal shares to Britain in 1875) and a brother of Tewfik (whose inability to govern Egypt had caused the British to occupy Egypt in 1883). Fuad became Sultan in 1917 and was proclaimed King in Cairo on 15 March 1923, the first anniversary of Britain's recognition of Egypt's independence. His reign was marked by conflict with the ►Wafd, uneasy relations with the British, expressions of admiration for Mussolini, and an uninhibited determination to acquire wealth for himself and his entourage. He was succeeded by ►Farouk, a son born when his father was already in his fifties.

G

Gaddafi (Qadhafi), Muammar Muhammed (1942–), Libyan President. Born at
Sirte and was a university student when, in 1963, he entered the Benghazi Military
Academy where, in emulation of ►Nasser, he formed a Free Officers Movement.
He attended a junior officers' course for signals specialists in England in 1966–7
but on his return to Tripoli concentrated on political issues and in September 1969
led the bloodless *coup* that forced King Idris into exile. He established a socialist
republic. Colonel Gaddafi evolved a curious form of direct democracy (►Libya)
which made him a virtual dictator. Libyan oil revenue enabled him to harbour
exiled Arab fanatics and, from 1980 onwards, the US and British governments
believed he was supporting terrorist hit squads operating in western European
cities and the Levant, often against American targets. On 15 April 1986 he survived
an American air-raid on Tripoli, part of a US campaign to topple his regime;
members of his family were among the civilian casualties. After 1979 Gaddafi
declined any formal post, content to be acknowledged as 'Leader of the Revolution'.
But as supreme military commander he kept tight hold on the armed forces.

Gagarin, Yuri Alexeyevich (1934–68), pioneer Soviet cosmonaut. Born at
Gzhatsk, near Smolensk, entered the air school in 1955 and was commissioned in
the Soviet Air Force in 1957. On 12 April 1961 he became the first man to travel
in space, completing an orbit of the earth in the satellite of the *Vostok* spaceship.
He was killed in an aircraft accident while supervising training in March 1968.

Gaitskell, Hugh Todd Naylor (1906–63), British Labour Party leader. Born in
London, educated at Winchester and New College, Oxford, becoming a socialist
while an undergraduate during the General Strike. Subsequently he became an
economist attached to London University. He was elected Labour MP for Leeds
South in 1945, his parliamentary skill leading him to be made Minister of Fuel and
Power two years later. In October 1950 he succeeded Cripps as Chancellor of the
Exchequer (the youngest since Austen Chamberlain in 1903). His introduction of
charges for the National Health Service antagonized the left of the party, especially
►Bevan and ►Wilson. Gaitskell was recognized as the outstanding representative
of a social democrat tradition within the Labour Party and, on Attlee's retirement
as leader in December 1955, he was elected his successor, convincingly defeating
Bevan and Herbert Morrison in the contest. Although united with Bevan in
denouncing Eden's policy in the ►Suez Crisis, Gaitskell remained in conflict with
other left-wingers over nationalization and unilateral nuclear disarmament and the
Labour Party failed to win the 1959 election. In 1961, however, Gaitskell gained

remarkable successes at the party conference, defeating moves by Wilson to oust him from the leadership and winning acceptance of his views on nuclear disarmament. Gaitskell's idealism re-fired Labour's sense of mission, helping to win the 1964 election, twenty-one months after his unexpected death.

Gallipoli. A peninsula forming the southernmost European shore of the ➤Dardanelles. When it proved impossible to force the Dardanelles by sea in March 1915, preparations were made to land an allied force (predominantly British and Australasian) on the peninsula so as to seize forts guarding the approaches to Constantinople. The initial landings were made on 25 April 1915, on five beaches around Cape Helles, by a French corps on the mainland of Asia Minor and by General Birdwood's Australians and New Zealanders, higher up the peninsula at Ari Burnu, subsequently known as ➤Anzac Cove. The Turks, under the command of the German general, Liman von Sanders, had anticipated the landings and offered strong resistance, whereas the British commander, General Sir Ian Hamilton, had expected a two-day advantage in which the Turks would be thrown into confusion. The Turkish 19th Division (under their commander later known as Kemal ➤Atatürk) fiercely contested the ridges around Anzac with the invaders. Further landings in early August came near to success but by the end of the summer the troops were pinned down to trench warfare. In seeking to gain 400 yards on a mile front 4,000 allied soldiers perished. ➤Kitchener visited the peninsula in November and recommended evacuation. Between 10 December 1915 and 9 January 1916 the troops were withdrawn, without loss. The expedition failed because of confused leadership, poor coordination, inadequate planning, and hostility from many British and French military chiefs at home who believed troops and firepower should be concentrated on the Western Front. The failure cost ➤Churchill, the expedition's principal champion in London, his predominant position on the War Council.

Gandhi, Mrs Indira (1917–84), Indian Prime Minister. Born in Allahabad, the daughter of ➤Nehru, educated at schools in Switzerland and England and at Somerville College, Oxford, married Feroze Gandhi in 1942 and was widowed in 1960. She joined the ➤Congress Party in 1939, spending over a year in prison for her political actions during the war. She was Minister for Broadcasting and Information from 1964 to 1966 in the government of ➤Shastri. On his death she stood for election to the leadership of Congress (19 January 1966), defeating her opponent Morarji Desai (1896–). Mrs Gandhi became Prime Minister five days later. She sought to combat mass poverty and encouraged birth control in order to check the rapid rise in population. In external affairs she found it impossible to collaborate with Pakistan, especially in the crisis over ➤Bangladesh during 1971. Her 'modern' views alienated older Hindu members of Congress, most of whom seceded in November 1969 to found a dissident Congress movement, led by Desai. Elections in March 1971 were a striking triumph for Mrs Gandhi. Subsequently the dissidents charged her with electoral corruption during the campaign. The

High Court at Allahabad declared her guilty on 12 June 1975, debarring her from public office for six years. A fortnight later, while an appeal was pending, 676 political opponents were arrested in pre-dawn raids under the Maintenance of Internal Security Act. In July most political organizations were banned and a measure giving Mrs Gandhi dictatorial powers was rushed through parliament, with communist support. Resentment at these unconstitutional measures threatened civil war throughout 1976. Political relaxation of tension was followed by an election in which Mrs Gandhi personally was defeated, while the Desai dissidents as a whole gained a landslide victory over the official Congress candidates. She resigned on 22 March 1977. Within eighteen months she was restoring her political fortune. A week's imprisonment in December 1978 for alleged breach of parliamentary privilege won her wide support in the country. She led the Congress Party to an electoral victory in 1980 but her third term of office was troubled by internal conflict, notably in Assam and the Punjab, where she was forced to use the army against Sikh extremists at ➤Amritsar. She was assassinated in Delhi by a Sikh member of her bodyguard on 31 October 1984. Her son, Rajiv Gandhi (1944–91), succeeded her as Prime Minister 1984–9, but was himself assassinated during an election campaign on 21 May 1991.

Gandhi, Mohandas Karamchand (1869–1948), Indian national leader. Born at Porbandar, a small princely state in western India on the Arabian Sea. He travelled to London in 1888 to study law, practised as a barrister in Bombay and then went to South Africa where from 1907 to 1914 he conducted passive resistance campaigns of protest at the Transvaal Government's discrimination against its Indian minority settlers. In 1915 he returned to India, and gradually emerged as leader of the ➤Congress movement. By boycotting British goods, Gandhi helped develop India's village industries, while, by preaching passive resistance, he curbed terrorist outrages, though he could not prevent them. He was imprisoned in 1922, 1930, 1933 and 1942, resorting to a hunger strike as part of his campaign of civil disobedience. In 1931 he came to London for an abortive round-table conference on the future of India. By 1942 he had reached a position where he believed that independence was the only possible solution for India's national grievances. He collaborated with the last viceroys (➤Wavell and ➤Mountbatten) in producing plans for the independence and partition of India, proclaimed 15 August 1947. Many of Gandhi's Hindu followers regarded him as a saint – the Mahatma, or 'great soul'. His asceticism and fasts of self-purification, his simple handspun loincloth and peasant's sandals marked him out as one of the masses. But some resented his acceptance of partition, rejecting his pacifist philosophy. He survived an attempt on his life on 20 January 1948, only to be shot dead by a young fanatical Hindu journalist in Delhi ten days later.

Gang of Four. Chinese radical opposition group denounced by Chairman ➤Hua in October 1976, and again in the eleventh congress of the Chinese Communist Party, August 1977.

GATT (General Agreement on Tariffs and Trade). A specialized agency of the ►United Nations seeking liberalization of tariffs and established in 1948 after a ►Geneva Conference from April to October 1947.

Gaza Strip. A disputed region of some 100 square miles on the Mediterranean coast around the town of Gaza, forming part of mandated ►Palestine but allocated to Egypt, along with Sinai, in 1948. The Egyptians administered Gaza from 1948 until October 1956, recruiting many anti-Israeli raiders from the Arab refugees around Gaza, which was only six miles from the Israeli frontier. The Israelis occupied the Gaza Strip during the ►Sinai Campaign of 1956, handing the territory over to a United Nations truce force on 7 March 1957, an Egyptian mayor accepting responsibility for civil administration. In May 1967 the United Nations force left, at the request of ►Nasser, who sent a joint force of Egyptians, Iraqis and Kuwaitans to the strip. The Israelis moved back in the Six-Day War of June 1967 and subsequently administered the Gaza Strip as an 'occupied territory'. The Palestinian ►Intifada began there in December 1987. A 'Declaration of Principles', agreed by Israel and the ►PLO after talks in Norway in 1993, included among its conditions a pledge of Israeli withdrawal in return for a Palestinian renunciation of terrorism. Israeli troops left Gaza in May 1994; the Palestinian National Authority, led by Yasser ►Arafat, thereupon made Gaza City the temporary administrative capital of an autonomous Palestinian state. Some 4,000 Jewish settlers living in the Gaza Strip remained under Israeli protection and jurisdiction.

General Strike (British), 4–12 May 1926. The General Strike was a climax to several years of industrial unrest, in which the miners' unions sought sympathetic support from workers in other major industries. The immediate cause of the strike was the report of a royal commission on the mining industry – the Samuel Report, March 1926 – which rejected nationalization, recommended more efficient organization, sanitary reforms, and a cut in wages. The mine-owners sought longer hours at the coal-face as well as lower wages. A special meeting of the Trades Union Congress (TUC) on 1 May agreed to call out transport workers, printers, builders, heavy industrial workers and, later, engineers to support the pledge of the miners' leader, A.J. Cook (1885–1931): 'Not a penny off the pay, not a minute on the day.' Baldwin's government recruited special constables, volunteers to run essential services, and used troops to maintain food supplies. The government's monopoly of information services, including for the first time broadcasting, prevented any general wave of panic. After nine days the TUC called off the strike, arguing that the government was better prepared for a General Strike than were the unions, and accepted a compromise, which the miners themselves rejected. The miners, resenting TUC 'betrayal', stayed out until August. In July 1927 Baldwin's government passed the Trade Disputes Act making general strikes illegal, a measure repealed by the Labour Government in 1946, the year in which the coal industry was at last nationalized.

Geneva Agreements (20 July 1954). Formally ended the French involvement in Indo-China (►Laos, ►Cambodia and ►Vietnam). The agreements were concluded at the end of a two-month-long conference, attended by the Foreign Ministers of Britain, France, America, Russia and communist China. A ceasefire line between North and South Vietnam was established along the 17°N parallel of latitude.

Geneva Conferences. The establishment of the ►League of Nations at Geneva in 1920 made the city a natural centre for international conferences. Between the wars there were important meetings on tariffs, trade and economic problems in May 1927, February 1930 and November 1930 as well as the ►Disarmament Conference. A further conference on tariffs and trade (April to October 1947) led to the conclusion of ►GATT, which provided the framework for the specialized agency on tariffs within the United Nations Organization. The best-known conferences since the Second World War have been: the conference on Korea and Indo-China (May–July 1954) which produced the ►'Geneva Agreements' but failed to stabilize the Korean situation; and the 'summit' conference of 18–23 July 1955, when President Eisenhower, the Soviet leaders Bulganin and Khrushchev, and the British and French Prime Ministers, Eden and Edgar Faure, sought a relaxation of 'Cold War' tensions, producing agreement on cultural exchanges and tacit recognition of each other's problems in the Far East. A conference on the detection of nuclear explosions was held in July 1958, followed by one on safeguards against surprise attack four months later. On 21 December 1973 a conference to seek a peace settlement in the Middle East opened at Geneva, under United Nations auspices: it was attended by representatives of Egypt, Israel, Jordan, USA and USSR, and when it was reconvened in May 1974 delegates from Syria were also present. An abortive conference on ►Rhodesia was held at Geneva, October–November 1976. Intermittent talks on the reduction of nuclear forces and strategic arms reduction were held at Geneva in 1983–8. So, too, was an abortive National Reconciliation Conference for the ►Lebanon in October 1983.

George V (1865–1936, reigned 1910–36), King-Emperor. Born Marlborough House, London, the second son of Edward VII and Queen Alexandra; served in the navy, 1877–92. The death of his brother, the Duke of Clarence, on 13 January 1892 made him second in succession to the throne. He was created Duke of York, marrying eighteen months later his dead brother's fiancée, Princess May of Teck (1867–1953), later Queen Mary. George V's reign, though overshadowed by the First World War and the downfall of European monarchs to whom he was closely related, was marked by growing affection between ordinary people and their sovereign: this was due in part to the felicity of his family life and the personal touch of his broadcasts in later years, but also reflects his diligence as a constitutional monarch. His interventions in politics – over the Parliament Act of 1911, the Irish Crisis of 1913–14, the choice of ►Baldwin as Prime Minister in 1923, the formation of the National Government, 1931 – were restrained. He was particularly conscious of his role in the Empire and was the only British Emperor of India to visit the subcontinent as its sovereign (►Delhi Durbar). The Silver Jubilee celebrations of May 1935 were a moving demonstration of popular loyalty. He died eight months later at Sandringham.

George VI (1895–1952; Duke of York 1920–36; King 1936–52; Emperor of India 1936–47). Born and died at Sandringham. He was the second son of George V and Queen Mary, succeeding to the throne on the ►abdication of his brother, Edward VIII. From 1909 to 1917 Prince Albert (as he was known) served in the Royal Navy, and was present in a turret of the battleship *Collingwood* throughout the battle of Jutland. He served in the Royal Air Force, 1918–19, and spent a year at Trinity College, Cambridge. In April 1923 he married Lady Elizabeth Bowes-Lyon. As Duke of York he took a keen interest in promoting social welfare, especially for young people of all classes. As King he remained above politics to an even greater extent than his father. In 1939 he became the first reigning British monarch to visit the United States, staying officially in Washington and privately with President Roosevelt at his Hyde Park home. During the war years the King's sense of service won him universal esteem, heightened by his courage in overcoming a chronic speech defect. He was succeeded by his daughter, ►Elizabeth II.

Georgia. Federal Republic in the western Caucasus, capital Tbilisi (Tiflis), an ancient state on the Black Sea, renowned in the twelfth century but absorbed into the Russian empire early in the nineteenth. From March 1918 to February 1921 Georgia experienced token independence, with at first German and later British troops supporting a moderate nationalist government against the Bolsheviks, and with the Turks occupying the port of Batum until March 1921. Georgia formally joined the ►Soviet Union in 1922, prospering under ►Stalin, who was born near Tbilisi. Despite an anti-Soviet uprising in Tbilisi in 1956 there was no serious challenge to rule from Moscow until March 1990, when the Georgian Soviet abrogated the 1922 treaty of union. Multiparty elections six months later were won by the nationalist spokesman Zviad Gamsakhurdia, who became President of an independent Georgia on 26 May 1991. He was, however, faced by civil war around his capital and by the secession of two northern regions – Abkhazia and southern Ossetia – which received arms and support from neighbouring Russians. Gamsakhurdia was forced to flee early in 1992 and an interim government was formed by Eduard Shevardnaze (1928–), Communist Party boss in Tbilisi from 1972 to 1985, subsequently serving as Soviet Foreign Minister for five years under ►Gorbachev. Shevardnaze was elected President on 11 October 1992. But Georgia was thrown into greater chaos in September 1993 when Gamsakhurdia returned and raised a rebellion west of Tbilisi, while the main Georgian military forces were fighting the northern secessionists. Shevardnaze was forced to seek help from ►Yeltsin in Moscow. Georgia joined the Commonwealth of Independent States in March 1994 and, with Russian aid, the rebellions were suppressed. The Georgian Constitution, promulgated in August 1995, provided for an elected executive President, a unicameral legislature, a special status for southern Ossetia (renamed

Tskhinvali) and autonomy for Abkhazia. A month later Shevardnaze narrowly escaped assassination in a car-bomb explosion; but he won the presidential election of 5 November 1995, his Citizens' Union gaining a massive majority in the legislature. Yet neither Abkhazia nor Tskhinvali was satisfied with the constitutional provisions: the basic problems of a shared economic structure remained unresolved.

German Democratic Republic ('East Germany'). A people's assembly convened in East Berlin in 1948–9 prepared a constitution which would be effective in the Soviet occupation zone, the former German provinces of Brandenburg, Mecklenburg, Saxony, Saxony-Anhalt and Thuringia (an area equivalent to one-fifth of the unified Germany established in 1871). This 'German Democratic Republic' was proclaimed an independent state on 7 October 1949, embarking on a programme of 'socialist construction' under the direction of the 'Socialist Unity Party', led by Walther ➤Ulbricht. The harsh conditions of industrial labour and suffering caused by collectivization of agriculture led to a general strike and mass demonstrations on 17 June 1953, an uprising met by the intervention of Soviet troops, with tanks. There followed a slight improvement in living conditions but by the end of the 1950s thousands of refugees were defecting to the West, especially in ➤Berlin. To halt this flow of people the Berlin Wall was erected in 1961. Economic reforms in 1962 marked a rise in living standards but Ulbricht remained in power until May 1971, the last of the Stalinists. The GDR became an important member of ➤Comecon and the ➤Warsaw Pact. Under Ulbricht's successor, Erich ➤Honecker, tension began to ease, both between the 'two Germanies' and in the relations of the GDR with the West, which had always refused to recognize Ulbricht's authority. A treaty of friendship with the ➤German Federal Republic was signed in December 1972. Significantly, an amendment passed by the parliamentary body (Volkskammer) in September 1974 erased all references to reunification of the German nation from the existing constitution. A new exodus of refugees began in the late summer of 1989, with East Germans travelling to the Federal Republic by way of Czechoslovakia and the newly opened border between Austria and ➤Hungary. After Honecker's resignation in October 1989, the GDR moved towards democratic socialism, with non-communists entering the government of Hans Modrow in November, and a Liberal Democrat, Manfred Gerlach, succeeding Egon Krenz as head of state. On 9 November 1989 free access through the Berlin Wall was conceded by the East German authorities. Elections on 18 March 1990 gave victory to a centre-right political alliance seeking German reunification. On 1 July 1990 the GDR entered into a currency union with the FRG. Political unification followed on 3 October 1990, when the GDR ceased to exist.

Germany, Federal Republic of (*Bundesrepublik Deutschland*). 'West Germany' was set up as a federation of ten provinces (*Länder*), covering an area slightly less than half the size of Bismarck's Germany of 1871. The republic was formally established on 23 May 1949, with its capital at Bonn, although the Americans, British and French retained certain rights over foreign policy under the 'Occupation

Statute', which was not finally abandoned until the week before the FRG joined ➤NATO in May 1955. From 1949 until 1963 the republic's policy was determined by Chancellor ➤Adenauer, who played a prominent part in securing West Germany's integration within the ➤European Community. His successor as Chancellor, Dr ➤Erhard, was an economist largely responsible for encouraging the 'miraculous' growth of the economy which, by 1968, was bringing the West Germans greater prosperity than they had known for eighty or ninety years. The third Federal Chancellor, Kurt Kiesinger (1904–88, in power from December 1966 to September 1969), was hampered by restraints imposed on EEC development by de Gaulle and by a mounting mistrust of his Christian Democrat Party. The electoral victory of the Social Democrats in 1969 brought Willy ➤Brandt to power. He was successful again in the elections of 1972, concentrating on an *Ostpolitik* which on 21 December 1972 even permitted the signing of a treaty of friendship with 'East Germany'. Brandt's coalition – a government in which the Social Democrats held eleven posts and the Free Democrat Party five – was maintained in essentials by his successor, Helmut Schmidt (Chancellor, May 1974 to October 1982). The most serious problems of the Schmidt Chancellorship were internal rather than external, in particular the anarchy threatened by the Rote Armee Faktion (the ➤Baader–Meinhof Group). The Christian Democrat leader, Helmut ➤Kohl, formed a coalition government in October 1982; further electoral successes in 1983 and 1987 consolidated his position. Integration with the GDR in October 1990 restored a single, free, sovereign and united Germany, one-third smaller in area than the German Empire at the start of the century. The General Election of December 1990 confirmed Kohl's coalition government in office, but by the following spring it was clear that the speed of social and economic change in eastern Germany had caused administrative chaos and a rapid growth of unemployment. Of the six parties returned in the October 1994 elections, the Social Democrats held most seats but were kept from office by a coalition of Kohl's Christian Democrats, Free Democrats and the Christian Social Union.

Ghana. Republic in the Commonwealth on the Gulf of Guinea, reviving the name of a West African empire which flourished from before 800 until 1240 in lands north-west of the modern republic. Swedes, Danes and Dutch established trading settlements along the Gulf of Guinea in the seventeenth century, the British acquiring the littoral in 1821, establishing the crown colony of the Gold Coast in 1874, adding to it Ashanti lands and further territories in the north (1901) and administering part of the former German colony of Togoland as mandated territory after the First World War. A constitution giving Africans a majority in the legislature of the Gold Coast Colony was introduced in March 1946, but demands for independence led to the creation in June 1949 of the Convention People's Party, led by Kwame ➤Nkrumah. Independence was conceded on 6 March 1957 and Nkrumah dominated Ghana for the following nine years, adopting a republican constitution on 1 July 1960, and establishing a one-party state in 1964. A severe slump, caused partly by government extravagance and partly by a fall in the world price of cocoa, led Nkrumah to strengthen links with the Soviet bloc; and he was overthrown by the army on 24 February 1966. A new, democratic constitution in 1969 was followed by elections won by the Progress Party of Dr Kofi Busia, who established a predominantly civilian government. A grave economic recession two years later led to further unrest. Once again the army intervened: General Ignatius Acheampong (1931–79) ruled as *de facto* head of state through a Supreme Military Council until overthrown by General Akuffo on 5 July 1978. Eleven months later the SMC was ousted by junior officers led by Flight Lieutenant Jerry Rawlings (the son of a Scottish father and Ewe tribe mother) who set up an Armed Forces Revolutionary Council (AFRC) pledged to stamp out corruption and hold elections. Acheampong, Akuffo and four senior officers were publicly executed outside Accra; drastic punishments inflicted on alleged racketeers; and a civilian government elected under Hilla Limann. Rawlings withdrew from active politics but emerged to lead another *coup* on 31 December 1981, establishing a Provisional National Defence Council to mask his personal rule. With help from the International Monetary Fund, the Ghanaian economy had improved by 1987. Inflation was at last held in check.

Gheorghiu-Dej, Gheorghe (1901–65), Romanian communist leader and President. Born Gheorghe Gheorghiu at Birlap, became tramway worker at Galati, joining the illegal communist movement in 1929. He was imprisoned from 1933 until escaping in August 1944, the hyphenated suffix added to his name commemorating years spent in prison at Dej in northern Transylvania. He became Minister of National Economy in the coalition established by King Michael in March 1945, assuming responsibility for all long-term planning when ➤Romania became a republic in 1948. As a 'home-grown' communist, not Moscow-trained like the formidable Ana Pauker (Foreign Minister 1947–52), Gheorghiu-Dej had to show himself ardently Stalinist and anti-Tito in order to survive. With the party administration in his hands, he risked an anti-Jewish purge in June 1952, which eliminated all Pauker supporters, and left him virtual dictator of the country. He was an early advocate of Khrushchev's doctrine of peaceful co-existence, speaking in favour of national variations in socialism two months earlier than the ➤Twentieth (Soviet) Party Congress of 1956. His close collaboration with Khrushchev led to the withdrawal from Romania of all Soviet troops in June 1958. From 1961 to 1965 he was President, pressing ahead with plans for industrial development which ran counter to the assignments of ➤Comecon and led him into verbal conflicts with the Soviet leaders. When he died in March 1965 he had recovered much of Romania's freedom of initiative, a trend intensified by his successor, ➤Ceauşescu.

Giap, Vo Nguyen (1912–), Vietnamese communist general. Born in Quang-binh Province, educated at the French Lycée in Hué and the University of Hanoi where he gained a doctorate in economics. He was a history master in Hanoi, joining the Communist Party in 1933 and participating in risings against the French. In

1939 he was arrested but escaped to China: his wife was sent to a prison in which she died; his sister was executed. From 1942 to 1945 he helped ➤Ho Chi Minh organize guerrilla resistance to the Japanese, serving as a minister in Ho's short-lived provisional government of ➤Vietnam in 1945. In 1946 he was given command of the Viet-Minh, with the rank of general, and led them in action against the French for eight years, opposing three distinguished commanders, Marshal de Lattre de Tassigny, General ➤Salan and General Navarre. Giap's greatest victory was at ➤Dien Bien Phu in 1954, which precipitated the collapse of French rule throughout Indo-China. He remained Viet-Minh commander-in-chief throughout the ➤Vietnam War against the Americans and their allies. With the Viet-Minh's entry into Saigon in 1975 and the formal establishment of the Socialist Republic of Vietnam in July 1976 General Giap became a deputy premier and retained the post of Minister of Defence which he had held in Hanoi since 1954. No other soldier has successively and successfully defied armies from Japan, France and the United States. He left the politburo in the spring of 1982 but unexpectedly emerged from retirement in 1988, as the Vietnamese prepared to withdraw from Kampuchea.

Gibraltar. Captured from the Spanish by Admiral Sir George Rooke in 1704 and ceded to Britain in perpetuity by the Treaty of Utrecht (1713); promised to Spaniards by George I in 1725; besieged by Spaniards, 1727, 1739, 1779–80; all claims formally renounced by Spain in the first Treaty of Versailles of 1783. The principal British dockyard and naval base for the western Mediterranean was established at the foot of 'the Rock' in the early nineteenth century, and was used as late as 1942 for assembling the allied invasion fleet for north Africa. Spanish demands for the return of Gibraltar were resumed by Franco in 1939, the question being taken up by the United Nations in 1963. Although Gibraltar had lost its former strategic importance to Britain, the people of the crown colony, voting in a referendum on 10 September 1967, sought to remain British rather than pass under Spanish sovereignty (for British rule 12,138, for Spain 44). Self-government was introduced into the crown colony in 1964 and expanded in May 1969, an action which prompted the Spaniards to close the land frontier between Andalusia and Gibraltar. Talks to reduce tension over the Gibraltar question were held in Madrid by the British and Spanish Foreign Ministers in September 1977. Agreement on easing frontier restrictions was reached at further talks in Lisbon in April 1980. The proposed re-opening in the spring of 1982 was postponed because of tension after the ➤Falklands Crisis and it was not until 5 February 1985 that free movement across the land frontier returned. Plans for the withdrawal of British troops from the Rock were announced in March 1991. Friction developed between the Gibraltar Assembly and the British and Spanish governments in 1994 over local resentment at European Union directives aimed at checking drug-smuggling and money laundering. In May 1995 the British threatened to rescind the powers of the Assembly if Gibraltar continued to defy the EU. In April 1998 direct talks between Gibraltarian leaders and the Spanish authorities in Madrid showed a wide divergence of political wishes; the Spaniards offered autonomy under Spanish sovereignty; the Gibraltarians sought a relationship to the United Kingdom similar to that possessed by the Channel Islands.

.

Giolitti, Giovanni (1842–1928), Italian Prime Minister. Born at Mondovi in Cuneo province, Piedmont, and educated in Turin, becoming a civil servant, before entering the Italian parliament as a Liberal in 1882. His first eighteen-month premiership, 1892–3, was cut short by a financial scandal which sent him into temporary exile; but his gifts as an astute parliamentary manager ensured his return to political life in 1900 and he headed four more governments: October 1903 to March 1905; May 1906 to December 1909; March 1911 to March 1914; June 1920 to June 1921. He was thus Prime Minister for more than eleven years, a longer period than any Italian except Mussolini. In foreign affairs he favoured friendship with the Austrians until 1915, seeking to keep Italy out of a European war. He was nevertheless primarily responsible for expansion into ►Libya and the establishment of the Italian hold on the ►Dodecanese after the Italo-Turkish War of 1911–12. His earlier ministries saw some success in combating left-wing strikes and disorders, but he was defeated by a General Strike in March 1914 and, in his final government, could neither satisfy nationalist groups over ►Fiume nor prevent the disorders in the streets which facilitated the rise of ►Mussolini.

Giscard d'Estaing, Valéry (1926–), third President of the Fifth French Republic. Born in Coblenz, where his father was Director of Finance to the High Commission for the (occupied) Rhineland. He was educated at a Paris *lycée* and the École Polytechnique. After military service, in which he won the Croix de Guerre, he entered the inspectorate of finance, before becoming a Gaullist Deputy for Puy-de-Dôme in 1956. He continued to represent either Puy-de-Dôme or Clermont in the National Assembly until 1974. After holding a number of minor governmental posts he was appointed Minister of Finance by ►Pompidou in 1962. He remained responsible for financial affairs throughout the Pompidou, Chaban-Delmas and Messmer governments (1962–74) until, on the death of Pompidou, he was himself elected President (19 May 1974), the youngest head of state in France since Louis Napoleon in 1848. Giscard's attempts to 'open up' political life lost him popular support in the traditionally conservative regions of France until after the parliamentary elections of March 1978 which gave the coalition of Gaullists and Giscardists (UDF) a majority. Friction then developed between Giscard's Prime Minister, Raymond Barr, and the Gaullist leader, Jacques Chirac, weakening the President's hold on political initiatives. Giscard suffered, too, from alleged political scandals, the most damning of which was that he had accepted gifts of diamonds, both as Finance Minister and as President, from the discredited Emperor ►Bokassa. Giscard was defeated by the socialist, ►Mitterrand, in the second round of the Presidential election on 10 May 1981. He retired into private life eleven days later.

Glasnost ('Openness'), a term used by ►Gorbachev in his report to the XXVII Party Congress in February 1986. From the context of the speech it is clear that Gorbachev was concerned with internal affairs, rather than the removal of external barriers. He spoke of the need for the Party 'to declare war on bureaucratic principles' and use 'openness and publicity' to let the people know what was taking place and to act as a check on abuses of authority.

Glenn, John Herschel (1921–), US pioneer astronaut. Born Cambridge, Ohio, served in US marines (air section), 1943–65, receiving decorations for bravery both in the Pacific during the Second World War and in Korea. In 1957 he made the first non-stop supersonic flight from Los Angeles to New York but his fame rests principally on a three-orbit flight in a *Mercury* space capsule which he made on 20 February 1962, completing a circuit of 81,000 miles in four minutes under five hours at a maximum altitude of 160 miles. In 1974 he stood as Democratic candidate for the US Senate in Ohio, and was elected.

Goebbels, Joseph Paul (1897–1945), German propagandist. Born at Rheydt, München-Gladbach, Westphalia, educated at Heidelberg, where he received his doctorate of philosophy in 1920. Goebbels, an embittered intellectual, self-conscious because of the lameness for which he had been rejected by the army, became a supporter of Gregor Strasser's wing of the ►Nazi Party, only attaching himself to Hitler in February 1926. From 1926 to 1930 he built up the Nazi following in Berlin, and was elected to the Reichstag in May 1928 and September 1930. He was given charge of the party's propaganda machine in 1929 and, when the Third Reich was established in 1933, Hitler appointed him Minister of Enlightenment and Propaganda, a post he held until 1945. His cynical understanding of mass psychology made him a formidable figure. His fanaticism led him to demand 'total war' after the defeat of ►Stalingrad and in August 1944 he was given special powers as Reich Commissioner for Total Mobilization, remaining loyal to Hitler. On 1 May 1945 he administered poison to his six children and then shot his wife and himself in Hitler's bunker in Berlin.

Goering, Hermann (1893–1946), German Nazi. Born at Rosenheim, Bavaria, his father being a member of the German colonial service in Africa. In the First World War Goering gained the highest award for bravery and was last commander of the crack Richthofen fighter squadron. He studied spasmodically at Munich University in 1920–21 and joined Hitler's ►Nazi Party in October 1922, being wounded in the ►Munich Putsch a year later. After spending four years in Sweden, he was elected to the Reichstag in 1928, becoming Reichstag Speaker (President) in 1932. On the establishment of the Third Reich he became Prime Minister and Interior Minister for Prussia and was appointed Reich Air Minister, building up the Luftwaffe (air force) and sometimes undertaking special diplomatic missions. The rank of *Reichsmarschall* was especially created for him in 1940. His personal vanity and ostentation, coupled in the later stages of the war with indolence and inefficiency, made him many enemies among the Nazi hierarchy, while his dependence on drugs accentuated his weaknesses. He surrendered to the Americans in Austria in May 1945, was brought to trial (►Nuremberg Trials), showing some of his earlier forceful character when he was in the dock and eventually cheating the gallows by swallowing poison a few hours before he was due to be executed, 15 October 1946.

Gold Standard. A system of currency in which money is held in the form of gold coins or of paper money convertible into gold on demand at the bank. The system was general in Europe and North America before 1914, but the gold market could not function freely during the First World War and Great Britain 'went off gold' from 1919 until Churchill's budget of 1925. In the late 1920s both Conservative and Labour politicians argued that the prosperity of the City of London as an international centre of finance depended on maintaining a gold standard even if this implied austere economy in government spending. Nevertheless, during the international economic crisis of September 1931, external pressure forced the coalition 'National Government' of ►MacDonald to suspend the gold standard by Act of parliament, a decision which devalued the pound sterling by 25 per cent within a few days, and Britain has remained off the gold standard ever since 1931. The French, forced off gold by the First World War, returned to it in 1926 but finally abandoned the gold standard in 1936, as also did the Netherlands, Belgium and Switzerland. The US Gold Standard Act of 1900 made a golden dollar 'the standard unit of value', and this system was maintained despite the 1929 panic (►Wall Street Crash). In April 1933, however, one of the first financial measures of the Roosevelt Administration was the formal abandonment of the gold standard. Subsequent monetary theories in America and Europe, in general, discounted the reliability of gold as a stable unit of currency, although by 1977 a group of economists within the University of California were prepared to defend gold as a check on world inflation.

Goldman, Emma (1869–1940), American anarchist. Born in White Russia of Jewish parentage, leaving her family and emigrating to New York at the age of sixteen. Disillusionment at the illiberal character of American society led her to advocate the idealistic ►anarchism of Kropotkin, favouring cooperative communes and instigating riots which led to her imprisonment in 1893. Through speeches and through a pioneering anarchist periodical *Mother Earth* she encouraged birth control, women's property rights and sexual freedom, while opposing wars, capital punishment and repressive violence by the police. By 1916, when her advocacy of birth control led to a second term of imprisonment, she had become the bogywoman of American family life (even though her personal moral standards were austerely high). Her extremism caused the authorities to deport her in 1919. She lived for two years in Russia but deplored Bolshevik illiberalism and spent much of the 1920s and early 1930s virtually stateless although respected by the European radical Left as a champion of women's emancipation. After three months in America in 1934 she settled in Canada, wrote an autobiography and travelled to Spain where she became a slightly incongruous pacifist anarchist among the republicans in the Civil War. She died in Toronto.

Goldwater, Barry Morris (1909–98), American Republican Party leader. Born in Phoenix, Arizona, into a merchant family of Polish origin, served as a pilot ferrying bombers from America to Asia, 1942–5, was elected Republican Senator for Arizona, 1953–65, and became accepted as the leading conservative political spokesman in the United States during the Kennedy administration. He was chosen as Republican candidate for the US Presidency in 1964, his campaign becoming notorious for his advocacy of increased opposition to world communism and his hostility to the powers of the federal government ('Extremism in the defence of liberty is no vice. Moderation in the pursuit of justice is no virtue'). These views, representing the extreme right of the Republican Party, won Goldwater only five states, a clear rejection of conservatism. Goldwater returned to the Senate in 1969 and, as a senior party leader, helped induce Nixon to step down from the Presidency after the ►Watergate Scandal in 1974. His role as elder statesman was also marked at the Republican Convention of 1976 when he nominated Gerald Ford as the Presidential candidate. He retired in 1986.

Gomulka, Wladyslaw (1905–82), Polish communist leader. Born at Krosno, then in Austrian Galicia, active as a trade unionist in the 1930s, becoming in 1943 secretary-general of a newly established clandestine Polish Workers' Party which played a major role in the resistance movement. Under the 'Government of National Unity' of 1945–7 he was made minister responsible for territories annexed from Germany but in the summer of 1948 he gave a speech on the 'historical traditions of the Polish labour movement' which was interpreted as nationalistic in Moscow. He was dismissed in December 1948 and kept in 'protective custody' from 1951 until October 1955. De-Stalinization after the ►Twentieth Soviet Party Congress brought Gomulka back into favour: he was readmitted to the party in August 1956, and became a popular leader after anti-Soviet riots in Poznań. In mid-October he was elected First Secretary of the party. While seeking a specifically Polish form of socialism, he retained defence links with the Soviet Union and therefore avoided the tragedies of the contemporaneous ►Hungarian National Rising. Agricultural collectivization was stopped, four-fifths of arable land remaining in private hands throughout the Gomulka era. Limited political reforms, curbing the prying powers of the secret police, were effective in 1957–8; but many of his reforms were abandoned in 1962–3 for fear of internal unrest. In December 1970 there were riots over the rising cost of food in Gdańsk, Gdynia and Szczecin and he was replaced as First Secretary by the party leader from Silesia, Edward Gierek (1913–).

Good Friday Accord (10 April 1998). ►Northern Ireland peace agreement, signed by representatives of the British and Irish governments and of eight political parties in the province, providing for constitutional changes. Agreement was reached after twenty-two months of discussion, under the chairmanship of the former US senator, George Mitchell. The Accord proposed the creation of a 108-seat Assembly, elected on a single transferable vote system of proportional representation. Subsequent decisions would be taken on a cross-community basis, with executive authority discharged by a First Minister and a Deputy First Minister from opposite sides of the community and by up to ten ministers with Departmental responsibilities. A North/South Ministerial Council would bring together representatives from London and Dublin for topics of joint concern; their work would be augmented by occasional meetings of a British–Irish Council and a British–Irish Intergovernmental Conference. Signatories of the Accord re-affirmed commitments made in September 1997 to the total disarmament of paramilitary organizations and accepted pledges safeguarding human rights and equal opportunities. It was agreed that a commission for policing Northern Ireland would be set up and that the British and Irish governments would gradually release prisoners convicted during the years of terrorism. A referendum across the whole of Ireland on 22 May showed voters' support for the Accord. The first session of the Assembly opened at Stormont on 1 July 1998.

Gorbachev, Mikhail Sergeyevich (1931–), Soviet leader. Born near Stavropol in the northern Caucasus. When he was eleven years old, his native village came in the war zone and was under enemy occupation for five months. After working on the land for several years, he went to Moscow University in 1949 to study law and became a party member in 1952. He returned to the Stavropol district in 1955, practising law, studying at an agricultural institute, organizing the local communist youth movement and serving as district Party organizer, 1970–78. He was summoned to Moscow as an expert on land problems in 1978 and admitted to the Politburo a year later, his rapid advancement helped by support from the KGB chief, Yuri ➤Andropov, who also came from Stavropol. When, in November 1982, Andropov succeeded ➤Brezhnev as General Secretary, he used Gorbachev as spokesman for his reform proposals in the state and the party. Andropov's death, in February 1984, left Gorbachev in a position of considerable influence, which he strengthened during the thirteen-month term of Andropov's successor, the ailing Konstantin Chernenko (1911–85). Gorbachev became General Secretary of the Communist Party on 11 March 1985, meeting Reagan at Geneva in November and subsequently in Reykjavik (October 1986) and in Washington (December 1987) where the two leaders signed an agreement to eliminate medium- and short-range nuclear missiles. Gorbachev's professed policy of 'openness' (➤glasnost) gave greater liberty to dissidents. At the same time he promised a major reconstruction (➤perestroika) of the Soviet state. On 28 June 1988 he addressed a special Communist Party conference in which he outlined reforms of the political structure, seeking to 'create a new image of socialism' by 'democratizing our government'. He was hampered by unrest among national minorities, notably in the Baltic republics, in Armenia and in Georgia, where a nationalist demonstration in Tbilisi (9 April 1989) was suppressed by army intervention, apparently contrary to his orders. At the end of September 1988 Gorbachev secured the removal from the Politburo of several old-style authoritarians and ousted ➤Gromyko from the presidency. Implementation of his reforms led to major constitutional changes in December 1988 and to the election of 2,250 Congress of People's Deputies, including liberal dissidents such as Andrei ➤Sakharov as well as Communist Party members. Although the People's Deputies criticized aspects of Gorbachev's policies, on 16 May 1989 the inaugural Congress confirmed his election as Soviet President for five years, with possible re-election for a further term. In 1990 he became the first Soviet statesman to be awarded a Nobel Peace Prize, but was unable to travel to Oslo to receive it because of increasing unrest in the Soviet republics. In October 1990 he urged a gradual transition to a market economy. A failure to ensure the distribution of adequate food supplies, together with a sudden jump in the cost of living, lowered his prestige at home. His policies were challenged in the Russian Republic by Boris ➤Yeltsin and in the Ukraine by a secessionist Opposition 'Republican' Party. Yet on 25 December 1990 the Congress of People's Deputies gave him greater executive powers than had been formally accorded to any previous Soviet leader. On 17 March 1991 he gained only limited success in a referendum on a continued unitary structure for the USSR, with six of the fifteen republics refusing to hold an official vote. He survived an abortive *coup* by Communist hard-liners on 19 August 1991, thereafter remaining in office with reduced authority and with the Communist Party outlawed until 25 December 1991, when he resigned as President, on the day before the ➤Soviet Union was dissolved.

Gottwald, Klement (1896–1953), Czechoslovak communist President. Born at Dedice in Moravia, fought in the Austro-Hungarian army on the Eastern Front in the First World War, joined the Czechoslovak Communist Party as a founder-member in 1921, becoming General Secretary in 1927 and representative of the Comintern in Czechoslovakia during the 1930s. After the Munich Agreement in 1938 he went to Moscow, holding discussions there with ➤Beneš in December 1943, returning with him to Prague in 1945 and, after communist successes in the elections of May 1946, heading a coalition government. The prospect of communist electoral defeat in 1948 prompted Gottwald to establish a one-party government, using the workers' militia and the police to carry through a *coup d'état* in the last week of February. Gottwald succeeded Beneš as President in June 1948, holding the office until he died from pneumonia contracted at Stalin's funeral in March 1953. The political development of Czechoslovakia during the Gottwald era was rigidly Stalinist, a five-year plan (1949–54) building up Czech industries as adjuncts of the Soviet economy while forced labour camps and political trials (➤Slansky Trial) created a sense of fear in the most westernized nation within the Soviet bloc.

Gramsci, Antonio (1891–1937). Born in Ales, near Cagliari; became the founder of the Italian Communist Party, showing himself, while imprisoned by Mussolini, a thinker of some originality who sought to harmonize historical materialism with the specifically Italian tradition in metaphysical philosophy (►Communist Parties).

Great Leap Forward. The slogan used in ►China to describe the radical innovations instituted in 1958 and continuing until 1961. Among these changes were the establishment of huge agricultural communes, to which light industries and local construction projects would be attached. Cuts in consumption, the withdrawal of material incentives and displays of regimented enthusiasm were calculated to emphasize the revolutionary zeal with which these innovations would speed up the establishment of a genuine communistic society. The programme was a failure, partly through three years of floods, bad harvests and other natural disasters, partly because of the withdrawal of Soviet technical advice and partly through managerial difficulties. A more normal system of communist economic planning was adopted in 1962.

Greece. Passed under Turkish rule in the mid fifteenth century. A cultural renaissance in the eighteenth century inspired the Greeks to rise against the Turks (1821–2) and a Greek kingdom was established in 1829, territorially extended in 1863, 1881 and 1913 (when parts of Macedonia and Thrace were added after the ►Balkan Wars). The political conflict of ►Constantine I and ►Venizelos led Greece to pursue a tortuous policy in the First World War, until Venizelist successes in 1917 enabled the Greek forces to join the allied army at ►Salonika and participate in the offensive of 1918. An attempt to secure Anatolia in the peace settlement failed disastrously at ►Smyrna in 1922. A republican interregnum from May 1924 until November 1935 was followed by the restoration of Constantine's son, George II (1890–1947), who had already reigned for eighteen months, 1922–4. In August 1936 George accepted the establishment of a right-wing dictatorship under General ►Metaxas which was still in power when Italy invaded Greece in October 1940. Although the Italians were defeated and thrown back into Albania, the Greeks could not sustain resistance after German intervention in April 1941. Rival monarchist and communist groups maintained a guerrilla war against the occupying powers from 1942 until the British liberated Athens in October 1944. Even before the complete liberation of the islands, these two resistance movements were fighting each other, notably at Christmas 1944 in Athens, despite the attempts of the Regent, Archbishop Damaskinos, to bring political stability. A plebiscite in 1946 brought George II back for a second time but the country was engulfed by civil war (►Greek Civil War) from May 1946 until October 1949. King George died in April 1947 and was succeeded by his brother, Paul (1901–64), whose seventeen-year reign was dominated by the right-wing 'Greek Rally' movement of Field-Marshal ►Papagos until 1955. The subsequent parliamentary regime was marked by contests between the conservative ►Karamanlis and the more radical ►Papandreou but was overshadowed by the problems of Cyprus and ►Enosis. The accession of the young king, ►Constantine II, in 1964 was followed by the discovery in May 1965 of a conspiracy by a secret army organization (Aspida), alleged to favour a left-wing dictatorship under Papandreou's son. Tension mounted between the royalists and the Papandreou supporters: and in April 1967 the right-wing elements in the army seized power, establishing the regime of the ►'Greek Colonels'. Constantine went into exile in December 1967 but it was only in June 1973 that the monarchy was formally abolished and Greece declared a republic once more. Unrest in Athens in 1973–4, intensified by the evident mishandling by the government of affairs in ►Cyprus, led the Colonels to surrender their power, and in August 1974 the veteran Karamanlis formed a new government, pending democratic elections in November. The elections gave Karamanlis's 'New Democracy Party' a good majority: but a referendum held three weeks later rejected a restoration of the monarchy by 69 per cent to 31 per cent. A constitution providing for a democratic 'Hellenic Republic' was debated in parliament during the early months of 1975, becoming valid on 11 June 1975, President Constantine Tsatsos (1899–1981) taking office nine days later. Greece became a member of NATO in 1952 and an associate of the ►EEC in 1962, becoming a full member at last on 1 January 1981, after Karamanlis's government sought increasing contact with the European Community, 1975–7. Tension between Greece and Turkey over the Cyprus question and over other disputes in the Aegean has threatened war on several occasions, notably 1955, 1959, 1964, 1967 (especially from 15 November to 8 December) and 1974. Karamanlis succeeded Tsatsos as President in May 1980. Widespread suspicion among the Greek electorate of the consequences of Greece's entry into the Common Market seems finally to have tipped the balance in favour of the Panhellenic Socialist Movement (PASOK) of Andreas ►Papandreou. The socialists won a Greek general election for the first time on 18 October 1981, and Karamanlis duly asked Papandreou to form a government. Although Greece remained in the EEC and NATO, Papandreou won a second electoral victory in 1985; scandals and internal feuds led to an electoral stalemate in 1989. Political deadlock was broken by elections in April 1990 which led to the formation of a right-wing 'New Democracy' government under Konstantinos Mitsotakis. Allegations of phone-tapping and other accusations discredited Mitsotakis, who resigned his party's leadership after it lost the 1993 election to PASOK, which continued to be led by Papandreou until his health finally gave way in February 1996. An election in September 1996 confirmed PASOK in office, led by the sixty-year-old lawyer, Kostas Simitis.

Greek Civil War (1946–9). During the occupation of Greece in the Second World War a communist-dominated resistance movement, EAM (National Liberation Front), recruited, trained and armed a guerrilla army, ELAS (National People's Army of Liberation). EAM wished to achieve in Greece a communist revolution similar to Tito's in Yugoslavia; and they opposed the return of the royalists. Civil strife in the winter of 1944–5 was followed by an agreement between the royalists and ELAS (the 'Truce of Varkiza', 12 February 1945) which left two-thirds of the country effectively under EAM authority. In October 1946 the former ELAS commander, Markos Vafiades, established a 'Democratic Army of Greece' in the northern countryside which called on all villagers for support. Markos received help in the subsequent Civil War from the Yugoslavs, Albanians and Bulgarians, while the Greek royalist army was supplied with arms (and advice) from the USA as part of the ➤Truman Doctrine. Without American backing Greece would have passed under communist control in the spring of 1947. Ultimately the 'Democratic Army' was defeated in the field when Marshal ➤Papagos trapped and eliminated its principal units on Mount Grammos, near the Albanian frontier (30 August 1949), the communists announcing a ceasefire seven weeks later. The communist failure in the Civil War sprang from three main reasons: (1) Markos's methods of intimidation aroused popular hostility and prevented the growth of support for a revolution; (2) the split between ➤Tito and ➤Stalin in 1948 led to the withdrawal of Yugoslav backing and left the 'Democratic Army' geographically isolated; (3) Markos's attempts to seize and hold large towns as territorial centres for a provisional government exposed the communist forces to conventional, pitched battles against the regular National Army, which was better equipped for such operations. The toll of the Civil War was heavy: some 21,000 soldiers and over 5,000 civilians killed, 12,000 homes lost, the judicial execution by the royalists of more than 1,200 communists, many of them former Resistance heroes. Psychologically the Civil War left a deeper wound on a generation of Greeks than had the Second World War itself.

Greek Colonels. A military *coup d'état* in Athens on 21 April 1967 suspended parliamentary government in Greece. The two strong men of the *coup*, George Papadopoulos and Stylianos Pattakos, were colonels; and the regime which they established and dominated for seven years was abused by liberals throughout Europe as 'the government of the Greek Colonels' (although both men rapidly reached the rank of general). The regime, which claimed to be saving Greece from communism, at first ruled by martial law. An attempt by King ➤Constantine II to overthrow the 'Colonels' in December 1967 was so inept that he was forced into exile in Rome, thus removing the last constitutional restraint on the regime. Papadopoulos became Prime Minister and Minister of Defence on the King's departure while Pattakos, as Minister of the Interior, was responsible for the imprisonment of conservative, liberal and radical politicians, for censorship of newspapers, the theatre and music, and for measures of social intolerance (no beards, no mini-skirts). Evidence of torture and brutality led the Dutch and Scandinavian Governments to arraign the regime before the European Commission on Human Rights. Papadopoulos became Regent in March 1972; allegations of a royalist plot within the navy in the summer of 1973 led him to proclaim Greece a republic, under his own Presidency. The joint burden of economic stagnation and denial of free expression caused student riots in Athens (November 1973), only suppressed by the use of troops and a strengthening of army control in the government, Papadopoulos handing over the Presidency to General Gizikis. This change in management failed to save a discredited regime. Fury at the part played by the Colonels in seeking to overthrow ➤Makarios and provoking the Cyprus crisis of 1974 brought Greece to the verge of revolution; and on 23 July 1974 the armed forces relinquished power, General Gizikis calling on ➤Karamanlis to form a constitutional government. Twenty leading figures of the Colonels' regime were put on trial in August 1975: both Papadopoulos and Pattakos were condemned to death, but the sentence was commuted to life imprisonment.

Green Parties. Concern over environmental issues led in 1979 to the formation in West Germany of *Die Grünen* (The Greens), a political party which extended its share of the vote from 1.5 per cent in 1980 to 8.3 per cent by 1987, sharing power with the socialists in several German states and holding forty-two seats in the Bonn Parliament from 1987 to 1990. This success encouraged the formation of Green parties in Finland, Switzerland, Austria, France, Belgium, Czechoslovakia, Holland, Ireland and Great Britain. The German Greens owed much of their success to the campaigning skills of Petra Kelly (1947–92), a Bavarian-born and American-educated ecologist with an international following. German support for the Greens fell in 1990, partly because of the party's indifference to the unification question and partly because Kelly's policies seemed too radical for the mood at that time. Her murder in October 1992, by a retired general who was a close associate, seemed fatally to weaken the movement. But at the German elections two years later the Greens won 49 of the 672 seats, and in the European Parliament there were Green members returned by seven member states.

Greenland. ➤Denmark.

Grenada, the southernmost of the Windward Islands, achieved independence from Britain in February 1974, remaining within the Commonwealth. The left-wing New Jewel Movement seized power in March 1979 and set up a People's Revolutionary Government, headed by Maurice Bishop (1944–83) who sought to collaborate with Cuba while also developing the island's tourist potential. But on 19 October 1983 Bishop was killed in a military *coup* by more strongly pro-Cuban Marxists. Appeals for intervention to President Reagan from Commonwealth Caribbean Islands led to the invasion of Grenada on 25 October by a US task force of 6,000 men, backed by 15 warships and token support units from the Caribbean islands. In overthrowing the Marxist regime, 45 Grenadans, 25 Cubans and 18 Americans were killed. The American invasion of Commonwealth territory aroused some resentment in London, especially as US bombing destroyed construction projects entrusted to a British company. The last invaders withdrew in 1985.

Grey, Edward (1862–1933, baronet 1882, created Viscount Grey of Fallodon, 1916). A member of one of the great Whig families of northern England, Liberal MP for Berwick from 1885 to 1916 and Foreign Secretary from December 1905 to May 1916, the longest-ever continuous tenure of that office. Grey continued the policy of Entente, initiated by the Conservatives under ➤Lansdowne, concluding the ►Anglo-Russian Entente of 1907 and authorizing ►military conversations with the French and the Belgians. While hating the idea of war and insisting that Britain must remain free from entangling alliances so as to retain a choice of peace in any crisis, Grey nevertheless made it clear to parliament in August 1914 that he considered Britain had an obligation to help Belgium, thus taking the country into the First World War. He believed strongly in international arbitration (which he used successfully in the Balkan Wars) and, despite failing eyesight, he vigorously championed the League of Nations in his later years. In 1919 he headed a special diplomatic mission to the United States. Grey was a keen fisherman and ornithologist who remained in active politics less from personal choice than from a sense of duty.

Grivas, George Theodoros (1898–1974), Greek army officer. Born in Cyprus, served in the Greek Army in the Second World War, organizing right-wing guerrillas. He fought with the royalists in the Greek Civil War, retiring as a colonel. In 1953 he discussed with Archbishop Makarios and with the Greek national leader, Marshal Papagos, the initiation of a guerrilla campaign in ►Cyprus in support of ►Enosis. Neither Makarios nor Papagos favoured the idea, but Grivas proceeded to create the terrorist movement EOKA which he led under the *nom de guerre* of Dighenis (a folk-hero who had defended the Greeks from Arab pirates). EOKA murders alienated British opinion, not at first unsympathetic to the Greek Cypriots. Against President Makarios's wishes Grivas was later given command of the Greek Cypriot National Guard, with the rank of general. Raids by his troops on Turkish Cypriot villages in November 1967 led to such international friction that he was recalled to Athens the following month. Grivas regarded Makarios's acceptance of Commonwealth membership and abandonment of Enosis as treason. In September 1971 Grivas returned secretly to Cyprus and reorganized his followers for action against Makarios. By now, however, Grivas was a sick man, suffering from cancer. He died in hiding at Limassol in January 1974. His divisive legacy contributed to the disastrous events in the island of the following July and August (►Cyprus).

Gromyko, Andrei Andreyevich (1909–89), Soviet President. Born in Byelorussia, studied economics at Minsk and Moscow, he edited the official economics journal during the ►*Yezhovshchina*, but was brought into the diplomatic service in 1939, succeeding ►Litvinov as Soviet ambassador in Washington, 1943–6. He took part in the conferences at ►Yalta and ►Potsdam and was Soviet delegate to the UN, 1946–9, thereafter serving as deputy foreign minister in Moscow and, briefly, as ambassador in London. From February 1957 until March 1985 he was Soviet Foreign Minister, a longer span of office than any predecessor since the Revolution. Although a master of detailed negotiations, Gromyko was primarily an interpreter of others' policies; he was not even admitted to the Politburo until 1973. When ►Gorbachev became General Secretary in March 1985, Gromyko succeeded Chernenko as head of state but without enjoying executive authority. He retired, in Gorbachev's favour, on 30 September 1988.

Guatemala. The most northerly Central American republic. A Spanish colonial administration ruled the region from 1543 until 1821. In 1823 Guatemala City was the capital of an independent federation, the 'United Provinces of Central America', which disintegrated in 1838, leaving Guatemala an independent republic dominated by a succession of military juntas. Attempts to revive the Central American Union in 1921–2 provoked revolution and were abandoned. The right-wing dictatorship of General Ubico, 1931–44, was followed by the first free election, 17 December 1944, and the establishment of a moderate reformist government under Professor Arevalo, succeeded as President in 1950 by Colonel Arbenz. Expropriation of the United Fruit Company by Arbenz's socialist administration alarmed the US Government, which backed a counter-revolution in June–July 1954. President Arbenz fled and a militaristic regime dominated the republic's politics until 1966. An interlude of parliamentary government under President Mendez was followed inevitably by reassertion of army control under Colonel Arana in 1970 and General Romeo Garcia in 1974. From 1960 onwards Guatemala reflected the conflicts in ▶Cuba, both as a refuge for anti-Castro conspirators and as a region where guerrilla groups sympathetic to Castro could operate. Garcia's use of 'death squads' with headquarters in an annex of the Presidential palace induced the United States to suspend military aid in 1977. On 23 March 1982 Garcia's junta was replaced by the first of several short-lived military governments, brutally repressive in character. The enforced resettlement of Indians caused several thousand deaths. In January 1986 civilian rule returned with the election of President Vincio Cerezo, a Christian Democrat lawyer who in October, under American pressure, agreed to peace talks with the left-wing guerrilla groups – the first in a quarter of a century of chronic insurgency. Little progress was made, however, until 1993, when sheer exhaustion led to agreements which the UN sought to enforce. An attempt in March 1993 to suspend the constitution and return to right-wing authoritarian government was thwarted by younger army officers advocating 'national advancement'. (▶Belize).

Guderian, Heinz (1888–1954), German general. Born at Kulm, on the Vistula, and educated at the Prussian cadet colleges before being commissioned in the infantry (1908). From 1914 to 1917 he served in Flanders, subsequently holding a General Staff post, specializing in motorized transport. As a pupil and admirer of ▶Seeckt, Guderian concentrated on developing a highly mobile mechanized army. From July 1934 onwards he was entrusted with the battle-training of armoured troops (*Panzers*), perfecting the technique of ▶*Blitzkrieg*. On 14 May 1940 Lt-Gen. Guderian's tanks broke through at Sedan and by a lightning advance reached the Channel coast within a week, thus virtually deciding the campaign in France. Guderian commanded the Second Panzer Army against Russia in 1941 but was dismissed at the end of the year for failing to break through to Moscow. In March 1943 he was reinstated as Inspector-General of Armoured Troops and became

Chief of the General Staff after the failure of the ►July Conspiracy in 1944. Although frequently critical of Hitler as a strategist, Guderian remained personally loyal to him, ultimately accepting dismissal on 28 March 1945 for his failure to check the Red Army's advance on Berlin.

Guernica. Ancient capital of the ►Basques, destroyed by bombing in the Spanish Civil War, 26 April 1937. The attack was made by Heinkel 111 and Junkers 52 bombers of the Kondor Legion, a German force sent by Hitler to support Franco. The raid outraged public opinion in Britain, France and the eastern seaboard of the USA. Pablo Picasso used Guernica as the theme for his mural on the horrors of war, commissioned for the Paris World Fair later that year. A vote offering apologies to the Basque people was carried in the Bundestag (German parliament) in April 1998.

Guevara, Ernesto 'Che' (1928–67), Latin American revolutionary. Born in Rosario, Argentina, of well-to-do parents, studied medicine at university and qualified as a doctor (1953). Subsequently he visited every mainland republic in Latin America and was turned into a revolutionary by anger when he witnessed American intervention in ►Guatemala in 1954. Crossing to Mexico he joined the exiled Fidel ►Castro, who was planning a revolution in Cuba (an island Guevara had never visited). Guevara accompanied Castro to Cuba in December 1956, taking a prominent part in the guerrilla campaign which led to Batistá's downfall in January 1959. In 1960 Guevara travelled in China and the Soviet Union, ostensibly as President of the Cuban National Bank. He also compiled a study of guerrilla warfare, arguing that in Latin America revolution must precede the propagation of communism and that therefore a guerrilla leader was more likely to inspire the peasantry to overthrow the existing order than a doctrinaire party member. From February 1961 until April 1965 Guevara was Minister for Industries but then resigned all his Cuban posts and turned to the jungle of Bolivia, hoping to test successfully his revolutionary theory. He believed he could rouse the tin-miners of ►Bolivia, who were living in terrible poverty, to insurrection, counting on support from the pro-Soviet and Maoist wings of a radical underground movement in the towns of Bolivia. His attempt was a disaster: few Bolivians supported him, and early in October 1967 he was wounded, captured and executed by Bolivian regular troops. Guevara's fame was created by his death. His rejection of both capitalism and orthodox communism made him a symbolic martyr for radical students throughout the world. Their adulation popularized the nickname 'Che' originally given to Guevara by his comrades in the Cuban Sierra Maestra because it was a familiarity he used in addressing others.

Gulf War, First (Iraq and Iran, 1980–88). The name given to the conflict which was begun after three weeks of border incidents by an Iraqi invasion of Iran on 22 September 1980. Iraq's immediate objective was control of the Shatt al Arab, the 120-mile waterway formed by the confluence of the Tigris and Euphrates at the head of the Persian Gulf. Instead of advancing deeply into Iran, the Iraqis besieged Khorramshahr and Abadan, thus enabling Iran to raise a substantial army of largely untrained young men who sustained heavy casualties in massive counter-attacks, especially around Dezful (March–May 1982). The conflict then became a war of attrition, resembling the Western Front of 1915–18. Both sides suffered heavily in mounting indecisive offensives, the war zone extending from Kurdistan south-wards to the marshes in front of Basra, where thousands of Iranians perished; Iraq resorted to poison gas and was censured by the UN for chemical warfare in 1984 and 1986. The Iraqi air force bombed Teheran; Iranian missiles struck Baghdad. Strategically the war was a stalemate, neither army having the resources to break the deadlock. On 20 July 1987 Resolution 598 of the Security Council instructed Iran and Iraq to implement the UN's repeated demands for a ceasefire or face an international arms embargo. Nevertheless the war dragged on into an eighth year, with Gulf shipping harassed by mines and attacks by Iranian gunboats; protection was given to convoys of tankers by American and British warships. The Iraqis were reluctant to agree to an armistice until they had increased their number of war prisoners, as bargaining counters in any final settlement. A ceasefire was at last enforced on 20 August 1988; subsequent peace talks in Geneva and New York made slow progress.

Gulf War, Second (Iraq and UN Coalition, 1991): was caused by a renewal in the summer of 1990 of Iraqi claims to ➤Kuwait, dormant for almost thirty years. When Iraqi–Kuwaiti talks in Jeddah broke down in late July, Saddam ➤Hussein sent the Iraqi army into Kuwait, which was overrun on 2 August. The UN Security Council demanded immediate withdrawal and imposed economic sanctions on Iraq; Saddam Hussein responded by detaining Westerners from both Iraq and Kuwait, many being held near strategic targets; but he ordered their release on 6 December. Iraq's defiance induced the UN to pass Security Council Resolution 678 in late November, authorizing members to use all means to enforce the demand for withdrawal. Troops, ships and aircraft from 29 countries concentrated in Saudi Arabia but delayed action in the vain hope that the crisis could be resolved peacefully. War began on the night of 16–17 January 1991, with the American General Norman Schwarzkopf as allied commander. American, British, French and Saudi planes attacked airfields and strategic bases. The Iraqis responded by firing Scud missiles at Riyadh and, despite Israel's non-belligerent status, at Tel Aviv. On 24 January a seaborne assault by the UN forces captured Qaruh Island, off Kuwait. The Iraqis mounted a limited offensive across the Saudi frontier on 29 January and captured Khafji, which was recovered two days later. More than 500,000 allied troops launched a ground offensive to liberate Kuwait on 24 February: American and French troops penetrated into southern Iraq, reaching the Euphrates near Nasiriyah, while the British 1st Armoured Division engaged Iraqi mechanized troops along the northern Kuwaiti frontier. Egyptian and Syrian troops captured the al-Salem air base, while Saudi troops, US Marines, and other Arab troops advanced into Kuwait City, which was fully liberated by 27 February, the Iraqis having set fire to hundreds of oil wells as they retreated. Saddam Hussein accepted a provisional ceasefire on 28 February, the active land campaign having lasted exactly 100 hours. A definitive ceasefire became effective on 12 April: Iraq abandoned claims on Kuwait, and undertook to pay reparations, to destroy chemical, nuclear and biological weapons, and to accept the presence of a UN peace-keeping force from countries which had not participated in the war. 200 allied troops were reported killed or missing; Iraqi deaths were estimated at more than 25,000, with several thousand civilian casualties from the bombing. The ecological effects of the burning oil wells were considered by many environmentalists to be disastrous. (►Iraq.)

Guyana, an independent cooperative republic in South America and within the British Commonwealth, formerly British Guiana. The region was settled by the Dutch in the seventeenth century, occupied by the British in 1796 and formally ceded to Britain in 1814, the sugar plantations being the colony's chief asset. Independence was granted on 26 May 1966 after British troops had been stationed in the colony for four years so as to check the violence between the rival parties of the Left, the People's Progressive Party of Cheddi Jagan (1918–97) and the People's National Congress of Forbes Burnham (1923–85). Jagan was supported by the Indian section of the population, Burnham mainly by the Negroes, and there were serious racial clashes. Burnham became Prime Minister in 1964 and built up the power of the PNC over the following sixteen years until in October 1980 he became executive President, with supreme authority under a newly promulgated socialist constitution. On Burnham's death in August 1985, Desmond Hoyle succeeded to the presidency and preserved the predominance of the People's National Congress by victory in a controversial election (9 December 1985). Criticism of voting procedures led to changes which in October 1992 enabled the PPP to win the election, Cheddi Jagan became President, with Samuel Hinds as Chief Minister. On Jagan's death (6 March 1997), Hinds succeeded to the presidency. The security of Guyana has at times been placed at risk by Venezuelan claims to some two-thirds of the republic's territory.

H

Haganah. Originally a secret protective force organized by the Jews in Palestine to defend their communities from Arab attacks in 1936. Subsequently Haganah became the military arm of the ➤Jewish Agency, as distinct from the two terrorist organizations, the Stern Gang and ➤Irgun Zvai Leumi, whose activities were officially condemned by the Haganah leadership. In April and May 1948 (immediately preceding British withdrawal from Palestine) Haganah engaged in pitched battles with Arab troops around Lydda and Ramla in order to keep communications open between Tel Aviv and Jerusalem. Haganah formed a nucleus for the Israeli Army.

Haig, Alexander Meigs (1924–), US General and Secretary of State. A distant cousin of Earl ➤Haig. Alexander Haig was born in Philadelphia and educated at the US Military Academy, West Point, and Georgetown University. He was commissioned in the army in 1947, rising to the rank of brigadier-general in 1969 and major-general in 1972. After holding a post in the Defence Department in 1964–5 and commanding a brigade in Vietnam (1966–7), he served as deputy commandant at West Point before joining President Nixon as military adviser in the White House from 1969 to 1973, when he undertook a special mission to Vietnam. General Haig was commander-in-chief of American forces in Europe from 1974 to 1979, and Supreme Commander NATO. On 25 June 1979 Haig survived an attempt on his life, near NATO headquarters in Belgium. Soon afterwards he retired from the army to enter political life as a Republican. He was duly appointed Secretary of State by ➤Reagan in January 1981 but at times his policy was at variance with the professed intentions of the President and other members of the administration. Haig made strenuous but vain efforts to solve the ➤Falklands Conflict peacefully in April 1982. Two months later he suddenly resigned after further differences with the President.

Haig, Douglas (1861–1928, knighted 1909, created an earl in 1919), British field-marshal. Born in Edinburgh, commissioned in the cavalry 1885, serving in the Sudan in 1898 and with distinction in South Africa, 1899–1902. From 1906 to 1909 he was at the War Office helping to implement the reforms of ➤Haldane. In August 1914 he crossed to France as general commanding the First Army Corps, fighting at Mons and later in the Ypres salient and at Loos. He succeeded Sir John French as British commander-in-chief on the Western Front in December 1915. Haig was an orthodox and unimaginative professional soldier, enjoying enormous prestige with his brother officers but distrustful of new ideas. He had been a personal friend of King George V for many years but was on bad terms with the Prime Minister, Lloyd George, who believed he wasted lives without tangible success. After being driven back by the Germans in March 1918, Field-Marshal Haig showed tenacity in rallying the defence 'with backs to the wall'. He secured the appointment of Foch as allied generalissimo in April 1918, and the two men collaborated closely until the final allied victory in November. Haig spent his last years in work for ex-servicemen, and especially for the disabled, instituting the 'Poppy Day' appeal associated with his name.

Haile Selassie (1892–1975). Emperor of Ethiopia. Born Tafari Makonnen, at Hurar, a cousin of the powerful reigning emperor, Menelek; educated by French mission priests. He showed such gifts that by the age of sixteen he was effective governor of one of the richest provinces in ➤Ethiopia. When he was twenty-four Ras Tafari (as he was known) was elected Regent by a council of notables. During the fourteen years of his regency, he improved health and education and visited Europe, taking Ethiopia into the League of Nations in 1924. Much of his time was spent in pacifying the country, asserting his claims to the throne against other, less gifted members of the dynasty. He was crowned Emperor in November 1930, taking the name Haile Selassie, with which he had been baptized. For five years he sought to modernize and centralize government but was forced into exile in 1936 when the Italians won the ➤'Abyssinian War'. He spent much of his exile at Bath, departing for Khartoum in 1940 in order to organize raids into Italian-held Ethiopia. The allied successes in 1941 allowed him to return to Addis Ababa. He then resumed his task of converting Ethiopia into a modern state, while asserting his empire's autonomous African entity and acting as elder statesman to the emergent African nations. Troops were sent, on his orders, to fight for the United Nations in Korea and help police the ➤Congo. From 1955 onwards, however, there was a tendency for him to encourage reforms at home which were more spectacular than real; he lost touch with the social problems of Ethiopia. His authority declined rapidly throughout 1973–4 and in September 1974 he was formally deposed by a committee of left-wing army officers. He was at first confined to a three-room mud hut but was later allowed back to his palace where he died in August 1975. In sixty years as Regent and Emperor he had built up a state in which, until the very close of his reign, he was the principal guarantor of stability, unity and cohesion.

Haiti. Republic on the western side of the island of Hispaniola, smaller than its neighbour, the ➤Dominican Republic. Originally Haiti was the French colony of Saint-Domingue, settled in 1697, and famous for the revolt of the slaves under Toussaint l'Ouverture between 1791 and 1802. Haitian independence was established in 1804. Frequent political upheavals culminated in occupation by the US Marines in 1915. They were withdrawn in 1934 but the Americans continued to control the republic's revenue until October 1947. The reformist government of President Estime from 1946 to 1950 was followed by a series of corrupt and largely military administrations. In September 1957 Dr François Duvalier was elected President, creating a system of personal rule dependent upon a mixture of voodoo magic and brutal repression by strong-arm agents. A new constitution in 1964 allowed him to be elected President for life and to nominate his successor. Dr Duvalier – 'Papa Doc' – died on 21 April 1971 and was succeeded on the same day by his twenty-year-old son, Jean-Claude Duvalier ('Baby Doc'), who was forced into exile in February 1986. The CNG, a council of army officers, perpetuated the corrupt system of government under four successive generals in the following three years. The promise of a democratic election provoked armed intervention; voters were killed at polling stations on election day itself (20 November 1987). Brutal repression during the presidency of General Henri Namphy culminated in the slaughter of worshippers in a church at Port-au-Prince on 11 September 1988. Presidential elections in December 1990 were won by a priest, Jean-Bertrand Aristide (1953–), to whom the Catholic hierarchy was unsympathetic. Aristide took office on 7 February 1991, at the head of a 'National Front for Change and Democracy' government, but within six months his anti-corruption campaign provoked a military *coup* and he took refuge in the USA. Despite trade sanctions and financial pressure, the junta remained in power. So brutal was the regime that in July 1994 the UN Security Council authorized the use of force to restore Haiti's elected Head of State. Under a threat of imminent American invasion the junta stepped down and Aristide returned on 15 October 1994. US troops policed Haiti, the last soldiers not leaving until April 1996. Aristide instituted some basic reforms during the remaining fifteen months of his term. He was succeeded in February 1996 by a close colleague, René Preval. Failure to carry out basic reforms made foreign investors reluctant to ease Haiti's chronic economic problems.

Haldane, Richard Burdon (1856–1928, created a viscount 1912), British statesman. Born and educated at Edinburgh, going to Göttingen University and specializing in German philosophy. He was a Liberal MP, 1885–1911, serving as War Minister 1905–12, and Lord Chancellor 1912–15 and again, in the first Labour Government, in 1924. At the War Office he was the first effective reformer in thirty years: he created the General Staff (1906), the Territorial Army (1907) and the Officers' Training Corps. While cutting military expenditure he made mobilization quicker and provided for the continental Expeditionary Force of six infantry and six cavalry divisions (with auxiliaries). Early in 1912 he went on a 'mission' to Berlin which, it was hoped, would halt the naval armaments race, but without success. In 1915 he was unjustly attacked by the sensationalist Press because of his knowledge of Germany and German affairs and was forced out of public life. He was never a popular personality, tending to obscure practical politics by his metaphysical erudition, but Field-Marshal Haig commended him as 'the greatest Secretary of State for War England has ever had'.

Halifax, Lord (1881–1959, Edward Wood, created Baron Irwin 1925, became third Viscount Halifax 1934, created Earl of Halifax 1944), British statesman.

Educated Eton and Christ Church, Conservative MP for Ripon 1910–25; entered Bonar Law's cabinet as President of the Board of Education in October 1922 and was Minister for Agriculture for a year under Baldwin before being appointed Viceroy of India in 1926. His five years in India were marked by growing tension with ➤Congress although he succeeded in reaching an agreement with Gandhi (March 1931). After three more years in charge of education and a few months as War Minister, Halifax was appointed Lord Privy Seal (November 1935), with special responsibilities in foreign affairs. In November 1937 he visited Hitler, seeking to assess his intentions for Neville Chamberlain, and was duly appointed to succeed ➤Eden as Foreign Secretary in February 1938. Although associated with Munich and 'appeasement', Halifax helped induce Chamberlain to take a stronger line with the Germans after March 1939. In May 1940 Halifax was considered by both King George VI and Chamberlain as a candidate for the premiership but he rejected the proposal, continuing to serve at the Foreign Office for seven months under Churchill. In January 1941 he was sent to Washington as ambassador, a post he held for ten years, achieving considerable success. He was Chancellor of Oxford University from 1933 to 1959.

Hammarskjöld, Dag (1905–61), second Secretary-General of the United Nations. Born at Jönköping, Sweden, and was Economics Professor at Stockholm University (1933–6), subsequently entering the Swedish Government service, becoming a deputy Foreign Minister in 1951. He succeeded Trygve ➤Lie as UN Secretary-General in April 1953 and was re-elected in 1957. The dignity and impartiality with which he conducted UN affairs, especially during the ➤Suez crisis, enhanced the standing of the UN itself. In 1960 his conduct of the ➤Congo crisis provoked hostility from the Soviet Union, including a personal verbal assault from Khrushchev who sought curtailment of the Secretary-General's authority. In seeking peace in the Congo, Hammarskjöld was killed when his plane crashed near Ndola on the borders of Zambia (northern Rhodesia) and Katanga. He was awarded the 1961 Nobel Peace Prize posthumously.

Hardie, James Keir (1856–1915), British socialist. Born near Holytown, Lanarkshire, worked in a coal-mine from the age of ten. From temperance societies, where he learned public speaking, he moved into trade unionism, first in Lanarkshire and later in Ayrshire. He established the Scottish Parliamentary Labour Party in 1888 and was elected independent socialist MP for West Ham South, in 1892, although he lost the seat in 1895. In 1893 he founded the ➤Independent Labour Party and was returned as MP for Merthyr Tydfil, 1900–1915. He played a leading part in setting up the Labour Representation Committee in 1900, becoming chairman of the parliamentary Labour Party in 1906. He opposed unconditional Labour support for the Liberal policy on trade unions. With his resolute insistence on independence from the major parties he was able to shape the political history of the British Labour movement more than any other person. He was a fervent nonconformist and pacifist, the most loved and respected figure among the Labour pioneers.

Harding, Warren Gamaliel (1865–1923), twenty-ninth President of the USA. Born in Morrow County, Ohio, studied law, became a newspaper-owner in Ohio and an orthodox Republican Senator (1900–1904 and 1915–21), fundamentally isolationist. His pledge for a 'return to normalcy' won him a landslide victory in the Presidential election of 1920, even though he was little known nationally. His administration was notable for the ▶Washington Conference, for continued rejection of the ▶League of Nations and for a high degree of political corruption among many of the President's personal friends, self-seekers known as the 'Ohio Gang'. Although Harding was not officially involved in the notorious ▶Teapot Dome scandal, the strain of humiliating revelations weakened his health and he died suddenly in August 1923, the Presidency passing to Vice-President ▶Coolidge.

Harriman, (William) Averell (1891–1986), US diplomat. Born in New York, the son of the railway and steamship magnate Edward H. Harriman (1848–1909), whose business interests he took over as a young man. Since Averell Harriman was a friend of Franklin Roosevelt, the President looked to him for advice under the 'national recovery' programme of 1934, and he was chairman of the Business Advisory Council. He was sent by Roosevelt to London in 1940 and again in 1941 to supervise ▶Lend-Lease administration. His calm and business-like skill as a diplomat led Roosevelt to send him to Moscow as ambassador in 1943 and he attended all the major international conferences of the Second World War. From 1946 to 1948 he was Secretary of Commerce in the Truman Administration and was Governor of New York State in 1954–8. From 1961 to 1965 he held high office in the State Department, with special responsibility for Far Eastern affairs, and in 1968 was nominated by President Johnson as US representative at the peace talks in Paris with the North Vietnamese. Harriman's long spell as 'ambassador-at-large' for the Democrat Administrations anticipated the more-publicized missions of ▶Kissinger under the Republicans.

Heath, Edward Richard George (1916–), British Prime Minister. Born at Broadstairs and educated at Chatham House School and Balliol College, Oxford. As an undergraduate he became President of the Oxford Union, attracting some attention as a reforming Conservative who opposed appeasement and was hostile to Franco (having visited republican Spain). From 1940 to 1946 he held a commission in the artillery, continuing with the territorials as a lieutenant-colonel until 1951. He was briefly a civil servant and news editor of the *Church Times* before being elected MP for Bexley in 1950, a seat he held until 1974 when he moved to the neighbouring Sidcup constituency. From February 1951 until 1960 he was involved in parliamentary management and was Conservative Chief Whip, 1955–9, with the difficult task of preserving party unity after Suez. His maiden speech in the Commons (June 1950) was a plea for European unity and, as Lord Privy Seal, he was given the task of seeking entry into the 'Common Market' (1961–3). These negotiations failed because of French obstruction but they made Heath's reputation. After a year with Trade and Industry under Douglas-Home (1963–4), he went into opposition and in the Conservatives' first democratic election of a leader (22 July 1965) defeated his rivals, Reginald Maudling and Enoch Powell. Heath formed a government when the Conservatives won the election of June 1970, the first bachelor Prime Minister since Balfour in 1902. He successfully reopened negotiations for British membership of the ➤European Community but was soon in difficulties with the trade unions, which deplored his Industrial Relations Act. His plans for limited naval collaboration with South Africa provoked hostile reaction at the ➤Commonwealth Prime Ministers Conference in Singapore. Ultimately he refused to amend his incomes policy to accommodate wage demands from the coal-miners. In January 1974 the miners' militant tactics forced Heath to put industry on a three-day week. Heath sought an appeal to public opinion by calling a general election in February, but failed to gain a majority, and resigned. On 11 February 1975 he was defeated in an election for the Conservative Party leadership by Mrs Margaret ➤Thatcher. He remained in the Commons, supported by his constituents in the elections of 1979, 1983, 1987, 1992 and 1997, even though he was critical of Thatcherism and of the Euroscepticism of many Conservatives. During the Gulf Crisis of 1990 he travelled to Baghdad and secured the release of sixty-nine ➤hostages. In 1992 he was made a Knight of the Garter.

Heligoland. A small isolated island in the North Sea, forty miles from Cuxhaven. The island was British from 1810 to 1890 when it was ceded to Germany in return for African colonial concessions (Zanzibar and Pemba). The Germans fortified Heligoland, establishing a naval base there at the turn of the century and therefore giving the island great strategic importance in the First World War. Although technically demilitarized under the terms of the Treaty of Versailles, the naval base was speedily restored in 1936, becoming a frequent target for RAF bombers in the subsequent war. The island, evacuated in 1946, was used for bombing practice until March 1952 when it was resettled and reconstructed by the German federal authorities.

Helsinki Conference (1975). From 30 July to 1 August 1975 a European Security Conference was held in the Finnish capital, attended by political leaders from thirty-five nations. The Conference was the final stage of negotiations aimed at reducing international tension which had begun at Helsinki in July 1973 and continued intermittently at Geneva, from September 1973 to 21 July 1975. The 'Final Act' of the Conference comprised three main agreements; methods to prevent accidental confrontations between the opposing power blocs; proposals for economic and technological collaboration; and an understanding on closer contacts between peoples of different nations, together with a reaffirmation of respect for human rights. A specific agreement was also concluded on Mediterranean problems. It was agreed that there would be 'follow-up conferences', reviewing new security problems and seeking to clarify older misunderstandings. The first 'follow-up' took place in Belgrade (October 1977 to March 1978) and revealed deep misgivings over opposing concepts of human rights.

Helsinki Human Rights Group. In May 1976 a number of Soviet dissidents, the majority of them Jewish, announced the formation of a 'Public Group' to seek fulfilment of the provisions for human rights set out in the Final Act of the ➤Helsinki Conference. Among members of the Group were writers, engineers, artists and the eminent Soviet physicist, Andrei Sakharov. Subsequently the Group sought to monitor instances of human rights being denied within the Soviet Union, protesting especially at prison conditions and at restrictions on movement. The founder of the Group, Dr Yuri Orlov, was charged with anti-Soviet agitation and in May 1978 sentenced to seven years' imprisonment. Two other founder-members, Alexander Ginsburg and Anatoly Shcharansky, were put on trial two months later; Ginsburg was sentenced to eight years in a labour camp, and Shcharansky (accused of treason) to thirteen years in prison and labour camps. Heavy sentences were also imposed on Roman Catholic members of the Helsinki Group in Lithuania and the Ukraine. This new wave of repression aroused strong protests outside the Soviet Union.

Hertzog, James Barry Munnik (1866–1942), Boer general and South African Prime Minister. Born in Wellington, Cape Colony, and became a farmer in the Orange Free State. Twice in 1900 he commanded Boer columns seeking to penetrate into Cape Colony. Subsequently he opposed Botha and ➤Smuts when they favoured reconciliation although he served as Minister of Justice in Botha's first Union of South Africa Government, 1910–12. In 1913 he founded the National Party and opposed South African participation in the First World War. His party, which believed in racial segregation, gained successes in the 1924 election and he became Prime Minister, governing for five years in coalition with the South African Labour Party and from 1933 to 1939 sharing power with the United Party of Smuts. He was not prepared to accept the republican beliefs of his colleague, ➤Malan, nor did he favour the rigid ➤apartheid of the later National Party leaders, but he was a strong advocate of South African isolationism. His reluctance to enter the Second World War led to his downfall, and in 1940 he retired from politics.

Hess, Rudolf (1894–1987), former deputy leader of the German Nazi Party. Born in Egypt, at Alexandria, educated at Bad Godesberg, enlisted in a Bavarian infantry regiment and fought at Ypres before transferring to the air corps as a pilot, enrolled at Munich University and met Hitler at a meeting of a society devoted to the study of Nordic myths. In 1920 he became Hitler's political secretary, participating in the abortive ➤Munich putsch and sharing Hitler's imprisonment at Landsberg, taking down *Mein Kampf* at his leader's dictation. He remained a close confidant of Hitler throughout the 1930s and was nominated deputy party leader (1934) and second in succession (behind ➤Goering) to Hitler as head of state in 1939. On 10

May 1941, apparently on his own initiative he flew his Messerschmitt 110 from Augsburg to Scotland in the hope of securing a negotiated peace with a British government (which, he stipulated on arrival, should not include Churchill). He was interned until 1945 when he was brought to Nuremberg as a major war criminal and sentenced to life imprisonment. From 1966 onwards he remained the sole prisoner in the four-power-controlled Spandau Gaol, Berlin, the Russians consistently refusing proposals from the British, French and Americans that he should be released. On 17 August 1987 it was announced that Hess had committed suicide in Spandau.

Hijacking. The crime of forcing the pilot of an aeroplane to fly to an unscheduled destination first acquired political significance in July 1968 when Palestinian terrorists seized an Israeli airliner and forced it to fly to Algiers. On 6 September 1970 four aircraft were hijacked by extremist guerrillas of the ➤PLO, operating from Jordan. The problem of terrorist hijacking and the taking of ➤hostages remained acute between 1970 and 1989, and on two occasions – at ➤Entebbe and ➤Mogadishu – provoked vigorous countermeasures by anti-terrorist commandos although sixty people were killed when, in November 1985, Egyptian commandos stormed a hijacked airliner at Malta. A month previously the Italian cruise liner, *Achille Lauro*, was hijacked by four Palestinians who boarded the ship in Genoa. After killing an American Jewish passenger, the Palestinians surrendered to the Egyptian authorities, whom the US Government accused of treating the hijackers lightly.

Himmler, Heinrich (1900–1945), German Nazi police chief. Born in Munich, the son of a Roman Catholic schoolmaster, served in the army in 1918, became a poultry farmer in Bavaria, associating with the Nazis from 1923 onwards. Hitler selected him in 1929 to build up his personal bodyguard of SS (Schutz Staffeln, stormtroopers). In April 1934 he was given command of the Prussian secret police (Gestapo), becoming commander of the unified political police forces in 1936 and gradually building up his power within Greater Germany until he became Minister of the Interior in 1943. Although personally shocked by the sight of executions, he was responsible for ordering systematic genocide in the concentration camps. He was arrested in hiding by British troops on 25 May 1945, committing suicide two days later.

Hindenburg, Paul von Beneckendorf und von (1847–1934), German field-marshal and President. Born in Posen (Poznan), entered the Prussian Cadet Corps in 1858, commissioned in a guards regiment in 1866, decorated for bravery both in the Seven Weeks War against Austria and in the Franco-Prussian War, represented his regiment at proclamation of German Empire, January 1871. He retired from active service in 1911 as general commanding the Fourth Army Corps but was recalled to command the Eighth Army in East Prussia on 22 August 1914, gaining a decisive victory over the Russians at ➤Tannenberg before the end of the month and a second victory at the Masurian Lakes, 6–15 September 1914. He became the military idol of Germany and was created field-marshal, securing command of the whole Eastern Front early in November 1914 although unable to deliver the final blow which would have knocked Russia out of the war. In August 1916 he became Chief of the Greater German General Staff, with his brilliant aide ►Ludendorff as First Quartermaster-General and his deputy. These two men, in effect, controlled German military and civil policy from July 1917 until the autumn of 1918. Together they were responsible for the harsh terms imposed on Russia at ►Brest-Litovsk and for mounting the final offensive on the Western Front in March 1918 which led to the second battle of the ►Marne. Foch's counter-offensive and the collapse of the Bulgarian, Austrian and Turkish fronts led Hindenburg to seek an armistice in October 1918. On 9 November 1918 Hindenburg advised Kaiser ►William II to abdicate and seek refuge in Holland. Hindenburg remained in command of the German Army until July 1919, when he retired once more. Although a monarchist at heart Hindenburg was induced by nationalist politicians to stand for the Presidency of the German Republic in April 1925. He won the election, although not convincingly, and was re-elected in 1931. Personally Hindenburg had little influence on policy during his Presidency, showing increasing signs of senility. Although at first contemptuous of Hitler, he appointed him Chancellor in January 1933 on the assurance of politicians whom he trusted, notably Papen. Hindenburg died on his estate at Neudeck on 2 August 1934 and was buried at Tannenberg.

Hirohito (1901–89), 124th Emperor of Japan. Prince Hirohito, the son of the Emperor Yoshihito (1879–1926), was the first member of the Japanese imperial family permitted to travel abroad, visiting Europe and the United States, March-August 1921. Three months after his return, the illness of his father led to his appointment as Prince Regent. He survived an assassination plot in December 1924 and succeeded to the imperial throne two years later. By temperament he was a moderate, by inclination a marine biologist, by tradition a Divine Ruler whose will was sacrosanct. The early years of his reign were marked by military aggression in Manchuria and China, association with Germany and Italy in the Anti-Comintern Pact, and territorial expansion in Greater Asia. In 1941 he accepted the demands of General ►Tojo for war against the United States and Britain but in the crisis of 1945 he came down firmly on the side of peace, commanding acceptance of the allied demand for unconditional surrender on 15 August. Chinese, Australian and New Zealand requests that he should be tried as a war criminal were refused by General ►MacArthur, the Supreme Commander in occupied Japan, who saw in the Emperor a pledge against radical revolution. Hirohito (who, by broadcasting on 16 August 1945, was the first Japanese ruler to address his subjects) abandoned his mystic authority and became a democratic and constitutional monarch, eventually paying state visits to a number of countries, including Britain, in 1971. On this occasion he had the curious distinction of becoming the first prince twice honoured with a knighthood of the Garter, having been deprived during the Second World War of the knighthood conferred originally by King George V. He fell gravely ill in September 1988; for the last four months of his reign the sovereign powers were exercised by Crown Prince Akihito (1933–) who acceded on 7 January 1989.

Hiroshima, Japanese city devastated by the first ►atomic bomb, dropped on 6 August 1945.

Hiss, Alger (1904–93). US diplomat. Born in Baltimore, entered the State Department in 1936, served as adviser at several international conferences, notably Yalta, before resigning from the US foreign service in 1947 to become president of the Carnegie Endowment for International Peace. He was then accused by a confessed Communist Party member, Whittaker Chambers, of having handed over to him 200 secret state documents. In August 1948 Hiss became the best-known victim of ►McCarthyism when he denied before the Un-American Activities Committee that he was himself a communist, associated with Chambers. Hiss was later charged with perjury and, after two trials in 1949 and 1950, sent to prison for five years. One of the principal prosecutors of Hiss was the future President, Richard ►Nixon; Governor Adlai Stevenson and the future Republican Secretary of State, Dulles, testified to Hiss's high character.

Hitler, Adolf (1889–1945). Born at Braunau-on-the-Inn, Upper Austria, educated at Linz and lived in Vienna, 1909–13, absorbing anti-Semitic prejudices, working as a casual labourer and third-rate commercial artist. In 1914 he crossed the frontier and enlisted in a Bavarian infantry regiment, fighting at Ypres, on the Somme and at Arras, receiving the Iron Cross (second class) in December 1914 and again (first class) in August 1918, ending the war as a corporal, temporarily blinded from a British gas attack in Flanders. In September 1919 he joined a small political group in Munich which shortly took the name 'National Socialist German Workers' Party' (NSDAP, derisively nicknamed ►'Nazi'). He discovered his demagogic gifts in open-air tirades against Jews and the Treaty of Versailles. In 1923 his abortive ►Munich putsch won him national fame and thirteen months' imprisonment, during which he wrote *Mein Kampf*. The world slump made him a prominent figure, enabling the Nazis to become the second largest party in Germany by September 1930. Disillusionment with existing parties, rising unemployment, superior propaganda techniques, the backing of leading industrialists afraid of communism and the provision of a scapegoat in the 'treacherous Jew' – all favoured the rapid growth of the Nazis. After the failure of three successive Chancellors President Hindenburg appointed Hitler head of the government on 30 January 1933, believing the non-Nazi Deputy Chancellor, Papen, would curb excesses. Four weeks later, the ►Reichstag Fire provided Hitler with the opportunity to establish a one-party system, and on 30 June 1934 he eliminated possible rivals in the ►'Night of the Long Knives', liquidating the SA (Sturm Abteilungen) group of Ernst Roehm and the supporters of Gregor Strasser. When Hindenburg died on 2 August 1934 Hitler was proclaimed 'Führer of the German Reich', to whom all officers had to take an oath of loyalty as head of state and supreme commander. From 1934 to 1937 he concentrated on rearmament at home, securing the military reoccupation of the Rhineland (March 1936) and achieving success in foreign policy by playing off potential enemies against each other. The ►Axis of 1936 gained him an ally in Mussolini. His expansionist policy began with the absorption of Austria in the ►Anschluss of March 1938, and continued with the occupation of Czechoslovakia in October 1938 and March 1939. The ►Nazi–Soviet Pact secured his eastern front and allowed him to overrun Poland, an action that led to the outbreak of the Second World War, which he considered he had won in the West when his troops occupied Paris (22 June 1940). In 1941 he moved the German army eastwards but in attacking the Soviet Union he encountered heavy opposition, personally assuming command in the field, 19 December 1941. A series of failures after ►Stalingrad culminating in the successful ►Normandy landings undermined the army's confidence in his leadership and led to the attempted assassination on 20 July 1944 (►July Conspiracy). At the end of the war Hitler was cornered in the ruins of Berlin where, as the Russians approached, he married his companion, Eva Braun, and entered into a suicide pact with her, shooting himself on 30 April 1945.

Ho Chi Minh (1890–1969), Vietnamese communist revolutionary. Born in the village of Kiemlien, central Annam, under the name of Nguyen Tat Thanh, became a primary schoolteacher (1907), a ship's steward (1912) and worked in the kitchens of the Carlton Hotel, London, during the First World War. In 1918 he settled in Paris and abortively sought to interest the American delegation to the Peace Conference in the cause of the Indo-Chinese peoples. He wrote articles for socialist newspapers under the name of Nguyen Ai Quoc (Nguyen the Patriot) and was a founder-member of the French Communist Party. From 1922 to 1925 he was in Moscow, subsequently accompanying the first Bolshevik advisers to China. In 1930 he was in Hong Kong and was arrested for sedition in 1931, his case arousing so much interest that it was taken by Stafford ►Cripps to the Privy Council, who ordered his release. The British refused to hand him over to the French colonial authorities who already regarded him as a dangerous revolutionary. In 1940 he tried to organize an uprising in Hanoi and Saigon but was forced to flee to south China, establishing among his fellow exiles the 'Viet-Minh' movement. On Chiang Kai-shek's orders he was kept in prison for much of 1941–2, but returned secretly to northern Indo-China in 1943 to encourage resistance to the Japanese. At this time he assumed the alias Ho Chi Minh ('Ho, the Seeker of Light'). On the defeat of Japan Ho declared a Democratic Republic of Vietnam (2 September 1945), but the French returned to southern Vietnam and Ho refused to accept the limited concessions offered by Paris. In consequence the Viet-Minh were forced to fight an anti-colonial war of independence from 1946 to 1954, culminating in the victory of General ►Giap at ►Dien Bien Phu. The Geneva Agreements of 1954 tacitly recognized Ho's Presidency of north Vietnam, but he claimed authority over the whole state, and encouraged the Viet-Cong resistance movement in south Vietnam from 1963 onwards, sending supplies down the hidden jungle road known as the 'Ho Chi Minh Trail'. When US troops intervened in the spring of 1965 Ho Chi Minh sent units of his regular army to support the Viet-Cong rebels, and was involved in military operations for the remainder of his life. At home he was able to initiate drastic land reforms and was re-elected President in 1960, while his Five-Year Plan (1961–5) increased the heavy industrial output of the north, despite American bombing. He was idolized by his people, who saw in him the Indo-Chinese equivalent of Mao Tse-tung (a leader to whose ideas and personality he was not always sympathetic). When Saigon fell to the Communists in April 1975 it was renamed Ho Chi Minh City in his honour.

Holland. ➤Netherlands.

Holocaust. The name widely used to describe the systematic attempt to annihilate the Jewish communities that fell under Nazi control before and during the Second World War by the re-establishment of ghettos, the expulsions from towns and villages and the establishment of ➤concentration camps, some of which were used for mass execution and others for slave labour. It has been calculated that at least six million Jews perished in this protracted act of genocide, euphemistically called *Endlösung* ('final solution') by the Nazis themselves. The word 'holocaust' was first publicly applied to the Nazi policy of extermination by the Liberal statesman Viscount Samuel (1870–1963), speaking in the House of Lords on 23 March 1943.

Holyoake, Keith (1904–83, knighted 1972), New Zealand Prime Minister. Born at Pahiatua on the north-eastern slopes of the Tararua Range, became a farmer and was elected to parliament as a Nationalist Party member in 1932. He was Deputy Prime Minister and Minister of Agriculture 1949–57, taking over as Prime Minister for four months in 1957 when his predecessor, Sir Sidney Holland (1893–1961), was taken ill, but losing the election of December 1957 to Labour and becoming leader of the Opposition. He won the 1960 election and remained Prime Minister until February 1972. His most important contribution to political life was as a Commonwealth statesman, firmly committed to multiracialism: he was strongly opposed to apartheid in South Africa and to the Smith regime in ➤Rhodesia. At the same time he accepted the need for close links with the USA and sent troops to Vietnam. The most bitter blow to him, as a farmer, was British desire for membership of the Common Market for he feared tariffs against New Zealand dairy produce and frozen-meat exports. His moderate and even-tempered advice won recognition by the European Community of New Zealand's difficulties, even though he could not gain substantial concessions. He was largely responsible for the development of the special Trade relationship with Australia (NAFTA).

Home, Lord. ➤Douglas-Home, Sir Alec.

Home Rule. The Home Rule Association, a movement favouring the establishment in Dublin of a parliament responsible for internal affairs, was founded in 1870 by Isaac Butt (1813–79). Under the leadership of Butt's successor, Parnell (1846–91), it succeeded in concentrating parliamentary attention on Irish grievances and induced the Liberals under Gladstone to introduce Home Rule Bills in 1886 and 1893. The first of these Bills was defeated in the Commons; the second in the Lords. Once the power of the Lords had been limited by the Parliament Act of 1911, the Liberals (under ►Asquith) introduced a third Home Rule Bill (1912). This aroused opposition in Protestant Ulster, which feared dominance by the Roman Catholic majority in Ireland: and when the Bill had its third reading in May 1914 it seemed as if Home Rule was bringing Ireland into civil war. The Home Rule proposals were shelved because of the First World War. After the war the situation changed. Northern Ireland gained Home Rule with a parliament at Stormont, Belfast, opened in June 1921, but southern Ireland wanted more and, by an agreement signed in December 1921, was conceded the status of a dominion, enjoying control over foreign affairs and representation in the League of Nations as well as the Irish parliament demanded by Butt and Parnell.

Honecker, Erich (1912–94), head of state, German Democratic Republic (DDR). Born at Neunkirchen in the Saar, where he joined the German Communist Party in 1929, organizing the youth movement in the early 1930s while working as a tiler and slater. He was imprisoned in 1937 by the Nazis and only released by the arrival of the Russians in 1945. After building up the East German Youth Movement 1949–58, he was promoted to the central committee of the ruling Socialist Unity Party becoming principal deputy for ►Ulbricht whom he succeeded as First Secretary in May 1971 and as head of state in October 1976. Unlike Ulbricht, Honecker was never a rigid Stalinist. He maintained close links with his Comecon partners but also improved relations with the West; he succeeded in lifting East Germany's industrial output and standard of living by reaching targets which he imposed in successive 'five year plans'. At a meeting with the Federal Chancellor, Helmut Kohl, in September 1987, the two leaders gave a joint pledge that 'war must never start again on German soil'. Despite failing health and violent demonstrations in Leipzig in favour of democratic reform, Honecker celebrated the fortieth anniversary of the DDR in early October 1989, but he resigned a few days later. When the DDR subsequently rejected communism, he found refuge in a hospital in the Soviet Union, but was extradited to Germany in July 1992 and put on trial for the manslaughter of thirteen escapees from the DDR. The trial was abandoned because of the gravity of Honecker's liver cancer. He was allowed to spend his last year of life with his wife and daughter in Chile.

Hong Kong (Xianggang). From 1841 to 1997 a British colony or dependent territory on the Pearl River estuary, eighty miles south-east of Guangzhou (formerly Canton), with which it was linked from 1912 by railway from Kowloon through the 'New Territories', leased by Britain from China in 1898. By 1940 Hong Kong had a population of 1.6 million, it was ranked third among commercial ports in the British Empire and served as the financial centre for British investment in the Far East. The colony was attacked by the Japanese on 8 December 1941 and forced to surrender on Christmas Day. The Royal Navy returned to Hong Kong on 30 August 1945 and British colonial administration was resumed a fortnight later. An influx of refugees from communist China made the population leap to 2 million by 1950 and over 5.3 million by September 1982, when talks began between the British and Chinese governments on the colony's future. A joint declaration, signed in the Chinese capital on 19 December 1984, provided for transfer of sovereignty on 1 July 1997, with the ex-colony becoming a 'Special Administrative Region' (SAR) within China, its social and economic system to be left unchanged for fifty years. From 1985 a Joint Liaison Group discussed arrangements for the transfer but ran into difficulties when, in 1992, the last colonial Governor, Christopher Patten (1944–), introduced constitutional reforms which made elections to the Legislative Council fully democratic. The first of these elections was held in September 1994. In December 1996 a nominated panel of local residents authorized the appointment of Tung Chee-hwa as Chief Executive-designate of the SAR. The (Chinese selected) legislature announced laws restricting political demonstrations a fortnight before the formal handover. British and American representatives boycotted the inauguration of the nominated SAR legislature on 1 July 1997, but the foreign ministers of Australia, New Zealand and Japan were present.

Hoover, Herbert (1874–1964), thirty-first President of the USA. Born of Quaker parentage in West Branch, Iowa, studied geology and engineering at Stanford University and became a mining engineer in Nevada, Australia and China, accumulating a considerable private fortune. During and after the First World War he directed relief work in Belgium, central Europe and Russia. He was Secretary of Commerce under Harding and Coolidge (1921–8), receiving the Republican nomination for the Presidency in 1928 and defeating the Roman Catholic Democrat, Al Smith. Within a few months of taking office Hoover's administration experienced a financial depression (▶Wall Street Crash) which many critics thought to be a consequence of unrestrained speculation during Hoover's years as Commerce Secretary. Hoover believed natural economic forces would bring about a revival of trade and, as President, he was reluctant to extend federal responsibilities. When the Depression spread to Europe he accepted a one-year moratorium on intergovernmental debts, a measure which relieved the reparations burden on Germany. He was decisively defeated by Franklin Roosevelt in the 1932 Presidential election. From 1947 to 1949 and from 1953 to 1955 he was chairman of two commissions to examine the functioning of the executive branch of government in the USA.

Hopkins, Harry Lloyd (1890–1946), American administrator and Presidential adviser. Born in Sioux City, Iowa, became a close friend of Franklin D. Roosevelt and was entrusted with administering federal relief in 1933–4. He was administrator of the Works Progress Administration in the ►New Deal from 1935 to 1938 when he became Secretary of Commerce. He was personal emissary for the President on wartime missions to London and Washington, despite increasingly poor health, and was present as adviser at the conferences of ►Casablanca, ►Cairo, ►Teheran and ►Yalta. His friendship with Churchill helped forge the close Anglo-American understanding of the war years.

Horthy de Nagybanya, Miklós (1868–1957), Austro-Hungarian admiral and Regent of Hungary. Born into a Protestant landed gentry family at Kenderes and trained for the navy. He was aide-de-camp to Francis Joseph, 1911–13, and served throughout the First World War in the Adriatic, distinguishing himself in action off Otranto in 1917 and becoming last commander-in-chief of the 'Imperial and Royal' fleet. On returning to Hungary he was largely responsible for organizing at Szeged the counter-revolution to the communist Béla ►Kun and entered Budapest triumphantly in November 1919. In March 1920 he became Regent of Hungary, an office he held for twenty-four years, refusing to surrender his powers to King ►Charles who twice returned to claim the crown in 1921. Horthy believed in maintaining the established social order at home while seeking revision of the Treaty of ►Trianon in foreign affairs. Although he recovered parts of Czechoslovakia and Romania in 1938–40 (►Felvidék and ►Vienna Awards) by grace of Germany, he was constantly on bad terms with Hitler. He helped dismember Yugoslavia in 1941 and, after the ►Kassa Incident, declared war on the USSR, but he maintained links with the western allies and on 15 October 1944 unsuccessfully sought a separate peace, being subsequently arrested and imprisoned by the Nazis. After the war his American liberators refused to hand him over to the Yugoslavs as a 'war criminal' and he went into exile in Portugal, where he died in February 1957.

Hostages. The ancient practice of the holding of an individual by an enemy as a pledge was revived in the twentieth century, originally to intimidate resistance movements in occupied territories in both world wars, and from 1970 onwards as a means of extracting political concessions. At first hostage taking was an aspect of ►hijacking, but it was used on a large scale by Iran when, on 4 November 1979, followers of Ayatollah ►Khomeini occupied the US embassy in Teheran and held sixty-six Americans hostage, because of an alleged attempt by President Carter's Administration to restore the exiled Shah, Reza ►Pahlavi. Despite economic pressure and an abortive rescue bid by helicopter in April 1980, the hostages were only released (through Algerian mediation) on 20 January 1980, the day Carter left office. The Archbishop of Canterbury's Assistant for Anglican Communion Affairs, Terry Waite (1939–), secured the release of three Anglican missionaries held in Iran in 1981 and, after a personal meeting with ►Gaddafi, negotiated the freedom of four British citizens held in Libya. He also won freedom for two churchmen in Beirut in 1985–6, but when he sought the release of further hostages in Lebanon by the Islamic Jihad he was taken prisoner on 20 January 1987 and held with them, partly because he was thought by his captors to be linked to a secret American project for supplying arms to Iran in return for the freeing of US hostages; Waite was not released until 18 November 1991. In Iraq, Saddam ➤Hussein held European and American hostages for four months during the Gulf Crisis of 1990, arrangements for their release being completed by a visit to Baghdad by Edward ➤Heath. Outside the Middle East hostages have been taken and used for political bargaining in Cambodia, Kashmir, Timor and ➤Chechnya.

Houphouët-Boigny, Félix (1905–93). President of the Ivory Coast Republic. Born in Yamoussoukro, the son of a chief in the French colony of the ➤Ivory Coast, studied medicine in Paris but returned to West Africa to supervise the family cocoa plantation, 1940–45, forming the first union of West African Negro farmers and entering politics as a member of the French National Assembly in Paris from 1946 to 1958. Boigny became the outstanding representative of French decolonization in equatorial Africa, believing in partnership with the former imperial power, and preaching personal and national self-discipline, as opposed to the extremism of some African leaders. In 1958 he was the first West African to hold ministerial office in Paris, resigning in order to lead the Ivory Coast into autonomy within the French Community. Full independence followed in August 1970, with Boigny elected President under a system of government modelled on the Fifth French Republic. Boigny greatly admired the political doctrines of de Gaulle and kept close commercial and cultural links with France. He was re-elected President on five occasions, but aroused criticism in later years by spending extravagantly on a palace and cathedral in the new political capital, Yamoussoukro.

Hoxha, Enver (1908–85), Albanian communist leader. Born at Gjirokaster (Argyrokastron), near the Greek border, studied in France in the early 1930s, joining the French Communist Party. He returned to Albania in 1936 and in 1941 took to the mountains, building up an Albanian communist movement ('Workers' Party') of which he became First Secretary, a post he never relinquished. He led the National Liberation Army in 1943–4, modelling his movement on the Yugoslav partisans, occupying all the main Albanian towns in October and November 1944 when the Germans began to pull out of the Balkans. He headed the Provisional Government of the Albanian Republic and established a dictatorship of strictly Stalinist principles. He refused to seek capitalist loans for ➤Albania, denounced the revisionism of Khrushchev at a Moscow communist congress in 1960 and was no less hostile to China's reconciliation (after 1968) with America and the West. From 1948 onwards Hoxha suffered from diabetes, the disease from which he died (11 April 1985). His chief deputy, Remiz Alia, succeeded him.

Hua Kuo-feng (Hua Guofeng, 1912–89). Chinese Prime Minister. Born in Human province, fought in the Communist Eighth Route Army under Chu Te (Zhu De), appointed Deputy Governor of Hunan in 1950, concentrating on increasing agricultural production in the province. He was criticized during the

➤'cultural revolution' but emerged unscathed and was elected to the Central Committee of the party in 1969, becoming a member of the ruling politburo in 1973 and deputy premier in 1975. Although little known outside China he was appointed successor to Chou En-lai (Zhou Enlai) as Prime Minister in February 1976. When Mao died seven months later Hua Kuo-feng won the ensuing struggle for control of the party, and he was recognized as Chairman of the Central Committee on 8 October 1976. Almost immediately he took action against the so-called ➤'Gang of Four', thus effectively countering the influence of the radicals, led by Mao's widow. In August 1978 Hua visited Romania, Yugoslavia and Iran and in October–November 1979 he made a much-publicized tour of Western Europe, spending a week in Britain as well as visiting Federal Germany, France and Italy. In retrospect it seems as if his power within China was not as influential as his hosts overseas believed at the time. Hua was succeeded as China's Prime Minister by Zhao Ziyang on 7 September 1980 and surrendered the chairmanship of the Party to Hu Yaobang in June 1981.

Huai–Hai, Battle of (November 1948 to January 1949). Decisive engagement of the Chinese Civil War. The battle takes its name from the two principal defensive positions of the Nationalists, the Huai river and the Lung Hai railway. Communist forces from Shensi and Honan in central China supported by a massive communist army coming down from the north successfully enveloped the Nationalists whose commander, General Tu Yu-ming (Du Yuming), had been ordered to hold the key railway junction of Suchow. Static defensive tactics led to the isolation of successive units of his army, Suchow itself falling on 1 December. The Chinese communist victory destroyed the will of the Nationalists to resist as well as much of their equipment and opened the traditional invasion route to Nanking and Shanghai, which fell to the communists in the following spring.

Hughes, William Morris (1864–1952), Australian Prime Minister. Born in London, educated in Llandudno, emigrated to Australia at the age of twenty, entered the state parliament of New South Wales as a Labour representative in 1894 and moved into the first Federal parliament in 1901, remaining a member all his life. He held minor office in the short-lived Labour Government of 1904, was Attorney-General in 1910 and succeeded Andrew Fisher as Prime Minister on 27 October 1915. He left the Labour Party in November 1916 but continued to head a coalition until February 1923. In 1931 he played the leading role in founding the United Australia Party, holding minor office again in 1934–5, serving as Minister for External Affairs, 1937–9, and Attorney-General, 1939–41, as well as being Minister for the Navy, 1940–41. Hughes was a controversial figure, respected and feared rather than liked. His demagogic skill and vituperative pen too often ran away with him so that he seemed a petty-minded antipodean Lloyd George, mercurially active but excessively emotional. He regarded hostility to his conscription proposals of 1916 as a personal insult and his reaction widened rather than healed the rift in the Australian ➤Labour Party. Outside Australia, and notably in London during the

First World War, he was accepted as a great imperial statesman preaching a hatred of the 'Hun' worthy of the newspapers of ►Northcliffe. He regarded the principles of Woodrow ►Wilson with suspicion, fearing that if the equality of nations was recognized in the League Covenant Australia would not be able to keep out Asian immigrants; and his attitude at the Paris Peace Conference caused particular resentment to non-white delegates, especially the Japanese. At times he seemed to favour transforming the British Empire into a closely federated white man's association: few agreed with him.

Hukbalahap Movement. Abortive left-wing movement in the ►Philippines, showing many of the characteristics of the Viet-Minh in Indo-China. The 'Huks' originated as the Anti-Japanese People's Liberation Army and carried out successful operations against the Japanese in the jungle in 1943–5. Their commander was Luis Taruc, and in the period 1946–50 the movement secured virtual control of Luzon, governing more than half a million people. The outbreak of the Korean War and the American need for bases in the Philippines led the United States to encourage the Filipinos to stamp out this left-wing revolutionary force, a task virtually achieved by the summer of 1954. The Huk failure emphasized the debt which successful communist movements on the Asian mainland owed to their interior lines of communication with Mao's China.

Hull, Cordell (1871–1955), American Secretary of State. Born at Olympus, Tennessee, sitting for six years in the state legislature before becoming a Democrat congressman from 1907 to 1921 and from 1923 to 1931. After two years as a Senator, he resigned in order to become Franklin Roosevelt's Secretary of State, an office he held until his health gave way in November 1944. During the pre-war period he concentrated on securing reciprocal trade agreements so as to reduce tariff barriers. He also improved US relations with Latin America, notably with ►Cuba and ►Haiti. From 1939 onwards he favoured as much assistance as possible to the western allies. Once America became a belligerent, he gave his mind to the problems of peace, helping to create the organization which became the United Nations. For this work he received a Nobel Peace Prize in 1945.

Hungarian National Rising (23 October to 4 November 1956). The posthumous denunciation of Stalin at the ►Twentieth Soviet Party Congress in February 1956 excited dissidents within the East European Communist Parties. In Hungary the ferment was swollen by a patriotic pride in the nation's history: left-wing intellectuals evoked the memory of Sándor Petöfi, the young poet and rebel martyr of 1849. Soviet attempts to appease the Hungarians by encouraging the hated Stalinist party leader ►Rákosi to resign (18 July) merely intensified demands for 'democratization'. A bad harvest and a fuel shortage in a wet and cold autumn led to increased unrest and demands for the withdrawal of Soviet troops. On 23 October students and workers in Budapest demonstrated, pulling down the massive statue of Stalin as a symbol of their protest. At first the Soviet authorities believed they could collaborate with a new government and a new party administration: Russian troops began to pull out of the country, and two former victims of Rákosi, Imre ➤Nagy and János ➤Kádár, were appointed respectively Prime Minister and First Secretary of the party. Nagy brought into his government former leaders of the Smallholders' Party and a courageous social democrat, Anna Kethly. He also lifted many restrictions, allowing the re-forming of the political parties of 1945 and the release of the Hungarian primate, Cardinal ➤Mindszenty, who broadcast to the nation on 31 October. Nagy announced that Hungary would withdraw from the ➤Warsaw Pact and seek a neutral status, similar to Austria and Switzerland. These changes were too rapid and drastic for the Russians or for Kádár, who left Budapest and established a new government in eastern Hungary to save the republic from 'Horthyite fascist counter-revolutionaries'. Soviet tanks supporting Kádár returned to Budapest early on 4 November and shelled insurgent centres in the city. Some 200,000 refugees escaped to the West, but there was never any likelihood of intervention from the Western Powers since the rising coincided exactly with the ➤Suez Crisis and the Anglo-French landings in Egypt. The Soviet authorities subsequently broke pledges of safe conduct and executed Nagy and other prominent figures in what was thereafter termed the 'counter-revolution'. Many reforms first mooted in 1956 were later carried through by Kádár but there was no major change in foreign relations.

Hungary. First occupied by semi-nomadic Magyars in 896. The kingdom enjoyed high respect in medieval Europe under a native dynasty before being overwhelmed by the Turks in 1526. The Austrian Habsburgs gradually began to expel the Turks at the end of the seventeenth century, incorporating Hungary in their empire. An abortive Hungarian National Revolution of 1848–9 under Kossuth created patriotic legends which remained an inspiration over a century later. In 1867 the Dual Monarchy of ➤Austria–Hungary was created. A powerful independence movement in the early years of the twentieth century triumphed briefly under ➤Károlyi in 1918, although his democratic republic was swept aside by the Soviet of Béla ➤Kun on 21 March 1919. The counter-revolution of Admiral ➤Horthy drove out the communists in November 1919 and re-established a Kingdom of Hungary, for which Horthy was Regent. Between the wars Hungarian policy was dominated by resentment of the Treaty of ➤Trianon, which reduced the kingdom to a third of its former area. Revisionist sentiment induced the Hungarians to collaborate with Nazi Germany against Czechoslovakia in 1938–9 (➤Felvidék) and against Romania and Yugoslavia in 1940–41. An alleged Soviet air raid on ➤Košice in June 1941 provided Hungary with reasons for joining Germany in the invasion of Russia. Half the trained soldiers in Hungary, and almost all of the army's tanks and modern equipment, were lost in battle, while seeking to defend a line along the river Don, south of Voronezh (12–25 January 1943). Subsequent attempts to secure a separate peace were unsuccessful. The Soviet Red Army crossed the Hungarian frontier early in September 1944, setting up a provisional government in Debrecen on 21 December 1944, and besieging Budapest from 27 December to 18 January 1945. Free elections in November 1945 gave a majority in the new Hungarian Republic to the Smallholders' Party, a non-communist movement of initiative and enterprise which had benefited from massive land reforms introduced by a communist minister, Imre ►Nagy, in the provisional government. Under Soviet pressure the secret police discovered 'nests of reaction' in 1946–7, discrediting the Smallholders' Party, which was edged out of the government by the 'United Workers' Party' under ►Rákosi. Hungary became a 'People's Republic' under a Soviet-type constitution, officially promulgated on 20 August 1949. Hostility to regimented Stalinization asserted itself in July 1953, when Imre Nagy replaced Rákosi as Prime Minister; but by March 1955 Rákosi had recovered full control of the party, which he only relaxed during the political uncertainties following the ►Twentieth Soviet Party Congress of February 1956. In the following autumn the ►Hungarian National Rising emphasized the failure of the existing socialist system to win support from the younger generation. Under the leadership of János ►Kádár a period of repression gradually gave way to collaboration with non-communists from 1959–61 onwards: educational reforms in 1961 were followed by experiments in decentralized economic planning in 1968. Despite cautious liberalization Hungary remained within the Warsaw Pact and Comecon, although growing increasingly resentful of the treatment by Ceauşescu's Romania of the Hungarian minority in ►Transylvania. In May 1988 the reformer Karoly Grosz succeeded Kádár as Party leader and secured the replacement of a third of the Party's central committee. In January 1989 Prime Minister Miklos Nemeth promised the removal of restrictions on other political parties by August, followed by multi-party elections. In October 1989 the Communist Party was reconstituted as the social-democrat Hungarian Socialist Party (MSzP) and Hungary was styled 'Republic' rather than 'People's Republic'; constitutional amendments provided for a national assembly of mixed first-past-the-post and proportional structure. The first elections brought to power on 23 May 1990 a right-centre coalition headed by the Hungarian Democratic Forum. Hungary joined the Council of Europe in November 1990 and the Forum encouraged the growth of a free-market economy. Concern over falling living standards enable the MSzP to poll more votes than other parties in the election of May 1994 and form a coalition government with the liberal-centrist Alliance of Free Democrats. Economic reforms, bolstered by welfare support provisions, continued. Hungary applied for membership of the European Union in 1994 and at the Madrid conference of July 1997 was invited to join a restructured ►NATO. Elections in May 1998 returned a right-of-centre government.

Hunger Marches. During the inter-war period unemployment in Britain was concentrated in certain 'depressed areas', which were allegedly ignored by the more prosperous regions in southern England, and especially by the propertied classes in London. As a propaganda measure a group of Glasgow socialists and communists organized a 'hunger march' to London in October 1922. This form of demonstration became common. There was an even bigger Glasgow–London March in January 1929 which was followed by the establishment of a National Unemployed Workers' Movement, created principally by a communist in his early thirties, Wal Hannington. When, in October 1932, unemployment in Britain reached 2¾ million the NUWM called the largest of all 'hunger marches': 3,000 men and women converged on London from South Wales, Glasgow, northern and central England, and the east coast ports. They demonstrated in Hyde Park and presented a petition to the Commons, with 1 million signatures, protesting at the iniquities of a 'means test', which made financial relief depend on the assessment of total income within a household. Hunger marches continued until trade began to improve in 1937–8: the most famous of the later hunger marches was the 'Jarrow Crusade' of 5–9 October 1936, when 200 unemployed workers from the Jarrow shipyards marched to London in a demonstration organized by their Labour MP, Ellen Wilkinson (1891–1947), who had at that time more than four-fifths of her constituents dependent on the dole.

Hussein, Ibn Talal (1935–), King of Jordan. Born in Amman, a grandson of King ►Abdullah who was assassinated in his presence in July 1951. Hussein, educated at Harrow and Sandhurst, assumed full sovereignty in May 1953 although he had become titular king in August 1952 when his father, King Talal, was deposed because of mental illness. Politically he steered a middle course, resenting any signs of British patronage, although sympathizing with many aspects of British life and policy. In his conflicts with Arab socialism he could count on his Bedouin subjects, who rallied to his support in 1958 (when Nasserite army officers murdered his ally, cousin and fellow-Harrovian, ►Feisal II, in Baghdad) and again in 1970 during the civil war in ►Jordan. From 1984 onwards he sought a general settlement in the Middle East and tried unsuccessfully to mediate in both ►Gulf Wars. He encouraged peace talks with Israel in 1993, dropping earlier demands for the return of the West Bank, lost after the ►Six-Day War of 1967. The King flew to Washington to sign a peace treaty with Israel's Yitzhak ►Rabin on 25 July 1994, the treaty acknowledging Hussein's custodianship of Islamic holy places in Jerusalem. The onset of cancer in 1996–7 led Hussein to give increased responsibilities to his brother and heir, Crown Prince Hassan (1947–).

Hussein, Sadisavan Saddam (1937–), Iraqi President. Born into a peasant family at Takrit and studied in Baghdad and Cairo. He joined the ►Ba'ath Socialist Party when he was twenty and in 1959 fled from ►Iraq to Syria after an abortive *coup* against the military dictator Brigadier Kassem. He returned to Iraq after Kassem had been overthrown and killed in 1963 and at first supported the new President Aref, but was imprisoned in 1964 for conspiring against him. He played a prominent role in the 1968 revolution and in the following year became Deputy Chairman of the ruling Revolutionary Command Council (RCC). Upon the resignation of President Bakr in July 1979, Saddam Hussein became the State President of Iraq and the Chairman of the RCC. He set up a ruthless dictatorship, promoting himself to the highest rank in the army and treating Kurdish separatists and Shi'ite fundamentalists with extreme harshness; in 1989 his regime of torture and imprisonment without trial was denounced by Amnesty International in a detailed report. Three of his bodyguard were killed when his car was ambushed outside Mosul in April 1987 and eighteen months later he survived a plot to shoot down his aircraft while he was returning from Cairo. He waged a bitter war against Iran from 1980 to 1988 (First ►Gulf War) and sent his troops into Kuwait in August 1990, thereby provoking the Second ►Gulf War. Subsequently he was faced with major rebellions in southern Iraq from Shia Muslims and from the ►Kurds to the north of Mosul. Both rebellions were suppressed with further barbarity. He survived several attempted *coups* in 1994–7, foiled an army rebellion in June 1995 and an assassination attempt by his own bodyguard in July 1996. A referendum in October 1995 showed 99.96 per cent of Iraqis backing him for seven more years of presidential office.

Hydrogen Bomb. Thermonuclear weapon of mass destruction. The first of these bombs was developed by the United States in 1950–51 and exploded in a 'test' at Eniwetok Atoll on 1 November 1952. The Russians tested their first H-bomb in August 1953, the British on 15 May 1957, the Chinese in June 1967, the French on 25 August 1968.

I

Ibarruri, Dolores (1895–1989), Spanish communist, 'La Pasionaria'. Born into a devout Catholic family near Bilbao, living in great poverty, married a miner from Asturias, accepting his communist beliefs and becoming a member of the Spanish Communist Party's central committee in 1930. Although twice imprisoned under the Spanish Republic she was elected to the Cortes, speaking dramatically in the parliamentary debates of early 1936. During the Spanish Civil War she became the best-known revolutionary heroine, with speeches of anti-fascist defiance, '*No Pasaran* – They shall not Pass', delivered in France as well as Spain. She escaped to the Soviet Union where she was acknowledged as leader of the exiled Spanish communists, her only son dying as a Red Army officer at Stalingrad. In May 1977 she was allowed to return to Spain, spoke at a rally in Bilbao and successfully stood as an election candidate in Asturias.

Ibn Saud, Abdul Aziz (1880–1953, King of Hejaz and Nejd 1926–32, King of Saudi Arabia, 1932–53), Arabian King. Born in Riyadh, of the Wahhabi dynasty. As a child he was forced into exile in Kuwait by the Turkish overlords of Nejd, but in 1902 he organized a Bedouin revolt which enabled him to seize Riyadh. By 1913 he had conquered the Turkish province of Al Hasa, on the Persian Gulf, and received recognition as Emir of Nejd and Hasa by the British in December 1915. Rivalry with Hussein of the Hejaz prevented him from joining the Arab Revolt associated with T.E. ➤Lawrence. From May 1919 to December 1925 Ibn Saud fought against Hussein and his dependent rulers on the Red Sea coast. In 1924–5 Ibn Saud's forces captured the key cities of Jedda, Medina and Mecca. Ibn Saud's proclamation as King of Hejaz and Nejd in Mecca on 8 January 1926 was recognized by the British in May 1927. Other powers recognized the unity and independence of his lands between 1927 and 1932 when he renamed his kingdom (which was four times as large as France) Saudi Arabia. He concluded an oil agreement with the Americans in 1933, although it was only in the last seven years of his reign that he enjoyed the wealth flowing from the oilfields in full measure. He showed strict loyalty to his British and American allies in the Second World War and his influence in the Arab world was recognized by both Roosevelt and Churchill, who received him independently in Egypt on their return from Yalta in February 1945. He retained complete personal rule over ➤Saudi Arabia until his death on 30 November 1953 and was succeeded by four of his sons: Saud, reigned 1953–64; Feisal, reigned 1964–75; Khalid, reigned 1975–1982; Fahd, from June 1982.

Iceland. Island in the North Atlantic with its northern shore bordering the Arctic Circle. Iceland was an independent republic in the tenth century but was subsequently linked to Norway and, later, Denmark. The Danes allowed the establishment of a local legislature in 1874, extending the Icelanders' rights in 1903 and 1918 so that the island virtually enjoyed home rule between the wars. When the Germans overran Denmark in 1940, British troops occupied Iceland. Although the United States was still non-belligerent, American forces relieved the British garrison in July 1941. A plebiscite in May 1944 declared in favour of independence and the union with Denmark was ended. Iceland became a member of NATO in 1949, but there were occasional anti-American demonstrations and the NATO presence within the island was strictly confined to specific areas by the left-wing coalition government of 1971–4. Attempts to protect the fishing industry by extending the limits of fishery jurisdiction led to disputes with Britain and West Germany, 1958–61, and more seriously between 1971 and 1976, in the so-called ➤'cod war'.

Imjin River, Battle of the (22–25 April 1951). Defensive action fought by the United Nations command in the ➤Korean War to halt the second wave of the Chinese–North Korean spring offensive against mountain positions along the Imjin. The battle was marked by the valiant resistance of the first battalion of the Gloucestershire Regiment, who were cut off by the Chinese on Hill 235. The commanding officer of 'the glorious Gloucesters', Lt-Col. James Carne, was subsequently awarded the Victoria Cross. Public feeling in Britain was deeply stirred by the action, which evoked parallels with deeds of valour in the previous century.

Immigration Acts (British). Until 1962 citizens of the British Empire and Commonwealth were allowed uncontrolled entry into the United Kingdom. This system was amended under the second Macmillan Government by the Commonwealth Immigration Act of 1962 which laid down the rule that Commonwealth immigrants needed to have a job to come to or be in possession of some 'special skill', of value to Britain. The sudden flight of Asians from Kenya in 1968, many of whom claimed United Kingdom citizenship, led the Labour Government to extend the controls established in 1962. The Heath Government's Act of 1971 set up a single system for aliens and Commonwealth citizens, with concessions for those who had parents or grandparents born in Britain. Later legislation tightened admission controls, especially from the Indian subcontinent and ➤Hong Kong.

Immigration Laws (USA). The first attempts to exclude immigrants to the United States were taken against the Chinese in 1882 and against the Japanese in 1900 and 1908. In 1917, despite a Presidential veto, the US Congress imposed a literacy test on all immigrants. Hostility towards immigrants increased under the predominantly isolationist Republican administrations of the 1920s, and a system of 'quotas' was introduced. The Law of 1921 limited the intake in any one year to 3 per cent of the number of each nationality in the 1910 census, with a maximum quota of 357,000. In 1924 the Johnson–Reed Act was even more drastic, halving the number admitted each year and amending the quota so as to allow only 2 per cent of the 1890 census, a device seriously restricting immigration from eastern Europe and Italy. This law was modified between 1927 and 1929. After the Second World War immigration restrictions were relaxed in 1948 and 1950 so as to admit some displaced persons and war orphans while in 1952 the McCarran–Walter Act regularized and codified procedure, placing a more liberal emphasis on the quotas established in 1924, especially towards the Asian people. In 1965 Congress enacted legislation to remove the national-origins quota system entirely from June 1968 onwards as it was held to be racially discriminatory in character.

Immigration Restriction Acts (Australian). From 1888 onwards there was a marked hostility to further immigration from labour unions in the Australian colonies, especially in Victoria where measures were taken to keep out Chinese settlers. When the federal parliament was established in 1901 one of its first measures was an Immigration Restriction Act (July 1902) which insisted that potential settlers must pass a test to show their ability to communicate in a European language (modified from 1905 to the phrase 'a prescribed language'). A further Immigration Restriction Act in September 1925 gave the Governor-General authority to ban the entry of any class or nationality of aliens whom he might specify either for economic or for racial reasons. Little use was made of this Act and it was intended mainly as a form of reserved power, caused by indignation in certain groups of workers who feared unemployment if there was cheap labour from southern Europe.

Imperial Conferences. Meetings of Prime Ministers of the Dominions within the British Empire held in 1911, 1921, 1923, 1926, 1930 and 1937. These meetings sprang from the five colonial conferences, which had begun when the colonial Prime Ministers came to London for Queen Victoria's Golden Jubilee in 1887. The second colonial conference in Ottawa in 1894 had been on a small scale, but the idea of imperial collaboration received a boost from the initiative of Joseph ➤Chamberlain who presided over the London colonial conferences of 1897 and 1902. A fifth colonial conference in the summer of 1907 showed a desire to substitute the term 'Dominions' for 'Colony' when applied to self-governing units; and for that reason the conferences were renamed in 1911. The first three Imperial Conferences were marked by growing evidence of the dominions' wish to control their external policy free from ties with the government in London and to define the precise character of a dominion. A formula proposed by A.J. Balfour at the 1926 conference was discussed at length in London in October and November 1930 and embodied in the ➤Statute of Westminster of 1931. The 1937 Imperial Conference was less formal than its predecessors, and was mainly concerned with the worsening international situation. An imperial economic conference of a different character was held at ➤Ottawa in 1932. (➤Commonwealth Conferences.)

Imperialism. A word often abused through use as a pejorative by political speakers and writers. In the late nineteenth century imperialism signified the urge of a nation to acquire, administer and develop less materially advanced territories, primarily for trade or prestige, sometimes to offset a strategic danger, real or imaginary. Overpopulation of the home country, the need for markets for mass-produced goods, the need for new sources of food and raw materials, the advantages of improved communications and better medical knowledge – all contributed to make the period 1880–1914 a climax of imperialist expansion marked by the 'scramble for Africa' of the British, French, Germans, Italians and Belgians. The imagination of newly educated millions was excited by the prospect of world empire, notably through the propaganda of imperial leagues in London and Berlin. Imperialist development was not limited to Africa: the USA acquired Pacific Ocean bases in the late 1890s; the French developed Indo-China; and the Russians expanded overland to Manchuria, provoking conflict with the Japanese who were establishing imperialist claims to Korea (►Russo-Japanese War). During the twentieth century imperialism has more frequently taken the form of economic penetration than of direct political domination. In Marxist theory, as developed by Lenin in 1915, imperialism was condemned as 'the highest stage of capitalism', competing with rival imperialisms to produce wars which would impose such a strain on the existing order that they would lead to world revolution and thus to the simultaneous downfall of capitalism and imperialism. Since the Second World War the terms 'neo-imperialism' or 'neo-colonialism' have been applied to situations in which a rich foreign power exploits a backward but nominally independent country, often to the resentment of a politically inarticulate majority among its peoples.

Imperial Preference. An economic doctrine by which the British dominions and colonies would form a self-contained trading unit, protected against foreign competition by high tariffs. The idea, originating in Canada, was canvassed by Joseph ►Chamberlain, first at the colonial conference of 1897 and later through the ►Tariff Reform League. Imperial preference ran counter to the Free Trade doctrines held by many Conservatives as well as the Liberals at the turn of the century, and Chamberlain could not convert his Conservative colleagues to his views. His resignation from Balfour's government in September 1903 over the issue of tariff reform and imperial preference severely split the party. Imperial preference was adopted by MacDonald's National Government in 1931 when Free Trade principles were abandoned during the Depression. The Ottawa Agreement (►Ottawa Conference) of 1932 applied imperial preference to the dominions, and it was extended to crown colonies a year later. The system was maintained, though with modifications, after the General Agreement on Tariffs and Trade of October 1947. It provided an obstacle to Britain's desire for membership of the European Economic Community in the 1960s, and was necessarily abandoned when the British signed the treaty of accession to the European Community in January 1972.

IMRO (Internal Macedonian Revolutionary Organization). Balkan terrorist movement, especially notorious between the wars, established in 1895 to secure autonomy for Macedonia. From 1921 onwards IMRO was dominated by a 'Supreme Macedonian Committee' which sought the absorption of Greek Macedonia and Yugoslav Macedonia by Bulgaria. IMRO organized acts of terrorism within Yugoslavia and gained considerable influence over the shaping of Bulgarian policies. In 1924, however, IMRO split into two militantly hostile factions, which indulged in an orgy of assassination tempered by raids across the Greek and Yugoslav frontiers. IMRO collaborated with the Croatian ►Ustaše and it was an IMRO assassin, in the Ustaše pay, who killed King Alexander of Yugoslavia at Marseilles in 1934. Thereafter IMRO activities died down, partly because of opposition from a new government in Sofia and partly because of the high casualty rate among IMRO's own leaders.

Independent Labour Party (ILP). In the 1880s and early 1890s working-class political candidates stood for parliament as 'Liberal-Labour'. Keir ►Hardie, seeking to free Labour candidates from Liberal connections, established the Independent Labour Party after a conference at Bradford in January 1893. The ILP did not have any direct link with the trade-union movement until, in 1900, it became one of the affiliated organizations in the Labour Representation Committee (►Labour Party). The ILP remained in uneasy partnership with the Labour Party until 1932, refusing to join the ►Third International or affiliate with the communists in March 1921, although collaborating with the communists and other dissident movements of the Left to champion a United Popular Front in January 1937. In James Maxton (1885–1946) the ILP possessed a chairman of firm principles who was also a gifted orator. On his death the party began rapidly to disintegrate: from three MPs in 1945 and four unsuccessful candidates in 1950 to three unsuccessful candidates in 1951. Although unrepresented in parliament since 1947 the ILP remains in being.

India Act (1909), also known as **Indian Councils Act.** Allowed Indians a share in the work of the legislative councils of British India and made them eligible for appointment to the Viceroy's executive council and to the advisory council of the Secretary of State in London. These measures – the ►Morley–Minto Reforms – did not imply responsible government, since the legislative councils could not eject the executive, but they were given an opportunity for gaining experience in the conduct of government.

India Act (1919). By establishing a bicameral parliament for all India this measure implemented the ►Montagu–Chelmsford report. The legislature still had no power to remove the executive, nor to prevent the Viceroy governing through emergency decrees. In the provinces, however, the Act accepted the principle of 'dyarchy' (rule by two bodies): 'reserved subjects' remained the prerogative of the permanent officials; 'transferred subjects' were handed over to the elected legislative councils.

This cumbersome system was much criticized in the ➤Simon Report of 1930, and virtually superseded by the ➤India Act of 1935.

India Act (1935). Proposed the transformation of the Indian Empire into a federation which would include native states as well as the provinces of British India. This proposal was never fulfilled because of divisions between the Indian communities which remained unresolved on the outbreak of the Second World War and the subsequent decision to give India dominion status. The Act also gave greater authority to eleven provincial assemblies in British India, allowing them fully responsible governments for questions falling within their own region. This section of the Act became effective on 1 April 1937 and facilitated the rise of ➤Congress. The Act also removed ➤Aden and ➤Burma from the jurisdiction of the British Government in India.

Indian Independence Act (1947). Long disputes over the form of government which should be established on the dissolution of the British Empire in India led to increasing communal violence in the spring of 1947. The Viceroy – Lord ➤Mountbatten – recommended an early grant of independence in the belief that clear evidence of governmental action in London would help to calm communal frenzy. The Indian Independence Act of July 1947 was accordingly hurried through parliament at Westminster between 10 and 18 July 1947, without a division. The Act provided for the creation on 15 August 1947 of two new dominions, a predominantly Hindu India and a predominantly Muslim Pakistan. All princely states in the subcontinent were left to choose their own fate, although advised to seek integration with India or Pakistan according to the racial and religious affiliation of their peoples and their geographical position.

Indian Princely States. From 1857 to 1947 Britain's Indian Empire was sustained by a system of shared rule by which more than 500 Indian princes accepted the concept of 'paramountcy', pledging loyalty to the sovereign in London (from 1877 titular Empress or Emperor of India) in return for varying degrees of autonomy. Treason or gross misrule led to a loss of autonomy. A Chamber of Princes served as consultative and advisory assembly for the Viceroy from 1921 onwards. On 25 July 1947 the Chamber was told that princes should formally accede either to ➤Pakistan or the new India within three weeks; by then two-fifths of the population lived within these princely states. Three of the larger states held out, mainly because the ruling prince belonged to a different religious faith from most of his subjects; of these states Hyderabad was absorbed into the India Republic in September 1949, Junagadh joined India when its Muslim Nawab went into exile, but the fate of ➤Kashmir remained long in dispute. Both Pakistan and India regarded the princely states as anachronistic and swept away their rulers' residual rights while also depriving them of much wealth. All princely titles were finally abolished in India in December 1971.

Indian Republic. For two and a half years after attaining independence India remained a dominion, accepting the former emperor, George VI, as king. The three immediate tasks facing the Indian Prime Minister, ►Nehru, were the need to increase food supplies, the political problem of integrating the princely states, and the long conflict with Pakistan over ►Kashmir. The only one of these problems to be solved without major difficulties was the problem of the princes, and even then there was serious opposition in Hyderabad and Junagadh. The constitution of 1950 established a centralized, quasi-federal republic, owing many of its features to the ►India Act of 1935. Nehru's ►Congress Movement won three-quarters of the seats in the first parliamentary election and the Prime Minister introduced the first of a series of five-year plans for expanding industry and achieving self-sufficiency in food. Industrial output doubled in ten years but although India succeeded in increasing food production, its gains could not meet the rising birth rate. At the time of Nehru's death in 1964 the population was still expanding annually by 15 million even though life expectation was only thirty-two years. The republic's world stature mounted with Nehru's reputation for statesmanship: he was accepted as an inspiring non-aligned leader of the anti-colonialists, willing to be arbiter in the ►Cold War. Sino-Indian relations, at first friendly, became tense with the Chinese absorption of ►Tibet in 1959 and were worsened by Chinese penetration of Assam in October 1962. Strained relations with Pakistan over Kashmir were followed in 1965 by a war, fought mainly over the disputed border region known as the Rann of Kutch. This conflict was settled at a meeting in Tashkent between Nehru's successor, ►Shastri, and the Pakistan President, ►Ayub Khan; but Indian concern for the Bengali people of ►Bangladesh led to a further war between India and Pakistan in December 1971, in which the Pakistani forces were defeated in a campaign of intensive fighting on three fronts. The premiership of Nehru's daughter, Mrs ►Gandhi, provoked widespread discontent in the period 1974–6, partly because of drastic attempts to encourage birth control, partly through a suspicion of mounting corruption, and partly through increasingly autocratic tendencies within the government. The election of March 1977 led to the first defeat of the Congress Party since independence and the establishment of a 'Janata' Government, headed by Morarji Desai. Janata was virtually a coalition and soon showed such signs of factionalism that Congress recovered its appeal to the Indian electorate – especially when communal rioting broke out in Uttar Pradesh and Bihar. The promise of firm government and a check in the rising rate of inflation brought Mrs Gandhi back to the premiership in January 1980. New internal security laws curbed the mounting disorders but prices of essential foods continued to rise as much under the new government as under the old. There was grave ethnic and religious violence in Assam in 1983; several hundred Bangladeshi immigrants were massacred in Nowgong. The Punjab was troubled by chronic terrorism, with the Sikhs demanding political rights which neither Mrs Gandhi nor her son and successor would concede. Sikh protests led to a virtual siege of the Golden Temple in ►Amritsar and ultimately in October 1984 to Mrs Gandhi's assassination. The five-year premiership of Rajiv Gandhi failed to restore order in the troubled provinces. A minority 'National Front' government, formed by V.P. Singh in December 1989, was weakened by a conflict with Hindus over a 'temple-mosque' in Uttar Pradesh. When in November 1990 Chandra Shekhar headed a new government (dependent on Congress Party support) he was confronted by insurgencies in Assam, Jammu, Kashmir and the Punjab. The election campaign of May and June 1991 was marked by unprecedented violence, including the murder of Rajiv Gandhi on 21 May. Congress returned to power from June 1991 to May 1996 but was faced by grave shortages of food and by a loss of monetary value of the rupee. After a month of political chaos a left-of-centre coalition took office in June 1996. The United Front government fell on 28 November 1997. Elections in February and March 1998 gave no party a clear majority and a coalition, dominated by the Hindu nationalists (BJP), took office, with Atal Behari Vajpayee as Prime Minister. In May 1998 he caused widespread dismay abroad by announcing that India had carried out a series of successful underground nuclear bomb tests.

Indo-China. An area of some quarter of a million square miles in south-east Asia colonized by the French between the early 1860s and 1893. The word Indo-China was first applied by the French to a union of their settlements and dependencies within Annam, Tonking, Cambodia and 'Cochin-China' (the area around Saigon) in 1887 and was extended westward in 1893 to the territories which they named ►'Laos'. The French developed the industries of the region and, by draining and reclaiming the lands of the Mekong delta, increased the cultivated area ten times over. While French businessmen dominated the industries and the civil administration most of the agriculture was managed by a small class of wealthy 'native' middlemen, employing tenant farmers who were unscrupulously exploited in many instances. Independence movements sprang up and there were local revolts, notably in 1930. A Vietnamese Nationalist Party, seeking the independence and unity of Annam, Tonking and Cochin-China, was founded by left-wing exiles in Canton (1925) and soon attracted young intellectuals such as the later ►Ho and ►Giap. French authority was undermined by the connivance of ►Vichy at the Japanese occupation of Indo-China in July 1941. The Viet-Minh resistance movement was created in 1941–2 and was for three years active in Annam and Tonking. When Japan surrendered a Vietnamese republic was proclaimed (September 1945) under the leadership of Ho Chi Minh. The French reasserted their control of Saigon and sought to negotiate with Ho for the establishment of an Indo-Chinese federation, including Laos and Cambodia as well as much of Vietnam, but excluding the area around Saigon which was to have been directly administered from Paris. In December 1946 fighting broke out between the French and the Viet-Minh near Hanoi: hostilities continued until after the disastrous French defeat at ►Dien Bien Phu in 1954. French sovereignty in Indo-China was formally transferred to governments in Cambodia, Laos and Vietnam by the ►Geneva Agreements of 20 July 1954.

Indonesia. In 1900 the Dutch possessed the third largest colonial empire in the world, most of it concentrated in the East Indies, where 65 million people of mixed races and religion lived in what is now the Indonesian archipelago. Apart from sporadic colonial warfare in ►Borneo there was little resistance to Dutch authority until the foundation in 1908 of Budi Utomo, a Dutch-sponsored Indonesian cultural society which stimulated nationalist sentiment, especially among the students. A communist-inspired revolt in 1926 was followed a year later by the formation of the PNI (Indonesian Nationalist Party), built up rapidly by ►Sukarno. The Dutch imprisoned and exiled PNI leaders, 1929–32, and established a severely repressive regime, especially after an Indonesian mutiny aboard a cruiser in 1933. Japanese forces began an invasion of the archipelago on 10 January 1942, the final unit of the Dutch East Indies army capitulating to the invaders in Java on 8 March. Most members of the PNI collaborated with the Japanese, who encouraged Indonesian nationalism so long as it was anti-Western in character. On Japan's surrender the PNI took the opportunity of proclaiming Indonesia's independence in the city they called Jakarta and the Dutch called Batavia (17 August 1945). The Indonesians were thus able to fill the power vacuum, for it was some weeks before Dutch colonial authorities returned. Fighting broke out between the PNI and the Dutch, notably at Surabaja in eastern Java. A truce was eventually arranged by the British and signed at Linggadjati on 15 November 1946. It was agreed that Indonesians and Dutch would establish a United States of Indonesia linked to the Netherlands in a special relationship. Dutch colonists and the PNI could not, however, collaborate; and in July 1947 the Dutch launched a 'police action' against the Indonesian republicans which seemed so brutal that several powers, including India and Australia, raised the matter at the United Nations. A ceasefire was established under American auspices in December 1947, but when a communist revolt against the PNI broke out at Madiun in September 1948, the Dutch massed their forces for a decisive blow against the republicans and heavily bombed the town of Jogjakarta (the provisional Indonesian capital) on 19 December 1948. This second 'police action' was condemned by most other countries, and the Dutch agreed in August 1949 to a conference on Indonesia at The Hague. The formal transference of all the Dutch East Indies (except western New Guinea) took place on 27 December 1949, although technically constitutional links remained with the Dutch crown until 1956. In August 1950 the original plan for a federation was cast aside in favour of a unitary state, dominated by Java, and by the first President, Sukarno. Disputes continued with the Dutch until western New Guinea was ceded to Indonesia in 1963. The dominance of the Javanese aroused resentment in the other islands and there was a serious revolt in Sumatra in 1956. Sukarno's ambitious foreign policy, and particularly the 'confrontation' with Commonwealth forces in ►Malaysia from 1963 to 1965, weakened the Indonesian economy. There were clashes between the Indonesian communists and the army in the autumn of 1965 which showed that the army had lost confidence in Sukarno. General Suharto (1921–), the Army Minister, took over the presidency from Sukarno on 12

March 1967 with the backing both of students and of the military leaders. The 'confrontation' with Malaysia was formally ended on 11 August 1966 and priority given to economic developments which had remained mere blueprints during the later years of Sukarno's Presidency. At the same time Indonesia resumed membership of the United Nations (from which Sukarno had withdrawn in 1965) and under President Suharto Indonesia became one of the chief contributors to the peace-keeping missions of United Nations troops. Suharto succeeded in stabilizing the currency in 1970: agricultural yield improved considerably between 1969 and 1974. The former Portuguese colony of East ▶ Timor was incorporated in Indonesia in 1976; strict military control was enforced by Suharto as there was a powerful Fretilin movement in favour of independence. Both Sukarno and Suharto encouraged the growth throughout Indonesia of a 'Pancasila' state ideology, at variance with the Islamic beliefs held by 90 per cent of Indonesians. A Muslim political party (PPP) challenged Suharto's ruling Golkar movement from 1984 onwards, with occasional riots in Jakarta, and came second in the 1992 elections, though Golkar had an overall majority of 162 seats. Sukarno's daughter, Megawati Sukarnoputri, emerged during 1996–7 as a leading critic of the Suharto administration, with considerable popular following. The principal Opposition, however, came from Muslim students, led by Amien Rais. When Suharto claimed a further electoral victory in March 1998, discontent was expressed with increasing violence, culminating in six days of rioting in Jakarta. Much of the central shopping area in the capital was set ablaze and there were more than 1,600 deaths. Suharto at last resigned on 21 May 1998, handing over authority to his Vice-President, Jusuf Habibie, who promised free, multi-party elections within a year.

Industrial Workers of the World (IWW). Sometimes known as 'the Wobblies' or 'the Bummery': was the most highly organized revolutionary labour movement in the USA. It was founded at a congress in Chicago in 1905, its members pledging themselves to the overthrow of capitalism by strikes and economic action. The conflict between syndicalist practice and social democratic principles divided the movement, one wing of which accepted the need for political action, at a conference in Detroit (1909), and continued to support the attempts of the pioneer American social democrat, Eugene V. Debs (1855–1926), to secure election to the Presidency. Other factions in the IWW indulged in sabotage, enabling the federal authorities to institute prosecutions and, from 1917 onwards, to work up feeling against the IWW as an example of 'red radicalism'. The IWW was strongest in the period 1912–15, with a membership of over 100,000. Although of little influence after 1918 the IWW left a double legacy: a preference in the USA for large industrial unions of skilled and unskilled workers; and a remarkably enduring collection of revolutionary songs.

Inkatha Freedom Party. Founded in the 1920s as a Zulu cultural association but discouraged in the early apartheid years, Inkatha was revived as a political movement in 1975 by Chief Mangosutu Buthelezi (1928–) to safeguard Zulu interests. It strongly opposed the ►African National Congress, mistrusted the partnership of ►Mandela and ►De Klerk, and was largely responsible for grave rioting in Natal and the Cape townships during 1991 and 1992. After gaining 10.5 per cent of the votes in South Africa's first multiracial election (April 1994), Buthelezi brought Inkatha into Mandela's ruling coalition and took office as Minister of Home Affairs.

Inönü, Ismet (1884–1974), Turkish soldier and statesman. Born Ismet in Smyrna (Izmir), commissioned in the Ottoman Army 1904, serving in Macedonia and the Yemen, winning distinction as a colonel at Gallipoli and promoted to a corps commander in 1916. After the Turkish collapse in 1918 he attached himself to Mustapha Kemal (►Atatürk), becoming Chief of the General Staff to the Kemalist armies in 1920 and commander of the Western Army fighting the Greeks in Anatolia in 1921–2. As a soldier Ismet was distinguished for the patience and efficiency with which he trained and built up the new Turkish armies and for his skill in winning two defensive battles against the Greeks around the village of Inönü, 160 miles west of Ankara, in 1921. (When surnames, on the European model, were introduced into Turkey in 1935 he took the name Inönü to commemorate his victories.) He was commander of Turkish forces at ►Chanak and subsequently headed the Turkish delegation at ►Lausanne. From 1923 to 1937 he was Turkish Prime Minister, supporting Atatürk's revolutionary policy of enforced westerniz-ation. On Atatürk's death in November 1938 he became Turkish President, and virtual dictator. During the Second World War he sympathized with the British and American cause, entertaining Churchill and three senior British generals on his Presidential train at Adana on 30–31 January 1943 although subsequently declining to enter the war until March 1945. Inönü gradually permitted greater freedom of speech and of the Press, tolerating the establishment in 1945–6 of an opposition party which defeated him in the 1950 election. For ten years Inönü led the opposition in the Turkish parliament, but after revision of the constitution returned as Prime Minister in October 1961, holding office for another four years before again being defeated in an election (largely on the grounds that he had cancelled a proposed Turkish invasion of Cyprus under strong pressure from President Lyndon Johnson). Inönu remained titular leader of the Turkish opposition until most of the republic was brought under martial law in July 1972.

International Labour Organization (ILO). Was created in 1919 as an adjunct of the ►League of Nations with responsibility for seeking improvements in labour conditions so as to maintain social stability by raising living standards. The pioneer work of the ILO was recognized by the United Nations in 1946, and the ILO was continued as a specialized agency of the United Nations, gaining additional importance in the 1950s and 1960s for its activity in protecting the interests of workers employed in countries other than their own. In 1960 the ILO was awarded the Nobel Peace Prize. American criticism that the Organization favoured left-wing political movements led President Carter to announce the withdrawal of the United States from the ILO on 5 November 1977.

International Monetary Fund (IMF). A specialized agency of the United Nations, proposed at the ►Bretton Woods Conference in 1944 and established on 27 December 1945. The IMF assists the expansion of world trade by providing cash reserves to offset national deficits in the balance of payments.

International Socialism. The concept of international solidarity among the proletarians of the world goes back to the *Communist Manifesto* of Marx and Engels in 1848. An international working-men's association was established by Marx in London in 1864. This 'First International' was weakened by disputes between Marxists and anarchists and was dissolved in 1876. The ►Second International was formed in Paris in 1889, and although weakened by the First World War, it was revived in the 1920s as a loose association of social democratic parties and still survives. The Third International, or ►Comintern, was established by the Bolsheviks in March 1919 to further the cause of world revolution. It was dissolved in May 1943 as a gesture of reassurance to the Soviet Union's wartime allies. The Second International worked closely with the International Federation of Trade Unions, founded at Amsterdam in July 1919. A 'Red International of Labour Unions', set up by the Third International in 1921 as a rival body, had some following in France and Spain but was never accepted as the mouthpiece of international labour.

Intifada. A name first given by the Arabs to their struggle against Jewish settlers and the British forces in ►Palestine in 1936–7. The word was revived half a century later to describe the risings against Israeli rule in the ►Gaza Strip and on the West Bank of the Jordan. This new Intifada began on 9 December 1987, with violence in the Gaza Strip.

IRA. ►Irish Republican Army.

Iran. From the later eighteenth century until 1925 Persia – as Iran was officially called before 1935 – was ruled by Shahs from the Qajar dynasty, with despotic powers, until a revolutionary movement in 1905–6 forced Shah Muzaffar al-Din to grant a liberal constitution. The agreement which established the ►Anglo-Russian Entente in 1907 divided Persia into Russian and British spheres of influence, separated by a neutral zone. Russian penetration of the area around Teheran (1909–11) and British exploitation of the littoral stimulated Iranian national sentiment. During the First World War Persia's neutrality was violated by British, Russian and Turkish troops, while a former German consul at Bushire, Wassmuss, organized raids by Persian irregulars on the British and sought, unsuccessfully, to bring Persia into the war as an ally of Turkey. The modernization of Iran dates from the *coup d'état* of Colonel Reza Khan (1878–1944), elected Shah on 13 December 1925 and reigning as Reza Shah until September 1941. He developed roads, railways, the army, built schools, imposed European costume, and superficially carried Iran into the twentieth century, although neglecting agriculture and accumulating personal wealth through appropriation of the best land. Suspicion that he favoured Germany led to a joint Anglo-Soviet invasion of Iran (26–29 August 1941) and the country remained occupied by British and Russian troops until the spring of 1946. Reza Shah abdicated in favour of his son, Muhammad Reza ►Pahlavi, who was proclaimed 'Shah-an-shah of Iran' on 16 September 1941. Anti-British and anti-American feeling grew rapidly between 1947 and 1951, crystallizing in demands for nationalization of the oil industry: the Shah was shot and wounded; and, within a few days of each other in March 1951, the Prime Minister and Education Minister were assassinated. The demagogic Mohammed ►Mussadeq became head of the government in May 1951 but in August 1953 lost his powers when arrested by the Shah, who believed he was seeking to overthrow the dynasty. The Shah concentrated power in his own hands, 1951–61, allowing a series of liberal reforms during the premiership of Ali Amini (1961–2) but reasserting his authority by appointing a personal friend, Asadollah Alam, as Prime Minister in July 1962. Thereafter land reforms and constitutional concessions were imposed by grace of the sovereign. Experiments in party government were permitted from 1964 until March 1975, when the Shah formed a single political movement, the 'National Resurrection Party'. Despite welfare programmes and the nominal emancipation of women (1963), much poverty and illiteracy remained under a dynasty made wealthy from oil. Student demonstrations in the autumn of 1977 were followed a year later by clashes in the holy city of Qom. Riots spread to Tehran; demands for the return of the exiled religious leader, Ayatollah ►Khomeini, forced the Shah to flee the country on 16 January 1979.

Throughout the period 1979–81 Iran was convulsed by revolution. Khomeini became the effective head of state in February 1979 and political affairs were administered by a Revolutionary Committee of Shia Muslim clergy, several of whom were assassinated in the general anarchy. Resentment at a constitution which confirmed Khomeini's spiritual leadership of the nation led to revolts in Khuzestan and Kurdistan. At the same time, student extremists in Teheran indulged in xenophobic exhibitionism which culminated in the seizure of the US embassy on 4 November 1979 and the holding of sixty-three Americans as ►hostages for the return of the exiled Shah to stand trial. The students' action led to protracted tension with the United States which dominated the last fourteen months of Carter's Presidency. The failure of a helicopter mission to rescue the hostages on 25 April 1980 intensified anti-American feeling in Teheran. Meanwhile the political anarchy worsened. At the end of January 1980 Abol Hassan Bani-Sadr was elected President but by mid-summer there were pitched battles between extremist groups in Teheran and other cities, and the situation worsened when ►Iraq launched a war to secure control of the Shatt al Arab waterway in September 1980. After the American hostages were released on 20 January 1981, Bani-Sadr was accused by his political enemies of wishing to appease the West, despite the payment by the Americans of a considerable sum to the Iranian authorities. Bani-Sadr's relations with Khomeini deteriorated. On 21 June 1981 the Ayatollah ordered Bani-Sadr's arrest and impeachment but the President escaped to France. Over 300 counter-revolutionaries were executed in the following six weeks. Bani-Sadr's successor as President, Muhammad Ali Rajai, was assassinated on 30 August, four weeks after taking office, in a bomb explosion in Teheran which also killed the Prime Minister and other prominent supporters of Khomeini. Ayatollah Sayyed Ali Khamenei (1939–), a pragmatic conservative pupil of Khomeini, was elected President on 2 October 1981 and thereafter the pace of revolution slackened. The ➤Gulf War took a heavy toll of largely untrained recruits. Diplomatic links with Britain were restored in October 1988. Five months later they were severed again by the Iranians after British protests at the action of Khomeini on 14 February in pronouncing a death sentence on the British author Salman Rushdie and his publishers for alleged blasphemy against Islam in the novel, *The Satanic Verses*. When Khomeini died (3 June 1989) President Khamenei was named as Spiritual Leader of the Islamic Republic. He never possessed his predecessor's prestige or moral authority. Ali Akbar Rafsanjani (1936–), Speaker of the *Majlis* (parliament), held executive power as President for two four-year terms, from July 1989, cautiously improving relations with the West and moving towards a free market economy, while maintaining the rigid discipline of an Islamic clericalist administration. In June 1997, however, the presidential election was won by a more moderate Muslim cleric, Mohammad Khatami (1943–).

Iraq. A state dominated by the Mesopotamian plain and the rivers Tigris and Euphrates, forming part of the Turkish Empire from 1638 until 1918, as the provinces of Mosul, Basra and Baghdad. Iraq became a British mandate after the First World War, with the Hashemite Emir, ➤Feisal I, elected King in August 1921. The early years of the kingdom were hampered by revolts of the Kurds (1922–32) and attempts to negotiate a favourable treaty with the British, ending the mandate and securing full independence. Such a treaty was signed in 1930, although it bound Iraq closely to the British Empire in a twenty-five year military alliance and did not become operative until Iraq entered the League of Nations as an independent state in October 1932. The first strike of oil in 1927 was followed by the commercial export of crude oil in 1934 and by the construction of pipelines to the Mediterranean coast (realigned in 1949 and 1952 to avoid Israeli territory). Pan-Arab political parties attained much influence during the reign of Feisal's son, Ghazi (king 1933–9), and a group of Iraqis established close links with the Germans and Italians. When their leader, Rashid Ali, set up a pro-German government in Baghdad, the British occupied the country (May 1941), remaining until October 1947 and continuing to lease an air base at Habbaniya for several more years. Under ➤Feisal II and the veteran Anglophile, ➤Nuri es-Said, Iraq became in the mid-1950s an alternative centre, for Arab feeling, to Cairo and its more radical teachings. Both Feisal and Nuri were murdered on 14 July 1958 in the Iraqi Revolution. The new left-wing republic was headed by Brigadier ➤Kassem, who was himself assassinated in a second *coup*, led by his former associate, Colonel Aref, in February

1963. Under Aref's Presidency the basic political creed was ➤Ba'ath Socialist. Most of Iraq's industries, including oil, were nationalized and close economic links were forged with Egypt. When Aref died in an air crash on 13 April 1966 he was succeeded briefly by his brother, but a third military *coup*, on 17 July 1968, brought to power General Hasan al Bakr who established a ruthlessly repressive system of government. In 1961 the ➤Kurds – a fifth of Iraq's population – had renewed their struggle for an independent Kurdistan, which would also include districts in Turkey and the Soviet Union. Iraqi army assaults on Kurdish strongholds in the north of the country were ably resisted by the *peshmerga* guerrillas, led by their mullah, Mustapha Barzani (*c.* 1920–79), who secured an Iraqi promise of Kurdish autonomy in March 1970. The failure of President Bakr to implement this concession led to further conflict, in which the Kurdish *peshmerga* were defeated by General Saddam ➤Hussein who, in July 1979, took over the presidency from the ailing Bakr. As Iraq's latest Ba'ath Socialist 'strong man', President Saddam had twenty-two leading Iraqi communists executed and then took action against Iraq's Shia Moslems, ordering the Shia Ayatollah and his sister to be hanged in April 1980. This 'affront to Islam' worsened relations with Khomeini's ➤Iran, already strained by Iraqi attempts to control the Shatt al Arab waterway. In September 1980 a major conflict began with Iran, generally called the First ➤Gulf War. Although Iranian counter-offensives in 1982 and 1984 nearly toppled Saddam from power, in 1988 he emerged from the long war with heightened prestige. Conflict with the Kurds continued. In July 1988 Iraqi aircraft and artillery attacked Kurdish villages in which the *peshmerga* had revived their movement for independence: poison gas was used; over 100,000 Kurds fled into Turkey, many suffering from chemical burns. By 1989 Iraq had the fourth largest army in the world. Saddam Hussein renewed old demands on ➤Kuwait in the early summer of 1990. After the failure of talks in Jeddah, he sent his army to occupy Kuwait on 4 August, precipitating the international crisis which resulted in the Second ➤Gulf War and the heavy bombing of Baghdad, Basra and other Iraqi towns. Despite defeat by the UN forces, the Iraqi army was still strong enough to crush a Shia revolt in the holy city of Najaf and to suppress a renewed rebellion by the Kurds. The flight of at least 400,000 Kurds to Turkey and a further 500,000 to Iran prompted international relief measures to help a submerged nation threatened with genocide. To protect Kurds in the north and Shias in the south air exclusion zones, patrolled primarily by the US air force, were established north of the 36th parallel and south of the 32nd parallel, while UN observers sought to preserve peace along the borders with Kuwait and monitored efforts to deprive Iraq of all weapons of mass destruction. Economic sanctions imposed on Iraq by the UN in August 1990 were slightly relaxed in 1996 so as to admit food and medicine in return for limited oil sales, with some revenue providing reparations for war victims, including Kurds. Mounting tension induced the Americans to make two pre-emptive cruise missile attacks on southern Iraq in September 1996. Saddam's refusal to allow UN inspectors access to sites suspected of concealing preparations for germ warfare led to the concentration of a US and British air and naval task force in the Gulf in January 1998, before Saddam accepted Russian mediation and relaxed his ban on inspection.

Ireland. The Act of Union between Great Britain and Ireland came into force on 1 January 1801. By the 1880s there was a strong demand in Ireland for ➤Home Rule, a concession wrung from the Westminster parliament in the summer of 1914 but formally suspended for the duration of the First World War. A treaty signed in London on 6 December 1921 gave dominion status to Ireland, apart from six of the nine counties in Ulster which were given limited self-government as ➤Northern Ireland. The Irish Free State, officially proclaimed on 6 December 1922, remained unacceptable to the republican supporters of ➤De Valéra, whose party, the Fianna Fáil, gained an election victory in 1932 and began progressively to remove the remaining restrictions on southern Ireland's independence. A new constitution, effective from 29 December 1937, established ➤'Eire' as a sovereign state which refused to acknowledge the fact of partition. Eire remained in the Commonwealth for another twelve years, officially becoming the Republic of Ireland in April 1949, but was the one dominion to observe neutrality throughout the Second World War. Economic links between Britain and the Irish Republic were intensified from 1966 onwards and Ireland became a member of the ➤European Community on 1 January 1973, as also did the United Kingdom. But the partition of Ireland has remained a source of governmental friction as well as of unrest and bloodshed, sympathy for the Roman Catholic minority in the 'six counties' being exploited by the ➤Irish Republican Army and other militants. The continuance of partition was the principal reason why the Republic of Ireland declined to become a member of NATO; but the Irish have been among the most active champions of the United Nations, with Irish troops serving on UN peace-keeping missions in the Middle East and central Africa. Talks in Dublin between the British and Irish Prime Ministers (Margaret Thatcher and Charles Haughey) on 8 December 1980 emphasized the close economic, social and political bonds linking the United Kingdom and the Irish Republic. In the following November the two governments agreed to establish an Anglo-Irish Council but mutual prime ministerial mistrust hampered further progress until the Haughey government was succeeded by Dr Garret Fitzgerald's coalition ministry in December 1982. Despite rebuffs from London, Dr Fitzgerald's experiment with a 'New Ireland Forum' (March 1983–May 1984) finally won British acceptance of an Anglo-Irish Agreement (November 1985); it set up an inter-governmental conference and provided for closer collaboration on security. Although the Agreement enhanced Fitzgerald's standing, he lost popularity by attempts to 'modernize' the constitution. Charles Haughey was able to form a minority government in March 1987. Anglo-Irish relations deteriorated once more after disputes over extradition procedures in the following winter. Ireland's first woman President, Mary Robinson, took office in November 1990. (➤Easter Rising, ➤Ulster, etc.) Haughey resigned in February 1992, after allegations of phone-tapping by his government. His successors as *taoiseach* (Prime Minister) – Albert Reynolds, in office until November 1994, and John Bruton, from December 1994 – came from opposing parties (Fianna Fáil and Fine Gael), but each led a coalition dependent on Labour support. Despite the weak structure of the governments, progress was made over EU affairs and over Northern Ireland, especially by Bruton. Economic success, marked by foreign investment and government-sponsored industrial development projects, prompted Bruton to call an election on 6 June 1997. The voters, however, preferred the more traditionalist Fianna Fáil, led by Bertie (Bartholomew) Ahern (1952–), who formed a centre-right coalition on 26 June. Close collaboration with the new Labour Government in London brought overwhelming support for the ➤Good Friday Accord on Northern Ireland from voters in the Republic in the referendum of 22 May 1998: a 'Yes Vote' from 94 per cent in a 55 per cent turnout of the electorate.

Irgun Zvai Leumi. Jewish terrorist organization operating in Palestine 1946–8, with Gideon Paglin (1923–) as chief of operations. The most notorious Irgun crime was the blowing up of the King David Hotel in Jerusalem on 22 July 1946. The British administration was housed in the south-west wing of the hotel. This wing was completely destroyed, with the loss of ninety-one lives. Irgun claimed responsibility for over 200 acts of terrorism, both against the British and against Arabs.

Irish Republican Army (IRA). The original IRA was organized by Michael ➤Collins in January 1919 to fight against the British until a unified republic was established in Ireland. They fought throughout the 'troubles' of 1919–22, provoking reprisals from the 'Black and Tans', and in June 1921 were responsible for shooting down the Chief of the Imperial Staff, Field-Marshal Sir Henry Wilson, on the steps of his Eaton Place home, the first political assassination in London for over a century. When Collins accepted the Irish Free State, the IRA regarded him as a traitor and waged civil war in Ireland until early 1923, recognizing the leadership of ➤De Valéra until he, too, took the Oath of Allegiance. IRA terrorism was so bad in 1930–31 that the army was outlawed by the government, although these measures were relaxed in 1932 when De Valéra became Prime Minister. By 1936, however, the IRA were such a menace to internal stability that De Valéra ordered the internment of many members. In January 1939 the IRA began a bombing campaign in England, hoping to force concessions from the Chamberlain Government over Northern Ireland. The worst incident during this wave of violence was at Coventry on 25 August 1939 when a bomb killed five people. Small-scale bombings continued until February 1940. Thereafter the IRA remained quiescent for many years, although raiding an armoury at Arborfield in Berkshire in August 1955 and engaging in a bombing campaign within southern Ireland in 1957. Civil-rights demonstrations in Northern Ireland in 1968 were exploited by the IRA whose chief of staff announced a resumption of activities on 18 August 1969. Early in 1971 terrorism intensified in Ireland, spreading to England on 22 February 1972 with a bombing outrage at Aldershot. Splits between the official IRA and the more radical 'provisional' IRA first became evident between January and March 1971 but gained new significance in May 1972 when the provisionals declined to accept a ceasefire announced by their 'official' leaders. Twenty-one people were killed in Birmingham by IRA terrorists on 21 November 1974 and an IRA gang was responsible for a series of bombings and murders in London during October–December 1975. The IRA continued to wage urban guerrilla warfare in Northern Ireland and to indulge in kidnapping and murder south of the border. Claims by convicted detainees in the Maze prison that they should be entitled to a special 'political status' led to demonstrations and ultimately to hunger strikes. Sympathy was aroused in America for the IRA by the deaths of nine hunger strikers in the Maze between May and September 1981. On 12 October 1984 an IRA bomb wrecked the Grand Hotel, Brighton, where Mrs Thatcher and many of her cabinet were staying for the Conservative Party Conference; there were five deaths and thirty-two serious injuries. After a lull in 1986 there was an escalation of violence in March 1987, with arms known to have reached IRA units from Libya. Eleven civilians were killed at a Remembrance Day parade in Enniskillen (8 November 1987). In 1988–9 the IRA was active in Germany and the Netherlands and killed eleven Royal Marine bandsmen at Deal, but three activists were shot by the SAS in Gibraltar (March 1988). Ian Gow, MP, a former junior minister for Northern Ireland, was killed by a car bomb in Sussex (30 July 1990). A mortar attack was made on Downing Street during a cabinet meeting on 7 February 1991 and eleven days later bombs exploded at Paddington and Victoria railway stations. One day after the 1992 General Election a powerful bomb devastated much of the centre of the City of London and in March 1994 four mortar bombs were fired at Heathrow airport. Under pressure from ➤Sinn Féin the IRA announced an end to military operations from midnight on 31 August 1994. The ceasefire was called off at 6 p.m. on 9 February 1996, an hour before a car bomb caused extensive damage and two deaths at South Quay and Canary Wharf in London's docklands. During the weeks preceding the 1997 election the IRA suspended attacks in Northern Ireland, but launched an effective campaign against communications in England, disrupting motorways and the railway system. There were further murders in Armagh in June, but on 20 July 1997 the IRA restored the ceasefire, in anticipation of talks between Sinn Féin and the Labour Government. Splinter groups of terrorists continued to defy the IRA leadership.

Iron Curtain. A term gaining general currency from the spring of 1946 onwards as a description of the border between Soviet-dominated countries and the West. The phrase was used by Churchill in a famous speech at Fulton, Missouri, on 5 March 1946, although he had also used it in a confidential telegram to President Truman nine months previously. The metaphor appeared earlier still, at the end of February 1945, in a propaganda article by ➤Goebbels which was quoted in two leading English newspapers, thereby probably subconsciously suggesting the phrase to Churchill. In popular usage 'iron curtain' came to signify ideological restraint, marked by an absence of freedom to move into and out of Bulgaria, Czechoslovakia, Hungary, Poland, Romania and Albania. Excessive use of the phrase has tended to exaggerate uniformity, obscuring local variations and ignoring instances of independent thought and action.

Islamic Fundamentalism. A comprehensive term used to explain, somewhat facilely, the return of Islamic militancy after decades of passive acceptance of Western encroachment on traditional values. The impact of fundamentalism was strongest in ►Iran under ►Khomeini, from 1979 to 1989, but the element of rejuvenation of Islam had already inspired the (Sunni) Muslim Brotherhood, founded by the Egyptian schoolmaster Hasan al-Bana (1906–49) in 1928 and becoming a secret paramilitary force by the end of the Second World War. The Brotherhood's ideology was expressed by Sayyid Qutb in *Islam and the Problems of Civilization*, a manifesto urging a return to strict Islamic law. Qutb and many others in the Brotherhood were executed for plotting against ►Nasser in 1955–6. The fundamentalist Brotherhood provoked rebellion and harsh repression in ►Syria under ►Asad, between 1962 and 1984. ►Gaddafi in Libya and ►Zia in Pakistan shrewdly exploited fundamentalist sympathies which they did not share, but which genuinely fired the enthusiasm of the Mujaheddin in ►Afghanistan. The Islamic Salvation Front of ►Algeria is also militantly fundamentalist; so, too, is the secret Turkish Islami Harekat which carried out assassinations in Istanbul in the early 1990s.

Isolationism. An American policy advocating non-participation in alliances or in the affairs of other nations. The concept, stemming from Washington's farewell address of 17 September 1796, was confirmed in the Monroe Doctrine of 1823 and observed by both Republican and Democrat administrations until the opening of the twentieth century. Isolationist sentiment remained strong, especially in the Mid-West and among communities of Germanic or Irish descent. Isolationism contributed to the American people's rejection of Woodrow Wilson's international ideal, the ►League of Nations, and helped revive the Republican Party's fortunes when ►Harding stood for President in 1920. Even under the Democrat Franklin ►Roosevelt isolationism in the Senate was strong enough to bring about a series of Neutrality Acts (1935–9) which, *inter alia*, banned loans to belligerents in civil or international wars, forbade the shipment of arms or munitions, and sought to prevent US citizens sailing in the ships of countries at war. Although these measures were gradually relaxed in 1940–41 – notably by the ►Lend-Lease Act – isolationism was only relinquished after the shock of Pearl Harbor. In the early 1960s a form of isolationism reappeared among the more conservative Republicans, who demanded the expulsion of the United Nations from American soil and urged the establishment of a 'fortress America', free from overseas obligations.

Israel. Was established as a Jewish state in ►Palestine on 14 May 1948, when the British mandate ended. The neighbouring Arab lands refused to recognize Israel and invaded the country on the following day. This 'War of Independence', technically ended by a series of ceasefires from January to March 1949, enabled the Israelis to enlarge the land under their control by a quarter. Tension continued with the Arabs and there was frequent loss of life, especially along the frontier with Jordan. Border warfare necessitated the establishment of defended settlements in uncultivated areas: thirty-one of the 'Nahal' settlements were created between 1951 and 1955, extending from the Lebanese border to the edge of the ►Gaza Strip. In 1955 an Egyptian blockade within the Gulf of Aqaba cut trade from Israel's only southern port, Eilat: this was the most important contributory cause of the ►Sinai Campaign in 1956. Despite the subsequent creation of a UN buffer force in Sinai, there were frequent actions near Gaza and also along Israel's northern frontier with Syria. The massing of Arab troops in May 1967 induced Israel to launch a preventive campaign, the ►Six-Day War, which won for Israel the whole of Sinai, the West Bank of the Jordan river, and the Golan Heights on the Syrian frontier. The establishment by the Israelis of a provisional administration on the West Bank of the Jordan and the continued presence of Israeli troops on the Suez Canal induced acts of terrorism, inside and outside Israel, as well as raids and counter-raids along the border. These activities were especially serious in the period 1968–70. In the autumn of 1973 the Egyptians and Syrians made a concerted surprise attack on the Day of Atonement (Yom Kippur), thus beginning the ►'October War'. Threats by the Arab states to the oil supplies of the western nations encouraged diplomatic intervention in Middle Eastern affairs; and Israel accepted an agreement with Egypt for the disengagement of forces along the Canal on 18 January 1974. Despite a conference at ►Geneva no general settlement could be reached, and tension continued along the borders with Syria and ►Lebanon.

In December 1948 Israel had a population of about 880,000, of whom 759,000 were Jewish. Immigration, at its peak in 1949–51 but again high in 1957 and 1962–3, brought 1½ million Jews to Israel in the first twenty-five years after Independence. Ingenious methods were found for meeting the shortage of water and oil so that industry could flourish, with greater concentration than elsewhere in the Middle East. Special attention was given to the development of the Kibbutzim, the settlements which formed basic pioneering units in Jewish farming methods even in mandated Palestine. Politically Israel at first accepted the traditions of ►Zionism, electing Chaim ►Weizmann as first President. The moderate socialism associated with ►Ben-Gurion, Mrs Golda ►Meir and the ►Labour movement became unpopular in the mid 1970s, partly because of high taxation but also because of a feeling that it was more inclined to appease the Great Powers than were the parties of the Right. The election of May 1977 gave a victory to the right-wing alliance, known as Likud, which was headed by Menachem ►Begin. Peace with Egypt was offset by annexationist policies on the Golan Heights and the West Bank of the river Jordan. From June 1982 the Israelis became increasingly involved in the ►Lebanon. There was widespread criticism in Israel of the army's role in the phalangist killings at Chabra and Chatila; the Kahane judicial commission

Italy

censured the Defence Minister, four senior army officers and, indirectly, Begin himself. Yitzhak Shamir (1925–) succeeded to the premiership in October 1983. The indecisive nature of the July 1984 election led to a coalition government, in which it was agreed that the Labour leader, Shimon Perez (1923–), should be Prime Minister from September 1984 until October 1986 when Shamir (Likud) would succeed him. The Shamir years saw increasing violence on the West Bank and in the Gaza Strip. A further indecisive election in November 1988 kept Shamir in office at the head of another coalition. Shamir resigned in March 1990 but, as Peres found it impossible to create a viable coalition government, he returned to office, dependent on Jewish Orthodox hard-liners for support. Under American pressure, Israel remained a non-belligerent in the Second ►Gulf War despite several Iraqi Scud missiles landing on Israeli soil. ►Rabin became head of a predominantly Labour coalition after the election of June 1992. Despite constant threats from Jewish extremists the government began negotiations with King ►Hussein and ►Arafat to settle Palestinian issues; an abortive approach was made to ►Syria. Agreement on autonomy for predominantly Arab regions in Palestine was reached with the PLO at Oslo (13 September 1993) and a peace treaty with Jordan was signed in Washington on 26 October 1994. After Rabin's assassination at a peace rally in November 1995 Peres returned to the premiership, but the electorate rejected his policies in May 1996 and an eight-party coalition government was formed by the right-wing Likud leader, Benjamin Netanyahu (1946–). Relations with the Arabs deteriorated rapidly because of his backing for Israeli settlers on the West Bank.

Italy. Became a unified kingdom under the royal House of Savoy in 1860. The assassination of the second king of Italy, Umberto I, on 29 July 1900 led to the accession of ►Victor Emmanuel III, who was on the throne for forty-six years. The first part of his reign was marked by syndicalist unrest and by a change in foreign policy by which Italy left the Triple Alliance (Germany, Austria–Hungary and Italy) and entered the First World War on the side of the Entente in May 1915. The Italians suffered a severe defeat at ►Caporetto, redeemed in the last days of the war in the battle of Vittorio Veneto. Disappointment at the peace settlement and fear of the revolutionary Left encouraged the rise of fascism and the appointment of ►Mussolini as Prime Minister on 30 October 1922. The fascist era (1922–43) was marked by extensive public works schemes to relieve unemployment (draining of the Pontine marshes, improved communications, farm settlements for ex-servicemen), reconciliation with the Vatican (►Lateran Treaties), and a vigorous foreign policy (►Corfu Incident, ►Abyssinian War) which was offset from 1936 onwards by growing dependence on Nazi Germany, Mussolini's partner in the ►Axis. Italy declared war on Britain and France on 10 June 1940 but, after defeats in Greece, East Africa and North Africa, was confronted by an Anglo-American landing in Sicily (10 July 1943). Mussolini was dismissed by the King a fortnight later and succeeded as Prime Minister by Marshal ►Badoglio who made peace with the western allies (8 September) and declared war on Germany (13 October). Fighting continued throughout Italy until 25 April 1945, the Italian partisans helping the British and Americans to clear German troops from the peninsula. The ending of the war led to the increased political influence of the ►Communist Party, although the outstanding postwar statesman was a Christian Democrat, ►de Gasperi. Victor Emmanuel abdicated in favour of his son, Umberto II (9 May 1946), but three weeks later a referendum decided by 12,717,923 votes to 10,719,284 in favour of a republic and the royal family left the country on 13 June 1946.

Rehabilitation and recovery under de Gasperi enabled the start of long overdue economic reforms intended to develop the south. Abroad, the Italian Republic helped create NATO and the embryonic ►European Community. A multiplicity of parties and splinter groups weakened political stability: in the first thirty years of the republic there were twenty-six governments under twelve prime ministers, dependent mainly on coalitions. In the 1960s overpopulation led to unemployment, only partially mitigated by the mobility of labour permitted under Common Market rules. Economic recession and financial crises benefited the communists, who gained spectacular successes in municipal elections, 1974–6. Urban violence, marked by political murders and kidnapping, seemed to foreshadow a period of constitutional anarchy when President Leone dissolved parliament on 1 May 1976. General elections held at the end of the following month gave the Christian Democrats 263 seats and the Communists 228 seats in a chamber of 630 members. The Christian Democrat leader, Giulio ►Andreotti, formed a minority government dependent for its survival on continued disunity among the four parties of the Left – a familiar constitutional phenomenon in the republic's history. The effective power of the 'Red Brigade' urban terrorists was shown in the spring of 1978 by the seizure and subsequent murder of the distinguished Christian Democrat, Aldo ►Moro. Terrorist kidnappings and outrages continued against a background of political instability. Despite electoral defeats, the rejection of proffered resignations and frequent parliamentary deadlock, Andreotti struggled on for three years. His fall, in July 1979, was followed by the longest political crisis since the establishment of the republic – twenty-nine days – and by a succession of short-lived governments. In July 1984 Bettino Craxi (1935–) became the republic's first socialist Prime Minister, at the head of a five-party coalition, which bravely put on trial leading members of the Red Brigade, the Sicilian Mafia and terrorists of the extreme Right. Craxi survived, with difficulty, until April 1987; two months later an indecisive General Election brought to office Italy's youngest Prime Minister, Giovanni Goria (1943–94); Goria, however, was forced from office in March 1988. Ciriaco De Mita then improvised a coalition which lasted for sixteen months, until in July 1989 Andreotti returned at the head of a five-party coalition. When conflict over budget proposals caused a new political crisis in March 1991, Andreotti was invited to try again. In April 1991 he formed his seventh government, the republic's fiftieth in forty-five years.

In 1992 allegations of corruption began to discredit leading political figures, including Craxi and Goria. Andreotti left office in May 1992 and the leaders of all five main political parties had resigned by the end of the following year. Evidence of acceptance of bribes and, in some instances, of ►Mafia protection or membership was cited to discredit more than half of the Chamber of Deputies and almost a third of senators in the Upper House, as well as over a thousand businessmen and civil servants. The scandal led to constitutional revision and to a revival of regionalism, including the growth of a Northern League, which sought to purify and protect Lombardy, Piedmont and the Veneto by autonomy within a loosely federated Italian state. Disenchantment with traditional politics favoured the rapid rise to power of the media tycoon Silvio ►Berlusconi, who became premier from May to December 1994. Experiments at government by non-party figures with apparently impeccable credentials were abandoned in time for the general election of April 1996, which was won by the Democratic Party of the Left, whose leader Romano Prodi formed a socialist coalition. By then Craxi had been sentenced to eight and a half years' imprisonment, Goria died while under investigation, and Andreotti was on trial in Rome. The Prodi government lowered inflation, recovered Italy's influence in the EU and, in 1997, sought to check ►Albania's descent into political anarchy.

Ito, Hiroboumi (1841–1909, created a prince 1901), Japanese statesman. Born into a peasant family, adopted by aristocrats close to the imperial family, sent to England in 1863 and returned to Japan as a convinced believer in westernization, later making further world tours to gain experience of modern government. He became Japanese chief minister in 1884 and virtually controlled the government 1884–8, 1892–6 and 1900–1901. He was largely responsible for summoning the first Japanese legislature in 1890 and for building up a modern fleet. Between 1901 and 1904 he strongly opposed the mounting nationalistic fever which sought war with Russia. His hostility to the Russo-Japanese War led to his disgrace and he spent the last three years of his life as Governor of Korea, vainly seeking to introduce liberal reforms. On 26 October 1909 he was assassinated by a Korean patriot fanatic. Ito was responsible to a greater extent than any other individual for the Europeanization of Japan's government, economy and armed services.

Ivory Coast. Independent West African republic on the Gulf of Guinea. French trading settlements were established in the region in the middle of the nineteenth century and the Ivory Coast, although not finally pacified until 1912, formally became a French colony in 1893. In December 1958 the colony received the status of an autonomous republic within the French Community, achieving full independence in August 1960. Under the Presidency of Félix ►Houphouët-Boigny the Ivory Coast became an outstanding example of the French system of benevolent decolonization, maintaining friendly relations with successive governments in Paris and taking the lead in the organization of a loose union of neighbouring states (Dahomey, Togo, the Niger Republic and Upper Volta, which changed its name in 1984 to Burkina Faso) in a Conseil de l'Entente to further political and economic collaboration between the former French equatorial colonies.

Iwo Jima, Battle of (19 February to 17 March 1945). Iwo Jima is a volcanic island in the Bonin archipelago 750 miles south of Tokyo, used as a major Japanese air base in the Second World War. US Marines landed on Iwo Jima in February 1945, intending to develop the base as a 'stepping stone' for the planned final assault on the Japanese mainland. Japanese defences on Mount Suribachi were so highly developed that the Marines lost 5,000 killed and 15,000 wounded in the three weeks of fighting to secure the island.

Izvolsky, Alexander R. (1856–1919), Russian statesman. Born into the lesser Russian nobility, educated at the Imperial Lyceum in St Petersburg, entered the diplomatic service in 1875, spending many years in the Balkan capitals before becoming ambassador in Tokyo in 1899. He was moved from Japan to Denmark in 1903. Dynastic links in Copenhagen strengthened Izvolsky's influence on the T'sar and he was an automatic choice as Foreign Minister, May 1906 to September 1910. Under his direction Russo-Japanese relations were improved and the ►Anglo-Russian Entente completed in 1907. His prestige suffered from the Bosnian Crisis of 1908–9, when he was skilfully outmanoeuvred by the Austrian Foreign Minister. In September 1910 he became Russian ambassador in Paris, where he remained for six years, strengthening the military aspects of the alliance between France and Russia and negotiating the abortive ►Constantinople Agreements of 1915. The repudiation of his achievements by the Bolsheviks hastened the end of his life. He died in exile at Biarritz. For German diplomatic historians in the inter-war period Izvolsky was the arch-intriguer, constantly scheming to complete the encirclement of the Reich. This view, however, assumes a greater continuity of purpose than Izvolsky's policy ever possessed.

J

Jajce Congress (29–30 November 1943). A meeting of delegates, from all over Yugoslavia, to the Anti-Fascist National Liberation Committee (AVNOJ), was held in the Bosnian town of Jajce (captured from the Germans and their allies by Tito's partisans in September 1942) at the end of November 1943. The Congress resolved to create a republican and federated Yugoslavia at the end of the war, and agreed that the Committee should assume the powers of a provisional government. Another motion bestowed on ►Tito the newly created title of 'Marshal of Yugoslavia'. The political decisions of the Jajce Congress were fundamental to the Yugoslav Revolution, and the anniversary of the Congress is celebrated as Yugoslavia's National Day. The most remarkable aspect of the Jajce Congress is its place and timing: within 'occupied' Europe; and eleven months before the first of the 'liberating armies' reached Yugoslav soil. The Federal People's Republic was proclaimed in Belgrade exactly two years later, 29 November 1945.

Japan. An isolated and largely feudal empire until the accession of the Meiji Emperor, Mutsuhito (reigned 1867–1912); became rapidly industrialized and emerged as a Great Power during the ►Taisho era, under the Emperor Yoshihito (reigned 1912–26). The early years of his successor, ►Hirohito, saw a constitutional recession in which army leaders and extreme nationalists used the Emperor's traditional divinity as a source of autocratic authority to minimize the effectiveness of the parliamentary liberalism encouraged during the Taisho era. The conquest of ►Manchuria was followed by the invasion of China in 1937, identification with Germany and Italy in the ►Anti-Comintern Pact and with an attempt to establish the so-called 'Greater East Asia Co-Prosperity Sphere', culminating in ►Pearl Harbor and war with the United States and the British Commonwealth in December 1941. The atomic bombs of 6 and 9 August 1945 on ►Hiroshima and Nagasaki led Emperor Hirohito to authorize Japan's surrender (15 August). Japan was then occupied mainly by American, British, Australian and New Zealand forces, commanded by the US General, Douglas ►MacArthur. The period of Occupation lasted officially until 28 April 1952 when a peace treaty signed at ►San Francisco the previous September came into force. During the Occupation a revised constitution (6 March 1946) extended the parliamentary powers originally granted by the emperors Mutsuhito and Yoshihito, while at the same time the Emperor Hirohito formally renounced his divinity, becoming a figurehead monarch with no executive power. This 'democratization' was accompanied by a series of land-reform measures (1946–50) and the spread of new ideas in education and social behaviour. From 1951 to 1960 Japan benefited economically from her close relationship with the USA, largely based on a bilateral 'Security Pact' signed on 8 September 1951. Anti-American feeling exploded in the first of many violent demonstrations in the summer of 1960, when the Pact was renewed for a further ten years, and there were other serious outbursts in March 1968 and November 1969. An amazing economic recovery led to an annual 10 per cent growth in the gross national product between 1953 and 1965. Middle-class consumer ideals stabilized political activity until 1968–9 when a new generation of militants, with anarchistic sympathies, began to demand radical reforms and a terrorist organization, the 'Japanese Red Army', came into being. Outwardly, however, Japan continued to benefit from her economic miracle and trade prospered. For the last fifty years political control has rested almost entirely with the centre-right Liberal Democratic Party. Allegations of corruption led to a ten-month interlude in 1993–4 when a seven-party coalition formed the government. This experiment ended in further scandals; the Liberal Democrats collaborated with a socialist Prime Minister from June 1994 until January 1996 when they again formed a government, dependent on support from the socialists and one of the smaller parties. Early in 1998 the Japanese economy entered the worst recession in fifty years, weakening the Liberal Democrat dominance of political life.

Jaruzelski, Wojciech (1923–), Polish soldier and head of state. Born at Kurow, near Lublin, his parents were devout Catholics. When he was sixteen the family was deported to the Soviet Union. Soon afterwards he was orphaned. He enrolled in a Polish division of the Red Army in 1943, graduating from Warsaw Military Academy after the war. By 1961 he was in charge of the army's political education and entered the *Sejm* (parliament). ►Gomulka and his successors, Gierek and Kania, advanced Jaruzelski's career rapidly in their terms as Party leaders: politburo member from 1964; Chief of the General Staff, 1965–8; Defence Minister, 1968–83. The threat from ►Solidarity led Kania to secure Jaruzelski's appointment as Prime Minister in February 1981, only to find the General displace him as the Party's First Secretary in September. On 13–14 December 1981 Jaruzelski carried through the first military *coup* in any people's republic, imposing martial law (until July 1983) and governing through a Military Council of National Salvation for twelve months. His political dexterity prevented a Soviet occupation; he held in check the security forces while seeking to collaborate with the Church. Although he remained Party Leader he relinquished the premiership in November 1985 and became Chairman of the Council of State. In this capacity – virtually Poland's President – he was invited to London in June 1989. He retired from office in December 1990. In March 1996 he was accused of ordering troops to fire on a demonstration in 1970, thereby causing forty-four deaths.

Jaurès, Jean (1859–1914), French socialist leader. Born of bourgeois parentage, at Castres, educated at the École Normale and Toulouse University, where he was a lecturer in philosophy. He represented Tarn in the Chamber of Deputies, 1885–9,

1893–8 and 1902–14. Jaurès was always a specifically French socialist rather than a Marxist, finding inspiration in his country's revolutionary tradition. Although the outstanding socialist writer and orator of his generation, his respect for the rights of the individual brought him into conflict with his more doctrinaire comrades. His sympathy for Dreyfus and hostility to ➤anti-Semitism won many converts to socialism. He was forced to accept the ruling of the Second International's Amsterdam Congress in 1905, which condemned the participation of socialists in 'bourgeois coalition governments' and he personally never held office. For the last eight years of his life he campaigned against excessive nationalism, favouring a 'citizen's militia' rather than a conscript army and trying to organize opposition by the workers in France and Germany to a war between their two nations. He was assassinated in a Parisian café on 31 July 1914 by a fanatical French nationalist. In 1904 he founded the first successful socialist daily newspaper in France, *L'Humanité*.

Jellicoe, John Rushworth (1859–1935, knighted 1907, created viscount 1919, earl 1925), British admiral. Born at Southampton, entered Royal Navy 1872, survived the disastrous collision between the battleships *Camperdown* and *Victoria* in June 1893, promoted captain in 1897, vice-admiral 1910, admiral 1915, Admiral of the Fleet 1919. Jellicoe was one of the officers trained by ➤Fisher to take high command in the war with Germany, which Fisher regarded as inevitable. Jellicoe served as Second Sea Lord from 1912 until the outbreak of war, when he was appointed commander-in-chief of the Grand Fleet. He gained small-scale victories in naval engagements in Heligoland Bight (28 August 1914) and on the Dogger Bank (24 January 1915). At ➤Jutland in 1916 he won the major naval battle of the war, although suffering heavier losses than the Germans and being criticized for his strategic rigidity and caution. He was First Sea Lord, 1916–17, and chief of the naval staff in the closing stages of the war. From 1920 to 1924 Jellicoe was Governor-General of New Zealand.

Jewish Agency. Originally a body representing the Jewish community in ➤Palestine established by the British (with encouragement from the League of Nations) as an essential institution under their mandate. The final form of the Agency was only settled in 1929, when half of its members came from outside Palestine, under the auspices of the World Zionist Organization. The Agency was responsible for promoting Jewish settlement within Palestine, administering funds of service to the community as a whole, and gaining experience in limited self-government. In 1948 the Palestinian members of the Agency became an embryonic government for the state of Israel, the members outside Palestine continuing to encourage investment in Israel and immigration of Zionists. The Arabs in Palestine resented the close collaboration between the Jewish Agency and the British High Commissioners in the 1920s. The first British High Commissioner, Herbert Samuel (1870–1963), wished to establish an Arab Agency, in order to strike a 'fair balance' between the communities, but he was overruled in London.

Jinnah, Muhammed Ali (1876–1948), founding father of Pakistan. Born in Karachi, joined the Indian National Congress (►Congress Party) but resented Hindu dominance of the independence movement and disapproved of Gandhi's civil disobedience campaign. He left Congress in 1934 to organize a rival political party, the Muslim League (originally a predominantly religious and cultural movement, dating from 1906). The remaining Muslim members of the Congress joined Jinnah in 1935. Relations between the two parties became strained in 1937 when, after the provincial elections, Congress declined to form coalition administrations with the Muslims in communally mixed areas. At a meeting in Lahore (March 1940) Jinnah led the Muslim League in demanding eventual partition of India and the creation of a 'Pakistan'. Jinnah increased his standing by giving support for the British cause in the Second World War, whereas the Hindu Congress refused any form of collaboration. Elections at the end of the war enabled Jinnah's followers to win almost every seat in the Muslim areas: he now demanded a six-province Pakistan, comprising Baluchistan, Sind, the Punjab, Bengal, Assam and the North-West frontier; and he rejected proposals which would have left most of Assam and much of the Punjab and Bengal in Hindu hands. Conflicts with Congress proposals led Jinnah, in August 1946, to favour 'direct action', and in riots between Muslims and Hindus around Calcutta some 4,000 people died. British opinion thereafter hardened against Jinnah, as he came to realize early in 1947; and he was forced to accept the 'maimed and moth-eaten' Pakistan which he had earlier rejected. He became Governor-General of Pakistan in August 1947, but his health was poor and he died thirteen months later with many ambitions still unrealized.

Joffre, Joseph Jacques Césaire (1852–1931), Marshal of France. Born at Rivesaltes in the eastern Pyrenees, near Perpignan, the son of a cooper, entered the army in 1870, helping defend Paris by taking command of a battery while still a cadet. Subsequently Joffre served in Indo-China and north Africa, winning distinction in 1894 when, as a lieutenant-colonel, he led a column on a gruelling march across the desert to capture Timbuktu. He showed gifts as an organizer when he was Director of Engineers, 1904–6, and he became Chief of the General Staff in 1911, automatically assuming command of France's armies in the field in 1914. He was responsible for the great counter-attack at the first battle of the Marne but later became identified with the long war of attrition on the Western Front. His imperturbability gave reassurance but sprang from a lack of imagination which limited his gifts as tactician and strategist. 'Papa' Joffre ('*Grandpère*') was respected by his troops and trusted, both by politicians and by his allies, but the failure to break through on the ►Somme discredited him. After twenty-eight months of 'blood and mud' he was promoted Marshal of France in December 1916 and succeeded as commander-in-chief by General Nivelle. Joffre served as president of the Allied War Council in 1917, and held sinecure posts at the Ministry of War from 1918 until 1930.

John XXIII (1881–1963, pontiff 1958–63), Pope. Born Angelo Giuseppe Roncalli at Sollo il Monte near Bergamo, ordained in 1904, served as army chaplain in the First World War, entered the papal diplomatic service and became apostolic delegate to Bulgaria (1925) and to Greece and Turkey (1935), before being appointed papal nuncio in liberated France (1944). He was created a cardinal in 1953, the year in which he also became Patriarch of Venice. On the death of ➤Pius XII he was elected Pope on the twelfth ballot (28 October 1958). His pontificate was marked by increased collaboration between Catholic and non-Catholic churches, by the progressive reforms of the second ➤Vatican Council, by more liberal social doctrines (as defined in the encyclical *Mater et Magistra* of 1961), and by his urgent pleas for world peace. He was a popular figure, of great humility; and, as pontiff, he continued to emphasize the importance of pastoral work by visiting prisons, hospitals and special schools within Rome.

John Paul II (1920–, pontiff 1978–), Pope. Born Karol Wojtyla at Wadowice, near Cracow in Poland. He entered the Jagiellonian University at Cracow in 1938 and was forced to work in a stone quarry during the German occupation of his homeland. In November 1946 he was ordained priest and, after studying in Rome, returned to Cracow as a parish priest. He spent most of the following twenty-nine years in that part of Poland, becoming auxiliary bishop in 1958, archbishop in January 1964 and cardinal in June 1967. To an understanding of communist governments he added wider experience through pastoral visits to Canada, Australia and America. When Pope John Paul I (Cardinal Albino Luciani) died from a heart attack only thirty-three days after taking up his 'supreme pastorship', the cardinals broke recent practice by looking for a successor outside Italy, and Cardinal Wojtyla became the first non-Italian pope since 1522. He was invested as John Paul II on 22 October 1978. His pontificate has been marked by a conservative approach to theological questions, moral problems and church discipline and by extensive travelling. In the first ten years of his pontificate he visited 75 countries on 40 international journeys, an average absence from Rome of 15 days in every 200. On three occasions he returned to his native Poland (1979, 1983, 1987). He was in Ireland on 29–30 September 1979, making a moving appeal at Drogheda for an end to violence. On 13 May 1981 he was shot and seriously wounded in St Peter's Square. When he recovered he was able to undertake a missionary journey to Nigeria in 1982 and to Portugal, where another attempt on his life was foiled at ➤Fatima. A few days later he came to England, participating in an ecumenical service at Canterbury Cathedral on 29 May 1982, before going to Scotland and Wales. Early in June he made a brief visit to Argentina, deploring in both London and Buenos Aires the conflict then reaching a climax in the ➤Falkland Islands. Several ➤encyclicals and synods emphasized concern for a moderate traditionalism in spiritual life and mistrust of permissiveness; critics complain that, in asserting the papacy's multi-national authority, he restricted the episcopate's local autonomy, which had often recognized the need within the Church for regional variations in social practice. His health began to fail in the winter of 1995–6, but he continued to travel widely; even in 1997 he was able to visit Sarajevo and Beirut and make an emotional return to Poland, and in January 1998 he was welcomed in Cuba.

Johnson, Amy (1903–41), pioneer British airwoman. Born at Kingston upon Hull, where she went to school, graduating at Sheffield University. She learnt to fly in her leisure hours (1928–9), while working for a firm of London solicitors; and she also studied aircraft maintenance, becoming the first woman to hold an Air Ministry ground engineer's certificate. In May 1930 she flew solo in a De Havilland Gipsy Moth from Croydon to Darwin, Australia (and ultimately to Brisbane) in twenty days. Her achievement made her the heroine idol of her generation, a schoolgirl's inspiration for the 1930s, and she was created a Commander of the British Empire. In July 1931 she flew from London to Tokyo by way of Siberia in ten days, a new record; and she later flew solo to Cape Town (1932). Her marriage to a rival air pioneer, Jim Mollison (1905–59), in 1932 did not stand the strain of newspaper publicity and she reverted to her maiden name when the marriage was dissolved in 1938. On the outbreak of the Second World War she joined the Air Transport Auxiliary. She was killed when her aircraft crashed in the Thames Estuary, 5 January 1941.

Johnson, Lyndon Baines (1908–73), thirty-sixth President of the USA. Born in Stonewall, Texas, worked his way through college, became a teacher and was a 'New Deal' Congressman from 1937 to 1948 although serving in the US Navy during the war. He was elected Senator in 1948 and was majority leader at the time of his selection by ►Kennedy as his running-mate in the 1960 Presidential election. Vice-President Johnson was Kennedy's host in Dallas on 22 November 1963 and, on Kennedy's assassination, was immediately sworn in as President, subsequently gaining 61 per cent of the popular votes in the 1964 election, giving him the biggest majority ever achieved by an American President at that time. His five years in the White House saw the completion of civil-rights legislation, a massive federal Education Act (1965), and the establishment of ►'Medicare' in pursuit of his professed ideal of a 'Great Society'. These achievements were offset by increasingly large-scale commitments to the ►Vietnam War, leading to mounting unrest and protests at home. Ill-health, and the sharp decline in his popularity because of the war, induced Johnson to announce his retirement from politics rather than contest the Presidential election of 1968 (when his chosen candidate, Hubert Humphrey, was narrowly defeated by the Republican, ►Nixon).

Jordan. Until 1918 the present Hashemite Kingdom of Jordan formed part of the Turkish Empire. The League of Nations accorded Great Britain a mandate for the region east of the Jordan river which was established as the Emirate of Transjordan, under the rule of ►Abdullah Ibn Hussein. The mandate expired in 1946 and Transjordan became a kingdom, changing its name to Jordan in June 1949 when it absorbed territory west of the Jordan river, a part of ►Palestine from 1918 to

1948. On the assassination of Abdullah in July 1951, his son Talal reigned for a year, even though he was mentally ill. Abdullah's grandson, ►Hussein, succeeded Talal on 11 August 1952, assuming full sovereignty the following May. King Hussein, educated at Harrow and Sandhurst, found strong suspicion of British influence among his younger subjects. Under pressure, he agreed in March 1956 to dismiss General Sir John Glubb (1897–1986) and other British officers whom his grandfather had employed to build up the Arab Legion, a highly efficient army. Although the King sympathized with the Arab cause, he distrusted Nasser, as also did the Bedouins among his subjects. From February until July 1958 Jordan and Iraq formed a union of kingdoms to oppose Nasser's ►United Arab Republic but the murder of ►Feisal II and the establishment of a radical Arab regime in Baghdad left Jordan isolated. A major split developed within Jordan over the Palestinian problem; the Jordanian Government claimed sole guardianship of the Palestinian Arabs, formally offering Jordanian nationality to any Palestinians in February 1960; but this claim was disputed by the militant refugees, who maintained a commando force (*fedayeen*) for raids from Jordan into Israel, and who established in 1964 the ►Palestine Liberation Organization (PLO). Threats from these militants induced the King to accept the risk of war in 1967 (►Six-Day War), although the fighting cost Jordan the whole of the West Bank. A new influx of refugees swelled the ranks of the *fedayeen* and the PLO, who persisted in guerrilla operations against Israel. In February 1970 the Jordanian Government sought to establish control over the guerrillas, who responded by provoking a civil war, which became general to Jordan 17–25 September 1970. The loyalty of his Bedouin regiments saved Hussein but there was heavy fighting in Amman and the northern region. The Jordanian Government gradually reasserted its authority and the last *fedayeen* military bases were broken up in July 1971. During the ►October War of 1973 eighty Jordanian tanks assisted the Syrians on the Golan Heights but there was no fighting along the Jordan river or the Dead Sea. Subsequently Jordan favoured a negotiated settlement of the whole Middle East problem, a policy strongly advocated by Hussein at an Arab League summit conference in Amman in 1987 and subsequently pursued with US backing. Jordan's relations with the PLO improved after 1974 and with Egypt from 1988. A final peace treaty with Israel was concluded on 26 October 1994, providing for the return to Jordan of the southern Wadi Araba, mutual recognition, Jordanian protection for Muslim holy places in Jerusalem, joint action against terrorist attacks, the opening of frontier posts, and cooperation over the use of waters from the rivers Jordan and Yarmouk. Political parties, banned in 1957 for fear of a socialist republican rising, were allowed freedom in 1991, provided they gave pledges of loyalty to the monarchy.

Juan Carlos I (1938–), King of Spain. Born in Rome, a grandson of ►Alfonso XIII. After receiving his earliest education in Switzerland and Portugal his father, the Count of Barcelona (1913–), was encouraged by ►Franco to send Juan Carlos to Madrid where he was trained in the armed services, studied in Madrid University

(1960–62) and spent five years gaining practical experience of civil service administration. The Franco Government recognized him as heir to a vacant throne in July 1969 and on Franco's death he was proclaimed King (22 November 1975). Within eighteen months he guided ➤Spain back to democracy after a lapse of 41 years, his firm control subsequently thwarting the right-wing *coup* of Colonel Molina and dissident generals in February 1981. Juan Carlos married Sofia of Greece (1938–) in May 1962; his heir-apparent, the Prince of the Asturias, was born in January 1968.

July Conspiracy (20 July 1944). Principal anti-Nazi attempt to overthrow the regime and secure a negotiated peace. A bomb, planted by Colonel von Stauffenberg, exploded beneath Hitler's conference table at his headquarters at Rastenburg, East Prussia. Stauffenberg, believing Hitler killed by the explosion, flew to Berlin, where Field-Marshal von Witzleben and General von Beck proposed to take over the capital and proclaim a government headed by Carl Goerdeler, formerly Lord Mayor of Leipzig and for many years a resistance leader. The conspiracy failed, partly because Hitler was only injured and no one cut telephone communications with his headquarters and partly because of energetic counter-measures taken in Berlin by Major Ernst Remer, of the SS. German officers opposed to the Nazis succeeded in gaining control of occupied Paris but were unable to take action because of the failure in Berlin. The Nazis inflicted savage reprisals: some 150 alleged conspirators were executed (including Witzleben, Goerdeler, thirteen generals and two ambassadors) while fifteen other leading figures committed suicide, including Field-Marshal ➤Rommel. The conspiracy was not merely an abortive putsch: young German liberals, known collectively as the 'Kreisau Circle', and idealists influenced by the teachings of the Lutheran pastor, Dietrich Bonhoeffer (1907–45), suffered as heavily as did the dissident officers from Nazi vengeance.

Jutland, Battle of (31 May to 1 June 1916). Principal naval engagement of the First World War. There were two distinct actions: the battle-cruiser squadrons of the Royal Navy (Admiral Beatty, 1871–1935) and the German High Seas Fleet (Rear Admiral Hipper, 1863–1932) engaged each other in the afternoon of 31 May, while the main fleets (Admiral ➤Jellicoe and Vice-Admiral Scheer, 1861–1928) met in the early evening, lost contact in the dark and resumed action briefly in the early hours of the following day. Tactically the battle was indecisive: despite British preponderance in vessels (151 to 99) and gunpower the Germans were able to return to port. The British lost three battle-cruisers, three cruisers, eight destroyers and suffered 6,100 casualties; the Germans lost one battleship, one battle-cruiser, four cruisers and five destroyers, with 2,550 casualties. Strategically Jutland was a British victory since, although not automatically giving the Royal Navy command of the North Sea, it led the German naval command to retain surface vessels close inshore for the remainder of the war. To Germans the battle is known as 'the Skagerrak'.

K

Kádár, János (1912–89). Hungarian communist leader. Born at Kapoly, secretly joined the communist underground movement in 1932, and as an active member of the resistance became a member of the central committee in 1942. He was Minister of the Interior (1948–50) but was arrested in April 1951, tortured by the secret police, and kept for several months in solitary confinement at Vác before being released from prison in July 1954. On the fall of his enemy, ►Rákosi, in July 1956, Kádár was given a high post in the party executive, and at first shared with Imre ►Nagy the reform programme of that autumn, becoming First Secretary of the party on 25 October. The pace of the ►Hungarian Rising, and in particular the emergence of the old political parties, alarmed Kádár who left Budapest on the night of 1–2 November and, with Soviet support, proclaimed a new 'revolutionary government of peasants and workers' in eastern Hungary, pledged to save the republic from 'Horthyite fascist reactionaries'. Kádár supported the Soviet intervention which crushed the rising and he remained Prime Minister until 1958, continuously retaining his hold on policy as First Secretary thereafter. Greater freedom of expression was allowed from 1959 onwards, and when Kádár held the premiership for a second term (1961–5) he took positive measures of reconciliation and cautious liberalization. This trend was maintained, despite intervention with the other Warsaw Pact powers in Czechoslovakia in 1968. The reformer Karoly Grosz (►Hungary) edged Kádár out as Party Secretary in May 1988 by creating for him the purely titular post of Hungarian Socialist Workers' Party President.

Kamikaze ('Divine Wind'). The name assumed by fanatical Japanese airmen prepared to pilot planes carrying bombs directly into American, Australian and British ships, sacrificing their lives for the certainty of a direct hit. The first attacks were made on US warships in Leyte Gulf on 25 November 1944 but they became severe on 4 January 1945, when the Americans landed two crack corps on Luzon in the Philippines. Further heavy *kamikaze* raids were made on the allied armada off ►Okinawa in April and May 1945, severe damage being inflicted on the British aircraft-carriers *Indefatigable*, *Formidable* and *Victorious*. The Japanese chose the name *kamikaze* from a legendary occasion in the late thirteenth century when a typhoon destroyed an invasion fleet of Kublai Khan preparing to invade the Japanese homeland.

Kampuchea. ►Cambodia.

Kapp Putsch. Abortive conspiracy by the right-wing German journalist Wolfgang Kapp (1868–1922), with backing from General von Lüttwitz (1859–1942) and irregular military *freikorps* recently disbanded after fighting in the Baltic provinces. On 13 March 1920 Lüttwitz seized Berlin and proclaimed a new nationalistic government of which Kapp would be Chancellor. The legitimate republican government escaped to the provinces and called a general strike. Kapp was supported by ►Ludendorff but the officer corps, in general, stood aside. No foreign powers recognized Kapp's authority, which speedily dwindled away because of opposition from the security police and the workers. Kapp and Lüttwitz fled on 17 March. Although a fiasco, the putsch has historical significance: it revealed the existence of disgruntled nationalists in Germany who were eager to destroy the 'Bolshevism' of the ►Weimar Republic; and the main fighting unit of Lüttwitz's force, the Erhardt Brigade, brought with them from the Baltic a new distinguishing symbol on their helmets – the swastika.

Karamanlis, Constantine (1907–98), Greek statesman. Born in the village of Proti, eastern Macedonia, he practised as a lawyer in Athens, entered parliament in 1935 and held numerous government posts from 1946 to 1955. He gained a reputation for efficiency as Minister of Public Works and also won the confidence of American officials with whom he collaborated in aid programmes after the Greek Civil War. On the death of ►Papagos in October 1955 King Paul appointed Karamanlis as Prime Minister and encouraged him to found a new conservative movement, the National Radical Union (ERE). He remained Prime Minister until June 1963 when he resigned in protest at the Greek King's state visit to Britain, with which he had conducted difficult negotiations over ►Cyprus. Large sums of American aid helped the Karamanlis government overcome basic weaknesses in the economy, although he was disappointed in his hope of joining the Common Market. After his resignation, the 1964 election showed a tendency towards the Left which was arrested by the establishment of the regime of the ►Greek Colonels in 1967. Karamanlis declined to associate himself with the Colonels and went into self-imposed exile in Paris, from which he was recalled at the end of July 1974 in order to preside over the reintroduction into Greece of parliamentary government. Karamanlis did not attempt to revive the ERE, preferring to create a 'New Democracy Party'. In elections held on 17 November 1974 this party won 220 of the 300 seats in parliament, and Karamanlis continued as Prime Minister, settling the form of the revised parliamentary constitution, adopted by the Hellenic Republic in June 1975. He was second President of the Republic from May 1980 until March 1985 when he retired into private life and was succeeded by Judge Christos Sarzetakis. Karamanlis agreed to become President once more in May 1990, holding office until March 1995.

Károlyi, Mihály (1875–1955). Hungarian reformer. Born in Budapest, a member of one of the great Magyar landowning families. Count Károlyi entered parliament in 1905 with liberal views which became increasingly radical. Throughout the

First World War he led the Independent Party, which favoured the allies. He was appointed Prime Minister by Emperor-King ➤Charles on 30 October 1918 and immediately sought an armistice, hoping the allies would treat an independent Hungary as the victim of German–Austrian domination. On 16 November he became provisional President of the Hungarian Republic and tried to carry through social and democratic reforms, personally supervising the splitting up of his estates among the peasantry. Lack of support for Károlyi among the allied governments left him politically isolated and in March 1919 he was forced out of office by Béla ➤Kun, who established a communist regime. Károlyi went into exile, not returning to Hungary until 1946. He then served for three years as a Hungarian diplomat, but the increasingly totalitarian character of the new Hungarian republic led him to resign in 1949, and he lived his last six years as a private citizen in voluntary exile.

Kashmir Dispute. Before the partition of India, the northern state of Kashmir was under the hereditary rule of a Hindu Maharajah, even though more than three-quarters of his subjects were Muslim. After several months of indecision, the Maharajah signed an act of accession by which his territories entered India rather than Pakistan (October 1947). Fighting at once broke out between the Hindus in Jammu and the predominant Muslim tribesmen and both India and Pakistan moved regular army units into the state. India denounced Pakistan as an aggressor in territory which had been ceded by its ruler to the Union and appealed to the United Nations. A UN supervisory commission established a provisional demarcation line in January 1949 which left most of Kashmir in India although allowing small enclaves in the west to be occupied by the Pakistanis. Attempts to arbitrate were frustrated by the Indian Government, especially since it was assumed that in any settlement based upon the principle of self-determination most of the region would pass to Pakistan. In January 1957 Kashmir was formally integrated within the Indian Union, despite protests from Pakistan supported by the United Nations. There was a major conflict between India and Pakistan over the Kashmir question in 1965, with open hostilities in April, May and June and again in August and September. A truce was agreed at Tashkent in January 1966 in conversations between the leaders of Pakistan and India, Ayub Khan and Lal ➤Shastri, under Soviet chairmanship; but in December 1971 fighting flared up once more, during the Indo-Pakistani conflict over ➤Bangladesh. In July 1972 the Indian and Pakistan Governments accepted that the Kashmir problem should be settled bilaterally, although the principal Kashmiri spokesmen, Sheikh Mohammed ➤Abdullah and his son Dr Farooq Abdullah (1937–), continued to press for a plebiscite under UN supervision. A Kashmiri uprising began in December 1989, with attacks on Hindus and the taking of Western hostages. After fifty years the Kashmir dispute remains unresolved.

Kassa Incident (June 1941). ➤Košice Incident.

Kassem, Abdul Karim (1914–63), Iraqi revolutionary. Born in Baghdad, the son of a carpenter, became an army officer and, as a brigadier, was largely responsible for the revolution in ►Iraq of July 1958 which led to the murder of King Feisal II. Kassem became Prime Minister and Minister of Defence in a republic which paid lip-service to 'Arab nationalism'. Within a few months, however, most of his Nasserite supporters had left him and he was bitterly opposed to the Egyptians both over their policy in Syria and because of a conspiracy of Nasserites at Mosul (March 1959). Kassem survived one assassination attempt but had little constructive to offer the Iraqis and, in February 1963, was executed after a *coup* led by dissident members of the ►Ba'ath Party and some of Kassem's former military supporters.

Katanga. The south-eastern province of the former ►Belgian Congo. The province was rich in mineral resources, especially copper and uranium. These resources were exploited by the Union Minière, which enjoyed exclusive rights by agreement with the Belgian Government until 1990. The sudden decision to give the Congo independence in 1960 provoked a vigorous reaction from companies which had received such concessions. With their backing Katanga seceded from the Congo Republic (11 July 1960) under the leadership of ►Tshombe. The ►Congo Problem remained acute for two and a half years, a United Nations force sent to restore order meeting armed resistance from Tshombe's largely white mercenary army. Katanga's secession was ended on 14 January 1963. The name of the province was changed to Shaba in 1971: its principal town, formerly known as Elisabethville, became Lubumbashi. In March 1977 5,000 members of the 'Congolese National Liberation Front' invaded Shaba from bases in Angola but were repulsed in twelve weeks of sporadic fighting. A second invasion in May 1978 led to anarchy in the mining centre of Kolwezi: more than 200 people were massacred, some by the invaders and some by Zairian regular troops. French and Belgian airborne units were flown to Shaba to restore order. ►Zaire conceded autonomy in 1993, when the name reverted to Katanga. In November 1996 Katanga served as a springboard for the rebellion which forced ►Mobuto to flee the country.

Katyn Massacre. On 13 April 1943 the Nazi Ministry of Propaganda announced that German troops had found mass graves of thousands of Polish officers killed by the Russians in 1940 and buried in the forest of Katyn, near Smolensk. General ►Sikorski, head of the Polish government-in-exile, asked the International Red Cross to investigate the German report, since the Russians had consistently refused to account for the disappearance of 10,000 Polish soldiers in 1939–40. Stalin was angered by this Polish move and, denying the German report, broke off diplomatic relations with the exiled Polish Government. The Soviet authorities continued to insist that the Katyn graves mark the burial place of Poles massacred by the Germans, an explanation accepted by post-war Polish governments in Warsaw. In 1989 a Soviet–Polish commission blamed Soviet security police, thus confirming the first reports.

Kaunda, Kenneth David (1924–), first President of Zambia. Born at Lubwa. Northern Rhodesia, trained as a teacher and was for three years a headmaster before working as welfare officer in copper-mines. He was imprisoned for organizing a Zambian African National Congress in 1958 but by 1960 he was free and able to lead the United Nationalist Independence Party in opposition to the Federation of Rhodesia and ►Nyasaland. His electoral successes heralded the end of the Federation in December 1963. In January 1964 Dr Kaunda was appointed Prime Minister of Northern Rhodesia, supervising the constitutional arrangements which won his country independence as the Republic of ►Zambia ten months later. As President, Dr Kaunda sought to hold in check militants, especially during periods of tension with the Smith regime in neighbouring ►Rhodesia. President Kaunda's Christian humanism has made him deplore racialism, whether the persecutor be black or white, a view not shared by the opposition politicians within Zambia. The threat of disintegration in a republic seeking to unite more than seventy tribes led the President to assume autocratic powers in February 1972, establishing a one-party state. A new constitution, introduced in July 1973, consolidated the privileged position of Kaunda's United Nationalist Independence Party. Elections held five months later under the revised constitution confirmed Dr Kaunda's hold on the Presidency. His persistence in maintaining one-party dictatorship aroused criticism in the Commonwealth. After nineteen years he bowed to external pressure and authorized the formation of parties and, on 31 October 1991, a contested presidential election, which he lost to the Democracy Movement's leader, Frederick Chiruba. When Kaunda returned to active politics in June 1995, a constitutional amendment required presidential candidates to be third-generation Zambians. This move by Chiruba disqualified Kaunda, whose missionary father had come from south of the Zambezi. On Christmas Day 1997 he was arrested for allegedly having plotted a *coup* in October. The case against him was dropped three weeks later.

Kautsky, Karl (1854–1938), German, European socialist. Born in Prague and was, as a young man, a friend of Marx. He was a prominent member of the German Social Democrat Party from 1901 to 1918, opposing both the revisionist theories of ►Bernstein and the extremists on the far Left. Although a pacifist, bitterly opposed to the First World War, Kautsky rejected Bolshevik appeals for a revolutionary peace, his independence of character inclining him to denounce the dictatorship of the proletariat as a distortion of Marx's teachings. In the early 1920s he helped edit German diplomatic documents which discredited the former monarchist regimes and he then settled in Vienna, where he was respected as the leading social-democrat theorist on the Continent. In 1934 he assumed Czechoslovak citizenship but continued to live in Vienna until the eve of the Nazi occupation, when he fled to Holland where he died later in the year.

Kekkonen, Urho Kaleva (1900–1986), Finnish President. Born at Pielavesi, studied law at Helsinki University, fought against the Bolsheviks (1918–19) and by 1935 was an Agrarian Party member of the Finnish Parliament, holding ministerial office

1936–9 and 1944. After heading four governments in the early 1950s, he was elected President on 15 February 1956, in succession to ►Paasikivi. As President he struck a careful balance between cautious friendship with the Soviet Union and fulfilment of Finland's obligations as an independent Scandinavian nation and, from 1961, a member of EFTA. His strict neutrality made it natural that in 1975 he should host the ►Helsinki Conference. Five years later he received the Lenin Peace Prize. So great was the respect he commanded in Finland that a constitutional amendment would have enabled him to remain in office until 1984 had not failing health forced his resignation on 27 October 1981, in his twenty-sixth year of office.

Kellogg Pact (27 August 1928). A convention formally renouncing war as an instrument of national policy and providing for the peaceful settlement of disputes. The Pact was signed originally by delegates to a nine-power conference in Paris, although subsequently another fifty-six governments adhered to the principles of the Pact. The idea for such an agreement originated in April 1927 with Aristide ►Briand who, as French Foreign Minister, proposed to the US Secretary of State, Frank B. Kellogg (1856–1937), that their two countries should set an example by making a declaration which outlawed war. Kellogg was opposed to a mere bilateral agreement and urged that the Pact should be broader in scope than Briand had envisaged. The resultant Kellogg Pact was regarded as a notable advance towards the pacific settlement of disputes, especially since its sponsors included not only Germany but two powerful non-members of the League of Nations, the USA and the USSR. The Pact was, however, limited for, although denouncing war, it made no provision for punishing aggressors, nor did it restrict the sovereignty of a signatory. Intensification of political nationalism in the following decade rendered its ideal nugatory.

Kennedy, John Fitzgerald (1917–63). Thirty-fifth President of the USA. Born Brookline, Massachusetts, educated at Harvard and the London School of Economics, won a high award for valour as commander of a torpedo-boat in the Pacific, served in the House of Representatives as Democratic congressman from Massachusetts, 1946–52, before being elected to the Senate in 1952, becoming prominent on the Foreign Relations Committee in 1957 and winning the Presidential nomination in 1960 largely through the excellence of his campaign machine. He won the election by a narrow margin over his Republican opponent, Richard ►Nixon, to become the youngest elected US President, and the first to be a Roman Catholic. His civil-rights and social-reform programme – attempts to cross the 'new frontier' of his nomination speech – met opposition from Congress and was not finally enacted until after his 'thousand days' of office. He achieved, however, spectacular successes in foreign affairs, his firmness in the ►Cuban Missiles Crisis of October 1962 leading to gradual relaxation of international tension, and in June 1963 he proposed talks which led to the limited ►Test-Ban Treaty. His programme of aid for Latin America – 'Alliance for Progress' – and his 'Peace Corps', which sought to develop assistance to underdeveloped countries, showed his breadth of interest and his skill in conveying a sense of mission within his policies. His instinctive susceptibility to public feeling (shown notably on a visit to the Berlin Wall, 26 June 1963 – '*Ich bin ein Berliner*') helped make him a symbol of hope and inspiration, especially to the young. On 22 November 1963 he was assassinated while driving in a motorcade into Dallas, Texas, apparently by Lee Harvey Oswald (who was himself shot at point-blank range while under police custody two days later). The grief and disillusionment at President Kennedy's premature death extended far beyond the United States.

Kennedy, Robert Francis (1925–68), US politician. Born at Brookline, Massachusetts, a brother of John ➤Kennedy. Robert Kennedy was educated at Harvard and the Law School of the University of Virginia; he served in the Navy 1944–6, before being admitted to the Massachusetts bar and prosecuting several trade-union leaders for 'improper activities' in the late 1950s. He acted as his brother's campaign manager in the 1960 Presidential election, served as Attorney-General 1961–4, and was strong in the championship of civil rights for Negroes. He was elected Senator for New York in 1964 and began the preliminary campaigning to secure the Democratic nomination for the Presidency in 1968, gaining wide support from the coloured people and the underprivileged. On 5 June 1968, after winning the Californian primary election, he was shot in Los Angeles by a Jordanian immigrant who alleged that Kennedy supported the Zionist cause against the Arabs. Robert Kennedy died the following day.

Kent State University Shootings (4 May 1970). Some 500 students from Kent State University, Ohio, staged a protest demonstration at US involvement in Vietnam and Cambodia. The Ohio State National Guard, summoned to the campus, were stoned by some students. The National Guard, believing that a sniper was shooting at them from the roof of the university, opened fire on the demonstrators, killing two men and two women and gravely wounding many more. The tragedy marked the climax of a long struggle between the authorities and protesting students at American universities and provoked a wave of sympathetic demonstrations both within and outside the United States. The protests only died down with the final withdrawal of American troops from Indo-China in 1973.

Kenya. An East African republic within the Commonwealth. The British developed trade with the East African coast in the 1840s, dominating the area around Mombasa by 1875. In May 1887 the British East African Company secured a formal lease of the coastal strip from the Sultan of Zanzibar, handing the region over to the British Government in 1893, as the 'East African Protectorate'. During the First World War the protectorate served as a base of operations against the Germans in ➤Tanganyika. In 1920 Kenya, as it was now called, became a crown colony. Legislative councils, established in 1906, were granted wider powers in 1919 and 1934 but authority remained a privilege of the white settlers, who had begun to farm the White Highlands at the turn of the century. The Kikuyu, the most powerful of Kenya's thirteen tribes, organized a Central Association, of which Jomo ➤Kenyatta, became Secretary as early as 1928. This association, a pioneer movement of Pan-Africanism, was concerned both with increasing white settlement and with Indian workers who flocked to Kenya in the 1920s as railway labourers and later as shopkeepers. Racial disturbances and killings threatened civil war in the early 1950s and the colonial authorities took emergency measures to deal with ➤Mau Mau terrorists in 1952. Indignation at the deaths of eleven Mau Mau inmates of the Hola prison camp (March 1959) hastened the inclination of the British Conservative government to change its Kenyan policy and in January 1960 the new British Colonial Secretary, Iain Macleod (1913–70), began to prepare Kenya for majority African rule. A multiracial constitution enabled Africans to win most seats on the Legislative Council in the February 1961 elections. Kenya gained self-government in June 1963 and became a republic, under Kenyatta's presidency, on 12 December 1964. The President sought to combat tribalism by a centralized constitution and by close collaboration with the young spokesman of the Luo tribe, Tom ➤Mboya, whose assassination in July 1969 led to major Luo demonstrations. Three months later the President banned the communist opposition party, the Kenya's People's Union, whose leader Oginga Odinga (1911–94) was also a Luo. 'Africanization' at the expense of Indian and other settlers helped distract rival tribes from persistent feuding while forcing many Kenya Asians to seek sanctuary in Britain, especially in the period 1966–8. On Kenyatta's death (22 August 1978) the Presidency passed to Daniel Arap ➤Moi, a former teacher, who had served as Vice-President for the previous eleven years. Moi came from the Kalenjin tribe but could count on the backing of the Kikuyu leaders and was able to consolidate his position after electoral successes in November 1979, launching an impressive four-year Development Plan (which was hampered by a general fall in the price of coffee and tea on the world markets). An abortive *coup*, by junior ranks in the Kenyan Air Force, threatened President Moi's position on 1 August 1982 and led to the imposition of a curfew, amid protracted tension in Nairobi. In 1991 Moi was warned that foreign funds would be cut unless political liberty was restored. The conduct of multi-party elections in December 1992 was criticized by Commonwealth observers. Moi was confirmed in office and the Kenya Africa National Union assured of a clear parliamentary majority. Racial clashes in Kikuyu lands caused some 1,500 deaths over the following five years. A further electoral victory claimed by Moi on 29 December 1997 seemed to outside observers even more blatantly rigged than its predecessor. Social and economic problems continue to increase; Kenya has the highest birth rate in the world.

Kenyatta, Jomo (*c.* 1897–1978), President of Kenya. Born into the Kikuyu tribe at Ngenda on the Thiririka river, educated at a Scottish mission school, found clerical work with the Nairobi Municipal Council in 1922. He interested himself in the political activities of the Kikuyu Central Association in 1928 and travelled to London to represent the tribe at talks in the Colonial Office, 1929–30, briefly visiting the Soviet Union (where he returned at greater length in 1932–3). After a few months back in Kenya in 1931 he settled again in London, studied anthropology and completed a book, *Facing Mount Kenya*, published 1938. During the Second World War he gave lectures on African affairs, practised freelance journalism and worked on the land in Sussex, living at Storrington. In October 1945 he was in Manchester for a Pan-African congress, at which ►Nkrumah was a fellow speaker. When Kenyatta returned to Nairobi in September 1946 he was accepted as a national leader and became president of the Kenya Africa Union (June 1947). Between 1948 and 1950 young militants organized the ►Mau Mau, a terrorist movement which Kenyatta denounced on 24 August 1952. The colonial authorities, however, distrusted him and he was arrested, charged with controlling Mau Mau, and sentenced to seven years' hard labour on 8 April 1953. When he completed his sentence (14 April 1959) he was still confined to a remote region and kept under restraint until the change in government policy of 1960, not receiving complete freedom until 22 August 1961. He was elected to the Legislative Council five months later and became the first Prime Minister of a self-governing Kenya on 1 June 1963, and President of the Republic of Kenya on its inauguration in December 1964 (►Kenya).

Kerensky, Alexander F. (1881–1970). Russian democratic socialist revolutionary. Born in Simbirsk, the son of a headmaster who, at that moment, numbered among his pupils the future Lenin. Kerensky studied law at St Petersburg University, and as a democratic socialist sat in the Duma, 1912–17, as well as becoming the (non-Marxist) deputy chairman of the Petrograd Soviet. On the outbreak of the ►Russian Revolution in March 1917 he became Minister of Justice in the Provisional Government, where his energy led to his rapid promotion, first as Minister of War (16 May) and then as Prime Minister (25 July). He sought the vigorous prosecution of the war against the Germans but his attempts to mount a formidable offensive ran counter to the feelings of the Russian people, who were anxious for peace. He was ejected from office by the Bolshevik *coup d'état* on 7 November (the 'October Revolution'). After seeking vainly to organize resistance, he escaped to France, settling in Australia in 1940 and for the last twenty-four years of his life in the USA.

Keynes, John Maynard (1883–1946, created a baron 1942). British economist. Born and educated at Cambridge, served as chief Treasury representative at the Paris Peace Conference, achieving fame with his *Economic Consequences of the Peace* (1919), a brilliant analysis of the leading statesmen and an attack on the idea of ►reparations. He was principal critic of established economic theory in the inter-war period, seeking a synthesis between socialism and capitalism by insisting that full employment could be attained through the production of capital goods, the adoption of a cheap-money policy, and a programme of public investment. These ideas he expressed definitively in his *General Theory of Employment, Interest and Money* (1936). He was a financial adviser to the government during the Second

World War and a strong advocate of a World Bank, to eliminate future international financial crises. Keynes was a member of the literary and aesthetic circle of friends known as the 'Bloomsbury Group' and was a patron of the theatre and the arts, marrying in August 1925 the Russian ballerina, Lydia Lopokova (1892–1981).

Khan. ➤Ayub and ➤Yahya.

Khomeini, Ruholla (1902–89), Iranian religious leader. Much is obscure about Khomeini's early life. He first became well known in 1963 when, as Ayatollah of Iran's Shia Moslems, he vigorously condemned the Shah's European-style reforms and especially the social emancipation of women. Khomeini was arrested in the holy city of Qom and exiled. He spent some time with the Shia community in Turkey but from 1965 to 1978 he established his personal headquarters with the Iraqi Shias at Najaf, a pilgrimage city for Shias only ninety miles from Baghdad. His activities alarmed Vice-President Saddam ➤Hussein of ➤Iraq who on 6 October 1978 sought to curry favour with the Shah by having Khomeini expelled from the country. By then there was already serious rioting in Isfahan, Shiraz and Teheran itself and, from his new sanctuary near Paris, the Ayatollah called on the Iranian Army to turn against the Shah and establish an Islamic Republic. Demonstrations in Iran induced the Shah to leave the country on 16 January 1979 and sixteen days later three million Iranians gathered around Teheran airport to welcome Khomeini's return. The Ayatollah was *de facto* ruler of Iran for the following twelve months, imposing a strict Islamic puritanism until the election in February 1980 of Iran's first President. Even then, Khomeini continued to enjoy a special, superior status as 'moral supervisor' (*Velayat Faqih*) of the nation; and when President Bani-Sadr offended the Ayatollah's narrow political creed, it was Khomeini who ordered his impeachment (➤Iran) and approved the selection of the two presidents who succeeded him. When in July 1988 he accepted the UN Security Council's Resolution ending the Gulf War, he likened it to having drunk a 'poisoned chalice'. On 14 February 1989 he issued a *Fatwa* edict calling on Islamic believers to kill the novelist Salman Rushdie for what Khomeini regarded as blasphemy against Islam in *The Satanic Verses*. Khomeini underwent an operation for stomach cancer two months later and died on 3 June.

Khrushchev, Nikita Sergeyevich (1894–1971). Soviet leader. Born at Kalinovka, on the borders of the Ukraine, the son of a mine-worker, fought with the Red Army in the civil war, and then himself became a miner while attending high school. He worked for the party in Kiev and later in Moscow, winning such respect that in 1935 he became secretary of the Moscow Regional Committee and was closely concerned with the construction of the Moscow Metro, working with the 'mayor' of Moscow, ➤Bulganin. From 1938 until 1947 he was primarily concerned with Ukrainian affairs, giving important assistance to the military commanders, notably in defence of the salient at ➤Kursk. He was Prime Minister of the Ukrainian Soviet Republic from its liberation until 1947, and in 1949–50 was appointed by Stalin to reorganize Soviet agricultural production. At the time of Stalin's death Khrushchev was a member of the party presidium and was formally appointed First Secretary of the party six months later (12 September 1953). This post enabled him to build up his position within the Soviet Union, securing the succession of his nominee, Bulganin, to the premiership in February 1955. Khrushchev was sufficiently strong to risk an attack on Stalin and the 'cult of personality' at the Twentieth Party Congress in January 1956 and to survive both the independent tendencies of the Poles under ►Gomulka and the ►Hungarian Rising later that year. On 27 March 1958 Khrushchev took over the premiership from Bulganin and held the supreme posts in party and state until 15 October 1964. Although willing to seek a relaxation of world tension by a series of foreign visits (including personal addresses at the UN Assembly in September 1959 and September 1960) he alternated peaceful gestures with threats, and in October 1962 came close to war with the United States during the ►Cuban Missiles Crisis. Khrushchev's deteriorating relations with Mao seemed to some of his party colleagues to threaten a Sino-Soviet War and it was primarily this aspect of his policy that induced them to oust him from office, ►Kosygin succeeding him as Prime Minister, ►Brezhnev as party secretary. He spent the last six and a half years of his life in retirement outside Moscow.

Kiaochow. A bay in the Gulf of Pechili, northern China, occupied by German naval units in November 1897 and leased from China under a ninety-nine year agreement. The Germans developed a naval base at Tsingtao in the bay, which was seized by the Japanese early in November 1914. Protests by China at the Japanese action led to the ►'Twenty-One Demands' of January 1915 and to long disputes with the Chinese authorities. The Japanese agreed at the ►Washington Conference of 1922 to evacuate Kiaochow, but they reoccupied the naval base in January 1938 and remained there until the end of the Second World War.

Kim Il Sung (1912–94), North Korean President. Born near Pyongyang but spent his formative years in Russia, returning home at the age of twenty to build up an anti-Japanese communist network before crossing back into the Soviet Union. He arrived in north Korea as a major in the Red Army in August 1945 and was founder-leader of the Korean Workers' Party. When the Korea People's Democratic Republic was set up in September 1948 he became Prime Minister, retaining control of North Korea for the remaining forty-six years of his life, becoming titular President in December 1972. He imposed a Stalinist system on North Korea while working consistently for Korean unification and acting as supreme commander of the armed forces. Like Stalin, he gave himself the rank of Marshal and enjoyed a personality cult. Within a week of Kim Il Sung's death in July 1994 his son, Kim Chong-Il (1942–), was accepted as head of the governing central committee, though until 1997 he did not become formal President.

King, Martin Luther (1929–68). Negro Baptist pastor and American civil-rights leader. Born at Atlanta, Georgia, the son of a Baptist minister, studied theology at Boston University, becoming minister of a church in Montgomery, Alabama, in 1954 and at once becoming nationally famous for his campaign against segregated seating in the town's buses. He led the ►civil-rights movement, insisting on non-violence. Although imprisoned in Birmingham, Alabama, for his civil-rights protests in the spring of 1963, he was able to lead (and control) a massive peaceful demonstration in Washington on 15 June. In October 1964 he was awarded the Nobel Peace Prize. The following March he headed a procession of 4,000 civil-rights demonstrators for sixty miles from Selma (where there had been much violence) to Montgomery, Alabama, with a petition on the grievances of the Negro population. He was assassinated while on a civil-rights mission to Memphis, Tennessee (4 April 1968). No public figure of his generation could match the skill with which he applied a mastery of the spoken word to the service of his cause.

King, (William Lyon) Mackenzie (1874–1950). Canadian Prime Minister. Born in Kitchener, Ontario, his mother's father being W.L. Mackenzie (1795–1861), the Scottish-born leader of the Upper Canada rebellion of 1837. Mackenzie King studied law at Toronto and, after a period as a civil servant, became a Liberal MP in the federal parliament in 1908, remaining a member for over forty years. He was especially concerned with industrial relations and was Minister of Labour, 1909–14, before succeeding ►Laurier as party leader in 1919. King was Canada's Prime Minister in all for twenty-one years: December 1921 to June 1926: September 1926 to August 1930: October 1935 to November 1948. During the inter-war years King was essentially an isolationist, eager to assert Canada's voice in foreign affairs but conscious of the need to prevent friction between the French-speaking and English-speaking communities at home. He carefully nurtured Canadian unity during the early years of the Second World War, avoiding the divisive topic of 'conscription' until April 1942 when he had rallied the dominion behind him. King saw himself as an intermediary between London and Washington, at times exaggerating his role and piqued that, although technically host for the ►Quebec conferences of 1943 and 1944, he was never entrusted with the shaping of military or political strategy for the allied cause as a whole. He attended the founding conferences of the ►United Nations, seeking especially to secure representation of the intermediate powers (i.e. neither 'great powers' nor 'small powers') on the Security Council.

Kissinger, Henry Alfred (1923–), US diplomat and Secretary of State. Born in Fürth, Germany, of Jewish parentage, settled in America and was educated at Harvard where he was Professor of Government from 1958 to 1971, completing a specialized study of Metternich, Castlereagh and the peacemakers of 1814–15, published as *A World Restored* (1957). He became an adviser to ►Nixon in the Presidential campaign of 1968 and from 1969 to 1973 was the President's Special Adviser on National Security, a post which made him a peripatetic ambassador, who visited China and the Soviet Union to sound out opinion on the possibilities for easing tension and who took pains to contain the Middle East conflicts. His efforts to secure peace in Vietnam won him the Nobel Peace Prize for 1973, an award shared with the Vietnamese delegate, Le Duc Tho (who declined the honour). On 3 September 1973 Kissinger was appointed US Secretary of State, holding the office for the remaining eleven months of Nixon's presidency and for the twenty-nine months of President Ford's administration. Kissinger practised a pragmatic, conservative style of diplomacy, less rigid than ►Dulles, less visionary than ►Kennedy.

Kitchener, Horatio Herbert (1850–1916, created a baron 1898, viscount 1902, earl 1914), British field-marshal. Born near Ballylongford, county Kerry, Ireland, gaining his baptism of fire with an ambulance unit attached to the French Army in 1871. He was commissioned in that year in the Royal Engineers and served in Palestine, Cyprus and the Sudan before becoming 'Sirdar', or commander-in-chief, of the army in Egypt in 1890, with the rank of major-general. He reconquered the Sudan (1896–9) gaining his greatest victory at Omdurman. In the Boer War he was Chief of Staff, 1899–1900, and commander-in-chief 1900 to 1902, arousing criticism by his policy of blockhouses and ►concentration camps, which were intended to isolate Boer resistance groups. From 1902 to 1909 he held the chief command in India, disputing administrative control of the Indian Army with the Viceroy, ►Curzon, 1903–5. He became virtual ruler of Egypt (i.e. British 'Agent') from 1911 to 1914. On 5 August 1914 he was appointed War Minister in Asquith's government, the first serving officer to hold such a post. Although invaluable as a morale-booster and for recruiting ('Your Country needs YOU'), he could not understand political considerations within the cabinet, distrusted the Territorial Army regiments, and was on bad terms with some commanders in the field. It was decided in the spring of 1916 to send him on a mission to Russia in the hope he could inspire the Russians with a more determined spirit of resistance to the invader. He was, however, drowned on 5 June when the cruiser in which he was travelling to Russia, HMS *Hampshire*, struck a mine off the Orkneys.

Kohl, Helmut (1930–), German Chancellor. Born in Ludwigshafen am Rhein, worked briefly in the chemical industry before studying law at Frankfurt and Heidelberg. He became Chairman of the Christian Democrats in the Rhineland at the age of 26. He led the Party in the federal parliament from 1976 to 1980, becoming caretaker Chancellor in 1982, consolidating his authority in the 1983 elections. Kohl's independent conservatism allowed him to make overtures to the East while remaining a pillar of the European Community. In May 1986 he was cleared of accusations of perjury and illegal funding of political parties. The electoral victory of his Christian Democrat and Christian Social coalition in January 1987 was followed by a meeting with ►Honecker, the East German head of state, in September. In 1989–90 Kohl supervised the negotiations which led to German reunification in October 1990 and on 2 December he won the first all-German democratic General Election for fifty-eight years. Although rapturously received in Leipzig during the spring of 1990, he rapidly lost popularity in the eastern provinces with the spread of unemployment in the following winter. Abroad he was criticized during the Gulf Crisis for limiting his response to financial aid rather than giving active German military assistance to the United Nations. The Bundestag election of October 1994 confirmed his personal ascendancy, though his party lost votes. Subsequently his vigorous campaign for ➤economic and monetary union received double setbacks, from a cautious German central bank and from his European partners at the Amsterdam summit meeting in June 1997.

Kolchak, Alexander Vasilievich (1870–1920), Russian admiral and anti-Bolshevik. Born in the Crimea of Tartar descent, played a distinguished role in the defence of Port Arthur during the Russo-Japanese War, and in 1916 was promoted vice-admiral and given command of the Black Sea Fleet. After the Revolution he joined an 'All Russian Government' in Siberia, acting as Minister of War and achieving considerable success along the central sector of the Trans-Siberian Railway. From November 1918 until December 1919 he officially styled himself 'Supreme Ruler' of Russia, although he resigned leadership of the 'White' forces to General ➤Denikin. Kolchak was captured by the Bolsheviks and shot at Irkutsk early in February 1920.

Korea. A peninsula east of China, became a tributary state of the Chinese Empire in 1637, gaining formal independence by the Treaty of Shimonoseki of April 1895. From 1898 to 1904 there was considerable rivalry in Korea between the Russians, who were penetrating the country from the north, and the Japanese, who virtually controlled the southern Korean ports. This rivalry precipitated the ➤Russo-Japanese War of 1904–5. In November 1905 Japan assumed responsibility for Korea's foreign relations, formally annexing the country in August 1910 and settling Japanese families there, especially around Seoul. The ➤Yalta Conference of 1945 agreed that Soviet and American troops would occupy Korea, with a demarcation line along the latitude 38° parallel, pending the establishment of a unified and independent democratic Korean government. Soviet forces occupied northern Korea from August 1945 until September 1948: a Korean People's Democratic Republic, with its capital at Pyongyang, was proclaimed on 9 September 1948, under the leadership of the Korean-born Red Army major ➤Kim Il Sung. US troops remained in southern Korea from August 1945 until June 1949: a Republic of Korea, with its capital at Seoul, was proclaimed on 15 August 1948, under the Presidency of a right-wing nationalist, Syngman Rhee (1875–1965). Rival claims to authority over the whole of the peninsula led the North to invade the South on 25 June 1950, thus beginning the ➤Korean War. The arrival of Chinese 'volunteers' to support the North Koreans in November 1950 introduced a new political force into the area and when the fighting was ended, in July 1953, the armistice was signed by military commanders representing the North Koreans, the Chinese and the United Nations forces, not by any spokesman for Syngman Rhee's South

Koreans. Attempts to secure unification of Korea at the ➤Geneva Conference of 1954 broke down. Kim Il Sung, as chairman of the Workers' Party and Prime Minister of the 'Democratic Republic', instituted Soviet-style economic planning but maintained a judicious neutrality in the ideological disputes between China and the Soviet Union. In southern Korea popular indignation at the corrupt character of Syngman Rhee's rule led to his overthrow in April 1960. After a year of weak government a military *coup* brought to power Major-General Park Cheng-hi (1918–79), who became President on 22 March 1962 and subsequently won elections in 1963, 1967, 1971 and 1972. North and South Korean emissaries concluded an agreement in July 1972 by which the two Korean Governments pledged themselves to seek unification of the peninsula by peaceful means. After the assassination of President Park by the head of his CIA in October 1979, there was further confusion in South Korea until General Chun Doo Hwan became President in August 1980. Demonstrations in Kwangju were put down with great brutality, over two hundred protesters being killed. Many prominent Opposition politicians remained banned from 1980 until 1985. Mounting concern over slow progress towards both democracy and reunification led to rioting in Seoul and other towns. But in December 1987, when South Korea had the first presidential elections for fourteen years, rivalry between the Opposition candidates (Kim Young-sam and Kim Dae-jung) led to the return of Chun's nominee, General Roh Tae Woo, with less than 35 per cent of the vote. Anti-government demonstrations died down during the ➤Olympic Games, but six days after their conclusion in October 1988 more than 3,300 students again rioted in Seoul and Kwangju. A new constitution eased tension. Kim Young-sam was elected President in December 1992 and three months later gave the republic its first entirely civilian government since Park's 1962 *coup*. North Korea suffered economically from the ending of barter trade with the Soviet Union after 1991, although it increased its industrial exports to other former Soviet dependencies.

Korean War (1950–53). Had its origins in the rival claims for sovereignty over a unified peninsula asserted by the Soviet-sponsored People's Democratic Republic in North Korea and the American-backed Republic of Korea in the south. United Nations attempts to hold all-Korean elections to establish a unified state were turned down by the Soviet Union. At dawn on 25 June 1950 the North Koreans launched a surprise attack with seven infantry divisions and one armoured division over the 38° parallel, the demarcation line between the two Koreas. The South Korean capital, Seoul, fell three days later. The Security Council – boycotted by its Russian member – recommended UN states to assist the Republic of Korea to repel the invasion. Fifteen nations sent troops to Korea, where they were organized under the 'unified command' of the American General, ➤MacArthur, since US forces bore the brunt of the fighting. The surprise character of the attack enabled the North Koreans to occupy all the South, except around the vital port of Pusan, by the end of August. On 15 September 1950 MacArthur landed American and

South Korean marines at Inchon, two hundred miles behind the North Korean lines, and on the following day launched an offensive from Pusan. The North Koreans, in danger of encirclement, hurriedly retreated, MacArthur carrying the war northwards, reaching Chosan on the Yalu river (the frontier between Korea and Chinese Manchuria) on 24 October 1950. Warnings from ►Chou En-lai of Chinese intervention were ignored and the military potential of the Chinese army underestimated. Small groups of Chinese volunteers were captured in mid-October. The main Chinese army was first encountered by a UN Turkish brigade at Wawon, seventy-five miles south of the Chinese frontier, on 27 November 1950. The Chinese succeeded in concentrating 180,000 men in North Korea, with another 100,000 in reserve. These huge numbers forced the UN troops rapidly south again. Seoul was lost a second time in January 1951 and the Chinese were only brought to a halt sixty miles south of the 38th parallel. A counter-offensive in the second half of January gradually recovered lost ground while the UN forces successfully contained two major attacks launched by the Chinese in April and May 1951, following this up with another counter-offensive in June which enabled the UN troops to establish a defensive line slightly north of the 38th parallel. Apart from a limited offensive to straighten the line in November 1951 the Korean War, hitherto so unusually mobile, became static, a matter of artillery duels and infantry engagements in front of fortified positions. Peace talks began at Kaesong on 8 July 1951 and were soon adjourned to the nearby village of Panmunjom. The talks were, however, less concerned with military objectives than with political aims, and the negotiations continued for two years. The change of US Presidents from Truman to Eisenhower and the death of Stalin led to a relaxation of international tension and an armistice agreement, maintaining the divided Korea, was signed at Panmunjom on 27 July 1953. Attempts to achieve a peaceful unification by international conferences have proved unsuccessful. Casualties in the war were very high: 142,000 Americans were killed and the other UN contingents lost 17,000 men, of whom 7,000 came from the Commonwealth divisions. It is possible that, including civilians, the Korean War cost the lives of between 3½ and 4 million people. (►Imjin River.)

Košice Incident (June 1941). Košice, the principal town in eastern Slovakia, was incorporated in Hungary as part of the ►Felvidék on 12 November 1938, being thereafter known for the next six years by its former Hungarian name of Kassa. On 26 June 1941 – four days after Hitler's attack on the Soviet Union – three aircraft bombed Košice/Kassa, even though Hungary was still a non-belligerent. It was officially assumed in Budapest that the planes were Russian and this 'act of unprovoked aggression by the USSR' was given as the reason for Hungary's declaration of war on the Soviet Union next day. Subsequently the Soviet authorities denied having made the raid, maintaining that the incident was fabricated by the Germans in order to secure Hungarian collaboration in their Russian campaign. The three planes were of German manufacture and bore a marking used to identify the aircraft of Germany and her allies. The Russian air force had more important strategic targets at that stage of the war.

Kosovo. A region of ➤Yugoslavia mainly inhabited by ethnic Albanians; principal town, Pristina. The region comprises a series of plateaux, surrounded by mountains, holding the potentially richest concentration of minerals in the Balkans. Kosovo Polje was the site of an epic battle against the Ottoman Turks on 28 June 1389 which, through alleged treachery, led to the destruction of medieval Serbia. Through many centuries Serbian patriots were fired by a need to avenge the Kosovo defeat, a task achieved militarily in November 1912 during the ➤Balkan Wars. After 500 years of Ottoman rule, few Serbs lived in Kosovo: most of the people were Albanian and Muslim. Between 1913 and 1940 several attempts were made by the government in Belgrade to 'colonize' the region with Serbs, but as late as 1991 a Serbian-sponsored census conceded that Albanians formed 82 per cent of the population. Under the 1946 Constitution of socialist Yugoslavia Kosovo, and the neighbouring Metohija district, became an autonomous province within federal Serbia. Tito gradually devolved increasing powers to the province, but in 1987 the revival of an aggressive Serbian nationalism under ➤Milošević reversed the process. As the 600th anniversary of the famous battle approached, the Serbian Government rescinded all autonomous rights. Resentment over this action, and at the later settlement in the region of subsidized Serbian refugees from Croatia and Bosnia, prompted the formation of a Kosovo Liberation Army and, in the first week of January 1998, to a confrontation with Serbian troops. The fighting intensified, with a fierce battle for the town of Orahovac in July. Attempts to curb Serb ravaging of the province and to force Belgrade to restore Kosovo's autonomy were made by the EU, with warning demonstrations of NATO air power along the Albanian frontier and with proposals for NATO military exercises in Albania and ➤Macedonia in the autumn. Russia sought to restrain NATO and to mediate in Belgrade.

Kosygin, Alexei Nikolayevich (1904–80), Soviet Prime Minister. Born and educated in St Petersburg, worked in textile mills in Leningrad, serving on political committees in the city, of which he was mayor in 1938–9. He became a member of the central committee of the party in 1939, when he was appointed Commissar for the Textile Industry. In the post-war Stalinist period he was successively Minister of Finance and Minister of Light Industry (1948–53), as well as being an inconspicuous member of the Politburo. In 1956–7 he was minister responsible for current economic planning, becoming chairman of the state economic planning commission in 1960 and first Deputy Prime Minister. In October 1964 he took over from ➤Khrushchev as chairman of the Council of Ministers (i.e. Prime Minister). In this capacity, he collaborated closely with ➤Brezhnev and with Andrei ➤Gromyko, Soviet Foreign Minister (1957–85). Kosygin's principal objective in home affairs, the decentralized control of industry and agriculture, was partially attained; his hopes of more consumer goods remained largely unfulfilled. Ill-health forced Kosygin to resign on 23 October 1980, Nikolai Tikhonov succeeding to the Soviet premiership. Kosygin died eight weeks later.

Kruger, Paulus (1825–1904), President of the Boer Republic of the Transvaal. Born in Cape Colony, accompanied the strictly Calvinist Boer emigrants who moved northwards across the Vaal river on the 'Great Trek' of 1836–7. He became President of the Transvaal in 1882, seeing his land suddenly enriched by the discovery of gold in the Witwatersrand in 1886. His anti-British sentiments were mingled with admiration for Germany, from whom he purchased arms in the mid 1890s, and, fearing a British invasion, he launched attacks on Cape Colony and Natal in September 1899 (►Boer War). In May 1900 Kruger left the Transvaal to seek aid in Europe. He found the Germans no longer interested and the French sympathetic but disinclined to take action. He settled in Holland, but died in Switzerland.

Krupp. German family of industrial magnates, settled in Essen since the sixteenth century and manufacturers of arms for over 300 years. Under the direction of Alfred Krupp (1812–87) the firm cast steel cannon from 1847 onwards, becoming the largest arms suppliers in the world while also controlling mines and other industrial enterprises in the Ruhr basin. His son, Friedrich Alfred Krupp (1854–1902), expanded the firm's undertakings so as to include shipbuilding and, in particular, the manufacture of armour plate. He committed suicide after accusations of immoral conduct and the firm passed into the hands of his daughter, Bertha (1886–1957). In 1906 she married Gustav von Bohlen und Halbach who was allowed to change his name to Gustav Krupp von Bohlen (1869–1950) and was effective head of the industrial empire from 1906 to 1943. In the First World War Gustav Krupp secured a virtual monopoly of arms supplies for Germany and her allies, converting his factories for the making of tractors and other agricultural implements under the Weimar Republic. From 1932 onwards he vigorously supported Hitler, as also did his son, Alfred Felix Krupp (1907–67), and Hitler introduced a special *Lex Krupp* in 1943 to ensure continued family control of the Krupp empire. In 1945 Gustav Krupp was indicted as a major war criminal at ►Nuremberg but was considered too frail and senile to stand trial. Alfred Felix Krupp was convicted in 1947 for inhumane treatment of foreign workers and for using concentration camp labour in his Essen factory and at Auschwitz: it was alleged that Krupps employed 130,000 'slave labourers' in 1944. Although sentenced to twelve years' imprisonment, Krupp was released in 1951 and assisted the economic recovery of the German Federal Republic so that, by 1963, he was the most powerful single industrialist in the Common Market. Shortly before his death, however, Krupps ran into financial difficulties and in 1968 ceased to be a family enterprise.

Kulaks. Former peasants able to become proprietors of medium-sized farms in Russia as a result of the agrarian reforms of Stolypin in 1906. Stolypin hoped he was creating a stable middle class as prosperous farmers who would form a naturally conservative political force. Only 15 per cent of Russian peasants had become *kulaks* by the outbreak of the ►Russian Revolution. As a class they became an embarrassment to Lenin and Stalin, vigorously opposing collectivization until 1929, when Stalin ordered 'the liquidation of the *kulaks*' as part of his first ►Five-Year Plan. Rebellious villages were machine-gunned: *kulak* families which survived were deported to unpopulated regions in Siberia, around Tomsk and Irkutsk. Stalin himself told Churchill in August 1942 that he had been forced to deal, in all, with 10 million people.

Kun, Béla (1886–1937). Hungarian revolutionary communist. Born, of Jewish parentage, at Szilagycseh. While serving with the Austro-Hungarian forces in the First World War Kun was captured by the Russians. After the Bolshevik Revolution he returned to Hungary as a communist agitator and secured the fall of the hesitant liberal republican ►Károlyi in March 1919. For four and a half months Kun ruled Hungary as a communist state, carrying through radical reforms but arousing fear and resentment through the cruelty of many of his supporters. Kun was faced by Czech and Romanian invasions and by the establishment at Szeged of a counter-revolutionary Hungarian regime under ►Horthy. Early in August 1919 the Romanians entered Budapest, forcing Kun to flee to Vienna, later seeking refuge in Russia. His government disintegrated with his flight. He perished in Stalin's purge, the ►Yezhovshchina. In 1958 he was formally rehabilitated.

Kuomintang (Guomindang). Chinese nationalist party founded in 1891 by ►Sun Yat-sen as a movement to encourage democratic government and social reform. Under ►Chiang Kai-shek (Jiang Jieshih) the Kuomintang became the effective government in China (1928–48) but departed from the principles of its founder and was, by 1946, riddled with corruption. Since 1949 it has been the ruling party of ►Taiwan.

Kurdish Question. The Kurds were first mentioned as warriors in Anatolia by Xenophon early in the fourth century BC. They long remained a pastoral people, converted to the Sunni sect of Islam soon after its inception, until in 1891 Sultan ►Abdul Hamid II recruited from them a force of irregular cavalry, not unlike Russian Cossacks and known as the *hamidiye*, used against the Christian ►Armenians. These *hamidiye* units stimulated a sense of political nationalism, heightened by mistrust of the post First World War frontiers, which cut across traditional routes of annual migration and separated urbanized kinsfolk in ►Iraq, ►Iran and French mandated ►Syria. Most strongly the Kurds resented Iraq's refusal to grant autonomy and the hostility of republican Turkey, where ►Atatürk denied their national identity, classifying them as 'mountain Turks'. They rose against the Persians (Iran) from 1919 to 1922, and against the Iraqis from 1922 to 1932, 1958 to 1974, 1984 to 1988 and they have maintained a rebellion from 1990 (►Iraq). There were also Kurdish revolts in northern Syria in 1937, and a chronic rebellion in Turkey, most effective in 1944–5, 1978–9, and intermittently from 1984, concentrated in the mountains around Diyarbekir and south to the Iraqi frontier. The PKK (Kurdish Workers' Party), established as an anti-Turk guerrilla group in 1978, operated from bases in northern Iraq and in Lebanon and received support from Kurds abroad, until it was banned as a terrorist association by the German and French governments in November 1993. Some of the suffering of the Kurdish people has been inflicted by their own groups: an embryonic Kurdistan, set up at Arbil in Iraq in October 1991, virtually disintegrated in 1995 after fighting between rival Kurdish parties in which at least 3,000 Kurds perished. In September 1996 the militia of the 'Kurdish Democratic Party', armed by the Iraqi government, occupied the 'autonomous' strongholds of Degala and Sulaimaniya, the surviving inhabitants fleeing to Iran, thus intensifying an already grave refugee problem.

Kursk. An important railway junction in the south of the central Russian plain, occupied by German troops on 3 November 1941 but liberated by the Red Army on 8 February 1943 in a counter-offensive following the German disaster at ►Stalingrad. The Russian success created around Kursk a salient 100 miles wide and 80 miles deep. In the summer of 1943 Hitler ordered the elimination of this salient in a pincer movement based on Orel to the north and Belgorod to the south. For this 'Operation Citadel' he concentrated seventeen armoured divisions (2,500 tanks and assault guns) around Kursk, supported by over 1,000 aircraft. The Russians, who had anticipated the German plan, filled the salient with even more tanks, guns and aircraft as well as establishing deep minefields. The battle for Kursk – which never came within fifty miles of the town – was the greatest clash of tank formations in history and lasted from 5 to 15 July 1943, with some defensive actions continuing for a further week. The German attack was especially severe around Prokhorova in the south of the salient where they made their deepest penetration, with the loss of over 300 tanks on one day alone. A Soviet counter-offensive ironed out the salient, capturing Orel on 4 August and Belgorod next day. The German losses were so heavy that it was impossible for them ever again to mount an offensive on the eastern front.

Kut-el-Amara. Fortified town in a loop of the river Tigris, seized by British forces advancing up river from Basra on 28 September 1915, at a vital moment in the campaign against the Turks in ►Mesopotamia. The British commander, General Townshend, sought to advance on Baghdad but was checked by Turkish defenders around the ancient ruins of Ctesiphon, 22–25 November, and fell back on Kut, where the British were encircled. The Turks besieged Kut from 7 December 1915 until 29 April 1916, three attempts to relieve the town failing, partly because of floods. The Turks captured 10,000 men when Townshend surrendered, many of them later dying as prisoners of war. In February 1917 the British imperial forces recaptured Kut, entering Baghdad a fortnight later.

Kuwait. A small independent state at the head of the Persian Gulf, ruled by a hereditary Emir. Kuwait was a British protectorate from 1899 to 1961, when full independence was conceded. Oil production, beginning in 1936, has made Kuwait rich and the city began in 1975–6 to develop as a banking centre for the whole Middle East. Iraqi claims to Kuwait, which produced tension between 1961 and 1963, were settled by Arab mediation on 4 October 1963. A defensive pact with Britain, signed in June 1961, was allowed to lapse in May 1971, partly because of the Kuwaitis' determination to pursue a policy of neutralism. A token force of Kuwaitis was sent to bolster the Syrian defence on the Golan Heights in the ➤October War of 1973. A thirteen-year experiment in parliamentary democracy was abruptly terminated in 1975, with the ruling Emir dissolving parliament and muzzling the media. In 1989 relations with Iraq deteriorated rapidly after Saddam Hussein's victory over Iran in the First ➤Gulf War. On 2 August 1990 Iraq invaded Kuwait, which was speedily overrun. Despite UN condemnation of this act of aggression, Kuwait was annexed to Iraq and its wealth plundered. UN troops from 29 countries participated in the Second ➤Gulf War and, in a 100-hour land campaign, liberated Kuwait on 27 Febraury 1991. Great destruction was caused in Kuwait City. The economy was weakened by the scorched-earth policies of the retreating Iraqis, who fired the oilfields. On returning from exile the Emir promised a speedy return to some form of representative government. Adult males in families resident in Kuwait for seventy years elected a legislative assembly in 1992; executive power remained with a nominated ministerial council.

L

Labour Party (Australia). When the Australian Commonwealth was instituted in 1901 the young Labour Party was better organized than its rivals, its strength being concentrated in small, urban areas. Labour formed short-lived minority governments in 1904 and 1908, gaining clear majorities in the elections of April 1910 and September 1914. During the government of ►Hughes the party split over conscription and was out of office for the next twelve years. In 1921 the party temporarily became syndicalist in outlook but by 1926–7 was showing greater moderation seeking, as it declared, 'Socialization of industry . . . by parliamentary and administrative machinery'. During the inter-war period the party both gained and lost voters through strong identification with the Roman Catholic Church, especially in New South Wales and Victoria. Labour was in power from October 1929 to December 1931 under James Scullin (1876–1953), a devout Catholic from Ballarat, but was plagued by the economic recession and had to wait another ten years for its most spectacular term of office, under ►Curtin from 1941 to 1945 and under ►Chifley from 1945 to 1949. Labour was then forced into opposition until the short-lived and controversial government of Gough ►Whitlam from 1972 to 1975. Under the leadership of Bob Hawke Labour returned to office in 1983, and won subsequent elections in 1984, 1987 and 1990. Hawke was succeeded in December 1990 by the more outspoken and republican Paul Keating, under whom Labour lost the election of March 1996. The party is generally called 'Labor' rather than 'Labour' in Australia nowadays.

Labour Party (Britain). Formed as the Labour Representation Committee in February 1900, a combination of all the socialist groups in Britain – the ►Independent Labour Party, the ►Fabian Society, the trade unions and the near-Marxist Social Democratic Federation (SDF). This first 'distinct Labour Group in Parliament' had as its secretary Ramsay ►MacDonald. Early resolutions of the Committee were moderate in character: they demanded better living conditions and condemned inequality of wealth but did not commit supporters to 'socialism' or the idea of a class war, and the SDF seceded in 1901. The Labour movement spread rapidly, winning support partly through the Balfour Government's hostility to the trade unions, as shown by the ►Taff Vale Case. Out of fifty Labour candidates in the 1906 election twenty-nine were returned to Westminster and the Committee decided later that year to assume the name 'Labour Party'. From 1906 to 1914 the party supported the social reforms of the Liberals. The Osborne Judgment of 1909, declaring against the use of trade-union funds for political objects, restricted the party's activities until after the introduction of payment for Members of Parliament in August 1911. During the First World War two Labour members gained cabinet experience in the coalition: Arthur Henderson (1863–1935) from December 1916 until August 1917; and George Barnes (1859–1940) from May 1917 until January 1919. In 1918 the Labour Party adopted a more openly socialist creed, declaring in its constitution that it sought, 'the gradual building up of a new social order based ... on deliberately planned cooperation in production and distribution'. Widespread post-war disillusionment (and internal feuds within the ►Liberal Party) allowed Labour to become the official Opposition in 1922, under MacDonald's leadership. The December 1923 general election was a stalemate – Conservatives 258, Labour 191, Liberals 158 – and MacDonald was invited to form a minority government on 23 January 1924. Ten months later (four days after publication of the ►Zinoviev Letter) a fresh general election cut Labour representation to 151, pushed up the Conservatives to 413 and reduced the Liberals to forty. Over the following five years rising unemployment improved Labour's prospects and MacDonald formed a second government in 1929. His decision to create a coalition in 1931 split the party, which was reduced to 56 members, led by ►Lansbury and after 1935 by ►Attlee. Although weak at Westminster the Labour Party was strong municipally, notably in London under ►Morrison. Two Labour members entered Churchill's coalition war cabinet in May 1940, five others receiving ministerial posts. The 1945 general election gave Labour a clear majority for the first time – Labour 398, Conservatives and allies 213, Liberals 12 – and Labour introduced some basic socialist reforms: the National Health Service; nationalization of coal, electricity, gas, transport, iron and steel; and several welfare measures as well as beginning the process of decolonization with the ►Indian Independence Act. Labour narrowly won the election of 1950 but was defeated in 1951, 1955 and 1959. A close examination of principles during the period of Opposition under ►Gaitskell and ►Bevan led to the emergence of a new style of Labour Party under Harold ►Wilson who was electorally victorious in 1964, 1966 and twice in 1974, although defeated by the Conservatives in 1970. On 5 April 1976 James ►Callaghan was elected Labour Party leader on Wilson's retirement. He was Prime Minister until the Labour Party defeat in the election of May 1979, finally resigning the party leadership on 15 October 1980. Four weeks later Michael Foot (1913–) won the election for a new leader, on the second ballot. He was soon faced with the defection of three prominent right-wingers to help found the ►Social Democratic Party. In 1983 the party fared worse at the polls than in any General Election since 1936. Foot was succeeded as Party leader by Neil Kinnock (1942–) in October 1983. The 1987 General Election brought Labour a gain of twenty seats and prompted an intensive re-examination of basic party principles, questioning both commitments to nationalization and unilateral nuclear disarmament. Although Labour attracted one and half million more votes in 1992 and won forty-one more seats, the Conservatives still had a majority of twenty-one. Kinnock resigned in July 1982, to be succeeded by the quiet reformer, John Smith (1938–94), upon whose sudden death Tony ➤Blair was elected leader (21 July 1994). Blair accelerated modernization, presenting 'New Labour' as a centre-left party: on 29 April 1995 a special Labour Party Conference amended the 1918 constitution, dropping the 'Clause 4' commitment to nationalization; later changes stressed Labour's independence of ➤trade unions; and pressure was exerted on constituencies so as to ensure that more women were selected as parliamentary candidates. The 1997 General Election, held on May Day, gave Labour a landslide victory, with 146 seats gained and none lost. In all, 418 Labour MPs were returned, giving an overall majority of 180, even greater than in 1945.

Labour Party (Israel). A 'Workers' Party of Israel', known by its initials as Mapai, was founded in Palestine in 1930 and was often called the Israeli Labour Party. The dominant political figure from the 1930s to 1965 was ➤Ben-Gurion. In January 1968 Mapai combined with two other democratic socialist splinter groups and formally constituted the Israel Labour Party, under the leadership of Levi Eshkol (1895–1969), who was then in his fifth year as Prime Minister. When Levi Eshkol died on 26 February 1969 he was succeeded as leader of the Labour Party and as coalition Prime Minister by Mrs Golda ➤Meir, who confirmed the status of the Labour Party as a centre group, of moderate democratic socialists. Mrs Meir resigned in April 1974 and the Labour Party chose General Itzhak Rabin as its leader. Internal conflicts weakened the party, which was defeated in the general election of May 1977, the first occasion since the creation of Israel in 1948 that Mapai-Labour was thrown into opposition. Mapai participated in coalition governments from 1984 to 1996, but never recovered the influence enjoyed in the 1960s.

Labour Party (Malta). One of the principal parties in ➤Malta since 1946: in office 1949–50, 1955–8 and 1971–87. The outstanding personality in the Party was Dom Mintoff (1916–), leader from 1950 until his retirement in December 1984.

Labour Party (Netherlands). Principal non-Catholic socialist party in the Netherlands, dominant in all post-war coalitions until 1959, out of office for twenty-one months, less influential in the 1960s, but recovering authority after the election of November 1972. The Party thereafter shared in coalition governments 1973–7, 1981–2 and since 1989. The trade unionist Wim Kok (1938–) was elected leader in 1987 and became Prime Minister of a centre coalition in August 1994.

Labour Party (New Zealand). Although Labour supporters of the Liberals stood for parliament from 1890 onwards and helped secure a series of basic social reforms in the government of Richard Seddon between 1893 and 1906, it was only in 1916 that an organized Labour Party was established. Despite the prominence of the farming community, urban Labour was recognized as the official opposition party in 1925 and won a majority for the first time in the general election of 27 November 1935. Labour remained continuously in power from 1935 to 1949, originally under Michael ➤Savage and, after his death in 1940, under Peter ➤Fraser. Among Labour Party reforms introduced between 1935 and 1938 were: nationalization of the Reserve Bank; a state mortgage system; compulsory arbitration and basic-wage measures; state control of railways; subsidies for the marketing of farm primary products in Britain; and an extensive social-security system. A state health service was introduced in 1941 but thereafter the reforming zeal of the party seemed to decline, and the electoral defeat of 1949 was caused as much by weariness as by the merits of the Opposition. In 1957 Labour regained office with a majority of one seat and for three years Labour formed a government, under Walter Nash, but the parliamentary situation was so unstable that no radical changes could be introduced. There were further Labour governments, under Norman Kirk and Wallace Rowling, from November 1972 until November 1975 and under David Lange and Geoffrey Palmer from July 1984 to October 1990.

Labour Party (Norway). Norway developed a socialist party on the British Labour model on the eve of the First World War. From 1919 to 1923, however, the Norwegian Labour Party belonged to the ➤Comintern, later shifting to a centralist, social-democratic position. After forming a minority government in 1928, lasting only eighteen days, Labour was in power continuously, 1935–63. Peculiarities in the electoral system left Norway with a succession of minority governments in the 1970s and 1980s, several with Labour leadership. The Party improved its standing in 1985 under Mrs Gro Harlem Brundtland (1939–), who had briefly been Norway's first woman Prime Minister in 1981 and was to lead minority governments 1986–9 and 1990–93. Labour emerged as the strongest party in Norway from the election of September 1993.

Lang, Cosmo Gordon (1864–1945). ➤Canterbury, Archbishop of.

Lansbury, George (1859–1940), British socialist. Born in Suffolk, active in local government in east London (Bow and Poplar). Labour MP 1910–12 and 1922–40, founder and editor of the *Daily Herald*, 1919–23. Lansbury was an individualist, ready to sacrifice his political career for his principles: thus he championed women's suffrage in 1912–14 and then opposed the war, at a time when neither of these causes would win him votes. He held major office under MacDonald from 1929 to 1931 but refused to join the MacDonald–Baldwin National Government coalition and was the only former cabinet minister in the Labour Party to retain his seat in the general election of 1931. From 1932 to 1935 he showed skill in leading the Labour Party, even though his simple and pacifist form of Christian socialism alienated many trade unionists, including ➤Bevin. He handed over the leadership of the Labour Party to ➤Attlee in 1935. Although loathing the Nazi dictatorship Lansbury visited Hitler in April 1937 in a vain attempt to assist Anglo-German understanding.

Lansdowne, Lord (1845–1927, born Henry Petty-Fitzmaurice, succeeded as fifth Marquess of Lansdowne, 1866). A great-grandson, through his mother, of the

French statesman, Talleyrand. Lansdowne, originally a Liberal, was appointed Governor-General of Canada by Gladstone in 1883 but five years later was nominated as Viceroy of India by the Conservative-Unionist Lord ►Salisbury. In 1895 Lansdowne returned to England and served as War Minister in Salisbury's Government and, as such, was blamed by the newspapers for British lack of success in the early months of the Boer War (1899). Lansdowne succeeded Salisbury as Foreign Secretary in November 1900. He failed to overcome Anglo-German prejudices sufficiently to achieve a settlement with the Kaiser's Germany but he successfully negotiated an alliance with Japan in 1902 and conducted the difficult negotiations culminating in the ►Anglo-French Entente of 1904. From 1905 to 1915 Lansdowne led the Conservative Opposition in the House of Lords, arousing much criticism by his use of the Conservative majority in the Upper House to reject measures passed by the elected Liberal majority in the Commons. Lansdowne became a minister without portfolio in the Asquith coalition cabinet of May 1915. By 1916 Lansdowne had come to favour a negotiated peace with Germany, a view he put forward first in the cabinet and later (29 November 1917) in a letter printed in the *Daily Telegraph*. His advocacy of a negotiated settlement made him extremely unpopular in England, although his views showed moderation and common sense.

Laos. A republic in northern Indo-China. From the fifteenth to nineteenth centuries the region was covered by two kingdoms and a principality (Luang Prabang, Vientiane and Champassac) administratively unified under French protection in 1893. In 1947 Laos was granted autonomy within the French Union and was recognized as an independent and neutralist monarchy by the ►Geneva Agreements of 1954. The country was thereafter weakened by chronic civil war, closely linked to the struggles in neighbouring ►Vietnam and ►Cambodia. There were three main contending parties striving for power: royalist-neutralists under Prince Souvanna Phouma; communists led by his half-brother, ex-Prince Souphan-ouvong, and generally known as the Pathet Lao movement; and a succession of army officers, pro-American but with little else in common apart from an inability to seize and retain power convincingly. By February 1973 the Pathet Lao controlled most of the region and a ceasefire was signed at Vientiane (the capital). After a final abortive *coup* by General Thoa Ma an agreement was concluded in September 1973 for the establishment of a joint government composed equally of royalist and communist delegates. But the fall of Saigon and the elimination of the South Vietnamese Government in the spring of 1975 was followed by a total communist takeover of Laos. The monarchy was formally abolished on 2 December 1975, Souphanouvong assuming office as President of a People's Democratic Republic. Over the following three years Laos came increasingly under the control of the Vietnamese government in Hanoi.

Lateran Treaties. Agreements concluded on 11 February 1929 between Mussolini's government in Italy and Pope Pius XI (pontiff 1922–39) which recognized the independent sovereignty of the Holy See in the Vatican city state and which included a concordat regulating the position of the Roman Catholic church in Italy. The Pope received a considerable indemnity for papal possessions seized when Italian unification was completed by the occupation of Rome in 1870.

Latvia. A ►Baltic republic, bounded by ►Estonia to the north and ►Lithuania and ►Belarus to the south; capital, Riga. Latvia was absorbed in the Russian Empire in 1795, the region falling within the provinces of Livonia and Courland. Until 1917 it was a land of large estates, owned by the 'Baltic Barons', Germans in Russian service. The Latvians proclaimed their independence on 18 November 1918 but had to struggle against both the Bolsheviks and German irregular troops before gaining international recognition in January 1921. Economic depression led in May 1934 to the suspension of the Latvian democratic constitution and to the establishment of an authoritarian dictatorship under Karlis Ulmanis, Prime Minister from 1934 to 1936 and thereafter President. Ulmanis vainly sought German protection against the increasing power of Russia. The ►Nazi–Soviet Pact left Latvia in the Soviet sphere of interest. Latvia was occupied by the Russians in June 1940, becoming a Soviet republic two months later. The German Army took Riga on 1 July 1941 and remained in Latvia until October 1944 but made no attempt to win support by establishing a puppet regime. Despite repression, and Russian immigration in the Brezhnev era, a strong sense of Latvian patriotism survived, manifesting itself in Lutheran church services during the *glasnost* thaw of 1988 (►Gorbachev) and subsequently in a determined movement favouring secession. An elected Supreme Council re-asserted Latvia's independent existence in May 1990. Clashes with Soviet troops and security police continued for seven months. A national referendum in March 1991 showed 73 per cent of the population favoured secession, which was conceded by the Soviet Union on 10 September 1991. The democratic constitution of 1921–2 was restored in 1993. Latvia joined the Council of Europe in February 1995 and applied for admission to the ►European Union eight months later.

Laurier, Wilfrid (1841–1919, knighted 1902). Born at St Lin, Quebec, educated in Montreal, became a barrister, entering the Ottawa parliament in 1874 as a Liberal and becoming leader of the Liberals in 1887. In 1896 he became Prime Minister, the first French Canadian and the first Roman Catholic to hold that office in the dominion. He remained Prime Minister until 1911, working assiduously for imperial collaboration although insisting on Canada's right to take decisions over foreign affairs and defence independently. He helped create a greater sense of Canadian unity, improved trade relations with Britain and was responsible for the decision to send Canadian troops overseas during the Boer War. His government fell in October 1911 because of general resentment at his attempts to strengthen trade links with the USA, and he was succeeded as Prime Minister by ►Borden. Sir Wilfrid Laurier remained Liberal leader and Leader of the Opposition until his death. While supporting Canadian participation in the First World War he declined to join the coalition government in 1917 because he could never approve of conscription.

Lausanne, Treaty of (24 July 1923). Final peace treaty with Turkey, necessitated by the refusal of the Turkish nationalists to be bound by the earlier treaty of ►Sèvres and by their victories against the Greeks in Asia Minor. Turkey surrendered claims to any territory formerly in the Ottoman Empire occupied by non-Turks. Greece retained all the Aegean islands, except Imbros and Tenedos which were returned to Turkey. Italian annexation of the Dodecanese and British annexation of Cyprus were confirmed. The Bosphorus and Dardanelles were demilitarized. The Greeks surrendered ►Smyrna and eastern Thrace. It was agreed that there would be an exchange of population between Greece and Turkey, 1 million Greeks being forced to leave Turkey and 350,000 Turks being expelled from Greece.

Laval, Pierre (1883–1945), French statesman. Born at Châteldon in the Auvergne, became a lawyer and joined the socialists in 1903 and was elected deputy for Aubervilliers, a working-class constituency north-east of Paris, in May 1914. He represented Aubervilliers in the Chamber, 1914–19 and 1924–7, as well as being Mayor from 1923 until 1944. From 1927 to 1936 he was Senator for the Seine and from 1936 to 1944 for his native department, the Puy-de-Dôme. After narrowly escaping imprisonment in 1918 for his anti-war policy, he left the socialists in 1920 and attracted support as an independent by astute political management of the smaller factions. He was Minister of Public Works in 1925, of Justice in 1926, of Labour in 1930, and Prime Minister, January 1931 to February 1932. His best-known spell of office was at the Foreign Ministry, October 1934 to January 1936, for the last seven months also serving as Prime Minister again: he was forced to resign because of an apparently cynical plan to appease Mussolini by partitioning Ethiopia. For the next four years he kept out of the forefront of politics but emerged as the main spokesman of ►Vichy after the defeat of 1940. He was chief minister of the Vichy Government from April 1942 until August 1944. His collaborationist policy sought to preserve France from civil war by neutralism: he avoided military undertakings to the Germans and, after D-Day, sought to reconvene the National Assembly as the only legal constitutional body in France, but he was arrested by the Nazis, who had never trusted him. After fleeing to Spain in 1945 he returned to France to face a charge of treason; after a trial of highly questionable legality, he was shot in the courtyard of Fresnes prison on 15 October 1945.

Law, Andrew Bonar (1858–1923), British Prime Minister. Born in Rexton, New Brunswick, the son of a Presbyterian minister, but left Canada for Scotland at the age of twelve. He was educated at Glasgow High School, entered the iron trade and was elected a Conservative MP for a Glasgow constituency in 1900, subsequently sitting for Dulwich 1909–10, Bootle 1911–18 and another Glasgow constituency 1918–23. He gained a following among the rank and file of his party who complained that their leader, ►Balfour, was remote, and in 1911 he became Conservative Party leader, strongly supporting the Ulstermen in the Irish crisis of 1912–14. In 1915 he entered the Asquith coalition as Colonial Secretary, becoming Chancellor of the Exchequer and Leader in the Commons under Lloyd George, 1915–19 and Lord Privy Seal 1919–22. In October 1922 he became Prime Minister but ill-health forced his resignation after seven months in office. Law's brief period of leadership set the fashion for tranquillity and 'safety first', which was to mark British conservatism throughout the inter-war period.

Lawrence, Thomas Edward (1888–1935), 'Lawrence of Arabia'. Born at Tremadoc but spent his childhood in Oxford, taking part in archaeological expeditions to the Middle East while still an undergraduate at Jesus College. In December 1916 his knowledge of the Arabs led him to be sent from Cairo to Jedda where he induced Emir ►Feisal and his father, Hussein, to maintain a revolt of Arabs against the Turks (which had begun, on a small scale, six months earlier). Colonel Lawrence's military expeditions consisted partly of raids on the Damascus–Medina Railway and partly of an advance to occupy key centres on the fringe of the main theatre of operations (e.g. the capture of the port of Aqaba, July 1917). Throughout the winter of 1917–18 the Arabs kept in close touch with the right flank of Allenby's army in Palestine, eventually entering Damascus itself on 1 October 1918. Lawrence considered that the Arab cause was betrayed by the peace treaties, and in particular by allowing the French a mandate in ►Syria. He served in the Middle East department of the Colonial Office, 1921–2, as special adviser on Arab affairs to the minister (Churchill), whom he accompanied to Egypt and Palestine in an attempt to ease the friction between Jews and Arabs and to consolidate the position of ►Abdullah in Transjordan. Lawrence's desire for anonymity led him to enlist under assumed names in the Tank Corps and the RAF. Eventually he changed his name by deed-poll to T.E. Shaw and served as an aircraftman, 1923–35, being stationed for more than two years on the north-west frontier of India. He was killed in a motor-cycle accident near his home in Dorset. His account of the Arab revolt. *Seven Pillars of Wisdom*, was printed privately in 1926 and published for general circulation soon after his death.

League of Nations. An international organization set up in 1919 to preserve peace and settle disputes by arbitration. Such a body had been advocated during the war by a number of Commonwealth statesmen (notably Viscount Cecil of Chelwood and Field-Marshal Smuts) and by President Wilson of the USA, who made formation of a League one of his ►Fourteen Points. The constitution of the League ('Covenant') was adopted by the Paris Peace Conference in April 1919 and written into each of the peace treaties. The League's headquarters were in Geneva but its first secretary-general (1919–32) was the British diplomat, Sir Eric Drummond (later Earl of Perth, 1876–1951). When the US Congress refused to ratify the Treaty of Versailles, America dissociated herself from the League and never became a member. Germany was a member only from 1926 to 1933. Soviet

Russia from 1934 to 1940. Founder members who were later criticized walked out of the League: Brazil, 1926; Japan, 1933; Italy, 1937. The League had no armed force to coerce members: it relied on the boycott known as ►'sanctions', discredited by the half-hearted way in which they were employed against Italy during the ►Abyssinian War of 1935–6. The League's successes include the settlement of several Balkan and Latin American disputes, assistance to refugees from Russia and Turkey in the 1920s, the provision of reconstruction loans for the Danubian states, and the encouragement of better working conditions by the International Labour Organization. The League also successfully supervised the system of ►mandates, the judicial administration of Upper Silesia, and the Free City of ►Danzig. It failed to check Japanese aggression in China, Italian aggression against Ethiopia or the Russian attack on Finland in 1939, although these three aggressors were member-states. In the pre-war crises of 1938–9 the Great Powers tended to ignore the League. During the Second World War the League maintained its non-political functions. Its remaining responsibilities were handed over to the ►United Nations in April 1946.

Lebanon. From 1516 until 1918 the Lebanon formed part of the Ottoman Turkish Empire, although its people enjoyed greater autonomy than their kinsfolk in neighbouring ►Syria. French protection from 1860 onwards brought commercial prosperity to the coastal towns and villages while perpetuating divisions between a privileged Christian governing class and a Muslim Arab rural proletariat. On the collapse of Turkey the Lebanese at first welcomed the French ►mandate, effectively established in 1920, and a Lebanese Republic was officially set up under French auspices in 1926 but slowness in making genuine political concessions destroyed much of the goodwill traditionally shown towards governments in Paris. From the summer of 1941 until December 1946 the Lebanon was occupied by Free French (Gaullist) forces, supported by British units. Despite serious friction between the authorities and the Lebanese (Christian and Muslim) in 1943, de Gaulle agreed, under British and American pressure, to transfer all remaining political powers to the Lebanese on 1 January 1944. Stability of government in the republic has depended on a constitutional compromise by which a succession of Maronite Uniat Christians held the Presidency while the Prime Minister was a traditional Muslim (Sunni) and the speaker of parliament a deviationist Muslim (Shia). This balance of sectarian interests failed on three occasions: on the assassination of Prime Minister Riyadh al-Sulh in July 1951; through the reluctance of the pro-American Camille Chamoun to surrender the Presidency to General Chehab, a Maronite trusted by the Muslims, in September 1958; and through the inability of President Franjieh to prevent fighting in Beirut between the principal Christian party (Phalangist) and Muslim supporters of the Palestinian guerrillas (April 1975 to April 1976). Each of these events caused outbreaks of civil war, the most disastrous being the protracted crisis of 1975–6. This led to widespread destruction in the capital, Beirut, to the loss of the Lebanon's position as the chief Middle East banking centre, and to the armed intervention of Syrian troops, who moved into the Lebanon in force in June 1976. A ceasefire was ordered in October 1976, but fighting between Phalangists and Syrians was resumed in Beirut in February 1978, continuing intermittently until July and beginning again in September. Attempts by successive Lebanese governments to remain neutral in the Arab – Israeli conflicts were hampered, from the autumn of 1967 onwards, by the growing activity of the ►Palestine Liberation Organization (PLO) in Arab refugee camps. Israel shelled Lebanese villages accused of harbouring PLO guerrillas in May and June 1968 and on 28 December 1968 carried out a helicopter-borne commando raid on Beirut airport as a reprisal for alleged Lebanese tolerance of Arab guerrillas. The civil war in ►Jordan led the Palestinians to move their headquarters to Lebanon in 1970 where they became a powerful revolutionary force and provoked frequent Israeli intervention, 1970–75. The Israeli air force resumed the bombing of Lebanese villages on 9 November 1977 after a two-year respite. Four months later Israeli troops occupied a segment of southern Lebanon allegedly to protect the villages from PLO infiltration. While a UN peace-keeping force moved into the Lebanon in a vain attempt to create a buffer zone, the Israelis intervened increasingly in the country's endemic civil war, playing off rival groups of Maronites against each other and giving full support to Major Sa'ad Haddad's Christian militia. In April 1979 Haddad proclaimed the segment which he occupied by grace of the Israelis to be 'Free Lebanon', and three weeks later ►Begin offered the Beirut authorities peace, provided that Syrian troops and the PLO left Lebanese territory. This offer was rejected, but it remained the basis of Israeli policy for the following three years. Repeated bombing raids by Israeli aircraft were backed up by large-scale raids of land forces, notably between April and mid-August in 1980. Fierce bombardments and ground fighting caused heavy casualties in July 1981 but were followed by eleven months of nominal peace. The ceasefire was broken in the first week of June 1982 with a full military invasion by Israel. The towns of Tyre and Sidon were severely damaged and several hundred Israeli tanks advanced on Beirut with the intention of finally eradicating the PLO threat. A military siege of Palestinian strongholds in west Beirut was maintained by the Israelis for ten weeks, the city suffering considerably from aerial bombing and from shelling by warships, tanks and artillery. The Palestinian guerrillas were evacuated in the fourth week of August 1982, with American, French and Italian troops seeking to keep peace in the city. On 16 September 1982 Phalangist forces in Israeli-occupied West Beirut massacred men, women and children in the Chabra and Chatila refugee camp. An American sponsored agreement for Israeli withdrawal in May 1983 was frustrated by the Syrian-backed Amal militia who carried the war into the Chouf mountains in September. Two National Reconciliation Conferences attended by the Lebanese factions with Syrian and Israeli observers met at Geneva (October 1983) and Lausanne (March 1984), and prepared the way for a gradual Israeli withdrawal from Beirut, beginning in February 1985. Beirut, however, remained divided, with 229 killed in car-bomb explosions in the city itself between

March and August 1985. The Bourj al Barajneh refugee camp in Beirut was besieged by the Amal militia for five months in the winter of 1986–7; a British surgeon, Dr Pauline Cutting, and Nurse Susan Wighton aroused widespread admiration for their courage in tending the sick and wounded in the camp. At the same time, rival factions took foreign ➤hostages. On 21 January 1987 Terry Waite, the Archbishop of Canterbury's envoy, was seized by Shia fanatics while trying to negotiate the release of others. The authority of the Lebanese President, Amin Gemayel (elected to succeed his murdered brother, Basir Gemayel, in September 1982), carried little weight in his capital and when his term expired in September 1988 no agreement could be reached on unifying the country. Fighting between rival Shia militias continued in Beirut throughout January 1989; a fortnight later there were clashes between Phalangist army factions too. Rene Muanad, elected President on 5 November 1989, was killed by a bomb on 22 November. Improved relations between Syria and the Western powers held out new hopes of peace at the close of 1990 under the Syrian-backed government of Umar Karami. The Beq'a valley, around Baalbek, remained under Syrian occupation, and a South Lebanon Security Zone was held by the Israelis. Sporadic fighting continued between Hezbollah (Palestinian guerrillas) and the Israelis, and in April 1996 Beirut again came under Israeli missile attack, aimed at alleged Hezbollah targets. Parliamentary elections were held for Lebanon in 1992 but were boycotted by Christian voters in areas still occupied by Syrians. The gradual recovery was marked in 1997 by a resumption of (strictly controlled) tourism and a visit by ➤John Paul II to Beirut.

Lebensraum. A doctrine, officially encouraged in Nazi Germany, which asserted the need to acquire 'living space' in order to offset the excessive concentration of Germany's population on a restricted area of arable soil. The phrase was introduced into politics from the biological sciences in the late 1870s but was first given wide usage by ➤Hitler and ➤Himmler. They assumed Germany would find the necessary 'space' in the east, especially in Poland, Byelorussia and the Ukraine, whose peoples were allegedly of inferior racial stock and thus, according to the Nazis, only fitted to serve as serfs under a master race.

Lend-Lease Act (11 March 1941). An act of the US Congress, passed while America was still neutral, authorizing President Roosevelt to lease or lend equipment to any nation 'whose defense the President deems vital to the defense of the United States'. In practical terms the Act permitted the immediate supply of arms, warships and other goods to Great Britain and later to China and the Soviet Union. The Act enabled American industry to be geared for war production eight months before Pearl Harbor. Critics have maintained that 'Lend-Lease' was a device which assisted US exports to force out British exports from the world markets: this, however, was already a likely consequence of wartime developments. The Act made America 'the arsenal of democracy'. Politically it ensured that, once the United States became a belligerent, American military and civilian leaders would have the predominant voice in strategic matters since they were ultimately responsible for 'delivering the goods'. Lend-Lease was abruptly terminated by President Truman on 17 August 1945, although American aid was resumed in a different form by the ➤Marshall Plan of 1947.

Lenin, Vladimir Ilyich (1870–1924, family name Ulyanov). Born in Simbirsk, on the middle Volga. In May 1887 his elder brother was hanged for complicity in a plot to assassinate Tsar Alexander III. Lenin was able to graduate in law from St Petersburg University although kept under surveillance 1,000 miles from the capital. He was arrested in December 1895 and exiled to Siberia from 1897 to 1900, eventually leaving Russia in July 1900. He lived successively in Brussels, Paris, London and Geneva. Through his pamphlets, with their penetrating analysis of post-Marxian socialism, and through his newspapers *Iskra* (The Spark) and *Vperyod* (Forward), Lenin was accepted as leader of the militant Russian Social Democrats, who assumed the name ➤'Bolsheviks' in 1903. Lenin returned to Russia in November 1905 and organized the Petersburg Soviet but was forced to escape to Finland and in 1907 settled again in Switzerland. After the Revolution of March 1917 Lenin travelled back to Petrograd, passing through Germany in a 'sealed train' provided by the German General Staff, who counted on the Bolsheviks spreading disaffection among the Russian soldiery. Lenin remained in Petrograd from 16 April to 18 July 1917, when the failure of an abortive Soviet *coup d'état* led him to escape once more to Finland. He returned on 23 October and, from his headquarters in the Smolny Institute, led the rising which captured the government offices (6–8 November – the 'October Revolution'). Lenin became head of the new government, the Soviet of Peoples' Commissars. He carried through a major distribution of land and nationalized property and the banks. He also ordered an armistice between Russia and Germany and in March 1918 authorized signature of the Treaty of ➤Brest-Litovsk, establishing Russia's capital in Moscow during the same month. Lenin's attempts to accomplish economic revolution while waging civil war against the 'Whites' led to famine and the virtual collapse of Russia's economy. In March 1921 he accordingly adopted the ➤'New Economic Policy', which was a retreat from his 'war communism'. He was wounded in an attempted assassination on 30 August 1918. Although he resumed his work less than three weeks later, his health suffered and he was partially incapacitated by a succession of strokes, May 1922 to March 1923: he died on 21 January 1924. Petrograd (St Petersburg) was renamed Leningrad in his honour five days later. The city reverted to its original name in 1991.

Leningrad, Siege of. German and Finnish forces encircled Leningrad at the beginning of September 1941 and the fall of the city seemed imminent. Desperate resistance induced the German command to depend on blockade and bombardment as a means of forcing the garrison to surrender. In a siege of nearly 900 days between 150,000 and 200,000 shells were fired at the city and over 100,000 bombs dropped by the Luftwaffe. The heaviest casualties were caused by famine and cold:

3,700 civilians perished in the month of December 1941, before supplies were brought into the city over the frozen waters of Lake Ladoga. Soviet counter-attacks early in 1943 partially relieved the city but it was not until 27 January 1944 that the Soviet High Command was able to announce the complete lifting of the siege and the reopening of the Leningrad–Moscow railway.

Liberal Party (Australia). Although Liberal parties, based on the traditions of the British ►Liberal Party were active in the Australian states before 1914 their representation in the federal parliament was small. The outstanding pre-war Liberal leader, Alfred ►Deakin, was forced to rely on fusion with Labour to form his three governments. In 1917 many Liberals joined ►Hughes in establishing a Nationalist Party which in 1931 became the chief component in the United Australia Party of ►Lyons. The election of 1943 left the UAP with only twelve representatives at Canberra: half of them, including the UAP leader ►Menzies, were from Victoria. In February 1945 Menzies accordingly revived the name 'Liberal', hoping to give the party a wider basis and to present it as an anti-Labour coalition, attracting conservative voters. This new-style Liberal Party gained fifty-five seats in the election of 1949 and was the dominant political group until 1972, tending to become increasingly Conservative while strongly upholding free enterprise and denouncing all forms of communism. The Liberals were in office again from 1975 to 1983 under Malcolm ►Fraser and returned to power in March 1996, within a Liberal–National coalition, headed by the party leader, John Howard.

Liberal Party (Britain). During the 1830s the political heirs of the Whig reformers came to refer to themselves as 'liberals', a term already in use on the Continent, but the first distinctly Liberal Government was not formed until 1868, under Gladstone. The 'National Liberal Federation', a centralized party organization, was established in 1877. Classical liberalism – in the Gladstonian tradition – favoured financial economy, political reform, Free Trade budgets, private initiative and a pacific attitude towards international and colonial disputes. The party was divided over ►Irish Home Rule; and when it came to power after the 1906 election showed more interest in social legislation than during the Gladstonian era. ►Campbell-Bannerman, ►Asquith and ►Lloyd George successfully presented the Liberal Party as the prime instigator of reforms (1906–12) but disputes between Asquith and Lloyd George weakened liberalism during the First World War and its radical traditions were inherited by the Labour Party. Liberal representation at Westminster fell continuously during the inter-war period and the slump continued after 1945. Only six Liberals were returned in the general elections of 1950, 1951 and 1955. Under Jeremy Thorpe (1929–), leader from January 1967 until May 1976, the party's fortunes improved: fourteen seats were gained at the election of February 1974; and Liberals were recognized as the champions of racial and religious minorities, of civil rights and of democratic decision-making machinery in politics and industry. By-election returns in 1976–7 suggested that the 'Liberal revival' was a temporary phenomenon, associated with Mr Thorpe, rather than a reversal of the general trend over the preceding half-century. A 'Lib–Lab Pact', arranged by the party leaders in March 1977, helped maintain in office the minority Labour Government of ►Callaghan in return for prior consultation between the two parties over aspects of government policy. The 'Pact' was unpopular with many rank-and-file Liberal Party members, and on 25 May 1978 the Liberal leader, David Steel (1938–), announced that the arrangement would not be renewed. In September 1981 the Liberal Party Conference voted in favour of an electoral alliance with the new ►Social Democratic Party. Disappointment at the working of this Alliance in the 1987 election led a year later to the merging of the Liberals and most SDP members in the Social and Liberal Democrat Party, under Paddy Ashdown's leadership. The 1988 Blackpool conference abandoned the historic 'Liberals' in favour of 'Democrats' as a short title for the Party but subsequent usage confirmed the name Liberal Democrats. After the 1992 election the number of MPs rose to twenty, and in May 1997 the Party had its greatest success for almost seventy years, winning in forty-six constituencies.

Liberal Party (Canada). One of the principal political parties in the dominion, believing in Free Trade, imperial interdependence and respect for the rights of minorities, especially the French-speaking Canadians. The Liberal Party has been in power 1896–1911 (►Laurier), 1935–48 (Mackenzie ►King and Louis ►St Laurent), 1963–84 (►Pearson and ►Trudeau) and since October 1993 (Jean Chretian).

Liberal Party (New Zealand). The New Zealand Liberal Party dominated colonial and dominion politics from 1890 to 1911, until 1909 in close alliance with a Labour Party. Richard Seddon (Prime Minister 1893–1906) was responsible for a succession of political and social reforms, anticipating the measures of the great British Liberal Governments on the eve of the First World War: factory acts, 1894 and 1897; trade-union legislation, 1894; old-age pensions, 1898. The Seddon Ministry also pioneered women's suffrage (1893). The growing political strength of the farmers in the North Island benefited the Reform Party (conservatives) and the Liberals never recovered their pre-war power, although participating in a wartime coalition, 1915–19. The Liberal leader, Sir Joseph Ward (1856–1930), sought to gain support in the North Island by broadening the base of the movement, which he restyled 'United Party', gaining a narrow electoral victory in November 1928. The impact of economic depression made this new political body hardly distinguishable from the Reform Party and in May 1937 the two merged to establish an anti-Labour front, the ►National Party.

Libya. A predominantly Arab state on the former Barbary coast, occupied by the Ottoman Turks in 1551 who administered it as the vilayet of Tripoli and sanjak of Benghazi (Cyrenaica). In November 1911 the two provinces were annexed by Italy during a war waged against the Turks for purposes of national prestige and colonial expansion (the 'Libyan War' of 29 September 1911 to 15 October 1912).

Civil government was established in 1919 but the Italians had to undertake military expeditions against Senussi tribesmen controlling the inland oases. Although Mussolini constructed military roads in the colony, his power suffered severe setbacks from the two British advances to Benghazi of December 1940 to January 1941 and again a year later. After the second battle of ►Alamein, the British Eighth Army conquered Libya (October 1942 to January 1943), placing the country under military administration until December 1951 when Libya became the first independent state created by a resolution of the General Assembly of the United Nations. The leader of the Senussi, Muhammad Idris al-Mahdi (1890–1972), was recognized as king of a federated constitutional monarchy. King Idris, a Cyrenaican, sought to rule impartially but his decision to abolish the federal system in 1963 was much resented in Tripoli, while the enfranchisement of women offended Muslim traditionalists. Although Libya joined the Arab League in 1953, King Idris permitted the maintenance of British and American military bases in return for economic aid. The discovery of oil in 1959, exported in quantity within two years, revolutionized the economic situation of the kingdom. A radical Pan-Arab movement deposed King Idris in September 1969 and established a socialist republic headed by ►Gaddafi. In September 1971 Libya joined Egypt and Syria in a Confederation of Arab Republics and followed a strongly anti-Israeli policy. The Anglo-Libyan Treaty of Friendship and Alliance concluded by King Idris in July 1953 was formally ended in January 1972 and was followed by immediate nationalization of British oil interests. The influence of the Soviet-bloc countries increased rapidly from 1971 onwards. Libyan relations with Sadat began to deteriorate in 1974–5 because of Egypt's contacts with the West. Skirmishes along the Egyptian–Libyan frontier in July 1977 were followed by a complete break between Tripoli and Cairo after the ►Sadat Initiative and the prospect of an understanding between Israel and Egypt. Libya began to interfere in the internal affairs of ►Tunisia, ►Chad and ►Morocco while Gaddafi gained international notoriety as the alleged patron of the extreme Arab terrorists. Assassination squads claimed victims among expatriate Libyans in London, Milan, Rome, Athens and Bonn between February and June 1980. Five African states and Saudi Arabia broke off relations with Libya in the course of 1980 because of Libyan intrigues in their internal politics. So, too, did Britain in April 1984 after Woman Police Constable Yvonne Fletcher was killed by a shot fired from the Libyan People's Bureau at a crowd protesting in St James's Square, London. Strained relations with the US were marked by air battles over the Gulf of Sirte in August 1981 and March 1986, and by an air raid on Tripoli by US F-111 fighter-bombers based in Britain (15 April 1986). The Libyans continued to supply arms to what were regarded, in Washington and London, as terrorist organizations. Reports that Libya was building a chemical weapons factory led to further tension with the US in the last four months of Reagan's presidency. The UN imposed sanctions in April 1992 after Libya's refusal to surrender two suspects allegedly involved in the bombing of the Pan-Am plane over Lockerbie in December 1988.

Lidice. A large mining village in Bohemia, west of Prague, destroyed with its inhabitants by German security forces on 9 June 1942 as part of a reign of terror established in the Czech lands in retaliation for the assassination of the ruthless 'Protector of Bohemia-Moravia', Reinhard Heydrich, five days previously. The village of Lezaky was also wiped out; but Lidice has remained a symbol of Resistance heroism and of the martyrdom of the innocent.

Lie, Trygve Halvdan (1896–1968), first Secretary-General of the United Nations. Born in Oslo, practised as a lawyer, entered the Norwegian parliament (Storting) as a social democrat and served in every government from 1935 to 1946, acting as Foreign Minister during the period of exile in London, 1940–45. His convinced internationalism secured his election as UN Secretary-General when the General Assembly had held its first session in London (January–February 1946). He was an early, though unsuccessful, advocate of the admission of communist China to the United Nations. On 6 June 1950 he was invited to complete a second term of office and took the opportunity of presenting a twenty-year peace plan to the UN. Within three weeks, however, the North Koreans crossed into South ►Korea and Trygve Lie took the initiative in organizing UN forces to assist the south Koreans to check the act of aggression and restore peace in the peninsula. Lie resigned as Secretary-General in March 1953 and later re-entered Norwegian politics, serving as Minister for Industry (1963–4) and as minister responsible for commerce and shipping (1964–8).

Lima Declaration (26 December 1938). A Pan-American conference met in Peru in December 1938 to emphasize the solidarity of the states of North and South America at a time of international tension in Europe and Asia. The conference accepted a declaration, issued in the Peruvian capital, that threats to the peace, security or territorial integrity of any republic in the Americas would be interpreted as a matter of concern for all the republics. This represented a victory for Roosevelt's policy of rallying support in the western hemisphere for the opponents of European totalitarianism, even though some signatories of the declaration were more sympathetically disposed to fascism than to the American democratic ideal.

Lin Piao (Lin Biao, 1908–71), Chinese communist soldier. Graduated from the Whampoa Military Academy with high honours but chose to fight with the communists rather than with ►Chiang Kai-shek and became a Communist Party member in 1927, commanding an army during the ►Long March and later fighting against the Japanese. Between January and November 1948 he gained a remarkable series of victories over Chiang's Kuomintang troops in Manchuria, capturing the vital city and arsenal of Mukden on 29 October, and carrying the war victoriously into central China in 1949. He commanded the Chinese 'volunteers' helping North Korea, 1950–52, but then suffered a breakdown in health. He was created a Marshal in 1955, Minister of Defence in 1959 and assisted ►Mao in organizing the 'cultural revolution' of the mid 1960s, by August 1966 being ranked second only to Mao in the list of party dignitaries. The Ninth Party Congress of April 1969 formally declared Marshal Lin to be Mao's designated successor. Two and a half years later it was announced he had been killed in an air crash over Mongolia in September 1971 while trying to escape from China after an unsuccessful attempt to seize power in Peking.

Lindbergh, Charles Augustus (1902–74), American airman. Born in Detroit, the son of a liberal and pacifist Republican congressman, identical in names. He was commissioned in the Army Air Corps Reserve in 1925. On 20 May 1927 he set off in a single-engined monoplane, 'The Spirit of St Louis', to fly from New York to Paris, the first non-stop solo flight across the Atlantic. Lindbergh covered 3,600 miles in 33½ hours, a feat of endurance which made him a popular hero on both sides of the Atlantic, and on his return to New York he was hailed as 'the lone eagle' and given an unprecedented ticker-tape reception. On 1 March 1932 his baby son was kidnapped and subsequently murdered. In 1938 Colonel Lindbergh was invited by Goering to inspect the German Luftwaffe. He returned from Europe full of admiration for Nazi Germany and he opposed Roosevelt's foreign policy for the next three years, although after Pearl Harbor he warmly supported the American war effort. Lindbergh was for many years the senior technical adviser of Pan American Airways. Towards the end of his life he was an enthusiastic conservationist, active in the World Wildlife Fund, and he was also one of the first inventors to perfect a pump for a mechanical heart. His fame, however, rests on the courage and navigational skills shown on his historic solo flight across the Atlantic.

Lithuania. A large state in the fifteenth century, extending from the Baltic to the Black Sea, united to Poland in 1569. Nearly all Lithuania was absorbed in the Russian Empire between 1793 and 1917. A Lithuanian national and cultural revival in the 1880s was belatedly exploited by Germany in the First World War; Kaiser William II recognized Lithuania's independence on 23 March 1918 and a Lithuanian assembly duly elected one of the Württemberg princes as ruler, King Mindaugas II, on 4 June. Five months later, when Germany was defeated in the West, this act was ignored and the Lithuanians established a republican government and were immediately faced by a Bolshevik invasion. The Russians captured the ancient Lithuanian capital of ►Vilna but soon lost it to the Poles, who held it until October 1939. The Russo-Lithuanian War was ended by the Treaty of Moscow of July 1920, and by the end of 1922 Lithuania was recognized as a democratic republic (capital, Kaunas) by all the Great Powers. From 1923 until March 1939 the Lithuanians occupied the predominantly German port of Memel, which they administered as an autonomous region until it was annexed to the Reich by Hitler. Conflict with Germany over Memel and Poland over Vilna left Lithuania exposed to the Soviet Union, especially after conclusion of the ►Nazi–Soviet Pact. A Soviet–Lithuanian mutual assistance pact (3 October 1939) permitted the Lithuanians to recover Vilna on condition the city was occupied by a Soviet garrison.

Russia continued to put pressure on Lithuania and in July 1940 a packed assembly voted for incorporation in the Soviet Union. On 8 August 1940 Lithuania – like her northern neighbours, ➤Latvia and ➤Estonia – became a constituent republic in the USSR. Relaxation of political pressure under ➤Gorbachev led to widespread patriotic demonstrations in October 1988, with demands for greater autonomy. In March 1990 the Lithuanian Parliament issued a unilateral declaration of independence. The Soviet Government responded by imposing an oil embargo. For over a year there were occasional clashes between Soviet troops and Lithuanian groups, with independence finally acknowledged by the Soviet Union on 10 September 1991. A new democratic constitution in 1992 established a unicameral parliament and confirmed Vilnius (Vilna) as capital of the republic. Lithuania applied to join the ➤European Union in December 1995.

Little Entente. The system of alliances between Czechoslovakia and Yugoslavia (1920), Czechoslovakia and Romania (1921) and Yugoslavia and Romania (1921), consolidated in a single treaty signed in Belgrade, May 1929. The alliances sought to preserve the central-European *status quo* as established by the Treaties of ➤St Germain and ➤Trianon; they were especially opposed to any Habsburg restoration either in Austria or Hungary. In February 1933 a permanent council and secretariat was established for the Little Entente, which began to encourage economic cooperation and thus became an early example of the international organizations prevalent after the Second World War. Regular military conversations were held, 1929–37, but the Little Entente's war plans were concerned only with a possible Hungarian war of revenge and never faced up to the growing German menace. The alliance was weakened by Yugoslav collaboration with Hitler's Germany, 1935–8, and disintegrated when Czechoslovakia was abandoned by the Western Powers in the ➤Munich Agreement of 1938. Formally the Yugoslavs and Romanians ended the Little Entente organization in February 1939. The term 'Little Entente' was coined, derisively, by a Hungarian journalist in the newspaper, *Pesti Hirlap*, 21 February 1920.

Litvinov, Maximilian (1876–1951), Soviet Foreign Minister. Born Meier Wallakh, of Jewish parentage, in Bialystok, became a revolutionary as a young man and, after imprisonment, escaped from Russia in 1902. His conspiratorial activities led to his deportation from France in 1908. He settled in London, worked for a publisher and married an Englishwoman. In 1917 he became the first Bolshevik representative in London but was deported in September 1918. From 1926 onwards he was in effective control of Soviet foreign policy, although he did not officially become Foreign Commissar until July 1930. Litvinov sought better relations with Russia's western neighbours and was largely responsible for the Franco-Soviet Pact of 1935 and for Russia's vigorous support of the League of Nations between 1934 and 1938. In May 1939 he was dismissed and replaced by ➤Molotov, since it seemed to Stalin unlikely that Litvinov could reach the agreement with Nazi

Germany which Russia needed at that moment (➤Nazi–Soviet Pact). From December 1941 until July 1943 Litvinov was Soviet ambassador in Washington.

Liu Shao-chi (Liu Shaoqi, 1898–1974), Chinese communist. Born into a peasant family in Hunan, went to Moscow as a student 1920–21, returning to work for the communist movement in Shanghai and Canton. He was elected to the Central Committee in 1927, appointed a Political Commissar during the ➤Long March and was accepted as a prominent Marxist theoretician, becoming principal vice-chairman of the party on the establishment of the Chinese People's Republic in 1949. In April 1959 he succeeded ➤Mao as Chairman of the People's Republic and therefore as Chinese head of state, although ranking second to Mao in the list of party dignitaries. In 1966, during the 'cultural revolution', he lost his position as heir-apparent to Marshal ➤Lin Piao (Lin Biao) and dropped in official ranking to eighth place. He was officially and publicly criticized for defending the importance of the industrial workers as a spearhead of revolution instead of accepting Mao's belief in the primacy of the peasantry. Both Liu and his wife were repeatedly denounced by Chiang Ching (Jiang Qing) (wife of Mao himself). A meeting of the Central Committee in October 1968 accused him of being 'a scab, renegade and traitor' and deprived him of all his offices, although it was impossible to remove him constitutionally from the chairmanship of the republic until early in 1969. He disappeared from public life, the Chinese Press announcing his death in November 1974.

Lloyd George, David (1863–1945, created an earl two months before his death). Born in Manchester, brought up near Criccieth in north Wales and articled to a solicitor at Portmadoc. In 1890 he was elected Liberal MP for the Caernarvon Boroughs, a constituency he represented for fifty-five years. He was denounced as 'pro-Boer' in 1899 but was brought into the government as President of the Board of Trade in 1905, becoming Chancellor of the Exchequer in April 1908. Lloyd George, as leader of the radical wing of Liberals, successfully advocated social reforms (Old Age Pensions Act, 1908, National Health Insurance Act, 1911) and was responsible for the 'People's Budget' of 1909. Since the budget proposed a super-tax and land-value duties it was thrown out by the House of Lords (30 November 1909), thus beginning the contest between the two Houses which culminated in the ➤Parliament Act of 1911. His name was cleared from allegations of corruption in the so-called ➤Marconi Scandal of 1913 and he remained Chancellor of the Exchequer until July 1915, when he became the first Minister of Munitions. He then collaborated with the Conservatives to overthrow ➤Asquith on the grounds that he lacked vigour. Lloyd George was coalition Prime Minister from December 1916 to October 1922. Although on poor terms with the generals in the field, Lloyd George was an energetic war leader and had some influence over the Admiralty, especially in the institution of the convoy system. He attended the ➤Paris Peace Conference in person, modifying the harsher proposals of the Treaty of Versailles. His Government of Ireland Act of 1920, establishing the Irish

Free State (►Ireland) and ►Northern Ireland, relieved the tension of the Irish problem and for long seemed to provide a settlement. The coalition became increasingly dominated by Conservatives, who took the opportunity of the ►Chanak Crisis to force him out of office. Although he led the Liberal Party from 1926 to 1931 (and then the Independent Liberals) his earlier treatment of Asquith left him an isolated figure and he was never again in office. He sympathized with German grievances 1932–8 and visited Hitler in September 1936 but opposed appeasement after the ►Munich Agreement. Throughout his life Lloyd George encouraged the cultural revival of the Welsh people, invariably speaking Welsh in his family circle.

Locarno, Treaties of (1 December 1925). A conference to ease international tension met at Locarno in the autumn of 1925 and produced a series of agreements, all signed on 1 December. The most important Locarno Treaty confirmed the inviolability of the Franco-German and Belgo-German frontiers and the demilitarized zone of the ►Rhineland: this Treaty was signed by France, Belgium and Germany and its terms were guaranteed by Britain and Italy. The Germans also concluded arbitration conventions with France, Belgium, Poland and Czechoslovakia. France signed Treaties of Mutual Guarantee with Poland and Czechoslovakia. The Locarno Treaties were a diplomatic triumph for ►Briand of France, ►Stresemann of Germany and Austen ►Chamberlain of Britain, all of whom were seeking a period of international cooperation based upon fulfilment of the peace treaties. The principal Locarno Treaty was violated by Hitler in March 1936 when he sent German troops into the demilitarized Rhineland: but, since the other signatories were preoccupied with the international crisis caused by the ►Abyssinian War, they contented themselves with formal protests at Hitler's action.

Lomé Convention (28 February 1975). A trade agreement reached in Lomé, the capital of Togo, between the ►European Economic Community and forty-six developing countries which thereby received free access for their products into the markets of all EEC members plus aid and investment. The Convention provides the basic post-imperialist economic understanding between Europe, Africa and the smaller political communities of the Caribbean and the Pacific. A successor to the original Convention was signed by the foreign ministers of sixty-seven countries at Lomé on 31 October 1979, after fifteen months of negotiation. 'Lomé II' (as the new Convention was called) provided for £3,650 million of aid from the EEC to be sent to the developing countries, spread over the period 1980–85. Lomé III (December 1984) and Lomé IV (December 1989) further revised arrangements between the EEC and the developing countries of the Third World.

London, Treaty of (26 April 1915). A secret agreement signed by Britain, France and Russia on one hand, and Italy on the other, guaranteeing the Italians generous territorial gains provided they joined the First World War on the side of the allies within one month. The Treaty promised Italy the acquisition of Italia Irredenta (the Austrian provinces of the Trentino, South Tirol, Istria, Gorizia, Gradisca and Trieste), a large stretch of the Dalmatian coast and its islands, a segment of Albanian territory around Valona, full sovereignty over the ex-Turkish Dodecanese Islands, the Turkish province of Adalia in Asia Minor, colonial gains in Africa, and a share in any war indemnity. The allies accepted these terms because they believed Italian intervention would rapidly destroy Austria–Hungary and thus 'open the back-door to Germany'. Italy duly entered the war on 24 May 1915 but without gaining the speedy and decisive victories for which the allies had hoped. When the Bolsheviks repudiated all the international obligations of Tsarist Russia early in 1918 they revealed the terms of the secret Treaty of London. The Treaty's flagrant disregard of the ethnic principle angered President ➤Wilson and he made it clear that the United States would not consider its terms as binding. At the ➤Paris Peace Conference the British and the French also opposed implementation of Italy's demands and she received far less than the Treaty had originally laid down. Italian popular resentment contributed to the rise of Mussolini's form of ➤fascism.

Long, Huey Pierce (1893–1935), Louisiana politician. Born at Winnfield, Louisiana: practised as a lawyer before building up a ruthless political machine within his home state. His demagogic skill enabled him to serve as State Governor (1928–31) and then to represent Louisiana in the Senate (1931–5). The state legislature passed a series of welfare measures in support of his 'Share the Wealth' campaign and by 1935 he had become a national figure, with a forceful and partially fascist programme, who did not disguise his ambition for the Presidency. 'The Kingfish', as he was known, was especially hostile to what he termed (in one word) 'lyingnewspapers' and succeeded in inducing the pliant state legislature to impose a discriminatory tax on any newspapers with a circulation in Louisiana of over 20,000. He was shot dead in Baton Rouge on 10 September 1935.

Long March. A migration of Chinese communists in the course of their conflict with the ➤Kuomintang. By the late summer of 1934 the position of the communist Soviet, set up in the Kiangsi province of ➤China in 1931, was becoming untenable because of a blockade instituted by Chiang Kai-shek, at the suggestion of his German military advisers. ➤Mao Tse-tung therefore decided to evacuate Kiangsi and establish a communist region in the north-west of China, protected by mountains. Some 100,000 men, and their dependants, set out from the area of Juichin, Hingkwo and Yutu in October 1934, under the leadership of Mao and the later Marshals, ➤Chu Teh and ➤Lin Piao. They headed westwards through mountainous areas where the local warlords were so backward that they could offer little military resistance. The marchers covered between forty and seventy miles a day, in an epic of human endurance, sweeping north-westwards through western Yunnan, Sikiang and Szechwan (where there was already a communist enclave) into Kansu and ultimately reaching Shensi on 20 October 1935, a year after setting out from Kiangsi. Only 30,000 of the original 100,000 communists survived the 8,000-mile march, although they were joined by further 'Route

Armies' over the following twelve months. Once in Yenan it was possible to establish a stronger position both for challenging Chiang and, from 1937 to 1945, for engaging the Japanese invaders. The Long March has provided the Chinese People's Republic with its greatest source of patriotic inspiration. Three episodes of heroism are especially remembered: the passage of the Tatu river on 30 May 1935 which required the overpowering of guards on a suspension bridge at Luting over a deep gorge; the crossing, a few days later, of the massive Tahsueh Shan mountains; and the march in August and September 1935 through the high, cold and untrekked swampland of Sikang, along the borders of Tibet.

Ludendorff, Erich (1865–1937), German general. Born at Kruszewnia, Posen (Poznan), received military training at Ploen and Lichterfelde, commissioned in the infantry in 1882, attracting attention by his hard work and mastery of detail. He became a major on the General Staff in 1906 and, as chief of operations planning, helped revise the famous proposals of ►Schlieffen for war in the west. In the early days of the 1914 campaign his initiative captured the citadel of Liège. He was then moved to the Eastern Front as Chief of Staff to the Eighth Army under ►Hindenburg, helping defeat the Russians at ►Tannenberg. The Hindenburg–Ludendorff partnership endured until 27 October 1918, and as Chief Quarter-master-General from 1916 to 1918 Ludendorff exercised greater authority in Germany than did the Chancellors. He planned the great offensive of 1918 culminating in the second battle of the ►Marne, but his nerve broke under the impact of the allied counter-offensive of August 1918. After urging Germany to conclude peace, he fled to Sweden, having resigned his post and disguised himself with blue spectacles and false whiskers. He later attached himself to right-wing groups, participating in both the ►Kapp Putsch and ►Hitler's Munich Putsch in March 1920 and November 1923 respectively. He sat as one of the earliest Nazi members of the Reichstag (1924–8). After gaining less than 1 per cent of the votes in the Presidential election of 1925, he broke with Hitler and entered a querulous retirement, rejecting Hitler's offer (1935) to create him a field-marshal and brooding over the way in which the Christian and Jewish religions, aided by the Freemasons, were, he thought, leading the world to destruction. These eccentricities of later years have tended to obscure the record of his genius as a staff officer.

Lumumba, Patrice (1925–61), Congolese politician. Born at Katako Kombe in the central Congo, spent most of his youth in Stanleyville (Kisangani), where he became a postal clerk. In 1957 he founded the MNC (Congolese National Movement). A year later he attended the Pan-African Conference in Accra, where he established contact with Nkrumah and Nasser, who saw in him a champion of left-wing anti-colonialism. The evident popular strength of the MNC led to Lumumba's appointment as first Prime Minister of the Congo Republic in July 1960 (►Congo Problem). He held office for only eleven weeks, being faced by mutinies, the secession of ►Katanga under ►Tshombe and political conflict in Léopoldville which culminated in a military *coup* organized by Colonel ►Mobutu on 14 September. Lumumbist political strength lay in Stanleyville. While he was on his way there, in December, Lumumba was detained by guards apparently loyal to the Léopoldville government. They handed him over to Katangese troops, who murdered him on 17 January 1961. A resolution by the UN Security Council on 13 February demanding an inquiry into the circumstances of his death was rejected by Tshombe. In the Soviet Union, Cuba and many parts of Africa Lumumba was regarded as a martyr in the struggle against 'colonialism and the rule of mercenaries'.

Lusitania. British liner sunk without warning by a German submarine off the Irish coast on 7 May 1915, with the loss of 1,153 passengers, including 128 Americans. The sinking led to anti-German riots in England, the victims being primarily shopkeepers with German-sounding names, especially in Liverpool and London. In America there was a widespread demand for a declaration of war on Germany, a mood so warlike that the peace-loving Secretary of State, ►Bryan, resigned. The German authorities claimed that the *Lusitania* had been carrying war material as part of her cargo and that advertisements in American newspapers had warned US citizens not to sail in allied ships. Informal assurances were given to President ►Wilson that such torpedoings would not recur, and the 'sinking vessels at sight' policy was abandoned on 18 September 1915, although resumed on 1 February 1917.

Luthuli, Albert John (1898–1967), Zulu tribal chieftain and African nationalist. Born near Bulawayo, educated at a Methodist mission school, becoming a teacher for fifteen years and chief of the Abasemakholweni tribe in 1936. He was an ardent worker for the ►African National Congress and in 1952 became President of the movement, consistently but peacefully opposing ►apartheid for the remainder of his life. The South African authorities officially deposed him as chieftain although the Zulu elders refused to nominate a successor. He was charged with high treason at Johannesburg in December 1956 but the charges were dropped in the course of the following year. The Suppression of Communism Act enabled the South African Government to banish him to a remote farm and severe restrictions were imposed on his freedom of movement. Chief Luthuli's struggle for African rights won him international respect, and he was elected Rector of Glasgow University, even though he could not leave Natal. The Nobel committee awarded him the Peace Prize for 1960 in recognition of his resolve to dedicate himself to non-violent methods in his fight against racial discrimination. His book *Let My People Go* (1962) emphasized his hostility to white repression and his rejection of black militancy. It was announced in September 1967 that he had died from falling in front of a railway train.

Luxembourg, Grand Duchy of. Established as an independent state of which the King of the Netherlands was Grand-Duke in 1815, a dynastic link broken in 1890 since at that time no woman could rule in Luxembourg (a constitutional tradition later amended). The Grand Duchy was invaded by Germany in 1914 and

1940 and was formally annexed to Germany from 1942 to 1945. From 1921 onwards Luxembourg has had close economic links with Belgium, an arrangement extended by the Benelux customs union of 1960. Luxembourg is a prominent member of the European Community, the home of the European Court, the secretariat of the European Parliament, and the European banking institutions, as well as being a member of NATO.

Luxemburg, Rosa (1871–1919), German socialist. Born of Jewish parentage at Zamość, Russian Poland; educated in Warsaw and at Zürich University, and became a German citizen when she went through a form of marriage with a German socialist *émigré* in Basle, 1898. She was an idealistic and independently minded socialist, contemptuous of any nationalistic trends among her fellow socialists and influencing the growth of both German and Russian communism. At first she worked for the union of socialist groups within the three areas of partitioned Poland, taking part in the anti-Tsarist riots of 1905. She then collaborated with Karl Liebknecht (1871–1919) in establishing a syndicalist wing of the German Socialist Party at the Jena party congress, September 1905. From 1910 onwards she organized regular Sunday-afternoon demonstrations in Berlin. In September 1914 Rosa Luxemburg and Karl Liebknecht published an open letter denouncing the war as an imperialist conflict and in the spring of 1915 organized the Spartacist group, socialists opposed to the war. Although imprisoned for most of the period between February 1915 and November 1918, she smuggled out letters calling for mass revolutionary action against the war. She criticized Lenin for having imposed a dictatorship over the proletariat rather than a dictatorship of the proletariat. By the end of December 1918 she was convinced that the German workers would have to stage a revolutionary upheaval throughout the country (not merely in Berlin) in order to overthrow capitalism. Although she tried to prevent the premature Spartacist disturbances of January 1919, she was captured by right-wing irregular troops (*Freikorps*) and – together with Liebknecht – murdered in west Berlin (15 January 1919) (►Spartacists).

Lyautey, Louis Hubert (1854–1934), Marshal of France. Born at Nancy, graduated from St Cyr, and saw active service in Algeria, Madagascar and Indo-China. General Lyautey was sent to Morocco as head of the military and civil administration when Morocco became a French protectorate in March 1912. Apart from a brief spell as Minister of War in 1916–17 he remained Resident-General of Morocco until September 1925, receiving his Marshal's baton in 1921. Lyautey was in many respects a model colonial governor, respecting the Sultan's authority, carrying out major engineering schemes (notably in Casablanca), and making arid lands fertile by expert scientific farming. Personally he remained a sincere Catholic, to whom many irreligious features of the Third Republic were antipathetic. He believed it was possible to assimilate the Islamic heritage of Morocco with Catholic culture and he sought to train a new type of colonial administrator who would accept his ideas. Many, however, failed to distinguish between assimilation and domination, and Lyautey's political legacy was thus almost exclusively to extremists of the Right who did not share his respect for Islamic traditions.

Lyons, Joseph Aloysius (1879–1939), Australian Prime Minister. Born at Stanley, Tasmania, taught in elementary schools for thirteen years and was elected to the Tasmanian Assembly as a Labour Party member in 1909, dominating the movement in the early 1920s and becoming a member of the federal parliament in 1929. He served briefly in the Scullin governments but was by temperament too conservative for his colleagues. In 1931 he seceded from Labour and, with a group of 'Nationalists', founded the United Australia Party, which won more seats than any other party at the general election on 19 December 1931, and Lyons became Prime Minister, holding office until his sudden death on 7 April 1939. Although a reformer in Tasmania, Lyons was an essentially non-constructive chairman as Prime Minister. He reassured people and conciliated temperamental colleagues with such geniality that cartoonists liked to depict him as the 'koala bear' of politics, a representation helped by his actual resemblance to a koala. He had come to office at a time of grim recession and, under his government, the Australian economy recovered. This recovery, however, sprang from rising gold and wool prices in the world market rather than from positive measures by Lyons. In July 1934 he launched a three-year defence programme to build up Australia's army and air force in the face of a mounting threat from Japan: it proved his most important decision.

M

Maastricht, Treaty of (7 February 1992). A treaty on ➤European Union agreed at a summit meeting at Maastricht in the Netherlands in December 1991 and signed there seven weeks later. The treaty created a common European citizenship, extended cooperation over foreign and security policy, provided for collaboration over juridical and internal social affairs, extended budgetary powers of the European parliament, and began preparations for a single currency and for ➤economic and monetary union. Separate protocols allowed the United Kingdom and ➤Denmark a right to 'opt out' of a single currency in January 1999; and Britain did not sign a protocol on social policy, adopted by eleven other members.

MacArthur, Douglas (1880–1964), US General of the Army. Born in Little Rock, Arkansas, and educated at the US Military Academy, West Point. Although commissioned in the Engineers in 1903 he was seconded for service in Tokyo in 1905, where his father was official US observer of Japan's military operations against Russia. MacArthur served in France, 1917–18, distinguishing himself at the second battle of the Marne. At the end of the war he was the youngest divisional commander in the field. He was Chief of Staff of the US Army from 1930 to 1935 when he was seconded to the Philippines to organize defence of the islands against the Japanese. From December 1941 to March 1942 he withstood the Japanese assault on Luzon, holding out on the Bataan peninsula and the island of Corregidor. As Supreme Allied Commander in the south-west Pacific he developed a strategy of throwing the Japanese back by 'island hopping' from Papua and Guadalcanal to Luzon, Iwo Jima and Okinawa, preparing for landings in Japan itself. This operation was rendered unnecessary by the ➤atomic bombs dropped on Hiroshima and Nagasaki which forced the surrender of Japan, formally accepted by MacArthur aboard USS *Missouri* in Tokyo bay. From 1945 until 1951 MacArthur, as commander of the occupation forces in Japan, was virtually a pro-consul, responsible for modernizing, neutralizing and rehabilitating the defeated nation. He gave Japan a democratic constitution and imposed reforms with Bonapartist vision, his autocratic and egotistical style arousing greater resentment in Washington than among the Japanese. In July 1950 he became commander-in-chief of UN forces in the ➤Korean War showing all his old strategic skill in the amphibious landings at Inchon (15 September 1950). Two months later he was surprised by the extent and strength of Chinese intervention. He wished to bomb Chinese bases in Manchuria and was prepared to risk a full-scale war with communist China. President ➤Truman sought to hold him in check, but MacArthur made public his advocacy of carrying the war into China. This defiance of official government policy led the President peremptorily to relieve him of his commands on 11 April 1951. MacArthur was given a hero's welcome on his return to Washington and delivered a moving speech to Congress, but his hopes of nomination for the Presidential election campaign of 1952 came to nothing, and he settled in honourable retirement in Manhattan.

McCarthyism. In February 1950 the junior Republican Senator from Wisconsin, Joseph McCarthy (1908–57), alleged that he had the names of fifty-seven 'cardcarrying communists' in the State Department and that 205 people employed by the Department were known communist sympathizers. This dramatic pronouncement came immediately after the conviction of Alger ►Hiss for perjury and was exploited by moderate Republicans to 'explain' the failure of the Truman Administration to halt the advance of communism in China. Although no evidence was produced to support the Senator's allegations he continued by means of smears, half-truths and leading questions to discredit prominent Democrats (such as ►Acheson and ►Marshall) and to attack intellectuals and universities throughout America. McCarthyism, the practice of accusing individuals of belonging to communist front organizations with little evidence for the accusation, created a sense of 'red menace' which helped win the 1952 election for the Republicans. In January 1953 McCarthy became chairman of the Senate Subcommittee on Investigations and for twelve months conducted a campaign against the alleged 'leftist' doctrines encouraged by US Information Service Libraries abroad. When in October 1953 McCarthy began to attack the institution of the army, seeking to discredit the US Secretary of the Army, Robert Stevens, he incurred the hostility of President Eisenhower. Counter-accusations by the army that McCarthy had sought preferential treatment for one of his aides called up for military service led to televised hearings which exposed the demagogic hysteria behind McCarthyism. A Senate Motion of Censure condemned McCarthy's conduct by 67 votes to 22 (2 December 1954). A few days later McCarthy rashly attacked President Eisenhower by name, thus finally discrediting his cause. Much of the early appeal of McCarthyism lay in its philistine contempt for intellectuals. By attacking 'twisted-thinking eggheads' who 'are born with silver-spoons in their mouths' McCarthy was appealing to widely held prejudices of social envy and resentment.

MacDonald, James Ramsay (1866–1937), British Prime Minister. Born in poverty in the small Scottish fishing village of Lossiemouth, settled in England in 1886, joined the ►ILP in 1894. He was able to devote his life to politics by marrying the daughter of an eminent scientist, who had a small private income of her own. MacDonald became honorary secretary of the newly formed ►Labour Party from 1900 to 1912 and was elected MP for Leicester in 1906, holding the seat until 1918. He led the parliamentary Labour Party with dexterity 1911–14, but lost influence during the war because of his alleged pacifism. After four years out of parliament he won Aberavon in 1922 and was re-elected leader of the parliamentary party, becoming also Leader of the Opposition since Labour had 25 more seats than the Liberals. In January 1924 he agreed to head a Labour minority government and was his own Foreign Secretary. The election of November 1924 (held under the shadow of the ►Zinoviev Letter) brought the Conservatives back to office but MacDonald returned as Prime Minister in 1929, having changed his constituency to Seaham. The world ►Depression, and the worsening financial situation, precipitated a split in his government in August 1931, and he formed a coalition (the 'National Government') which most Labour members refused to support. He headed the coalition for four years, maintaining a considerable influence in foreign affairs and questions of defence but being overshadowed by the Conservatives, who were predominant in his cabinet. He resigned as Prime Minister in June 1935 and was succeeded by ►Baldwin but he was elected MP for the Scottish Universities in 1936 and remained a member of Baldwin's cabinet. He died on a cruise in the south Atlantic, November 1937. His decision to form a coalition in 1931 was seen as a betrayal by the party he had built up and it was said that as the first Prime Minister to come from the working classes he had easily been seduced by ambition for social success. In retrospect, however, it is clear that he was, until his last years, a leader of exceptional administrative skill and international vision, hoping for peace and collective security through the League of Nations.

Macedonia. A region of the Balkans, heart of a great empire in the fourth century BC, later a Roman province, colonized by the Slavs (Bulgars) in the eighth century AD, and overrun by the Ottoman Turks in 1380. With Russian backing the Bulgarians sought to recover Macedonia by the short-lived Treaty of San Stefano in 1878. Bulgarian claims were disputed by the Greeks and Serbs (later Yugoslavia), and became a major issue in the ►Balkan Wars. In 1919 the Treaty of ►Neuilly constituted most of Macedonia as 'southern Serbia'; eastern Macedonia, including the port of ►Salonika, was confirmed as Greek; Bulgaria was left with a district around Petritch. Bulgarian attempts to secure more of Macedonia led to intermittent fighting during the inter-war period, mostly instigated by the terrorists of ►IMRO. Bulgaria occupied the Yugoslav and Greek regions, 1941–4, but the ►Paris Peace Treaties in 1947 restored the inter-war frontiers. The Yugoslav constitution of January 1946 created a Federal Republic of Macedonia, comprising the 26,500 square miles within Yugoslavia, with its capital at Skopje. The Yugoslavs gave the Macedonian language a literary form, publishing the first grammar in 1952 and the first scholarly dictionary in 1961. The Greek prefecture of Macedonia (larger in population than the federal republic) also encouraged Macedonian cultural studies in Salonika. Some 300,000 Macedonians live in south-west Bulgaria, and Bulgarian revisionist claims have been asserted at appropriate historical anniversaries, largely, it would seem, as a conventional patriotic gesture. When Yugoslavia disintegrated, the federal republic's parliament declared Macedonia independent (18 September 1991); the Yugoslav army peacefully withdrew to Serbia seven months later. Complaints from Athens that the new republic had territorial designs on northern Greece and disputes with Albania heightened tension in the region; the United Nations deployed a peacekeeping force (known from March 1995 as UNPREDEP) along the republic's frontier with Serbia and Albania. European recognition of the republic came only in December 1993, and then as 'Former Yugoslav Republic of Macedonia' (FYROM). To the Greeks, who imposed a trade embargo until October 1995, it remained the 'Skopje Republic'.

Macmillan, (Maurice) Harold (1894–1986), British Prime Minister. Born in London, the grandson of the founder of the famous publishing house. Harold Macmillan was educated at Eton and Balliol College, Oxford, served in the Grenadier Guards throughout the First World War and was wounded three times. He was Conservative MP for Stockton 1924–9 and 1931–45 and for Bromley 1945–64. In the 1920s he was regarded as one of the progressive social reformers within the Conservative Party and from 1935 onwards he was critical of both Baldwin and Chamberlain over foreign affairs and defence, becoming a firm supporter of Churchill. After two and a half years of junior ministerial posts he was appointed Minister Resident in North Africa in December 1942, with cabinet rank. He remained principal political spokesman in the Mediterranean until May 1945, handling problems of Italy, Greece and Yugoslavia as well as difficulties between the Americans and de Gaulle. On the return of Churchill to office in 1951 Macmillan became Minister of Housing, a post he held for three years, successfully fulfilling party promises. He was Minister of Defence (October 1954 to April 1955), Foreign Secretary (April 1955 to December 1955), Chancellor of the Exchequer (December 1955 to January 1957). As Foreign Secretary he completed negotiations leading to the signature of the ➤Austrian State Treaty and participated in the summit conference at ➤Geneva. As Chancellor he presented only one budget – April 1956 – which introduced 'premium' savings bonds. He was appointed to succeed Eden as Prime Minister in January 1957, successfully winning the 1959 general election and holding office until forced to resign through ill-health in October 1963. Economic boom and stable prices in the early years of his government were followed by rising unemployment and uncertainty over balance of payments. In foreign affairs Macmillan's role as a middleman between Moscow and Washington was hampered by Khrushchev's switches of policy, notably after the ➤U-2 Incident, but Macmillan strengthened Anglo-American collaboration, knowing Eisenhower well and achieving an easy friendship with Kennedy. Macmillan was far-sighted over African affairs, accepting the emergence of independent states, and he wished for British participation in the ➤EEC, an initiative frustrated by de Gaulle's veto of 29 January 1963. The institution of life peerages (1958) and the creation of a planning authority – 'Neddy', the National Economic Development Council, 1961 – were among progressive reforms uncharacteristic of traditional Conservative political philosophy. In his last year of office Macmillan's position was weakened by the ➤Profumo Affair and by Press speculation that his habitual imperturbability showed he was out of touch with the contemporary scene. He declined a peerage in 1963 and, although active as Chancellor of Oxford University (from 1960), he remained out of political life until he was created Earl of Stockton in 1984.

McNamara, Robert Strange (1916–), US Secretary of Defence. Born in San Francisco; served in US Army Air Force (1943–6) before becoming an executive of the Ford Motor Company, eventually accepting presidency of the company. Although he was a registered Republican voter until 1960, President Kennedy appointed him Secretary of Defence in January 1961, an office he held until resigning to become president of the World Bank, 1968–81. McNamara's term at the Defence Department was marked by ruthlessly efficient coolness and by dispassionate assessment of the cost of continuing or escalating the ►Vietnam War. During the period of tension over ►Cuban Missiles in November 1962 he defined his task as being not so much the conduct of strategy as 'crisis management', a concept seen as complementary to the ►'brinkmanship' allegedly pursued by ►Dulles.

Mafia. Originally a small private army protecting family possessions and interests in late medieval Sicily. After the French Revolution it became a secret society extorting protection money and developed into a crime syndicate, with offshoots among Italian immigrants to the USA (the Cosa Nostra) and in Naples, where the syndicate was known as the Camorra. ►Mussolini effectively curbed the Mafia. The US Navy received help from Mafia members in New York in 1943 and through them contacted anti-fascist Mafia groups in Sicily on the eve of the allied landings in the island. Subsequently the Mafia penetrated allied military government in southern Italy, extending its influence into the reconstruction industry and eventually drug trafficking. The extent of Mafia-induced corruption only began to emerge in 1987. After two magistrates were murdered in August 1992, an Anti-Mafia Investigation Directorate was set up in Rome which soon discovered the close links of the syndicate with political parties and top politicians (►Italy and ►Andreotti).

Maginot Line. The fortifications constructed in the period 1929–34 along the eastern frontier of France from Longwy (facing Luxembourg) to the Swiss frontier. They were named after the Minister of War, André Maginot (1877–1932). Belgian objections prevented the continuance of the fortifications along the Franco-Belgian frontier. Many senior French officers also believed the Germans would never penetrate the Ardennes. In May 1940 the Germans successfully turned the Maginot Line by their thrust through Belgium and around Sedan. Apart from outlying defences facing Saarbrücken the forts of the Maginot Line were intact when France concluded her armistice with Germany (22 June 1940). The Maginot Line is often taken as a symbol of the defensive mentality within the French high command between the wars.

Major, John (1943–), British Prime Minister. Born and educated in London, he served in a merchant bank before being elected Conservative MP for Huntingdonshire in 1979, the constituency becoming Huntingdon in 1983. In 1986 Mrs Thatcher appointed him Minister of State responsible for social security and he entered her Cabinet in 1987 as Chief Secretary to the Treasury. He became Foreign Secretary in July 1989 and Chancellor of the Exchequer three months later. When Mrs Thatcher announced her impending resignation he defeated Michael Heseltine and Douglas Hurd in the contest for the Party leadership and on 28 November 1990 he became Prime Minister. He led the ►Conservatives to victory in the 1992 General Election but was soon faced by criticism from 'Eurosceptic' Thatcherites. A 'back to basics' campaign, launched in October 1993, failed to excite interest in the Party or with the general public. He tackled the Irish Question with greater patience than his predecessor, but as his government lost by-elections he became increasingly dependent on Unionist support at Westminster. In July 1995 he successfully defeated a challenge to his leadership from the right-wing John Redwood. Thereafter he was hampered by media revelations of 'sleaze', which discredited some of his colleagues, eleven of whom resigned office in the course of his government. When Britain went to the polls on 1 May 1997, after the longest electoral campaign on record, the Conservatives were heavily defeated, losing more than half the seats they had held. He resigned as Party leader, handing over to William Hague (1961–) on 19 June 1997.

Makarios III, Archbishop (1913–77), President of the Cypriot Republic. Born at Ano Panayia, near Paphos, into the peasant family of Mouskos and baptized Mikhail Christodoulos; became a monastic novice at the age of thirteen and studied divinity at the University of Athens during the German occupation, being ordained priest in 1946 before going to Massachusetts to study theology and sociology. He was elected Bishop of Kitium in 1948 and head of the self-governing Orthodox Church in Cyprus two years later, assuming the name Makarios ('Blessed') borne by his predecessor as archbishop, and accepting the traditional role of Ethnarch, a national as well as spiritual leader of his people. In this capacity he brought fresh life to the movement for ►Enosis. The British military authorities thought he was director of the EOKA terrorists and he was arrested and deported to the Seychelles in March 1956. His personal fate was thereafter linked for the remainder of his life to developments in ►Cyprus. He helped create the Cypriot Republic, of which he was elected first President on 14 December 1959, assuming office 16 August 1960. He survived several assassination plots by extremists still seeking union with Greece. In March 1970 his private helicopter was shot down in Nicosia but he escaped unhurt. On 15 July 1974 Greek officers in the Cypriot National Guard attacked the Presidential palace with aircraft and armoured vehicles, forcing him into a five-month exile. He returned to a Cyprus partially occupied by the Turks and was unable to reassert Greek primacy in the island. In June 1977 he was the senior Commonwealth leader at the Queen's Silver Jubilee celebrations in London. Soon after his return to Nicosia he suffered a heart attack and died on 3 August.

Malan, Daniel François (1874–1959), South African Prime Minister. Born in

Riebeck West, Cape Colony, educated at Stellenbosch and the University of Utrecht, serving as a *predikant* (preacher) in the Dutch Reformed Church in South Africa, 1905–15. His intensive Boer patriotism, hardened by Calvinist convictions of being among the Elect of God, led him to champion Afrikaner nationalism, at first in his newspaper, *Die Burger*, and from 1918 onwards as a nationalist MP. He held office in the Hertzog coalition of 1924–33, introducing measures making Afrikaans an official language and seeking to repatriate South Africa's Indian minority. In 1934–9 and 1940–48 he was leader of the Opposition, hostile to Smuts's internationalism and to participation in the Second World War. The Nationalist Party victory in the elections of May 1948 led to Dr Malan's appointment as Prime Minister (3 June), an office he held until December 1954, when he was succeeded by ►Strijdom. Malan was responsible for introducing the segregationalist policy of ►apartheid, separating South Africa into white, black and coloured zones. The repressive and racially divisive policies of Malan were held to be unconstitutional by the South African Supreme Court (20 March 1952), a judgement which prompted Malan to introduce legislation constituting parliament a High Court, thus ensuring continuance of the apartheid programme to which he held himself committed by divine will. He died at Stellenbosch after four years of austere retirement.

Malatesta, Enrico (1853–1932), Italian anarchist. Descended from one of the great families of the Romagna and born on family estates in Campania, studied medicine at the University of Naples until expelled for fomenting anarchist unrest. He gave away his personal wealth, working as an electrician in many European capitals. His enterprise and ingenuity (aided by his small stature) enabled him to gain legendary fame among the continental Left for his escapes from Italian prisons. He preached anarchism in London from 1900 to 1913, respected as a hard-working individualist whose ideal was essentially pacific rather than violent. An attempt to deport him for having had contact with the 'Sidney Street' anarchists (who shot three policemen, 1911) proved unsuccessful. He was able to return to Italy and pass the last years of his life at variance with society but unmolested by the fascists, probably because Mussolini had, in his youth, respected Malatesta's revolutionary idealism.

Malawi. Central African republic within the Commonwealth known as ►Nyasaland until it gained independence on 6 July 1964. Under the Presidency of Dr Hastings ►Banda Malawi pursued a moderate and cautious policy towards South Africa, partly because of the loss of traditional economic links with Rhodesia since ►UDI. Banda became increasingly autocratic, establishing in 1971 a one-party state in which he was proclaimed President for Life. Pressure from foreign banks, with loans made conditional on improved civil rights, led to a restoration of democracy in 1993 and to Banda's downfall in May 1994. President Bakili Muluzi's United Democratic Front restored personal freedom and sought to tackle the widespread corruption.

Malaya. The earliest British settlement in the Malay peninsula was Penang (1786). Singapore and other settlements in the south of the peninsula were founded early in the nineteenth century while areas further north became British protectorates between 1874 and 1909. Administratively the peninsula – rich in rubber and tin – was divided into the Straits Settlements (a crown colony 1867–1946), the Federated Malay States and a group of unfederated but protected states on the Siamese frontier. The Japanese occupation, 1942–5, stimulated nationalist sentiment. The British response, an experimental 'Union of Malaya', in 1946 was unpopular for its excessive centralization and colonialist traditions; and a 'Federation of Malaya' was set up in 1948 to include Johore, Kedah, Kelantan, Labuan, Malacca, Negeri Sembilan, Penang, Perlis, and Selangor and Trengganu. (➤Singapore enjoyed separate status, 1946–63.) The Chinese minority resented Malay dominance of the Federation, complaining especially of unfair food distribution. Some Chinese communists waged a guerrilla campaign (the ➤'Malayan Emergency') for over ten years. During the Emergency the Federation was given sovereign independence within the Commonwealth (31 August 1957) but was expanded into ➤Malaysia in 1963.

Malayan Emergency. Communist guerrillas began attacking estate owners and rubber planters in Malaya in June 1948. The British responded by proclaiming a state of emergency and by organizing military resistance to the 'Malayan Races' Liberation Army' of Chen Ping, which was assisted by a supply network, the 'Min Yuen'. Troops from Australia, New Zealand, East Africa and Fiji helped the British and local units to wage a 'jungle war', intensive at times from 1950 to 1953 and not officially ended until 1960. Resistance was led in 1950–51 by General Sir Harold Briggs and in 1952–4 by General Sir Gerald Templer (1898–1979, created field-marshal 1956). The 'Liberation Army' was defeated for five main reasons: the use of helicopters and specially trained jungle-warfare platoons; the establishment of 'new villages', easily policed and protected; supervision of the sale and supply of foodstuffs in rural areas so as to cut off Min Yuen sources; the acceleration of plans for full independence; and the failure of Chen Ping's followers to convince the (mainly non-Chinese) villagers that they would benefit materially from communist rule.

Malaysia. An independent federation in the Commonwealth established on 16 September 1963 and comprising ➤Malaya, Sabah (the former British colony in north ➤Borneo) and Sarawak. ➤Singapore originally joined the Malaysian Federation but seceded in August 1965. Western Malaysia is separated from Eastern Malaysia (Sabah and Sarawak) by 400 miles of the South China Sea. This union was resented by ➤Indonesia and from 1963 to 1966 intermittent warfare continued between Malaysia and the Indonesians in what ➤Sukarno called the 'Confrontation'. There was also friction between Malaysia and the Philippines, which claimed sovereignty over northern Borneo in 1968. The tin and rubber resources of the Federation ensure one of the highest standards of living in southern Asia. Fear that the founder

Prime Minister, Tunku Abdul ►Rahman, would be unable to protect the Malays against commercial exploitation by the Chinese minority led to serious race riots in May 1969 and parliamentary government was suspended until February 1971. A cohesive Malaysian loyalty is evoked only in response to external pressures.

Malenkov, Georgy Maximilianovich (1902–88), Soviet Prime Minister. Born at Orenburg on the borders of European and Asiatic Russia; joined the Communist Party in 1920, assisted Stalin to enforce collectivization on the ►*kulaks* and became his close party associate in the late 1930s, with a prominent position in the party secretariat by 1939. From 1942 to 1944 he was a member of the State Defence Committee, the inner war council, but was regarded as Stalin's mouthpiece. He was a Deputy Prime Minister in 1946 and, from 1948 onwards, was marked out by Stalin as his successor, making the main five-hour speech to the Nineteenth Party Congress on 5 October 1952. When Stalin died in March 1953 Malenkov became both First Secretary of the Party and Prime Minister. He was edged out of his party post by ►Khrushchev a fortnight later but remained Prime Minister until February 1955 when he resigned on the grounds that he found his experience inadequate for such responsibility. His successor as Prime Minister was ►Bulganin who appointed Malenkov Minister for Electrical Energy In July 1957 Malenkov and ►Molotov were denounced as members of an 'anti-party group' and were expelled from the Central Committee and all government posts. Malenkov became manager of a hydroelectric plant near his birthplace and disappeared from the public eye, although he was reportedly living in retirement in Moscow ten years later. The fact that he was deposed and disgraced but not tried and executed (as were earlier 'anti-party conspirators') was interpreted abroad as evidence of greater self-confidence among the Soviet party chiefs.

Malta. An island in the narrowest part of the central Mediterranean with a population allegedly Carthaginian in origin and speaking a Semitic language. The island was held by the Knights of St John of Jerusalem 1530–1798, by the French 1798–1800 and by the British thereafter, becoming formally annexed to the British crown in 1814 and developed as the main base of the Mediterranean fleet. A Legislative Assembly was established in 1921 but there were disputes between the administrations and the Roman Catholic Church during the inter-war period and the rights of the assembly were suspended on three occasions. Between 1940 and 1943 the island was severely bombed and threatened with starvation. The valour of the Maltese people led King George VI to bestow the George Cross on the island (16 April 1942). In 1947 Malta was given internal self-government, but from 1957 onwards the naval economy programme led to unemployment and uncertainty. There was rioting on the island and political confusion since, in a referendum held in February 1956, three-quarters of the voters had asked for integration in the United Kingdom with a similar status to Northern Ireland. Hesitancy at Westminster led the rival political groups to favour independence, which was conceded on 21 September 1964. Financial difficulties made the ►Labour

Party under Mintoff press for aid from NATO between 1972 and 1979 on the understanding that no naval concessions would be offered to Warsaw Pact countries. Malta remains within the Commonwealth.

Manchuria. The north-eastern and most highly industrialized province of modern China; developed by the Russians, 1895–1905, and subsequently by the Japanese, who occupied the whole province in 1931. In February 1932 the Japanese established an 'independent' puppet state in the province, which was known as Manchukuo from 1932 to 1945, but was recognized only by Germany, Italy and Japan. The last Chinese Manchu emperor, Henry ➤Pu-yi, was installed as ruler of Manchukuo. With Soviet support, the Chinese communists gained control of Manchuria on Japan's collapse in 1945 and used the province as a key centre in their struggle with the ➤Kuomintang, 1946–8. Soviet military and naval units reoccupied ➤Port Arthur, 1945–55. From the late 1950s onwards the Chinese concentrated on developing still further the fuel and mineral resources first harnessed by the Japanese in the inter-war period.

Mandates. Former German colonies and non-Turkish areas of the Ottoman Empire were ceded to the allied powers in 1919–20 under the ultimate responsibility of the League of Nations, to whom annual reports on conditions were submitted. Some were intended for early independence: ➤Iraq, ➤Palestine, Transjordan (Jordan) under British mandate; ➤Lebanon and ➤Syria under French mandate. Others were seen as requiring longer administration because of the backward state of the peoples: Cameroons, New Guinea, Samoa, South-West Africa, Tanganyika and Togoland. Detailed questions were settled by the Permanent Commission of the League. In 1946 the functions of this commission were taken over by the Trusteeship Council of the United Nations. South Africa, which in 1919 was given mandated responsibility for the former German protectorate in South-West Africa, refused to acknowledge the right of the United Nations to inherit the duties of the League and maintained that, since the League no longer existed, South Africa would continue to administer South-West Africa in the original 'spirit of the mandate'. The matter was taken to the International Court of Justice at The Hague which, by 13 votes to 2, ruled that the continued presence of South Africa in 'Namibia' (South-West Africa) was illegal (21 June 1971). This ruling was rejected by the South African Premier, ➤Vorster. ➤Namibia.

Mandela, Nelson (1918–), southern African President. Born the son of a chieftain, studied and practised law in Johannesburg until 1952 when hostility to apartheid led him to accept membership of the executive of the ➤African National Congress. Throughout the 1950s he travelled as widely as he could through South Africa championing his ideal of a free, multiracial, democratic society. When the African National Congress was banned in 1961, he evaded arrest for a year but in November 1962 was jailed for five years. Before this sentence expired he was charged under the 'Suppression of Communism Act' and, after a trial lasting from October 1963 to June 1964, was sentenced with seven other defendants to life imprisonment. His incarceration in a maximum-security island prison deprived black southern Africans of their wisest and most respected leader. In August 1988 he was admitted to hospital in Cape Town suffering from tuberculosis. His conditions of internment were subsequently eased. He has remained, both inside and outside Africa, a heroic symbol of black resistance. Nelson Mandela was released on 11 February 1990 and took part in talks aimed at ending the apartheid laws and bloodshed in the townships between ANC supporters and the Zulu 'Inkatha Freedom Party'. He secured the establishment of a Transitional Executive Council in December 1993 which, for the first time, ended exclusive white rule. Mandela was awarded the Nobel Peace Prize in 1993 jointly with President ►de Klerk. After the election victory in April 1994 he was chosen by parliament as State President, taking up office on 10 May. His principal political initiative was to promote legislation providing for restitution of land rights lost during the years of white supremacy and to set up a 'truth commission' to examine injustices committed under apartheid and assess compensation to surviving victims or the relatives of those killed. Subsequently President Mandela used his personal prestige and authority to mediate in African conflicts, notably in 1997 in ►Zaire.

Manhattan Project. The code-name given to the development of the ►atomic bomb after the establishment of a large community of workers at the 'Manhattan District', a site at Oak Ridge, Tennessee, in August 1942. The Project was marked by the international collaboration of scientists from Canada, Great Britain and the USA.

Manley, Michael Norman (1923–97), Jamaican Prime Minister. Born in Kingston, the son of Norman ►Manley, educated in Jamaica and at the London School of Economics, held important posts in the sugar-workers' trade union, was a Senator 1962–7 and subsequently a member of the Jamaican House of Representatives, succeeding his father as head of the People's National Party in February 1969 and becoming Prime Minister in February 1972. Economic misfortunes and violence in the streets led the Jamaican electorate to turn against Manley in the general election of October 1980, the People's National Party retaining only 9 of the 60 seats in the House of Representatives. Manley remained leader of the Opposition, Edward Seaga's 'Jamaica Labour Party' forming the government.

Manley, Norman Washington (1893–1989), Jamaican Prime Minister. Born in Kingston, studied law, becoming a respected QC. In 1938 he successfully defended his cousin, ►Bustamente – who was his political opponent – against charges of sedition. Manley founded the People's National Party in 1938. He became Prime Minister of Jamaica in 1955 and was a vigorous supporter of the short-lived ►West Indies Federation. Its collapse in May 1962 led to his fall as Prime Minister but he continued to lead the parliamentary opposition until handing over the People's National Party to his son, Michael ►Manley, in 1969.

Mannerheim, Carl Gustaf Emil (1867–1951), Finnish soldier and President. Born at Villnaes, of partly Swedish descent, commissioned in the Russian Imperial Army, 1889, serving with distinction in the Russo-Japanese War (1904–5) and as a general in the First World War. When Finnish communists occupied Helsinki in the spring of 1918, Mannerheim organized a 'White' counter-revolution and, with German help, drove the 'Reds' out of the country. He was acting head of state 1919–20 and fought against the Bolsheviks until the Soviet Government recognized Finnish independence (1921), when he retired from active service with the rank of field-marshal. As President of the Finnish Defence Council he retained great influence and was responsible for the construction of the 'Mannerheim Line' fortifications, close to the Soviet frontier and within twenty miles of the suburbs of Leningrad. When the Russians attacked Finland in the winter of 1939–40 he resumed command of the Finnish army, the Mannerheim Line keeping out the Red Army for thirteen weeks. In June 1941 he accepted co-belligerency with Germany for a third campaign against Russia. Faced by imminent defeat in 1944 the Finnish Parliament elected Mannerheim as President and he was able to secure an armistice with the Russians (September 1944), eventually bringing Finland into the war against Germany (March 1945). He retained the Presidency until March 1946 when failing health prompted his retirement.

Mao Tse-tung (Mao Zedong, 1893–1976), Chinese communist leader. Born in Chaochan, Hunan province, the son of a peasant farmer; educated at Changsha, discovering Marxism while working as a library assistant at Peking University. He was a founder-member of the Chinese Communist Party (▸Communist Parties) in 1921, soon developing his characteristic contribution to Marxist–Leninist thought – the need, in Asiatic society, to concentrate on the countryside rather than the towns, finding a revolutionary élite within the peasantry and not within the urban proletariat. With ▸Chou En-lai (Zhou Enlai) and ▸Chu Teh (Zhu De) he established a revolutionary base on the border of Hunan, seeking to set up a Chinese Soviet republic in Kiangsi, 1931–4, before being compelled to trek to northern Shensi on the epic ▸Long March, 1934–5. He collaborated with the ▸Kuomintang (Guomindang) against the Japanese, 1937–45, resuming the struggle against the nationalists of ▸Chiang Kai-shek (Jiang Jieshih), 1945–6, switching decisively from guerrilla warfare to set battles in the spring of 1948 and accepting office as Chairman of the People's Republic of China on its proclamation in Peking in October 1949. In home affairs Mao favoured radical and original solutions of traditional Chinese problems, communicating his ideas in metaphors which lent themselves naturally to striking slogans (▸'Great Leap Forward'). Mao had always shown independence of Moscow (which he never visited before 1949) and he rejected the expediencies of post-Stalinist Soviet thought, vigorously criticizing ▸Khrushchev. Mao relinquished his post as head of state to ▸Liu Shao-chi (Liu Shaoqi) in April 1959, though retaining chairmanship of the party and concentrating on ideological matters. Differences with Liu over the relative importance of industrial workers and peasants formed part of the ➤'Cultural Revolution' which reasserted Mao's primacy in the People's Republic, 1965–6, his earlier essays ('*Thoughts*') now becoming the dogma of the Chinese masses. For much of the last five years of his life he was a figurehead, with Chou En-lai managing the unexpected reconciliation with President ➤Nixon and the West. In a struggle for the succession at Peking, Marshal ➤Lin Piao (Lin Biao) was eliminated (1971) and a group of Shanghai 'radicals' – including Mao's fourth wife, the actress, Chiang Ching (Jiang Qing) – gradually discredited in favour of the ultimate victor, ➤Hua Kuo-feng (Hua Guofeng).

Maoris. Members of a race of Polynesian origin, established in New Zealand by the time of Captain James Cook's first visit of discovery, 1769. Conflict between the Maoris and the white settlers, 1843–5, and intermittently 1860–70, drastically reduced the size of the Maori population, which was little more than 45,000 in 1896 (by contrast, the 1966 census gave a figure of 201,000, rising to 227,000 five years later, about 9 per cent of the total New Zealand population). New Zealand governments have traditionally shown multiracial tolerance and there has been a Maori revival throughout the twentieth century marked by the initiative of such men as Sir James Carroll (a half-Irish and half-Maori minister in the governments at the turn of the century), Sir Maui Pomare (1876–1930, a Maori chief's son who became Minister of Health in 1923) and Sir Apirana Ngata (1874–1950, land reformer and exponent of Maori culture). The Native Land Settlement Act of 1929 – a triumph for Ngata and his 'Young Maori' political party – provided the Maori people with state-directed and financed land to settle and develop, thus helping the Maoris to survive as a flourishing community enjoying equal civic rights while amplifying their cultural heritage rather than merely preserving it as a tourists' curiosity. Maori units fought in both World Wars, the 28th Maori battalion distinguishing itself in the battle for ➤Cassino in 1944. Improved living conditions in recent decades led to a rise in Maori numbers; by 1993 they formed 13 per cent of the total population. Claims of restitution for lost land rights led to occasional demonstrations, and in 1994 the Maoris were offered 1,000 million New Zealand dollars (some £478 million), spread over ten years, as compensation. In a symbolic act while attending the ➤Commonwealth Conference at Auckland, Queen Elizabeth II signed the Waikato-Raupatu Claims Award, compensating the Maori peoples of North Island for land seized by settlers in 1867 (2 November 1995).

'March on Rome', 1922. A fascist-inspired myth of the way in which ➤Mussolini came to power in Italy. The threat of civil war in Italy in the autumn of 1922 led Mussolini, in the last week of October, to demand the formation of a fascist government in order to save the country from socialism and anarchy; and fascist supporters began concentrating between Bologna and Rome. On 29 October Mussolini was invited by King Victor Emmanuel III to come from Milan to Rome: next day he formed a government. The phrase 'March on Rome' is a characteristic over-dramatization of events: Mussolini personally travelled to Rome by express overnight; his followers never marched on the city although some 25,000 'blackshirts' were brought by rail to Rome and participated in a ceremonial parade on 31 October.

Marconi, Guglielmo (1874–1937), Italian inventor. Born at Bologna, of part Irish descent, experimented with wireless telegraphy in England and Italy 1895–1900, transmitting and receiving signals between Newfoundland and Cornwall. His companies subsequently played a leading part in the commercial development of wireless telegraphy and ►broadcasting.

Marconi Scandal (1913). In the summer of 1912 the British Government commissioned the British Marconi Company to construct a network of wireless stations linking the empire. The managing director of the company was a brother of Sir Rufus Isaacs, the Attorney-General, and it was rumoured that Sir Rufus and other cabinet ministers had benefited by using previous knowledge to speculate in Marconi shares. In June 1913 the report of a Select Committee of the House of Commons found that Sir Rufus, Lord Murray of Elibank (a former Chief Liberal Whip) and ►Lloyd George, the Chancellor of the Exchequer, had purchased shares in the American Marconi Company but not in the British company, and cleared them of corruption. Both Sir Rufus Isaacs and Lloyd George offered the Prime Minister their resignation but Asquith refused to accept the offers.

Marcos, Ferdinand Edralin (1917–89), President of the Philippines. A lawyer, born at Caviter, in 1939 he successfully defended himself on a charge of killing a personal enemy of his father. He had a good war record in the resistance to the Japanese invaders and in 1949 began ten years as a right-wing Congressman, followed by six years as an 'anti-Reds' Senator, much favoured by the Americans. He became President on 30 December 1965, with widespread popular backing, and was re-elected in November 1969. His second term was marked by brutal repression of liberals, by flagrant abuse of foreign aid funds, and by the imposition in 1972 of martial law. A year later he imposed constitutional changes which heightened the dictatorial character of the Presidency and removed from it any fixed term of office. In August 1983 the murder of the liberal leader Benigno Aquino at Manila airport began a popular revolt, centred on the widowed Cory ►Aquino, which forced Marcos to seek refuge in Hawaii in February 1986. Corruption charges against Marcos were never pressed home because his health gave way and he died in the USA three years after going into exile. His widow, Imelda Marcos, though herself accused of financial mismanagement, later returned to the Philippines and in 1995 was elected to Congress.

Marne, Battles of the. The river Marne, a 325-mile-long tributary of the Seine with its confluence ten miles east of Paris, marked the point of farthest penetration into France by the German army in the First World War and gave its name to two major battles: (1) 5–11 September 1914, a series of interrelated actions fought along a front of 125 miles as part of a general manoeuvre, executed by General ►Joffre, to force the invaders to retire from Paris and reaching a successful climax on 9 September; (2) 15–20 July 1918, the last offensive thrust by ►Ludendorff, enabling the Germans to cross the river east of Château-Thierry, only to be forced back by a vigorous French counter-offensive, launched by Marshal ►Foch on 18 July. Each Marne battle represented a turning-point in the war: the retreat of the Germans in 1914 marked a transition from a war of movement to a war of attrition, stabilized in opposing trenches; and Foch's attack in 1918 began the general Franco-British-American advance which forced Germany to sue for peace fifteen weeks later.

Marshall, George Catlett (1880–1959), US General of the Army and Secretary of State. Born at Uniontown, Pennsylvania, graduated from the Virginia Military Institute in 1901, fought as a colonel on the Western Front, being chief of operations to the US First Army at the battle of Saint-Mihiel (13–18 September 1918). He was Chief of Staff of the US Army, 1 September 1939 to 20 November 1945, and thus responsible for enlarging the army and for overall strategic military planning throughout the period of American participation in the Second World War. In December 1945 he was sent to ►China on an abortive diplomatic mission to end the civil war. He was appointed Secretary of State by President Truman (16 January 1947), holding office until succeeded by ►Acheson on 7 January 1949, subsequently taking over as Secretary of Defence, 1950–51, during the Korean War. Marshall's name is especially associated with the European Recovery Programme (►Marshall Plan), but he also held much responsibility for the firm attitude taken by the Western Powers in the blockade of ►Berlin and he helped create ►NATO. He is the only General of the Army to have been Secretary of State and the only general of any nation to have won a Nobel Peace Prize (1953), awarded for his sponsorship of European recovery.

Marshall Plan. The proposal made by General ►Marshall in a speech at Harvard on 5 June 1947 to offer American financial aid for a programme of European economic recovery, on condition that the European governments themselves took the first steps towards economic collaboration. The plan, warmly supported by the British and French Foreign Ministers, ►Bevin and Bidault, was rejected by the Soviet Foreign Minister, ►Molotov, after long consultations. The Western Powers organized a conference in Paris, July 1947, and in April 1948 set up the OEEC (►Organization for European Economic Cooperation), a body representing eighteen European countries, together with the United States and Canada. 'Marshall Aid', totalling $17,000 million, was administered through the OEEC, 1948–52, and the US 'Economic Cooperation Administration' (ECA). More than any other enterprise, the Marshall Plan stimulated the speedy recovery of Europe from the dislocation of war.

Martov, Julius (1873–1923), leader of the Russian ►Mensheviks.

Masaryk, Jan (1886–1948), Czechoslovak diplomat and Foreign Minister. Born in Prague, the son of Tómaš ➤Masaryk, educated at the universities of Prague and Vienna; served briefly as an Austro-Hungarian army officer, principal assistant to ➤Beneš in the Czechoslovak delegation to the Paris Peace Conference of 1919–20, Czechoslovak Minister (i.e. diplomatic envoy) to London, 1925–38. Jan Masaryk resigned after ➤Munich but spent most of the war years in London, as Foreign Minister and Deputy Prime Minister of the Czechoslovak government-in-exile, 1941–5. His excellent English and charm of manner made him a popular broadcaster in Britain. On the liberation of Czechoslovakia he continued as Foreign Minister in the coalition government of ➤Gottwald even though he was out of sympathy with the increasingly pro-Soviet policy imposed on the coalition by its communist members. He remained in office after the communist *coup* of February 1948 but a few days later (10 March) he was killed in a fall from the window of the Foreign Ministry in Prague. It is assumed that, finding himself the lone dissentient in a cabinet of time-servers, he committed suicide.

Masaryk, Tómaš Garrigue (1850–1937), founder-President of Czechoslovakia. Born at Hodonin, Moravia, the son of a coachman on a Habsburg estate. He was educated at Brno, Vienna and Leipzig, and was Professor of Philosophy at the Czech University in Prague, 1882–1914. He championed the Czechs in the Vienna Parliament, 1891–3 and 1907–14, but he was also a strong believer in reconciling all western and southern Slav groups, Czechs with Slovaks and Croats with Serbs. He achieved European fame by defending Croats accused of treason at Zagreb (then known as Agram) in 1908 and by showing that the Austrian Foreign Ministry was using forged documents to discredit the political leaders of nationalist minorities within the Habsburg monarchy. When in December 1914 Professor Masaryk escaped to London his academic reputation assured him of a sympathetic hearing from leading politicians and journalists. He stressed the need for nation states to replace the multinational anachronism of Austria–Hungary. As chairman of the Czech National Council and as a lecturer at King's College, London, he had considerable opportunity to disseminate his views and, from October 1916 onwards, he did so through an influential monthly periodical, *The New Europe*. In 1917 he travelled to Russia and organized a Czech Legion from among prisoners of war. Later he crossed Siberia and went to the United States where he influenced the formulation of President Wilson's views on the post-war world. While in America he received such backing from Czech and Slovak immigrants that the US Government officially recognized him as leader of an allied country (3 September 1918). He returned to Europe as President-elect of Czechoslovakia in December 1918. Although twice re-elected President, he considered he should remain aloof from party politics, retiring in favour of ➤Beneš in December 1935 when his health gave way and dying twenty-one months later.

Massey, Vincent (1887–1967), Canadian diplomat and statesman. Born in Toronto, served as Canada's diplomatic representative in Washington, 1926–30, and as high commissioner in London, 1935–46. In 1949 he was appointed chairman of a royal commission on the arts and sciences in Canada which held public hearings in every province and in May 1951 presented the Massey Report, recommending, in detail, a more positive approach by the federal government to the encouragement of the arts and to the development of university education in Canada. On 28 February 1952 Vincent Massey became the first Canadian-born Governor-General of Canada, holding the office until September 1959. This appointment was seen as recognition of Canada's distinctive nationhood.

Massey, William Ferguson (1856–1925), New Zealand Prime Minister. Born in Ulster, emigrated to New Zealand in 1870, farmed in the North Island, becoming the political spokesman of the small dairy farmers and serving in the New Zealand parliament from 1894 until his death. He was leader of the anti-Liberal opposition 1903–12 and Prime Minister from July 1912 to May 1925. Massey virtually founded the conservative Reform Party, reflecting the views of the North Island agrarian community among whom he lived. The most notable 'Reform' was the conversion of all crown leaseholds into freeholds (1912). From August 1915 to August 1919 Massey headed a wartime coalition but thereafter reverted to Reform Party rule, winning substantial majorities in the elections of December 1919 and November 1922. Massey was a strong supporter of the Empire ideal, favouring collaboration in the Imperial War Cabinet of 1917 and urging continued naval links between the United Kingdom and the dominions. He doubted the wisdom of establishing a League of Nations and, though he accepted the responsibilities of membership of the League, he distrusted the system of mandates.

Matteotti Affair (1924). On 10 June 1924 a wealthy thirty-nine-year-old socialist deputy, Giacomo Matteotti, who was an outspoken critic of fascism, disappeared from Rome. Three days later his body was found in a shallow grave twelve miles from the city. His death provoked anti-fascist demonstrations in the Italian parliament, the socialists hoping King Victor Emmanuel would use the reaction against ►Mussolini in Italy and abroad as an excuse for re-establishing democratic government. The King did not intervene: a number of fascists were arrested as accomplices in the crime and, in 1926, received light sentences; but Mussolini used the agitation as an excuse to ban socialist meetings and impose a strict Press censorship. Matteotti became the chief martyr of the anti-fascist socialists: 'Matteotti Brigades' were organized in the Resistance movement of 1943–5. Mussolini consistently maintained that he had known nothing of any plot to kill Matteotti and that the murder ran counter to his own immediate policy. An anti-fascist inquiry of 1947 laid the blame on extremists over whom Mussolini had little control and who may have intended to beat up Matteotti rather than kill him.

Mau Mau. A secret society established among the Kikuyu tribe in Kenya, 1948–52, which sought by restoring ancient customs of oath-taking and murder to drive white farmers and their labourers out of the traditional Kikuyu lands. Mau

Mau-instigated violence began on 20 October 1952, with arson and killings. The Kenyan authorities proclaimed a state of emergency, arrested Jomo ►Kenyatta on charges of managing the movement, and used troops and aircraft to stamp it out. A massacre at Lari in the Rift Valley (March 1953), in which there were more than eighty victims, mostly African, led to a revulsion of feeling against Mau Mau among the Kikuyu as well as among other tribes. The Mau Mau rebellion was virtually crushed by the end of 1954 although the state of emergency remained in force until 1960. It is calculated that 11,000 Kikuyu Mau Mau were killed: the security forces lost 167 men; sixty-eight Europeans (mainly farmers and their families) were brutally murdered, as also were over 1,800 Africans opposed to Mau Mau. More Mau Mau were killed by Africans than by white troops.

Mauritius, an independent member of the British Commonwealth, is a volcanic island in the Indian Ocean, 550 miles east of Madagascar. The island was discovered by the Portuguese, named by the Dutch (who held it from 1598 to 1710) and developed by the French in the eighteenth century. Mauritius was the last of Napoleon I's colonies to be seized by the Royal Navy (July 1810). It was ceded to Britain in 1814 and was a crown colony until 1967 when Mauritius and its dependencies were granted internal self-government, leading to independence seven months later, on 12 March 1968. In 1965 the atoll dependency of Diego Garcia, 1,200 miles north-east of Mauritius, and neighbouring islets were detached from Mauritian administration so as to become the 'British Indian Ocean Territory'. The deportation of the Creole population of Diego Garcia became a standing grievance in Mauritius after independence. Feelings were further incensed by the lease of Diego Garcia to the United States in order to give the Americans a military base in the Indian Ocean. For the first fourteen years of independence Mauritius was governed by the Mauritian Labour Party of Sir Seewoosagur Ramgoolan (1900–1985) but in the general election of 11 June 1982 all sixty-two seats in the legislature were won by a left-wing alliance, with the barrister Sir Aneerood Jugnauth (1930–) becoming Prime Minister. A high level of unemployment and the failure of the sugar crop were the chief reasons for the dramatic change of government, but there was also resentment of Sir Seewoosagur's apparent acceptance of a mounting American military presence in the Indian Ocean. Jugnauth proved less militantly radical in office than in opposition. He won further elections in 1986 and 1991 but was defeated in December 1995 by Navin Ramgoolan, son of his old rival.

May Events (France, 1968). ►Student Demonstrations (Paris).

Mboya, Tom (1930–69), Kenyan nationalist leader. Born, a member of the Luo tribe, on a sisal plantation in the Kenyan White Highlands; educated at Roman Catholic missionary schools and at Ruskin College, Oxford. He served as treasurer of the Kenya African Union and was the principal trade-union organizer in Kenya in the late 1950s, attending a conference on the future of Kenya in London in

1960 and gaining wide respect for his intellect, moderation and perspicacity. After Kenya gained independence he was successively Minister of Labour, Minister of Justice and Minister of Economic Planning. He seemed heir apparent to ►Kenyatta and rival leader to the more radical Oginga Odinga among the Luo, but on 5 July 1969 he was shot dead in the centre of Nairobi. A Kikuyu was charged with the murder and later hanged. The assassination was followed by Luo demonstrations against President Kenyatta at Kisumu and the republic narrowly escaped civil war.

Medicare. A US programme of medical benefits for the aged, originally proposed by President Kennedy and passed by Congress under Johnson (30 July 1965). Federal support of this character – with its implication of state responsibility for health – was an innovation in American social and political affairs.

Meinhof, Ulrike (1934–76), West German anarchist. ►Baader–Meinhof Group.

Meir, Golda (1898–1978), Israeli Prime Minister. Born Golda Mabovich in Kiev, her parents emigrating to America in 1907 and sending her to school in Milwaukee. She married Morris Mayerson in 1917, the couple hebraizing the name to Meir when they settled in Palestine in 1921. The Meirs worked on a kibbutz in Lower Galilee and she became active in Jewish socialist politics, undertaking secret diplomatic missions in 1947–8 and, on independence, being appointed the first Israeli ambassador to the Soviet Union. She returned to Israel to serve as Minister of Labour, 1949–56, and Foreign Minister, 1956–66. In January 1966 she left the government and spent three years organizing the Mapai socialist party before being elected Prime Minister in February 1969. Her basically doctrinaire socialism made her distrust the forceful measures consistently urged by General ►Dayan, although she retained him as Minister of Defence until after the ►October War of 1973. Mrs Meir won the general elections of 1969 and 1973 but governed through coalitions. A prolonged crisis over the formation of a new coalition ministry in March 1974 seemed resolved in Mrs Meir's favour when, on 10 April, she unexpectedly announced her resignation. General Rabin succeeding her as Prime Minister a month later.

Menderes, Adnan (1899–1961), Turkish Prime Minister. Born near Aydin, studied law and practised farming before entering politics in 1932 as a cautious critic of ►Atatürk. He was a founding father of the Democratic Party in 1945, winning the general election of May 1950 and becoming Prime Minister, an office he held for exactly ten years. Menderes strengthened his country's links with the West, taking Turkey into NATO in 1952, and he controlled the mounting Greco-Turkish tension over Cyprus, travelling to London (February 1959) to help conclude agreements on Cypriot independence (narrowly escaping death in an air crash at Gatwick). Severe inflation from 1954 onwards provoked discontent in Turkey, especially in the towns. Menderes relied on peasant support but was forced in April 1960 to set up a dictatorial regime. Army officers under General Gürsel overthrew his government on 27 May 1960. Menderes was charged with having broken the constitution and, after a long political trial at Yassiada, sentenced to death with two of his ministers. They were hanged at the prison on Imrali island on 17 September 1961. In September 1990 Menderes was rehabilitated and given a state funeral attended by the Turkish President.

Mendès-France, Pierre (1907–82), French statesman. Born in Paris of Jewish parentage; had a brilliant career as a law student at Paris University; joined the Radical Socialist Party in 1923 and in 1932 was elected to the Chamber, at twenty-five the youngest Deputy. He was an Under-Secretary at the Treasury, March–April 1938, served in the air force 1939–43 (escaping to join de Gaulle 1941), and was principal adviser to de Gaulle on financial questions until 1945, representing France at the ►Bretton Woods Conference. He disliked the right-wing trend of Gaullist policy after the liberation and was a Radical opponent of successive governments, 1945–54. In June 1954 his formation of a Radical–Gaullist–Socialist coalition was widely welcomed as promising stability to the ►Fourth Republic and as bringing fresh blood into the government. Mendès-France showed skill and initiative in checking inflation and collaborating with the British over defence questions. He also tackled the problems of ►Tunisia and ►Indo-China with courage. The coalition succumbed, however, to the Algerian question: Mendès-France's appointment of Jacques Soustelle as governor and his dispatch of many more troops to Algeria offended the Left in his coalition and he resigned (5 February 1955) after a mere 230 days of power. He served for four months as Minister of State in 1956 but resumed his role as critic of the government, subsequently voting against the return of de Gaulle as Prime Minister in 1958, and remaining opposed to Gaullist policies under the ►Fifth Republic. No French Radical leader since Gambetta in 1881 has enjoyed such wide esteem while having so little opportunity to shape policy.

Mensheviks. The moderate faction in the Russian Social Democrat Party, opposed to the ►Bolsheviks after a split at the Party Congress in London in 1903. The principal Menshevik was a Jewish intellectual from Odessa, born Julius Cedarbaum, but taking the conspiratorial name of Martov (1873–1923). The Mensheviks were themselves divided: some favoured representation in the ►Duma after 1906, and some were prepared to assist Kerensky to fight the Germans in 1917 (►Russian Revolution). After the October Revolution, they hoped to constitute a legitimate opposition to Lenin but were treated with suspicion and formally suppressed in 1922. Martov was banished in 1920 and died in exile.

Menzies, Robert Gordon (1894–1978, knighted 1963), Australian Prime Minister. Born the son of a storekeeper in Jeparit, Victoria, educated at Melbourne University, practised as a barrister in Victoria and was a member of the state Legislative Assembly from 1928 to 1934, when he was elected to the Canberra parliament as United Australia Party member for Kooyong. He served as Attorney-General under ►Lyons from 1935 until 20 March 1939 when he resigned because the government would not support a national-insurance scheme to which he felt committed. Lyons died eighteen days later and Menzies won a bitter fight for the party leadership, accepting office as Prime Minister on 24 April. He devoted all his energies to preparing for the World War, which he held to be inevitable, setting up new ministries and reintroducing compulsory service. His preoccupation with the war (particularly after a visit to London early in 1941) cost him popularity at home and he failed to control members of his own cabinet, who deposed him in August 1941. The establishment of a Labour Government under ➤Curtin two months later left Menzies in opposition for the rest of the war. Between 1943 and 1945 he reorganized the UAP, creating the more democratic and widely based ➤Liberal Party which won the 1949 election, enabling him to return to the premiership (12 December 1949), an office he held until his retirement in 1966. At home Menzies favoured the encouragement of spectacular industrial programmes. Abroad he collaborated closely with the United States (➤ANZUS and ➤South East Asia Treaty Organization) and gained a reputation as the senior wise counsellor of the British Commonwealth. In 1956 he presided over the abortive five nations committee which sought agreement with Nasser over ➤Suez. Respect for Menzies' qualities as an elder statesman led in 1965 to his appointment to succeed Churchill as Lord Warden of the Cinque Ports, a largely honorific dignity never before bestowed on a non-resident of the United Kingdom.

Mers-el-Kébir. Former French naval base in the Gulf of Oran, Algeria, finally evacuated by the French in 1968. On 3 July 1940 a British naval force of two battleships, a battle-cruiser, an aircraft-carrier, two cruisers and eleven destroyers arrived off Oran. The admiral in command had orders to prevent French warships at anchor from falling into German or Italian hands, following the French armistice concluded eleven days previously. The senior French naval officer refused proposals that his fleet should continue to resist, sail for the West Indies and be entrusted to the Americans, or be scuttled in port. The British vessels accordingly bombarded the French squadron, which was also attacked by carrier-based aircraft. Shore batteries returned the fire. Three French capital ships were put out of action and 1,300 French seamen killed. This tragic event intensified the traditional hostility shown by the French navy for France's oldest enemy and marked the end of the ➤Entente Cordiale. It eased the conscience of many natural collaborators at ➤Vichy and hampered the attempts of the 'Free French' to rally support behind General de Gaulle. No French warships fought on the side of Germany or Italy although, in retaliation, French aircraft bombed Gibraltar on 7 July and again on 24 September 1940.

Mesopotamia. The area between the rivers Tigris and Euphrates, now forming part of ➤Iraq. British and Indian forces established a front against the Turks in Mesopotamia early in November 1914 and maintained military operations there until the end of October 1918. Originally the campaign was intended to safeguard oil supplies from the Persian Gulf and divert Turkish troops from other battle zones.

Command was exercised from Delhi until February 1916 when the authorities in London assumed responsibility in the hope that the rivers would make possible an advance into the heart of Turkey. This hope was not realized: Baghdad fell on 11 March 1917, and at the time of the Turkish surrender the British imperial forces had reached the outskirts of Mosul. The principal fighting was around the town of ►Kut-el-Amara on the lower Tigris.

Metaxas, Joannis (1871–1941), Greek soldier and dictator. Born on the island of Ithaka, commissioned in the army in 1890, fought against the Turks in 1897 and in the ►Balkan Wars, becoming Chief of the General Staff in 1913. Metaxas had received his staff training in Germany and, with King ►Constantine I, opposed Greek entry into the First World War, going into voluntary exile in Italy, 1917–21. He led the Monarchist Party in republican Greece during the late 1920s and early 1930s, opposing his old rival, ►Venizelos. Metaxas helped restore the monarchy in November 1935 and was rewarded by being appointed Minister of War on 5 March 1936 and Prime Minister six weeks later (13 April). Faced by a communist threat, Metaxas secured the adjournment of parliament (which did not meet again for ten years) and formally established a dictatorship (4 August 1936). While his rule copied many outwardly fascist trappings, he improved the social services, reduced corruption, increased agricultural productivity, carried through ambitious public works and made the army the most efficient military force in south-eastern Europe. His powers of personal application to work were phenomenal but tended to produce dutiful servants rather than men of initiative. His death on 29 January 1941, after a short illness, left Greece with no natural successor as leader.

Mexican Revolution (1910–24). In November 1910 Francisco Madero (1873–1913), an exiled democratic reformer, published his San Luis Potosi Plan in which he called for an armed uprising in Mexico to end the long dictatorship of Porfirio ►Díaz and the return to the peasantry of holdings appropriated by landowners. Although Díaz fled the country and Madero became President his radical programme unleashed social anarchy which engulfed Mexico for fourteen years. Revolutionary armies led by Emiliano Zapata (1879–1919) in the south and by Francisco 'Pancho' Villa (1877–1923) in the north clashed with the professional soldiery under General Victoriano Huerta (1854–1916), whose troops turned against President Madero, and later murdered him. The US Government, though hostile to Zapata and Villa, mistrusted General Huerta and gave armed support to the moderate Venustiano Carranza (1859–1920), who overcame his rivals but fell foul of the USA over his neutrality in the First World War and his curbs on US oil investment in Mexico. Further chaos followed Carranza's assassination in April 1920, until the revolutionary upheaval was checked from 1924 onwards by General Plutarco Calles (1877–1945), who secured the implementation of long promised social and agrarian reforms, though incurring the lasting enmity of the Church.

Mexico. Conquered by the Spaniards under Cortés in the years following 1519, recovered independence from Spain 1821; resisted attempts by the French to establish a Mexican Empire ruled by Maximilian of Habsburg from 1863 to 1867. The country only began to progress economically under the dictatorship of Porfirio Díaz. With his fall in 1911 a series of short-lived regimes struggled for recognition (►Mexican Revolution). The US Government sent punitive expeditions into Mexico, 1914 and 1916, and encouraged the Mexicans to adopt a new constitution (5 February 1917) providing for a bicameral elected Congress and an elected President, with full executive powers. From 1924 to 1934 Mexico was virtually controlled by General Plutarco Calles (1877–1945), President from 1924 to 1928 and political boss thereafter. Calles was a rabid anticlerical and sought to limit foreign influence in the oil industry, although he succeeded in remaining on good terms with his American neighbours. General Lázaro Cárdenas (1895–1970), President 1934–40, instituted social reforms including land redistribution and nationalization of the oil companies (1938), imposing a strain on relations with the USA. Mexico declared war on Germany and Japan in May 1942, thereby increasing American investment and influence in the republic, the United States absorbing more than three-fifths of Mexican trade ever since. Apart from the Presidency of Adolfo López Mateos from 1958 to 1964 (when there were stirrings of socialism) successive governments since the Second World War have been fundamentally right-wing but less overtly dictatorial than during the inter-war period. Contempt for a government which paid lip-service to revolutionary ideals but tolerated social abuses prompted student unrest in 1968 on the eve of the opening of the Olympic Games in Mexico City. The apparent stability of the Mexican Republic was not, however, seriously affected. Despite the fall in world oil prices in the mid-1980s, a rapidly rising birthrate and a severe earthquake in the capital (19 September 1985), between 1988 and 1994 President Salinas de Gortari was able to stimulate the economy by a privatization programme. His reforms failed to satisfy the southern 'Indian' peasantry who, in January 1994, formed a Zapatista National Liberation Army (ZNLA) which for two years sustained an insurrection to recover and safeguard traditional land rights.

Midway Island, Battle of (4 June 1942). A defensive naval victory gained by the US fleet to frustrate an attempted Japanese amphibious operation to seize two islands off the atoll of Midway, where there were advance air bases protecting Hawaii, 1,500 miles to the east. Good intelligence work by the Americans enabled them to anticipate the plan of Admiral ►Yamamoto and to strike early at the Japanese carriers. The battle was remarkable in being fought almost entirely between naval aircraft, with the opposing fleets out of sight of each other and initially 250 miles apart. The Japanese lost four carriers to the Americans' one. The battle marked a turning-point of the war since it ended Japanese expansion into the central Pacific.

Mihailović, Draža (1893–1946), Yugoslav royalist officer. Born at Ivanjica in southern Serbia, served with distinction in the Serbian Army in the First World

War and was seconded to study guerrilla warfare in the 1930s, serving with the rank of colonel in the Yugoslav Army in 1941. After the fall of Yugoslavia he organized ➤Chetnik resistance in the forests and hills of western Serbia: he was appointed Minister of War by the Yugoslav government-in-exile and promoted general. British support, given originally to Mihailović, was withdrawn early in 1944 because Chetnik forces were reported to be collaborating with the Germans in actions against the communist partisans under ➤Tito. Mihailović remained in arms, on the border of Serbia and Bosnia, until captured by armed police in March 1946. He was charged with collaboration and war crimes and put on trial at military barracks outside Belgrade on 10 June. The trial lasted for five weeks and observers were impressed by Mihailović's courage and fortitude. He was sentenced to death and shot on 17 July 1946.

Military Conversations, 1906–14. During the first ➤Moroccan Crisis the French asked the British Government to authorize Anglo-French military staff talks in order to determine a common strategy in case of war with Germany. The Foreign Secretary, ➤Grey, obtained approval for these talks from the Prime Minister (➤Campbell-Bannerman), the War Minister and the Chancellor of the Exchequer. The conversations were accordingly held, confidentially, between 17 January 1906 and the outbreak of hostilities in 1914. The cabinet as a whole were not informed until 1912, when naval talks were also authorized, but an exchange of letters emphasized the hypothetical character of all undertakings. Despite these reservations, the military conversations extended the scope of the ➤Anglo-French Entente. Talks in Brussels with Belgian staff officers also began in 1906. Anglo-Russian naval conversations, authorized in June 1914, had made virtually no progress when war began.

Milner, Alfred (1854–1925, created a viscount 1902), British imperial statesman. Born in Hesse-Darmstadt, of mixed Anglo-German parentage, educated at Tübingen and Balliol College, Oxford, serving as a civil servant in Britain and Egypt before being sent to Cape Colony as High Commissioner in 1897. He remained in South Africa until 1906, acting as civil Governor of Cape Colony before and during the Boer War and serving as Governor of the defeated Boer territories, the Transvaal and the Orange Free State, 1902–6. He was able to accomplish much material reconstruction. In December 1916 he entered Lloyd George's war cabinet, where he maintained links with the overseas empire and checked the rasher decisions of the Prime Minister. Milner headed an important delegation to Petrograd in February 1917 and eased obstacles hampering Anglo-French military collaboration, March 1918. He was Colonial Secretary, 1919–21, but had no sympathy with any major reshaping of Europe and deplored many decisions of the Paris Peace Conference. His rigidity of outlook and his liking for bureaucratic methods cut him off from the masses, to whom he remained an enigmatic figure. His belief in the need to educate colonies for self-government and his hope of establishing some supra-imperial council in London made Milner the principal inspirer of the last generation of servants of empire.

Milošević, Slobodan (1941–), Serbian President. Although born at Požarevac, in north-eastern Serbia, Milošević made the Belgrade municipality his base to rise to power in the post-Tito Communist Party of federal ►Yugoslavia. His Serbian nationalist hostility to the Hungarian and Albanian minorities gained him popular support in the capital and he became Serbia's President (within the old Yugoslavia) in May 1989. A year later he imposed constitutional changes, depriving both minorities of autonomous provisions made by Tito. His Greater Serbian patriotism clashed with the Croat nationalism of ►Tudjman and hastened the disintegration of the federation. During 1992 he encouraged Serb military intervention in the republic of ►Bosnia-Herzegovina and was accused of tolerating 'ethnic cleansing' there and among the Albanians in ►Kosovo. The threat of NATO military intervention and the cumulative effect of several years of sanctions against Serbia weakened Milošević's readiness to back the Bosnian Serbs, and he accepted the compromise imposed by the ►Dayton Accord. His persistence in keeping Serbia a police state, and a conviction that he was mismanaging election results, led to three months of street demonstrations against Milošević in Belgrade in winter 1996–7. His fall seemed imminent, but his political skills secured a compromise. He then exploited differences between his opponents, and by midsummer 1997 had regained popular respect, ahead of elections later in the year. The European Union continued to mistrust him.

Mindszenty, Jósef (1892–1975, created a cardinal 1947), Primate of Hungary. Born József Pehm (later Magyarizing his name as an anti-German gesture); ordained priest 1915, Monsignor 1937, Bishop of Veszprém 1944. His courageously anti-Nazi views led to his arrest on German orders in the winter of 1944–5; and he insisted on being taken to prison in full canonicals. In October 1945 he was installed as Prince-Primate of Hungary. Although clashing with the Hungarian republican authorities over their dissolution of a church youth movement, he was allowed in 1947 to visit America, where in Chicago he held a long conversation with the claimant to the Hungarian throne, Archduke Otto of Habsburg. On 28 December 1948 Mindszenty was arrested, charged with treason and currency offences. At his trial in Budapest (February 1949) he acknowledged his hostility to communism and his Habsburg legitimist sympathies. He was sentenced to penal servitude for life, commuted to house detention in July 1955. During the ►Hungarian National Rising of October 1956 he was freed by the insurgent militia, brought back to the capital and allowed to broadcast to the nation. When the rising was suppressed he sought refuge in the American Legation, remaining there for almost fifteen years since he consistently declined to acknowledge the reconciliation between the Hungarian Government and the Vatican, formally achieved in 1964. In September 1971 he was induced to leave Budapest for Vienna and ultimately Rome. To some liberal believers he long seemed a twentieth-century Becket, denied the accepted form of martyrdom but vindicating a traditional faith by his fortitude. Others, however, regretted his obstinate championship of an unyielding and socially conservative order of society.

Minorities Treaties. Most central and eastern European nations were required to sign treaties, or make declarations, protecting minorities as part of the peace settlement of 1919–20. The treaties, guaranteed by the League of Nations, promised racial minorities equal treatment in law, use of their languages and religious freedom. German commitments were limited to Upper Silesia; Italy, as a Great Power, was not asked for undertakings either for the ➤Alto Adige or for the Slovenes of Istria. Several states – notably Poland and Romania – disregarded their obligations, and the League proved powerless to enforce the treaties.

Mitterrand, François (1916–96), fourth President of the Fifth French Republic. Born the son of the station-master at Jarnac, in south-western France, educated at Angoulême and the University of Paris, he became a prisoner of war in 1940 but escaped and joined the ➤Resistance, being sent on a special mission to ➤de Gaulle in London in 1943, later crossing to Algiers. For his war service Mitterrand gained the Croix de Guerre. He entered politics in 1946 and was elected a socialist deputy for the Nièvre department. Apart from three years as a Senator, 1959–62, he remained a deputy until 1980, holding several ministerial appointments between 1947 and 1957. He was the left-wing candidate against President de Gaulle in the election of 1965, polling 44 per cent of the votes. Disagreement among the French socialist parties led to his eclipse in November 1968, but at the socialist congress at Épinay in 1971 he recovered his political authority and was accepted as leader of the democratic left in France throughout the decade, again unsuccessfully contesting the Presidential election in 1974. Mitterrand was selected as the candidate of the left once more in 1981. On this occasion he received 51.7 per cent of the vote in the second round of the election on 10 May; and he duly succeeded Giscard ➤d'Estaing in the Presidency eleven days later. His programme of nationalization was delayed by the Senate; austerity budgets, though checking inflation, were so unpopular with the electorate that from 1986 to 1988 Mitterrand had to accept a National Assembly dominated by parties of the Right, with the neo-Gaullist Jacques Chirac (1932–) as his Prime Minister. This political 'cohabitation' ended in 1988 when Mitterrand defeated Chirac to win a second presidential term, while the electorate returned a predominantly left-of-centre Assembly. Five years later, however, the voters again backed a right-wing alliance and Mitterrand had to accept economic reforms which favoured private initiative and ran counter to his socialist principles. Though in failing health, he completed his term of office, handing over to a victorious Chirac after the presidential election of May 1995. Mitterrand's fourteen years as President made him the longest-serving French Head of State since the fall of Napoleon III in 1870.

Mobutu, Sese Seko (1930–97), President of Zaire. Born at Lisala, on the north bank of the Upper Congo, christened 'Joseph Désiré' and educated at a Catholic mission school. He served as an NCO in the Belgian colonial army, briefly practised journalism, and with the rank of colonel became Chief of Staff to the Force Publique, the embryonic Congolese Army, in June 1960. His ruthlessness helped him quell mutinies and by September he was sufficiently sure of his authority to oust ►Lumumba from office, receiving backing from both the United States and Belgium. The threat of a renewal of the ►Congo problem led Mobutu – by now a general – to take over the Presidency at the end of November 1965. Once again he imposed discipline harshly but he gradually brought into the administration better-trained officials and achieved an orderly government in ►Zaire, which had seemed impossible in the early 1960s. While satisfying the demands of his supporters for 'Africanization', he shrewdly concluded sound trading agreements with the foreign companies engaged in exploiting the republic's copper deposits and completed the important hydro-electric power scheme at the Inta Dam, near Matadi. His inability to prevent massacres in Shaba province (►Katanga) in May 1978 led to widespread criticism of his conduct of government, especially by the Belgian authorities. The despotic character of Mobutu's rule increased with the passage of time. Unrest in central Zaire prompted him to summon a constituent assembly in April 1991. A formidable political Opposition, the Sacred Union, forced concessions from him over the following eighteen months but, though his term of office had expired, he remained President, adroitly exploiting divisions among his opponents in the capital. From 1992, however, he was faced by renewed secessionist insurgency in Katanga which in the closing months of 1996 was absorbed in a general rebellion, directed by Laurent Kabila, whose Alliance of Democratic Forces forced an ailing Mobutu to flee the country on May 1997 and seek medical treatment in Morocco, where he died in early September.

Mogadishu Raid (18 October 1977). A rescue operation, mounted by twenty-eight police commandos of the West German anti-terrorist squad, Grenzschutz-gruppe 9, on the airport at Mogadishu, Somalia, to free eighty-six hostages held by members of the ►Baader–Meinhof Group aboard a hijacked Lufthansa Boeing 737 airliner, taken over on a flight from Palma to Frankfurt five days previously. The rescue lasted less than a minute: three hijackers were killed, a fourth wounded. A hostage and a commando were also injured. In contrast to the Israeli raid on ►Entebbe this operation was undertaken with the collaboration of the airport authorities. News of the raid appears to have caused the suicide of Andreas Baader and two others of his group, held in Stammheim high-security gaol near Stuttgart.

Moi, Daniel Arap (1924–), second President of Kenya. Ethnically of Kalenjin origin, born in a Rift Valley village near Kartonjo, where he attended a mission school. By 1950 he was a school teacher and became Minister of Education after colonial Kenya's first multiracial elections in February 1961. Although originally a federalist in politics he supported the ruling centralist Kenya Africa National Union (KANU) from 1964 and served ►Kenyatta loyally as Home Affairs Minister and as Vice-President from 1967 until his death eleven years later. Moi assumed office as President on 14 October 1978. He encouraged foreign investment in public works and industrial enterprises but politically he made Kenya a police state. An abortive attempt by air force officers to overthrow Moi in August 1982 led him to strengthen the executive powers of the presidency and for the following nine years to outlaw all political movements apart from KANU. The suspension of aid from the International Monetary Fund 1991–3 induced him to make democratic concessions as well as promising measures to curb corruption. These promises were not fulfilled. The electoral processes by which Moi was assured further five-year terms of office in 1992 and 1997 were viewed by impartial outsiders with some suspicion. Criticism by Commonwealth observers of Moi's style of government and his poor civil rights record continued to influence foreign bankers.

Moldova. Independent republic comprising historic ➤Bessarabia and a disputed region to the east of the river Dniester; capital, Kishinev. From 1940 until 1991 the region constituted the Moldavian Soviet Socialist Republic and geographically formed the south-western corner of the USSR, with most of the people west of the river Dniester being ethnically Romanian. When independence was declared on 27 August 1991 most Moldovans in the capital demonstrated in favour of union with ➤Romania. The Ukrainians and Russians, racially a majority in the more industrialized lands east of the Dniester, set up a Transdniester Republic, which seceded in December 1991. Former Red Army units and Cossack volunteers supported the secessionists and open warfare with Moldovan troops along the lower Dniester caused great destruction, until a ceasefire was reached in August 1993. Moldova refused to concede federal status or independence for the Transdniester region, but promised autonomy. On 6 March 1994 a referendum in Moldova rejected unification with Romania; the republic joined the ➤Commonwealth of Independent States a month later. The Moldovan Constitution of July 1994 provided for a strong presidential executive, a unicameral parliament chosen by proportional representation, and autonomy for the Transdniester and for a small region known as the Gagauz. The Transdniester rejected its proposed status in a referendum in December 1995 and reaffirmed its claim to independence, a problem left unresolved. Although Moldova's government was a left-of-centre coalition, it hastily embarked on a privatization programme in 1994–5, striving to counter poverty caused by the disruption of pre-independence trading links, war damage along the Dniester and a drought in 1992, which crippled wine-producing and fruit-growing enterprises.

Mollet, Guy (1905–75), French socialist leader. Born at Flers, the son of a textile worker. In the 1930s he was an English teacher at Arras. During the Second World War he joined the Resistance, survived three interrogations by the Gestapo, and was the official government representative in the liberated Pas-de-Calais, 1944–5. He was elected a Socialist Deputy for that region in October 1945, and was

Secretary-General of the French Socialist Party, 1946–68. From January 1956 until May 1957 he headed the longest-lived coalition government under the ►Fourth Republic, failing to secure the peace he desired in Algeria, allowing his military advisers to push him into the ►Suez episode, but sustaining defeat ultimately over a minor financial detail. He tried, but failed, to organize a unified, democratic socialist opposition to the Fifth Republic, retiring from public life in 1971. He was the archetypal socialist politician of the Fourth Republic, torn between socialist principles and the practical needs of *ad hoc* coalitions constantly under internal and external pressure.

Molotov, Vyacheslav Mikhailovich (1890–1986), Soviet Russian statesman. Born into the Skriabin family at Kukaida, educated at Kazan, became a revolutionary Bolshevik in 1905 and assisted in the editing of *Pravda* from 1912 onwards, assuming the name 'Molotov' (i.e. 'hammer') for conspiratorial purposes. He was the top-ranking Bolshevik in Petrograd in March 1917, before the return of Lenin, and was a member of the military committee which helped plan the October Revolution, becoming in 1921 the youngest member of the Politburo, the chief executive body of the ruling party. He was a staunch Stalinist from 1921 onwards, helping to launch the first Five Year Plan in Moscow (1928) and serving as Prime Minister, 1930–41, taking over foreign affairs from ►Litvinov on 4 May 1939 and gaining international recognition by the part he played in concluding the ►Nazi–Soviet Pact of 23 August 1939. He remained Foreign Minister until 4 March 1949, cautiously and suspiciously collaborating with the British and Americans, 1941–5, building up the network of treaties linking the Eastern European republics to the Soviet bloc, 1945–9, rejecting ►Marshall Aid, and declining to relax tension in the so-called ►'cold war'. On Stalin's death in 1953 he again took charge of foreign affairs, negotiating the ►Austrian State Treaty of 1955, but he opposed Khrushchev's reconciliation with ►Tito and in June 1956 he was demoted, serving as Minister of State Control for a year until expelled from his party posts for 'anti-party' activity. He was sent as ambassador to the Mongolian People's Republic, 1957–60. At the age of seventy he was appointed Soviet delegate to the International Atomic Energy Agency in Vienna but was thereafter intermittently denounced by Khrushchev in public speeches for his loyalty to Stalin in the 1930s. In 1983 he was readmitted to the Communist Party.

Monnet, Jean (1888–1979), French economist. Born at Cognac and largely self-educated. While a civil servant in the Ministry of Commerce, 1915–19, he prepared abortive plans for economic collaboration between western Europe and America. He was a consultant economist at the Peace Conference, 1919–20, and later for the League of Nations. In 1939–40 he chaired a committee promoting Anglo-French economic collaboration and was attached to the British Supply Council in Washington 1940–43 before preparing reconstruction plans for General de Gaulle in Algiers. On 21 December 1945 he was put at the head of a commission to prepare the modernization and re-equipment of French industry, evolving the Monnet Plan which within five years enabled France to outstrip its pre-war industrial level. He established close contact with Robert Schuman, Prime Minister in 1947 and Foreign Minister 1948–53. Monnet was responsible for working out details of the ►Schuman Plan for supranational coal and steel integration. It was therefore appropriate that Monnet should serve as first President of the ►European Coal and Steel Community, from 1952 to 1955. Monnet's vision of Europe ran counter to Gaullist ideas and in the early 1960s he became a severe critic of the foreign policy pursued by ►de Gaulle.

Montagu–Chelmsford Report (1919). Recommended the establishment in British India of an elected central legislature, enjoying partially responsible powers of government. This proposal formed a basis for the ►India Act of 1919. The report was jointly submitted by the Secretary of State for India, Edwin Montagu (1879–1924), and Lord Chelmsford (1868–1933).

Montenegro (Crna Gora). A mountainous region in south-western ►Yugoslavia, a principality from the late fourteenth century, maintaining effective independence from the Turks because of the difficulties of terrain, and producing a remarkable dynasty of warrior princes of whom the last, Nicholas Petrović Njegoš (1841– 1921, Prince 1860–1910, King 1910–18), modernized the state, ruling as an almost enlightened despot. Montenegro was granted a constitution in 1905 and Cetinje was built up as a capital city. Judicious intervention by King Nicholas in the ►Balkan Wars considerably extended his territory. Montenegro supported Serbia in 1914 but was overrun by the Austrians at the end of 1915, King Nicholas escaping to France (where he lived out his last six years of life). Suspicion that Nicholas had not resisted the Austrians with sustained energy led the allied Great Powers in 1918 to accept the decision of an arbitrarily convened assembly at Podgorica which deposed the dynasty and voted for union with Serbia, whose effective ruler, Prince-Regent ►Alexander, was a son of the deposed Nicholas's daughter. Between the wars Montenegro lost its identity in Yugoslavia. After the Axis invasion of 1941 Montenegrin guerrilla resistance ensured that, in the communist constitution of 1946, Montenegro reappeared as a federated republic within Yugoslavia. Subsequently several public figures have shown the traditional independence of spirit of the Montenegrin people, the best-known of them being Milovan ►Djilas. No attempt was made to re-assert Montenegrin independence when the Yugoslav federation broke up in 1991. New federal links were established with Serbia in April 1992 with joint membership of the parliament in Belgrade, as well as a separate multiparty assembly in Podgorica, the capital. Relations with Belgrade became strained in the early months of 1998 through resentment at Milošević's attempts to impose his nominees on Podgorica.

Montgomery, Bernard Law (1887–1976, created viscount 1946), British field-marshal. Educated at St Paul's School and Sandhurst, commissioned in the Royal Warwickshire Regiment in 1908, serving on the Western Front throughout most of the First World War. A succession of staff and command postings at home and in India were followed by promotion to the rank of major-general in 1938. He commanded the Third Division of the British Expeditionary Force in 1939–40 until the evacuation from Dunkirk. His fame as a field commander was established with the Eighth Army, July 1942 to January 1944, from ►Alamein across North Africa and into Sicily and southern Italy. He commanded allied ground troops in the ►Normandy Landings, holding the main weight of German forces with British and Canadian units and thereby enabling the US Twelfth Army Group to fight its way deeply into France. Subsequently Montgomery wished to mount a 'pencil-thrust' advance of some forty divisions on Berlin by way of the Ruhr, but his plans were overruled by the Supreme Commander, ►Eisenhower. 'Monty' was promoted field-marshal on 1 September 1944, during which month his Twenty-First Army Group captured Antwerp but failed to roll back the German right flank at ►Arnhem. Subsequently Montgomery played a decisive role in checking the German counter-offensive in the ►Ardennes and crossed the Rhine on 24 March 1945. Six weeks later (4 May) he formally accepted the surrender of all German forces in north-western Europe at Lüneburg Heath. From 1946 to 1948 he served as Chief of the Imperial General Staff and he was Deputy Supreme Commander of NATO forces in Europe, 1951–8. His outstanding characteristics were his professional thoroughness in planning set-piece battles and the projection of his self confidence so as to arouse enthusiasm among his troops. He was the most successful British general against European adversaries since Wellington, and arguably since Marlborough.

Montreux Convention (20 July 1936). At Turkey's request an international conference was held at Montreux in the summer of 1936 to consider revision of the Treaty of ►Lausanne because of Turkish fears that Mussolini wished to acquire colonial settlements for Italy in Asia Minor. The resulting Convention (signed by the Black Sea powers, Britain, France, Greece and Yugoslavia) permitted Turkey to refortify the Dardanelles and the Bosphorus and imposed new regulations on the aggregate tonnage of warships passing through the Straits in time of peace.

Morgenthau Plan. A proposal made at the ►Quebec Conference of 1944 by the US Secretary of the Treasury, Henry Morgenthau (1891–1967), for the postwar removal of all industry from defeated Germany. This plan for 'pastoralization', originally accepted by Churchill and Roosevelt, was soon rejected as absurd by the State Department and the Foreign Office who emphasized the burden of maintaining a pastoralized Germany on foreign subsidies from the victorious powers. News of the plan was leaked to Germany, where it provided the propaganda machine of ►Goebbels with material to encourage prolonged German resistance to the allied invasion armies.

Morley—Minto Reforms. The name generally given to the ►India Act of 1909, which established Indian councils. Lord Morley (1838–1923) was Secretary of State for India at the time: Lord Minto (1847–1914) was Viceroy, 1905–10.

Moro, Aldo (1916–78), Italian Prime Minister. Born at Maglie in south-eastern Italy, studied law at Bari University and became a prominent member of the non-fascist Catholic students movement, attending the constituent assembly of the Italian Republic in 1946 and sitting as a Christian Democrat parliamentary deputy from 1948 onwards. He was Foreign Minister briefly in the winter of 1965–6, from August 1969 until January 1972, and from July 1973 until October 1974, playing a leading role in EEC affairs. From 1963 until 1968 and from November 1974 until July 1976 he was Prime Minister, and was thereafter much respected as elder statesman of the Christian Democrats. On 17 March 1978 his car was ambushed in Rome by 'Red Brigade' anarchists, who killed his bodyguard and held him as a hostage while they sought the release of terrorists already in Italian custody. The government declined to bargain with the kidnappers, and Moro's body was found riddled with bullets in an abandoned car near the Rome headquarters of the Christian Democrat Party on 9 May.

Moroccan Crisis (1905). French agreements with Britain (April 1904) and Spain (October 1904) secretly provided for the eventual partition of Morocco. Although Germany had little direct economic interest in Morocco, Chancellor Bülow believed it would be possible to weaken the ➤Anglo-French Entente by championing Moroccan independence, since he was confident Britain would not support France to the brink of war over Morocco. Bülow accordingly induced Kaiser ➤William II to land at Tangier on 31 March 1905 and show sympathy for the Moroccans. The Germans demanded an international conference, which the French at first declined, and there was a diplomatic crisis throughout the summer and autumn of 1905. As a gesture of appeasement the French jettisoned their Foreign Minister, Delcassé, but agreed to an international conference at ➤Algeciras when they were sure of British backing and American goodwill. The conference was a diplomatic defeat for Germany, strengthening rather than weakening the Entente. A second Moroccan crisis – ➤Agadir – occurred in 1911.

Morocco. Independent Muslim state in north-west Africa. At the turn of the century tribes were in revolt against the Sultan, conditions were backward and the French were eager to colonize the area. International crises in 1905 and 1911 (➤Moroccan Crisis) retarded French policy, but protectorates were set up by the French in the south and the Spanish in the north (1912). A free port was established at ➤Tangier in 1923. French Morocco was rapidly westernized by ➤Lyautey. Riff rebels under ➤Abd-el-Krim engaged the Spanish and the French garrisons in the early 1920s. In November 1934 a Moroccan reform programme, presented by young Arab students to the French Chamber of Deputies, was rejected out of hand, but Moroccan nationalism grew in intensity until the local patriotic party, Istiqlal, began to demand full independence, 1943. Consultative assemblies were authorized in 1948. Serious anti-French riots continued intermittently 1953–5, complicated by clashes between Berber tribesmen and supporters of Sultan Muhammed Yusuf. Morocco became a unified and independent kingdom, under the former Sultan, in November 1956. On Muhammed Yusuf's death in February 1961 his son succeeded to the throne, taking the title Hassan II (1929–). Serious disturbances in March 1965, mainly in Casablanca, led to the establishment of a royal dictatorship, although eventual restoration of a unicameral legislature was promised under a new constitution, promulgated in March 1972. King Hassan pursued a cautious policy, seeking close collaboration with France, but conscious of the pro-Soviet inclination of neighbouring ▸Algeria. Claims on the Spanish Sahara, vigorously asserted by King Hassan in October and November 1975, led to tension with Spain and to armed clashes with Algerian troops in February and March 1976. The international recognition subsequently accorded by some states to the nationalist guerrillas (Polisario) in the western Sahara angered King Hassan, who insisted that the Saharan Arab Democratic Republic (formally proclaimed in February 1976) would soon be swept away. Major battles were fought by the Moroccans against the Polisarios in January, August and November in 1979 and March 1980, with Hassan mobilizing an extremely large army and the Polisarios receiving sophisticated weapons from ▸Libya. None of these battles was conclusive. The Saharan War dragged on until 1988, seriously damaging Morocco's economy, but keeping the country united in an almost fanatical loyalty to the sovereign, 'Commander of the Faithful'.

Morrison, Herbert Stanley (1888–1965, created Baron Morrison of Lambeth 1959). Born in Lambeth, educated at elementary school, helped build up the London Labour Party, becoming its general secretary in 1915 and holding pacifist beliefs at that time. He was Mayor of Hackney 1920–21, and entered the London County Council in 1922, eventually leading the LCC, 1934–40, unifying the transport system and creating a 'green belt' around the suburbs. In 1923 he was elected Labour MP for South Hackney, representing the constituency again in 1929–31 and 1935–45 and sitting for East Lewisham, 1945–59. He was in MacDonald's cabinet as Minister of Transport, March–August 1931. As Minister of Supply in Churchill's coalition government, May–October 1940, he stimulated industrial production and was Home Secretary for the remaining years of the coalition, accepting responsibility for civil defence and creating the National Fire Service. He sat in the war cabinet, October 1942 to May 1945. Morrison drafted the programme of nationalization and social services successfully offered by Labour to the electorate in the 1945 election. He was Deputy Prime Minister 1945–51, was Lord President of the Council and, briefly in 1951, Foreign Secretary. Morrison stood as candidate for the party leadership after the 1935 election but lost to Attlee who was, by temperament, a more natural unifier of the party. Internal conflicts also frustrated his hopes of replacing Attlee 1945–55. He stood for the leadership again in 1955 but was defeated by ▸Gaitskell, a much younger man. Morrison, an able organizer, left his principal mark on municipal socialism in London rather than on the party as a whole.

Mosley, Oswald Ernald (1896–1980, succeeded his father as a baronet, 1928), British politician. Educated at Winchester and Sandhurst, fought with the 16th Lancers at Ypres before transferring to the Royal Flying Corps. He entered the House of Commons as Conservative member for Harrow, 1918–22, continuing to sit as an Independent until 1924 when he joined the Labour Party, and was Labour MP for Smethwick, 1926–31. MacDonald appointed him Chancellor of the Duchy of Lancaster in June 1929, a member of the government but not of the cabinet. Mosley proposed to solve the ►Depression by stimulating foreign trade, directing industrial policy so as to avoid needless competition, and using public funds to promote industrial expansion. The cabinet rejected these proposals and Mosley resigned, 21 May 1930. Nine months later he founded a progressive socialist movement, which he called the 'New Party', which contested twenty-one seats in the 1931 general election without success. Mosley visited Rome in January 1932 and was impressed by Mussolini. He dissolved the New Party in April 1932 and six months later announced the establishment of the British Union of Fascists. In 1934–6 the movement became anti-Semitic and Hitlerite rather than fascist in character, staging provocative marches and rallies in the East End of London, although its following declined after the Public Order Act of 1936 banned political uniforms and private armies. Mosley was interned under the wartime 'Regulation 18b', 1940–43. He founded the 'Union Movement' in 1947, unsuccessfully seeking election to parliament in Kensington North (1959) and Shoreditch and Finsbury (1966). He was an early advocate of British integration in an economically united Europe.

Motor Vehicles. Although there were 3,000 cars in France in 1900, and Britain had held a motor show at Tunbridge Wells as early as 1895, on both sides of the Atlantic motor vehicles remained a rare novelty at the start of the century. The invention of the Daimler Mercedes model in 1901 shaped the definitive form of the motor car. Yet when car licensing was introduced in Britain in January 1904 there were still only 24,000 registered cars, their quality bolstered in April by the marketing of the earliest Rolls-Royce. By then, Olds in the USA were turning out 5,000 motor vehicles a year though it was Henry ►Ford who revolutionized the car market by mass production of a people's car, the Model T, in 1908: a million Model T cars went off the production line by 1915. France remained the chief motor vehicle producer in Europe until 1930, although Renault at first specialized in taxis (in particular for Paris and London). Austin and Morris followed the US lead on a smaller scale in the United Kingdom before the First World War, while Citroën and Peugeot in France, and Fiat in Italy, provided effective rivals. The British were the first to organize the racing of motor vehicles as a sport, with the opening of the world's pioneer racetrack at Brooklands (Surrey) in July 1907. The number of trucks and lorries increased dramatically during the First

World War, especially after the USA entered the war. Although in continental Europe the car remained an expensive luxury between the wars, 'family' motoring became popular in Britain and the USA in the 1920s; a surge of buying in Britain, which began in the spring of 1922, was only momentarily checked when petrol rose to two shillings (10p) a gallon in 1924; and in America both cars and gasoline were cheaper. Hitler recognized the appeal of cheap motoring in 1936 when he backed Ferdinand Porsche's design for the Volkswagen 'people's car'; ironically, more than 40 million were sold on the world market after Hitler's downfall. Despite the success of Alec Issigonis's Mini Minor for Morris and Austin between 1959 and 1970, the British car industry shrank rapidly in the face of American, Japanese and German competition. Significantly in September 1986 it was the Japanese company, Nissan, who opened a new car plant in Sunderland. Alarm over the rapidly rising rate of road deaths led to a series of experimental safety measures in Britain and America from 1931 onwards, but concern over the pollution caused by car fumes only became widespread in the late 1970s. Measures to reduce car pollution were among pledges given at the ►Rio Earth Summit of 1992. Five years later a UN summit conference in New York regretted that little had been achieved, particularly in the USA, where the 'oil' and 'automobile' lobbies retained great political influence.

Mountbatten. The anglicized form of the Battenberg dynasty, adopted at the request of King George V in June 1917 when British royalty abandoned foreign-sounding names. At that time Admiral Prince Louis of Battenberg (1854–1921), who as First Sea Lord was responsible for ensuring that the British fleet was ready and at war stations in August 1914, became Marquess of Milford Haven. His second surviving son became Lord Louis ►Mountbatten. The Admiral's second daughter's son, born (in 1921) Prince Philip of Greece, was naturalized as Lieutenant Philip Mountbatten early in 1947, becoming Duke of Edinburgh in November 1947 on his marriage to Princess Elizabeth.

Mountbatten, Albert Victor Nicholas Louis Francis (1900–1979), Earl, of Burma, Admiral of the Fleet. Served with the battle-cruisers in the North Sea in the First World War; commanded fifth destroyer flotilla in 1939, the flotilla leader HMS *Kelly* being badly damaged off Norway (1940) and sunk off Crete (1941). Lord Louis became chief of combined operations in 1942, planning raids on St Nazaire and ►Dieppe as well as beginning work on technical preparations for the eventual ►Normandy Landings. In October 1943 he arrived in Delhi as Supreme Allied Commander, South-East Asia, introducing new ideas and techniques into the ►Burma Campaign, ultimately accepting the surrender of all Japanese forces in south-eastern Asia in September 1945. He was appointed the last Viceroy of India on 20 February 1947, speeding up the transition to independence and becoming the first Governor-General of India, 15 August 1947 to 21 June 1948. He later resumed his naval career, principally in the Mediterranean, and was First Sea Lord, 1955–9, and Chief of the Defence Staff 1959–65. In 1922 he married the Hon.

Edwina Ashley (1901–60), who was much respected because of her work for the Red Cross and in social welfare. Earl Mountbatten was assassinated by Irish terrorists in his boat while on holiday in County Sligo on 27 August 1979.

Mozambique. A republic on the east coast of southern Africa, bordered by Tanzania, Malawi, Zambia, Rhodesia and South Africa. Mozambique was a Portuguese colony, 1498–1975. A Marxist liberation group, ►Frelimo, organized a guerrilla campaign against the Portuguese from September 1964, using bases in Tanzania. The strain of colonial military operations in Mozambique and ►Angola demoralized Portuguese army units and contributed to the revolution in ►Portugal in 1974. The new Portuguese Government held talks with Frelimo leaders in September 1974, establishing a joint transitional government which prepared for the proclamation of the independent People's Republic of Mozambique on 25 June 1975. The Mozambique President, Samora Machel (1933–86), announced total nationalization of private property in February 1976, also changing the name of the capital from Lourenço Marques to Maputo. Raids and border skirmishes broke out between Frelimos, Zimbabwe nationalists and Rhodesian security forces along the 800-mile Rhodesia–Mozambique frontier and there were several 'hot pursuit' attacks by the Rhodesians into Mozambique notably at the end of February and the beginning of August 1976. Rhodesian airborne troops killed over 1,000 alleged guerrillas in raids against camps more than 100 miles inside Mozambique on 23 and 26 November 1977. A further Rhodesian attack was made on the lower Limpopo valley in September 1979, and when the fighting ended in ►Zimbabwe President Machel reported that his country had sustained, in all, 350 raids by the Rhodesian forces. South African troops raided targets in the suburbs of Maputo, the capital of Mozambique, on 30 January 1981, claiming that they were seeking to destroy the headquarters of the ►African National Congress. Thereafter the greatest threat to Mozambique's multi-racial system of village democracy came from South African backing for a 'nationalist' guerrilla force, controlled by former wealthy businessmen from the Portuguese colonial era, said to number 10,000 well-armed troops by May 1982, known as the MNR ('Remanos'). A further raid by South African commandos on Maputo in October 1983 was followed by a formal peace agreement concluded by Machel and President ►Botha outlawing guerrilla attacks across the border (February–March 1984). Nevertheless the Remanos were growing rapidly in strength when, on 19 October 1986, President Machel was killed. The Soviet-built aircraft in which he was returning from a meeting with the Presidents of Zambia, Zaire and Angola struck a mountain just inside South African territory. Machel was succeeded by his Foreign Minister, Joachim Chissano (1940–), who checked Remano penetration, began peace talks in 1990, and secured a formal end to the civil war in October 1992. Delay in demobilizing the rival armies led to postponement of multi-party elections for another two years; but on 29 October 1994 the voters backed Chissano as President, for a five-year term, with an elected Frelimo government. A programme of rural development and land reform in the war-ravaged republic needed foreign aid and technical assistance, notably from South Africa. In November 1995 Mozambique was admitted to the ►Commonwealth as 'a unique and special case' with the backing of her neighbours, all of them Commonwealth members.

Mubarak, Mohammad Hosni (1928–), Egyptian President. Born near Cairo, he married an Egyptian whose mother was Welsh. Mubarak was an air force officer who, after leading fighter-bomber squadrons in the Yemen, was commander of the Egyptian Air Force, 1973–5. Mubarak was appointed Vice-President by ►Sadat in April 1975 and became Head of State on 14 October 1981, after Sadat's assassination. Mubarak allowed greater political freedom than his two predecessors and in 1984 and 1987 there were genuine multi-party elections. By 1990 his 'Western' foreign policy and continuation of Sadat's attempts to reach a peace settlement aroused such anger among his opponents that the Opposition parties boycotted the elections in protest. From 1992 ►Islamic fundamentalist terrorist attacks endangered his life on more than one occasion, but they restored respect for his policies and resolution of purpose.

Mugabe, Robert Gabriel (1924–), first Prime Minister of Zimbabwe. Born at Kutama, educated at missionary schools and Fort Hare University College, South Africa, as well as in London. From 1952 to 1960 he was a teacher in Rhodesia. He became Deputy Secretary General of ZAPU (the Zimbabwe African People's Union) on its foundation by ►Nkomo in 1961. Mugabe was detained by the Rhodesian authorities in September 1962, but he escaped to Tanzania seven months later and set up ZANU (the Zimbabwe African National Union) there. Mugabe was detained in ►Rhodesia from 1964 to 1974. In October 1976 he became joint-leader with Nkomo of the Patriotic Front, leading the guerrilla group known as the Zimbabwe African National Liberation Army from Mozambique until a ceasefire was agreed in London, to end the seven-year international conflict in Rhodesia–Zimbabwe, on 21 December 1979. Mugabe attended the Lancaster House Conference in London (September–December 1979) and returned to Rhodesia on 27 January 1980 to lead the ZANU election campaign. He survived two assassination attempts in the following three weeks and ZANU gained an overall majority in the election. Mugabe became the first Prime Minister of ►Zimbabwe on 4 March, five weeks before the country became formally independent. Despite internal tension between black and white and difficulties with Nkomo's ZAPU supporters, Mugabe proceeded cautiously until constitutional changes enabled him to become executive President on 30 December 1987. He was re-elected in 1990 and 1996 when, as two rival presidential candidates withdrew, less than a third of the voters went to the polls.

Mujibur Rahman, Sheikh. ►Rahman, Sheikh Mujibur.

Mukden Incident (18 September 1931). Japanese troops, sent to guard the South

Manchurian Railway in accordance with treaty rights, seized the key city of Mukden, alleging that the Chinese had blown up a section of the railway while the Japanese Army was on manoeuvres. This incident, condemned by the League of Nations, was followed by a complete Japanese occupation of ▸Manchuria by the end of the year. These operations were undertaken by a group of army staff officers without reference to the civil government of Tokyo and mark the beginning of a period of militaristic dominance which led to the end of party government in Japan (May 1932) and to the forward policy culminating ten years later in ▸Pearl Harbor.

Munich Agreement (29 September 1938). A settlement of the crisis over the ▸Sudetenland in Czechoslovakia reached in conference at Munich by the heads of government of Germany, Britain, France and Italy (▸Hitler, ▸Chamberlain, ▸Daladier and ▸Mussolini). No Czechoslovak representative was present, the conference taking place under a German threat of war. The Agreement transferred to Germany the fortified frontier region, inhabited by a German-speaking minority, and provided for settlement of Polish and Hungarian claims on Czechoslovakia. What remained of Czechoslovakia was guaranteed by the four Powers against further unprovoked aggression. Most people in Britain, France and Germany were relieved by 'Munich', hoping the statesmen had saved European peace. A minority, in France and Britain, held it to be a betrayal of democratic Czechoslovakia: Churchill said in the House of Commons, 'We have sustained a defeat without a war.' Defenders of 'Munich' maintain that, even if it did not give 'peace for our time' (as Chamberlain predicted), it gave the West twelve months in which to improve aircraft and armaments: critics reply that Germany was better prepared for war in 1939 than in 1938 and that the Czech defences would have kept out the Germans for several months. By ignoring the Soviet Union (which, like France, was an ally of Czechoslovakia) Chamberlain and Daladier convinced Stalin that the West was prepared to make an 'imperialist deal' with Hitler, thus encouraging him to seek his own bilateral settlement, the ▸Nazi–Soviet Pact.

Munich Olympics Killings (5 September 1972). During the twentieth ▸Olympic Games in Munich, Palestinian guerrillas of the 'Black September' movement attacked the quarters of the Israeli team, killing two athletes outright and taking nine others hostage. An attempted rescue bid at an airport outside Munich failed: the remaining nine athletes were killed. Two Germans and five terrorists also died. Surviving Arab guerrillas were flown to Libya and set free six weeks later when a Lufthansa aircraft was hijacked by other terrorists.

Munich Putsch (8–9 November 1923). Abortive attempt by Hitler to seize the state government of Bavaria as a prelude to a march on Berlin (▸'March on Rome') and the establishment of a Nazi government. The putsch was ill-planned and collapsed when Bavarian police opened fire on a Nazi procession in the Odeonsplatz, killing sixteen of Hitler's supporters but not injuring either Hitler himself or his prestigious companion, General ►Ludendorff. Hitler was sentenced to five years' imprisonment on a charge of treason, Ludendorff acquitted. The sixteen victims were the leading Nazi martyrs, while Munich – and the beer-cellar used as headquarters for the putsch – became accepted as the legendary shrine of Nazism.

Murray, (John) Hubert (1861–1940, knighted 1925), Australian colonial administrator. Born in Sydney, a member of a Roman Catholic family of Irish descent. He was educated in Sydney and at Magdalen College, Oxford, serving with distinction in the Boer War, and becoming a barrister and circuit judge in New South Wales before being appointed judicial officer in Papua in 1907. His humanitarian and sympathetic understanding of native problems induced the Australian Government to appoint him Lieutenant-Governor of Papua in 1908 and he held the post until his death, thirty-two years later, a longer term of office than any other colonial governor in the modern British empire. He was responsible for bringing a Stone Age native population into the twentieth century without causing the suffering and spreading the diseases which had weakened Australia's aboriginal population in the previous century. Murray inherited an indentured labour service which he disliked as being near to slavery, but he succeeded in restraining the economic greed of the white enterprises which employed the natives. His policy won widespread respect outside Australia but was criticized by conservative administrations in Canberra. Sir Hubert was an elder brother of Professor Gilbert Murray, OM (1866–1957), great classical scholar and liberal internationalist.

Mussadeq, Mohammed (1881–1967), Prime Minister of Iran. Born in Teheran, becoming a rich landowner although by nature an ascetic man. He served as Foreign Minister, 1922–4, and held other government posts in the 1920s but then withdrew from politics until 1942 when he was elected to the Iranian parliament, the Majlis. He soon attracted a wide following for his violent speeches against the Anglo-Iranian Oil Company, maintaining that if the oil industry were nationalized all mass poverty in Iran would disappear. His militantly nationalistic following triumphed in the spring of 1951 when, following the assassination of the Prime Minister, General Razmara (7 March), the Majlis nationalized the oil industry and after a fortnight's rioting in Abadan induced Shah Reza ►Pahlavi to appoint Mussadeq Prime Minister (27 April). The withdrawal of western experts left the Iranians unable to produce the oil upon which Mussadeq had counted. In August 1952 the Majlis gave him dictatorial powers for six months, extending these powers subsequently for another six months. Failure to secure the expected oil revenue made Mussadeq, a natural and tearful hysteric, lose his political common sense. Promises of social revolution by the break-up of large estates were not realized; he quarrelled with political leaders, the army, the judiciary and finally the Shah, who dismissed him on 13 August 1953, appointing General Zahedi as his successor. Mussadeq refused to accept dismissal and there were five days of civil unrest before he was arrested on a charge of unconstitutional behaviour and sentenced to three years' solitary confinement. His Foreign Minister, Hussein Fatemi, was executed for treason.

Mussolini, Benito (1883–1945), Italian Prime Minister. Born near Forlì in the Romagna; briefly a schoolteacher, fled to Switzerland in 1902 to evade military service and, while working as a manual labourer, became interested in socialism, especially ►syndicalism. He returned to Italy in 1904 and was an able left-wing agitator and journalist before resigning from the Socialist Party (1915) because it criticized his support for war with Austria-Hungary. Mussolini fought on the Isonzo front, was wounded and returned to Milan to edit *Il Popolo d'Italia*, forming the right-radical groups which were later merged into the Fascist Party (►Fascism). Mussolini's anti-communist followers demanded full implementation of Italy's demands at the Paris Peace Conference and vigorously supported Gabriele ►d'Annunzio at ►Fiume. From February 1921 Italy was in a state of incipient civil war, with serious riots in Bologna, Florence and Milan. In October 1922 King ►Victor Emmanuel III appointed Mussolini Prime Minister in order to forestall a communist revolution (►'March on Rome'). As Duce – 'Leader' – Mussolini headed a coalition of fascists and nationalists, allowing muted parliamentary government until after the murder of ►Matteotti in 1924. Full fascist government was established in 1928–9: Italy became a single constituency in which the electorate voted for or against 400 candidates nominated by the Fascist Grand Council; disputes between workers and employers were settled by a National Council of Corporations. Mussolini carried out an extensive public-works programme, improved Church–State relations by the ►Lateran Treaties, and from the ►Corfu Incident in 1923 to the ►Abyssinian War in 1935 pursued an aggressive foreign policy. At first he was hostile to Hitler's Germany, because of its ambitions to absorb his northern neighbour (Austria); but the similarity between the Nazi and fascist systems, together with the international ostracism caused by the Abyssinian War, encouraged collaboration between the two dictators, who formed what Mussolini described as an ►'Axis' in 1936. At Easter 1939 Mussolini annexed Albania; he declared war on Britain and France (10 June 1940); and invaded Greece (28 October 1940). Defeats in the Greek campaign, in Libya and in East Africa, weakened Mussolini's prestige, especially since he had encouraged fascists to admire the military virtues. By the winter of 1941–2 Mussolini was virtually a German pensionary. The imminent invasion of the Italian mainland led Victor Emmanuel and Marshal ►Badoglio to force Mussolini's resignation (25 July 1943). He was imprisoned but rescued from his place of internment in the Apennines by German airborne troops (12 September 1943) and set up a republican fascist regime which administered German-occupied northern Italy. On 28 April 1945 Mussolini was captured and shot by Italian partisans on the shore of lake Como, while attempting to escape to Switzerland. His corpse was taken to Milan and hung in the Piazzale Loreto amid a display of public execration.

Myanmar. Name officially substituted for historic ➤Burma by General Saw Maung in 1989 after his military *coup* in September 1988.

My Lai Massacre (16 March 1968). In November 1969 it was announced in Washington that investigations were taking place into allegations that US troops had killed all the inhabitants – men, women and children – living around the hamlet of My Lai in Vietnam twenty months previously. A Lieutenant William Calley was subsequently charged with the murder of at least 109 Vietnamese at My Lai and, after a four months' court-martial, found guilty on 29 March 1971. His immediate superior, Capt. Ernest Medina, was acquitted. Defence counsel argued that the crimes had been committed as part of a major punitive operation against an area harbouring Viet-Cong guerrillas. Lieut. Calley was sentenced to life imprisonment, a penalty later substantially reduced. The incident, contrary to the accepted traditions of the US Army, raised doubts within America on the problems of military duty and respect for justice while also illustrating the decline in morale and standards of conduct among troops required to fight the ➤Vietnam War.

N

Nagorny-Karabakh. An Armenian-populated autonomous region within ►Azerbaijan, which from 1988 to 1994 fought an inconclusive war of secession in the hope of joining the neighbouring republic of ►Armenia.

Nagy, Imre (1896–1958), Hungarian communist Prime Minister. Born in Kaposvár, a railway junction in southern Hungary; captured while serving on the Eastern Front in the First World War, returning to Hungary from Russia as a secret communist in 1921, escaping to Austria in 1928. From 1930 to 1944 he lived in the Soviet Union, studying agriculture. As republican Hungary's first Minister of Agriculture Nagy was responsible for major land reforms in 1945–6, dividing up the great estates. He was briefly Minister of the Interior, although removed by ►Rákosi who wished the post to be held by the more ardently socialist ►Rajk. Nagy succeeded Rákosi as Prime Minister in July 1953, with the backing of ►Malenkov in Moscow, and instituted a more liberal regime, encouraging the manufacture of consumer goods and relaxing agricultural collectivization. Eleven days after Malenkov's resignation as Soviet Prime Minister, Nagy was forced out of office (February 1955) and expelled from the Communist Party in the following November. He remained popular, however, and with the relaxation of tension after the ►Twentieth Party Congress the Hungarian Press urged his reappointment. He was entrusted with the formation of a government on 24 October 1956, after the anti-Stalinist demonstrations which marked the start of the ►Hungarian National Rising. Nagy included three non-communists in his coalition, announced Hungary's withdrawal from the Warsaw Pact and sought a neutral status for the country, similar to the neutrality of Austria and Switzerland. Soviet intervention overthrew Nagy's government on 4 November 1956. He took refuge in the Yugoslav embassy, emerging eighteen days later under what he believed to be a safe conduct. He was, however, arrested, secretly tried and executed on 17 June 1958.

Namibia. Territory colonized in 1884–90 as German South-West Africa, comprising the protectorates of Damaraland in the north and Namaland in the south. The German colony was conquered by South African troops in a campaign lasting from 14 April to 9 July 1915 and subsequently administered by ►South Africa as a ►League of Nations mandate. From 1948 onwards the South African Government sought to integrate the territory with its other sovereign lands, despite protests from the United Nations and condemnation by the International Court of Justice. Guerrillas belonging to SWAPO (South-West African People's Organization for

Namibia, founded in 1960 by Sam Nujoma and Herman Toivo Ja Toivo) began fighting South African units in the Damaraland bush country in 1966, the UN recognizing SWAPO as 'the sole authentic representative of the people of Namibia' in 1971. On 30 January 1976 the UN Security Council accepted a five-nation proposal for elections, under UN supervision, of a constituent assembly for the establishment of an independent Namibia. The sponsors of the resolution (Britain, USA, Canada, France and West Germany) put pressure on the South African Government in August 1977 to implement the proposal, but the South Africans held their own 'Turnhalle Talks', 1975–7, with white and coloured moderates in Namibia seeking to reach a settlement independent of SWAPO (which, its opponents claimed, was representative only of the Ovambo tribe). Improved relations with South Africa permitted the UN to send a Finnish observer, Martti Ahtisaari, on a fact-finding visit to Namibia in August 1978. Deadlock persisted throughout most of the following year, the South Africans rejecting compromises proposed by the UN. The SWAPO guerrilla attacks in Namibia became so serious in 1980 that the South African army mounted a major invasion of ►Angola in June to destroy guerrilla bases, an operation repeated in November 1981. Subsequently the South Africans agreed to talks with SWAPO but reimposed direct rule from Pretoria in January 1983. The Reagan Administration sponsored talks in Lusaka in 1984 and 1988 aimed at securing Namibian independence and, at the same time, Cuban withdrawal from Angola. Ahtisaari's mission in 1978 was followed over the next ten years by two other UN delegations 'preparing for Namibian independence' and in December 1988 South Africa agreed to implement the UN resolution of 1976 providing for Namibian independence. SWAPO won an electoral victory in November 1989 and on 21 March 1990 Namibia, the last remaining colony in Africa, attained independence.

Nansen, Fridtjof (1861–1930), Norwegian explorer, diplomat and internationalist. Born at Store-Fron, near Oslo; led the first expedition to cross Greenland (1888) and in 1893 allowed his ship, *Fram*, to be locked in the ice so that it could drift across the polar basin. During the eighteen-month expedition Nansen and a companion travelled by sledge and ski to a more northerly point than any earlier explorer. Nansen's exploits made him a national hero at the turn of the century and facilitated his entry into politics. He worked for Norwegian independence (►Norway) and became Norway's first diplomatic envoy to London in 1905. He was an ardent champion of the League of Nations and organized relief work in Russia during the famine which followed the Civil War in 1920–21. For these services Nansen was awarded the Nobel Peace Prize for 1922.

Nassau Agreement (18 December 1962). The outcome of a meeting between President Kennedy and the British Prime Minister, Harold Macmillan, at Nassau in the Bahamas. The meeting was intended to strengthen Anglo-American collaboration. The principal aspect of the agreement was the provision by the United States of Polaris missiles for Royal Navy submarines, normally operating under

NATO command. Such Anglo-American nuclear collaboration was resented by President de Gaulle, who cited the Agreement as proof that the British were not yet sufficiently Europe-minded to enter the Common Market. His veto on Macmillan's application to join the ►European Community followed within four weeks of the Nassau Agreement.

Nasser, Gamal Abdel (1918–70), Egyptian national leader. Born on the middle Nile at Beni Mor, near Asyut, and educated at Cairo Military Academy where he subsequently became an instructor. From 1942 onwards he secretly encouraged among the cadets and junior officers a republican, anti-British and patriotic movement, hostile to the great landowners. This movement – known from 1948 onwards as the Free Officers Movement – spread rapidly after Egypt's failure against ►Israel in 1948, a war in which Nasser fought as a major and in which he was appalled at the corruption and inefficiency of his countrymen. Brigadier Mohammed ►Neguib, as spokesman of the Free Officers, forced the abdication of King ►Farouk and set up a ruling junta of which Colonel Nasser was the dominant figure (23 July 1952). On the proclamation of the republic in the following June Nasser became Minister of the Interior and deputy to President Neguib, taking over the premiership on 17 April 1954 and succeeding Neguib as President on the following 17 November. Nasser secured British withdrawal from their bases on the ►Suez Canal and achieved a limited social revolution by breaking up the great estates. His main hopes rested on industrialization and the extension of arable lands, both of which he believed could be accomplished by the building of a High Dam at Aswan. When he failed to get Anglo-American financial backing for the Dam, Nasser announced the nationalization of the Suez Canal Company (26 July 1956). There followed the ►'Suez Crisis' and the ►Sinai Campaign of Israel, which increased Nasser's prestige and popularity among all Arab peoples since he appeared successfully to defy the West. This prestige enabled him to enjoy three years (1956–9) when Nasserism as a Pan-Arab force dominated the Middle East, establishing the ►United Arab Republic, a federation with Syria, in February 1958 and also securing links with the ►Yemen and with the new republic in ►Iraq. By 1961, however, Nasserism had lost much of its appeal outside Egypt although Nasser was still accepted as protector of socialist independence movements in Africa. By 1966 left-wing extremists among the Arabs were forcing Nasser to take an increasingly hostile stand against Israel, action which prompted massive retaliation by the Israelis in the ►Six-Day War of 1967. Egypt's staggering defeat led Nasser to resign, on 9 June, a decision reconsidered next day after large-scale demonstrations of support in the Egyptian cities. Although Nasser remained the head of a reconstruction government and kept close links with Moscow, he also improved relations with the United States and was criticized by the Palestine Liberation Organization for his cautious statesmanship (1969–70). He died suddenly from a heart attack on 28 September 1970 after mediating in the civil war in ►Jordan. His friend and coeval, Anwar ►Sadat, succeeded him as President.

National Health Service. The British National Health Service Act, introduced by Attlee's Labour Government, became law on 6 November 1946. It instituted a comprehensive state health service, effective from 5 July 1948. The Act was intended to provide free diagnosis and treatment of illness, at home or in hospital, and included dental and ophthalmic services. The Act – a personal triumph for the Minister of Health, ➤Bevan – realized a long-standing demand within the Labour movement. Although private practice was maintained, the Act revolutionized medical and dental service; the Minister of Health became responsible for 2,688 hospitals in England and Wales, leaving only 352 outside governmental control. The National Health Service was expensive, and successive governments had to impose charges for spectacles, prescriptions, dental treatment and amenity beds in hospital. The first of these charges was introduced as early as April 1951 by the Labour Chancellor of the Exchequer, Gaitskell – a shilling on every prescription and half the cost of dentures and spectacles. Rising costs have subsequently placed the service in considerable difficulty and the Thatcher administrations looked critically at the basic concept of the NHS. Legislation in 1990 established NHS Trusts; further reforms changed community care administration (1993) and set up new regional NHS Executives and new Health Authorities, while also creating two levels of fundholding for general practitioners, dependent on their number of patients. Blair's Labour Government proposed a major restructuring of the NHS and, to mark its fiftieth anniversary in 1998, promised to inject £21 billion pounds of public funds into the service over seven years.

National Party (New Zealand). A combination of the United and Reform Parties in New Zealand, created as an anti-Labour conservative bloc in 1936 and forming governments, 1949–57, 1960–72 and 1975–84. The best-known National Party leader was Sir Keith ➤Holyoake.

National Party (South Africa). Originally formed by General ➤Hertzog in 1914–15 and shared in the coalition government of 1924–33 which instituted an industrial colour bar throughout the Union of South Africa. The party was totally reformed by ➤Malan in 1935; many of its members sympathized with Nazi Germany and were anti-British and neutralist; all favoured Afrikaner dominance and accepted ➤apartheid. The election of 1948 gave Malan a firm majority and the party remained in power from that date, ➤Strijdom, ➤Verwoerd and ➤Vorster succeeding Malan as leaders and Prime Ministers. Secession from the Commonwealth and the establishment of an Afrikaner Republic – long a tenet of the more-committed party members – was achieved in May 1961. P.W ➤Botha succeeded Vorster as party leader and later State President, handing over both posts to F.W. ➤de Klerk in 1989.

National Works Council (Australian). A body established by the government of John ➤Curtin in January 1944 to supervise a joint federal and state public-works programme for implementation at the end of the war. The project aroused criticism since it proposed considerable public investment, principally financed by the states.

Native Land Settlement Act (1949). A reform carried through the New Zealand parliament of considerable benefit to the ➤Maoris.

NATO. ➤North Atlantic Treaty Organization.

Nazi Party. Abbreviated form of the National Socialist German Workers' Party (NSDAP), adopted by a political movement in Munich (October 1920) which had been founded as a German Workers' Party a year earlier, ➤Hitler becoming the seventh party member. Nazism was a German manifestation of the right-wing romantic authoritarianism which produced ➤fascism in Italy. But Hitler, while using the ritual of fascism, imposed his personality on the Nazi Party: members of the party had to accept his anti-Semitism, his belief in the superiority of the Aryan peoples (of whom the Germans were the 'master race'), and his determination to secure revision of the 'iniquitous' Treaty of ➤Versailles. Mass unemployment caused by the economic ➤Depression allowed the Nazi Party to expand rapidly in the period 1930–32, redeeming the fiasco of the ➤Munich Putsch of 1923 and enabling Hitler to become Chancellor on 30 January 1933. Party membership in Germany grew from 176,000 in 1929 to 2 million in February 1933 and to 6 million in 1944. The Nazi Party disintegrated in 1945, and its revival is officially forbidden by the constitution of the German Federal Republic.

Nazi–Soviet Pact. A treaty of non-aggression signed by ➤Molotov and ➤Ribbentrop in Moscow on 23 August 1939. The published terms included pledges to maintain neutrality if either country was at war; secret clauses gave a free hand to Germany in Lithuania and western Poland and to Russia in Latvia, Estonia, Finland, ➤Bessarabia and eastern Poland. A later secret agreement (28 September 1939) extended the German area in Poland and transferred Lithuania to the Soviet sphere of influence. The Pact was a major change in policy for both countries: the Russians were affronted by the ➤Munich Agreement, angered by the failure of Britain and France to accept Soviet terms for an alliance, and willing to precipitate war between 'the two imperialist camps' while expanding westwards. The Germans were willing to postpone ambitions for ➤*Lebensraum* in the Ukraine, so as to secure the isolation of Poland. Hitler regarded the Pact as such a diplomatic triumph that he was prepared to risk a European war, which followed within a fortnight. Friction developed between Germany and the Soviet Union in the late summer of 1940 when the Russians enlarged their sphere in south-eastern Europe. 'Operation ➤Barbarossa', the German invasion of the USSR on 22 June 1941, broke the Pact.

Neguib, Mohammed (1901–84), Egyptian President and general. Born in Khartoum of half-Sudanese origin, and achieved international fame as the brigadier responsible for overthrowing King ➤Farouk in July 1952. He was titular head of a junta of Egyptian officers, the real leader of whom was Colonel ➤Nasser. When the Egyptian republic was proclaimed on 18 June 1953 General Neguib became the first President. He lacked the political skill of Nasser and was gradually isolated by the younger army officers, resigning and retiring from public life in November 1954.

Nehru, Jawaharlal (1889–1964), Indian Prime Minister. Born at Allahabad, educated at Harrow and Trinity College, Cambridge, reading chemistry but practising as a barrister on his return home in 1912. Together with his father, the distinguished lawyer and journalist Motilal Nehru (1861–1931), he became active for the Indian Congress movement after the ➤Amritsar shootings of 1919. He was arrested and imprisoned in 1921, spending more than nine of the next twenty-five years in gaol and long periods under partial restraint. In 1926–7 he visited continental Europe and, as a Soviet guest in Moscow, was impressed by Marxism. The support of ➤Gandhi gained him the Presidency of the Congress movement in 1929, and he was the chief tactician of the campaign for independence until 1947 when he became Prime Minister and Foreign Minister. His anti-colonial and non-aligned foreign policy owed much to his perception that the 'cold war' would inevitably lead to a thaw. He mediated in Korea (1951) and Vietnam (1954), as well as sending Indian troops on UN peace keeping missions in Palestine, the Congo and Cyprus. Conservative critics in the West attacked his inactivity when the Chinese entered Tibet in 1960, his unwillingness to compromise over ➤Kashmir and his forceful annexation of Portuguese Goa in 1961. Many of his followers thought he was excessively restrained in the Kashmir dispute, but he was blamed for the defeat of Indian forces in border warfare with the Chinese in 1962. Possibly his agnosticism made him at times minimize the strength of religious sentiment among the peoples of the Indian subcontinent. His successes include the rationalization of Hindu laws and the acceptance, among individualistic and suspicious rural communities, of economic plans for a mixed economy. His death, at the end of May 1964, deprived India of moral leadership of the developing 'third world'. Lal ➤Shastri, who became India's Prime Minister on Nehru's death, was himself succeeded by Nehru's daughter, Mrs Indira ➤Gandhi, twenty months later.

Netherlands. A constitutional kingdom under the House of Orange, existing within its present frontiers since 1839 although dynastically linked with ➤Luxembourg until 1890: neutral in the First World War, invaded by Germany on 10 May 1940 and liberated September 1944 to March 1945. Entry into the customs union ➤Benelux of 1947 was followed by membership of the ➤European Economic Community from January 1958 onwards. The kingdom was also a founder member of ➤NATO in 1949. Until the Second World War the Dutch were the third largest colonial power: the loss of most of the Dutch East Indies (➤Indonesia) created economic and social problems at home, among them the discontent of South Moluccan exiles who were responsible for terrorist outrages in December 1975 and September 1977. The last Dutch East Indian possession, West Irian on ➤New Guinea, became Indonesian in May 1963. A 'Statute of the Realm', effective from 29 December 1954, allowed the remaining Dutch overseas territories in South America and the West Indies to enjoy autonomy in domestic affairs. Surinam (formerly Dutch Guiana) became fully independent, 25 November 1975.

Neuilly, Treaty of (27 November 1919). The peace treaty with Bulgaria after the First World War: western Thrace was ceded to Greece (thereby cutting off Bulgaria from the Aegean) and two small areas were ceded to Yugoslavia. Romania retained the southern ►Dobrudja acquired after the Balkan Wars. Bulgaria was liable for ►reparations and had to limit her army to 20,000 men. These terms were less severe than those imposed on the other defeated states, partly because Bulgaria had influential British sympathizers and partly because it was accepted at the peace conference that major territorial changes in the Balkans would provoke war rather than help keep the peace.

New Deal. The social and economic reforms of President Franklin Roosevelt's first and second administrations. The first New Deal programme (1933–5) sought financial recovery and relief of unemployment: a Federal Emergency Relief Administration, an Economy Act and an Emergency Banking Relief Act stimulated confidence after the economic ►Depression. The Civilian Conservation Corps (1933–41) found work for 2 million in reforestation projects; the Civil Works Administration (CWA) employed 4 million people on public-works projects; the Tennessee Valley Authority (TVA), an independent public corporation, was responsible for building dams and hydroelectric power plants to serve parts of seven states; and industrial competition was regulated under federal supervision by the National Industrial Recovery Act. The second New Deal (1935–9) concentrated on social security for the working population and on protecting small farmers. At the same time it included the setting up of the Works Progress Administration (WPA) to coordinate many earlier projects. The New Deal aroused opposition as a form of 'creeping socialism', and in 1936–7 there was a conflict between the Administration and the Supreme Court caused by the judiciary's attempt to block social federal legislation as 'unconstitutional', but the federal protection afforded by the programme found work for 10 million unemployed.

New Economic Policy (NEP). A relaxation of communist economic practice in Russia introduced by ►Lenin at the Tenth Party Congress in March 1921 after peasant disturbances and riots caused by a shortage of food. The NEP allowed some freedom of internal trade, permitted limited private commerce and re-established state banks. These measures principally benefited the peasants and improved the efficiency of food distribution. Doctrinaire Marxists did not approve of the NEP and it was formally abolished in January 1929 after the Fifteenth Party Congress had backed Stalin's desire for collectivization of agriculture under the first ►Five-Year Plan.

Newfoundland. An English colony was established in Newfoundland by Sir Humphrey Gilbert in 1583, but the colony was neglected, except by the fishing trade, until the middle of the nineteenth century, when responsible government was conceded to the island (1855). Newfoundland was granted dominion status in 1917. The world ➤Depression of 1929–31 led to the complete financial collapse of Newfoundland. A Royal Commission reported in February 1933 on the seriousness of the economic situation and recommended that the island should lose dominion status, accepting control from a nominated commission of seven. This system was instituted in February 1934: British loans helped the island acquire new economic strength and enjoy great prosperity during the Second World War, when many US bases were established there. The British Labour Government authorized the election of a Newfoundland Convention in June 1946 to discuss the future position of the island. A referendum held on 3 June 1948 was indecisive: 64,900 voters wanted responsible self-government; 64,100 wanted integration with Canada; 23,300 wished to remain under a nominated commission, with British financial aid. A second referendum on 22 July, omitting the third possibility, gave 78,323 in favour of federation with Canada and 71,334 for the return of responsible government. Negotiations continued in Ottawa for several months and Newfoundland became the tenth province of Canada at midnight on 31 March 1949.

New Guinea. Island four times the size of Great Britain, the eastern half forming ➤Papua New Guinea. The western half was part of the Netherlands East Indies until 1963 when it joined ➤Indonesia as West Irian, the name later changing to Irian Jaya. There was continuous fighting in New Guinea against the Japanese invaders from January 1942 until the surrender of the last jungle units in September 1945.

New Zealand. Captain James Cook first visited New Zealand in October 1769 but it was only with the foundation of the New Zealand Company in London in 1826 that any attempt was made to settle the islands and, even then, no progress was made until the establishment of a second company by Edward Gibbon Wakefield (1796–1862) in 1839. The colony was granted a constitution in 1852, with responsible government in 1856 and remained a self-governing colony until after the turn of the century, the conferment of dominion status being officially celebrated on 26 September 1907. The following years were marked by the growth in political influence of the farming communities in the North Island, especially in the premiership of W.F. ➤Massey, and the closer integration of the ➤Maoris in the life of what remained predominantly an Anglo-Scottish dominion. New Zealand troops distinguished themselves in both World Wars, notably at ➤Gallipoli and Messines, at the Olympus Pass and Thermopylae in April 1941, in Crete and Libya, and at ➤Cassino. After the Second World War the New Zealand Governments concentrated on the Pacific and the Far East, participating in ➤ANZUS and sending a contingent to Vietnam. Under ➤Savage and ➤Fraser, the Labour Governments of the period 1935–49 brought in extensive social legislation. Under ➤Holyoake the New Zealanders, who feared that their economy would suffer from British entry into the Common Market, achieved recognition of their problems from the European Community and strengthened free-trade links with Australia. From 1976 to 1984 the National Party Government of Robert Muldoon (1921–) was hampered by mounting inflation and rising unemployment and by a highly articulate anti-nuclear lobby. Over the following five years Labour, under David Lange (1932–), carried hostility to nuclear power to such lengths that New Zealand virtually opted out of its ANZUS commitments. Lange supported a South Pacific Forum, which brought together Fiji, Western Samoa and other Commonwealth islands in opposition to ►nuclear tests in the Pacific. Domestic issues in New Zealand were dominated by the ►Maori land-rights campaign and by demands for modernizing the constitution. A referendum in 1992 supported the introduction of proportional representation for the House of Representatives. The General Election of 12 October 1996, the first to use the new system, produced no outright winner. Jim Bolger, the National Party Prime Minister since 1990, continued in office, forming a coalition with the New Zealand Party two months later. He was succeeded on 8 December 1997 by Jenny Shipley, who thus became New Zealand's first woman Prime Minister.

Nicaragua, the largest and most thinly populated of the Central American republics. The region was under Spanish rule from 1522 to 1821. Like ►El Salvador it then joined the Central American Federation until gaining independence in 1838. Rival factions in two of the main towns, 'Liberals' in Leon and 'Conservatives' in Granada, long prevented any real sense of political unity in the republic. Pressure from successive administrations in Washington kept US marines in Nicaragua from 1916 to 1933. From 1936 until 1979 the republic was controlled by the immensely wealthy Somoza family: Anastasio Somoza Garcia was President from 1936 until his assassination in September 1956, except for a brief interlude in 1947; his son, Luis, followed him in the Presidency, but it was a second son, General Anastasio Somoza Debayle, who gained most notoriety for the family, as President from 1967 to 1973 and from 1974 until July 1979. American business interests, which had made many Americans supporters of the Somozas as anti-communists, were officially discouraged by the Carter Administration because of Somoza's violation of human rights in a long campaign against the guerrillas of the Sandinista Liberation Front. This was a radical movement which won the backing of the Church, the middle classes and the trade unions in opposition to Somoza's personal rule. Heavy fighting in June and July 1979, including the bombardment of Managua (the capital) by troops loyal to Somoza, cost some 50,000 lives. Somoza himself fled the country. He was assassinated in Paraguay (17 September 1980). By then Sandinista supporters were in a majority on the ruling junta and on the nominated Council of State. The Reagan Administration backed and armed a Somocista insurgent movement, the National Democratic Front ('Contras'), who attacked oil installations in Nicaragua in January and February 1984 to begin a civil war which took a heavy toll of civilian life over the following four years. A free presidential election in November 1984 was won by the Sandinista candidate,

Daniel Ortega, who began a six-year term on 10 January 1985 and who, from February to June 1988, played a patient role in talks designed to end the fighting. Opinion in the US Congress had turned against armed support for the Contras. In the election of February 1990 Ortega's Sandinistas were defeated. A ceasefire, achieved in the same month, was frequently broken during the rest of the year but the new right-wing President, Violeta Barrios de Chamorro, continued to pursue a policy of national reconciliation. Political tension in Managua brought Nicaragua once more to the verge of civil war in December 1992, but the ceasefire survived and, in July 1995, President Chamorro accepted curbs on his powers as head of the executive.

Nicholas II (1868–1918, reigned 1894–1917), Tsar of Russia. Son of Alexander III and the Danish-born Marie Feodorovna, a sister of Queen Alexandra of England. As Tsarevich Nicholas undertook a world tour, opening the terminus of the Trans-Siberian Railway in Vladivostok (1891) and narrowly escaping assassination in Japan. Interest in Far Eastern affairs continued into his reign. Soon after his accession he married Alexandra of Hesse (granddaughter of Queen Victoria), who became a fanatical believer in the religious and autocratic traditions of Tsardom, urging Nicholas to show a strength of character he did not possess. Nicholas had no sympathy with what he called the 'senseless dreams' of political reform. Industrial unrest, bad harvests and defeat by Japan led to a state of ►revolution in 1905. The Tsar summoned a ►Duma but continued to distrust representative government and, being a bad judge of men, listened to poor advisers. From 1906 both Nicholas and his consort were unduly influenced by the charlatan ►Rasputin. Although unsuited for high military office, Nicholas assumed supreme command on the Russian front in September 1915; and it was at his headquarters in Pskov that he was forced to abdicate, on 15 March 1917 (►Russian Revolution). The imperial family were kept under guard at Tsarskoe Selo until August 1917, then at Tobolsk in Siberia for eight months and, from 30 April 1918, at Ekaterinburg (now Sverdlovsk) in the Urals. The possibility of rescue by 'White' counter-revolutionaries appears to have prompted the execution of Nicholas, on the orders of the local Bolshevik commander (16 July 1918). His wife, three daughters and son were reported killed at the same time. Eighty years later their remains were interred in the small cathedral within the fortress of St Peter and St Paul, the traditional burial place of the Tsars at St Petersburg. The ceremony on 17 July 1998 was attended by President ►Yeltsin who declared, 'By burying the innocent victims we want to expiate the sins of our ancestors'. Although DNA tests had authenticated the bones, the Russian Orthodox Patriarchate declined to accept scientific evidence and took no part in the funeral rites, which were conducted by priests whose prayers never mentioned the victims by name.

Nigeria. Became a British protectorate in 1899, although the British military conquest of northern Nigeria was not completed until March 1903 and the protectorate did not come under a unified administration until January 1914.

Between the wars Nigeria was the largest British colony in Africa; administration was peaceful but education and the economy backward; a few privileged Nigerians from the south became rich on trading concessions and secured the opportunities for an elitist education, mainly abroad. One of these beneficiaries, Dr ➤Azikiwe, was able to establish a newspaper chain and gain a moral leadership that made him a natural choice as Governor-General (later President) when Nigeria received independent dominion status on 1 October 1960, becoming a republic within the Commonwealth three years later. The government was headed by Azikiwe's rival, Tafawa ➤Balewa, Prime Minister from August 1957 until his assassination in January 1966. The Nigerian Republic was based on a federal structure, with separate regional constitutions for the Northern, Eastern, Western and Mid-Western regions. This system tended to emphasize regional differences, arousing resentment, most frequently on a tribal basis (Ibo, Yoruba, Aro, Angas, Hausa) but sometimes as conflict between the Islamic north (Kano, Borno, Sokoto) and the richer south-eastern lands, where prices began to soar after the discovery of oil in 1958. Strikes, corruption and urban anarchy led to a military *coup* on 14 January 1966, originally staged by junior officers but taken over by the army commander, Major-General Ironsi, who was himself ambushed and killed on 29 July 1966. Ironsi's chief-of-staff, Colonel Yakubu Gowon (1934–), quelled a mutiny in the north and became head of a federal military government. Two months later many Ibos were massacred in further violence in northern Nigeria: the chief military commander in eastern Nigeria, Colonel Ojukwu, began preparing for the secession of his Ibo people, an act formally undertaken on 30 May 1967 with the creation of ➤Biafra. General Gowon countered the Biafran movement politically by creating a new federal structure for the republic, with twelve divisions rather than four, but when this move failed to satisfy the Ibos, he ordered federal troops into Biafra (7 July 1967). The Nigerian Civil War continued until mid-January 1970. Reconstruction and rehabilitation weakened the economy still further, and a major development programme of public works linked financially to anticipated oil revenues ran into difficulties. On 29 August 1975, while General Gowon was attending a meeting of the ➤Organization of African Unity in Kampala, he was ousted as President by a military *coup* which proclaimed Brigadier Murtala Mohammad as Head of State. Further constitutional reforms, cutting across tribal boundaries by increasing the states of the Federation to nineteen, were announced in January 1976, but a month later President Murtala Mohammad was killed in an abortive *coup*. General Olusegun Obasanjo, who succeeded him, announced that free elections would be held in October 1979 and summoned a constituent assembly to debate the future form of government, although insisting that no political parties should be organized and no political meetings held until twelve months before the proposed election. This strict programme was, in essentials, fulfilled. On 1 October 1979 General Obasanjo voluntarily ceased to exercise the powers of the Federal Military Government, handing the executive over to President Shehu Shagari, leader of the NPN (National Party of Nigeria), the most successful of the five political organizations which had contested the Presidential election seven weeks before. President Shagari cautiously restored civilian rule, seeking to encourage respect for human rights in all communities. There was, however, serious rioting by Muslim fanatics in December 1980, with extremists killing so many 'infidels' that the Nigerian army had to be sent to Kano in force; a thousand civilians were killed, and a few months later there were widespread complaints of corruption. The total collapse of the economy in 1983 prompted a bloodless coup on New Year's Eve which overthrew Shagari. There followed a period of harsh military rule under Mohammad Bubari until August 1985 and thereafter under Ibrahim Babangida, who stressed the Islamic links of Nigeria even though there were few Muslims in the southern half of the Federation. In July 1987 General Babangida promised a return to civilian rule by 1992. In 1993 a civilian Transitional Council prepared for a return to non-military rule. A presidential election in June 1993 appears to have been won by the Social Democrat candidate, Chief Moshood Abiola, but the military refused to accept the verdict of the voters. General Sanni Abacha (1943–98) seized power on 17 November 1993, imprisoned Abiola and other dissidents and, despite protests from other Commonwealth countries, executed nine human rights activists of the Ogoni people, including the eminent playwright Ken Saro-Wiwa. Nigeria was accordingly suspended from membership of the Commonwealth on 11 November 1995. General Abacha died from a heart attack on 8 June 1998. His deputy, General Abdusalam Abubaka, succeeded him as Nigeria's Head of State, amid hopes of release for Chief Abiola. But on 7 July Abiola himself died from a heart attack while talking to an American envoy. Although a post-mortem by foreign medical specialists confirmed he had died from natural causes, there was widespread unrest. On 20 July General Abubaka announced that Nigeria would return to civilian rule on 29 May 1999, following democratic elections; all charges against political prisoners were quashed; army officers were told to encourage their troops to accept the concept of democracy.

'Night of the Long Knives'. The events in Germany on the night of 29–30 June 1934, and the following two days, when Hitler used the SS units in the private army of ▶Himmler to murder the older and more radical Nazi private army known as the SA (Sturm-Abteilung), or brownshirts, led by Captain Ernst Roehm. At the same time other rivals within the Nazi Party were shot, as also were some non-party figures including General Kurt von Schleicher, Hitler's immediate predecessor as German Chancellor (2 December 1932 to 28 January 1933). Hitler later announced that seventy-seven people were summarily executed that weekend, for an alleged conspiracy: some were shot at the Stadelheim Prison in Munich, some at the Lichterfelde Military Academy near Berlin. Almost certainly the killings claimed more than 100 victims. They made Hitler indisputable leader of the Nazi Revolution while, at the same time, ridding the movement of followers unacceptable to the principal members of the German officer corps. Without this purge, Hitler would not have been able so rapidly to win acceptance from the officer corps as head of state when the ailing President ➤Hindenburg at last died, five weeks later. The dramatic name, 'Night of the Long Knives', was first used publicly by Hitler himself in a speech at the Kroll Opera House, Berlin, 13 July 1934.

Nixon, Richard Milhous (1913–94), thirty-seventh President of the USA. Born in Yorba Linda, California; educated at Duke University, North Carolina, practised as a lawyer, served in the US Navy 1942–6, and was then elected as a Republican representative to Congress, where he became well known for his zeal in hounding those suspected of 'Un-American Activities', notably ➤Hiss. Nixon was elected to the Senate in 1950 and became Vice-President under ➤Eisenhower in January 1953. Difficult visits to Peru, Venezuela and the Soviet Union, together with a statesmanlike approach to the settlement of a steel strike, won Nixon wide popular support, and he was preferred to Nelson Rockefeller as Republican candidate for the 1960 election, losing narrowly to Kennedy. Two years later he was again unsuccessful in a contest for the Governorship of California: he ascribed his defeat to the hostility of 'the media', and it seemed as if his political career was over. The poor showing of the Republicans in the 1964 election encouraged his supporters to 'run' him for 1968, when he gained the nomination and, campaigning endlessly and vigorously, defeated Hubert Humphrey, largely through the Democratic administration's unpopularity over the Vietnam War. As President (1969–74) Nixon sought to stimulate the economy and check inflation while, in foreign affairs, gradually reducing involvement in Vietnam, easing tension with the Soviet Union, and improving diplomatic contacts with communist China. The brilliance of his aide and later Secretary of State, ➤Kissinger, ensured that Nixon's most lasting achievements were concerned with world politics: the Vietnam ceasefire in January 1973; personal visits by the President to Peking (February 1972) and to Moscow (May 1972); agreement on limiting strategic weapons of aggression. At home, the Democratic control of Congress prevented four-fifths of his legislative programme becoming law. But Nixon's prestige was sufficiently good for him to gain a remarkable electoral triumph in 1972 against the Democrat, George McGovern: Nixon won forty-nine of the fifty states and 61 per cent of the popular vote. His second term was marked, in the first instance, by a financial scandal which led to the resignation of Vice-President Spiro Agnew (December 1973) and then by the mounting criticism of the President for having connived at illegal practices in the ➤Watergate Scandal. Steps were taken to secure Nixon's removal from office by impeachment, but before this process was far advanced, he became the first US President to resign from office (9 August 1974) having received from his successor, President Gerald ➤Ford, a comprehensive pardon. Nixon retired immediately to private life in California.

Nkomo, Joshua (1917–), Zimbabwean nationalist. Born at Matopos, Matabeleland, and educated in Natal and at Johannesburg before working for several years as a welfare officer and trade-union organizer on the Rhodesian railways at Bulawayo.

He was President of the African National Congress from 1957 to 1959, when it was banned in Rhodesia. After spending some months in London, he returned to his homeland where, in 1960, he founded the National Democratic Party, which was promptly proscribed by the authorities. Next year he set up ZAPU (Zimbabwe African People's Union) which he continued to lead secretly when it was declared an illegal body in 1962. These activities brought Nkomo a six-month prison sentence in 1963 and he was then detained as a subversive agitator in Rhodesia from November 1964 to December 1974. British emissaries recognized his standing in the community when they visited him in detention during their abortive quest for a Rhodesian settlement in 1968 and 1971. He led a delegation from the African National Council in talks with Ian ➤Smith at Geneva in October 1976. But from 1976 until 1979 Nkomo encouraged guerrilla operations in Rhodesia as joint-leader with Robert ➤Mugabe of the Patriotic Front. ZAPU's revolutionary army (ZIPRA) operated from Zambia, and on 13 April 1979 Rhodesian commandos destroyed Nkomo's house in a raid on ZAPU headquarters near Lusaka. Five months later Nkomo was in London, participating in the Lancaster House Conference which agreed, at the end of the year, to establish a Zimbabwe–Rhodesian state and to conclude a ceasefire in the guerrilla war. Nkomo returned home in triumph in January 1980 but ZAPU did not match the success of Mugabe's ZANU in the new Zimbabwe's first election, and it was Mugabe rather than the better-known Nkomo who became Zimbabwe's Prime Minister. Mugabe appointed Nkomo his Minister of Home Affairs, but there was mounting friction between the supporters of the two men. Serious skirmishing in old ZIPRA strongholds around Bulawayo in November 1980 was followed two months later by the removal of Nkomo from his department, although he remained a minister without portfolio in the government. The uneasy Nkomo–Mugabe partnership finally broke down when caches of arms were allegedly found in Nkomo's farms. There was, however, a reconciliation in December 1987, with the merger of ZAPU and ZANU and the return of Nkomo to the government.

Nkrumah, Kwame (1909–72), President of Ghana. Born at Nkroful, near Axim, in what was then the western Gold Coast, educated at Achimota College, Lincoln University in Pennsylvania, and the London School of Economics. In 1949 he founded the Convention People's Party, seeking immediate self-government for the Gold Coast, which he renamed ➤Ghana. His party won the general election of June 1954 and he became Prime Minister of the Gold Coast which, as Ghana, achieved dominion status in March 1957. Nkrumah became President when Ghana became a republic within the Commonwealth on 1 July 1960. He was respected as a Pan-African leader throughout the central and western regions of the continent, encouraging closer union with neighbouring states, supporting Nasser and the Arabs, remaining technically non-aligned but showing great hostility towards South Africa and some sympathy for the Chinese and Romanian forms of socialism. He distrusted French-oriented groupings among the African states and resented the mounting influence of other independence leaders who did not respect him as 'the Redeemer' and 'Africa's Gandhi'. At home, his rule became increasingly dictatorial and from 1963 to 1965 he interfered with the conduct of the judiciary. Governmental extravagance, both personal and for public works, together with a slump in cocoa prices, led to inflation and economic chaos in 1965–6. At the end of February 1966 Nkrumah travelled to China on an official visit. While he was out of the country, his government was overthrown by the army. He enjoyed sanctuary briefly in Guinea, later travelling to Romania for medical treatment, dying in a sanatorium there at the end of April 1972. Ghana acknowledged its debt to him as a national leader at a funeral in his birthplace three months later.

Normandy Landings. The Allied invasion of Europe began with landings on the Normandy coast between the river Orne and St Marcouf on 6 June 1944 (D-Day). US troops landed on the western beaches: British and Canadian on the eastern, General ➤Eisenhower was Supreme Allied Commander, the immediate field command devolving on General ➤Montgomery. Artificial harbours ('Mulberries') were towed across the Channel and linked to the shore by articulated steel roadways so that armoured vehicles, guns and equipment could be landed on the beaches. Heavy fighting continued in Normandy for a month, the US First Army capturing the port of Cherbourg on 27 June and the British and Canadians entering Caen on 9 July, thus enabling tanks to break through the German defences. Paris was liberated on 25 August, Brussels on 2 September and the German pre-war frontier crossed near Aachen on 12 September (D-Day + 68).

North African Campaigns. When Italy entered the Second World War in June 1940 Mussolini wished Marshal Graziani to advance from Libya to Cairo and the Suez Canal, thus achieving imperial prestige for the fascist regime and opening the route to the Middle East and the Persian oilfields. British strategy, at first defensive, became later concerned with clearing the southern Mediterranean shores and securing a stepping-stone to the Italian peninsula. Graziani's offensive began on 15 September 1940 but petered out after penetrating some sixty miles across the Egyptian frontier. A major British offensive on 9–11 December 1940 destroyed the Italian threat and in two months occupied most of Cyrenaica. In the spring of 1941 ➤Rommel and the Afrika Korps again advanced into Egypt, to be checked by ➤Wavell in June and repulsed by ➤Auchinleck, November 1941 to January 1942. In May and June 1942 Rommel's second offensive inflicted a severe defeat on the British Eighth Army, although Cairo and the Nile delta were saved by Auchinleck at the first battle of Alamein in July 1942. The ➤Alexander and ➤Montgomery offensive, which began with the second battle of Alamein on 23 October 1942, carried allied forces across Libya and into ➤Tunisia within four months. British and American forces landed in French north-west Africa (➤'Torch') on 8 November 1942. The two armies converged on Tunis, where the Germans offered a sustained defence. All Axis troops in North Africa formally surrendered on 12 May 1943.

North Atlantic Treaty Organization (NATO). A 'North Atlantic Treaty' was signed in Washington on 4 April 1949 by the Foreign Ministers of Belgium, Britain, Canada, Denmark, France, Iceland, Italy, Netherlands, Norway, Portugal and the United States, providing for mutual assistance should any one member of the alliance be attacked (although not automatically providing for immediate military action). Greece and Turkey joined NATO on 18 February 1952, the German Federal Republic on 9 May 1955. The treaties were a product of the ➤'Cold War' and the blockade of ➤Berlin, but the organization itself was built up as an integrated military force under the later tensions imposed by the Korean War from September 1950 onwards. Friction has developed at times between American policies, which aimed at using NATO as a means of creating a political and economic 'Atlantic Community', and the needs of the growing European Community. President de Gaulle's suspicion of American intentions led to the withdrawal of French forces from NATO command in the spring of 1966, requiring the removal of NATO headquarters from Fontainebleau to Brussels. Disputes between two NATO members, Greece and Turkey, have at times weakened the effectiveness of the organization in the Mediterranean, the Greeks withdrawing all their units from NATO on 17 August 1964 because of tension with Turkey over ➤Cyprus. A compromise over the alliance's responsibilities in the Aegean enabled Greece to re-enter NATO in October 1980. Spain joined in May 1982. With the ending of the Cold War, a series of conferences in the winter of 1990–91 recommended major cuts and redeployment, including the setting up of a multinational 'rapid reaction' force of some 100,000 men, able to be transported by air to potential danger-spots. NATO forces were deployed in ➤Bosnia-Herzegovina and the Adriatic from 1992 until 1995 supporting UN peacekeeping, and remaining to seek implementation of the ➤Dayton Accord. At the same time a 'Partnership for Peace' programme, outlined in 1994, extended associate membership to twenty-seven states, each of whom collaborates with NATO at its headquarters in Belgium and may seek aid from full members if there is a direct threat to its territorial integrity. Proposals to extend full NATO membership to former Warsaw Pact countries angered Russia. However, in late May 1997 ➤Yeltsin travelled to Paris for a meeting with Western political leaders and signed the 'Founding Act on Mutual Relations, Co-operation and Security between NATO and the Russian Federation'. Six weeks later, at a summit conference in Madrid, the Czech Republic, Hungary and Poland were invited to join NATO; it was anticipated that eventually Slovenia and Romania would become members; a 'special relationship' was established with ➤Ukraine.

Northcliffe, Lord (Alfred Charles William Harmsworth, 1865–1922, created a baron 1905, viscount 1917), British newspaper magnate. Born the son of a Dublin barrister, became a journalist on leaving school in 1880 and founded *Answers* in 1888, the first weekly to use a crisp style and sensationalism. Assisted by his younger brother, Harold (in 1913 created Viscount Rothermere, 1868–1940), he built up a successful business in periodicals, branching out into daily journalism with the *Evening News*, 1894. In May 1896 he founded the *Daily Mail*, on sale at a halfpenny, half the price of most dailies. By 1899 the *Mail* had twice the circulation of any other newspaper. He founded the *Daily Mirror*, 1903, and was proprietor of the *Observer*, 1905–11, and *The Times*, 1908–22, but always regarded the *Daily Mail* as his most important enterprise. Largely for publicity purposes he financed new ventures in motoring, aviation and polar exploration. Throughout the First World War he pressed for vigorous leadership, heading a diplomatic mission to America in 1917, and became director of propaganda to enemy countries on his return. In this role he encouraged the subject-nationalities of Austria–Hungary to demand independence. In later years Northcliffe suffered from megalomania, but his style and methods transformed British journalism, introducing the tendentious headline and the bright story which would appeal to a huge reading public.

Northern Ireland. In the seventeenth century Protestant immigrants, many of them Scottish Presbyterians, settled in parts of ➤Ulster, imposing a social pattern on certain areas different from the rest of the country: this division was unfortunately perpetuated by rival commemoration of the religious–dynastic conflicts in 1689–90. Irish Home Rule was opposed by the Protestants in the late nineteenth and early twentieth centuries ('Home Rule means Rome Rule') and civil war was endemic, 1913–14 and 1918–20. ➤Lloyd George established a separate parliament and executive government for six of the nine Ulster counties in 1921, thus creating 'Northern Ireland' as a distinctive part of the United Kingdom, returning members to the House of Commons but enjoying limited self-government. Friction developed within Northern Ireland during the late 1960s primarily over electoral laws which, by favouring owners of property, discriminated against the largely Catholic working-class population in Londonderry, Belfast and other towns. Legitimate grievances over special security powers, housing and social conditions also fed the Civil Rights movement, which staged a major demonstration in Londonderry on 5 October 1968. Fear of further disturbances forced the Belfast Government to ask for troops in April 1969. Bombings and shootings, encouraged by the ➤Irish Republican Army in the first instance, produced numerous outrages and led, in August 1971, to the internment of people suspected of membership of the IRA or of giving aid to it. The situation deteriorated early in 1972, with troops firing on a demonstration in favour of a unified Ireland at Londonderry on 30 January (➤'Bloody Sunday'). Eight weeks later the British Conservative Government suspended the Northern Ireland Constitution and imposed direct rule (31 March 1972) in the hopes of achieving a political settlement acceptable to both political–religious factions. A Northern Ireland Assembly was elected on 28 June 1973 but collapsed, through extremist Protestant intransigence, on 29 May 1974. A constitutional convention, meeting from 3 February to 5 March 1976, was no more successful. Direct rule continued, with outrages committed by both sides, the gloom relieved only by the hopeful overtures of the ➤Ulster Peace Movement, itself born of tragedy. Political initiatives by successive governments in London failed to satisfy the contending parties in Northern Ireland. At the same time, from the autumn of 1979 onwards, closer collaboration was established with the authorities in the Republic of ➤Ireland culminating in the inter-governmental Anglo-Irish Agreement concluded at Hillsborough in November 1985. The economic recession of 1979–82 hit Northern Ireland harder than any other part of the United Kingdom, producing a constantly higher level of unemployment. The first initiative taken by John Major's Government led, in the early summer of 1991, to ten weeks of all-party talks on the future of the province. The talks broke down because of Unionist opposition to Anglo-Irish governmental cooperation. But on 15 December 1993 the British and Irish prime ministers issued the joint Downing Street Declaration, a bilateral agreement on the need to end the Northern Ireland conflict. This undertaking advanced the peace process sufficiently for a ceasefire to be announced by the IRA on 31 August 1994 and by the 'loyalist' paramilitary command on 13 October. A second Downing Street Declaration on 28 November 1995, backed by President ➤Clinton, set up a commission chaired by the former US Senator George Mitchell, to secure the surrender of weapons before multi-party talks. When Clinton visited Belfast and Londonderry on 30 November he hoped the province would serve as 'a model of peace through tolerance'. The IRA broke the ceasefire ten weeks later; ➤Sinn Féin spokesmen were, in consequence, barred from peace talks at Stormont in June 1996. Soon after Labour's electoral victory in May 1997 Tony Blair and his Irish Secretary, Mo Mowlam, visited the province and said that government officials were ready for talks with Sinn Féin. 'Final' multi-party peace talks began at Stormont on 15 September, but with the Unionists treating with considerable suspicion Sinn Féin pledges to abide by George Mitchell's principles of democracy and non-violence. By the end of the month the talks were concentrating on constitutional issues, but it was not until the second week of April 1998 that last-minute concessions by spokesmen for both communities produced the ➤Good Friday Accord. Referenda in Northern Ireland and the Irish Republic on 22 May accepted the peace agreement: 81 per cent of the province's electorate went to the polls, with 71 per cent giving a 'Yes' vote. The Assembly Election was held on 25 June 1998: the Ulster Unionists emerged as the largest single party and when the Assembly held its first session six days later their leader, David Trimble, took office as Northern Ireland's First Minister. John Hume, the leader of the Social Democratic and Labour Party, became Deputy First Minister.

Norway. United to Denmark from fourteenth century until 1814 and to Sweden from 1814 until 1905. The Norwegians retained their own parliament (Storting) from 1807 onwards. A national consciousness, accompanied by a literary revival, in the late nineteenth century led to demands in the Storting for complete independence, especially after the adoption of universal suffrage in 1898. Dissolution of the union with Sweden, announced in the Storting on 7 June 1905 and confirmed by a plebiscite in August, was accepted by the Swedes and became effective, 26

October. Prince Charles of Denmark accepted the Norwegian throne, ruling as Haakon VII (1872–1957) until his death. Norway, neutral in the First World War, was surprised by a German air and naval invasion on 9 April 1940. Resistance continued until 10 June, especially in Narvik, held by Anglo-French forces against German attacks for eight weeks. A puppet administration was set up in Oslo under Vidkun ➤Quisling while King Haakon and his ministers continued to inspire resistance from their exile in London, the government returning to Oslo on 31 May 1945, the King a week later. Norway joined NATO in April 1949 and signed the treaty of accession to the European Economic Community in January 1972 but subsequently withdrew when a referendum in Norway showed a majority against membership of the Common Market. The outstanding statesman of the post-war era was the ➤Labour Party leader, Einar Gerhardsen (1897–1986), Prime Minister 1945–51 and 1955–65; his governments ensured that Norway became a largely self-dependent welfare state. The economy was transformed in the late 1970s by the rapid exploitation of Europe's largest offshore-oil and natural-gas deposits. In 1992 Norway for a second time applied to join the EEC, but a referendum on 28 November 1994 showed that the electorate again rejected membership of the ➤European Union with only a slight change of feeling since 1972.

Novibazar, Sanjak of. A corridor of mountainous territory which, in the nineteenth century, separated the principalities of Serbia and Montenegro, remaining a Turkish possession until 1912–13. The corridor, which extended for about 120 miles from the river Drina in the west to the river Ibar in the east, was constituted a sanjak (minor province) by Turkey in 1856. Austrian troops occupied the Sanjak from 1878 to 1908, partly to protect Bosnia-Herzegovina but mainly because the Austrians hoped to construct a continental trunk railway through the region linking the existing lines, Vienna–Sarajevo and Mitrovica–Constantinople. Technical difficulties made the route impossible. As soon as Austrian troops withdrew, Serbian nationalists claimed the Sanjak, which was overrun by Serbian and Montenegrin troops in the first Balkan War and was later absorbed in Yugoslavia. It is now within Serbia.

Novotný, Antonin (1904–75), Czechoslovak President. Born at Letnany, near Prague, a bricklayer's son, worked in an armaments factory, becoming a communist in 1921, and being detained in Mauthausen concentration camp, 1941–5. He was promoted within the Czechoslovak Communist Party after the disgrace and trial of Rudolf ➤Slansky in 1951–2, becoming First Secretary early in 1953, an office he held until replaced by ➤Dubček in January 1968. Novotný was also President of the Czechoslovak Republic from November 1957 until March 1968. He was, at heart, a dedicated Stalinist, never able to readjust to the peasant tantrums and folksy expedients of Khrushchev and his successors, and therefore increasingly isolated and unpopular in Czechoslovakia. In seeking to make the republic a 'machine works' for the entire socialist camp, he concentrated too much on heavy industry and there was a severe economic recession in 1961–3, with student demonstrations at the end of 1962. Novotný jettisoned a number of veteran ministers and officials, abandoned the third Czechoslovak five-year plan, and began to make political concessions to the less rigidly socialist Slovaks, seeking more flexibility for the economy. Mountingly intensive student discontent in Prague, backed by protests from Czech intellectuals, forced Novotný on the defensive from the early autumn of 1967. On 25 February 1968, in a last bid to check liberalization and assert his presidential powers, he sought the backing of Czech army officers for a march on Prague. When they refused, Novotný prepared his own withdrawal from political life. He resigned the Presidency on 22 March 1968: General ►Svoboda was elected his successor eight days later.

Nuclear Tests. The first ►atomic bomb test explosion was made, in great secrecy, near Alamogordo, New Mexico, on 16 July 1945. Subsequently the British tested atomic bombs on the Monte Bello islands, off north-west Australia, in October 1952, with further tests at Woomera in South Australia, at Emu and at Maralinga. The Soviet Union also developed an atomic bomb, beginning tests in Siberia in 1949. The Americans tested a hydrogen bomb at Enwetok atoll in mid-Pacific in May 1951 and, with greater publicity, at Bikini atoll in the Marshall Islands on 1 March 1954. The British, too, exploded a test thermo-nuclear bomb over Christmas Island in the south-western Pacific on 15 May 1957. French tests in the Pacific began in 1960, while the Chinese tested an atomic bomb in 1964 and a hydrogen bomb in 1967. By then there was mounting medical evidence of appalling consequences of atmospheric explosions, and a partial ►Test-Ban Treaty was concluded in August 1963, with the USA, USSR and Great Britain as the first signatories. Underground testing continued in the United States and the Soviet Union, while France and China refused to sign the treaty. Indignation at French testing on the Pacific atoll of Muroroa in French Polynesia led to strained relations between ►New Zealand and France, especially when French saboteurs mined the Greenpeace protesters' vessel *Rainbow Warrior* in Waitemata harbour, Auckland, on 11 July 1985. Later that year the New Zealanders and their South Pacific neighbours concluded the Treaty of Raratonga, declaring the southern Pacific Ocean a nuclear-free zone. In July 1995 President Chirac caused widespread hostility by authorizing a series of further underground nuclear tests in French Polynesia. In September 1996 Britain, America, China, France and Russia signed a Comprehensive Test-Ban Treaty. India – as yet a non-nuclear power – was invited to sign, but refused. Fresh international tension was caused by India's first series of nuclear tests, in May 1998. Pakistan responded by a series of tests announced a fortnight later.

Nuremberg Rallies. Nazi Party rallies were held on a site near the Dutzendteich, south-east of the north Bavarian city of Nuremberg, each September from 1933 to 1938. The rallies were carefully staged propaganda exercises: competitive games, torchlight processions and oratorical displays culminating in a major policy speech each year from Hitler. It was at one of the rallies (15 September 1935) that Hitler announced legislation reducing all Jews in Germany to second-class citizens. These 'Nuremberg laws' defined Jews, closed professions to Jews and denied them the right of marriage with non-Jews, forbidding sexual relations between Jews and non-Jews.

Nuremberg Trials. Thirteen trials of major war criminals were held in Nuremberg, 1945–7, presided over by American, British, French and Soviet judges. One hundred and seventy-seven Germans or Austrians were indicted: twenty-five were sentenced to death; twenty to life imprisonment; ninety-seven to shorter terms of imprisonment; thirty-five were acquitted. The charges were based on accepted principles of international law and conventions governing the conduct of war but the notion of a trial of vanquished by victors offended, and has continued to offend, many jurists. The principal trial (November 1945 to September 1946) involved the prosecution of twenty-one former Nazi leaders, of whom ten were subsequently hanged in the small hours of 16 October 1946 in the Nuremberg prison gymnasium: an eleventh war criminal – ➤Goering – committed suicide a few hours before execution. ➤Hess, sentenced to life imprisonment, was never released from Spandau prison.

Nuri-es-Said (1888–1958), Iraqi general and politician. Born at Kirkup in Mesopotamia and sent as a cadet to the staff college in Constantinople, fled to Egypt on the eve of the First World War, and became an early participant in the Arab Revolt, serving under T.E. ➤Lawrence and as Chief of Staff to Emir ➤Feisal. He maintained this connection with Feisal on the establishment of the mandated kingdom of ➤Iraq and was virtually the founder of the Iraqi Army, becoming Prime Minister in 1930 and dominating a succession of governments over the following ten years. Nuri-es-Said was fundamentally pro-British and strongly anti-communist. The hanging of four leading Iraqi communists in 1949 created martyrs and unified differing strands of opposition to Nuri in a common front, although ultimately it was his hostility to Nasserism which led to his downfall. On the outbreak of the revolution of Brigadier ➤Kassem he tried to escape from Baghdad disguised as a woman but was captured and revoltingly butchered (14 July 1958).

Nyasaland. The name by which ➤Malawi was known between 1907 and 1964. The region became a British protectorate in 1891 and was developed as a tea-producing and tobacco-growing agricultural area, largely dependent on the neighbouring ➤Rhodesias, with whom it was linked in a Federation, 1953–63. The political initiative of Dr Hastings ➤Banda led the British Government to permit Nyasaland to secede from the Federation, and the country became self-governing in February 1963, and independent on 6 July 1964.

Nyerere, Julius Kambarage (1922–), President of Tanzania. Born the son of a chief at Butiama village on lake Victoria, educated at Makarere University College and Edinburgh University, teaching at a Roman Catholic school near Dar es Salaam before organizing the Tanganyika African National Union in 1954–5. The Union won electoral successes in 1958 and 1960, ensuring that Nyerere was recognized as Prime Minister on 1 May 1961, when Tanganyika prepared for independence. He surrendered the premiership after a month of independence, concentrating for the remainder of the year 1962 on building up a socialist and distinctively Christian political movement. He was elected President of the Tanganyika Republic in November 1962, becoming President of the United Republic of Tanzania when Tanganyika and Zanzibar formed a common sovereign state in April 1964. President Nyerere was re-elected in 1965, 1970 and 1975. He tended to treat contacts with China and the Soviet Union cautiously. A quiet but effective style of public speaking won him respect as a Commonwealth statesman. While President he translated into Swahili (and published) Shakespeare's *Julius Caesar* and *The Merchant of Venice*. He retired as President in October 1985 and was succeeded by Ali Hassan Mwinyi.

O

OAS. ➤Organisation de l'Armée Secrète and ➤Organization of American States.

October Revolution (1917). The climax of the ➤Russian Revolution when Lenin led the Bolsheviks against Kerensky's government in Petrograd (6–7 November 1917). By the old-style Julian calendar, in use in pre-Bolshevik Russia, these events took place on 25–26 October.

October War (1973). Egyptian and Syrian forces launched a surprise attack on Israel in the early afternoon of 6 October 1973, when Jews were keeping the religious observance of ➤Yom Kippur. Within two days the Egyptians had crossed the Suez Canal and penetrated some fifteen miles beyond the front Israeli positions, while Syrian troops advanced a similar distance in the Golan Heights. Israeli troops counter-attacked on 8 October, crossing the Suez Canal south of Ismailia and advancing along the Suez-Cairo road to within sixty-five miles of the Egyptian capital. In the Golan Heights Israeli counter-attacks recovered territory occupied in the early days of the campaign and the advance along the old Tiberias–Damascus road reached a point about thirty-five miles from the Syrian capital. A ceasefire was established under UN auspices on 24 October, followed by a disengagement of forces along the Suez Canal, 18 January to 5 March 1974. UN forces established a peace-keeping unit of 1,200 men on the Golan Heights in May 1974, thereby creating a buffer zone between the Syrians and Israelis. An interim agreement between Israel and Egypt in September 1975 declared the willingness of the two countries to settle their differences by peaceful means. This cautious move towards reconciliation – which was encouraged by the diplomacy of Dr ➤Kissinger – marked the beginning of a change in Egyptian policy, shown to the world dramatically in the ➤'Sadat Initiative' of 1977.

Oder–Neisse Line. The frontier between Poland and Germany, following the river Oder southwards from the Baltic to its confluence with the river Neisse, and then along the western Neisse to the Czechoslovak frontier. The line was provisionally agreed at ➤Yalta and confirmed at ➤Potsdam. Six million Germans were ejected by the Poles from these newly acquired territories. The German Democratic Republic (East Germany) accepted the frontier in 1949, but refugee organizations in West Germany maintained a campaign against the loss of traditionally Prussian farmland east of the Oder and the Neisse; and the German Federal Government in Bonn did not formally recognize the Oder–Neisse frontier until

18 November 1970, as part of the policy of reconciliation, the *Ostpolitik*, of Chancellor ►Brandt.

Okinawa. Largest of the Ryukyu Islands, between Taiwan and Japan. An amphibious attack was mounted by US forces on Okinawa at the beginning of April 1945 and continued until 21 June. A Japanese garrison of 120,000 men defended the island fanatically, suffering 103,000 casualties. Allied shipping sustained heavy losses from Japanese ►*kamikaze* aircraft. The Americans lost some 12,500 men in securing Okinawa, which was intended as the principal base for the final attack upon the Japanese mainland.

Olympic Games. In 1894 the French aristocrat, Baron Pierre de Coubertin (1863–1937), presiding at an international congress of sportsmen in Paris, proposed the revival of the four-yearly Olympic Games, known to have been celebrated in Greece from 776 BC to AD 393. Baron de Coubertin wished the revived Games to be an amateur championship of individual sportsmen, not a competition between nations: 'May the Olympic flame shine through all generations to the benefit of a purer and more valiant humanity, with ever higher aspirations,' Coubertin declared. The first modern Olympiad was celebrated at Athens in 1896 with competitors from twelve nations participating. It was not until the sixth Olympic Games at Antwerp in 1920 that ceremonies, including the taking of an Olympic oath and the unfurling of an Olympic flag, were introduced. Politics intruded at the eleventh Olympiad in Berlin (August 1936), largely because racialists in the Nazi Press derided the 'use' made by the Americans of 'black auxiliaries' and Hitler was affronted by the successes of the great Negro athlete, Jesse Owens (1913–80). After the Second World War the Olympics were revived in London (1948). At the eighteenth Games in Mexico City (1968) some Negro sportsmen emphasized intrusive feelings of racial resentment by giving the clenched fist salute of the 'Black Power' movement on the victory rostrum. The 1972 ►Munich Olympics were tragically marred by the murder of Israeli competitors and again showed depth of feeling over racial matters by a threatened withdrawal of the African states if Rhodesia competed. The twenty-first Olympic Games were held in Canada (primarily Montreal) from 17 July to 1 August 1976: nineteen African and Arab nations withdrew in protest at the participation of New Zealand, since the New Zealanders had agreed to send a rugby team to apartheid-divided South Africa. The twenty-second Olympiad at Moscow in July 1980 was disrupted by the campaign launched by President Carter to have the Games 'abandoned, postponed or boycotted' in protest at Soviet military intervention in ►Afghanistan. The United States, West Germany, New Zealand, Canada, Japan, Turkey, Tunisia and Kenya were among the nations who boycotted the Olympiad. A call by Mrs Thatcher for British sporting groups to stay away from Moscow was defied by the British Olympic Association. The twenty-third Olympiad at Los Angeles in 1984 was boycotted by all the Warsaw Pact countries except Romania and by several other governments critical of US policies; but there was less political pressure on participants at the Seoul Olympics of September 1988. Barcelona successfully hosted the Olympic Games in 1992, and Atalanta less smoothly in 1996. The Games will be held in Sydney in 2000.

Open-Door Policy. A system of economic development of China, proposed in September 1899 by the US Secretary of State, John Hay (1838–1905), and accepted in principle by the European Great Powers and Japan. The policy, which sought to preserve Chinese political unity and independence, affirmed that all nations should enjoy equal commercial and tariff rights in China, together with equal rights to bid for the construction and management of railways. Hay assumed the continued weakness of China. The revival of Chinese national feeling and the incursions of Japan effectively destroyed the policy, although it was formally reaffirmed at the ➤Washington Conference in 1921–2.

Oran, Bombardment of (3 July 1940). ➤Mers-el-Kébir.

Organisation de l'Armée Secrète (OAS). Secret terrorist organization threatening the survival of the French ➤Fifth Republic, 1961–2. The effective leader was General ➤Salan and most of his supporters were former settlers from Algeria, disillusioned by President de Gaulle's Algerian policy. The OAS plotted de Gaulle's assassination on several occasions, notably by machine-gunning his car at Petit Chamart in March 1962. The OAS was eliminated by the capture or flight of its leaders and ceased to pose a threat from the spring of 1963 onwards.

Organization for Economic Cooperation and Development (OECD). Succeeded ➤OEEC on 14 December 1960, by adding the United States and Canada to the eighteen member states of that body. OECD is an attempt by the world's leading industrial nations to provide development aid for developing countries and to assist the economies of the less highly developed member states by providing financial stability and encouraging world trade. Japan joined OECD in 1964, Finland in 1968, and Yugoslavia, New Zealand and Australia enjoy a special status of associate membership.

Organization for European Economic Cooperation (OEEC). An intergovernmental organization formally established on 16 April 1948 to ensure methods of liberalizing trade and encouraging the growth of industrial and agricultural production in western Europe. The original sixteen member states were Austria, Belgium, Britain, Denmark, France, Greece, Iceland, Ireland, Italy, Luxembourg, the Netherlands, Norway, Portugal, Sweden, Switzerland and Turkey. The German Federal Republic joined in 1955, Spain in 1959. The Organization continued the collaboration foreshadowed in the ➤Marshall Plan, while providing an association from which the members developed the ➤European Economic Community ('Common Market') and the ➤European Free Trade Association. In December 1960 a new statute, signed in Paris, extended the scope of the OEEC by forming the ►Organization for Economic Cooperation and Development and OEEC ceased to function at the end of September 1961.

Organization of African Unity. A body established at a Pan-African conference in Addis Ababa in May 1963 in order to maintain solidarity among the African states and eradicate colonialism in the African continent. Heads of member states meet annually, a Council of Ministers every six months: specialized commissions were founded to concentrate on health, education, and economic and social affairs. Politically the Organization succeeded in settling border disputes between Algeria and Morocco, but failed to solve the problem of ►Biafra or the conflict between ►Ethiopia and Somalia, and was for long divided over the Angolan civil war. Only seven of the forty-eight member nations sent their heads of state to the 1976 conference in Mauritius: the prestige of the Organization was higher in the days of ►Nkrumah, ►Nasser and Haile ►Selassie than in later years.

Organization of American States (OAS). Was created at the ninth Pan-American Conference in Bogotá, Colombia (30 March to 30 April 1948) as a regional agency of United Nations members to promote the joint welfare of nations in the western hemisphere, specifically through the peaceful settlements of disputes and the promotion of economic development. The OAS built on the foundations established by the International Bureau of American Republics in 1890, the name of the Bureau being changed to Pan-American Union in 1910. Latin American states have criticized the dominance of the USA in its affairs and especially the anti-communist trend of US resolutions at the conferences from 1952 to 1962, culminating in the expulsion of Castro's Cuba. Conversely, OAS members unanimously supported the US blockade of Cuba when Soviet missiles were installed on the island at the end of 1962 (►Cuban Missiles Crisis). The OAS has eased political tension between Bolivia and Chile and promoted new agreements over the ►Panama Canal. Headquarters remain at the former Pan-American Union buildings in Washington, DC. Canada has never been a member of the OAS or its predecessors.

Organization of Petroleum-Exporting Countries (OPEC). Established after negotiations, during 1960, at a conference in Caracas, attended by delegates from Iran, Iraq, Kuwait, Qatar, Saudi Arabia and Venezuela. Abu Dhabi, Indonesia, Libya and Nigeria joined later in the decade, Egypt, Syria and Algeria were associated from 1967 onwards. Originally OPEC was an intergovernmental organization seeking to check overdevelopment by the oil companies and to maintain steady prices. Government power increased during the 1960s because of a rise in demand, a change in geographical emphasis to accommodate Libya, and the political action of Arab oil-producing states against Israel, together with problems caused by the closing of the Suez Canal and restrictions on some Middle East pipelines. The biggest problems have been caused by a conflict between member governments and western oil companies over price, commission and output, together with the threat of nationalization of western holdings. The Arab oil-producing states – exporters of two-thirds of the oil consumed by western Europe in the early 1970s – put political pressure on other governments by cutting supplies of oil in protest at Israel's expansion beyond the 1967 ceasefire lines by the ►October War of 1973. This political action was, however, criticized by other members of OPEC.

Orlando, Vittorio Emmanuele (1860–1952), Italian Prime Minister. Born at Palermo, where he became a professor of law, entered the government as Minister of Justice in 1916, and was appointed Prime Minister at the height of the ►Caporetto disaster, October 1917. His government saw a strengthening of Italian morale, ending in the final victory at Vittorio Veneto a year later. Orlando was one of the 'Big Four' national leaders at the Paris Peace Conference in 1919, but was soon on bad terms with Woodrow ►Wilson, who rejected Orlando's territorial demands as inconsistent with national self-determination. This failure to secure Italy the prizes she expected, together with the absence of any remedy for mounting social unrest, led to Orlando's rapid political eclipse. Moreover his excitable Sicilian temperament aroused scorn, both in Paris and Rome. He resigned on 20 June 1919, totally withdrawing from politics when Mussolini came to power in 1922.

Osborne Judgement. A railway employee, Walter Osborne, took legal action in 1908 to restrain his union from giving financial support to a political party of whose principles he did not approve. The case was taken to the House of Lords where judgement was given in Osborne's favour, 21 December 1909. The judgement restricted Labour Party funds. In 1913 legislation made it possible for Labour again to take money from unions, by giving individual unionists the option of choosing not to pay a 'political levy'.

Ottawa Conference (21 July to 20 August 1932). A British imperial economic conference convened on the initiative of the Canadian Conservative Prime Minister, R.B. ►Bennett. The Conference met the challenge of world Depression by partial ►imperial preference, following the switch to protective tariffs by the British in February 1932. The Conference was an assertion of the imperial connection rather than a means of guaranteeing wheat prices as the host-dominion had hoped.

Ottoman Empire. The name given to the Turkish Empire, deriving from the Ottoman dynasty, the reigning house until the abolition of the Sultanate in 1922. Although in decline throughout the nineteenth century the Ottoman Empire was bolstered up by one or other of the Great Powers until suffering defeat, as the ally of Germany, in 1918.

'Overlord.' The Anglo-American military code-name for the ►Normandy Landings of June 1944. The name was first used at the ►Quebec Conference of August 1943 to describe plans for the invasion of France worked out by General Sir Frederick Morgan (1894–1967) and a small staff over the previous eight months.

P

Paasikivi, Juho Kusti (1870–1956), Finnish statesman. Born in Tampere and as a Senator of the Grand-Duchy of Finland he sought reconciliation with Tsar Nicholas II, 1906–9. In May 1918 he became chief minister in what he believed would become a Finnish Kingdom, with a German on the throne, but he accepted republicanism and negotiated frontier demarcation with Soviet Russia in 1920 and in 1930–40. From November 1944 to March 1946 he was again Prime Minister, initiating what was called the 'Paasikivi Doctrine', that strict neutrality was the only means of keeping Finland independent of the Soviet Union. This doctrine he practised skilfully as President in succession to ➤Mannerheim from 1946 until his death. It was developed further by Paasikivi's successor, ➤Kekkonen.

Pahlavi, Mohammed Reza (1919 80), Shah of Iran 1941–79. Born in Teheran, the eldest son of Colonel Reza Khan (1878 1944), who overthrew the Kajar dynasty in a *coup d'état* on 30 October 1925 and was proclaimed Shah six weeks later. When German infiltration into Iranian affairs led the British and Russians to intervene in August 1941, Shah Reza Khan abdicated. Mohammed Reza Pahlavi was duly proclaimed Shah-an-Shah on 16 September 1941. A comparatively liberal and westernized system of government at first made the Shah popular with his subjects, although he was fortunate to survive gunshot wounds in an assassination attempt in 1951, during the radical hysteria aroused by ➤Mussadeq. A phase of liberal experiment, in 1961–2, was followed by a series of autocratic reforms imposed from above. Attempts to secure the social emancipation of Iranian women were denounced by the Moslem leaders, notably Ayatollah ➤Khomeini who was arrested and exiled in June 1963. Repressive measures, displays of imperial grandeur, lack of sympathy with the Arab cause and appalling inflation won support for the Shah's enemies, whether they were young students or an older generation of puritanical religious zealots. Rioting throughout the last four months of 1978 induced the Shah to leave Iran 'on holiday' on 16 January 1979. He was formally deposed two months later, at a time when he was already gravely ill with cancer. He found refuge briefly in Morocco, Mexico, the United States and Panama, dying as a guest of President Sadat in Cairo on 27 July 1980.

Pakistan. A predominantly Islamic state in the Indian subcontinent, the idea of ➤Jinnah and his Muslim League in British India, constituted as a dominion under the Indian Independence Act of 1947, becoming a republic on 23 March 1956, and leaving the Commonwealth in protest at the recognition of ➤Bangladesh, 30 January 1972. From its inception Pakistan suffered from disunity, since it consisted of two geographical regions, West and East Pakistan, separated by 1,100 miles of Indian territory: and it was the failure of West Pakistan to appreciate the distinctive problems of its eastern Bengali province that led to the secession of Bangladesh under Mujibur ➤Rahman. Conflict with India over ➤Kashmir and other frontier areas weakened the prospects of good neighbourly progress. Pakistan's parliamentary constitution was abrogated in October 1958 by General ➤Ayub Khan who ruled principally through martial law. Riots and massed strikes in March 1969 forced him to surrender authority to the commander-in-chief, General ➤Yahya Khan, who permitted 'one man, one vote' elections for the first time in Pakistan (December 1970). The victory in the elections of the People's Party under Ali ➤Bhutto led to seven years of civilian government; but four months of unrest culminated, on 5 July 1977, in a bloodless *coup* by the chief of the army staff, General Muhammad Zia-ul-Haque, who arrested the cabinet (including Bhutto) and the opposition leaders. General ➤Zia then became leader of an administrative Military Council, assuming the Presidency in July 1978 and imposing harsh Islamic penalties in a new legislative code. In March 1985 he strengthened the President's powers, but in December lifted martial law for the first time in eight years. Discontent mounted, especially in Sind and Karachi. On 17 August 1988 Zia, the US ambassador and twenty-one senior army officers were killed, when the President's plane blew up in mid-air after taking off from Bahawalpur. The chairman of the Senate, Ghulam Ishaq Khan, took over the presidency. Elections three months later were followed by the formation of a government in which the Pakistan People's Party, led by Benazir ➤Bhutto, was predominant. Her government was overthrown in August 1990 by a *coup* backed by President Ishaq Khan and the army. Mohammed Nawaz Sharif's Islamic Democratic Alliance won the General Election of October 1990 and proposed a series of economic reforms aimed at the privatization of state enterprises. Complaints of maladministration allowed Benazir Bhutto to win another General Election in October 1993 but she was faced by mounting ➤Islamic fundamentalism among the Shia Muslims of the north and around Karachi. Political confusion was intensified in November 1996 when President Farooq Leghari dismissed the Bhutto Government amid allegations of corruption. Few voters bothered to go to the polls when an election was called three months later; the Muslim League was returned to power. Pakistan became a nuclear power with a series of tests carried out in late May 1998, in response to India's tests a fortnight previously.

Palestine. Absorbed in the Ottoman Empire in 1517 and under Turkish rule until conquered by ➤Allenby in 1917–18, becoming a British mandated territory, 1920–48. The British administrators were hampered by the claims of the Arabs and obligations implied to the Jews in the ➤Balfour Declaration but sought to hold a balance between the two communities. Despite disturbances in 1921, communal relations improved until 1928–9 but then deteriorated rapidly with over 200 deaths in fighting around Jerusalem, 23–26 August 1929. The chief reason for these riots was Arab alarm at a doubling of the Jewish population in ten years: Arab nationalism was fanned by insidious propaganda from the Mufti of Jerusalem, Haji Amin al-Husseini (1900–1975). Jewish immigration rose from 4,075 in 1931 to 61,854 in 1935, reaching one-third of the Arab population and, in the Mufti's opinion, threatening to give the Jews a majority in Palestine by the early 1940s. Continuous Arab–Jewish skirmishes from May to October 1936 led to British intervention during which thirty-four soldiers were killed: the ➤Peel Report, favouring partition, was followed by further open warfare from November 1937 until July 1938. Jewish extremists began to attack British forces from resentment at the imposition of a quota of immigrants and at restrictions on land purchase, while the Arabs complained that the British were lax in preventing unauthorized landings by Jewish immigrants along the coast. Terrorism, suspended during the war, broke out again in 1946, the activities of the Jewish extremist bodies, ➤Irgun Zvai Leumi and the Stern Gang, alienating many Labour sympathizers in Britain. The hope of Ernest ➤Bevin that it might still be possible to create a bi-national state in Palestine failed because of Jewish terrorism, Arab intransigence and a Democratic Administration in Washington which was sensitive to Jewish voting pressure. In November 1947 the United Nations accepted the idea of partition. The British mandate officially ended on 14 May 1948 but the Arabs refused to recognize the new State of ➤Israel and the enlarged ➤Jordan. War engulfed Palestine from May 1948 until January 1949 and was followed by an uneasy truce. Thereafter Palestinian Arab hopes rested at first with the Mufti who, having spent the years 1942–5 in Germany, installed himself at Gaza as head of an 'All Palestine Government' which encouraged guerrilla raids by groups of *fedayeen* ('fanatics'). From 1956 onwards the Mufti's influence declined, being replaced by the Syrian-dominated Al Fatah and by the ➤PLO. An embryonic Palestinian state re-emerged after talks between Israeli and PLO representatives in Oslo during September 1993. Full autonomy was conceded by Israel to the ➤Gaza Strip and the Jericho area, and partial autonomy to a larger region of the West Bank, including the towns of Bethlehem, Hebron, Nablus and Ramallah. The 'Palestine National Authority', headed by Yasir ➤Arafat, began effective government from Gaza City in May 1994.

Palestine Liberation Organization (PLO). Set up in May 1964 in Jordan as a movement seeking to reconcile various Palestinian Arab groups. From 1967 it was dominated by Al Fatah, the Syrian wing associated with Yasir ➤Arafat, but even more extreme groups such as the 'Popular Front for the Liberation of Palestine' and the 'Black September' terrorists emerged to pursue a course of murder, hijacking and bombing, both inside and outside Israel. It is not always clear how far the main PLO body was responsible for such actions as the ➤Munich Olympics killings or the events culminating in the ➤Entebbe raid. Attempts by King Hussein to restrain the fanatics in the PLO led to a civil war in ➤Jordan in September 1970, and to the withdrawal of the PLO guerrilla units to Syria and ➤Lebanon. A meeting of representatives from the Arab states at Rabat in October 1974 announced that the PLO was henceforth to assume complete responsibility for all Palestinians at national and international level, and on 22 March 1976 PLO representatives in New York were admitted to a United Nations debate on conditions in the Israeli-occupied west bank of the Jordan. Internal feuds between Arafat and the extremists led in 1978 to several killings in London, Paris and other cities far from the Middle East. Despite these splits the PLO improved its international standing with the West during 1979–80. Arafat was a prominent mourner at Tito's funeral in May 1980; his representatives were accorded a hearing at the British Foreign Office; and the PLO was given diplomatic status by several governments (including India, Austria, and Cyprus) as well as receiving a degree of recognition by Japan. The growing strength of the PLO in the Lebanon led to Israeli attacks on Palestinian refugee camps in July 1981. The Israeli advance on Beirut in June 1982 was primarily intended to destroy the PLO bases and discredit Arafat by inflicting a major defeat on the Palestinian cause at a time when it was receiving more sympathetic attention than ever before in the West. The PLO evacuated Beirut in late August 1982 and was ordered out of Lebanon (under Syrian pressure) in June 1983, although Arafat and 4,000 supporters did not finally leave until December. They established new headquarters at Hammam, east of Tunis, which were bombed by Israeli aircraft on 1 October 1985. Israeli agents also assassinated Arafat's deputy, Khalil al-Wazir (Abu Jihad), in Tunis in April 1988. Arafat proclaimed a Palestinian State in exile in December 1988. Shortly afterwards he recognized Israel and renounced terrorism but the PLO strongly supported Iraq throughout the Second Gulf War. Most of the PLO supported Arafat's negotiations with ►Rabin in 1993–4, subsequently helping him establish the Palestine National Authority.

Palme, Olof (1927–86), Swedish Prime Minister, was a member of a banking family. After graduating in law at Stockholm university, Palme became personal assistant to Tage Erlander, Sweden's socialist Prime Minister 1946–69. He entered parliament in 1957, becoming Minister of Communications (1965), Minister of Education (1967), and succeeding Erlander as Prime Minister in 1969. Palme was defeated in the elections of October 1976. While out of office he undertook considerable work for the UN and, as chairman of the Commission on Disarmament and Security, sought to mediate in the ►Gulf War, 1980–81. He became Sweden's Prime Minister again in 1982 and had a third electoral victory in September 1985, although his government became dependent on support from nineteen Communist members. On 28 February 1986 he was shot dead as he walked home from a cinema in Stockholm with his wife. Ingvar Carlsson (1933–), his successor, ordered several enquiries into the murder, but no satisfactory explanation was reached.

Panama Canal. A waterway, fifty miles long, linking the Atlantic and Pacific, and saving vessels a voyage of 6,000 miles around South America. A canal through the isthmus was envisaged in the sixteenth century but it was not until 1879 that a French company began work on the project. Gross mismanagement, malaria and yellow fever contributed to the failure of the project in 1889, after 22,000 workers had died. Improved medical knowledge induced President Theodore ►Roosevelt to encourage Americans to construct the canal. At the beginning of the century the isthmus lay within Colombia. With American support a separatist movement established the Panamanian Republic in November 1903; the republic then leased to the United States territory extending five miles on either side of the projected canal (except for the cities of Panama and Colon). Work began in 1908 and the canal was opened for vessels on 15 August 1914. Throughout the 1960s the Panamanian people continued to agitate in favour of retrocession of the Canal Zone, and relations were broken off between the republic and the USA from May 1963 until April 1964 over the question. Eventually, on 7 September 1977, President Carter and the Panamanian national leader, General Omar Torrijos, signed a Treaty in Washington pledging return of the Canal Zone (about 1 per cent of the total territory of Panama) on 1 January 2000. The signing of the Treaty was witnessed by twenty heads of government from South America. It was, however, ill-received both in the US Senate and in Panama, whose people could not see why there should be a delay of twenty-two years in securing transfer of the territory. Conflict with the Panamanian authorities over drug trafficking led President Bush to authorize an invasion of the republic on 20 December 1989; the Panamanian President, General Norriega, was captured in Panama City on 3 January 1990 and taken to the USA to face drug charges.

Panay Incident (12 December 1937). Japanese aircraft bombed and machine-gunned the US gunboat *Panay* in a twenty-minute attack as she was sailing down the Yangtze with refugees from Nanking, which fell to Japanese troops on that same Sunday. The *Panay* sank within two hours. Although the Japanese Foreign Ministry apologized for a 'terrible blunder' the bombing appears to have been an act of deliberate policy by Japanese militarists anxious to minimize American influence in Chinese affairs. The restraint shown by American public opinion after this sinking of a warship was interpreted by foreign observers as evidence of the extent of isolationist sentiment.

Pankhurst, Mrs Emmeline (1858–1928), champion of women's political rights. Born Emmeline Goulden in Manchester, married Richard Pankhurst, a barrister who advocated the social and political emancipation of women, but who died in 1898. Mrs Pankhurst continued to lead the Women's Franchise League, which she had formed, in collaboration with her husband, in 1889. Her eldest daughter, Christabel (1880–1958), persuaded her mother to found the more militant Women's Social and Political Union in 1903. After talks with the Prime Minister in May 1906, Mrs Pankhurst decided that the Liberals would not give women the vote, and the ►suffragettes resorted to more violent tactics. She was arrested twice in 1908 and 1909, again in 1911 and 1912, when she went on hunger strike and was released. A campaign of arson in 1913 led her to be sentenced to three years' penal servitude, from which she was released within a year. During the war she encouraged women to join the armed forces or go into industry. After women were enfranchised in 1918, she left the ►Independent Labour Party to which she had belonged for twenty-six years. She lived in Canada, 1919–26, encouraging child welfare. Shortly before her death she was adopted as prospective Conservative parliamentary candidate for Whitechapel. Her daughter Christabel controlled the WSPU from exile in Paris while her mother was in prison: she spent most of her later life in Canada and America and was created a Dame of the British Empire in 1936. Mrs Pankhurst's second daughter, Sylvia (1882–1960), was a pacifist in the First World War, a socialist, and from 1935 a champion of Ethiopia, where she spent the last four years of her life. A third daughter, Adela (1885–1961), emigrated to Australia, where she remained a consistent feminist, socialist and pacifist.

Papadopoulos, George (born 1918). Leader of the regime of the ►'Greek Colonels'.

Papagos, Alexander (1883–1955), Greek soldier and Prime Minister. Born in Athens, served in a succession of campaigns 1912–22, became a political general in the 1930s, and was Minister of War in 1936, before being ousted by ►Metaxas, who appointed him Chief of the General Staff. Papagos was largely responsible for organizing the Greek counter-attacks after the Italian invasion of 1940, but he was slow to respond to the German invasion in April 1941. With the rank of marshal, he was made commander-in-chief of the royalist forces in the final stages of the ►Greek Civil War. In May 1951 he resigned all military appointments and two months later founded a political party, the 'Greek Rally', which won a large majority at the elections of November 1952. He became Prime Minister, holding office until his death on 5 October 1955, when he was succeeded by his Minister of Public Works, ►Karamanlis. Papagos headed a strongly right-wing, but not totalitarian, government, which enjoyed the confidence of the Americans from whom he obtained substantial credit for physical reconstruction work.

Papandreou, George (1888–1968), Greek Prime Minister. Born in Salonika, became a lawyer and entered politics as a moderate socialist republican. He served in several governments, 1923–35, escaped from occupied Greece in 1942 and returned as head of a coalition government on the liberation of Athens in 1944. Within a few weeks he was in opposition, since he was suspect to the influential right-wing militarists. As a gifted and popular orator, Papandreou commanded a large following on the mainland and became a formidable political force when he founded the Centre Union Party of radicals and democratic socialists in 1961. He was Prime Minister for fifty-five days late in 1963, but after electoral successes in February 1964 looked forward to a ministry of progressive reforms. In this he was largely disappointed. Unresolved problems over ►Cyprus, hostility from the army, resentment at the way in which he was advancing the political power of his son, and a clash of personalities between the Prime Minister and the young King, ►Constantine II, led to Papandreou's downfall in July 1965. Support continued for the Centre Union, especially in northern Greece, and it was to prevent the opening of an election campaign with a Centre Union rally in Salonika that the ►Greek Colonels staged their *coup d'état* on 21 April 1967. Papandreou himself was briefly detained: his health was bad, and he died the following year. His son, Andreas Papandreou (1919–96), a former associate professor of economics in California, was kept in custody until he was allowed to leave for America in January 1968. Andreas Papandreou returned to Greece in 1973 and became the leader of the principal opposition party to ►Karamanlis, the Panhellenic Socialist Movement (PASOK). When the socialists won the general election of October 1981 Andreas Papandreou became Prime Minister, heading the Government until 1989 and returning to office from October 1993 to February 1996.

Papua New Guinea. The south-eastern part of the island of ►New Guinea; was constituted a British colony in 1887, the Australian Federal Government taking over control in 1901, completing the political transfer in 1905. The region was officially known as the 'Territory of Papua' from September 1906 and was administratively integrated with the mandated ex-German colonies to form ►Australian New Guinea from 1920 onwards. Papua benefited considerably from the enlightened administration of Sir Hubert ►Murray until his death in 1940. Formal administrative union of the area as 'Papua New Guinea' (PNG) was achieved in 1968, internal self-government following on 1 December 1973. The transfer of authority was completed by recognition of full independence within the Commonwealth on 16 September 1975, the capital being Port Moresby. Australia relinquished powers over defence and foreign affairs in March 1975, but would still assist PNG in repelling an invasion. PNG covers a considerable area of the south-west Pacific, including not only the eastern New Guinea mainland, but ten other islands formerly under Australian mandate, including the largest of the Solomon islands, Bougainville (although most of the Solomons, lying south of Bougainville, form a separate monarchical state, also within the Commonwealth and centred on the island of Guadalcanal). Resentment at alleged exploitation of the northern Solomons' considerable mineral resources led to a secessionist rebellion in which a Bougainville Revolutionary Army established an independent government at Arawa on the island in May 1990. For three and a half years the PNG armed forces were engaged in conflict on the island. In April 1993 there were clashes between naval patrol boats belonging to PNG and to the Solomon Islands monarchy after the New Guineans raided islands said to be aiding the Bougainville secessionists. Intermittent guerrilla fighting has kept Bougainville's copper mine closed since 1989. Several thousand New Guineans were drowned on 17 July 1998, when a tidal wave caused by tremors swept up the northern coast of the island.

Paraguay. Landlocked South American republic, bordered by Argentina, Brazil and Bolivia. The area was administered by Spain from 1535 until 1811. Hopes of gaining territory and access to the sea led Paraguay into a major war against Brazil, Argentina and Uruguay from 1865 to 1870 which decimated the population.

Political instability continued until 1912, when the four-year presidency of the liberal Edvard Schaerer attracted foreign capital and led to economic improvements which were maintained through the seven short-lived presidencies of the following twelve years. A long dispute with Bolivia over the territory of the ►Chaco erupted in war (1932–5), which resulted in a Paraguayan victory but at considerable economic cost. For most of the years since 1940 Paraguay has been under military dictatorships. General Morinigo controlled Paraguay from 1940 to 1947; General Alfredo Stroessner (1912–), the son of a German immigrant, seized power on 11 July 1954 and remained President until overthrown by General Alfredo Rodriguez in February 1989. Stroessner carried through a series of public works programmes, notably some major hydro-electric projects. Paraguay's economy prospered; civil liberty did not. Constitutional amendments under President Rodriguez allowed the election of a civilian President, Juan Wasmosy, in May 1993. The customary military *coup*, staged in April 1996, was (unusually) defeated.

Paris Peace Conference (1919–20). A congress of 'allied and associated powers' in Paris, 18 January 1919 to 20 January 1920, determining the settlement embodied in the Treaties of ►Versailles (Germany), ►St Germain (Austria), ►Neuilly (Bulgaria), ►Trianon (Hungary) and ►Sèvres (Turkey). Until July 1919 the Conference was dominated by the 'Big Four' – ►Clemenceau of France, ►Wilson of America, ►Lloyd George of Britain, and ►Orlando of Italy. Decisions were later taken by a 'Council of Heads of Delegations', generally Foreign Ministers, while the final delineation of the Hungarian and Turkish frontiers was left to a 'Council of Ambassadors'. Expert commissions were sent from Paris to report on disputed areas. The Conference achieved a higher degree of ethnic self-determination than had existed before, and it was hoped that weaknesses or injustices would be rectified by the ►League of Nations. There were five chief obstacles to the making of a just peace: (1) conflict between the objectives of the Big Four; thus Wilson and Clemenceau differed over the League, Wilson and Orlando over the Adriatic, Lloyd George and Clemenceau over Poland; (2) domestic pressure groups seeking harsher terms; thus 370 British MPs telegraphed Lloyd George urging higher ►reparations on Germany, and French army leaders wanted Clemenceau to detach the Rhineland from Germany; (3) American isolationism, eventually leading Congress to reject Wilson's undertakings; (4) impatient nationalist groups which used force of arms to secure and hold disputed regions (►Fiume, ►Teschen, ►Vilna); (5) the uncertainty over Russia's frontiers caused by the Civil War. The defeated states resented the fact that the terms were dictated to them rather than settled by agreed compromises between victors and vanquished.

Paris Peace Treaties (10 February 1947). At the end of July 1946 a peace conference of twenty-one nations which had fought against Hitler and his allies met in Paris to draft a settlement with Germany's principal supporters in Europe – Italy, Bulgaria, Finland, Hungary and Romania. Committees of the conference sat intermittently until mid October and the Treaties were signed in the following

February. The chief terms were: Italy to cede parts of the Istrian peninsula, Zara and some Adriatic islands to Yugoslavia, to surrender the Dodecanese islands to Greece, to accept a minor frontier adjustment with France, to allow ►Trieste to become a free city, and to renounce sovereignty over all African colonies; Bulgaria to recover her frontiers of January 1941; Finland to cede Petsamo to the USSR and to revert to the frontiers of 1940; Hungary to be limited to her ►Trianon frontiers, with cession of a small region on the Danube to Czechoslovakia; and Romania to recover her inter-war frontiers apart from ►Bessarabia and the northern ►Bukovina which remained in the Soviet Union and the southern ►Dobrudja which remained in Bulgaria. These terms were mild, largely because all five countries had made a separate peace and participated in operations against the Germans before the end of the war. Thus Romania lost 150,000 men fighting on the side of the allies, 1944–5, and Bulgaria similarly lost 32,000 men. Only Trieste later proved a serious and unresolved problem.

Parliament Act, 1911. Reform passed by the Asquith Liberal Government depriving the House of Lords of any powers over 'money bills' and restricting it to a suspensive veto on other legislation of three sessions. The Act also reduced the maximum duration of the elected Commons from seven years (as enacted in 1716) to five years. Limitation of the Lords' power was necessitated by Opposition tactics which used the Conservative majority in the Upper House to prevent reform measures carried by the elected Liberal majority in the Lower House, a procedure culminating in the rejection of the 1909 'People's Budget' of ►Lloyd George. The Parliament Bill was introduced in May 1910, after a Liberal victory in the general election. When the Lords maintained opposition to the Bill, parliament was again dissolved and the Liberals returned with a slightly increased majority. The Bill was only passed, in August 1911, after George V had guaranteed his willingness to create 250 Liberal peers so as to swamp the Conservative majority in the Lords and ensure passage of the reform. The Parliament Act of 1949 reduced the number of delaying sessions from three to two.

Partisans. Armed groups offering resistance behind the enemy lines, a word originating with the Russians who raided Napoleon's supply-line during the 1812 campaign. The word was used again in the American Civil War, in the Caucasus in 1905, and in the Russian Civil War, assuming thereafter a specifically left-wing connotation. Partisan groups were encouraged by Stalin to operate within occupied territory 1941–2. Communist-led partisan organizations were established about the same time in Albania, Slovakia, Moravia and Greece, and a little later in Italy. The name is, however, most closely associated with resistance in Yugoslavia: communist forces accepting the leadership of ►Tito called themselves 'partisans' (as distinct from non-communist ►Chetniks) in July 1941, concentrating in the mountain strongholds of Bosnia-Herzegovina and Montenegro. The small partisan units were organized into 'the National Army of Liberation and Partisan Detachments of Yugoslavia' during a respite from fighting in central Bosnia, November

1942, at the Bihać Assembly. In general the Yugoslav partisans remained isolated and largely self-sufficient units, though capable of resisting seven major offensives by the occupation armies, and collaborating with the Red Army which advanced up the Danube 1944–5.

Pašić, Nikola (1845–1926), Serbian statesman. Born at Zaječar, on the borders of Serbia and Bulgaria, became a radical politician, and was Prime Minister of Serbia 1891–2, 1904–8, 1910–18 and of Yugoslavia 1921–6. He was largely responsible for the restoration of the Karadjordjević dynasty in ►Serbia in 1903 and for Serbia's political success in the ►Balkan Wars. He was too moderate for the militarists in the ►Black Hand and too exclusively Serbian for the Yugoslav exiles who secured the ►Corfu Pact from him. Although he achieved much as chief spokesman for the Serbs at the Paris Conference, his tendency to treat the kingdom established in 1918 as a mere territorial extension of Serbia perpetuated internal conflicts which ultimately weakened ►Yugoslavia.

Passchendaele. A village on a ridge eight miles east of Ypres, being the furthest point reached by British and Empire troops in the third battle of ►Ypres, 31 July to 10 November 1917. The Passchendaele Ridge was among the first objectives in the plan of ►Haig for a breakthrough in Belgium, but it was not possible to launch an attack on Passchendaele itself until 12 October, a second attack failing on 26 October and the ruins of the mud-caked village falling to the Canadians only on 9 November, when it was too late to sustain an offensive in appalling weather with weary and demoralized troops. A wet August, with twice the normal rainfall, combined with the low-lying Flanders plain to make Passchendaele a battlefield of mud. Allied troops suffered 300,000 casualties in creating a dangerously exposed salient of five miles, speedily evacuated five months later when the Germans launched their spring offensive. Passchendaele, in which the German defenders used mustard gas for the first time, remained the supreme hell-hole of horror among the British and the Canadians much as did ►Verdun for the French.

Patton, George Smith (1885–1945). American general. Born at San Gabriel, California, educated at West Point and commissioned in the US Army, 1909. He became an enthusiast for armoured vehicles, and as a colonel on the Western Front sent the first American tanks into action at St Mihiel (12 September 1918). He continued to specialize in tanks during the inter-war period, commanding an armoured corps in 1941, fighting in Tunisia early in 1943 and becoming widely known for the rapidity of his thrust with tanks to seize Palermo. This enterprise, at times carried through with no regard for other units, was shown at its most flamboyant in 1944 when his Third Army cut rapidly across France in a sweep through Brittany, round Paris, up the Marne and the Moselle, across the Rhine and into northern Bavaria, eventually entering Czechoslovakia (18 April 1945). Patton was killed in a road accident while commanding the US Fifth Army in occupied Germany, 21 December 1945. The nickname 'Old Blood and Guts', bestowed on him by his troops, testified to his reputation for daring and recklessness.

Paul VI (1897–1978, elected pontiff in June 1963), Pope. Born Giovanni Montini at Concesio, near Brescia, his father being editor of a Catholic newspaper and a member of the Italian parliament. He was ordained priest in 1920, serving in the papal secretariat of state from 1924 until 1954, with a brief interlude as nuncio in Warsaw. For nine years he was Archbishop of Milan, being created a cardinal in 1958. As Pope he continued the ecumenical tendencies of his predecessor, ➤John XXIII, presiding over the closing stages of the ➤Vatican Council. Pope Paul was the first pontiff to travel outside Europe: he went as a pilgrim to Jerusalem in January 1964 as well as visiting Bombay (December 1964), the United Nations headquarters in New York (October 1965), Latin America (1968), Uganda in August 1969 and Australia and the Philippines in November 1970. In Europe (in 1967) he called on the Ecumenical Patriarch in Istanbul and celebrated mass at the shrine of ➤Fatima in central Portugal. In the Vatican itself Pope Paul simplified the ritual of state, proposed reform of the Curia, and in 1970 imposed restraints on the active rights of cardinals who attained the age of eighty. He attempted to mediate in Vietnam and in the Nigerian Civil War and offered to take the place of hostages held by terrorists in a hijacked aircraft. His social policy, notably on birth control, was traditionalist but his support for the increased use of the vernacular gravely offended conservative churchmen, who found a leader in the French archbishop, Marcel Lefebvre. During the later years of Paul's pontificate, second thoughts seemed frequently to make him reverse difficult decisions. He died from a heart attack at Castelgandolfo on 6 August 1978. His successor was the Patriarch of Venice, Cardinal Albino Luciani (1913–78), who took the title John Paul I. He died thirty-three days after his election as Pope.

Pearl Harbor. Main US naval base in Hawaii. Japanese carrier-borne aircraft, from a fleet which had secretly left the Kurile Islands twelve days previously, attacked the anchorage early on Sunday, 7 December 1941, without a declaration of war. Within two hours the Japanese sank or disabled five battleships and fourteen smaller vessels, destroyed 120 aircraft and killed more than 2,000 seamen and almost 400 other people. Of 353 Japanese planes taking part in the attack, only twenty-nine were lost. Diplomatic negotiations between America and Japan were in progress when news of the attack reached Washington. Congress declared war on Japan next day: Germany and Italy, as allies of Japan, declared war on the United States on 11 December. American losses at Pearl Harbor gave an initial advantage to Japanese sea power, although no US aircraft-carriers were in port at the time and three of the five battleships took part in operations later in the war.

Pearson, Lester Bowles (1897–1972), Canadian statesman. Born at Newtonbrook, Ontario, and educated at the Universities of Toronto and Oxford; entered the Canadian diplomatic service, distinguishing himself as ambassador in Washington, 1945–6, and playing a major role in setting up the United Nations Organization.

He was Canadian Secretary of State for External Affairs (1948–57), presiding over the UN General Assembly, 1952–3. In 1957 he became the first Canadian to win the Nobel Peace Prize, for his role as a mediator in the tensions of the preceding year. He led the Opposition in the Canadian parliament 1958–63, and became Prime Minister at the head of a Liberal government on 22 April 1963. His premiership was troubled by increasing signs of conflict between English-speaking and French-speaking Canadians and his legislative programme was hampered by the fact that he did not enjoy a clear majority. In foreign affairs he continued to give authoritative support for the United Nations peace-keeping enterprises, as well as showing a readiness to mediate over Vietnam. After exactly five years as Prime Minister he retired in favour of Pierre ►Trudeau. His statesmanship was recognized by conferment of the Order of Merit in 1971.

Peel Commission (1936–7). A series of Arab attacks on Jews in Palestine early in 1936 induced Baldwin to appoint a royal commission to consider the working of the mandate. The Commission was headed by Earl Peel (1867–1937), a former Indian Secretary. The report of the Commission (7 July 1937) recommended partition into separate Arab and Jewish states, with the British supervising a corridor inland from Haifa and including Jerusalem, Nazareth and Bethlehem. This drastic solution was rejected by most Arabs and most Zionists, exceptions including Emir ►Abdullah and Chaim ►Weizmann. It was also rejected by the House of Lords and, although technically accepted by the government, was never implemented. The report is historically significant for three reasons: it was the first public proposal of partition; it represented the most earnest attempt of any inter-war government to solve the Palestine problem; and it brought from the Jews the implacable objection that a Zionist state was impossible 'without Zion'.

Perestroika. A Russian word meaning 'restructuring' that first came into general political parlance after its use by ►Gorbachev in his speech to the Twenty-Seventh Congress of the Soviet Communist Party on 25 February 1986. The word has been applied to the reform programme which he wished to introduce into Soviet social and economic life. Significantly, coinciding with the 70th anniversary celebrations of the Bolshevik Revolution eighteen months later, he gave the title *Perestroika and New Thinking for Our Country and the Whole World* to his first book, which updated Leninist theory.

Perón, Juan Domingo (1895–1974), Argentinian general and President. Born at Lobos, Buenos Aires, helped plan the military *coup d'état* of 1930, studied fascism in action in Italy and Germany and, as a colonel, was one of the Group of United Officers who seized power on 4 June 1943, remaining powerful in the government as Minister of Labour and Social Security and surviving a clumsy attempt, inspired by US agents, to oust him in October 1945. He was elected President on 24 February 1946 and re-elected with a decisive majority on 11 November 1951. From 1946 onwards his personal fate is part of the general history of ►Argentina.

Much of his success depended on the magnetic appeal, and social common sense, of his wife Eva Duarte Perón (1919–52). Her death on 26 July 1952 was followed by a conflict with the Church over which Perón lost considerable support. He survived an attempted uprising in June 1955, but was forced into exile three months later. The Peronista Party recovered strength in the early 1970s and Perón returned as President from October 1973 until his death in July 1974. His second wife, Maria Estela Perón, succeeded him, but was overthrown on 24 March 1976.

Persia. Ancient empire, becoming a nation state under the Safavid dynasty in the late sixteenth century and officially changing its name to ►Iran in 1935.

Peru. South American republic. The Inca inhabitants of Peru were overwhelmed by Pizarro (1478–1541) early in the sixteenth century and the land formed part of the Spanish empire until 1821. A democratic republican constitution was adopted in 1856, subsequently being drastically amended and occasionally suspended: effective control rested with a small group of businessmen in Lima. Augusto Leguia, President 1919–30, introduced material reforms with the help of substantial American loans but his government became corrupt and fell during the Depression. The following fifteen years saw improvised conservative regimes rigorously suppressing the 'Popular Revolution Alliance' (APRA) movement, which was strongly supported by students and by the Indian population. Although APRA had a parliamentary majority from 1945 to 1948 it was unable to carry out any fundamental reforms. The army intervened in 1948 and again in 1962 to check any movement towards a liberal regime. Elections in June 1963 led to the victory of a reformist and Catholic movement, the 'Popular Action Party', whose leader, Fernando Belaúnde, was President for the next five years. Currency deflation and concessions to an American oil firm made the Belaúnde Government unpopular. On 3 October 1968 it was replaced by a military regime under General Velasco which suspended the legislature, expropriated the oilfields and promised land reforms. In a bloodless *coup d'état* on 29 August 1975 General Velasco was replaced by General Morales Bermúdez. Although the pattern of Peruvian government was at first unchanged, Bermúdez gradually recognized the need for a return to democratic forms. Elections for a constituent assembly were held in June 1978, the first sounding of public opinion in Peru for fifteen years. An election for the Presidency and a bicameral legislature (contested by fifteen parties) took place on 18 May 1980. It brought back the 'Popular Action Party', and Bermúdez duly handed over the Presidency to its old leader, Fernando Belaúnde (28 July 1980). With the APRA movement gaining the second largest number of votes in the election, Peruvian party politics seemed set in a traditional mould to a greater extent than is customary in Latin America. The APRA candidate, Alan Garcia (1949–), won the election of 1985; but, from 1982, the civilian presidencies of both Belaúnde and Garcia suffered from the intimidating guerrilla activities of the Sendero Luminoso Marxists, who were, in their turn, treated brutally by the Peruvian security forces. When the Sendero Luminosa began to have links with drug cartels in northern Peru, revolutionary enthusiasm passed to the smaller Tapac Amara movement (MRTA). The impact of these two groups weakened the economy and so discredited APRA that the election of 1990 brought back a right-wing government under President Alberto Fujimori, from a Japanese immigrant family. In order to combat terrorism, Fujimori suspended and amended the constitution so as to rule by decree and lengthen his term of office. MRTA gunmen seized the Japanese embassy in Lima during a reception on 17 December 1996 and held 460 guests as ➤hostages for the release of Marxist prisoners. Fujimori refused the terrorists' terms but secured the release of more than half the hostages under promise of negotiations. After five months of siege and talks crack Peruvian troops stormed the embassy, freed the remaining hostages and shot dead their fourteen captors (22 April 1997).

Pétain, (Henri) Philippe (1856–1951), Marshal of France and head of state. Born at Cauchy-à-la-Tour, near St Omer, educated locally and at the Dominican college at Arceuil before entering St Cyr and being commissioned in the infantry in 1878. He followed an orthodox military career, teaching at the École de Guerre from 1906, being promoted colonel in 1912 and general soon after the outbreak of war. His indomitable tenacity as commander of the French Second Army at ➤Verdun won wide esteem. When mutinies weakened the French Army in May 1917 he was appointed commander-in-chief, with the immediate task of raising morale. He held this post until the end of the war although from April 1918 he was subordinate to ➤Foch, who had been made supreme allied generalissimo. He received his Marshal's baton at Metz in December 1918. In 1925–6 he commanded the forces which defeated ➤Abd-el-Krim in Morocco, and in 1929 he became Inspector-General of the Army, much respected as one of the most humane commanders of the First World War, anxious to avoid heavy casualties and believing in defence rather than attack. He was Minister of War from February to November 1934, his political ideas being well to the Right. After a period of retirement he became France's first ambassador to Franco's Spain in March 1939, but was summoned back to France and appointed Prime Minister on 16 June 1940, concluding an armistice with Germany six days later. At ➤Vichy on 10 July he secured from the National Assembly the right to rule unoccupied France by authoritarian methods, which he believed would purge the country of its 'moral decadence'. He sought to put his ideas into practice as head of state until the Germans occupied the whole of France (November 1942), when he became virtually a German puppet forced to accompany the German Army back across the Rhine in 1944. He was tried for treason in Paris in July 1945, deprived of his military rank and sentenced to death, a penalty subsequently commuted to life imprisonment, served on the Île d'Yeu in the northern Bay of Biscay where he died and was buried. Successive governments ignored appeals that he should be reinterred, as he had wished, at Verdun.

Philippines. Islands conquered by the Spanish in 1565 and remaining in Spanish hands until ceded to the United States by the Treaty of Paris (10 December 1898) after the Spanish–American War. A Filipino national leader, Emilio Aguinaldo (1869–1964), who had already led an anti-Spanish rebellion in 1896, maintained a resistance movement from February 1899 until April 1902. The Americans conceded self-rule and recognized the rights of the Filipinos to independence by the Jones Act of 1916. The Tydings–McDuffie Act of March 1934 established a 'commonwealth' administration in which the Philippines had autonomy under a President, Manuel ►Quezon, but in which the US High Commissioner retained certain rights of veto. The Japanese invaded the islands in December 1941, capturing the capital, Manila, on 2 January 1942: General ►MacArthur continued resistance at Corregidor in Manila bay until May. US troops returned in June 1944, recapturing Manila in February 1945, and liberating all the Philippines, except for some remote mountain areas, by July. The independent republic of the Philippines was established on 4 July 1946, the US retaining certain military and air bases. The communist-dominated ►Hukbalahap movement posed political and economic problems, 1946–50, and from 1953 onwards the republic was dominated politically by right-wing nationalists. In 1965 President Ferdinand ►Marcos established a repressive dictatorship and a revised constitution was proclaimed in 1972 by Presidential decree under martial law. In February 1986 the Marcos government was overthrown by a popular church-backed, liberal movement headed by Mrs Cory ►Aquino, widow of Benigno Aquino, former leader of the People's Power Movement who was assassinated at Manila airport on his return from three years' exile in the United States (21 August 1983). Mrs Aquino became President on 24 February 1986 but was forced to take sweeping emergency powers a month later in order to safeguard the democratic revolution and had difficulty in foiling plots to overthrow her government in November 1986 and August 1987. She was succeeded by Fidel Ramos in June 1992. He began talks aimed at curbing the insurgency of both Muslims and Maoist communists in Mindanao, promising in 1996 the creation of an autonomous Muslim region on the island. On 21 December 1987 the Philippines suffered the worst peacetime shipping disaster when a ferry sank off Manila, with the loss of more than 1,550 lives.

Pilsudski, Józef (1867–1935). Polish soldier and statesman. Born near Vilna: studied at the University of Kharkov and spent the years 1887–92 in Siberian exile as a socialist agitator. On his return to Russian Poland he founded and edited an underground left-wing newspaper, *Robotnik*, which combined socialist and nationalist views. He travelled to Tokyo in 1904 to seek Japanese aid for a Polish revolt during the Russo-Japanese War. In 1914 he recruited a Polish legion of 10,000 men who fought with the Austrians against the Russians but he was interned in 1917 by the Germans, who did not trust him. On his release in 1918 he went to Warsaw where the authorities gave him command of all Polish troops and made him provisional head of state. He successfully defended Poland against the Bolsheviks in 1919–20 and was the dominant figure in Poland until 1921, continuing as head of the army until May 1923. After three years of retirement he staged a military *coup* in May 1926, largely because he was exasperated by the instability of the democratic governments. From 1926 until his death on 12 May 1935 he was virtual dictator, serving as Prime Minister 1926–8 and briefly in 1930 and remaining Minister of War throughout the period. He was one of the first European statesmen to see the menace of Nazi Germany. After vainly seeking to arouse his French allies, he authorized the signing of a ten-year Polish–German non-aggression pact (January 1934).

Pius XII (born Eugenio Pacelli, 1876–1958, elected pontiff in March 1939), Pope. Born and educated in Rome, ordained priest 1899, entering the papal secretariat in 1901, spending the next thirty-eight years in the papal diplomatic service. He was created a cardinal in 1930, becoming papal Secretary of State at the same time. For much of his life he was concerned with German affairs, nuncio to Bavaria in 1917 (where he tried unsuccessfully to promote a negotiated peace) and nuncio to the Weimar Republic in the 1920s, as well as being responsible for an agreement with Nazi Germany in 1933. This record, and his natural sympathy as Pope with the people of Rome during the allied bombings of the Second World War, led to much criticism of his political attitudes, and in particular of his failure to protest vigorously at Germany's persecution of the Jews. His condemnation of the post-war governments in Yugoslavia, Poland, Romania and Hungary left little room for compromise. He supported attempts to relieve distress among prisoners and refugees, both during and after the war.

Plate, Battle of the River (13 December 1939). First major naval engagement of the Second World War. The German pocket battleship, *Graf Spee*, commerce-raiding in the South Atlantic, was sighted by a cruiser squadron commanded by Commodore Harwood (later Admiral Sir Henry Harwood, 1888–1959) in HMS *Ajax*, accompanied by the slightly larger cruiser *Exeter* and the New Zealand light cruiser *Achilles*. Although inflicting heavy damage on *Exeter*, the pocket battleship was forced into Montevideo for repairs. Before a larger naval force could reach the Plate Estuary the *Graf Spee* put to sea again. It was scuttled on Hitler's orders, rather than risk a renewal of the battle, off the coast of Uruguay on the evening of 17 December. Inactivity elsewhere in the first winter of war caused news of the naval victory to be received with particular elation in Britain: the ships' companies of *Ajax* and *Exeter* were inspected by King George VI on Horse Guards Parade and entertained by the Lord Mayor of London at the Guildhall on their return to England (23 February 1940).

PLO. ➤Palestine Liberation Organization.

Poincaré, Raymond (1860–1934), French President. Born at Bar-le-Duc, was a lawyer in Paris when elected a Deputy in 1887, remaining in the Chamber until 1903 and thereafter serving as a Senator, 1903–13 and again 1920–29. He was briefly Minister of Education, 1893–5, and Finance Minister for a few months in

1906. From January 1912 to January 1913 he headed a Republican–Radical coalition, preoccupied with electoral reform and raising France's international prestige. In February 1913 he became President of the Third Republic, vainly hoping he could assert the President's authority and thus provide stronger government for France. A state visit to St Petersburg in July 1914 furthered military collaboration between the two allies during the war, but Poincaré's relations with the principal wartime premier, Clemenceau, were strained, and they remained uneasy during the Paris Peace Conference when, once again, Poincaré tried to be an active President and not a mere figurehead. His Presidential term expired in February 1920 and in January 1922 he became the first ex-President to head a government, of which he was Foreign Minister as well as Prime Minister for much of his ministry. He pursued a nationalistic and conservative policy, marked by the occupation of the ➤Ruhr. His cabinet broke up in January 1924 but he was summoned back to office in July 1926 as Prime Minister of a 'Government of National Union' which carried through stringent financial economies, stabilizing the franc. Poincaré finally retired in July 1929.

Poland. In the eighteenth century, Poland was a weak kingdom with an elective monarchy. Encroachments by powerful neighbours led to the partitioning of Poland between the Russians, Prussians and Austrians (1772, 1793, 1795, boundaries revised 1815). This division persisted and hostility to Polish nationalism formed a common bond between the Russian, Austrian and Prussian autocracies up to the eve of the First World War. During the war both sides attempted to gain Polish national support, a situation astutely exploited by the Polish leader, Marshal ➤Pilsudski. An independent Poland was reconstituted in 1918, finally absorbing so much former Russian territory that the new republic became the biggest state in eastern Europe, and larger in area than Italy. Germany and Russia combined again in 1939 (➤Nazi–Soviet Pact) to overrun inter-war Poland and inflict a fifth partition. Polish–Soviet relations remained strained even after Hitler's invasion of Russia (➤Katyn, ➤Sikorski, ➤Warsaw Rising) and at the end of the war, the Soviet Union thrust the new Poland's western frontier to the ➤Oder–Neisse Line, retaining the ➤Curzon Line as the Soviet boundary. After a period of coalition, Poland was established as a communist-dominated state under Boleslaw Bierut (1892–1956) by December 1948, with the Soviet Marshal, Rokossovsky, as Minister of War from November 1949. Dissatisfaction with the cost of living and with Soviet 'exploitation' led to strikes and rioting in Poznań at the end of June 1956 in which fifty-three workers were killed. To forestall a serious rebellion the pragmatic conservative communist, ➤Gomulka, was put in office in order to accomplish an austere and controlled series of reforms. A further sharp rise in food prices in the closing months of 1970 led to riots in Gdańsk, Gdynia and Szczecin and to Gomulka's replacement as head of the party by Edward Gierek (1913–94). Gierek attempted to raise living standards by producing more consumer goods. When in June 1976 he sought to increase food prices, rioting in Polish cities once more made the government drop its proposals. Gierek found himself unable to meet agricultural and industrial production targets. He was faced by mounting opposition, especially from dissident students. The election of Cardinal Wojtyła of Cracow as Pope (►John Paul II) increased the already powerful influence of the Church, and his 'religious pilgrimage' back to his homeland in June 1979 emphasized the historic links between catholicism and the Polish nation. Over the following fourteen months communist leadership faltered, with admissions by Gierek that the economy had been mismanaged. Another wave of strikes in the summer of 1980 was followed by the emergence of an independent trade union, ►Solidarity, whose leader, Lech ►Wałęsa, began to demand political as well as economic concessions. Gierek was taken to hospital with a heart attack on 5 September and replaced as party leader by Stanislaw Kania. A bad harvest and poor distribution of food led to continued unrest throughout the winter of 1980–81, foreign observers fearing armed intervention by the Soviet forces. On 9 February 1981 General ►Jaruzelski was appointed Prime Minister but he found it expedient to make even more concessions. Early in May Solidarity won the right to broadcast its own radio and television programmes while the communist leaders complained ominously of 'serious deterioration' in public order. Seven of the eleven members of the Polish Politburo failed to be re-elected in mid-July, a demonstration of dissidence followed by a trebling of the price of bread and by strikes of protest by women workers. On 18 September 1981 Jaruzelski ousted Kania as party leader. He at once ordered troops to use tear gas against strikers at Katowice. This hardening of attitude on the part of the Polish authorities, under Russian pressure, was followed on 14 December 1981 by a proclamation of martial law and by the arrest and internment of Solidarity leaders. Strict repression was gradually relaxed in May and June 1982 but the easing of the curfew restrictions was followed by new demonstrations, notably in Poznań. A planned visit by the Pope to Czestochowa in August 1982 for the 600th anniversary of the shrine was postponed but he was able to return to Poland in June 1983 and June 1987. Martial law was relaxed towards the end of 1982 and lifted entirely in July 1983. In December 1986 Jaruzelski, who had become head of state in 1985, established a Consultative Council which included several senior Catholic laymen and a human rights lawyer. State-run enterprises were promised greater autonomy in 1987 and in January 1988 an ombudsman was appointed. Inflation again forced up the price of food during 1988, causing further discontent. Early in 1989 talks between the Solidarity leaders and the government were followed by constitutional revision in April and by a General Election on 4 June for 35 per cent of the seats in the parliament, a ballot won overwhelmingly by Solidarity candidates. After several weeks of political and economic crisis, Tadeusz Mazowiecki – a noncommunist Solidarity nominee and Roman Catholic – became Prime Minister of a coalition government. In December 1990 Lech Wałęsa won the first democratic election for the presidency. During the five-year Wałęsa presidency tension developed with the *Sejm* (parliament) over the pace of economic reform and the need for constitutional revision; and the presidential election of November 1995 was won by a former communist, Alexander Kwasniewski (1954–). Nevertheless, Poland strengthened links with Western Europe, reaching agreement over cooperation with the EEC in 1991 and applying for membership of the ►European Union in 1994; the West reciprocated with an invitation to join NATO in July 1997. After eight years of intermittent debate a new constitution, recognizing the Catholic traditions of the country but refusing to endorse papal social teachings on family ethics, won popular backing in a referendum on 25 May 1997. Solidarity won the parliamentary elections held on 21 September 1997.

Pompidou, Georges Jean Raymond (1911–74), second President of the Fifth French Republic. Born at Montboudif in the Auvergne, schoolmaster in Marseilles and Paris, fought with the Resistance, joined de Gaulle's staff as an adviser on economics and education in 1944, served as a director of the Rothschild Bank and was de Gaulle's principal administrative adviser in May 1958. In 1961 he became chief contact with the Algerian nationalists in France and was largely responsible for the ►Évian Agreements. He was appointed Premier in May 1962, showing much political tact and dexterity, notably in the crisis caused by the ►student demonstrations of 1968. Resentment at his rising prestige and authority seems to have induced President de Gaulle to drop him as Prime Minister in early July 1968. Pompidou announced that he would be a candidate for the next presidential election. When ►de Gaulle resigned in April 1969, Pompidou was the obvious successor. He was elected President by the National Assembly at the second ballot, on 15 June 1969, the communists abstaining. Although Pompidou did not have the legendary appeal of his predecessor he showed distinctive statesmanship, especially in questions concerning the European Community. His health began to give way rapidly in 1973 and he died from a form of cancer on 2 April 1974.

Popular Front. A coalition of left-wing and centre parties in opposition to fascism in the 1930s. The French Popular Front was in power from June 1936 to October 1938, led by ►Blum, Camille Chautemps and ►Daladier. Extensive social reforms went side by side with the suppression of fascist groups. The Senate, in France always conservative, hampered the reforms and showed wide suspicion of the coalition, which eventually broke up because of left-wing criticism of Daladier's role at ►Munich. In Spain the Popular Front governments of ►Azaña, Caballero and Negrin were in office from February 1936 until March 1939; and it was against these governments that Franco and the Nationalists waged the ►Spanish Civil War. A Popular Front government in ►Chile, established by President Aguirre in 1938 and marked by genuine social welfare reforms, survived until the emergence of a wave of anti-communist sentiment in 1947.

Port Arthur (also known as Lushunkow, Dairen and Lu-ta). Chinese seaport in a key position commanding the Gulf of Pechili, captured by the Japanese 1894, returned to the Chinese 1895, and leased to the Russians in March 1898. The Japanese began the ►Russo-Japanese War with a surprise attack on warships at

419

Port Arthur (February 1904) and proceeded to occupy the neck of the peninsula, imposing a ten-month siege on the town. From 1905 to 1945 the Japanese leased Port Arthur, using it as an important naval base. The Soviet Union controlled the port from 1945 to 1955, when it was at last handed back to China.

Portsmouth (New Hampshire), Treaty of (September 1905). Ended the ➤Russo-Japanese War. Both countries agreed to evacuate ➤Manchuria, which was restored to Chinese rule. The Russians transferred to Japan their lease over ➤Port Arthur and its hinterland, as well as ceding the southern half of Sakhalin and acknowledging Japanese predominance in Korea. The Treaty ended Tsarist Russia's forward policy in the Far East but it was unpopular in Japan as it did not provide for a war indemnity. Signature of the Treaty in the United States confirmed the emergence of America as a world power prepared to mediate in the affairs of other continents.

Portugal. A monarchy since 1128, Portugal became a republic on 5 October 1910 after a three-day insurrection which forced King Manuel II (1889–1932) to flee to England, only two and a half years after the assassination of his father, Carlos I, and his elder brother (1 February 1908). Portuguese republicanism sprang from resentment at royal extravagance, hostility to a reactionary Church, and acute poverty among the workers. Anti-clerical laws, a liberal constitution and other palliatives introduced by the republicans did not change conditions: Portugal remained poor, backward, inefficiently governed and corrupt, with the republicans as dependent on the military as the monarchy had been. Improved social conditions came with the virtual dictatorship of Dr ➤Salazar from 1928 onwards, although at the cost of lost personal liberties in his 'New State' (Estado Novo). Salazar was succeeded as Prime Minister in September 1968 by Dr Marcello Caetano, who failed either to liberalize the political structure or to halt the demoralizing wars in Portugal's colonies of Angola and ➤Mozambique. Protests by two senior army commanders, Generals Spinola and Gomes, in February 1974 were taken up by a secret left-wing group of junior officers, the 'Captains' Movement' which, turning itself into the 'Armed Forces Movement', staged a military *coup* on 25 April 1974 'to save the nation from the government'. This 'Revolution of Flowers' led to administration by the Junta of National Salvation, a coalition headed by General Spinola, who was President from 15 May to 30 September 1974. The Junta allowed socialist and communist exiles to return and throughout 1975 a *coup* by the extreme left seemed probable. The President (General Costa Gomes, from September 1974 until July 1976) collaborated with the moderate socialist leader, Mario Soares (1924–), and forestalled a communist takeover on 25 November 1975. The situation was sufficiently stable for Portugal's first free elections in fifty years to be held on 25 April 1976, the socialists gaining 35 per cent of the vote. Dr Soares formed a minority government which was faced by a grave economic crisis. He survived defeats in parliament in December 1977 but finally resigned in July 1978. There followed a period of political confusion, with elections in December 1979 and

October 1980 and with five Prime Ministers in two and a half years, among them Senhora Maria Pintassilgo, the first Portuguese woman to enter high politics. Not until July 1987, when Anibal Cavaco Silva (1939–) gained an electoral triumph for the Social Democrats, did a government enjoy an absolute majority. By then Soares, who served as President from 1986 until March 1996, could regard the 'transitional stage of democracy' as over. Portugal joined the EEC in January 1985 and improved relations with the former colonies in Africa while, in 1987, negotiating a treaty with Peking for Macao to follow neighbouring Hong Kong to become a Special Administrative Region of China on 20 December 1999. The socialists won a parliamentary majority in Lisbon in the election of October 1995 and a socialist Jorge Sampaio (1938–) succeeded Soares as President.

Potsdam Conference (16 July to 2 August 1945). The last of the wartime summit conferences, held in the former Hohenzollern palaces at Potsdam, outside Berlin. Truman and Stalin were present throughout the Conference. The results of the British general election were announced while the Conference was in session. Churchill and Eden (Foreign Secretary) headed the British delegation but were accompanied by ➤Attlee who was Leader of the Opposition at the start of the Conference but Prime Minister for the final sessions. Churchill and Eden did not attend any of the meetings after 24 July: ➤Bevin replaced Eden. The main questions discussed were allied control in Germany, reparations, the ➤Oder–Neisse Line and Russian intervention in the war against Japan. Stalin was informed by Truman of the existence of the ➤atomic bomb.

Poujadism. An independent conservatively minded political movement, violently active in France 1954–8, and taking its name from its founder, Pierre Poujade (1920–), a bookseller from central-southern France. It was an anti-intellectual, anti-socialist and anti-European body, technically known as the Union de Défense des Commerçants et Artisans, and recruited its members primarily from small shopkeepers whose profits had been hit by rapid inflation. In the French elections of January 1956, fifty-two Poujadist Deputies were returned to the National Assembly, but the protest movement quickly declined with the return to political life of ➤de Gaulle and the new challenges of the ➤Fifth Republic.

Powell, (John) Enoch (1912–98), British politician. Born Birmingham, educated King Edward VI School and at Trinity College, Cambridge, where he was a classics don 1934–8. After two years as Professor of Greek at the University of Sydney he served in the Second World War, finishing with the rank of brigadier. He was elected Conservative MP for Wolverhampton, South West, in 1950 holding the seat until February 1974. From October 1974 to 1987 he was Ulster Unionist member for South Down. He served under Macmillan for three years as Minister of Health (1960–63), but was recognized as a strongly right-wing and individualistic member of the cabinet, hostile to British membership of the European Community. Later he became widely known (and much reported) for his desire to check the growth of the coloured population within Britain by ending Commonwealth immigration and by supporting repatriation.

Prague. Principal city in Bohemia and, after 1918, capital of ►Czechoslovakia. Like ►Munich and ►Suez, Prague is an emotive place-name in contemporary history, recalling three separate international crises: March 1939, when Hitler's occupation of the Czech capital in defiance of the Munich Agreement finally discredited ►appeasement; February 1948, when mass demonstrations of workers in the streets formed a background to the establishment of one-party rule by ►Gottwald; August 1968, when Soviet tanks entered the city to check the movement of liberalization – sometimes called the 'Prague Spring' – initiated by Prime Minister ►Dubček.

Primo de Rivera, Miguel (1870–1930), Spanish general and dictator. Born at Jerez de la Frontera, near Cádiz, the son of a Spanish Governor-General in the Philippines, a Spanish possession which Primo helped unsuccessfully to defend as a major in 1898. He thereafter saw active service in Morocco and was a full major-general by 1910. Anarchism and demands for Catalan autonomy so weakened the Spanish monarchy that, on 13 September 1923, ►Alfonso XIII encouraged Primo to seize power and establish a fascist-type dictatorship. The Cortes was dissolved, and the country placed under martial law, while the censored newspapers printed Primo's appeals for loyalty to 'Country, Religion and Monarchy'. Increasing discontent among workers and students forced a relaxation of the dictatorship in December 1925, but for more than four years Primo continued as Prime Minister until his health gave way at the end of January 1930 and he resigned, to die six weeks later. His son, José Antonio Primo de Rivera (1903–36), founded the ►Falange, developing his father's ideas into a paternalistic and strongly Catholic fascism, but was executed by extreme left-wing militants at Alicante, soon after the start of the ►Spanish Civil War.

Profumo Affair (1963). In March 1963 rumours were circulating at Westminster concerning the relationship between the War Minister, John Profumo (1915–) and a call-girl, Christine Keeler, who allegedly also associated with a Soviet naval attaché. In a statement to the Commons on 22 March the War Minister denied impropriety in his acquaintance with Christine Keeler, but on 4 June he admitted that he had misled the House and resigned from office, from the Privy Council and from parliament. A subsequent inquiry, headed by Lord Denning, concluded that the 'Profumo Affair' had not endangered national security. These revelations, which were given relentless publicity by the newspapers, damaged the standing of the Conservative Government, not least because the whole episode seemed to have taken the Prime Minister, Harold Macmillan, by surprise. The popularity of the Conservatives (in power for thirteen years) was already declining: the Profumo Affair merely accelerated that decline. John Profumo subsequently undertook philanthropic works in the poorer areas of London. For these services he was created CBE (Commander of the British Empire) in 1975.

Progressive Conservative Party (Canada). A party of free enterprise and strong Commonwealth links, in power in Canada under ►Bennett from 1930 to 1935 and ►Diefenbaker, from 1957 to 1963. The party's strength comes from the traditional Conservative regions in the Eastern Provinces (though not in Quebec). There was a strong, separate and individualistic Progressive Party, mostly Liberal dissidents, in 1921−5; some of these voters subsequently supported the Conservatives of Bennett, thus justifying the name under which the party campaigned from 1930 onwards.

Prohibition. The term applied to the period between January 1920 and December 1933 when the manufacture, sale or carriage of alcoholic drinks was prohibited by the 18th Amendment to the constitution throughout the United States. Temperance societies began urging prohibition on state legislatures in the 1830s, and by 1920 there were restrictions in nineteen states. The national agitation, started by the Anti-Saloon League in 1895, received wide backing during the war when it was alleged that 'liquor' was unpatriotic because of the control exercised by German-born citizens over the drink trade. The 18th Amendment was proposed on 3 December 1917, but not ratified until the war was over. Prohibition was evaded on a large scale throughout the 1920s: illicit distilling and distribution ('bootlegging') fell under the control of major criminals and led to a rise in gangster warfare, especially in Chicago. Repeal of Prohibition became a plank in the platform of the Democrats in 1928 and in 1932, and a proposal to repeal the 18th Amendment was put to Congress three weeks after Franklin Roosevelt's inauguration as President. The 21st Amendment, ratified on 5 December 1933, duly abandoned federal Prohibition, leaving states the right to determine anti-drink laws of their own.

Propaganda. The use of the Latin word 'propaganda' originated in late sixteenth-century Rome and was employed by Pope Gregory XV in 1622 when he established the Sacred Congregation of Propaganda, a commission of cardinals with responsibility for spreading the faith in heathen lands. Modern propaganda techniques were first widely used by the opposing combatants in the First World War to convince doubters at home and abroad of the righteousness of their respective causes and to denigrate their opponents by spreading tales of alleged atrocities. Propaganda subsequently became the chief ideological weapon of the new dictatorships in Russia, Italy and Germany. It was also used by governments with a sense of major national grievance (for example, Hungary's resentment of the Treaty of ►Trianon). ►Broadcasting and the ►cinema were natural instruments of propaganda. So, too, in the hands of Hitler's propaganda minister, ►Goebbels, were the Olympic Games of 1936 and the annual ►Nuremberg Rallies. During the Second World War allied propaganda concentrated on the ideological appeal of individual rights, such as

Roosevelt's 'four freedoms' – *of* speech and worship, *from* fear and want. Goebbels stressed the evils of Bolshevism and the alleged 'poisonous conspiracy of world Jewry'. There is no evidence that the war of words undermined opposing governments or shook morale but it may have bolstered acceptance at home of the existing order. Propaganda has deviated more and more from its original objective, the spread of a faith abroad. Since the Second World War rival propaganda machines have tended principally to laud the merits of one or other 'way of life', an exercise in contentment rather than in subversion.

Provisional Government (Russia). The name given to the liberal, republican and democratic form of government established in Russia on 12 March 1917 and remaining in power until the Bolshevik rising of 6 November (➤Russian Revolution). The Provisional Government – headed by Prince Lvov until 20 July and then by ➤Kerensky – favoured continued commitment to the war against Germany. Its authority was continuously hampered by conflicts with the Bolshevik-dominated Soviet in Petrograd.

Pu-yi, Henry (1906–67), last Manchu Emperor in China and sole Emperor of Manchukuo. Born in Peking, succeeded to the imperial throne as a child of two, a regency being established under a reactionary warlord prince while the child was given the title Emperor Hsuan T'ung. The Chinese republican revolution in October 1911 led to the nominal abdication of the boy-emperor on 12 February 1912, and he was allowed to live in a summer palace near Peking, receiving his education from an English tutor. He remained a toy of the warlords, one of whom reinstated him on the throne for eleven days in 1917. Mounting disorder in northern China in 1928 induced him to find sanctuary in the Japanese zone of Tientsin. When the Japanese occupied ➤Manchuria in 1931 they appointed him nominal head of their puppet government, and he was proclaimed Emperor K'ang Te of Manchukuo on 1 March 1934, although he was no more than a figurehead sovereign. He abdicated again on 19 August 1945, was captured by Soviet troops and interned in Siberia until 1950 when he was handed over to the Chinese People's Republic. After a period of political re-education, he spent his last years as a private citizen in Peking who was invited occasionally, as a social curiosity, to official receptions for distinguished foreign guests.

Q

Quebec Conferences (1943, 1944). Two conferences between Roosevelt and Churchill and their combined chiefs of staff were held in Quebec during the Second World War. The first conference (code-named 'Quadrant'), 19–24 August 1943, was concerned with plans for the Normandy landings, with land operations in south-east Asia (particularly the ►Burma campaign) and with the development of the Italian campaign. The second conference (code-named 'Octagon'), 13–16 September 1944, was primarily concerned with shifting the naval balance to the Pacific in order to finish off Japan after the defeat of Germany, but it also discussed the most effective military routes of advance into Germany, the ►Morgenthau Plan and operations in the Philippines.

Québec Libre. The independent aspirations of the French-speaking electorate in Quebec have long been a familiar feature of Canadian politics. Traditionally French Canadians have supported the Liberals: three Liberal Prime Ministers – ►Laurier, ►St Laurent and ►Trudeau – have been of French Canadian origin. By the mid sixties, however, Liberal support for French Canadian culture and patronage of the French language failed to satisfy the younger generation. A specifically separatist movement, the Parti Québécois, was created, under the leadership of the ex-Liberal, René Levesque. Their separatism received wide publicity when President de Gaulle, addressing a crowd from the balcony of Montreal town hall, exclaimed, '*Vive le Québec libre!*' (24 July 1967). In 1968 and 1969 the Canadian Government complained at attempts by the provincial government of Quebec to deal directly with foreign governments, an issue revived in November 1977 when M. Levesque was received during a visit to Paris with dignities normally reserved for a head of state. Political support for the Parti Québécois grew rapidly in the 1970s: in the provincial election for the 110-member Quebec National Assembly, the party gained six seats in 1971 and seventy seats five years later. This remarkable victory of 15 November 1976 was regarded by some observers as evidence that Quebec, in which four-fifths of the population were French-speaking, would soon secede, either by agreement or unilaterally, from the dominion.

Quemoy. The largest of several 'offshore islands' (of which the others are in the Matsu and Pescadores groups) included in the territory of ►Taiwan since 1949, despite the proximity of the Chinese communist mainland. Quemoy is little more than six miles from the mainland port of Amoy, and was used by the Nationalist armies of Chiang Kai-shek as a base for amphibious guerrilla raids, especially in the period 1953–8. Communist batteries shelled the islands heavily in August and

September 1958, threatening an invasion or a blockade, and the defenders were assisted by supply vessels escorted by US warships. A further invasion threat in June 1962 was again countered by strong American support for the Taiwan authorities.

Quezon, Manuel Luis (1878–1944). President of the ►Philippines, born near Manila, becoming a plantation manager for the Church and joining Aguinaldo in rebellion against Spanish colonial rule. He became an attorney in 1903 and was sent to Washington in 1909 where, for seven years, he championed Filipino claims for complete independence. From 1917 until 1934 he presided over the Philippine Senate. President Franklin ►Roosevelt sympathized with his political ideals and supported Quezon when, in 1935, he was elected the first President of the Philippine Commonwealth. His attempts to establish a corruption-free administration were cut short in 1942 by the Japanese invasion. Quezon escaped and for the last two years of his life had a seat on the Pacific War Council in Washington, where he died. A district of Manila was named after him and, from 1949, served as the administrative centre of the independent republic of the Philippines.

Quisling, Vidkun (1887–1945), Norwegian traitor. Born at Fyredal, in the county of Telemark, the son of a Lutheran pastor. After an exceptionally brilliant career at the military academy he became a General Staff officer in 1911, was military attaché in Russia and Finland 1918–21, and retired from the army as a major in 1923. In 1931–3 he served as Minister of Defence in an Agrarian Party Government but his dislike of democratic methods led him in May 1933 to establish the Nasjonal Samling ('National Unity') movement, in imitation of the German Nazis. He visited Hitler in December 1939 to discuss a possible *coup d'état* in Oslo and he revealed secrets concerning Norwegian defences to German agents in Copenhagen on 3 April 1940, six days before the surprise German occupation of Norway began. Under his leadership the 'National Unity' movement administered Norway under German protection from April 1940, and he became puppet 'prime minister' on 1 February 1942. At the end of the war he was charged with high treason and executed (24 October 1945). His name became an eponym for the leader of an enemy-sponsored regime, a usage current in the British Press even before the end of April 1940.

R

R.101 Disaster. The largest airship in the world, the British R.101, crashed on a hillside near Beauvais, France, on 5 October 1930 killing forty-eight passengers and crew on her maiden commercial flight, from Cardington in Bedfordshire to Egypt and India. Among the dead was the Secretary of State for Air, Lord Thomson. This disaster led the British authorities to abandon the construction of airships for military or commercial flights, relying on aircraft – especially flying-boats – to 'link the Empire together'. Germany, however, persisted with the commercial ➤Zeppelins until 1937.

Rabin, Yitzhak (1922–95), Israeli soldier and Prime Minister. Born in Jerusalem of Russian immigrants, he studied agricultural engineering but became a soldier and completed an officer cadet course in England early in the Second World War. He fought in defence of the newly independent Israel in 1948–9 and rose to become a general and to serve as Chief of Staff from 1964 until after the ➤Six-Day War in 1967. Rabin was ambassador in Washington, from 1968 to 1973, and then entered Israeli Labour politics. In 1974 he succeeded Golda ➤Meir as Prime Minister, the first *sabra* (native-born Israeli) to head a government. He went out of office after the 1977 election but was Defence Minister in the coalition of 1984. With US backing he became Prime Minister again in July 1992 and concentrated on securing a settlement of the Palestinian Problem, concluding agreements with both King ➤Hussein of Jordan and the PLO leader, Yasir ➤Arafat. His policies of reconciliation angered Orthodox Jewish extremists, and on 4 November 1995 Rabin was shot dead by a Jewish student as he was leaving a peace rally in Tel Aviv.

Radical Parties. In British politics the 'radicals' were believers in thoroughgoing reform, generally members of the Liberal Party, as during the period of Lloyd George's reforms. Continental countries had specific Radical Parties, many of them originally representing individualistic protests at the power of the Church or of the great landowners, and several of them becoming conservative bodies by the 1920s, especially in eastern Europe. The most famous of the continental radical parties was the Parti Radical, later the Parti Radical-Socialiste, in France, founded in 1875, and having several associated political groups in the Senate and the Chamber of Deputies, so that the best-known French radical of the twentieth century, ➤Clemenceau, was not technically a party member from 1909 onwards. French Radicalism was fundamentally negative: hostile to the Catholic Church, hostile to political authoritarianism, hostile to economic collectivization (whether in the form of socialist nationalization or of big capitalist combines). This was the party of ►Caillaux, whom Clemenceau regarded as a political enemy, and later of ►Daladier; it survived into the Fourth Republic, achieving some distinction again under the leadership of ►Mendès-France.

Rahman, Tunku Abdul (1903–90), Prime Minister of Malaya and Malaysia. Born at Kuala Kedah, the son of the Sultan and his sixth wife (a Siamese princess). The Tunku was educated at St Catharine's College, Cambridge, and qualified as a barrister in London. In 1952 he founded a Malayan national party ('Alliance') which won the elections of 1955 and he became Prime Minister of an independent Malaya two years later and of the new Federation of ►Malaysia in 1963. The Tunku had the remarkable facility of securing collaboration between the Malay, Chinese and Indian peoples in the peninsula, largely by consultation between committees of national associations within the Alliance Party. This system held together until 1969 when protests at alleged privileges for Malays led to electoral reverses for the Alliance and to grave ethnic riots at Kuala Lumpur (14–15 May 1969) in which there were many deaths. The Tunku remained in office for another eighteen months, trying to restore better community relations by emergency government, finally retiring in January 1970.

Rahman, Sheikh Mujibur (1920–75), Bangladesh national leader. Born at Tongipara in East Bengal, studied law, became leader of the Awami League in 1954, campaigning for a ►Bangladesh state. He was arrested on several occasions under the rule of ►Ayub Khan. When talks on the future of ►Pakistan broke down he was charged with treason (August 1971) but was released after Indian military intervention in Bangladesh and returned to a hero's welcome in Dacca on 10 January 1972. He declined to serve as President of Bangladesh, an office to which he had been elected *in absentia*, but he became Prime Minister. The problem of creating a socialist state and parliamentary democracy in the area was too much for him. He assumed dictatorial powers in January 1975 but landowning officers in the army staged a military *coup d'état* on 15 August 1975 in which Mujibur Rahman and his immediate family were murdered.

Rajk, Laszlo (1909–49), Hungarian communist. Born near Budapest, becoming a communist while studying at the university, escaped to Spain and fought with the 13th International Brigade in the Civil War, being wounded in 1938 and secretly returning to Hungary through France. In Hungary he served as a go-between for the 'Peace Party' and the Soviet command, before being entrusted with building up the party organization in Budapest in 1945. He was Minister of the Interior, February 1946 to August 1948, when he became Foreign Minister. In May 1949 he was charged with having treasonable links with Tito and with having served as a secret police agent in the 1930s. At his trial in September 1949 (which was given wide publicity throughout the Soviet bloc) he pleaded guilty and was hanged a few days later. The evidence presented in the accusations was clearly fabricated:

in March 1956 he was officially rehabilitated by ➤Rákosi in a speech at Eger; and six months later his remains were solemnly reinterred in an official ceremony. His 'crime' seems to have been an un-Stalinist independence of spirit.

Rákosi, Mátyás (1892–1971), Hungarian communist leader. Born of Jewish parentage in Budapest, held minor office under Béla ➤Kun in 1919, escaped to Austria and to Russia whence he secretly returned to ➤Hungary in 1925, hoping to re-form an underground communist resistance. He was arrested, put on trial in 1927, jailed for eight years, re-arrested in 1935 and sentenced to life imprisonment. In November 1940 Rákosi and another arrested communist were allowed to return to Moscow in exchange for Hungarian patriotic flags held in Russian museums since their capture in 1849. He was immediately appointed chairman of a foreign committee of Hungarian communists and was recognized as the 'party boss' until July 1956, ruthlessly presiding over the establishment of a Stalinist regime in Hungary, 1945–9. He subsequently described the methods by which he induced rivals in the coalition to 'slice off' opposing factions: these 'salami tactics' left only orthodox communists. Rákosi's unwillingness to relax the controls of the secret police was one of the principal causes of the ➤Hungarian Rising of 1956, three months after his return to the USSR for a health cure.

Ramsey, Michael (1904–88). ➤Canterbury, Archbishop of.

Rapacki Plan. Adam Rapacki (1909–70), the Polish Foreign Minister, made a speech to the UN General Assembly on 2 October 1957 in which he proposed the creation of a zone free of nuclear weapons in central Europe. The Plan, as developed in a note issued to diplomatic representatives in Warsaw on 2 February 1958, suggested that there should be no nuclear weapons manufactured or 'stockpiled' in an area to include Poland, Czechoslovakia, the German Federal Republic and the German Democratic Republic. Joint inspection by NATO and Warsaw Pact states would ensure observance of the Plan, and Rapacki hoped it would be followed by reductions of conventional forces and by the creation of similar zones elsewhere in Europe and Asia. The Plan was supported by Khrushchev for the Soviet Union but rejected by the Americans and the British, who thought that, strategically, it would favour the Soviet-bloc countries with their greater number of conventional weapons and of conscripts. The Western Powers also distrusted the Plan since the Russians argued that it should be followed by direct talks over the future of the two Germanies and their relationship to each other, a proposal at that time unacceptable in Bonn.

Rapallo, Treaties of. There were two treaties of Rapallo, signed within a short period of each other but between different states and entirely unconnected: (1) 12 November 1920. A temporary bilateral agreement between Italy and Yugoslavia settling Adriatic disputes and pledging collaboration to prevent a Habsburg restoration. This pact is of much less importance than the following Rapallo Treaty, of 1922. (2) 16 April 1922. A Russo-German Treaty, unexpectedly concluded by delegations to a World Economic Conference at Genoa, twenty miles from Rapallo. The German and Soviet Governments re-established diplomatic relations, renounced financial claims on each other and pledged cooperation. The real significance of the Treaty lay in its conclusion rather than in its terms: it showed the recovery of both former empires from the diplomatic isolation caused by revolution and defeat, and foreshadowed five years of good German–Soviet relations, to the chagrin of the British and French.

Rasputin, Grigory (1871–1916), Russian 'holy man'. Born at Pokrovskoye, Tobolsk, accepted as a holy man at the Tsar's court because of the hypnotic healing power he exercised over the haemophiliac heir to the throne, Alexis (1904–18). Rasputin, confident of the Tsarina's protection, interfered in politics from 1911 onwards, securing high appointments in Church and State for his nominees and the dismissal of those of whom he did not approve, including at least one Prime Minister. His alcoholic excesses and debauched private life became common knowledge in St Petersburg society and provoked adverse Press comment on his influence. During the First World War it was widely believed he received German payment, and in December 1916 he was assassinated by exasperated aristocrats in a plot initiated by Prince Felix Yusupov (who was married to a favourite niece of the Tsar). Rumours of Rasputin's activities discredited the imperial couple – and, indirectly, the Orthodox Church – among the Russian people as a whole.

Rathenau, Walther (1867–1922), German industrialist and statesman. Born of Jewish parentage in Berlin, studied engineering and became director of the great electrical trust, AEG, which his father had founded. From 1916 to 1918 he was responsible for organizing Germany's war economy, countering the British blockade by control of labour and raw materials. His knowledge of economics was invaluable to the ►Weimar Republic and he entered politics as founder of a Democratic Party. In May 1921 he became Minister of Reconstruction and, at the end of the year, Minister of Foreign Affairs. He secured financial settlements with France and America and was largely responsible for the 1922 Treaty of ►Rapallo with Soviet Russia, whose regime he distrusted but was willing to exploit. On 24 June 1922 he was assassinated in a Berlin suburb by anti-Semitic nationalists. Rathenau's intellectual interests gave him understanding of Europe and a sense of international dependence, without lessening his conviction of Germany's ability to gain leadership of the Continent.

Reagan, Ronald (1911-), fortieth President of the USA. Born at Tampico, Illinois, educated at Eureka College and became a sports reporter and a Hollywood actor, appearing in some twenty-five films between 1937 and 1964, their titles ranging from *Accidents will Happen* to *Law and Order*. He served in the US Air Force from 1942 to 1946, entered politics as a Republican and was Governor of California from 1967 to 1974. In 1968 and 1976 he failed to gain the Republican Presidential nomination but a well-organized campaign pushed aside eleven other contenders in 1980 and he was acclaimed candidate at the party convention in Detroit in July. Four months later he won forty-four states in the Presidential election, although only 53 per cent of the electorate voted. On 20 January 1981 Reagan became the oldest American to take office as President for the first time, with markedly right-wing and strictly monetarist policies. In foreign affairs he was not always in agreement with his first choice as Secretary of State, Alexander ➤Haig, who resigned in June 1982. Within ten weeks of taking office, President Reagan was shot and wounded in the lung as he was leaving a Washington hotel (30 March 1981). His assailant, John Hinckley, was later found to be insane and unable to face trial. In the 1984 presidential election he won every state except Minnesota (and Washington, DC), defeating the Democrat candidate, Walter Mondale, by 525 electoral votes to 13. His second administration saw a rearguard action to stave off internal inflation and, outside the United States, heavy involvement in ➤Nicaragua, continuous tension with ➤Libya and in the Persian Gulf but a gradual thaw in the Great Power relationship, especially after the rise of ➤Gorbachev in 1985. His personal following remained high, despite an Iranian arms deal scandal in November 1986 which involved a White House aide (Colonel Oliver North) and the Contra rebels in Nicaragua. He was succeeded in January 1989 by his Vice-President, George ➤Bush.

Referendum. The practice of referring particular political questions to a direct popular vote. This procedure has been followed in many states and municipalities in the USA since 1898, when it was introduced by South Dakota. Referenda were favoured by General ➤de Gaulle and introduced in May 1946, although anticipated in the plebiscites of Napoleon III in the 1850s and 1860s. The ➤Fifth Republic made greater use of referenda than its predecessor. The practice has been followed in Switzerland and, among Commonwealth countries, especially in ➤Australia. In Britain a referendum was held for the first time over membership of the ➤European Economic Community, 5 June 1975.

Reichstag Fire (27 February 1933). The parliament (Reichstag) building in Berlin was destroyed by arson four weeks after Hitler became Chancellor. The police arrested a Dutch worker of low intelligence, Marinus van der Lubbe, who was put on trial at Leipzig, condemned and beheaded. The Nazi Government maintained that the fire was the first move in a communist conspiracy: three communists (including the Bulgarian exile, ➤Dimitrov) stood trial with van der Lubbe, but were acquitted largely through Dimitrov's brilliant defence which suggested that the fire was instigated by Nazis who wished to take emergency measures against parties of the Left. This explanation was accepted and endorsed by anti-Nazi exiles: after the fire Hitler used the 'red peril' as an excuse for rushing through an enabling law (23 March 1933) which conferred totalitarian powers on the Chancellor and his ministers. Later evidence made it seem probable that van der Lubbe started the fire on his own initiative but that prominent Nazis exploited the incident, possibly hampering the fire services.

Reparations. A form of war indemnity imposed on Germany and her allies by the peace treaties of 1919–20. The wisdom of requiring large sums from defeated countries which had lost markets was criticized by contemporary economists, notably ➤Keynes, but German reparations were fixed at £6,600 million plus interest in April 1921. A first instalment of £50 million was rapidly paid. The inflation of 1922 led the Germans to halt payments, prompting a Franco-Belgian occupation of the ➤Ruhr. The ➤Dawes Plan in 1924 helped Germany secure a loan to meet payments; and the ➤Young Plan in 1929 led to substantial cuts in the required sum and gave Germany until 1988 to complete her obligations. The general financial collapse in 1931 stopped all payment of reparations. In all, Germany paid one-eighth of the original figure, though foreign loans over the period 1924–30 to assist Germany's financial recovery were considerably greater than the amount of reparations received. Austria and Hungary were helped by loans backed by the League of Nations, specifically for 'reconstruction' but also to help meet the demand for reparations.

Republic of Ireland Act (1949). ➤Eire.

Republican Party. One of the two main political parties in the USA. The first Republican Party was founded by Thomas Jefferson in defence of agrarian interests and states' rights in 1792, but split into several factions in the 1820s. A second Republican Party was formed as an anti-slavery coalition in 1854, coming to power in 1861 with the victory of Abraham Lincoln and forming Administrations from 1861 down to 1913, apart from the years 1885–9 and 1893–7. At the turn of the century the party was accepted as representing 'big business' and as favouring high tariffs, economic imperialism and federal action. After the First World War the Republicans returned to power under Presidents Harding, Coolidge and ➤Hoover, giving free rein to business interests and free voice to ➤isolationism. The 'Grand Old Party' accepted international obligations after the Second World War and the victory of ➤Eisenhower in 1952 marked the emergence of a less sectional type of Republican sentiment. Traditional Republican beliefs – updated by Senator ➤Goldwater – had little appeal to the electorate, which has returned a predominantly Democratic Congress since 1932 (with brief Republican successes in 1946 and 1952). Under Richard ➤Nixon the Republican Party won the Presidential elections of 1968 and 1972 but was discredited by the ➤Watergate Affair and failed to break new ground in the 1976 elections. Four years later the successful Presidential campaign of Ronald ➤Reagan was accompanied by remarkable victories in the Congressional elections, giving the Republicans control of the Senate for the first time since 1954 and gaining them thirty-three seats in the House of Representatives. The Republicans controlled the Senate from 1981 to 1987 but never had a majority in the House of Representatives. In 1988 George ➤Bush and his running-mate, Senator J. Danforth Quayle of Indiana, won forty-three states for the Republicans. The election of November 1992 brought the Democrat ➤Clinton to the White House and the Republicans lost control of both houses of Congress. But in 1994 the Republicans recovered sufficiently to secure majorities in both Senate and House. Their presidential candidate in 1996, Robert Dole (1923–), fared badly but once again the Party kept a tight hold on the Congress.

Resistance Movement. The unwillingness of the other European peoples to accept the dominance of Nazi Germany and Fascist Italy in the Second World War was manifested by a resistance movement, diverse in character from country to country but intended to weaken the hold of Hitler and Mussolini either by direct action or by a passive defiance intended to sap confidence in the governing system. The best known acts of resistance were carried out in countries under enemy occupation but there were also instances of resistance within Italy and Germany, notably gestures of proud hostility in the concentration camps. Para-military operations were encouraged from London by SOE (Special Operations Executive) and, in Eastern Europe, from Moscow. The resistance movements helped prepare the way for the invading armies, notably in ►Yugoslavia, ►Slovakia and along the Rhône valley in France. Some resistance movements accomplished remarkable acts of sabotage, especially in Norway. Often there were political divisions within the resistance, not always a simple confrontation of 'left' and 'right'. In Warsaw, for example, the desperate revolt in the ghetto which ultimately cost the lives of some 30,000 Jews in April 1943 was an action totally distinct from the famous ►Warsaw Rising of Poland's 'Home Army' sixteen months later. The French resistance bands, known as the 'Maquis', were divided into guerrilla groups equally split between supporters of General ►de Gaulle and his ►'Free French' and communists who regarded him as a tool of London capitalism, someone who should be used, exploited and, in the end, discredited. The latent antagonisms within the resistance movements emerged after the liberation to help shape the political alignment in France and other Western European states

Revisionism. A term applied by orthodox and conventional Marxists to condemn attempts at critically reassessing the basic tenets of revolutionary socialism. The term originated in the 1890s and 1900s over the writings of ►Bernstein but it was revived after the 1948 breach between Stalin and ►Tito and has subsequently been used so freely in left-wing polemic that it has become battered beyond recognition. In a different sense and context the word 'revisionism' was used during the inter-war period to describe German, Hungarian and Bulgarian attempts to secure by inter-national agreement territorial changes in the boundaries imposed by the Treaties of ►Versailles, ►Trianon and ►Neuilly.

Revolution of 1905 (Russia). The refusal of Tsar ►Nicholas II to grant liberal concessions on his accession in 1894 was followed by mounting distress among the peasants (who bore a heavy burden of taxation) and the industrial workers. Defeat in the ►Russo-Japanese War brought discontent into the open. The disorders began on 22 January when troops opened fire on a peaceful demonstration in St Petersburg (►'Bloody Sunday'). The Tsar's promise in March to summon a 'consultative assembly' was insufficient to calm the mounting agitation. Throughout the spring and early summer there were strikes, outrages and assassinations. A serious mutiny broke out aboard a battleship in the Black Sea fleet, the *Potemkin* (28 June), and other units in the army and navy were affected. At the end of October all European Russia was paralysed by a general strike, directed in the capital by the first workers' Soviet. Tsar Nicholas yielded on 30 October, granting Russia a constitution which promised a legislative ➤Duma and, for the first time, a Prime Minister (➤Witte) was appointed. This so-called 'October Manifesto' split the revolutionaries. Most willingly accepted the Tsar's concessions, believing their revolution had triumphed. The Soviet still sought a total overthrow of the system and continued resistance for several weeks: from 21 December until 2 January 1906 there was grim street fighting in Moscow, with over 1,000 deaths; and there was less serious rioting at Rostov-on-Don. Order was restored by drastic methods in the countryside.

Reynaud, Paul (1878–1966), French Prime Minister. Born at Barcelonnette in the Basses-Alpes. After winning the Croix de Guerre in First World War, he entered politics and was a Deputy from 1919 to 1924 and 1928 to 1940 as well as in the post-war National Assemblies. Reynaud acquired widespread respect in the 1930s as a consistent opponent of Nazi Germany but his independent convictions – slightly to the right of centre – denied him any large following. Although he held ministerial posts in the 1930s he did not have the opportunity to form a government until 20 March 1940, too late to counter the defensive defeatism of France's military leaders. He was Prime Minister for only twelve and a half weeks, his authority weakened by his deputy and successor, Marshal ➤Pétain, who sought an armistice with the victorious Germans. On 28 June 1940, twelve days after his resignation, Reynaud was injured in a car crash, an accident which necessarily prevented him associating himself with the ➤'Free French' had he wished to do so. He was subsequently imprisoned by ➤Vichy France and interned by the Germans in Austria from 1943 to 1945. After the war he was Minister of Finance in 1948, failed to form a government when invited to become Prime Minister again in 1953 but remained President of the Finance Committee of the National Assembly for the early years of the Fifth Republic.

Reza Khan (1878–1944). Persian soldier who, as Reza Shah Pahlavi, ruled ➤Iran from 1925 to 1941.

Reza Pahlavi, Mohammed. ➤Pahlavi, Mohammed Reza.

Rhineland. Became Prussian in 1815, having its rich mineral deposits developed and exploited in the mid nineteenth century. The Treaty of ➤Versailles provided that the Rhineland should be occupied by allied troops for fifteen years and permanently demilitarized. An independent Rhineland Republic was encouraged by the French and the Belgians and technically existed, with Aachen as its capital and Dr Heinz as its President, from 21 October 1923 until Heinz's murder by

German nationalists three months later. The ►Locarno Treaties affirmed the permanence of demilitarization but ►Stresemann secured the evacuation of the Rhineland by the British in November 1926 and by the French in June 1930. International relations were again strained over Rhenish problems after Hitler's advent. In March 1936 Hitler alleged that the French were planning the encirclement of Germany and that the Reich required a fortified Rhineland for security. He ordered German troops to enter the demilitarized zone, thus violating both the Versailles and Locarno Treaties. The French and British Governments, preoccupied with the crisis over the ►Abyssinian War, contented themselves with protests. (►Ruhr and Saar.)

Rhodes, Cecil John (1853–1902). British imperialist. Born and educated at Bishop's Stortford and later at Oriel College, Oxford. As a young man he acquired a fortune in diamonds and gold in South Africa and, in 1887, founded the British South Africa Company to develop the area later known as ►Rhodesia. He was Prime Minister of Cape Colony, 1890–96, resigning because of his connection with attempts to overthrow the Boer republic in the ►Transvaal. He remained an influential figure in world politics, dying shortly after the end of the Boer War. Much of his £6-million fortune was left to Oxford University, some of it to endow scholarships tenable by men of high character from the British overseas empire, the USA or from Germany.

Rhodesia. Occupied, settled and administered by the British South Africa Company from 1890 until after the First World War, the white minority holding many views in common with white South Africans, though declining a proposal of union in October 1922. The territory became known as Southern Rhodesia and was granted limited powers of self-government in October 1923, London retaining a right to veto legislation concerning the African peoples. This restriction caused resentment by the dominant white minority although from 1934 to 1956 the premiership of Sir Godfrey Huggins (later Lord Malvern, 1883–1971) gave the country over twenty years of mildly paternalistic businessman's administration. Huggins, like ►Welensky in Northern Rhodesia, favoured the Federation of Rhodesia and Nyasaland (see below) and when this experiment failed his moderation gave way to the more right-wing attitudes of the Rhodesian Front, which won an electoral victory in 1962. When Ian ►Smith became Prime Minister in 1964 it was clear that his opposition to sharing power with the African majority ran counter to the liberal principles of other Commonwealth countries. Smith's ►Unilateral Declaration of Independence in November 1965 was condemned by the British, who imposed trade restrictions and an oil embargo, although declining to use armed force to put down Smith's defiant act of rebellion, as many African states demanded. The United Nations supported the British decision to impose a naval blockade off Portuguese Mozambique to prevent oil supplies reaching Rhodesia, although Smith was able to rely on the South African Government to aid him by sanctions-breaking. Attempts to reach a compromise by personal meetings between Harold Wilson and Smith in HMS *Tiger* and later in HMS *Fearless* were abortive. Missions by other British, United Nations and American intermediaries revealed few points of contact between Smith and majority opinion outside Rhodesia. On 2 March 1970 the Smith Government declared Rhodesia a republic and adopted a new constitution, supported by almost all the white voters in the country. On 26 October 1976 a conference on Rhodesia opened at Geneva attended by Ian Smith as well as by the Rhodesian African leaders and chaired by a British diplomat, Ivor Richard, but no agreement could be reached. Guerrilla actions by supporters of ►Zimbabwe and Rhodesian commando 'hot pursuit' raids on alleged guerrilla bases in Mozambique continued even while the Geneva Conference was in session. Anglo-American proposals for achieving a transition to majority rule in a legally independent Rhodesia were published on 1 September 1977: they included the appointment of a British resident high commissioner to take over authority from the Rhodesian Government during the transition. The commissioner-designate, Field-Marshal Lord Carver (1915–), travelled to Rhodesia on an exploratory mission at the end of November 1977. Meanwhile Ian Smith began negotiations with three moderate African leaders, Bishop Muzorewa, the Reverend N. Sithole and Chief Chirau. On 24 November 1977 Smith announced his willingness to accept the principle of adult universal suffrage; and on 1 March 1978 Smith and the three moderates reached agreement on achieving independence under black majority rule by 31 December 1978, the proposed legislative assembly to contain seventy-two blacks and twenty-eight whites. These proposals were rejected by the Anglo-American mediators and by the United Nations since they were unacceptable to the 'Patriotic Front' guerrillas of ►Nkomo and ►Mugabe. While Smith, Muzorewa, Chirau and Sithole formed an Executive Council to govern Rhodesia, guerrilla attacks and counter-violence by the Rhodesian Army continued until December 1979, when it was calculated that seven years of warfare had cost the lives of 20,000 black and white Rhodesians. The ►Commonwealth Conference at Lusaka (1–7 August 1979) provided an opportunity for contact with black African intermediaries, and a conference was convened at Lancaster House, London, in September at which Smith, Muzorewa, Mugabe and Nkomo negotiated a settlement, under the chairmanship of the Foreign and Commonwealth Secretary, Lord Carrington. It was agreed in November that the country would once again become the British dependency of Southern Rhodesia under a British Governor for a transitional period, pending the establishment of an independent Zimbabwe, with a multi-racial parliament. Lord Soames arrived as Governor in Salisbury on 12 December 1979, supervising the restoration of peace and the organizing of elections in the country within twelve weeks of his taking office. This remarkable achievement allowed the proclamation of the Zimbabwe Republic at midnight on 17–18 April 1980, thus ending ninety years of white rule in Rhodesia.

Rhodesia and Nyasaland, Federation of (1953–63). Abortive central African federation comprising Southern ►Rhodesia, Northern Rhodesia and Nyasaland.

The Federation was especially championed by Sir Roy ➤Welensky and Sir Godfrey Huggins (see above) who thought that the agriculture of Nyasaland, the copper-belt industries of Northern Rhodesia and the more sophisticated economy of Southern Rhodesia would be profitably balanced within a single political community. The Federation failed, primarily because of suspicion in Northern Rhodesia (the future ➤Zambia) and Nyasaland (the future ➤Malawi) of the attitude in the capital, Salisbury, to specifically African affairs. An advisory commission sent from London with Viscount Monckton as chairman published a report on 11 October 1960 which condemned racially discriminatory legislation, recommended more African participation in the Federal Assembly and emphasized the natural right of a territory to secede. A constitutional conference in London in 1961 showed major divergences between the three member territories, and the Federation was officially dissolved in December 1963.

Ribbentrop, Joachim von (1893–1946), German Foreign Minister. Born at Wesel, served as a cavalry officer in the First World War and later as a wine salesman. He joined the Nazi Party in the mid twenties and, boasting of his contacts abroad, was encouraged by Hitler to establish a foreign-intelligence information service, effective both before and after the Nazis came to power (1933). Ribbentrop was appointed German ambassador in London in October 1936, holding the post until recalled to Berlin to become Foreign Minister in February 1938. He was responsible for giving German foreign policy a specifically Nazi bent, of which the climax was the ➤Tripartite Pact of 1940. His most original and unexpected achievement was the ➤Nazi–Soviet Pact of August 1939. He was tried as a war criminal at ➤Nuremberg and hanged, 16 October 1946.

Rio Earth Summit. The name generally given to the UN Conference on the Environment, held at Rio de Janeiro in June 1992. An earlier UN conference on human environment at Stockholm in 1972 achieved so little that the UN Secretariat was determined to emphasize the importance of the issues raised by inviting 100 national leaders to attend, making Rio 'the biggest ever gathering of heads of government'. The conference considered problems of pollution of seas, rivers, lakes and the atmosphere, deforestation, the effects of climate change, the preservation of wild life, overconsumption of fossil fuels, the recycling of industrial waste. A 'Rio Declaration' of good intent was signed by most leading powers and supported by a 720-page 'blueprint for action' suggesting practical ways of implementing conference resolutions. Five years later a special meeting in New York deplored the lack of progress made since the Rio summit, noting that of the heavily industrialized nations only Germany and Great Britain had come close to the targets set over industrial pollution (➤Motor Vehicles).

Rivera, Primo de. ➤Primo de Rivera.

Roberts, Lord (Frederick Sleigh Roberts, 1832–1914, created viscount 1892, earl 1902), British field-marshal. Born at Cawnpore, educated at Clifton, Eton and

Sandhurst, gained the VC in the Indian Mutiny, and was one of the idols of Victorian England for his exploits in the Afghan War, 1879–80. After the first reversals in the Boer War he was appointed commander-in-chief in South Africa. His victorious advance ended with the capture of Pretoria in June. He returned to England at the end of the year 1900 and served as commander-in-chief of the army until the post was abolished in 1904. In his retirement he became a passionate and vociferous advocate of compulsory military service. He died on 14 November 1914 while inspecting Indian units newly arrived for service in France.

Rockefeller, John Davison (1839–1937), US oil magnate. Born in New York, settled near Cleveland, Ohio, in 1853, subsequently establishing an oil refinery which in 1870 was incorporated as the Standard Oil Company: within ten years he had gained a virtual monopoly of oil refining throughout America, dominating the world market by 1890. Despite legislation seeking to break the monopoly 'trust' character of the Rockefeller empire, his enterprises survived as one unit under different names. From 1890 onwards he was interested in philanthropic undertakings, notably medical research and education, establishing and richly endowing the University of Chicago (1891–2). These enterprises were further developed by his son and namesake (1874–1960). A grandson of the original oil magnate, Nelson Aldrich Rockefeller (1908–79), was a prominent liberal Republican Governor of New York State, 1959–74, and Vice-President of the United States under President Ford, 1974 to 1977.

Romania. Autonomous principality within the Ottoman Empire until 1862, gradually achieving independence which was fully recognized in 1877, with the reigning Prince, Charles of Hohenzollern-Sigmaringen, ruling as King Carol I from 1881 until his death in October 1914. Romania more than doubled her size, 1913–20, acquiring southern ►Dobrudja after the second Balkan War, and gaining ►Transylvania, ►Bessarabia, the ►Bukovina and much of the Hungarian plain in recognition of her role as an ally of France and Britain, 1916–18. (Although forced to make a separate peace on 5 March 1918, Romania redeclared war on Germany two days before the final armistice and thus ensured her seat among the victorious peacemakers.) Between the wars internal politics were notoriously corrupt and frequently marred by anti-Semitism, which was encouraged by the local variant of ►fascism, the 'Iron Guard' movement. King ►Carol II sought deviously to balance support for the ►Little Entente with a commercial understanding with Hitler's Germany, a good customer for Romania's oil. Although forced to surrender some territorial gains to the Soviet Union, Hungary and Bulgaria during the period of Nazi–Soviet collaboration (1939–40), the Romanians remained in the Axis camp under the leadership of General ►Antonescu. The Romanians suffered heavily in the invasion of Russia. When the Red Army reached the Romanian frontiers in 1944, King Michael (1921–, reigned 1927–30 and 1940–47) arrested Antonescu, made peace and declared war on Germany (15 August 1944). The Romanians sustained 150,000 casualties fighting against the Germans for the last nine months of the war in Europe and received lenient terms by the ►Paris Peace Treaties of 1947. King Michael was at first regarded with favour by the Soviet authorities, who awarded him the Order of Victory, but he was forced to make concessions to a communist-dominated Democratic Front from March 1945 onwards, and abdicated on 30 December 1947, Romania becoming a 'People's Republic' (a status changed to 'Socialist Republic' in 1965). Under ►Gheorghiu-Dej and ►Ceauşescu, Romania was able to play an increasingly independent role within the communist bloc, although a member of the ►Warsaw Pact and ►Comecon. Serious disputes arose in 1987–8 between Romania and Hungary over the treatment of the Magyar minority in ►Transylvania. The increasingly harsh dictatorship of Ceauşescu and the brutality of his secret police ('Securitate') led to widespread unrest. On 15 December 1989 an attempt to arrest Pastor Laszlo Tokes, champion of the Magyar minority, sparked off a rising in Timişoara (Temesvar) which spread to other cities while Ceauşescu was on a visit to China. When he flew back to Romania he was unable to restore his authority and, with his wife, was executed after a summary trial on 25 December. Four days later Romania dropped the 'Socialist' status of the republic and erased all communist insignia; an interim 'National Salvation Front' government promised early democratic elections, while charitable aid from the West sought to relieve social distress, particularly in the state orphanages. Twenty political parties contested the elections, held on 20 May 1990; the National Salvation Front won a landslide victory. Subsequently complaints that the Front retained too many office-holders and institutions from the Ceauşescu era led once more to anti-government demonstrations in Timişoara at the turn of the year. In 1991 a democratic constitution was adopted, which guaranteed human rights and a free market economy. Discontent at the slowness of reform caused further strikes and demonstrations but by 1996 parliamentary government was stable and settlements made with Hungary, Moldova and the Ukraine over frontier problems and minority rights. Romania joined the Council of Europe in 1993, applied for membership of the ►European Union in 1995, sent peacekeeping troops to Bosnia and Albania. Romanian citizenship was restored to King Michael in 1991. He was allowed to make an official visit to the country in February 1997 after fifty years in exile, and subsequently gave his support to Romania's (unsuccessful) bid to join NATO.

Rome, Treaties of (25 March 1957). Two Treaties were signed in Rome on the same day by representatives of Belgium, France, the German Federal Republic, Italy, Luxembourg and the Netherlands. They set up the ►European Economic Community, or 'common market', and ►Euratom. The Treaties were the product of discussions begun at a conference in Messina in 1955: they provided for the abolition of the remaining internal tariffs between the six states, the achievement of uniform external tariffs, and the establishment of free movement for workers, capital and goods between the member states. These changes were to be carried out in three successive stages of four years each. The Rome Treaties have remained the basic foundation of the European Community, providing later applicants for membership with an institutional framework and a standard of acceptance.

Rommel, Erwin (1891–1944), German soldier. Born at Heidenheim and educated at Tübingen, distinguished himself in the German Third Army early in the First World War and was awarded the highest military decoration later in the war. He remained an infantry regimental officer and instructor between the wars, attracting Hitler's attention by his efficiency and organizational gifts in 1938. His enterprise in the 1940 campaigns led Hitler to appoint him commander of the 'Afrika Corps' in 1941, where he restored Axis fortunes after a series of Italian defeats and won respect for his intuitive strategy, becoming known as the 'desert fox'. Defeated at the second battle of ➤Alamein and recalled to Germany before the end of the ➤North African Campaigns he was made responsible for improving the defences of the Atlantic Wall in February 1944, and commanded the key 'Army Group B' in France at the time of ➤D-Day. On 17 July 1944 he was severely wounded when aircraft machine-gunned his staff car near St Lô. The Gestapo believed he was implicated in the anti-Hitler conspiracy of 20 July 1944 (➤July Conspiracy) and he died suddenly and mysteriously, apparently being compelled to commit suicide, on the following 14 October. He was a daring and much-admired general, his personality and his fate creating an enduring legend denied to many orthodox, and ultimately more successful, commanders.

Roosevelt (Anna) Eleanor (1884–1962), American 'first lady'. Born in New York, the niece of President Theodore Roosevelt and married her distant cousin, Franklin ➤Roosevelt in March 1905. Throughout her life she was interested in social work and humanitarian causes, her faith in moral principles bringing a didactic quality to the numerous newspaper columns and lectures she wrote both during her husband's political career and after his death. Among many Republicans her vigorous personality aroused resentment: 'Nor Eleanor Either' was an electoral slogan of her husband's opponents in 1940. But her concern for the rights of minority groups and her belief in international understanding made her a natural choice as a delegate to the UN Assembly in 1946, and she served as chairman of the UN Human Rights Commission from 1947 until 1951.

Roosevelt, Franklin Delano (1882–1945), thirty-second President of the USA. Born at Hyde Park, New York, studied at Harvard and Columbia Law School and married his fifth cousin once removed, Eleanor, a niece of President Theodore ➤Roosevelt. 'F.D.R.' sat as a Democrat State Senator in New York, 1910–13, was Assistant Secretary to the Navy under ➤Wilson, 1913–20, but was crippled by infantile paralysis in 1921. He was elected Governor of New York in 1928 and was nominated as the Democrat candidate against Hoover in the 1932 election, gaining a majority of more than 12 million popular votes and winning forty-two states against six for the incumbent President. Roosevelt promised 'direct, vigorous action' against the ➤Depression and his Administration was therefore primarily concerned with the ➤'New Deal', a programme of public works, support to the farmers, legislation to improve labour relations. In 1936 Roosevelt won every state except Maine and Vermont: his radio 'fireside chats' made him more widely known than any earlier President, but he lost some popular support by his plans to alter the structure of the Supreme Court, which had ruled against some of the New Deal legislation. Roosevelt shaped his own foreign policy, steering cautiously away from ➤isolationism. He was personally responsible for the decision to recognize Soviet Russia (November 1933): once war came to Europe he carried formal neutrality to the point of co-belligerency in support of Britain, notably by the ➤Lend-Lease proposals, meeting Churchill to issue the ➤Atlantic Charter in August 1941. His close links with Churchill after ➤Pearl Harbor and America's entry into the war (December 1941) contributed considerably to inter-allied unity. He attended the wartime conferences of ➤Casablanca, ➤Quebec and ➤Cairo as well as meeting Stalin at ➤Teheran and ➤Yalta. He has been criticized for a naive faith in Stalin's word, for overrating the hold of Chiang Kai-shek on China, for distrusting General de Gaulle, for insisting on ➤'unconditional surrender' and for favouring a frontal assault across the Channel rather than a northward penetration of Europe from the Mediterranean and the Adriatic. These criticisms frequently ignore the circumstances of the time and minimize the occasions on which he overruled his chiefs of staff in the interests of allied collaboration. In American constitutional practice, he is unique in standing for a third and a fourth term of office: he defeated Wendell Willkie in 1940 and Thomas Dewey in 1944. Roosevelt's ideals inspired the foundation of the United Nations: he died suddenly at Warm Springs, Georgia, on 12 April 1945, a fortnight before the ➤San Francisco Conference, and was succeeded by his Vice-President, ➤Truman.

Roosevelt, Theodore (1858–1919), twenty sixth President of the USA. Born in New York City, educated at Harvard and spent two tough years on a cattle ranch in Dakota. He was influential in Republican circles in New York and was Assistant Secretary to the Navy, 1897–8. In the Spanish American War of 1898, he gained fame as a colonel of 'Rough Riders' in Cuba. He was Governor of New York, 1899–1900, combating corruption so vigorously that the Republican Party bosses there backed him as Vice-Presidential candidate in the 1900 election so as to get him to Washington. On the assassination of President McKinley in September 1901, 'TR' succeeded to the Presidency, beginning an unorthodox Republican Administration which sought to destroy monopolistic 'trusts' in the major industries. He preached what he called 'the doctrine of the strenuous life', acting on his axiom that 'to go far' one must 'speak softly and carry a big stick'. In international affairs he pursued a forward policy, sending warships to Panama to back up his attempts to wrest concessions for American construction and control of a ➤Panama Canal. Yet in 1904–5 he successfully mediated in the ➤Russo-Japanese War and sought to arbitrate over the first ➤Moroccan Crisis: he became the first head of state to receive the Nobel Peace Prize (1906). He won the election of 1904 with an overwhelming majority but withdrew from politics in 1908, spending two years on a world tour. In 1912 he sought unsuccessfully to gain the Republican nomination against the incumbent President, ➤Taft, whom he then opposed in the election, standing as an independent Progressive ('Bull Moose') candidate. He polled more votes than Taft, but his intervention allowed the Democrat, ➤Wilson, to win. Indefatigable, Roosevelt then travelled to Brazil and explored the 'river of doubt', now known as the 'Rio Teodoro' after him. He was a forceful critic of US neutrality, 1914–17, his sympathies being on the side of the British, with whose Foreign Secretary, ➤Grey, he was on terms of personal friendship. He died a fortnight before the opening of the Paris Peace Conference.

Rosenberg Case. Wide protests, reminiscent of the Sacco–Vanzetti Case, were aroused in America and Europe when a husband and wife in their mid thirties, Julius and Ethel Rosenberg, followed each other to the electric chair at Sing Sing Prison on 19 June 1953 for selling wartime atomic secrets to the Soviet Union. The case evoked protests for three reasons: doubts over the reliability of an important prosecution witness; the fact that the spying was carried out on behalf of a government then allied to the United States; and fear that the execution – the first carried out in peacetime for espionage in the USA – reflected the 'anti-Red' prejudices aroused by ➤McCarthyism and the witch-hunts dominating the newspapers during the Rosenberg trial.

Round Table Conferences. Meetings were held in St James's Palace, London, to discuss the future of India from November 1930 to January 1931 and again from September to December 1931, with a brief and unproductive third session in 1932. The conferences accepted the need for Indian federation and tacitly acknowledged that India would eventually receive the status of a dominion (similar to Canada and Australia). The second session was attended by ➤Gandhi, who aroused much interest in London but failed to convince the British Government of any urgency in making concessions over Indian home rule. A similar round table conference on ➤Palestine in March 1939 failed to agree over proposals to partition the mandated territory into Arab and Jewish regions.

Rowell–Sirois Report. Disagreement over the raising and distribution of national revenue in Canada in the mid 1930s seemed to threaten the disintegration of the dominion into nine separate provinces. In 1935 the Prime Minister, ➤King, accordingly appointed a royal commission to examine relations between the dominion and provincial governments. The commission was chaired first by N.W. Rowell and second by Joseph Sirois, who published its Report in 1940. The Report emphasized the uneven level of wealth and resources between provinces and urged the assumption of greater responsibility by the federal authorities in Ottawa so as to maintain the unity of Canada. The report was unpopular with Ontario, Alberta, British Columbia and Quebec and its main proposals were rejected in a two-day conference in January 1941. The Report, and its fate, form a significant commentary on the rivalry between 'centralism' and provincial rights within Canada.

Ruhr. The leading manufacturing and mining region of western Germany, occupied by French and Belgian troops in January 1923 when Germany failed to fulfil quota payments of ►reparations. The occupation was condemned by the British and Americans and aroused passive resistance among the Ruhr workers. Little benefit and much expense came to the French from the occupation but, rather than lose face, troops were stationed in the Ruhr until the summer of 1925, withdrawing only on the eve of the ►Locarno Pact with its promise of better Franco-German relations.

Rumania. ►Romania.

Rusk (David) Dean (1909–93), US Secretary of State. Born on a cotton farm in Georgia, educated at Davidson College, North Carolina, and St John's College, Oxford, served as a senior staff officer with American troops in southern China and on the Burma Road, 1944–5, before joining the US diplomatic service in 1946, taking over responsibilities with the United Nations previously held by Alger ►Hiss in 1947. From 1949 to 1951 he was employed by Truman almost exclusively in questions relating to Korea and the Far East. Kennedy appointed him Secretary of State in 1961 and he held the office until January 1969. Although Kennedy personally concerned himself with many aspects of foreign policy, he left Far Eastern affairs to Rusk, a practice which continued under the Johnson Administration, thus involving Rusk closely with the ►Vietnam War.

Russell, Bertrand (1872–1970, succeeded as third Earl Russell in 1931, although he did not use the title), English philosopher and intellectual leader. Born in Monmouthshire, spending his infancy in the household of his grandfather, Lord John Russell (1792–1878). Bertrand Russell was educated at Trinity College, Cambridge, his principal works of logic and mathematics being published in 1900, 1910 and 1914. During the First World War he was deprived of his fellowship at Trinity because of his pacifism and was imprisoned in 1918. Between the wars he pioneered progressive education and challenged outmoded concepts of moral behaviour. Hatred of fascism led him to abandon his pacifist principles in the Second World War. He was awarded the Order of Merit in 1949, the Nobel Prize for Literature in 1950. From 1949 onwards he became a vigorous champion of nuclear disarmament, helping found the ►Campaign for Nuclear Disarmament in 1956. In September 1961 he was imprisoned for two months at Brixton for 'inciting members of the public to commit a breach of the peace', as part of the protest movement against nuclear weapons. He corresponded directly with Kennedy and Khrushchev during the ►Cuban Missiles crisis and joined in demonstrations against the Vietnam War when he was in his nineties.

Russia. In 1900 Russia was an autocracy covering more than a sixth of the land surface of the world. It was a multi-national empire in which ethnic Russians formed only 44 per cent of the population, although a further 29 per cent were other Slav peoples. The ➤Russo-Japanese War, closely followed by the ➤Revolution of 1905, exposed the weaknesses of the Tsarist system; the subsequent experiment in parliamentary government (➤Duma) failed, largely because of the repugnance felt towards it by Tsar ➤Nicholas II. The strain of a long European war finally precipitated the ➤Russian Revolution. Russia formally became a 'Republic of Soviets of Workers', Soldiers' and Peasants' Deputies' on 25 January 1918, although the constitution proclaimed on 10 July 1918 set up a 'Russian Soviet Federal Socialist Republic' (RSFSR). Sixteen autonomous Soviet republics were established within the RSFSR. In December 1922 the RSFSR joined the ➤Ukraine, ➤Belarus and Transcaucasia to form the ➤Soviet Union.

With the loosening of Communist Party control under ➤Gorbachev, Russian nationalism re-emerged as a political force and was harnessed by ➤Yeltsin, who led resistance to an attempted *coup* by Party hardliners in Moscow on 19 August 1991. The Soviet Union formally dissolved on 26 December 1991, foreign governments thereupon recognizing Russia as an independent state under Yeltsin's presidency. Conflict arose with several of the autonomous republics, who were critical of the treaty which established a new Russian Federation in March 1992: the worst dispute culminated in long and bitter fighting in ➤Chechnya in 1994–5. Russia's initiative in establishing the ➤Commonwealth of Independent States as a successor to the Soviet Union also ran into difficulties. Yeltsin's two principal assistants in foiling the 1991 *coup*, the Parliament Speaker, Ruslan Khasbulatov, and the Afghan war hero Alexander Rutskoi, led opposition to his socio-economic reforms and to the 1993 Federal Constitution which, though safeguarding private ownership and multi-party rule, gave the President supreme executive powers. When Yeltsin dissolved parliament on 21 September 1994, Khasbulatov and Rutskoi denounced his action and formed an alternative government in the parliament building (White House) which, after several days of fighting in Moscow, was stormed by troops loyal to Yeltsin. Elections to the Duma three months later gave a majority to the pro-reform movement, but disillusionment with the new system induced the voters to reverse this trend completely in December 1995 when the communists became the largest single party, with over a third of the seats. The communist candidate (Zyuganov) also mounted a powerful challenge to Yeltsin in the presidential elections of June–July 1996. Urban crime (with the spread of Mafia-style racketeering), hyperinflation and confusion over the restructuring of enterprises created for a centrally planned system left the new Russia's economy stagnant until 1995 when the effects of substantial loans from the International Monetary Fund stimulated a gradual recovery. But a fall in oil prices, uncertainty over Asian markets and the burden of crippling interest rates checked this improvement. Yeltsin dismissed the government in March 1998 and appointed a young banker from Nizhni Novgorod, Sergei Kiriyenko (1963–), as Prime Minister. Four months later Russia had to seek further aid from the IMF and the World Bank to stave off an economic disaster of great concern to three continents. For even in its attenuated form, the Russian Federation still covers an eighth of the world's land surface.

Russian Revolution and Civil War. The origins of the 1917 Revolution lay in the incompatibility between the mystic authority of Tsardom and an increasingly industrialized society, but the immediate cause of the revolt was the inability of the existing order to manage a world war. Shortage of ammunition and food, a chaotic transport system, the burden of 5½ million casualties all contributed to demoralization. The Tsar's government was so divided by petty feuds and intrigue that in twelve months there were four different Prime Ministers, three different War Ministers and three different Foreign Ministers. There were two main groups of revolutionaries: liberal intelligentsia, hoping to transform Russia into a democratic republic and win the war against Germany; and Bolsheviks and Social Revolutionaries, who believed the 'imperialist war' lost and wished to transform Russia's economy and society as a first step towards the world proletarian revolution. The liberals carried through the February Revolution, the Bolsheviks the October Revolution (the name of each of these events is taken from the Julian calendar, which was in 1917 thirteen days behind 'western' reckoning).

1. *The February Revolution*. Strikes and riots broke out in Petrograd (the former St Petersburg) on 8 March, the troops siding with the rioters two days later. The ▶Duma appointed a Provisional Government, under Prince Lvov, which secured the abdication of Tsar Nicholas II at Pskov on 15 March. The Bolsheviks, meanwhile, revived the Soviet of Workers', Peasants' and Soldiers' Deputies which had been originally established during the ▶Revolution of 1905. The Soviet challenged every move of the Provisional Government, especially after ▶Lenin arrived in Petrograd on 16 April. An abortive attempt by the Bolsheviks to seize power on 16–17 July weakened the Soviet and forced Lenin into hiding. But the Provisional Government, seeking to continue the war, was also weakened especially by misunderstanding between the new Prime Minister, ▶Kerensky, and the commander-in-chief, General Kornilov, who unsuccessfully tried to seize power in September.

2. *The October Revolution*. Since the mass of the Russian people were apathetic, short of food and dreading another winter of war, Lenin led a Bolshevik revolt from Soviet headquarters in the Smolny Institute against Kerensky's government in the Winter Palace, 6–7 November 1917. Next day an All-Russian Congress of Soviets gave authority to the Bolsheviks to organize a 'Council of People's Commissars' as the executive body. Lenin promised 'Peace, Land, Bread'. Local Bolshevik representatives established administrations in other key cities, giving workers control of factories, prohibiting private trade and confiscating the property of the Church and of 'counter-revolutionaries'. A ceasefire was arranged with the Germans on 5 December, followed by the Treaty of ▶Brest-Litovsk on 3 March

1918. A Soviet Constitution was promulgated in July 1918, Lenin having moved the capital from Petrograd to Moscow on 10 March.

3. *The Civil War*. The October Revolution was at first received with apathy, but counter-revolutionary armies ('Whites') began organizing resistance in December 1917: they were opposed by the Red Army, a force hastily improvised by ➤Trotsky. Civil war continued for nearly three years in five main regions, the lack of cohesion between the various counter-revolutionary movements contributing to the ultimate Bolshevik success:

(a) The Caucasus and Southern Russia. The Don Cossacks were organized by General Kornilov, who was killed in action in May 1918, and then by General ➤Denikin. In the Crimea resistance continued until November 1920.

(b) The Ukraine. A puppet German ruler, the Ukrainian Hetman, Skoropadsky, held the region until the collapse of November 1918, when there followed months of unparalleled confusion. Denikin held the Ukraine, August to December 1919; ➤Pilsudski captured Kiev for the Poles briefly in May 1920, before the Red Army recovered the region in the summer of 1920.

(c) The Baltic. The Bolsheviks were faced by nationalist revolts from ➤Latvia, ➤Estonia, ➤Lithuania and ➤Finland, with all of whom peace was concluded, on bases of recognition of independence, February–October 1920. Earlier Petrograd had been threatened by the White Army of General Yudenich, thrown back from the outskirts of the city by the Bolsheviks in October 1919.

(d) Northern Russia. A Franco-British expeditionary force landed at Murmansk in June 1918, seized Archangel a month later and conducted sporadic operations against the Bolsheviks until October 1919.

(e) Siberia. A Czech Legion (of released prisoners of war) supported Admiral ➤Kolchak at Omsk and in 1918–19 exercised some authority over the central section of the Trans-Siberian Railway. In the Far East the Japanese landed at Vladivostok in December 1917 and held the eastern sector of the Trans-Siberian Railway, as well as the port, until November 1922.

The Bolsheviks were also faced by peasant risings, caused by famine in 1920, and by a mutiny of sailors at Kronstadt, 21 February to 17 March 1921, put down with heavy loss of life. Many governments long withheld recognition of the Soviet regime: it was accorded by Britain in January 1924; by the USA in November 1933; by Yugoslavia (where there were many 'White' refugees) not until 24 June 1940.

Russo-Japanese War (1904–5). Caused by rival attempts to penetrate ➤Manchuria and ➤Korea. The Japanese Navy launched a surprise attack on the Russian fleet at ➤Port Arthur without declaring war (8 February 1904). Although the Russians recovered from initial disasters to hold the Japanese armies along the Yalu river and in Manchuria, they could not challenge Japan's mastery of the seas, their attempts to use the Baltic fleet in Far Eastern waters ending in total defeat at ➤Tsushima. American mediation led to the conclusion of peace at ➤Portsmouth,

New Hampshire. Russia's loss of prestige contributed to the ➤Revolution of 1905.

Rutherford, Ernest (1871–1937, created Baron Rutherford of Nelson 1931), British scientist. Born near Nelson in New Zealand, educated locally and at Trinity College, Cambridge. As a professor at McGill University, Canada, he was one of the first scientists to explain radioactivity by a disintegration theory (1904). In 1911, at Manchester University, he was able to bombard the atom with particles discharged by radioactive substances. From 1919 he supervised experiments in the Cavendish laboratories at Cambridge which led Cockroft and Walton to split the atom, May 1932.

Rwanda. Central African republic; capital Kigali. Although the population is overwhelmingly Hutu, a tribe of settled farmers rather than warrior pastoralists, Rwanda was linked with neighbouring ➤Burundi under Tutsi rule for 400 years. Both were part of German East Africa from 1890 to 1919 and then came under Belgian mandate and trusteeship. Rwanda gained independence on 1 July 1962, after a Hutu revolt in 1959 ended centuries of Tutsi dominance. In 1973 the Hutu soldier Juvenal Habyarimana (1937–94) set up a military dictatorship, though with a partial return to civilian rule in 1980. Tutsi incursions from Burundi and Uganda supported dissident Hutu in a Rwandan Popular Front (RPF). This first civil war caused some 30,000 deaths, notably in October 1990 when Habyarimana summoned Belgian and French airborne troops to help him put down the rebellion. When Habyarimana was killed in a plane crash in April 1994, Hutu soldiers systematically massacred the Tutsi minority, causing a second civil war. Within two months the RPF secured control of Rwanda; over one and quarter million Hutus fled the country. Some found refuge in Tanzania, but many perished from disease in camps in ➤Zaire. In August 1995 Zaire began forcibly repatriating the Hutus, who were said to be provoking unrest in ➤Katanga. Humanitarian aid and UN-sponsored voluntary repatriation were hampered by the growing anarchy in Zaire and Burundi during 1996–7.

S

Saar. A German district on the left bank of the Rhine, rich in coal deposits and covering an area of nearly 1,000 square miles in the basin of the river Saar. The League of Nations accepted responsibility for administering the Saar, 1919–35, with the mines controlled by France as a form of reparation. A League plebiscite held in the Saar, 13 January 1935, voted overwhelmingly for restoration of the area to German authority and the transfer was carried out seven weeks later. French occupation after the Second World War was marked by a form of economic union and local autonomy, 1947–56, but the Saar was integrated in the German Federal Republic on 1 January 1957, the last French economic concessions being ended by direct Franco-German talks in the autumn of 1959.

Sacco–Vanzetti Case (1920–27). Two Italian-born American anarchists, Nicola Sacco, 1891–1927, and Bartolomeo Vanzetti, 1888–1927, were arrested in May 1920 on charges of armed robbery and the murder of two men at a shoe factory in Massachusetts. Although the evidence against them was inconclusive, the judge conducted their trial with great prejudice, and appeals were at once launched against their conviction. These appeals lasted for more than six years, rallying liberals and intellectuals to support Sacco and Vanzetti in Britain and continental Europe as well as in America. Finally the Governor of Massachusetts appointed a commission, headed by the president of Harvard University, which sustained the verdict, though deploring the conduct of the trial judge. Sacco and Vanzetti were sent to the electric chair on 23 August 1927. Their execution, which was attributed to 'anti-Red hysteria', provoked hostile demonstrations in many countries.

Saddam Hussein. ➤Hussein, Sadisavan Saddam.

Sadat, Mohammed Anwar el (1918–81), President of Egypt. Born at Abu el-Kom. He was an officer cadet with ➤Nasser, becoming his close companion and colleague. After serving as secretary of the ruling Egyptian National Union (1957–61), he became Speaker of Parliament and in 1969 Vice-President. On Nasser's death in October 1970 Sadat was elected President and followed his policies closely until the disastrous ➤October War of 1973 brought Israeli troops across the Canal. Sadat subsequently broke links with the Soviet Union and Syria, concentrated increasingly on African problems and improved relations with the USA. Four years after the war he was able to take the so-called ➤'Sadat Initiative', the first step towards a Middle East peace settlement. Arab militants, angered by this change of policy, exploited every grievance against Sadat's home policies; there were riots over cuts in food subsidies in January 1977 and Islamic fundamentalism spread among students and junior officers. On 6 October 1981 he was assassinated at a military parade in Cairo by Islamic extremists within a crack regiment.

Sadat Initiative (19–21 November 1977). Faced by a mounting economic crisis, caused by high expenditure on defence, President Sadat of ►Egypt sought to hasten a Middle East settlement by offering to go to Jerusalem and plead the Arab cause before the Israeli parliament, the Knesset. His offer was accepted by the Israeli Prime Minister, Menachem ►Begin, and the visit took place over the third weekend of November 1977. This courageous peace initiative marked the first tacit recognition of Israel's sovereignty by an Arab head of state, and brought strong condemnation of President Sadat from the ►Palestine Liberation Organization and from the governments of Syria, Libya and Algeria. Intricate negotiations continued between Egyptian and Israeli spokesmen in Egypt itself, at Leeds Castle in Kent, and in September 1978 at ►Camp David, where President Carter sought to settle differences between Sadat and Begin in private talks.

St Germain, Treaty of (10 September 1919). Peace treaty concluded between the allies and the Austrian Republic. Austria lost the South Tirol and the Julian March to Italy; Dalmatia, Slovenia and Bosnia-Herzegovina to Yugoslavia; Bohemia and Moravia to Czechoslovakia; Galicia to Poland; the Bukovina to Romania. The Austrian Army was limited to 30,000; the republic was made liable for ►reparations and was forbidden to unite with Germany. The Treaty deprived Austria of about one-third of her German-speaking population. In 1914 there were 28 million people in the 'Austrian' part of Austria–Hungary: the St Germain Treaty left the Austrian Republic with a population of less than 8 million.

St Jean de Maurienne Agreement (1917). A secret understanding reached by British, French, Russian and Italian representatives in April 1917 promising Italy a segment of Turkish territory around ►Smyrna after the war. The agreement was never implemented, partly because it clashed with Greek ambitions but even more because of the Turkish national resurgence under Kemal (►Atatürk). The revelation by the Bolsheviks in 1918 that this secret agreement had been concluded intensified suspicion of the Italians among the Greeks and Turks.

St Laurent, Louis Stephen (1882–1973), Canadian Prime Minister. Born at Compton, Quebec, educated at Laval University, Quebec, practising as a lawyer before entering the dominion parliament as a Liberal in 1941 and serving almost immediately as Attorney-General. After two years as Minister for External Affairs (1946–8) he became Liberal leader and Prime Minister in succession to Mackenzie ►King on 15 November 1948. Probably the most lasting achievement of his ministry was the agreement between the dominion government, the provincial governments and the USA on construction of the ►St Lawrence seaway. St Laurent continued the Canadian Liberal tradition of social reforms with the Old Age Security Act of 1951. He won the general election of 1953 but opinion began to swing against the Liberals – partly because they had been in office since 1935, but specifically because they kept tight checks on the flow of money and seemed unwilling to subsidize western farmers in the great wheatlands. After losing the election of June 1957, St Laurent continued as leader of the opposition for a year before handing over the Liberal Party to Lester ➤Pearson.

St Lawrence Seaway. A waterway along the upper St Lawrence river of great commercial value to Canada and the United States. It extends from Montreal to Lake Ontario and permits the passage of deep-draught ships between the Atlantic and the Great Lakes. Hydroelectric collaboration between the two countries began in 1952. Work began on the canal and locks system at the end of 1954 and the Seaway was jointly opened by Queen Elizabeth II and President Eisenhower at a ceremony at St Lambert, Quebec, on 26 June 1959.

Sakharov, Andrei Dimitrievich (1921–89), Soviet physicist and dissident. Born and educated in Moscow, serving as director of the research team which perfected the Soviet Union's hydrogen bomb (1947–54). Seven years later he publicly opposed atmospheric nuclear tests, calling for a test-ban treaty. In 1968 his *Progress, Coexistence and Intellectual Freedom* was published outside the Soviet Union. His courageous campaign was recognized abroad by the award of the 1975 Nobel Peace Prize, which the Soviet authorities would not allow him to receive. He backed the ➤Helsinki Human Rights Group in 1976, his persistent dissidence leading to his exile in the closed city of Gorki in 1980. Knowledge that Sakharov was enduring hunger strikes and forced feeding intensified the campaign abroad for the restoration of his liberty; his return to Moscow in 1987 was interpreted as a sign of Gorbachev's genuine desire for ➤*glasnost*. In April 1989 he was elected to the Congress of People's Deputies as an independent representing the Academy of Science.

Salan, Raoul Albin Louis (1899–1984), French general. Born at Roquecourbe, educated at Nîmes and St Cyr, commissioned in the French Army 1919, serving under ➤de Gaulle in French West Africa in the Second World War and from 1945 to 1953 in Indo-China. He was senior officer in Algiers in November 1956 and commander-in-chief Algeria, June to December 1958. Although welcoming de Gaulle's overthrow of the Fourth Republic, General Salan was soon disgusted by the President's proposed settlement of the ➤Algerian War. From February 1959 until June 1960 he held a strategically important post as Military Governor of Paris, an office which made him a potential threat to civil government in the republic. He spent the remaining months of 1960 and the beginning of 1961 in Spain, setting up the OAS (➤Organisation de l'Armée Secrète). His OAS revolt in Algiers on 22 April 1961 was a failure and forced him into hiding. He was arrested in Algiers almost exactly a year later and sentenced to life imprisonment for treason. After serving six years in Tulle prison he was released and formally pardoned by President de Gaulle, June 1968.

Salazar, António de Oliveira (1889–1970), Portuguese Prime Minister. Born at Vimieiro, a village some forty miles north of Lisbon, the son of an innkeeper. He was educated at a seminary, where he took minor orders, but never became a priest. Later he was a student of the university at Coimbra, lecturing there in economics and becoming a professor at the age of twenty-nine. In April 1928 he was appointed Minister of Finance and showed such skill at a time of political and economic crisis that he was made Prime Minister on 5 July 1932, and given virtually dictatorial powers. Although personally ascetic, quiet and unambitious he ruled Portugal firmly, through a corporative system which used the ideas of fascism without its style and insignia. Salazar was Prime Minister continuously until September 1968, when he was incapacitated by a stroke. He was also Foreign Minister, 1936–47, War Minister 1936–44, and retained a tight hold on the Ministry of Finance, as well as being leader of the only permitted political party, the Portuguese National Union. He carried through a series of reforms at home, improving living conditions and education (strictly Catholic) as well as public-works projects, of which the most spectacular was a new bridge across the Tagus at Lisbon. His hostility to political change at home and in the African colonies left a difficult legacy for his successor, Marcello Caetano (1906–), a right-hand man of Salazar for over thirty years. (►Portugal.)

Salisbury, Lord (Robert Gascoyne-Cecil, 1830–1903, succeeded as third Marquess, 1868), British Prime Minister. Born at Hatfield, educated at Eton and Christ Church, Oxford: member of the House of Commons as Lord Robert Cecil, 1853–65 and as Viscount Cranborne, 1865–8. He was Indian Secretary 1866–7 and Foreign Secretary, 1878–80, subsequently heading three Conservative Governments, 1885–6, 1886–92 and 1895–1902. Except for a few months in 1886 and from October 1900 until his final retirement in July 1902, Salisbury always combined the offices of Prime Minister and Foreign Secretary. His old-fashioned conservatism made him fear the rise of democracy and he was more interested in imperial and foreign affairs than in domestic reforms. Since he avoided long-term diplomatic commitments his policy is often, misleadingly, described as one of 'splendid isolation'. He was succeeded as Prime Minister, in 1902, by his nephew, ►Balfour. Lord Salisbury's heir, the fourth Marquess (1861–1947), was a prominent Conservative and leader of the House of Lords in the 1920s, while the fifth Marquess (1893–1972) was a member of the Conservative Governments, 1951–7, leader of the Lords, and an influential elder statesman of the party. Another son of the third Marquess, Lord Robert Cecil (1864–1958, created Viscount Cecil of Chelwood in 1923), helped draft the League of Nations Covenant, supported the League's ideals and was an active believer in disarmament, receiving the Nobel Peace Prize in 1937.

Salonika Campaign (1915–18). In October 1915, when it was clear that Germany, Austria–Hungary and Bulgaria were about to launch an offensive against ►Serbia, the British and French landed an expeditionary force in Salonika, hoping to aid the Serbs. King ►Constantine I protested at this breach of Greek neutrality, although the principal Greek statesman, ►Venizelos, supported the allies. Little effective aid was given Serbia but a new 'Macedonian Front' was established, using Salonika as an armed camp, from which it was intended that an eventual Balkan offensive should be launched against the Austrians, Bulgars and Turks. The strategy of maintaining this 'sideshow' was much criticized by 'westerners' in London and Paris, notably by ►Clemenceau. Eventually an army of French, British, Serbs, Italians, Russians and Venizelist Greeks was concentrated around Salonika. General ►Franchet d'Esperey mounted a major offensive in the mountains along the Greek-Serbian frontier in September 1918 which led to the defeat of Bulgaria by the end of September and enabled troops from Salonika to reach the Danube in the north and Constantinople in the east as the war ended.

SALT Talks. Abbreviated form used for the Soviet–American talks on ►Strategic Arms Limitation, which began in November 1969.

Samoa. A group of islands in the central Pacific, colonized by Germans and Americans in the late 1890s. Since 1899 the seven eastern islands have formed American Samoa, administered from 1900 to 1951 by the US Navy Department, and subsequently by the US Department of the Interior, with the assistance of a bicameral legislature. Western Samoa, and in particular the island of Upolu, formed a German dependency, 1899–1914. A New Zealand expeditionary force occupied the German Samoan islands on 30 August 1914. They were administered by New Zealand under a League of Nations mandate from 1920 to 1946 and thereafter, until the end of 1961, as a UN trusteeship territory. The New Zealanders established internal self-government in 1959. Western Samoa became the first independent decolonized Polynesian state on 1 January 1962, enjoying 'native sovereignty' while remaining within the Commonwealth.

Sanctions. An economic boycott of a country undertaken in order to fulfil international obligations. The chief coercive instrument of the ►League of Nations lay in such sanctions, which League members were empowered to apply under Article XVI of the Covenant. Sanctions were imposed on Italy after Mussolini's invasion of Ethiopia, becoming binding on members from October 1935. As a compromise gesture oil, iron and steel were excluded from the boycott, and non-League members were free to trade normally with Italy. These concessions made sanctions ineffective and they were raised in July 1936, never again to be applied by the League. Attempts were made, from 1965 onwards, to put pressure on Rhodesia after the ►Unilateral Declaration of Independence by a similar resort to sanctions; but again there were too many ways of evading the sanctions for them to prove crippling.

San Francisco Conference (15 April to 26 June 1945). A meeting of delegates from fifty nations, all of whom had declared war on Germany before 1 March 1945, at which the design and structure of the United Nations Organization were finally determined. The Conference drafted the UN Charter, signed on 26 June and formally ratified at the first session of the General Assembly of the ➤United Nation in London on 24 October 1945.

Sarajevo. Principal city of Bosnia. On 28 June 1914 Archduke Francis Ferdinand and his wife were assassinated in Sarajevo by a Serbian student, Gavrilo Princip (1894–1918), a member of a secret nationalist movement, 'Young Bosnia', which hoped for the liberation of ➤Bosnia–Herzegovina from Austrian rule. Princip's weapons were supplied by a Serbian terrorist organization, known as the ➤'Black Hand', and the Austrians believed that the Serbian Government had instigated the plot, although in reality the Black Handers and the government were engaged in a struggle for power. Austria–Hungary sent a harsh ultimatum to Serbia on 23 July and, although the Serbs conceded most of the demands contained in the ultimatum, war followed on 28 July, spreading to the major Powers of Europe within days because of Russian support for Serbia and Germany's alliance with Austria–Hungary. The assassination led to rioting in Sarajevo and to the trial and execution of many Serbs living in Bosnia: Princip was too young for the death penalty but he died from tuberculosis on 28 April 1918 in hospital at Theresienstadt, where he had been confined in a fortress. Princip was regarded as a heroic martyr by both the inter-war and the communist rulers of Yugoslavia. Sarajevo, in 1914 still an old Turkish town of 52,000 inhabitants, was by 1991 a westernized city, population 453,000. When Yugoslavia disintegrated it was besieged on 4 April 1992 by Serb forces of the Federal army and Bosnian Serb troops. Not until September 1995 could food convoys reach the city, which was frequently bombarded from the surrounding hills. A lull in the closing months of 1993 was followed by a callous mortar attack on Sarajevo market in February 1994 which killed sixty-eight civilians. Only when NATO aircraft destroyed the Bosnian Serb munitions dump at Vogošća on 12 September 1995 did fighting die down. The ➤Dayton Accord reaffirmed the war-ravaged city's status as capital of Bosnia Herzegovina.

Saudi Arabia. The largest Middle East kingdom (four times the size of France) was the creation of ➤Ibn Saud and dates from 20 September 1932 when the Sultanate of Nejd, the Kingdom of the Hejaz and their conquered dependencies were unified in a single kingdom dominating the Arabian peninsula. In 1932 Saudi Arabia was a backward state: half the population was engaged in primitive agriculture, a quarter were nomadic and the remaining quarter were town dwellers, many of them concerned with the holy cities of Mecca and Medina and the Moslem pilgrim-trade, the principal source of income for the kingdom. The country became wealthy in the 1950s because of the exploitation and export of oil: the first oil concession was granted in 1933 and the first exports were made in 1938 but the oilfields were not developed fully until 1946–50. Within twenty years Saudi Arabia was exporting more petroleum than any other Middle East state. During Ibn Saud's last illness, and immediately after his death in 1953, attempts were made to create a form of ministerial government and to modernize the administration. A series of new codes of conduct were decreed, reconciling twentieth-century developments with Islamic traditions: a code of commerce (1954), labour and work (1970), social insurance (1970), civil service (1971). Television was introduced in 1958, the education of women formally permitted in 1960, the final abolition of slavery decreed in 1962. From 1974 onwards the Saudi Arabian Minister of Petroleum and Mineral Resources, Sheikh Ahmad Zaki Yamani, showed great astuteness at meetings of ►OPEC. From 1975 to 1982 the effective ruler of the country was Crown Prince Fahd (1921–), who succeeded his half-brother, Khalid, as King on 13 June 1982. Between August and November 1981 Fahd attempted to take the initiative as a mediator over the Middle East, summoning an abortive Arab summit conference which met at Fez, but his endeavours were hampered by Arab suspicion of his close links with the United States and by the hostility of President Assad of ►Syria towards any Saudi peace plans. Shiite Islamic fundamentalism in the Eastern Province of Saudi Arabia has at times threatened the reforming dynasty with the type of challenge which overthrew the Shah in Iran. Tension was acute in August 1987 when riots provoked by Islamic fundamentalists within Mecca caused the deaths of more than four hundred pilgrims. The Iraqi annexation of Kuwait in August 1990 induced King Fahd to seek an inter-allied UN presence to protect his frontier in the crisis leading up to the Second ►Gulf War. In 1993 a consultative council from which members of the ruling family were excluded was set up, and thirteen regional councils were also established. For several months in 1996 King Fahd was incapacitated by a stroke, with the royal authority passing temporarily to his brother, Crown Prince Abdullah.

Savage, Michael Joseph (1872–1940), New Zealand Prime Minister. Born in Australia, emigrated to South Island, becoming a trade unionist but keeping politically to the Right. He became leader of the New Zealand ►Labour Party in 1933 and at once began to seek support from the agricultural districts, traditionally conservative but alienated by neglect of farming interests in recent governments. This policy resulted in a Labour victory in the New Zealand general election of 27 November 1935 and Savage formed the first Labour Government a week later. Basic social reforms, including a marketing Act to help the farmers, redeemed most of the party's election pledges and Savage gained another electoral victory in October 1938. He was a popular figure and his death in office (March 1940) caused widespread sorrow. Peter ►Fraser succeeded him.

Schlieffen Plan. Operational war plan prepared in December 1905 by General Count Alfred von Schlieffen (1833–1913), Chief of the German General Staff. With regular annual revision the Plan formed the basis for the German attack in 1914. Schlieffen argued: (1) that in the coming war the decisive theatre would be in the West, and that the Russians could be held by defensive operations during the first weeks; (2) that, if France were speedily defeated, her allies (among whom Schlieffen included Britain) would soon conclude peace; (3) that the French forts facing Germany should be outflanked by a scythe-like attack through Holland, Belgium and Luxembourg. Schlieffen's successor as Chief of the General Staff, the younger Moltke (1848–1916), modified the Plan by limiting the sweeping movement to Belgium and Luxembourg (ignoring treaty obligations requiring Germany to respect their neutrality). The Plan nearly succeeded in 1914 but was defeated by Joffre's counter-offensive on the ►Marne, by lack of direct contact between German headquarters and the field army commanders, and by the decision to withdraw forces from the Western Front because of a new panic in Berlin at the advance of the Russians into East Prussia. The Plan minimized the effectiveness of Belgian resistance and of the British Expeditionary Force as well as neglecting the value of the French railway system in rapidly bringing reserve divisions to the front. Basically the Plan formed a blueprint for the victorious German 'lightning-war' in the West in 1940, when armoured columns and aircraft gave the invaders even more mobility than in 1914.

Schuman, Robert (1886–1963), French statesman. Born in Luxembourg, elected to the Chamber of Deputies in 1919 as a moderate conservative, remaining a Deputy until 1940. He joined the more liberal Catholic party, MRP (Mouvement Républicain Populaire) soon after its foundation in 1944 and was an MRP Deputy from 1945 until 1962, serving as Prime Minister from November 1947 until July 1948. Schuman's 'Germanic' accent – in reality a Luxembourger accent – lost him popularity with the French public but he was an efficient and far-sighted Foreign Minister from the summer of 1948 until January 1953, passionately advocating European integration and becoming widely known from the so-called ►Schuman Plan of May 1950. French hostility to his proposed European Defence Force caused his downfall, but he remained actively concerned with the European Parliament at Strasbourg until shortly before his death.

Schuman Plan (9 May 1950). A proposal put forward by the French Foreign Minister, Robert ►Schuman, for pooling the coal and steel industries of France and Germany under a supranational 'High Authority', to which other European nations might accede. Details of the plan were worked out by ►Monnet and implemented by the establishment in 1952 of a ►European Coal and Steel Community, to which Italy and Benelux belonged as well as France and Germany. Schuman's initiative is seen as the first positive proposal leading to the creation of the European Community (EEC).

Schweitzer, Albert (1875–1965), German theologian, musician and medical missionary. Born at Kaisersberg, Alsace, studied theology, philosophy and music at the Universities of Strasbourg, Paris and Berlin, and from 1902 to 1906 taught theology at Strasbourg, also winning renown as an organist and interpreter of J.S. Bach. His theological studies, notably *The Quest of the Historical Jesus* (1906–10), stimulated critical appraisal of accepted ethical teaching. In 1911 he took a degree in medicine and two years later abandoned his academic career in order to devote his life to serving humanity. He set up a hospital at Lambaréné in French Equatorial Africa where he sought to combat leprosy and sleeping sickness. Apart from the years 1917–24, which he spent in Europe, he lived for the remainder of his life at Lambaréné, preaching the concept of paternalistic service as an act of atonement to the African peoples. He was awarded a Nobel Peace Prize in 1952, largely because his belief in 'reverence for life' was an ethical corrective to the destructive spirit prevalent throughout the century.

Scientific Management. A term applied to the assembly-line method of industrial production originally perfected in the USA between about 1908 and 1923: the term was coined in 1911 by F.W. ➤Taylor.

Scotland. Dynastically linked to England and Wales in 1603, Scotland remained an independent kingdom with a unicameral parliament in Edinburgh until the Act of Union of 1707. Unlike ➤Wales, Scotland retained a separate and distinctive legal system and an established church which was presbyterian in structure and teaching rather than episcopalian. External respect for Scottish traditions, emphasized by King George IV and his niece Queen Victoria, was matched within Scotland by demands for autonomy, especially when intensive industrialization of a comparatively small belt of land raised unique social problems. Until 1885 administration was conducted through Under-Secretaries at the Home Office in London, and it was not until 1926, when a Secretary of State for Scotland was appointed for the first time, that separate Scottish departments were created for education, health, fisheries etc. Politically the industrialized lowlands were a cradle for the British Labour movement (Keir ➤Hardie, Ramsay ➤MacDonald). Although a member of the Scottish Nationalist Party, Dr Robert McIntyre, was returned at a by-election in Motherwell on 12 April 1945, he failed to hold the seat in the general election three months later and the nationalists did not become electorally effective until the 1960s. Less than 22,000 people voted for SNP candidates in the 1959 general election, but Mrs Winifred Ewing was returned as MP for Hamilton in November 1967 and eleven Scottish Nationalists were elected in October 1974, when the party polled over 839,000 votes. The three principal reasons for this apparent change in voting habits were: fear that London did not understand the nature of Scotland's economic depression; concern over the development of the offshore oil industry; and (1969) extension of the franchise to eighteen-year-olds, the young being especially impatient with remote and largely alien government. In November 1973 the Kilbrandon Report recommended some form of Scottish assembly. Devolution measures were discussed in parliament intermittently, 1976–8. A bill providing for an elected assembly received the royal assent in July 1978: devolution was made dependent on support from at least 40 per cent of the Scottish electorate. A referendum, held on 1 March 1979, was indecisive: a majority of voters favoured devolution, but they formed only 32.85 per cent of the total electorate. After the 1997 General Election (in which the Conservatives failed to win any seat in Scotland) a second referendum was held. Almost two-thirds of the

Scottish electorate went to the polls on 11 September 1997: 74.3 per cent voted for a Scottish parliament; and 63.5 per cent wished it to be given tax-raising powers. Preparations began for the return of a parliament to Edinburgh in 1999.

Scott, Robert Falcon (1868–1912). Antarctic explorer. Born near Plymouth, entered the Royal Navy in 1881. While serving with the rank of commander in the Channel squadron he was appointed to lead the National Antarctic Expedition which explored the Ross Sea area of ►Antarctica in *Discovery*, 1901–4. Captain Scott (as he became in 1906) was given command of a second expedition, which sailed for Antarctica in *Terra Nova*, 1910. With four companions Scott reached the South Pole by sledge, 17 January 1912, only to discover that this feat had already been achieved a month earlier by the Norwegian, Amundsen. Illness and blizzards delayed the return of Scott's party from the Pole to *Terra Nova*, and by the end of March all had perished, their bodies and diaries remaining undiscovered for eight months. Scott's heroism made a deep impression on the British public and he was posthumously knighted. His son, Sir Peter Scott (1909–89), was an outstanding commander of small naval craft in the Channel in the Second World War and won distinction as an artist and ornithologist.

Second Front. In August 1941 Stalin asked the British authorities to open a 'Second Front' as soon as possible, by invading the European mainland, so as to relieve pressure on the Red Army. A widespread agitation, beginning in Britain early in 1942, also urged the government to 'Open a Second Front Now', a concept supported in the war cabinet by ►Beaverbrook. Later in the year, the Americans, too, favoured a landing in Europe. Churchill was reluctant to commit himself to a second front before 1944, hesitating to support combined operations on a large scale without long planning and specialized equipment because of the lesson of ►Gallipoli in 1915. The decision to launch a second front was finally taken at the ►Quebec Conference of August 1943 and the front was established by the ►Normandy landings on 6 June 1944.

Second International. The second attempt at the organization of ►International Socialism, effective from 1889 to 1914. Reformed in 1923 as the 'Labour and Socialist International', it was revived in 1951 as the 'Socialist International', to which more than forty social democratic parties were affiliated.

Security Council Principal executive organ of the ►United Nations. The Council was first proposed at the ►Dumbarton Oaks Conference, when it was felt that the United Nations needed a stronger executive than the old League of Nations. At Yalta, the principle of a veto was established, opposition to major issues by one permanent member being seen as sufficient to negate a decision or resolution otherwise approved by the Council. Permanent members were the 'Big Five' of 1945: the USA, the USSR, China, France and Britain. Until 1965 six other countries served two-year periods on the Council: in 1965 the number of non-permanent members was increased from six to ten. 'Nationalist' China – the government of Chiang Kai-shek, on ►Taiwan since 1949 – held the Chinese permanent seat on the Council until 25 October 1971, when expelled from the UN by a vote in the General Assembly. Chinese representation was thereafter accorded to the People's Republic.

Seeckt, Hans von (1866–1936), German general. Born in the town of Schleswig, a member of a Prussian military family, commissioned in the Guards in 1885, transferring at the end of the century to the General Staff, where he showed perception and wide interests. In the First World War he served mainly on the Eastern Front, achieving a remarkable breakthrough at Gorlice (May 1915). From 1919 to 1926 he was responsible for circumventing the disarmament clauses of the Versailles Treaty, notably by cooperating with Soviet Russia for secret training and the acquisition of forbidden weapons. As commander-in-chief of the Reichswehr during these years, he was prepared to use troops dispassionately against left-wing or right-wing trouble-makers. The jealous hostility of President Hindenburg forced Seeckt's retirement in October 1926, but his secret building-up of the army made possible the rapid transformation under Hitler of a force, nominally limited to 100,000 men, into the conscript armies which gained the victories of 1940. In 1934–5 Seeckt served as principal military adviser to Chiang Kai-shek in China.

Serbia. The medieval Serbian Empire was overthrown by the Turks at the battle of ►Kosovo in 1389. Although the Serbian Orthodox Church kept together a cultural and religious tradition, Serbian nationalism did not erupt until the revolt of Karadjordje Petrović in 1804–13. Serbia remained a disturbing and assertive influence in Balkan politics down to the ►Sarajevo crisis of 1914. Constitutionally Serbia was an autonomous Ottoman principality 1830–78, an independent principality 1878–82, an independent kingdom 1882–1918, a constituent kingdom with ►Croatia and ►Slovenia in Yugoslavia 1918–41, a German-occupied puppet state 1941–4 and, since 1945, a socialist republic within a federal ►Yugoslavia. Two autonomous provinces were created within Serbia in 1946: the Vojvodina (capital, Novi Sad), with a considerable Magyar population; and Kosovo-Metohija (capital, Pristina) where there were many 'Shqiptars' (Albanians). By 1988 the Serbs were protesting at Shqiptar oppression in Kosovo; and a Serbian nationalist revival, under the demagogic leadership of Slobodan ►Milošević, threatened federal unity. Milošević induced the Serbian Federal Assembly to abolish the autonomous rights of Kosovo-Metohija and the Vojvodina in March 1989 and was elected President of the Serbian Republic two months later. Free elections in December 1989 gave victory to his Serbian Socialist Party; over the following eighteen months Milošević's 'Greater Serbian' nationalism intensified mistrust between the Yugoslav republics. Croatia's secession from Yugoslavia in June 1991 was followed by open warfare between the two republics from September 1991 to January 1992. Milošević's support for the ethnic Serbs within Croatia and Bosnia led to the imposition of UN sanctions on Serbia from May 1992 to November 1995. Serbia and Montenegro formed a new Yugoslav Federation in 1992. Although seven political parties won seats in the parliament (*skupština*) after the 1993 elections, effective power remained in the hands of Milošević's Socialist Party. During the winter of 1996–7 anger at Serbia's slow progress towards genuine democracy prompted protracted street demonstrations in Belgrade. In the first six months of 1998 the chronic crisis in Kosovo erupted in virtual civil war.

Sèvres, Treaty of (10 August 1920). Abortive peace settlement accepted after the First World War by the Sultan's Turkey but rejected by the republican movement of Kemal (➤Atatürk), largely because it gave the Greeks extensive rights in the ➤Smyrna area of Asia Minor and placed the Dardanelles and Bosphorus under the League of Nations' administration. The settlement was later revised by the Treaty of ➤Lausanne of 1923; but the recognition of the independence of non-Turkish peoples in Arabia, Mesopotamia, Palestine and Syria, originally included in the Sèvres Treaty, was retained in the revised settlement.

Shaba Province (Zaire). ➤Katanga.

Sharpeville Shootings (21 March 1960). South African police, using automatic weapons, opened fire on a demonstration against pass laws in the township of Sharpeville, near Vereeniging and south-west of Johannesburg. Sixty-seven Africans were killed and nearly 200 wounded. There was widespread international condemnation of this gravest incident since the introduction of the ➤apartheid laws and a state of emergency was proclaimed in South Africa, which was thought to be on the verge of civil war. Three weeks later a European farmer attempted to assassinate the Prime Minister, ➤Verwoerd, but there was no sustained rebellion. The abhorrence felt towards South Africa in the Commonwealth countries after Sharpeville was one of the reasons why the South African Government chose to break all links with London and become an independent republic in 1961.

Shastri, Lal Bahadur (1904–66), Indian Prime Minister. Born in Benares, his father being a clerk in the law office of Nehru's father. Shastri joined the Congress Party in 1920 and was, on several occasions, sent to prison for his activities. He was a good organizer, and was brought by Nehru into the cabinet with ministerial responsibilities for railways and transport (1952–8), later serving as Minister of Commerce and Minister for Home Affairs. In 1963 he embarked on a plan for establishing contact with the masses on behalf of the Congress Party and was out of office for several months, but he was brought back into the government when Nehru's health began to fail in 1964 and succeeded him as Prime Minister (2 June 1964). There was fighting between India and Pakistan in September 1965 over the Rann of Kutch area after Shastri had reiterated his government's belief that ➤Kashmir must remain part of India. The Soviet Prime Minister, Kosygin, arranged a meeting between ➤Ayub Khan and Shastri at Tashkent to settle these Indo-Pakistani disputes. At the end of the meeting Shastri died suddenly from a heart attack (11 January 1966).

Shidehara Kijuro (1872–1951), Japanese conservative reformer. Born at Osaka, studied law and entered the Japanese diplomatic service in 1895, serving in the USA before 1914 and collaborating closely with the allies as deputy Foreign Minister during the First World War. Family links with the Mitsubishi financial institution increased his natural pro-Western policies; he showed moderation both as a delegate to the ►Washington Conference and as Japan's Foreign Minister in 1924–7 and 1929–31, when he sought to fulfil Japan's obligations to the ►League of Nations. He could not, however, check the growing influence of the army leaders and he withdrew from political life after 1931 in protest at Japan's occupation of ►Manchuria. With the backing of General ►MacArthur he formed a 'Progressive Party' government in October 1945. Shidehara persuaded the Americans to support the retention of the Emperor as a guarantee of Japan's sovereign unity and he also proposed the insertion into the new constitution of Article 9, which renounced war as an instrument of policy and rejected the retention or raising of an army, navy or air force. His 'Progressives' were defeated in the first post-war election (April 1946). He presided over the Japanese parliament for the last two years of his life.

Siegfried Line. A name originally used by the Germans to describe defences from Lens to Rheims on the Western Front in September 1918. It was later applied by Hitler to the fortifications erected along Germany's western frontier, emulating the ►Maginot Line although less extensive. French patrols were in contact with the outer defences of the Siegfried Line around Saarbrücken in the first week of the Second World War, but lacked the heavy field artillery needed to penetrate farther towards the Rhine. US forces reached the Siegfried Line on 1 February 1945 and British and Canadian troops broke through the northern and weaker sections of the Line to cross the Rhine near Milingen on 8–9 February 1945. The Siegfried Line did not prove such a formidable defensive obstacle as Nazi propaganda had maintained.

Sierra Leone. West African republic within the Commonwealth: capital, Freetown. Sierra Leone was founded by Wesleyan missionaries as a haven for emancipated slaves at the end of the eighteenth century. It became a British crown colony in 1808 and Freetown served as the Royal Navy's base in West Africa until after the Second World War. Not until 1951 was Freetown administratively linked to the hinterland; Africans joined the legislative assembly two years later; independence followed in April 1961, with the country becoming a republic in 1971. Sierra Leone has been a one-party state since 1978, a promise of multi-party elections given in 1991 provoking a military *coup* in April 1992 which brought a Supreme Military Council to power. The Council proved unable to check the spread of insurgency in the eastern and southern provinces headed by a xenophobic Revolutionary United Front. There were more than 10,000 deaths in a civil war which continued for five years. Multi-party elections finally returned a civilian government in March 1996, but a year later renewed revolutionary violence brought anarchy to Freetown and the hasty evacuation of foreign residents. The elected President, Ahmad Kabbah, was ousted by a military *coup* on 25 May 1997, and a brutal, repressive regime established. President Kabbah was restored to office by a counter *coup* nine months later.

Sikorski, Wladyslaw (1881–1943), Polish general and Prime Minister. Born at Tuszow in Galicia, studied engineering at the universities of Cracow and Lvov, served under ➤Pilsudski, commanded divisions against the Bolsheviks at Vilna and Warsaw (1919–20). From December 1922 to May 1923 he headed a non-parliamentary coalition but was distrusted by Pilsudski (and his successors) for associating with democrats and peasant parties' leaders, and was retired from the armed forces in 1926. His offer to take command again in 1939 was declined by the Polish Government. He escaped to France, organized a Polish army and became head of a liberal-centre coalition government-in-exile, earning great respect in London. After the revelations and allegations about the ➤Katyn Massacre, the Soviet Government severed diplomatic relations with Sikorski's government (25 April 1943). Ten weeks later (4 July), Sikorski was killed in an air crash at Gibraltar while flying to inspect Polish troops in the Mediterranean.

Simon, John Allsebrook (1873–1954, knighted 1910, created viscount 1940). Born in Manchester, the son of a Congregational minister, educated at Fettes College and Wadham College, Oxford, becoming a barrister in 1889. He sat as Liberal MP for Walthamstow 1906–18 and for Spen Valley 1922–31, when he became a 'Liberal National', although continuing to sit for Spen Valley until 1940. He was Solicitor-General, 1910–13, and entered Asquith's cabinet as Attorney-General in 1913. At first he opposed entry into the First World War and tendered his resignation, but then withdrew it. In 1915–16 he was Home Secretary, resigning because his conscience was opposed to conscription, although he served in France as a major in the Royal Flying Corps, 1917–18. From 1927 to 1930 he was chairman of a commission on Indian affairs and returned to the cabinet as MacDonald's Foreign Secretary, 1931–5, favouring disarmament and international reconciliation. In March 1935 he became the first member of the British cabinet to visit Hitler. Subsequently he served as Home Secretary, 1935–7, Chancellor of the Exchequer, 1937–40, and Lord Chancellor in the Churchill coalition, 1940–45.

Simon Report (1930). Report of the Indian Statutory Commission established in 1927 under the chairmanship of Sir John ➤Simon. The Report recommended increases in responsible government and indirect election to a central legislature. Subsequent round-table conferences on India, meeting in London in 1931–2, went further than the Simon proposals, advocating an Indian Federation. The ➤India Act of 1935 accepted many of the criticisms of the existing system contained within the Simon Report but was based on the conferences rather than on the Report itself.

Sinai Campaign (1956). Tension between Egypt and Israel mounted during 1955 and early 1956 because of a series of *fidayeen* terrorist raids launched from within the Egyptian frontier, notably from ►Gaza. The establishment by ►Nasser of an Egyptian blockade in the Gulf of Aqaba sealed off the Israeli port of Eilat. The setting up of a combined Egyptian–Syrian and Jordanian military command, announced early in October 1956 and coinciding with violent anti-Israeli propaganda in Cairo, led the Israelis to strike first, having held secret talks with the British and French Governments. On 29 October Israel launched a surprise attack, with four main tank thrusts westwards: one column seized Gaza, another struck at El Arish; a third penetrated the Sinai desert through Abu Aweigila towards Ismailia; the fourth seized the frontier post of Kuntilla and rapidly occupied the whole of southern Sinai, supported by airborne assaults at the Mitla Pass and on the garrison at Tor and occupying the base at Sharm el-Sheikh from which the Egyptians had blockaded the Gulf of Aqaba. The campaign coincided with Anglo-French intervention in the ►Suez Crisis. American and UN pressure halted the Israelis on 5 November, and in March 1957 Israeli troops evacuated the Sinai peninsula while a UN force was established near Gaza, at Kuntilla and at Sharm el-Sheikh in order to keep peace along the Egyptian–Israeli border. The peace-keeping task was beyond the resources of the UN force: tension mounted from 1964 to 1967, culminating in the ►Six-Day War and a second Israeli invasion of Sinai.

Singapore. Island republic south of the Malay peninsula, acquired for the East India Company by Sir Stamford Raffles (1781–1826) in 1819, remaining under British Indian authority until 1867 and thereafter forming part of the Straits Settlements, the main British colony in ►Malaya, until 1946 when the island became a separate colony, enjoying internal self-government as the 'State of Singapore', 1959–63. In September 1963 Singapore joined the Federation of ►Malaysia but seceded within two years on the grounds that the Federation discriminated against citizens of Chinese racial origin (who form three-quarters of the island's population). Singapore became an independent republic within the Commonwealth on 9 August 1965, maintaining close commercial and defence links with Malaysia, and surviving commercially as the fourth largest port in the world. For the first half of the twentieth century Singapore was a British naval base of strategic importance for all south-east Asia. Its defences faced seawards and when, on 8–9 February 1942, Japanese troops under General ►Yamashita crossed the Johore Straits from the Malayan mainland, Singapore was able to resist for only a week. Churchill described the fall of Singapore (15 February 1942), with the surrender of over 70,000 British and Commonwealth soldiers and airmen, as 'the worst disaster and largest capitulation in British history'. British troops landed again at Singapore on 5 September 1945.

Sinn Féin ('Ourselves Alone'). Irish republican party, founded in 1902 by Arthur Griffith (1872–1922), influential from the time of the Irish disorders of 1913–14 onwards and closely associated with James Connolly (1870–1916), the Dublin socialist leader, ►de Valéra, and the ►Easter Rising of 1916 which gave the party its martyrology. Sinn Féin regarded itself as at war with the British in 1919–20. A split in the movement in 1922, between those who (like Griffith) accepted the Irish Free State and those who (with de Valéra) wished to continue the old traditions in the ►IRA, led to the virtual disintegration of Sinn Féin, although it recovered influence as the political front of the official IRA from 1969 onwards. Under the Presidency of Gerry ►Adams the party won increasing support in Northern Ireland, though was denied full participation in talks at Stormont on the province's future so long as the IRA refused to accept a lasting ceasefire. Although Sinn Féin will not sit in the Commons at Westminster, Adams was returned as MP for Belfast West in 1983, 1987 and also in 1997, when Sinn Féin won a second seat. Talks with British government officials took place in May and June 1997; and from September Sinn Féin delegates cooperated in the 'peace process', subsequently backing the ►Good Friday Accord. In the Northern Ireland Assembly Election on 25 June 1998 Sinn Féin received 17.6 per cent of first preference votes.

Sino-Japanese War, 1937–45. Japanese militarists had been manoeuvring for an extension of Japan's sphere of influence on the Chinese mainland ever since the ►Mukden Incident of 1931. A clash between Japanese and Chinese forces near the Marco Polo bridge across the Hun river, ten miles west of Peking, on 7 July 1937, was followed by full-scale hostilities, no formal declaration of war being made by either side. The Japanese tended to advance along the main railway routes: they overran northern China in the autumn of 1937, capturing Shanghai and penetrating up the Yangtze in November. Nanking fell in December 1937, Canton and Hankow in October 1938. The regular resistance of the Kuomintang Army, under ►Chiang Kai-shek, was supplemented by increasingly effective guerrilla resistance by the 'Eighth Route Army' of communists inspired by ►Mao Tse-tung. The British and Americans supplied Chiang along the Burma Road to his capital at Chungking until the Sino-Japanese conflict was engulfed in the Second World War after ►Pearl Harbor, when the Japanese forces cut the Burma Road. The Chinese armies kept 1 million Japanese soldiers tied down on the mainland and, in July 1942, inflicted a serious defeat on the Japanese near Fuchow in Kiangsi. Japanese forces in China formally surrendered to Chiang Kai-shek at Nanking on 9 September 1945.

Sirois Report (Canada, 1940). ►Rowell–Sirois Report.

Six-Day War (5–10 June 1967). A preventive campaign initiated by General ►Dayan, as Israel's Minister of Defence, against Egypt, Jordan and Syria. The War was caused by the gradual erosion, under Egyptian pressure, of the UN peace-keeping force established after the ►Sinai Campaign in 1956, by the concentration of Arab armies around the Israeli frontiers (May 1967) and by a new Egyptian naval blockade, thus again closing the Gulf of Aqaba to Israeli shipping. Militarily the War was a remarkable success for Israel: attacks on airfields in Egypt, Syria, Iraq and Jordan virtually destroyed the Arab air forces on the ground on 5 June, the attacks ranging as far south as Luxor and Ras Banas; Egyptian tanks were destroyed in Sinai and the Suez Canal reached on 7 June, the whole West Bank of the Jordan river being cleared the same day: finally the Israelis overran the Golan Heights, captured the town of Quneitra and penetrated some thirty miles into Syria. Politically the defeat of Egypt temporarily weakened the position of ➤Nasser. While the Israeli victory reopened the Gulf of Aqaba and removed the immediate danger of a concerted Arab war of encirclement, it left the Israelis with 600,000 more Arabs under their administration on the occupied West Bank of the Jordan. The Arab–Israeli conflict was renewed in the ➤October War of 1973.

Slansky Trial (17–30 November 1952). On 24 November 1951 Rudolf Slansky, Czechoslovak Vice-Premier and until two months previously Communist Party secretary, was arrested on treason charges by the security police in Prague. Subsequently thirteen other communist officials, eleven of them Jewish (as was Slansky), were also arrested: among them was Vladimir Clementis, who had succeeded Jan ➤Masaryk as Foreign Minister and held the post until March 1950. The fourteen men were arraigned in a 'show trial', which was given great publicity, on 27 November 1952 and were accused of being 'Trotskyist, Titoite, Zionist, bourgeois, nationalist traitors' who were 'in the service of American imperialism'. Eleven of the accused, including Slansky and Clementis, were found guilty on all charges and hanged on 2 December: the remaining three minor offenders were sentenced to long terms of imprisonment (and pardoned in 1963). The trial marked the greatest purge of communists outside the Soviet Union and coincided with the peak period of Stalin's anti-Semitism. As in the case of ➤Rajk in Hungary, the evidence seems to have been a total fabrication.

Slim, William Joseph (1891–1970, knighted 1944, created a viscount 1960), British field-marshal. Born and educated in Birmingham, served in France, Gallipoli and Mesopotamia in the First World War, becoming a regular officer only in 1920 when he transferred to the Gurkha Rifles. In 1940–41 he led British–Indian troops in Eritrea, Syria, Iraq and Iran. He was sent to Burma early in 1942, maintaining morale and discipline during the long retreat from Rangoon to Imphal. He was appointed commander of the Fourteenth Army in December 1943, leading it throughout the ➤Burma campaign and liberating Mandalay and Rangoon. Later he served as Chief of the Imperial General Staff, 1948–52, and as Governor-General of Australia, 1953–60.

Slovakia . The Slovaks, a western Slav people, were subjects of the rulers of Hungary from 906 to 1918. As their capital city Bratislava (Pressburg in German; Pözsöny in Hungarian) is less than forty miles from Vienna and served as a political capital for Hungary from 1723 to 1848, Slovak life was shaped by non-Slavonic traditions until the gradual growth of a national cultural identity in the later nineteenth century. Before 1914 only a minority group of Slovak Protestants favoured cooperation with the Czechs, in distant Prague. Slovak exiles in France (notably the pioneer airman, Milan Stefanik, 1880–1919) and the large Slovak immigrant community in Pittsburgh forged political links with the Czech spokesman ►Masaryk during the First World War. Their expectation of autonomous status for Slovakia was denied by the centralist structure of the new ►Czechoslovakia. Slovak resentment at apparent Czech domination was exploited by Hitler who accepted the proclamation of an independent Slovak Republic by the Catholic priest ►Tiso on 14 March 1939, after much of southern Slovakia was retroceded to Hungary (►Felvidék). Slovakia was a German protectorate from October 1939 until 1945. Hopes of autonomy were again frustrated during the ►Gottwald era. However ►Dubček, himself a Slovak, secured equal federal status for the Czech lands and Slovakia in 1969. With the restoration of free elections in Czechoslovakia in 1989 the Movement for Democratic Slovakia (HZDS) became the principal party to favour both secession and gradual transition to a market economy. The HZDS leader, Vladimir Mečlar (1942–), formed a government in June 1992 which negotiated independence and dissolved the federal bond in January 1993. Over the following four years there was uneasiness abroad over the increased authoritarianism of the HZDS and over the treatment of the Hungarian minority in southern Slovakia. In 1995 Slovakia applied for membership of the European Union.

Slovenia. The Slovenes are a South Slav people, speaking a distinctive language and first settling in the upper Sava valley in the late sixth century. Until 1918 they lived under Austrian rule in the provinces of Carniola, Carinthia, Styria and the Küstenland of Istria. The principal Slovene city was Ljubljana, then known as Laibach. Although by nature less demonstrative than their neighbours in Croatia, the Slovenes accepted the need for a South Slav State – ►'Yugoslavia' – in the first decade of the century but remained distrustful of the Serbs, who were Orthodox in religion, whereas the Slovenes were Catholics and politically clericalist by tradition. Most Slovenes were included within Yugoslavia after the First World War, although there remained Slovene minorities in Carinthia (around Klagenfurt) and in Italy. At the end of the Second World War the Slovene minority in Istria was incorporated in Yugoslavia and a 'People's Republic of Slovenia' set up as one of the new federal units. Free elections in April 1990 gave victory to a centre-right coalition which three months later formally asserted a parliamentary right to declare independence, which was backed by a Slovene referendum in December. Independence was proclaimed on 25 June 1991 but was followed by a week's intermittent fighting between Slovene militia and Yugoslav federal forces, backed by tanks. A truce was imposed by European Community mediators on 7 July. Slovenia was admitted to the ►Council of Europe in May 1993, and in 1996 applied to join the European Union. By then a stable and democratic Slovenia seemed to enjoy more prosperity than other ex-communist states and was attracting considerable foreign investment and developing its only port, Koper, as a trade rival to neighbouring ►Trieste and more distant Venice and Rijeka (►Fiume).

Smith, Ian Douglas (1919–), Rhodesian Prime Minister. Born at Selukwe, in central Rhodesia, educated at Gwelo and Rhodes University, Grahamstown, and became a farmer, serving in the Royal Air Force, 1941–6. He was a member of the Southern Rhodesia legislature from 1948 to 1953 and then of the Federal Parliament for the Rhodesias (►Rhodesia and Nyasaland, Federation of), 1953–62. When the Federation disintegrated he was a founder of the Rhodesia Front Party in 1962. In April 1964 he became Prime Minister, implacably hostile to the concept of majority rule. A decisive electoral victory for the Rhodesia Front in May 1965 strengthened his position, and on 11 November 1965 he defied the British authorities by making what he termed a ►'unilateral declaration of independence'. After unsuccessful talks with Harold Wilson aboard HMS ►*Tiger* in December 1966 and HMS *Fearless* in October 1968, Ian Smith announced his intention of establishing a republic in Rhodesia and introducing restrictions similar in spirit to the apartheid regime in South Africa. He declared Rhodesia a republic on 2 March 1970, remaining as Prime Minister thereafter. In October–November 1976 he travelled to Geneva for a conference on Rhodesia's future with the principal Rhodesian African leaders but the conversations were abortive. Thereafter he sought to divide his opponents among the black Rhodesians by seeking agreement with the moderates, led by Bishop Muzorewa, with whom he collaborated in the establishment of a joint white and black government in March 1978. Smith became Minister without Portfolio in the 'Zimbabwe–Rhodesia' government under Bishop Muzorewa's premiership in May 1979 and came to London in the following September for the talks which finally settled the Rhodesia crisis. Smith was returned as one of the white members of the first parliament of independent ►Zimbabwe.

Smuts, Jan Christian (1870–1950), South African soldier and statesman. Born at Bovenplaats, Cape Colony, educated at Stellenbosch and Christ's College, Cambridge, became a lawyer in the Transvaal and was general commanding commando forces within Cape Colony in 1901. Smuts collaborated with ►Botha in reconciling Boers and British and was responsible for South African defence policy as soon as the Union was created in 1910. He was second in command of the army which occupied German South-West Africa in June–July 1915 and commanded the allied force that took Dar es Salaam in December 1916. In March 1917 he travelled to London on a political mission, served in the Imperial War Cabinet, 1917–18, carrying out secret negotiations with Austrian representatives in Switzerland in the hope of securing peace with Austria–Hungary (midwinter 1917–18). Smuts attended the Paris Peace Conference, assisted in the preparation of the League Covenant, and travelled to Vienna and Budapest in April 1919 on a fact-finding mission for the peacemakers (meeting Béla ►Kun). On returning to South Africa, he succeeded Botha as Prime Minister and was in office from August

1919 until June 1924, seeking unsuccessfully to induce Southern Rhodesia to join the Union of South Africa (1922). From 1933 to 1939 he was Minister of Justice under General Hertzog. On the outbreak of the Second World War, Smuts again became Prime Minister and was treated as the elder statesman of the Commonwealth: he was created a field-marshal in 1941 and made four visits to London during the war, as well as participating in the ►Cairo Conference and conducting delicate negotiations with Eisenhower in Algiers (1943). Smuts helped draft the UN Charter. His sense of world statesmanship was at variance with the prejudices of many of his countrymen who, in the elections of May 1948, rejected Smuts in favour of ►Malan, the ►Nationalist Party and ►apartheid. Apart from his political activities Smuts was a botanist and philosopher, the creator of the theory of holism: he was Chancellor of Cambridge University for the last three years of his life.

Smyrna (now known as Izmir). An ancient port on the west coast of Asia Minor, captured by the Turks in 1424 but settled by many Greek traders. There were nearly half a million Greeks in Smyrna in 1914 and the city with its hinterland was ceded to Greece for a trial period of five years by the Treaty of ►Sèvres, in 1920. The Turkish Nationalists of Kemal (►Atatürk) resisted Greek military occupation of Asia Minor and there was fighting between Greeks and Turks from June 1920 until August 1922 when the Greeks suffered a major defeat. Turkish forces reoccupied Smyrna a month later, ruthlessly killing such Greeks as had not fled the city, which was then set on fire. The Treaty of ►Lausanne formally restored Smyrna to Turkey, providing for the settlement of the surviving Greek families from the Smyrna area in new townships in Greece. War, massacre and forced emigration reduced Smyrna's population from 1 million in 1914 to under 200,000 in 1939.

Social Credit Parties. At the time of the ►Depression a British economist, Major Clifford H. Douglas (1879–1952), advanced the theory that the weakness of modern capitalism is a lack of purchasing power, and he argued that this deficiency could be countered by a monetary reform, in which 'social credit' would be made available to consumers. Parties advocating this system developed in several countries but most markedly in Canada: a social-credit party came to power in Alberta in 1935, and (apart from the years 1972–5) has remained in power in British Columbia since 1952. These parties, however, represented a narrowly provincial particularism rather than a revolutionary form of capitalism and their electoral successes were essentially gestures of protest, akin to ►Poujadism under the French Fourth Republic.

Social Democratic Party (SDP). Discontent with the alleged infiltration of the ►Labour Party by militant Marxists in 1979–80 led a group of four former Labour cabinet ministers (Roy Jenkins, Mrs Shirley Williams, Dr David Owen and William Rodgers) to set up a Council for Social Democracy on 25 January 1981. Dr Owen and eleven other dissident Labour MPs resigned the Labour Party whip five weeks later and on 26 March 1981 formally launched a new centre party in British politics, the Social Democratic Party. In the following September the SDP formed an electoral alliance with the ➤Liberal Party and it subsequently gained striking successes at by-elections: Shirley Williams took Crosby from the Conservatives on 26 November 1981; Roy Jenkins won the Conservative seat of Glasgow Hillhead, on 25 March 1982. The SDP, free from rigid adherence to any familiar party programme, seemed an influential force in British politics during the early months of 1982 but lost ground with the hardening of traditional attitudes during the ➤Falklands Crisis. After a three-week postal ballot among 62,000 SDP members Roy Jenkins was elected as the first leader of the new party on 2 July 1982. Dr Owen succeeded him a year later. The Alliance won fewer seats than anticipated at both the General Elections of 1983 (6 SDP MPs returned) and 1987 (5 SDP MPs returned). After the 1987 electoral setback a resolution was carried at the Party Conference in favour of a merger with the Liberals. As Dr Owen opposed this policy he resigned the leadership and was succeeded by Robert Maclennan. When in 1988 the Social and Liberal Democrat Party ('Democrats') was formally constituted, Dr Owen resumed the leadership of the remaining SDP independents. But the SDP was formally dissolved in June 1990.

Social Democrats. Originally all Marxist political parties assumed the name 'Social Democrat' but from 1905 onwards the term was applied to socialist groups believing in evolutionary reforms through parliament rather than in revolution. The German party (the Social Democratic Workers' Party) was founded at a congress of socialist groups in Eisenach in 1869, and polled 4¼ million votes in 1912. Parties on the German model were founded in Belgium (1885), Austria (1889), Hungary (1890), Bulgaria (1891), Poland (1892), Romania (1892–1900, refounded 1910), Holland (1894), Russia (1898), Finland (1903) and Serbia (1903). British socialism developed along different lines (➤Labour Party), which were broadly followed by the Scandinavian Social Democratic parties and by Socialist parties in the British Empire. French social democracy had an entirely separate origin: socialist sects (some of them pre-Marxist) coalesced in 1899 into two main groups, the Parti Socialiste Français of ➤Jaurès and the Parti Socialiste de France of Jules Guesde (1845–1922) who was more influenced by ➤syndicalism than was Jaurès. These groups united in 1905 to form the Section Française de l'Internationale Ouvrière, reverting to the name of the earlier Jaurès group in the inter-war period. Representatives of all three strands of social democracy met in the congresses of the ➤Second International. Orthodox Marxists tended to secede and form ➤Communist parties from 1919 onwards.

Solidarity, the name given to the independent, self-governing trade union which emerged in ➤Poland under the leadership of the Gdańsk electrician Lech ➤Wałęsa in August 1980. Agreements signed with representatives of the Polish Government in Szczecin, Gdańsk and Katowice provided for a relaxation of censorship, reduction of the working week, the promise of increased food supplies and greater freedom of expression in the media, including the broadcasting each Sunday of a catholic mass. Further concessions over access to the media were granted in May 1981. Food shortages led to renewed tension between Solidarity members and the Polish authorities in the autumn of 1981. Under Soviet pressure the Polish leader, General ➤Jaruzelski, imposed martial law on the country on 14 December 1981. This action deprived Solidarity of many of the gains it had made over the previous fifteen months. Solidarity leaders, including Wałęsa, were imprisoned or interned; Wałęsa was released on 12 November 1982 although Solidarity itself remained banned even after martial law was lifted in July 1983. Father Jerzy Popiełuszko, a young Warsaw priest sympathetic to Solidarity, was abducted on 19 October 1984; his tortured body was recovered eleven days later from the river. The moderation urged on Polish Catholics by the Pope, by Cardinal Josef Glemp and by Wałęsa prevented irresponsible acts by angry Solidarity supporters; four secret police agents were given long prison sentences in February 1985 for Popiełuszko's murder. Solidarity banners were again displayed in 1988 when there was renewed trouble in Gdańsk, with closure of the Lenin shipyard threatened by the Polish authorities. There was, however, a series of talks between Solidarity leaders and the Polish Government from February to April 1989; the ban was lifted on Solidarity, whose candidates gained spectacular successes in the General Election of 4 June 1989. Subsequently, a Solidarity nominee, Tadeusz Mazowiecki, became prime minister of a coalition government. Marian Krzaklewski succceeded Wałęsa as Chairman early in 1991.

Solzhenitsyn, Alexander (1919–), Russian writer and dissident. Born at Kislovodsk in the Caucasus, educated at the University of Rostov and the Moscow Institute of History, served as an artillery battery commander in the Red Army, 1942–5, and was twice decorated for bravery, imprisoned 1945–53, in exile in Siberia, 1953–6, rehabilitated 1957. His novel *A Day in the Life of Ivan Denisovich* was published in 1962 and won approval from ➤ Khrushchev as well as in the West, since it exposed the misery of prison-camp life under Stalin. Later novels, published after the fall of Khrushchev, were banned in the Soviet Union for suggesting the path to socialism was paved with corruption. His award of the Nobel Prize for Literature in 1970 was attacked by the Soviet authorities, who continued to persecute him, despite protests from abroad, after his publication of the major works, *August 1914* and *The Gulag Archipelago*, in 1971–3. He was expelled from the Soviet Union in 1974, eventually settling in California (1975). When Soviet citizenship was restored to him in 1990 he repudiated the action, but later returned to visit the new Russian Federation.

Somalia. Territory on the north-east horn of Africa. The British established a protectorate over the coast facing ➤Aden in 1884, administered at first by the government in India, but transferred to the Colonial Office in 1905. Italy colonized a larger area, 'Somalia Italiana', further south, overrun by British and British Empire troops in 1941 and administered by the British until 1950 when the United Nations allowed Italy to assume trusteeship for the region, pending the establishment of a Somali state. The British and Italian protectorates were united in 1960, becoming the independent Somali Republic, with its capital in Mogadishu. President Shermarke was assassinated in a left-wing military *coup* on 15 October 1969 which brought General Siyad Barre to power. The 'Somali Revolutionary Socialist Party' later showed independence of Moscow and Peking, seeking territorial expansion in the Ogaden region of ►Ethiopia, which it invaded on 23 July 1977 in support of guerrillas of the 'Western Somali Liberation Front'. These incursions were repulsed by Ethiopian troops, supported by Soviet and Cuban weapons and advisers, 21 January to 5 March 1978. In 1980 President Barre granted the US Navy facilities in the port of Berbera and the Americans gave the Somalis military and financial aid when renewed fighting with Ethiopia broke out in 1982. Early in 1986 there was a rapid improvement in relations with Ethiopia. Food shortages and accusations of corruption caused riots in Mogadishu in January 1991, forcing President Barre to flee the country. His departure led to a final breakdown of government, with rival warlords devastating southern Somalia, including Mogadishu, and a rival Somaliland Republic established in the north-west around Berbera. An American-led UN Task Force landed at Mogadishu in December 1992 but found it impossible to restore order. The last UN troops – from India, Pakistan and Egypt – were withdrawn in March 1995, after suffering casualties from repeated attacks from rival Somali factions. The combinations of protracted famine and fighting has left up to half a million Somalis dead. Anarchy persists.

Somme, Battle of the (1 July to 18 November 1916). After a week's intensive bombardment the British Fourth Army, with the French Sixth Army on its right, launched the first of a series of attacks on German positions along a twenty-mile front north of the river Somme between the towns of Albert and Péronne. Twenty thousand British soldiers perished on the first day of the battle (1 July), more than were killed in action during the five years of Wellington's peninsular campaign (1809–14). The offensive was intended to relieve pressure on the French at ►Verdun. During twenty weeks of successive offensives the allies advanced some ten miles and lost 600,000 men, two-thirds of them British. Use of tanks for the first time (by the British on 15 September) was not entirely successful because of the muddy and marshy terrain. Although the Germans were forced back to new positions, they held the vital railway junction of Bapaume, threatened by the British attacks. Subsequently German military historians claimed that the Somme, together with Verdun, so weakened their army that it was never again possible to find a trained nucleus upon which to build an efficient fighting force: hence it has been argued that the Somme, despite its futile costliness, was the turning-point of the war in France.

South Africa. In September 1909 the British parliament approved a 'South Africa Act' establishing a new dominion of the British crown, the Union of South Africa, comprising the former colonies of the Orange River, ►Transvaal, the Cape and

Natal and assuring equal status for people of British and Dutch Boer descent. The Union came into being on 31 May 1910, with General ►Botha as first Prime Minister. The ►National Party formed by ►Hertzog and reformed in 1935 by ►Malan was more illiberal and discriminatory than the South Africa Party of ►Smuts and its successor, the United Party. The Status of the Union Act of June 1934 emphasized that South Africa was 'a sovereign independent state' with the right to secede from the British Commonwealth and the Representation of Natives Act in April 1936 defined the limited political status of the coloured population: an advisory representative council, and in Cape Province the right to elect three whites to parliament. These concessions were too much for Malan, who came to power after the elections of May 1948 and instituted a strict system of ►apartheid. This fanatical belief in racial segregation ran contrary to the governing principle of human rights throughout the Commonwealth and was repeatedly condemned by the United Nations, notably in a resolution of the General Assembly on 14 December 1973. A referendum held among white voters in the Union on 5 October 1960 decided by a narrow majority (52 per cent in a poll from which 9 per cent of the electorate abstained) to leave the Commonwealth and the Union became the independent Republic of South Africa on 31 May 1961. South-West Africa, ►'Namibia', became a mandate of South Africa under the League of Nations but has been a cause of dispute ever since the establishment of the United Nations: South Africa has refused to submit to international supervision of its system of administration, despite condemnation by the International Court of Justice at The Hague (June 1971). South African moves to establish independent Bantu homelands – the first of them in the ►Transkei, the second being Bophuthatswana (November 1977) – were denounced outside the republic as fraudulent. The white South Africans, unmoved by foreign criticism, gave the Nationalists their biggest ever majority in the general election of November 1977. Soon afterwards the Nationalists found themselves in great difficulty because of rumours of corruption in a government department. The new Prime Minister, P. ►Botha (who succeeded ►Vorster in September 1978), ordered a judicial commission of inquiry which, on 5 December 1978, revealed the misuse of secret propaganda funds by the South African Department of Information. The Minister of Information, Dr Connie Mulder, resigned in what became widely known as the 'Muldergate Scandal'. This affair distracted public attention at home from the problems of Namibia and, to some extent, also distracted world opinion from the continued brutality of the security police. Underground black resistance to apartheid perpetrated acts of terrorism, the most dramatic being the sabotage of oil storage tanks at Sasolburg in June 1980. Prime Minister Botha appeared in 1979–80 to be inclining towards a more liberal interpretation of apartheid, a tendency which strengthened right-wing groups more extremist than the National Party, who found their majority greatly reduced after the general election of April 1981. New security measures intensified repression in June 1986. Although Botha won a further election in May 1987, there were striking gains by conservative dissenters in his own party and a growth in support for the neo-Nazi Afrikaner Resistance Movement. F.W. ►de Klerk succeeded Botha as party leader in February 1989 and took office as State President in October 1989. Talks with black leaders led to relaxation of the 1986 emergency regulations and, by the end of June 1991, to the formal abandonment of apartheid. In the second week of July 1991 the USA lifted economic sanctions against South Africa and the Republic was re-admitted to the Olympic Games and to international Test cricket. Bitter conflict continued within South Africa during the period of transition. Hostility towards ANC led to violence from the ►Inkatha movement among the Zulus and from a neo-Nazi Afrikaaner movement. Agreement was reached in November 1993 on an interim constitution which enabled the first multi-racial democratic general election to be held in April 1994; ANC received 62.7 per cent of votes; National Party 20.4 per cent; Inkatha 10.5 per cent. Nelson ►Mandela became President on 10 May 1994. At first the National Party joined a coalition 'government of national unity' and helped to draft a definitive constitution, agreed in May 1996 but not effective until 1999, the principal innovation being a National Council of Provinces to replace the Senate as the Upper House of Parliament. In June 1996 the National Party left the Government; Mandela's reformed cabinet contained twenty-two ANC ministers and three from Inkatha.

South East Asia Treaty Organization (SEATO). A treaty was signed at Manila on 8 September 1954 by representatives of Australia, Britain, France, New Zealand, Pakistan, the Philippines, Thailand and the United States providing for collective action if any of the signatories should be attacked or should be weakened by internal subversion. Although SEATO sought to base its character on ►NATO, several members early evaded long-term commitments, including France and Britain (neither of whom believed that the Manila Treaty operated in Vietnam, Laos and Cambodia). Pakistan formally withdrew from SEATO on 7 November 1973, France on 30 June 1974. At a meeting of ministers in New York at the end of September 1975 it was resolved to 'phase out' the organization because of changed conditions in the region.

South Tirol (Sudtirol). The area formerly belonging to the Imperial Austrian province of the Tirol, but ceded to Italy by the Treaty of St Germain in 1919 so as to give Italy a strategic frontier on the Brenner Pass. Austro-Italian disputes over the area continued intermittently from 1920 to 1971. (►Alto Adige.)

Soviet Union. The founding treaty of the Union of Soviet Socialist Republics (USSR) was adopted at a Congress of Soviets in Moscow on 30 December 1922 attended by delegates from the Russian, Ukrainian, Byelorussian and Transcaucasian SSRs. By 1941 there were fifteen constituent republics in the Union, with autonomous rights which had to conform to directives from the governing body of the Union, the central Presidium. The definitive Soviet Constitution of December 1936 recognized a bicameral Union assembly; an elected Council of the Union, with every deputy being a member of the Communist Party; and a nominated Council of Nationalities. In practice, from 1923 until 1953, all policy was determined by Joseph ➤Stalin, as General Secretary of the Party until May 1941 and thereafter as Prime Minister as well (➤Five-Year Plans; Yezhovshchina; Kulaks; Molotov; Beria; Nazi–Soviet Pact). Victory over Germany in 1945 left the Soviet Union controlling Eastern Europe and much of Germany, a confrontation with the West long perpetuated in the ➤Cold War. On Stalin's death in 1953 his successor, ➤Malenkov, was soon replaced by ➤Bulganin as head of the government, and as Party leader by the more accommodating ➤Khrushchev, who denounced the cult of Stalin at the Twentieth Party Congress in January 1956. The hostility with which his cautious reforms were viewed by communist ➤China led to Khrushchev's increasing isolation in the Politburo (the Party executive) and to his replacement in October 1964 by ➤Brezhnev in Party affairs and by ➤Kosygin as Prime Minister. While the Soviet Union remained a super-power in world affairs, spending vast sums on defence and on a prestigious space programme (➤Gagarin; Sputnik; Tereshkova), the standard of living remained poor and the secret police (KGB, Committee of State Security) probed increasingly into people's conduct. From 1973 onwards the extent to which 'dissidents' were punished by GULAG (Chief Administration of Corrective Labour Camps, established originally in 1930) was made known through the writings of ➤Solzhenitsyn and others abroad. The failure of the Soviet invasion and occupation of ➤Afghanistan in Brezhnev's later years demoralized sections of the army at a time when there was clear evidence of corruption in government and the Party. On Brezhnev's death in 1982 his immediate successors, ➤Andropov and Chernenko (1911–85), realized the need to 'clean up' the Party, but both were old men, in poor health, whose combined span of office was only twenty-eight months. Attempts were made to restore confidence in the Party in some regions, notably by Shevardnaze (1928–) in ➤Georgia. But it was left to ➤Gorbachev, as General Secretary of the Party from 1985 to 1991, to promise long-overdue radical reform by his double policies of ➤glasnost and ➤perestroika. Such changes needed financial aid and support from the West which were not forthcoming. Disillusionment at Gorbachev's failure to raise standards, coupled with a diminution in police surveillance, stimulated resurgent national feelings originally outside the Russian republic but subsequently exploited by ➤Yeltsin, whose power base was in Moscow itself. By August 1991, when the people of Moscow defeated a *coup* by Party hardliners, the autonomous republics were already seceding from the Soviet Union in the belief that independence would free them from a bankrupt system. On 8 December 1991 new bonds of association linked Russia, Ukraine and Belarus in a ➤Commonwealth of Independent States; and on 26 December 1991 the Soviet Union ceased to exist.

Soweto. Predominantly black township, south-west of Johannesburg. Riots broke out in Soweto on 16 June 1976 after demonstrations by non-whites against legislation proposing to make Afrikaans the compulsory language of instruction in all schools. On the first day of rioting two black children and four black adults were killed when police opened fire, and two whites were killed by the rioters. More than forty casualties were reported in rioting on the following day. After three days of riots in Soweto and a further three days elsewhere in the Transvaal, it was officially reported that 236 non-whites had been killed and more than 1,100 injured. On 6 July the South African Minister of Bantu Education announced that plans for compulsory teaching in Afrikaans would be dropped. Tension remained high in Soweto, and there was further rioting on the first anniversary of the original demonstrations. Services to commemorate the 1976 riots – in which the blacks consistently claimed that 600 people died – have themselves provoked violence every year in June.

Spaak, Paul-Henri (1899–1972), Belgian statesman and internationalist. Born at Schaerbeek, became a lawyer in Brussels in 1922 and was elected to the Belgian parliament as a socialist Deputy for one of the districts of the capital in 1932. Six years later (13 May 1938) he became Belgium's first socialist Prime Minister, holding office for eleven months. After the invasion of Belgium in 1940 he came to London and was Foreign Minister of the government-in-exile, playing a great part in establishing ➤Benelux. He presided over the first General Assembly of the United Nations, as well as serving as Belgium's Prime Minister again, March 1947 to June 1949. From 1949 to 1951 he was president of the consultative assembly of the ➤Council of Europe, showing himself a strong champion of the European idea. After serving as Belgian Foreign Minister, 1954–7, he was secretary-general of NATO, 1957–61, before resuming his tenure of the Belgian Foreign Ministry from 1961 until his retirement from politics in 1966.

Spain. Throughout the nineteenth century Spain was weakened by political disunity, which culminated in a series of outrages by ➤anarchists. King ➤Alfonso XIII tried a succession of political expedients, including a right-wing dictatorship under ➤Primo de Rivera, but was faced by an ominous mounting of republican sentiment shown by the municipal elections of 1931, leaving the country in April. Alcalá Zamora (1877–1949) became provisional head of state, pending the adoption of a republican constitution in December, the assembly then confirming his appointment as President and recognizing Manuel ➤Azaña as Prime Minister. The republic was hampered by regional demands for autonomy, notably by the Catalans and the ➤Basques; anti-clericalism led to several outrages against priests, nuns and church property; a communist-inspired rising of the miners in the Asturias was suppressed with considerable brutality (October 1934); and the army leaders were appalled at the ineffectual lead given by the parties in parliament (Cortes). The ➤Spanish Civil War led to the institution of General ➤Franco as 'Caudillo of the Realm and Chief of State', and his views determined Spain's political evolution until his death in 1975. In July 1969 Franco nominated the grandson of King Alfonso XIII, Prince ➤Juan Carlos, to succeed him as head of state, the transition being peacefully made on 22 November 1975. King Juan Carlos relaxed the restraints of the Franco years, permitting the legal re-establishment of political parties (including the ►Communist Party) and autonomous concessions in Catalonia. On 15 June 1977 the first general election since February 1936 was held in Spain, giving the moderate Democratic Centre Party an overall majority with 166 seats to the Socialist Workers' 116 seats and Communists' 20 seats. The Democratic Centre Party (UCD) formed a government under Adolfo Suarez who remained Prime Minister until January 1981, winning another general election in March 1979. The UCD programme envisaged devolution, with a degree of autonomy in the Basque provinces, Catalonia and eventually Andalucia, and also sought the entry of Spain into NATO and the Common Market. Basque and Catalan regional parliaments were duly elected in March 1980 but mounting hostility caused the UCD to drag its feet over Andalucia, where there was a strong socialist tradition. Right-wing movements, especially within the army, were a constant threat to Suarez; in November 1978 Lieutenant-Colonel Tejero Molina was arrested after the discovery of a plot to kidnap the Prime Minister and other members of the cabinet. But the gravest crisis for the UCD government came after Suarez was succeeded as Prime Minister by Calvo Sotelo: on 23 February 1981 Colonel Tejero Molina (having served a sentence of imprisonment for his earlier plot) entered parliament with 300 Civil Guardsmen and held the Deputies hostage for 17 hours, while General del Bosch in Valencia staged an (abortive) military coup. Subsequent inquiries led to the arrest of the deputy Chief of the Army Staff and the military governor of Corunna as well as del Bosch and the Colonel. The sentence of thirty years' imprisonment imposed on the two leading rebels in June 1982 aroused much sympathy for them in Spain. The General Election of 28 October 1982 brought victory to the socialists; and Felipe Gonzalez formed the first left-wing government in Madrid since the Civil War. Spain joined the EEC in 1985. The election of March 1996 brought the centre right Populist Party to power, under Jose Maria Aznar (1953–).

Spanish Civil War (1936–9). Began as a revolt of army commanders in Spanish Morocco prompted by resentment at the growing socialist and anti-clerical tendencies of the republican government of ►Azaña. The insurgents were led by Generals José Sanjurjo (1872–1936) and ►Franco. Cádiz, Saragossa, Seville and Burgos declared for the insurgent nationalists: Madrid, Barcelona, Bilbao and Valencia remained in republican control. The Civil War was an ideological battleground for all Europe. The insurgents were assisted by German air power, the pilots perfecting dive-bombing techniques used in 1940–41 in other campaigns; and 50,000 Italian 'volunteers' assisted Franco on land. Russia sent advisers and technicians to the republicans, who were also assisted by International Brigades, made up of communists and left-wing sympathizers from many countries. There were four main military phases of the Civil War: (1) 1936: surprise and superior military strength enabled Franco, by the end of the year, to gain control of half of Spain, including the length of the Portuguese frontier, a vital supply link, but the ►Basques and Catalans rallied to the government forces and held the east and the north;

(2) Franco sought to drive a wedge through republican territory by advancing from Teruel on Valencia in 1937, but a largely Italian army was defeated at Guadalajara while the republicans recaptured Teruel; in June the nationalists were successful in the north, capturing Bilbao; (3) in 1938 greater German–Italian assistance enabled the nationalists to resume the offensive throughout Spain; a six-month thrust to the sea severed republican territory in August, and in December they broke through on the Catalan front, but Madrid withstood attacks throughout the year; (4) intrigues between rival factions amid the republicans and the end of Soviet support led to a rapid collapse of republican forces; Barcelona fell on 26 January 1939; Valencia and Madrid on 28 March; all fighting ceased three days later. Probably over half a million lives were lost during the war, three-fifths of them killed in action. Official Spanish estimates place the figure higher, at 1 million.

Spartacists. A group of German radical socialists, led by Rosa ►Luxemburg and Karl Liebknecht, and functioning from the early summer of 1915 until January 1919, when its leaders were killed or arrested after a week of street violence in Berlin, sometimes incorrectly called 'the Spartacist Rising'. Members of the group founded the German Communist Party (30 December 1918). The name was derived from Spartacus, leader of the slave revolt against Rome in 73 BC.

Sputnik. The name given by the Russians to their original earth satellites. On 4 October 1957 the Russians launched Sputnik I, a sphere weighing 184 lb (80 kg), into space. It circled the globe in ninety-five minutes, sending out 'bleep-bleep' radio signals which shattered complacency over the alleged lead of the western world in technological matters. A month later – 3 November – Sputnik 2 carried a husky bitch, 'Laika', in order to study conditions of life in space. The Russian successes spurred the Americans to complete arrangements for the launching of their own scientific satellite, Vanguard I, on 17 March 1958. The scientific achievement represented by Sputnik raised Soviet prestige in the world at large, an opportunity ably exploited by the Soviet leader, ►Khrushchev.

Sri Lanka. The name, meaning 'Resplendent Island', assumed by ►Ceylon on becoming an independent republic within the Commonwealth in 1972 during the second administration of Mrs ►Bandaranaike. In July 1977 an electoral contest marred by riots and arson culminated in the defeat of Mrs Bandaranaike's supporters by the United National Party, led by Junius Jayewardene (1906–94). A new constitution in 1982 set up 'the Democratic Socialist Republic of Sri Lanka' and increased the executive power of the Presidency, a post to which Jayewardene had acceded in February 1978. Tension between the Sinhalese and Tamil communities developed into virtual civil war, and a state of emergency, giving unlimited powers to the security forces, was imposed in May 1983. Despite Indian attempts at arbitration in 1984, the Tamil Tiger guerrillas established control of most of the Jaffna Peninsula and inflicted terrorist killings on Trincomalee, Anuradhapura, Colombo and smaller towns and villages. Sri Lankan attempts to recover the Jaffna

Peninsula led to Indian intervention in July 1987, with the Indian forces themselves having to take action against the Tamil Tigers. At the same time the government faced a new challenge from the JVP (People's Liberation Front), Marxist dissidents in the south of the island. The presidential election of November 1988 was won by the government candidate, Ranasinghe Premadasa. In January 1989 he risked ending the state of emergency after nearly six years and secured agreement on the phased withdrawal of 50,000 Indian troops policing the predominantly Tamil areas of the island. On 15 February 1989 Sri Lanka's first general election in twelve years gave the United National Party 128 seats in a 225-seat chamber, and the party leader, D.B. Wijetunge, became Prime Minister. Violence, however, continued with terrorist outrages both by Tamil guerrillas and the JVP. By the spring of 1991 the civil war between Tamils and Sinhalese was estimated to have caused the deaths of 20,000 Sri Lankans and had resulted in an exodus of over 100,000 refugees. A suicide bomber assassinated President Premadasa in May 1993. Elections in August 1994 were won by the People's Alliance, a movement headed by Mrs Chandrika Bandaranaike Kumaratunga (1945–) who, after forming a government, was elected President in November 1994. She then handed over the premiership to her mother, the veteran Sirimavo Bandaranaike. A proposed federal restructuring of the island, promising regional autonomy, failed to satisfy Tamil extremists. The Sri Lankan army accordingly launched two offensives against Tamil Tigers on the Jaffna Peninsula, in the spring of 1995 and the summer of 1996, twice capturing Tiger headquarters. But terrorist outrages continued, particularly in Colombo and also at Kandy, where the ancient Buddhist shrine, the Temple of the Tooth, was severely damaged by a bomb. By June 1998 some 55,000 people had died in fifteen years of insurgency.

Stalin, Josef Vissarionovich (1879–1953, original name Djugashvili), Soviet Marshal and Prime Minister. Born in the village of Didi-lilo, near Gori, in the Caucasian mountains of Georgia; educated in a seminary at Tiflis, from which he was expelled for holding revolutionary views (1899); twice exiled to Siberia, escaping each time. He was in London in 1907 and Vienna in 1913, imprisoned 1913–16. He became editor of *Pravda* in 1917, assisted Lenin in Petrograd (October 1917) and became the first Commissar for Nationalities, 1917–22. In the Civil War he helped defend Petrograd and distinguished himself at Tsaritsyn (later known as Stalingrad). At the Twelfth Party Congress (April 1923) Stalin secured control of the party machine, allying with other old Bolsheviks to keep out ➤Trotsky, whose theory of revolution he denounced. From 1928 Stalin began his policy of achieving 'Socialism in One Country' through the ➤Five-Year Plans. He enforced his views through trials in 1935–8 in which many veteran revolutionaries and army leaders were charged with treason and condemned (➤Yezhovshchina). On 7 May 1941 Stalin (who had previously relied on indirect political control) became Prime Minister, holding the post until his death. As Commissar of Defence and a Marshal of the Soviet Union he directed the Soviet war effort, attending allied conferences in Teheran,

Yalta and Potsdam, and emerging as the dominant figure in eastern Europe. After 1945 he retained as rigid a grip on the newly socialist states as on the Soviet political machine. He failed only in the case of Yugoslavia where ➤Tito refused to accept criticisms from Stalin (March 1948) and survived a formal break, made by Stalin in June 1948. In his last years Stalin was obsessed with suspicion of Jewish doctors. He died on 9 March 1953, having anticipated that ➤Malenkov and ➤Beria would succeed him. The Twenty-second Party Congress, having heard criticism of his persecutions in the 1930s, ordered his embalmed body to be removed from Lenin's mausoleum and reburied in a plain grave beside the Kremlin wall (31 October 1961).

Stalingrad, Battle of (1942–3). On 5 September 1942 General von Paulus, commanding the German Sixth Army with the Fourth Panzer Army, advanced from the Don Basin on Stalingrad, a city on the lower Volga. The Russians resisted street by street until in the third week of November General ➤Zhukov mounted a counter-offensive with six Soviet armies which cut the German communications by defeating largely Romanian units north and south of the city. Besiegers thus became besieged. Despite stubborn German resistance the Russians gradually closed in on the city, capturing Paulus and his staff on 31 January 1943. Twenty-one German divisions fought at Stalingrad and the Russians took 90,000 prisoners. The German defeat marked the turning-point of the war on the Eastern Front. The city of Stalingrad – known as Tsaritsyn until 1928, when it was renamed to commemorate the role played by Stalin in defending the region against White armies in the Civil War – had its name changed to Volgograd in November 1961, as part of the anti-Stalinist reaction of the Khrushchev era.

Stamboliisky, Alexander (1879–1923), Bulgarian peasant leader. Born near Radomir into a peasant farming family rich enough to send him to Germany to study agriculture. He became an active agrarian agitator, soon widely known as a brilliant demagogue, 1908–15. After a term of imprisonment during the First World War he was briefly President of a Bulgarian republic in 1918 and was then appointed Prime Minister by King ➤Boris. Stamboliisky's premiership (October 1919 to June 1923) was a unique instance of a peasant dictatorship, equally hostile to the traditional liberal parties and to communism. Stamboliisky imposed burdens of taxation and labour both on the bourgeoisie and on the urban proletariat, leaving the peasantry almost free from taxes. He was murdered in a right-wing *coup d'état* which was protesting, not at his one-sided agrarian policy, but at attempted collaboration with the Yugoslavs in suppressing the Macedonian terrorist organization, IMRO.

Stavisky Scandal (1934). A discreditable episode bringing France to the verge of civil war. Serge Stavisky, a French citizen of Russo-Jewish origin, was accused of issuing fraudulent bonds on the security of a municipal pawnshop in Bayonne. Before the charges could be pressed, he committed suicide (3 January 1934).

Inquiries revealed that Stavisky had been protected in other dubious enterprises by well-disposed ministers and deputies. An official in the Public Prosecutor's office in Paris was found murdered, allegedly to protect well-known figures of the Third Republic. Both communists and fascist-royalist groups exploited the scandal, maintaining that it showed the corrupt character of French democratic government. Serious riots in Paris on 6, 7 and 9 February were followed by a general strike, and the republic was only saved by the formation of a National Union coalition headed by the much-respected former President, Gaston Doumergue (1863–1937). The Stavisky riots had a lasting effect on French politics: the ideology of the right-wing demonstrators, despising the republic, became the official doctrine of ►Vichy.

Stepinac, Aloysius (1898–1960), Archbishop of Zagreb and Primate of Croatia. Born at Krasić, in Croatia. As a young man he supported the movement for a unified Yugoslavia, but became disenchanted with the ideal between the wars, resenting Serbian dominance over the Catholics of Croatia and ►Slovenia. He welcomed the establishment of an independent Croatia by the ►Ustaše in April 1941, although by 1943 he was protesting to their leader, Pavelić, at the atrocities they had committed in Bosnia. In 1945–6 he sought at first an understanding with ►Tito who met him for talks on the relations of Church and State, but there was no agreement. Stepinac was arrested on charges of war-time collaboration, and in October 1946 sentenced to sixteen years' imprisonment. He was released in December 1951 and allowed to exercise his priestly office (but not archiepiscopal duties) living in a village near Zagreb. The Vatican treated Stepinac at the ►Mindszenty of Yugoslavia, and Pope Pius XII created him a cardinal in 1952. Stepinac refused to travel to Rome to receive his red hat, because Tito was not prepared to allow him back into the country. His health gave way and he died of leukaemia early in 1960. Stepinac's successor, Archbishop Seper, was able to bring about a reconciliation between the Catholic authorities and the government in Belgrade.

Stevenson, Adlai Ewing (1900–1965), US Democratic politician. Born in California but the family had long associations with the Democrats in Illinois, where after editing a newspaper he practised law. Stevenson worked on ►New Deal legislation for Roosevelt and, after two years as assistant head of the Navy Department, helped establish good relations between the State Department and the fledgling ►United Nations. After becoming Governor of Illinois in 1948 Stevenson won a high reputation for tackling corruption and also for his firm handling of 'anti-Red' ►McCarthyism. He was the Democrat candidate for the presidency in 1952 and 1956 but his intellectual probity failed to win over the American voters; on both occasions they 'liked Ike' (►Eisenhower). Later Stevenson was to serve President ►Kennedy as Special Ambassador to the UN. What his opponents derided as 'Harvard lace-cuff liberalism' made Stevenson receptive to British ideas and he was much respected in London. Fittingly he died suddenly while walking in a London street on a visit to clarify the policies of his friend and colleague Dean ➤Rusk.

Stimson, Henry Lewis (1867–1950), US Secretary of War and Secretary of State. A law graduate from Yale and a vigorous campaigner for the Republicans in New York, he served as Taft's Secretary of War, 1911–13, distinguished himself as a reconciler of Filipinos and Americans during a term of office as Governor-General of the Philippines, 1927–9, and was recalled to the Administration by Hoover as Secretary of State, 1929–33. His knowledge of the Far East made him wish to pursue a more resolutely anti-Japanese line than the isolationists could accommodate. He was, however, permitted to formulate the Stimson Doctrine of 7 January 1932, informing the Japanese that the United States would never recognize treaties impairing the integrity of the Chinese Republic. In 1939–40 Stimson broke away from the main body of the Republican Party by advocating aid to the British and he was appointed Secretary of War by Roosevelt, holding office until the autumn of 1945, and thus being the first American politician to have served in the cabinets of two Republican and two Democrat Presidents.

Stockholm Accord (21 September 1986). A treaty concluded at a 35-nation conference on ➤disarmament that agreed the giving of advance notice of NATO and Warsaw Pact troop movements and manoeuvres to lessen the risk of accidental conflict.

Strategic Arms Limitation Talks ('SALT Talks'). A series of conversations aimed at restraining the arms race, held between Soviet and US representatives, the first round beginning in November 1969 and continuing until May 1972, when a treaty was signed ('SALT-1') on limiting defensive anti-ballistic missile systems and agreement was reached over certain other measures. Further talks began at Vladivostok in November 1974, seeking agreement over the numbers and types of missiles possessed by the two Great Powers. A second agreement ('SALT-2') was concluded by Presidents Brezhnev and Carter when they met in Vienna in June 1979 but it fell short of American hopes and the Carter Administration found it impossible to persuade the Senate to ratify the agreement. The Reagan Administration abandoned the SALT talks but in May 1982 the President himself indicated that he favoured discussions on limiting intermediate nuclear forces in Europe. At Geneva on 1 July 1982 Soviet and American representatives accordingly began 'Strategic Arms Reduction Talks', exchanges given the acronym START as an optimistic substitute for the discredited SALT. These START talks paved the way for the agreement on intermediate missile cuts reached by Gorbachev and Reagan in Moscow (29 May 1988). A further round of START talks opened in January 1991 and a treaty was signed in Moscow in July 1991.

Stresa Conference (September 1932). A meeting of delegates from sixteen governments at Stresa, on Lake Maggiore in Italy, to discuss means of assisting the central and eastern European states to meet the economic difficulties caused by the world ➤Depression.

Stresa Conference (11–14 April 1935). A summit meeting between the Prime Ministers of Italy, Britain and France (Mussolini, MacDonald and Flandin) with their Foreign Ministers in order to discuss forming a common front against Germany following Hitler's announcement that Germany would no longer be bound by the Versailles Treaty's limitations imposed on her armaments. The Conference issued a strong protest at Hitler's action. This was the last demonstration of unity by the three former allies against their former common enemy. The so-called 'Stresa Front' disintegrated when Italy was ostracized for launching the ➤Abyssinian War in October 1935, and Mussolini proclaimed the ➤Rome–Berlin Axis on 2 November 1936.

Stresemann, Gustav (1878–1929), German Chancellor. Born in Berlin, became a Reichstag deputy in 1906 and leader of the National Liberals in 1917 (renaming them 'People's Party', 1919). Stresemann, an ardent nationalist during the war, moderated his views under the Weimar Republic. He believed Germany's best prospect of dominating Europe lay in 'fulfilment' of the Versailles peace terms, thus winning the confidence of her former enemies in the West. Stresemann was Chancellor only from August until November 1923 but he continued as Foreign Minister until his death and secured a reversal of Germany's diplomatic position. His greatest successes were a reduction in the figure of ➤reparations, the Pact of ➤Locarno and the admission of Germany to the League, with a seat on the League Council (1926). His work for Franco-German collaboration led him to be awarded the Nobel Peace Prize for 1926, jointly with Aristide ➤Briand.

Strijdom, Johannes Gerhardus (1893–1958), South African Prime Minister. Born at Willowmore in Cape Province and educated at Stellenbosch and Pretoria, was a farmer and a lawyer in the Transvaal before becoming Nationalist MP for Waterberg in 1929, emerging as the extreme Afrikaner leader in 1934. He succeeded ➤Malan as South Africa's Prime Minister on 2 December 1954, holding office until his death in September 1958. Strijdom was responsible for an Act which destroyed the liberal traditions of South Africa's older and multi-racial universities, for legislation removing Cape coloured voters from the lists, for the harassment of Albert ➤Luthuli and for the initiation of the great Treason Trial (preliminary hearings, December 1956 to January 1958) when 156 supporters of a 'Freedom Charter' were charged with treason. He was a fanatical believer in apartheid, more contemptuous of world opinion than either his predecessor or his successor, ➤Verwoerd.

Student Demonstrations (Paris, 1968). Discontent in France at the contrast between high expenditure on defence (especially on the independent nuclear deterrent) and on education and the social services led to the formation of a revolutionary student group in the spring of 1968, taking its name from the date of foundation, '22 Mars'. Demands for higher expenditure on education and for modernization of the curricula were put forward at demonstrations by students in Nanterre on 2 May and on the Paris Left Bank a day later. Police attacked the demonstrators, brutally in Paris: the demonstrations became riots – in which an anarchist element, the *gauchistes*, participated – and rioting students were supported by the most sustained general strike in France's history, as the workers took the opportunity of condemning the policy of ➤de Gaulle in the Fifth Republic. These 'May events' as they were called, lasted until the end of the third week in June, paralysing the French economy and threatening the survival of the Fifth Republic. The students were promised reforms: the workers received an increase of 33⅓ per cent in the minimum wage and other concessions; and the government sensed that the demonstrations were a warning that orthodox Gaullism was out of date.

Succession States. The countries established after the First World War on territory formerly belonging, wholly or in part, to the Habsburg Monarchy, ➤Austria–Hungary, also known as the Dual Monarchy. These states were: ➤Czechoslovakia, ➤Romania, ➤Poland, ➤Yugoslavia, the ➤Austrian Republic and what was often called 'Trianon' Hungary (➤Trianon, Treaty of). Italy, although acquiring former Habsburg territory, is not generally considered a Succession State.

Suchow, Battle of (November–December 1948). ➤Huai-Hai.

Sudan. In 1896–8 ➤Kitchener reconquered the Sudan, which had been ruled by the fanatical Muslim Khalifa, Abdullah al Taashi, since the death of the Mahdi, Mohammed Ahmed, in 1885. Four months after Kitchener's victory at Omdurman, the Sudan was organized as an Anglo-Egyptian condominium, which continued until 14 December 1955. Affairs in the country remained unsettled: there were numerous short-lived governments and military *coups*, and in southern Sudan a state of civil war lasted until February 1972. General Mohammed el Nimeri, who established a revolutionary council of government in May 1969, was formally elected President in October 1971, and re-elected for a five-year term in May 1977. Nimeri's introduction of an Islamic code of law in 1983 led to his overthrow in a bloodless *coup* by a military council in April 1985. Civilian government was restored twelve months later, with Sadiq el-Mahdi as Prime Minister of an uneasy coalition, weakened by its dependence on the fundamentalist National Islamic Front. The chief threat, however, came from the rebel leader of the SPL (Sudan Peoples' Liberation) movement in southern Sudan, Colonel John Garang, who was supported by the Marxist government in Ethiopia. Severe fighting between the Sudanese regular army and SPL troops around Wau (1986) and Pibor (1987) intensified the sufferings of the Sudanese from ➤famine, and the plight of the refugees worsened after the Nile floods of September 1988. Implementation of a peace agreement negotiated in Addis Ababa two months later was frustrated by the hostility of the Islamic Front. The Sudanese regular army made a determined offensive early in 1994, but the SPL recovered territory in 1995–6, only to suffer a heavy defeat in August 1997. None of these battles brought any prospect of peace. By July 1997 most of the Sudan had experienced forty-two years of war during the century, leaving at least 2 million dead. Hundreds of thousands of non-Muslims in southern Sudan were believed to have been killed by troops of the Islamic extremist government. The chronic famine, in which drought followed rains so heavy that crops had been destroyed, was so severe that in mid-July 1998 a UN estimate predicted 1.2 million deaths from malnutrition.

Sudetenland. A highly industrialized region of some 11,000 square miles in northern Bohemia, east of the mountains which form the natural strategic frontier between Germany and Czechoslovakia. In 1919 most of the population were Germans but they had never been part of Germany and, by the Treaty of ➤St Germain, were transferred from Austrian rule to form part of Czechoslovakia. Until after Hitler's coming to power in 1933 most Sudeten Germans were content to remain in Czechoslovakia but in 1935 a Sudeten-German Party, financed from within Germany and led by Konrad Henlein (1898–1945), began an active campaign against the Czechoslovak state, increasing their demands after the absorption of Austria in Germany (March 1938). By the ➤Munich Agreement of September 1938, the Sudetenland (in which the Czechs had constructed their principal defensive positions) was annexed by Germany. Czechoslovakia recovered the region in 1945, expelled more than 3 million all-German-speaking inhabitants and organized the settlement within the area of Czechs from other parts of Bohemia–Moravia.

Suez Canal. The Suez Canal was constructed between 1859 and 1869, largely by French engineers under Ferdinand de Lesseps (1805–94). In November 1875 the initiative of Disraeli secured, for Britain, the largest single holding (40 per cent) of the shares in the Suez Canal Company, whose headquarters remained in Paris. In 1888 the Suez Canal Convention was signed by the Great Powers at Constantinople: it recognized concessionary rights to be held by the Canal Company until 1968 but provided for 'free and open' navigation of the canal 'in time of war as in time of peace' for all vessels. This right was denied to vessels at war with Britain, 1914–18 and 1939–45, and to Israeli vessels from 1948 onwards, as the Egyptian authorities refused to recognize the existence of Israel. British troops guarded the canal from 1882 until 13 June 1956, when the last units were withdrawn in accordance with an Anglo-Egyptian Treaty signed on 19 October 1954. Six weeks after their departure, President ➤Nasser announced the nationalization of the Suez Canal Company, an event which precipitated the ➤Suez Crisis. Anglo-French forces held the canal, 5 November to 23 December 1956, and Egyptian block-ships prevented the passage of any vessels until April 1957. The Israeli advance in the ➤Six-Day War of 1967 brought Israel's tanks to the eastern bank on 9 June, again closing the canal. An Israeli force crossed the southern sector of the canal in the ➤October War of 1973, some units remaining on the western bank until 21 February 1974.

Disengagement enabled Egyptian, American and British vessels to begin clearing the canal, which was officially reopened by President Sadat on 5 June 1975.

Suez Crisis (1956). On 26 July 1956 President ►Nasser of Egypt nationalized the Suez Canal Company, whose shares were mainly held by the British Government and French investors. Nasser claimed he wanted canal dues to pay for the Aswan Dam project on the Nile, which Britain and America had announced their unwillingness to finance a week previously. The Egyptians were uncooperative over several compromise proposals put forward in August, September and October, Nasser resenting financial retaliation imposed on Egypt jointly by Britain, France and the USA. The British and French Governments gained advance knowledge of an Israeli plan for preventive operations against Egypt in a ►Sinai campaign which began on 29 October. When Nasser rejected an Anglo-French ultimatum demanding that both Israel and Egypt should halt military operations, British and French planes attacked Egyptian bases (31 October) and airborne forces landed around Port Said on 5 November. The Anglo-French invasion aroused indignation among many sections of British and French public opinion, and was condemned by the United Nations as well as by the United States, Canada and other Common-wealth governments. The value of sterling collapsed dramatically; and the combi-nation of diplomatic and economic pressure – especially the resolute hostility of the US Secretary of State, ►Dulles – led the Anglo-French operations to be halted on 7 November, a United Nations emergency peace-keeping force being sent to the canal. The crisis showed the impossibility of British and French Governments trying to play Great Power politics against the will of America, Russia and most other nations. Anglo-French 'collusion' with Israel increased Nasser's reliance on the Soviet Union and raised his prestige among the Arab peoples. The crisis destroyed the reputation for statesmanship of the British Prime Minister, ►Eden, who resigned in poor health two months later. The episode distracted international attention from Soviet intervention to suppress the ►Hungarian National Rising.

Suffragettes. Women who seek the right to vote. In Britain the word is especially associated with the activities of Mrs ►Pankhurst, her supporters enduring imprison-ment and forcible feeding in support of their cause. British women over the age of thirty were enfranchised in 1918; women between twenty-one and thirty in 1928. The American Woman Suffrage Association was established in Cleveland, Ohio, in November 1869; and it seems as if the word 'suffragette' was of American origin. In 1890 the AWSA fused with the more aggressive 'National Woman Suffrage Association', led by Susan Brownell Anthony (1820–1906). Wyoming had female suffrage from its inception as a state (1889), and women had the vote in Colorado (1893), Idaho (1896) and Utah (1896). Militant tactics by the first woman Methodist minister, Anna Howard Shaw (1847–1919), and Carrie Chap-man Catt (1859–1947) helped to swing Democrat opinion behind the idea of votes for women, which was supported by President ►Wilson. The 19th Amendment to the US Constitution gave general female suffrage, 28 August 1920. The earliest country to give the vote to women was New Zealand (1893). In Europe women first gained the vote in July 1906, for elections to the Finnish Diet – a concession made by Tsar Nicholas II, as Finland was still within his empire. Norwegian women gained the vote in 1907. Frenchwomen had to wait until 1944, the Swiss until 1971.

Sukarno, Achmed (1901–70), first President of Indonesia. Born at Blita in eastern Java, educated at Dutch schools in Surabaja and studied engineering in Bandung. He was a founder-member of the national movement for ➤Indonesia in 1927, preaching non-cooperation. In 1929 he was arrested and jailed as a trouble-maker, spending thirteen of the next fifteen years either in prison or in exile. His astute conduct during the Japanese occupation of the Dutch East Indies enabled him to emerge as *de facto* President of an Indonesian state, a title he claimed formally on 13 November 1945. Despite conflict with the Dutch he retained this office and was recognized by the Netherlands Government as President of an independent Indonesia in 1950. Sukarno's stature was at its peak in 1955 when he was host at the ➤Bandung Conference. His authoritarian tendencies – a belief in what he called 'guided democracy' – aroused increasing resentment from 1956 onwards, especially in Sumatra. 'Confrontation' with ➤Malaysia, 1963–5, coincided with a period of economic stagnation, and the army leaders began to turn against him. He lost executive power to General Suharto on 12 March 1967, although he clung to the title of President for another twelve months.

Summit Conferences. Meetings between heads of government among major powers, intended to agree on future policy in a war or to ease mutual antagonism and promote understanding so as to avoid conflicts. Summit conferences have long been a familiar form of personal negotiations, but the term only became common after Churchill's call for 'parley at the summit' on the eve of the general election in February 1950. In retrospect the wartime meetings of Stalin with the US President and the British Prime Minister at Teheran, Yalta and ➤Potsdam have been called 'summit conferences'. A successful summit meeting was held at ➤Geneva, 18–23 July 1955, attended by Bulganin and Khrushchev (USSR), Faure (France), Eden (Britain) and Eisenhower (USA). A further summit conference in Paris, 16–19 May 1960, and attended by Khrushchev, Eisenhower, Macmillan and de Gaulle was a failure, largely because of the ➤U-2 incident.

Sun Yat-sen (1867–1925). Chinese nationalist revolutionary. Born the son of a peasant near Macao, educated in Honolulu and was for several years an American citizen, accepting Christianity and training as a doctor in Hong Kong. From 1894 to 1905 he led a 'Save China League', a propaganda organization primarily among exiles. He proclaimed his 'Three Principles' – Nationalism, Democracy, Socialism – in 1898 and these formed the ideological basis of his 'League of Common Alliance' and later of the party he founded, the ➤Kuomintang. The Chinese Revolution of 1911, which overthrew the Manchu dynasty, found him in America but he hastily returned to China. An assembly in Nanking elected him 'President of the United Provinces of China' in January 1913 but he resigned office within a few months in the hope that this gesture might encourage unity in a country divided by rival claimants to power. He retained considerable influence around Canton and, from 1922 to 1924, sought to modify his teachings so that communists could be accommodated within the Kuomintang, a change which brought him some Soviet assistance. In March 1925 he succumbed to cancer, dying before he could attain the national authority for which his life seemed a preparation. Both the later nationalists of ►Chiang Kai-shek and the Chinese communists claimed to be his political heirs. His widow, Soong Ching-ling (1890–1981), became a vice-chairman of the Chinese People's Republic in 1950.

Svoboda, Ludvik (1895–1979), Czechoslovak general and President. Born near Bratislava, fought in a Czech Legion on the Eastern Front in the First World War, became a professional soldier in the Czechoslovak Army in 1919 and a senior instructor at the staff college in 1937–8. He escaped from Czechoslovakia into Poland, and eventually into the Soviet Union, in 1939 and became commander of the Czechoslovak Army Corps attached to the Red Army in the winter of 1943–4. Svoboda's corps, part of Marshal Koniev's army group, liberated Košice and Brno and reached Prague on 9 May 1945. Until 1950 Svoboda himself was Minister of Defence, joining the Communist Party in 1948, but Stalin distrusted Svoboda's prestige and, early in 1952, he disappeared from public affairs, spending a brief period in prison, before being released to serve as an accountant in an agricultural collective. He was rescued from obscurity by Khrushchev, who remembered him as a commander in 1944–5. In the period 1963–5 Svoboda was built up as a legendary figure from Czechoslovakia's past: he was proclaimed a Hero of the Czechoslovak Republic and a Hero of the Soviet Union shortly after his seventieth birthday. By 1968 General Svoboda was accepted as a 'safe' father-figure; for this reason he was elected President in succession to ►Novotný on 30 March 1968. He collaborated closely and loyally with ►Dubček and appears to have restrained the repressive regime established after Soviet intervention in August 1968, personally leading a delegation to Moscow (►Czechoslovakia). He remained President until the spring of 1975, but was little more than a distinguished figure-head for most of his term of office.

Sweden. A dominant power in the Baltic in the seventeenth and early eighteenth century, falling in influence with the rise of Russia. In 1815 Sweden exchanged her last Germanic possession, part of Pomerania, for ►Norway, which remained dynastically united with Sweden until 1905. The Swedish Estates elected the French Marshal Bernadotte as heir to the throne in 1810: he reigned as King Charles XIV from 1818 until his death in 1844, and his descendants have held the Swedish crown ever since. Sweden has remained at peace since 1814, basing her foreign policy on principles of neutrality although collaborating with her Scandinavian neighbours and conscientiously observing her obligations to the United Nations, with Swedish troops serving on peace-keeping missions in the Middle East, Cyprus and the Congo. Sweden was a founder-member of the European Free Trade Association (1959) at a time when the country was rapidly becoming one of the most highly developed industrial communities on the Continent. In 1924 the Swedish Socialist Party (under Hjalmar Branting and Rickard Sandler) introduced the first of a series of social reforms, a legislative programme taken up by later governments. The Social Democrats were in office from September 1932 until October 1976 (apart from fifteen weeks in the summer of 1936). They returned to power in 1982 under Olof ►Palme and, after his murder in 1986, under Ingvar Carlsson. During an interlude of centre-right coalition government from 1991 to 1994 Sweden completed negotiations to join the European Union, and on 1 January 1995 duly acceded. The Øresund tunnel and bridge, linking Malmö and Copenhagen and due to be completed in the summer of 2000, will provide Sweden with a direct road and rail route to Europe's major trading centres.

Switzerland. A confederation based on the traditional cantonal union, loosely binding from the fifteenth century onwards but with the basic Federal Pact providing for a centralized Diet agreed only in 1815. A constitution, democratic in character and reconciling central and cantonal government, was adopted in September 1848 and with slight variations has remained binding ever since. Frequent use is made of referenda, but women were not allowed to vote on a federal basis until 1971 and remain restricted in some cantons. At the Vienna Congress of 1815 the Great Powers and the representatives of Switzerland accepted the principle of the confederation's 'Perpetual Neutrality'. This ideal has been scrupulously maintained: Switzerland has fought in no external war since Napoleonic times; has no foreign alliances; and has never been a member of the United Nations, although housing the 'Palace of the Nations' and other international institutions at Geneva. The Swiss parliament considered it possible to reconcile neutrality with membership of the League of Nations until 1938, although insisting that Switzerland could never participate in any collective action, apart from the imposition of ►sanctions. During the Second World War the commander-in-chief of the army, General Henri Guisan (1874–1960), provided common leadership for the disparate confederation with a constantly modified defensive strategy. Although never tested, it inspired such confidence that the Federal Council felt no need to appease Switzerland's belligerent neighbours.

Sykes–Picot Agreement (16 May 1916). A secret agreement concluded by British and French diplomats, Sir Mark Sykes and Georges Picot. The agreement outlined partition of the Turkish Empire, in the eventual peace settlement: the French to be pre-eminent in Syria, Lebanon, Turkish Cilicia; the British in Palestine, Jordan, around the Persian Gulf and in Baghdad. In addition the north of Syria and Mesopotamia were regarded as within a French sphere of influence, while Arabia and the Jordan valley were within a British sphere; Russia was to have a free hand in Turkish Armenia and northern Kurdistan: Jerusalem would be established under an international administration. This agreement clashed with Lawrence's assurances to the leaders of the Arab Revolt and with pledges given to ➤Ibn Saud of the Nejd. After the Bolshevik revolution in Russia, the communist authorities found a text of the agreement in the Petrograd archives and published it (November 1917). This action led to friction with the Arabs and strengthened Turkey's will to resist. Moreover, although the agreement was not completely fulfilled in the Peace Treaties, the Arab leaders continued to suspect British and French motives in the Middle East.

Syndicalism. A movement seeking ownership of industry by workers' unions through 'direct action' (strikes and, in particular, the general strike). The most influential syndicalist thinker and writer was Georges Sorel (1847–1923) whose *Reflections on Violence* was published in 1908. Syndicalism was powerful in France before the First World War, had some following in Britain, 1911–14, and had a double impact on Italy, partly encouraging ➤anarchist groups and influencing ➤Mussolini. Syndicalism survived in Spain until the Civil War and found an American form in the ➤Industrial Workers of the World. In general, syndicalism left a legacy of direct action for trade unionists although it faded away in the 1920s as a specifically political movement.

Syria. Part of the Turkish Empire until 1918, becoming a French mandate in 1920 after the French had expelled the Arab leader, the Emir ➤Feisal. The French maintained that Syria fell into their sphere of influence as defined in the ➤Sykes–Picot agreement. The Syrians resented the French military presence and Druse insurrections in 1925–7 twice forced the French to withdraw from the capital, Damascus. French policy was changed on the eve of the Second World War and the Syrians were promised independence, against the wishes of France's senior officers. In July 1941 British and Free French troops entered Syria in order to oust supporters of ➤Vichy and prevent the establishment of German air bases in the Middle East. Syrian independence was duly proclaimed on 1 January 1944, but French officers were still reluctant to concede the loss of a land with Bonapartist associations and there was renewed fighting in Damascus, May–June 1945. The last French troops were withdrawn in April 1946. The rise of the ➤Ba'ath Party was accompanied by mounting Pan-Arab sentiment, culminating in the experimental union of Syria and Egypt in the ➤United Arab Republic from February 1958 until September 1961. Arrogant behaviour by Egyptian officials and the threat of greater loss in Syria's autonomy turned the Syrians against any formal union with Nasser, although a common intense hatred of Israel led to collaboration in the guerrilla activities which provoked the Six-Day War of 1967 and in the ➤October War of 1973. Israeli dominance of the Golan Heights west of Damascus has increased the hostility of President ➤Asad for the neighbour whom he refuses officially to recognize, and Syria opposed the ➤Sadat Initiative of November 1977. A revised constitution, promulgated in March 1973, declared the 'Syrian Arab Republic' to be a 'democratic, popular, socialist state'. Syria has given support to the Al Fatah wing of the ►Palestine Liberation Organization, intervening in the ►Lebanon and incurring heavy losses in the Israeli incursions of 1981 and 1982. President Asad has, from time to time, collaborated closely with 'Gaddafi' in ►Libya and has effectively blocked proposals for a Middle Eastern settlement emanating from King Fahd in ►Saudi Arabia. A reconciliation with the USA under the Bush administration in 1990 eased tension with Israel, both in the Lebanon and along the Golan Heights. Syria sent troops to Saudi Arabia during the Second ►Gulf War and in February 1991 they took part in the UN coalition's land campaign in Kuwait. Elections in both 1990 and 1994 confirmed support for the National Progressive Front, dominated by the Ba'ath Party.

T

Taff Vale Case. In 1901 the Taff Vale Railway Company in South Wales brought a legal action against the Amalgamated Society of Railway Servants for damage to railway property caused by its members during a strike. The courts found the ASRS responsible for the action of its members and the union was ordered to pay £23,000 compensation. Trade unionists regarded this judgement as a deliberate attempt by the propertied classes to weaken the strike weapon. After the Liberal electoral victory in 1906 a Trade Disputes Act gave unions immunity from such actions.

Taft, William Howard (1857–1930), twenty-seventh President of the USA. Born in Cincinnati, educated at Yale, practised law, served as civil governor in the Philippines (1901–4) and was Secretary of War under Theodore Roosevelt, 1904–8, winning the Presidential election of November 1908 for the Republicans. Although he was a good lawyer and an able administrator he was too conservative and too cautious for politics, proving unable to maintain smooth relations with Congress, even though his party controlled both Houses. A breach in the Republican Party, intensified by Roosevelt's desire for a return to office, led to Taft's defeat in the Presidential election of 1912 by Wilson. Taft taught law at Yale for eight years before being appointed Chief Justice of the US Supreme Court by President Harding in 1921, an office he held until his death nine years later. He was an admirable jurist though conservative in his judgements.

Taft–Hartley Act (1947). Officially termed the Labor-Management Act, this was the strongest anti-union measure carried by the first US Congress in fifteen years to have a Republican majority in both Houses. The principal author of the measure, which was carried by Congress against President Truman's attempted veto, was Senator Robert Taft (1889–1953). The Act forbade closed shops, outlawed certain strikes or boycotts (including sympathy strikes and strikes by federal employees) and restricted the amount unions could pay on political activity. The Act has never been repealed.

Taisho Era. The period of Japanese history covered by the reign of the Emperor Yoshihito, 1912–26. Japan emerged as one of the five world Great Powers during this era partly because of her successes as an allied combatant in the First World War, partly because of penetration of eastern Russia after the Revolution, but mainly through the application of modern techniques to her economic resources. Yoshihito personally took no active part in politics. Imperialism abroad was matched with political liberalism at home: a Reform Act in 1919 doubled the electorate, which was increased still further by the grant of universal male suffrage in March 1925. There was, however, mounting industrial unrest (intensified through the suffering caused by the great Tokyo earthquake of 1 September 1923) and conservative militarists helped meet open rebellion in ➤Korea.

Taiwan. Chinese traditional name for the island of ➤Formosa, from 1949 onwards the refuge of the Chinese nationalist forces under ➤Chiang Kai-shek (Jiang Jieshih). The Government of the Republic of Taiwan claimed to be the legitimate government of China and its representatives sat in the United Nations and even on the Security Council until expelled by a resolution of the other UN members in October 1971. The US Seventh Fleet long protected Taiwan from the communist Chinese under a Mutual Security Pact concluded between the Eisenhower Administration and Chiang Kai-shek on 2 December 1954. After President Nixon's visit to communist China in February 1972, US forces on Taiwan were gradually reduced in strength although the Security Pact remained valid until the end of 1978 and the recognition of 'Red China' by President Carter. When Chiang Kai-shek died in 1975 he was succeeded as President by his son, General Chiang Ching-Kuo (Jiang Qingho, 1910–88). In March 1984 Lee Teng-Hui (Lee Denghui), who was born in Taipeh, was elected Vice-President, and he duly succeeded to the Presidency four years later amid prospects of improved relations with communist China.

Tanganyika. A German settlement was established near Dar es Salaam in 1884 and the area was developed by the German East Africa Company, 1885–90, and thereafter became a protectorate of the German Empire. General von Lettow-Vorbeck resisted allied invasions, 1915–16, carrying the war into Mozambique in 1917 before finally surrendering on 25 November 1918. German East Africa was assigned by the Versailles Treaty to Great Britain as a mandated territory under the League of Nations, and was renamed Tanganyika in 1919. A moderate socialist national party, the Tanganyika African National Union, was organized by Julius ➤Nyerere in the 1950s. The British granted Tanganyika internal self-government on 1 May 1961, independence following on 9 December. A year later Tanganyika became a republic within the Commonwealth. By uniting with Zanzibar in April 1964 the Republic became known as ➤Tanzania.

Tangier. City and port in north-west Africa, facing Gibraltar. Kaiser William II, on a Mediterranean cruise, made a spectacular and much-publicized visit to Tangier on 30 March 1905, his support for Moroccan independence on that occasion marking the start of the ➤Moroccan Crisis. From 1912 to 1923 Tangier was within Spanish Morocco but was neutralized and declared an international free port in 1923, a status it enjoyed until reunited with an independent Morocco in 1956 (although Spanish troops occupied Tangier as a wartime emergency, 1940–45).

Tangier was declared a free port again, by command of King Hassan II of Morocco, in 1962, although remaining an integral part of his kingdom.

Tannenberg, Battle of (26–30 August 1914). Two Russian armies, commanded by Generals Rennenkampf and Samsonov, penetrated East Prussia at the start of the First World War. A plan for destroying these armies was worked out by Colonel Max Hoffmann (later a general) and submitted by him to the two commanders sent to check the Russian advance, ➤Hindenburg and ➤Ludendorff. The plan rested on Hoffmann's knowledge of a deep personal feud between the Russian generals, and his conviction that Rennenkampf would do little to relieve Samsonov. The Germans thus concentrated their forces in the region around Tannenberg and, aided by intercepted wireless signals, were able to rout Samsonov, taking more than 100,000 prisoners. Hindenburg then gave his attention to Rennenkampf's army which was virtually destroyed near the Masurian lakes in the second week of September. These victories made it impossible for the Russians to launch another invasion of German territory during the First World War.

Tanzania. On 25 April 1964 ➤Tanganyika united with the former Sultanate and British protectorate of Zanzibar, becoming officially known later in the year as Tanzania. Originally it had been anticipated that the independent republics established in the area (Kenya and Uganda as well as Tanzania) would form an East African Federation but tribal and religious difficulties ruled out the creation of any larger political entity. President ➤Nyerere was elected head of the United Republic, with the principal Vice-President also serving as President of Zanzibar. Ali Hasan Mwinyi succeeded President Nyerere in October 1985. President Mwinyi legalized multi-party politics in June 1992, ending fifteen years of dominance by the CCM (Chama Cha Mapinduzi), the movement Nyerere had created. Multi-party elections in October and November 1995 were nevertheless won by the CCM, amid allegations of vote-rigging from their opponents. The CCM leader, Benjamin Mkapa, succeeded President Mwinyi after the election.

Tariff Reform League. A movement led by Joseph ➤Chamberlain in the period 1903–6 to press for ➤Imperial Preference and ultimately for moderate protection of British industry in the face of German competition. The League's activities divided and embarrassed the Conservative-Unionists in the 1906 election.

Taylor, Frederick Winslow (1856–1915). American industrial engineer and an early graduate of the Stevens Institute of Technology. While serving as a foreman in a steel-mill in the 1880s, he pioneered time-and-motion studies so as to increase efficiency. Taylor's analyses and reports became basic material for the techniques of industrial management perfected in America during the early years of the century and he attempted to summarize his conclusions in an influential book, *The Principles of Scientific Management*, published in 1911. His work facilitated the rapid growth of the impersonal and regimented mass production particularly associated, in the first instance, with Henry ➤Ford.

Teapot Dome Scandal. The management of US naval oil reserves at Teapot Dome, Wyoming, was transferred by President ►Harding from the Secretary of the Navy to the Secretary of the Interior, Albert Fall, an old friend of the President from his early political days in Ohio. In 1922 Fall leased other reserves at Elk Hill, California, to a second oil developer. Senate investigation led to the cancellation of the leases, to the imprisonment of Fall in 1929, and to posthumous criticism of the President's handling of affairs, although Harding was never officially accused of corruption.

Teheran Conference (28 November to 1 December 1943). The first inter-allied summit meeting attended by Stalin as well as by Roosevelt and Churchill. The conference discussed coordination of the eventual ►Normandy landings with a Soviet offensive against Germany, the possible entry of the Soviet Union into the war against Japan, and the need to establish an international organization to keep peace in the post-war world.

Television. The principal means of communicating distant events and scenes in the second half of the century. Television was developed in Britain by John Logie Baird (1888–1946), who first publicly demonstrated the medium in Soho on 26 January 1926. New York had a small television service operating in 1928 and there were some 30,000 viewers in twelve separate metropolitan areas of the United States by 1932. The ►BBC began regular transmissions from Alexandra Palace, London, on 2 November 1936, and the French established a service in Paris early the following year. The Second World War delayed development of television: the BBC, for example, transmitted no television between 2 September 1939 and 7 June 1946. The boom in television began in America in 1948, spreading to Europe in the early 1950s. Colour television, available in America in 1951, was slower coming to Europe, although Cuba had a regular colour television service in 1959 and Japan in 1960. The first transatlantic pictures were transmitted by Telstar artificial satellite on 11 July 1962 and it was possible by 1969 to receive live pictures from the surface of the moon. The rapidity with which visual news can be transmitted has influenced the public response to world affairs in recent years, notably over the ►famine in Africa in 1985, the Tiananmen Square massacre in ►China in 1989, and during the Second ►Gulf War in 1991 and the subsequent Kurdish emergency. The launch, in December 1988, of a television satellite from French Guiana gave an opportunity for sixteen new channels in Europe, and in February 1989 the first satellite television service opened in Great Britain. Multi-channel digital television spread across the USA in 1995. Soon afterwards it was developed so as to cover the African continent. In June 1997 it was announced that digital television would begin transmissions in Britain within eighteen months.

Temple, Frederick (1821–1902) and William (1881–1944). ►Canterbury, Archbishop of.

Teresa, Mother (Agnes Gocha Bedjanxhiu, 1910–97), nun. Born in Skopje (now

Macedonia) of Albanian Catholic parentage, she became a nun with the Sisters of Loreto in 1928, joining the sisterhood in Dublin but settling in India before the end of that year. Until 1946 she taught, mainly in Calcutta where she was deeply moved by the poverty around her. A vocation to live among the desperately poor and help them enabled her to gain permission for medical training (1948) and for setting up a new order, the Missionaries of Charity (1950). By 1960 the order had spread from Calcutta to every densely populated city in India; by 1965 Mother Teresa had established centres in Latin America and within a few years in every other continent. The houses of the order cared for the destitute, lepers, abandoned children, drug addicts, and – especially in the 1980s – for the victims of ➤famine and civil war in Africa. Such world-wide charitable enterprise was recognized by the award of the Nobel Peace Prize (1979) and by distinctions from many governments, including an honorary Order of Merit bestowed personally by Queen Elizabeth II when she visited India in November 1983.

Tereshkova, Valentina Vladimirovna (1937–), Soviet astronaut. Became the first woman to fly in space, when she piloted spacecraft Vostok 6 for forty-eight orbits of the earth (16–19 March 1963), twenty-three months after the first space flight by ➤Gagarin. This achievement exploded an American myth that biological tensions made space flights necessarily a male preserve. Valentina Tereshkova subsequently married another astronaut and became a mother in 1967.

Teschen Dispute. The Duchy of Teschen formed part of the Habsburg Empire from 1772 to 1918. On the disintegration of Austria–Hungary this rich, industrial region was claimed by both Poland and Czechoslovakia, between whose troops there was sharp fighting for a week in January 1919. The frontier, as finally determined by the 'Conference of Ambassadors' in Paris (July 1920), awarded the town of Teschen to Poland, leaving Czechoslovakia with the suburb of Freistadt and a valuable coalfield. The Poles complained that the settlement favoured the Czechs and the dispute over the Teschen area prevented Polish–Czech collaboration between the wars, even though both Poland and Czechoslovakia were allies of the same Western Power, France. The opportunity to acquire the rest of the region induced the Poles to collaborate with Hitler in 1938, and after the ➤Munich Agreement Germany insisted on the cession of the Czech area to Poland. The dispute was renewed in June 1945, but was peremptorily settled by Stalin and Molotov, who summoned the Polish and Czechoslovak Foreign Ministers to Moscow and imposed a return to the 1920–38 frontier.

Test-Ban Treaty (5 August 1963). An agreement, concluded originally by the United States, the Soviet Union and Britain, prohibiting the testing of nuclear weapons in the atmosphere, in outer space or under water, but permitting underground testing. The Treaty was the fruit of five years' negotiations, for the first three of which the nuclear powers had voluntarily abstained from tests. More than ninety other governments signed the Treaty in the two years 1963–5, but France and China declined to sign and continued to carry out nuclear tests in the atmosphere.

Tet Offensive (29 January to 25 February 1968). The principal counter-offensive mounted by General ►Giap in the ►Vietnam War. The name is derived from the word for the lunar new-year celebrations, during which the attack was launched. The offensive took the form of major operations by guerrillas and North Vietnamese regular troops against Saigon, Hué and more than ninety other towns and fifty small villages. Losses were heavy on both sides and the material gains of the attackers were small, but the extent of the offensive finally turned the Administration in Washington against involvement in Vietnam. The 'Tet' was therefore decisive for the war as a whole.

Thailand. From 1781 until 1939 Thailand, known for 400 years as the Kingdom of Ayuthia, was called Siam, a name taken from the ruling dynasty. The Kingdom's independence rested largely on the assumed need in Europe for a neutral buffer zone between British-dominated Burma and French Indo-China, a position regularized by Anglo-French diplomatic agreements in 1896 and 1904, although the British obtained concessions from Siam at the northern tip of the Malay peninsula in 1909. The Siamese King granted a constitution in 1934 and the rise of political parties in a parliament, 1935–9, coincided with a new popular nationalism and bestowal on the country of the title Muang Thai, 'Land of the Free', to emphasize its avoidance of colonial rule. While the Thais technically allied themselves to Japan, they retained American sympathy by mounting a persistent guerrilla campaign. After a period of chaos in 1946 the country was effectively governed from 1946 to 1957 by Marshal Pibul Songgram, a former collaborator with the Japanese. Military rule, frequently corrupt, continued until February 1969 and was resumed in November 1971, the threat of communist infiltration from Laos being used as an excuse for martial law. There were grave riots and demonstrations in September and October 1973, and an interim civilian government summoned a constituent assembly which promulgated a democratic constitution in October 1974. Elections held in January 1975 and April 1976 returned predominantly civilian coalition governments. Further constitutional experiments in 1978 strengthened the hand of the right-wing army leaders. The presence of Vietnamese forces in Cambodia (Kampuchea), within 150 miles of Bangkok for much of 1979–80, inevitably increased the military hold on the country, the Thai authorities supporting any anti-Vietnamese regime beyond their frontier. A brief rebellion in Bangkok (31 March–3 April 1981) was put down by loyalist forces who marched on the capital from Nakhon Ratchasima. The threat of communist infiltration from Laos led to the establishment of a military dictatorship under General Prem Tinsulanonda. A two-and-a-half year interlude of civilian rule under Chatichai Coonhavan ended in February 1991, when a further military *coup* suppressed an allegedly corrupt system of parliamentary government. Mass anti-government demonstrations in Bangkok in May 1992 secured a return to parliamentary democracy, but the threat of intervention by the army inhibits reform.

Thant, U (1909–74), third Secretary-General of the United Nations. Born in Pantanaw, became a high-school headmaster, entered the Burmese diplomatic service in 1948, serving at the United Nations from 1957 onwards. When ➤Hammarskjöld was killed in 1961 U Thant assumed responsibilities as acting Secretary-General, a position confirmed by election on 30 November 1962, after he had successfully sponsored a plan to reconcile ➤Katanga and the ➤Congo and helped to ease tension over the ➤Cuban Missiles Crisis. His initiatives included the establishment of UN peace-keeping forces in Cyprus (1964), the ceasefire arrangements after the ➤Six-Day War of 1967, and the acceptance of the communist Chinese as members of the UN and the Security Council. He resigned at the end of 1971 and was succeeded by Dr Kurt ➤Waldheim.

Thatcher, Margaret Hilda (née Roberts, 1925–), British Prime Minister. Born at Grantham, educated at Grantham High School and Somerville College, Oxford, and became a barrister. Mrs Thatcher was elected Conservative MP for Finchley in 1959, held minor office 1961–4, and was appointed Minister of Education and Science by Edward ➤Heath in 1970, a post she held until the fall of the Conservative Government in February 1974. A year later (11 February 1975) she was elected leader of the Conservatives in succession to Edward Heath, thus becoming the first woman to lead a major political party in Britain. She became Prime Minister after the Conservative victory in the election of May 1979. The first achievement of the Thatcher Government – the transition from ➤Rhodesia to ➤Zimbabwe – owed more to the tact and skill of two members of her cabinet, Lords Carrington and Soames, than to the Prime Minister herself. Mrs Thatcher's concern with the economy induced her to adhere closely to monetarist principles which, at first, failed to halt inflation or to stimulate the growth of industry. Unemployment reached two million in August 1980 for the first time since 1935 and three million eighteen months later. Mounting criticism of her rigidity of purpose was allayed by the resolute way in which, during the ➤Falklands Crisis, she rejected any compromise over the islands' sovereignty. This achievement, together with a curb on ➤Trade Union power and the creation in southern England of a surface prosperity, helped her to win the June 1983 election with an increased parliamentary majority. By encouraging home-ownership and the purchase of shares in de-nationalized industries she broadened the class of property defenders, traditionally upholders of conservatism. Shares in thirteen publicly owned enterprises were floated on the stock-market in the first ten years of her premiership. At the same time the hectoring style with which she upbraided Britain's European partners appealed to a strong xenophobic inclination among the electorate. The General Election of June 1987 returned her to power for an unprecedented third consecutive term, with a majority of over a hundred seats, despite losses in Scotland. In January 1988 she became the longest serving British prime minister of the century. Criticism within the Party of her style of cabinet government and her insistence on distancing Britain from the ►European Community culminated in the resignation of the Deputy Prime Minister, Sir Geoffrey Howe, on 1 November 1990 and to a challenge to her leadership by Michael Heseltine. Although 204 Conservative MPs voted for Mrs Thatcher, Heseltine was backed by 152 members. The size of the revolt induced Mrs Thatcher to resign. After a further leadership election (in which she did not stand) Margaret Thatcher was succeeded by John ►Major on 28 November 1990. She received the Order of Merit, was created Baroness Thatcher of Kesteven in 1992, and three years later became the first non-royal Lady Companion of the Order of the Garter. No Conservative since Disraeli has made so personal an impact on Party doctrine and practice.

Third International (Comintern). The Russian Bolshevik form of ►international socialism established in March 1919 to promote revolutionary Marxism as opposed to the reformist socialism of the ►Second International. Until 1925–6 the movement was dominated by Zinoviev (►Zinoviev Letter): by 1928 it had become a vehicle for Stalin's ideas with the influence of ►Trotsky and his adherents eliminated. Throughout the 1930s the Third International obediently followed the changes of Soviet foreign policy and was eventually dissolved, as a gesture of assurance to Russia's western allies, in May 1943.

Third Reich. The Nazi style of describing their regime in Germany, January 1933 to May 1945. The phrase was invented early in the 1920s by a nationalist writer, Moeller van der Bruck, who used it as a title for a book, and was speedily adopted by the Nazis in order to stress their continuity with the 'First Reich' (the medieval empire) and the 'Second Reich', 1871–1918.

Third Republic (French). Generally held to have been the governmental system in France between the defeats by Germany in 1870 and 1940. Technically, however, the Third Republic dates from the passage of a constitutional law on 30 January 1875 and nominally lasted until the establishment of the ►Fourth Republic in 1946. By the beginning of the twentieth century the republic had survived a conservative phase in the 1870s, a series of scandals culminating in the Dreyfus Case of 1894–9, and a colonial rebuff inflicted on French ambitions in Africa by the British at Fashoda on the upper Nile in 1898. Politically the period between 1900 and 1914 was marked by a contest between the ►Radical Party and the socialists, led by ►Jaurès. The republic narrowly survived the First World War, finding its archetypal leader in ►Clemenceau. During the inter-war years weak party structures and a sense of political irresponsibility led to a multiplicity of factions and to short-lived governments. Between military victory in 1918 and military defeat in 1940 there were forty-four governments, headed by twenty different Prime Ministers (among them ►Poincaré, ►Briand, ►Laval, ►Daladier, ►Blum, ►Reynaud). The weakness of the political system led to extra-parliamentary demonstrations by extremists on the Left and on the Right, especially after the

➤Stavisky Affair of 1934, but it was the shock of military defeat in the German invasion of 1940 which led to the final eclipse of the republic and the interim regime of ➤'Vichy'.

Tibet. A mountainous wilderness between India and China proper, Tibet was nominally under Chinese suzerainty from 1715 onwards with the Dalai Lama, the spiritual and temporal leader, as a Chinese vassal. By 1900, however, Tibet was virtually independent. Rumours of a Russian presence led the British to send an expedition, commanded by Colonel Francis Younghusband (1863–1942), to Lhasa which was entered on 3 August 1904 after a confused skirmish in which several hundred Tibetan peasants were mown down by British machine-guns. No Russians were in Lhasa: an Anglo-Tibetan Treaty providing for trade with India revived Chinese concern for the region. Chinese troops occupied Lhasa from 1910 to 1913, forcing the Dalai Lama to flee to India. He returned in 1913 and Tibet continued in unmolested independence until October 1950 when Chinese communist troops crossed the eastern frontier. Chinese troops occupied the whole of Tibet in 1951, the Indian Government recognizing Tibet as an integral part of the People's Republic in 1954. In March and April 1959 a major rebellion led to heavy fighting between Tibetans and Chinese, the Dalai Lama and some 9,000 of his subjects subsequently fleeing to India. Tibet was administered as a Chinese province from 1959 until September 1965 when it was constituted an autonomous region within the People's Republic. There was renewed unrest in Lhasa in the winter of 1988–9, countered by armed repression.

Tiger **Talks** (2–4 December 1966). Abortive conversations between the British Prime Minister, Harold ➤Wilson, and the Rhodesian Prime Minister, Ian ➤Smith, aboard the cruiser HMS *Tiger* at Gibraltar. Proposals for a constitutional settlement of the Rhodesian question, following Rhodesia's unilateral declaration of independence thirteen months previously, were rejected by Smith's cabinet since the British Government wished for guarantees of Rhodesian progress towards African majority rule. Further talks aboard the assault vessel, HMS *Fearless*, in October 1968 met a similar fate.

Timor. The most southern island of the East Indies, it was colonized by two European Powers from the seventeenth century. The Lisbon Convention of 1904 confirmed western Timor as part of the Dutch East Indies, while the eastern third of the island was Portuguese. Dutch Timor became a province of ➤Indonesia in December 1949. East Timor remained a Portuguese colony until November 1975, when a left-wing nationalist movement, Fretilin, proclaimed independence. The Soares Government in ➤Portugal at once recognized the colony's secession, but troops from the west of the island invaded East Timor ten days after independence and declared it an Indonesian province. Fretilin resistance to the Indonesians has continued for more than twenty years, and the United Nations refuse to acknowledge the annexation. The fighting has been brutal and reports of atrocities have shocked world opinion, the worst incident being a massacre of anti-Indonesian demonstrators in Dili, the capital, in 1991.

Tirpitz, Alfred von (1849–1930), German grand-admiral. Born at Kustrin; joined the small Prussian Navy as a cadet in 1865, later specializing in torpedoes. While serving in the Baltic squadron he prepared a memorandum on the importance of developing a battle fleet which won him the support of Kaiser ➤William II. Tirpitz maintained that Germany needed a fleet as a bargaining counter with Britain over colonial questions and insisted that the German Navy need not be the strongest in the world but that it should be sufficiently large to deter a greater naval power from risking the losses which would be entailed by any attack upon it. After a spell of service in the Far East, Tirpitz was recalled to Berlin as Minister of Marine in June 1897 and held the post until resigning in March 1916. He built up the German High Seas Fleet by a series of 'Navy Laws' of which the most important were in 1898 and 1900, and he also encouraged enthusiasm for a large fleet through the German Navy League, the first organization for mass propaganda in Germany. In 1906 he resolved to construct super-capital ships to rival the British ➤Dreadnoughts, thus bringing the expensive naval arms race to a climax in the years 1909–12. When the First World War began, Tirpitz found the Kaiser's veto prevented his fleet from undertaking offensive operations in European waters, and he became an early advocate of unrestricted submarine warfare. When his recommendations were rejected by the Kaiser, he resigned and spent the last two and a half years of the war in retirement, though seeking to organize a new nationalistic political party. He sat as a Nationalist Deputy in the republican Reichstag, 1924–8, and was responsible for persuading ➤Hindenburg to stand for the German Presidency.

Tiso, Josef (1887–1947), Slovak priest and autonomist. Born near Bratislava, ordained priest in 1910, assisted two other priests, Monsignor Hlinka and Dr Jehlicka, to build up the Slovak People's Party in Czechoslovakia, a movement bitterly opposed to Czech centralism. Tiso gained political experience as Minister of Health in a Czechoslovak coalition government, 1927–9, but on Hlinka's death in August 1938 he assumed leadership of the Slovak People's Party, becoming Prime Minister of the autonomous Slovak Government set up after ➤Munich, in October 1938. On 14 March 1939 he proclaimed the independence of ➤Slovakia, becoming President of the Slovak Republic, established as a German protectorate on 26 October 1939. The willingness with which he declared war on the Soviet Union and the United States lost him support from his compatriots, who traditionally looked to one or other of these Great Powers for encouragement or sanctuary. On 22 May 1945 Monsignor Tiso was arrested in hiding in Austria, tried for wartime collaboration and sentenced to death by a Czechoslovak court in April 1947. The sentence provoked an internal crisis in Czechoslovakia. His nationality and his priestly office induced democrats and socialists in Slovakia to press for a reprieve. The coalition government of ➤Gottwald insisted on execution and he was hanged on 18 April.

Titanic. This British liner, then the largest ship in the world (46,300 tons) and held to be unsinkable, struck an iceberg in the North Atlantic on her maiden voyage (15 April 1912), and sank with the loss of 1,513 lives. In August 1985 salvage experts located the wreck.

Tito, Josip Broz (1892–1980), President and Marshal of Yugoslavia. Born at Kumrovec, Croatia, a village on the borders of Slovenia, then in Austria–Hungary. Josip Broz served with the Austrian infantry in the First World War, and as a sergeant-major was wounded and captured by Russian troops in the Carpathians on 4 April 1915. By midsummer 1917 he had escaped and joined the revolutionaries in Petrograd, subsequently helping 'Reds' against 'Whites' in Omsk, returning to Croatia in September 1920 and finding employment in a metal works at Zagreb. While working for the illegal Yugoslav Communist Party he fell into a police trap (1928) and was gaoled for six years. He visited Moscow in 1935, 1938 and 1939, serving as General Secretary of the Yugoslav party from the summer of 1937 onwards. 'Tito', as Broz was now called, came to Belgrade a few weeks after the German invasion in 1941, making his way to southern Serbia at the end of June to lead the ➤Partisans in their resistance to the invaders. His successes brought him the title of 'Marshal of Yugoslavia', bestowed on him at the ➤Jajce Congress in November 1943, and won him international recognition. He narrowly escaped death or capture in a German airborne attack on his headquarters at Drvar, 24 May 1944, but finished the war as head of the new federal government in ➤Yugoslavia. His prestige enabled him to defy Stalin in 1948, by refusing to follow a policy in Balkan affairs dictated by Moscow. The independence he thus gained allowed him to experiment with workers' self-government and to achieve recognition as leader of the non-aligned countries, especially after his election as President on 14 January 1953. Subsequently he was re-elected on five occasions before a constitutional amendment in May 1974 created him President for life. Despite a reconciliation with the Soviet Union in 1955, Tito refused to accept uncritically every shift in Soviet policy: he denounced Russian intervention in Hungary in 1956 and in Czechoslovakia in 1968. He died in hospital at Ljubljana on 4 May 1980 after four months of illness. His funeral in Belgrade four days later was the most impressive ceremony in Yugoslavia's history, with three kings, the Soviet President, thirty other heads of state and sixteen Prime Ministers among the mourners.

Togo, Heihachiro (1847–1934, created a count 1907), Japanese admiral. Born at Kagoshima, and became one of the first Japanese naval officers to be sent to Britain for training at Greenwich. He served against China, 1894–5, and was commander of the Japanese navy in the ➤Russo-Japanese War of 1904–5, becoming famous for his bombardment of Port Arthur and his overwhelming naval victory at ➤Tsushima.

Togoland. A German protectorate, 1884–1918, occupied by British and French forces from neighbouring Gold Coast and Dahomey in August 1914. One-third of the former German protectorate ('Trans-Volta-Togoland') became a British mandated territory in 1919, and was administered in close association with the Gold Coast. Following a referendum in May 1956, the British mandate entered the dominion of ►Ghana, established in March 1957, and became known as the Volta region. The remaining two-thirds of Togoland, including the capital Lomé, became a French mandate, which was granted independence on 27 April 1960, becoming the Republic of Togo.

Tojo, Hideki (1884–1948), Japanese general and Prime Minister. Born in Tokyo, graduated with distinction from the military college and served as military attaché in Germany shortly after the First World War. He was a leader of the militarist party in Japan from 1931 onwards, serving in Manchuria and as Chief of Staff of the Kwantung Army (1938–40), becoming War Minister in the summer of 1940 and urging closer collaboration with Germany and Italy. As War Minister he switched intelligence planning southwards, securing Vichy French acquiescence in the occupation of strategic bases in Indo-China (July 1941). His appointment as Prime Minister on 14 October marked the final triumph of the militarists, and he established what was virtually a military dictatorship, authorizing the attack on ► Pearl Harbor. American successes in the Marianas in the summer of 1944 brought Japan within easy bombing range of captured airfields and Emperor ►Hirohito sensed that Tojo had lost the ability to shape events. Tojo duly resigned on 9 July 1944. After the allied occupation he was put on trial as a major war criminal in November 1948; he was found guilty of instigating 'Japan's criminal attacks on her neighbours' and of permitting 'barbarous treatment' of prisoners of war, and was hanged, together with six other Japanese war leaders.

Tonkin Resolution (7 August 1964). A resolution of both Houses of the US Congress, following attacks by North Vietnamese torpedo-boats on the destroyer USS *Maddox* and other vessels in the Gulf of Tonkin on 2 August. The resolution approved retaliatory raids by American aircraft on North Vietnamese naval bases and oil refineries and authorized President Johnson 'to take all necessary steps, including the use of armed forces' to help members of ►SEATO defend their freedom. This resolution was interpreted by the Johnson Administration as a blanket authorization for American military commitment in the ►Vietnam War. From 1968 onwards many members of Congress followed the lead of Senator J. William Fulbright (1905–), an influential Democrat from Arkansas, in seeking the repeal, or restrictive clarification, of the Resolution.

Tonypandy Riots (November 1910). Tonypandy, a mining village in one of the Rhondda valleys of South Wales, was the scene of rioting during a coal strike early in November 1910. A request from the Chief Constable of Glamorgan for the dispatch of troops to the region was turned down by the Home Secretary (►Churchill) who feared the presence of soldiery would cause bloodshed. He agreed to send 300 extra police from London to the Rhondda: a cavalry squadron was kept in reserve at Cardiff and infantry units at Swindon. The police reinforcements kept peace in the valleys, sometimes by vigorous use of their truncheons. Troops encamped at Penycraig, a few miles south of Tonypandy, after the strike was over. The allegation that Churchill 'sent the army against the miners at Tonypandy' is technically incorrect. Nine months later, troops mobilized by Churchill to safeguard key routes during the war scare caused by the ►Agadir Crisis opened fire on strikers attacking a train at Llanelli and four men were killed. It is possible that Churchill's opponents have frequently confused Tonypandy with the tragic incident at Llanelli.

'Torch'. Military code-name for the Anglo-American landings in French North-West Africa (8 November 1942), designed to secure Morocco, Algeria and Tunisia, linking up with the British offensive which had begun a fortnight previously in the second battle of ►Alamein. Operation Torch assumed a rapid victory in north Africa, so as to open up Mediterranean sea-routes and prepare for an assault on the southern shore of what German propaganda called 'Fortress Europe'. Although the operation was successful in Morocco and Algeria, the Vichy French authorities in Tunis called on Axis support and north Africa was not cleared of Germans and Italians until May 1943, at least five months later than the allied planners had hoped.

Trade Unions. The first trade unions in the modern world were organized in the British woollen industry at the end of the eighteenth century, but it was not until after Disraeli's legislation of 1875, allowing peaceful picketing and clarifying contractual obligations between employers and workmen, that the union movement began to grow rapidly, partly because of the rising prestige of the Trades Union Congress (TUC), which had been established in Manchester in 1868. The ►Taff Vale Case in 1901 showed the need for further legislation, achieved under the Liberal Government in 1906 and 1913 (►Osborne Judgement). There was an outcrop of grave strikes, 1911–14, influenced by ►syndicalism. Amalgamation of unions, both in these years and immediately after the war, increased their bargaining power. Railwaymen, miners and transport workers collaborated in the 'Triple Alliance', 1914–21, which broke down when other workers failed to support the miners. British unionism suffered a setback over the failure of the ►General Strike in 1926, but regained much power and sense of corporate responsibility under the inspiration of Ernest ►Bevin. After the Second World War unionism was endangered by the 'wrecker tactics' of militant cells, active minorities able to shape policy through the passivity and complacency of a majority of members. The influence of trade unions grew during the 1960s, and the decision by the Conservative Government of Edward ►Heath to establish an Industrial Relations Court in August 1971 aroused bitter hostility from the TUC, which was consistently opposed to any restriction of trade-union rights. A rash of strikes in 1972–3 (miners, gas workers, train drivers, etc.), culminating in a fuel crisis from October 1973 to February 1974, led to an early general election (21 February 1974), in the first occasion upon which union pressure effectively overthrew a British government. A bargain, known as the Social Compact (and frequently inaccurately called 'social contract'), was then struck between the Labour Government of Harold ➤Wilson and trade-union leaders by which Labour would introduce social policies desired by the trade-union movement in return for a moderation of wage demands. A sequence of strikes, with much 'secondary picketing', in the winter of 1978–9 encouraged Mrs Thatcher's newly elected Conservative Government to amend trade-union law by the Employment Act of 1980, which gave the Secretary of State the right to issue codes of practice for the improvement of industrial relations. Trade-union membership in Britain grew from 1½ million in 1895 to 9½ million in 1955 and 11½ million in 1975, but fell to 10 million by 1985 and 9 million by the end of the Thatcher government.

Until the rise of Hitler, Germany was second to Britain in strength of trade unions, with status well defined and legalized between 1881 and 1899, and with a membership of 3½ million in 1914. French unions were organized secretly in the 1830s but were not given formal recognition until 1884: syndicalism was strong, the Confédération Générale du Travail (CGT) deciding in congress at Amiens in October 1906 to work by 'direct action' for revolution; and it was only with the growth of 'Christian' trade unions under the Fourth Republic that analogies could be drawn with the British movement. American unionism was dominated by the AF of L (American Federation of Labour) established by a Dutch-Jewish immigrant, Samuel Gompers, in 1881, but being essentially a craft union. The CIO (Congress of Industrial Organizations) existed as an independent movement of skilled and unskilled industrial workers from 1935 to December 1955, when the two organizations came together. In Tsarist Russia an attempt was made to set up police-regulated unions in 1902, without success: subversive unions came to the surface in 1907 and after the Revolution workers were required to belong to a union, though denied any right to strike. Among Commonwealth countries, unionism has been strong in Australasia, especially in New South Wales: the first Australian TUC gathered as early as 1879. Canadian unionism has tended to follow American practice. Attempts have been made to establish supranational union organizations, the earliest being the International Federation of Trade Unions (1901–45). From 1945 until January 1949 the labour movement in forty-five countries collaborated in the World Federation of Trade Unions, but the TUC, CIO and several other bodies seceded in protest at the undemocratic character of the movement in the communist bloc, forming the breakaway International Confederation of Free Trade Unions, February 1949. The rise of ➤'Solidarity' in Poland in 1980 significantly modified the traditional role of trade unions in a communist society.

Transkei. An area within ➤South Africa of some 16,000 square miles – about twice the size of Wales – forming the first of nine 'Bantu homelands' constituted as part of the apartheid policy of the South African Government. Transkei received self-government in 1962 and its own 'Bantu'-elected parliament in November

1963. Formal independence was granted on 26 October 1976 but was not recognized by any country other than South Africa. Transkei repealed immorality laws imposed by the South African Government forbidding sexual relations between whites and non-whites. The South African authorities (in February 1977) announced that Transkei citizens employed within the republic would receive some of the status enjoyed by white foreigners, such as not being restricted by pass laws. Resentment at the continued influence of South African officials led the Transkei Government to break off relations with the South African Republic early in 1978. The Bantu homelands experiment was a failure. Transkei, together with the other homelands, was reincorporated in South Africa by the transitional constitution of December 1993.

Transvaal. Province of ➤South Africa, settled by Boers who migrated across the Vaal river in the Great Trek of 1836–7, self-governing 1853–77, 1881–4 and existing as a Boer Republic free from British suzerainty, 1884–1902. Conflict between the British and the Boers of President ➤Kruger led to British reannexation of the Transvaal in 1902 although responsible government was restored in 1906. Boers from the Transvaal played a notable role in establishing the Union of South Africa in 1910. Subsequently the Transvaal became a centre of extreme Afrikaner feeling and a stronghold of the ➤National Party. The 1996 Constitution abolished all the historic provinces, but the name 'Eastern Transvaal' survives as one of South Africa's nine regions.

Transylvania. A mountainous and wooded region in eastern Europe, long disputed by Romanians and Hungarians. The region passed under Habsburg rule at the end of the seventeenth century and from 1867 to 1918 formed part of the Kingdom of Hungary, the urban population being predominantly Magyar while most of the peasants were Romanian. The offer of Transylvania was the chief inducement for Romania to enter the First World War on the Entente side and the Treaty of ➤Trianon duly assigned the region to Romania: 2 million Magyars, and a sizeable German minority, remained hostile to the Romanian rule imposed on them. Since many Magyars lived in a compact territorial block in south-eastern Transylvania, far from the Hungarian frontier, it is difficult to see how any redrawing of the map could have satisfied their wishes and the wishes of the other nationalities around them. Relations between Hungary and Romania remained bad from 1920 to 1940 because of the Transylvanian question. In August 1940 Germany and Italy imposed arbitrary revision, the second ➤Vienna Award, restoring two-fifths of Transylvania to Hungary. Even so, over half a million Magyars remained within Romania. The ➤Paris Peace Treaties in 1947 re-established the inter-war frontiers. In 1952 the Romanian Constitution established a Magyar Autonomous Area in Transylvania, and a Hungarian university was permitted in Cluj. Many of these concessions had lapsed by 1960, Magyar autonomy was not mentioned in the revised constitution of 1965, and the autonomous Magyar districts disappeared in a new county administrative structure imposed on Transylvania and the rest of Romania in 1967.

The Romanian constitution continued to guarantee the Magyar minority 'free use of their mother tongue'. An ethnic Hungarian from Transylvania, Janos Fazekas, became a Deputy Prime Minister of Romania in 1965. In general, however, under ➤Ceauşescu the Magyar minority was forcibly assimilated to Romanian rule, a policy which in 1987–8 led, once again, to strained relations between the governments of Hungary and Romania.

Trenchard, Hugh Montague (1873–1956, created Baron in 1930 and Viscount in 1936). Marshal of the Royal Air Force. Born in Taunton, he was commissioned in the Royal Scots Fusiliers, saw service in India and was seriously wounded in the Boer War. As a thirty-nine-year-old major he went on a flying course, gaining his wings after thirteen days of training in 1912. A year later he became assistant commandant of the Central Flying School. From 1915 to 1917 he was general officer commanding the Royal Flying Corps in the field. His experiences on the Western Front convinced him of the need for treating military aviation as an independent branch of the armed services. His arguments prevailed and, with some justice, he was later known as the 'Father of the RAF', which came into being on 1 April 1918. Trenchard served as Chief of the Air Staff from 1919 to 1929. Two years after his retirement he became Commissioner of the Metropolitan Police in London (1931–5), drastically reforming the force and establishing a Police College, at Hendon.

Trianon, Treaty of (4 June 1920). Peace treaty with Hungary after the First World War. The Hungarians lost more than two-thirds of their pre-war territory: the area ceded to Romania – ➤Transylvania and half the Banat – was in itself larger than the area left to Hungary. Slovakia and Ruthenia were included in Czechoslovakia, and Croatia and the Vojvodina in Yugoslavia. Italy eventually gained ➤Fiume, Poland gained a small area in northern Slovakia, Austria acquired a section of western Hungary, later called the ➤Burgenland. The Treaty made Hungary liable for reparations and limited the Hungarian Army to 35,000 men. The Trianon settlement caused sustained resentment in inter-war Hungary, whose foreign policy was shaped by a desire for treaty revision. The Kingdom of Hungary in 1914 had a population of 21 million: Trianon Hungary had under 8 million. Defenders of the Trianon settlement maintained that the old Kingdom had been multinational and claimed that the new frontiers accorded more closely with the principles of national self-determination, a claim denied in Budapest. Hungary recovered some of the lost lands, 1938–41 (➤Felvidék and ➤Vienna Awards) but in 1947 the ➤Paris Peace Treaties restored the Trianon frontiers, apart from a small adjustment in Czechoslovakia's favour on the Danube, facing Bratislava.

Trieste. The railway system of the Habsburg Monarchy enabled Trieste to develop from a fishing village in 1840 to become the principal port and third most populous city in Austria–Hungary by 1910. Most of the banking and commercial facilities were in Italian hands, while Slovenes predominated in the surrounding countryside.

Trieste became Italian after the First World War, despite protests from Yugoslavia. At the end of the Second World War the city was seized by Tito's Yugoslav partisans but disputed by the 2nd New Zealand Division, under General Freyberg, VC, which had advanced up the Italian peninsula. The New Zealanders, supported by British and American units, faced the Yugoslavs for three months before the future of Trieste was referred to international settlement. The ►Paris Peace Treaties of 1947 established Trieste as a Free Port with a British and American military presence in Zone A (the city and main harbour) and Yugoslav troops to the south, Zone B. Tension remained high, and there were occasional riots, until signature of an agreement between Britain, USA, Italy and Yugoslavia on 5 October 1954 which, with a minor border adjustment, handed over Zone A to Italy, leaving Zone B within Yugoslavia, and guaranteeing the Yugoslavs rights within the Free Port. Uncertainty over Trieste's future led to its decline as an Adriatic port in the 1950s, challenged both by Venice within Italy and by Rijeka (►Fiume) in Yugoslavia. An Italo-Yugoslav friendship treaty was concluded in 1975 to settle residual claims in the Trieste region.

Tripartite Pact (27 September 1940). The basic document of collaboration between Germany, Italy and Japan, signed at Berlin. The signatories undertook to assist each other if attacked by a Power not already in the war, and the Pact was therefore seen as an anti-American gesture. It was, however, used as a basic form of union between the 'New Order' in Europe and 'Greater East Asia', and appears to have been given an anti-Soviet twist by the German Foreign Ministry, which required and obtained the adhesion to the Pact of Hungary, Romania and Slovakia (November 1940), Bulgaria and Yugoslavia (March 1941). The Yugoslavs subsequently overthrew the government which had signed the Pact. After Yugoslavia was overrun the puppet state of Croatia adhered to the Pact (15 June 1941).

Trotsky, Lev Davidovich (1879–1940, original surname Bronstein). Born of Jewish parentage at Ianovka in the Ukraine, arrested as a revolutionary at the age of nineteen and, after three months' solitary confinement, sent to Siberia whence he escaped to join Lenin in London (October 1902). He showed much independence of thought, notably in 1904, but was back in Petersburg early in 1905 and organizing the first Soviet. He was again arrested and sent to Siberia, escaped and spent several years as an itinerant revolutionary organizer in central Europe and beyond. In May 1917 he returned to Petrograd from America and was chairman of the Petrograd Soviet during the October Revolution. At first he took charge of foreign affairs, travelling to ►Brest-Litovsk where his brilliant debating skills long delayed signature of the harsh treaty. On the outbreak of the Civil War he became Commissar for War and created the Red Army. His preoccupation with military and external affairs during Lenin's illness enabled ►Stalin to gain control of the party administration and gradually undermine Trotsky's authority. Trotsky's fundamental belief in 'Permanent Revolution' conflicted with Stalin's more opportunist backing for 'Socialism in One Country'. By 1925 Trotsky had lost all share in the direction of policy. He was expelled from the party in 1927, and deported in January 1929. He settled briefly in Turkey, later in France where he wrote an epic *History of the Revolution*, and finally in Mexico where he was murdered by a Spanish-born Stalinist agent on 20 August 1940.

Trotskyists. Originally supporters of Lev ►Trotsky and, as such, regarded as perverters of the Revolution by conventional communists, whether supporters of Stalin and his successors, Tito or Mao. In the late 1960s and early 1970s the term began to be applied loosely to any radical-left movement uncompromisingly committed to revolutionary, rather than evolutionary, beliefs. Some of these factions were more syndicalist and more anarchistic than their eponym himself.

Trucial States. The name by which the seven emirates of the lower Persian Gulf were known from the early 1820s until 1972, when they were established as the ►United Arab Emirates. The term 'Trucial States' sprang from the practice of the British Resident Agent at Sharja, who from 1823 onwards, sought and gained an annual 'Truce', an assurance from the local rulers that they would abstain from piracy.

Trudeau, Pierre Elliott (1919–), Canadian Prime Minister. Born in Montreal, the son of a millionaire, educated at a Jesuit college, University of Montreal, Harvard and London School of Economics, practising briefly as a barrister in Quebec. From 1950 to 1960 he was associated with moderately left-wing movements for reform in the province, opposed to old-fashioned clerical policies. In 1965 he entered the federal parliament as a Liberal member for one of the Montreal constituencies, serving as Minister of Justice and Attorney-General in the government of Lester ►Pearson in 1967, and becoming well known for his up-to-date style of life and his firm opposition to separatist tendencies in Quebec, whether provincial or federal in character. He succeeded Lester Pearson as Prime Minister in April 1968; his Liberal Party increased its majority at a general election ten weeks later. He was left as head of a minority government after the election of October 1972 but regained a decisive majority in 1974. Criticism of his heavy expenditure of federal funds on grandiose projects weakened his hold on the electorate. He was defeated in May 1979 and contemplated retirement. The Liberal Party executive body induced him to stay in politics and fight another general election in February 1980, which the party duly won. The main achievement of his second term of office was to 'bring home the Constitution from Britain' (►Canada), a controversial and divisive political measure which left his future leadership of Canada in question. His critics pointed out that, while attention was concentrated on the constitutional issue, the Canadian economy was falling into greater difficulties. In June 1984 he was succeeded by John Turner as Prime Minister and Party Leader.

Trujillo (y Molina), Rafael Leonidas (1891–1961), President of the Dominican Republic. Born at San Cristóbal; by the end of the 1920s had secured dominance of the underworld politics of the ➤Dominican Republic of which he made himself President in February 1930. Ambitious public works mainly benefited his own family and he ruled by terrorism, corruption and murder. Technically he was President only between 1930 and 1938 and between 1942 and 1952. In reality he was an absolute dictator for thirty-one years, largely responsible for the deaths of 10,000 Haitian immigrants in October 1937 and finally seeking to provoke revolution in Venezuela and other American states. He was assassinated when his car was machine-gunned by unknown assailants on a lonely road outside the capital (which he had renamed Trujillo City) on 30 May 1961.

Truman, Harry S (1884–1972), thirty-third President of the USA. Born at Lamar, Missouri, in a farming community, served as a captain in the US Artillery on the Meuse and in the Argonne 1918, running a haberdashery business on demobilization, before studying law at Kansas City and entering Democrat Party circles, serving as a county judge for eight years. He was a US Senator 1935–44 and head of the committee keeping check on wartime expenditure. In the 1944 election he was Roosevelt's running-mate, becoming Vice-President in January 1945 but having no experience of executive decision-making when, eleven weeks later, he succeeded to the Presidency on Roosevelt's death. Truman had immediately to assume responsibility for the conduct of the war in its final months, attending the ➤Potsdam Conference and authorizing the use of ➤atomic bombs on Japan. After the end of the war his administration began to show greater leniency over ➤civil rights than any recent administrations and Truman himself gained a surprising victory in the 1948 Presidential election, but he suffered from a hostile Congress which prevented passage of his 'Fair Deal' reforms and from 1947 onwards his authority was weakened by the 'anti-red' hysteria encouraged by ➤McCarthyism. In foreign affairs ➤Truman evolved the doctrine associated with his name, following it up by support for the ➤Marshall Plan, by resolute backing for the airlift to ➤Berlin and by carrying the United States into its first peacetime military alliance, ➤NATO. Truman seized the initiative in rallying United Nations support for South Korea in June 1950 and the last two and a half years of his Presidency were overshadowed by the ➤Korean War. His strength of character led him to dismiss General Mac-Arthur (April 1951) for exceeding the authority of a subordinate commander in his public statements on the Korean War; and Truman did not hesitate to seize (unconstitutionally) steel-mills in order to prevent a strike harmful to the whole economy (8 April 1952). In 1953 he retired into private life in Independence, Missouri.

Truman Doctrine (12 March 1947). A message from President ➤Truman to the US Congress pledged American support for 'free peoples who are resisting attempted subjugation by armed minorities or by outside pressures'. This message, prompted by the need to give military and economic aid to Greece (and, it was believed, Turkey), marked a switch to a positive anti-communism on the part of the Administration.

Tshombe, Moise (1919–69), Congolese politician. Born at Mushoshi near Elisabethville (Lubumbashi) in the ►Belgian Congo and educated at an American Methodist mission. The Tshombe family were wealthy and in 1951 he took over a chain of stores and a hotel, becoming president of the native Katangan Chamber of Commerce. Close association with the 'Union Minière' of ►Katanga enabled him to found a political party, the Conakat, which advocated an independent but loosely federal Congo, as opposed to the unitary state favoured by his rivals. When the Congolese Republic came into being in the summer of 1960, Tshombe declared Katanga's secession and for two and a half years sought to keep the province independent. The ►Congo Problem necessitated UN intervention, and United Nations forces finally overthrew his regime in January 1963. Tshombe's use of white mercenaries, and his apparent involvement in the murder of ►Lumumba, made African nationalists regard him as a Judas. American and European businessmen, however, saw him as a resolute opponent of communism; and it was in this guise that Tshombe returned from exile in July 1964 to become Prime Minister of the Congo Republic. Once again he used mercenaries, to stamp out a radical secessionist movement in Stanleyville (Kisangani). Blatantly corrupt elections in 1965 led to his flight, and he found refuge in Spain. President ►Mobutu had him placed on trial for treason in his absence, and he was condemned to death. This sentence was not carried out. In July 1967, however, he was kidnapped in his private aircraft and taken to Algeria, where he languished in prison until, on 29 June 1969, it was announced he had died from a heart attack.

Tsushima, Battle of (27–28 May 1905). An engagement in the Straits of Tsushima separating Korea from Japan, in which Admiral ►Togo intercepted the Russian Baltic Fleet at the end of a seven-month voyage intended to restore Russian sea power in the Far East after Japan's surprise attack on Port Arthur. The battle was an overwhelming victory for Togo and his Japanese fleet, which suffered little damage while virtually destroying the Russians and thereby determining the government in St Petersburg to seek an end to the ►Russo-Japanese War.

Tudjman, Franjo (1922–), Croatian President. Born in Zagorje, he joined the Partisans under ►Tito in 1941 and became a regular officer in the Yugoslav army after the war, serving mainly at the Ministry of Defence in Belgrade and retiring as a Major-General in 1961. For six years he was director of the Historical Institute in Zagreb. His own research convinced Tudjman that Yugoslav historians exaggerated the extent of ►Ustaše atrocities. He also believed that the predominantly Serb literary establishment in ►Yugoslavia discriminated against Croat writers. His views led to his dismissal from the Institute, expulsion from the ruling League of Communists, and ultimately, in 1972 and again in 1981, to imprisonment with hard labour. Such treatment made General Tudjman a martyr-hero to many Croats. As tension mounted within federated Yugoslavia, Tudjman was able in June 1989 to found a home rule party, the Croatian National Union (HDZ), which won free elections to a Croatian assembly in May 1990. A month later the Assembly elected Tudjman President of Croatia, paving the way for formal secession and independence on 30 May 1991. Tudjman used his military skill as commander-in-chief of the army, although it was not until the summer of 1995 that two brilliantly executed campaigns destroyed the Serbian puppet state in the Krajina and recovered much of western Slavonia. Tudjman – who, like Tito, made a practice of wearing smart uniforms – wished to impose an authoritarian constitution on Croatia. But, though in 1992, 1995 and June 1997 Croatian voters supported HDZ and Tudjman personally, they did not give him sufficient backing to make himself a virtual dictator. Moreover, by 1997 he was known to be gravely ill with stomach cancer.

Tunisia. Independent republic in North Africa. Although technically under the suzerainty of Turkey, the local ruler (Bey) of Tunis retained considerable monarchical powers throughout the eighteenth and nineteenth centuries. French economic penetration was followed in May 1881 by the establishment of a French protectorate. Apart from a period of German administration during the North African campaign of 1942–3, Tunisia remained a protectorate until March 1956. Nationalist agitation developed in the early 1930s, finding a natural leader in Habib ibn Ali ►Bourguiba, who shaped and dominated Tunisian affairs after 1954–5. The monarchical powers of the Bey were abolished on 25 July 1957 and Bourguiba was elected President on the same day, being re-elected at five-yearly intervals and proclaimed President for life in March 1975. There were occasional clashes with French military and naval units, holding bases in Tunisia during the Algerian War, and it is estimated that 1,000 Tunisians were killed between 1958 and 1961. The last French stronghold in Tunisia, the port of Bizerta, was handed over on 30 June 1962: French trading links with Tunisia, inevitably close, fluctuated with nationalization measures undertaken by the Tunisian Government in the mid 1960s. Tunisia concluded special treaties with the European Economic Community in 1969 and 1976. In 1970 the astute financier Hedi Nouira became Prime Minister. His austere policies led to much resentment and political repression. There were major strikes and some rioting by trade unionists in January 1978, with over a hundred deaths. On 26 January 1980, the second anniversary of the riots, armed detachments fitted out with modern weapons in Libya attacked and seized the southern town of Gafsa, threatening Tunisia with civil war. After a twenty-hour battle the Tunisian Army recovered Gafsa. The strain of these events gave Hedi Nouira a heart attack and he died in February 1980. His successor as Prime Minister, Mohammed Mzali (1924–), was a respected international amateur footballer; and he brought a more liberal approach to Tunisia's press laws and greater freedom of expression to the social democrats. Unemployment, however, remained high and poverty widespread. The first multi-party election in independent Tunisia was held on 1 November 1981. It was won by Mzali's ruling 'National Front' coalition. The threat of Islamic fundamentalism in 1983–4 brought the army once more into politics with General Zine el-Abidine Ben Ali (1926–) succeeding Mzali and in November 1987 deposing the senile Bourguiba as President. Although Ben Ali confirmed the right of Opposition parties to contest elections, in practice his Democratic Constitutional Rally (RCD) won all the seats in two elections; the President was re-elected in 1989 and 1994.

Turkish Republic. The defeat of Turkey in the First World War and the humiliating Treaty of ►Sèvres finally discredited the ►Ottoman Empire, dubbed 'the sick man of Europe' more than seventy years before. Mustapha Kemal – ►Atatürk – was chosen as President of a provisional government in Ankara on 23 April 1920, and given executive authority as head of the administration of a 'national' Turkey in January 1921: he accordingly decreed the abolition of the Sultanate in November 1922 and proclaimed a Turkish Republic on 29 October 1923. The religious headship exercised by the Sultan as Caliph was abolished in March 1924 and a constitution establishing the republic as a lay state published a month later. Kemal Atatürk ruled the republic as a reforming – but at times despotic – President until his death in 1938. He was succeeded by his right-hand man, ►Inönü, who tolerated the growth of a political opposition party. Free elections were held in May 1950 and they were won by the opposition leader, ►Menderes, who dominated Turkish political life for ten years before being overthrown by a committee of army officers. Although a new constitution was introduced in 1961, and elections held in 1969, 1973 and 1977, governments have failed to inspire respect in the outlying provinces of the republic or abroad. Occasionally – notably in ►Cyprus – a vigorous foreign policy has distracted attention from economic grievances and political frustration at home. Feuds between left-wing and right-wing students, religious conflicts in which the minority Shiites sought to assert an Islamic puritanism alien to the republic's tradition, and fighting between Turks, Kurds and Armenians all contributed to a breakdown of authority within Turkey in 1978–80. On 12 September 1980 the Turkish army – which had intervened at crises in public order in May 1960 and March 1971 – seized power, established a six-man National Security Council under General Kenan Evren and imposed martial law on the country. A puppet civilian administration was installed by General Evren eight days later. A new constitution in November 1982 gave increased power to Evren, who was elected President for a seven-year term. Twelve months later the Motherland Party of Turgut Ozal (1927–93) won a general election victory and President Evren formally dissolved the National Security Council in December 1983. During the following five years Turkey made great economic progress, despite continued resistance from the Kurds and the consequent imposition in 1987 of emergency government in eight of Turkey's seventy-one provinces (►Kurdish Question). At the same time, there was a rapid revival of Islamic observance, marked in 1983 by the foundation of a specifically strict Islamic political party, Refah (Welfare), decentralized and ably led by Necmettin Erbakan (1926–). In November 1989 Ozal became Turkey's first civilian President for thirty years but was faced by parliamentary difficulties in October 1991 when the True Path Party defeated Motherland in the general election and his political rival, Suleyman Demirel (1924–), formed a coalition. On Ozal's sudden death, Demirel was elected President (for a seven-year term) on 16 May 1993, and his deputy, the distinguished economist Tansu Çiller (1946–), became Turkey's first woman Prime Minister. This development accelerated the growth of Refah in the Anatolian heartland. Refah gained most seats in the elections of December 1995 but was kept out of government by a secularist coalition until June 1996 when its leader, Erbakan, became Prime Minister. His advocacy of Islamic reforms was curbed by a political pact in which he was to alternate the premiership with Çiller and by the General Staff who, distrusting both party leaders, gave clear warnings in April and June 1997 of an imminent military *coup*. This threat induced Erbakan to resign. A new coalition was formed on 20 June 1997, with the Motherland Party's leader, Mesut Yilmaz, as Prime Minister. The Yilmaz coalition was weakened by the European Union's rejection of Turkey's application for membership in December 1997, by foreign pressure on Turkey over ➤Cyprus, and by the insistence of the army leaders that the political activities of the Islamists be curbed. In January 1998 Turkey's constitutional court outlawed Refah, maintaining that it threatened 'to bring the country to the brink of civil war'. Erbakan and six colleagues were barred from political activity until 2004. A new 'Islamic Virtue Party' won support from ex-Refah followers. An early election was anticipated.

Tutu, Desmond Mpilo (1931–), South African religious and political leader. Born at Klerksdorp in the Transvaal and educated at a Bantu high school, he was a teacher before being ordained an Anglican priest in 1962. When in 1975 he became the first non-white Dean of Johannesburg, he insisted on living in ➤Soweto, sharing the deprivations imposed by apartheid. As Bishop of Lesotho and General Secretary of the South African Council of Churches from 1978 he led a civil disobedience campaign against apartheid. His support of non-violent passive resistance won Tutu the Nobel Peace Prize for 1984. His prestige and authority as Bishop of Johannesburg, 1984–6, and as Archbishop of Cape Town and Primate, 1986–96, enabled him to promote the movement towards multiracial democracy in ➤South Africa in partnership with ➤Mandela while seeking to check the communal violence. After retiring as Primate, Tutu became chairman of South Africa's 'Truth and Reconciliation Commission'.

Twentieth Party Congress (February 1956). A meeting of the Communist Party of the Soviet Union, attended by representatives of other national parties, and made famous by a speech of ➤Khrushchev, 'leaked' by US intelligence sources in June 1956. The speech denounced Stalin and his methods, maintained that the 'cult of personality' was fundamentally anti-socialist in character, accepted the principle of 'different roads to socialism' and emphasized the need for 'peaceful coexistence'. These drastic ideological revisions had important consequences in eastern Europe, encouraging the re-emergence of ➤Gomulka in Poland, reforms in Bulgaria, the removal of some unpopular ministers in Czechoslovakia and, above all, the revulsion in Hungary towards ►Rákosi ending in the ►Hungarian National Rising of October 1956.

Twenty-One Demands (18 January 1915). An attempt by the Japanese Government of Count Okuma to impose a virtual protectorate on China. Japanese forces had seized the German territory of ►Kiaochow, on the mainland of China, on 7 November 1914, thereby winning favour with the British, French and Russians. The Japanese listed twenty-one 'outstanding questions' over which they demanded satisfaction from the Chinese, threatening war if the demands were not met. The Chinese duly made concessions increasing Japan's hold on Manchuria and Shantung, gave assurances that no further coastal regions would be leased to a foreign power, and conceded a half-interest to Japan in the most valuable Chinese iron and steel company. The British persuaded the Japanese not to enforce further demands which would have led to the appointment of Japanese political, military and financial advisers by the Chinese authorities. The demands aroused lasting resentment among all Chinese, irrespective of their political affiliation, and provoked suspicion of Japanese imperialism in Washington.

U

U-2 Incident. On 1 May 1960 a high-altitude American photographic reconnaissance aircraft, a Lockheed U-2, was shot down over Sverdlovsk, and the pilot, Francis Gary Powers, taken prisoner. Although these flights had been made for three years the episode was exploited by Khrushchev, who demanded an apology from President Eisenhower at the ►summit conference in Paris a fortnight later. The President's refusal to give an apology led Khrushchev to break off the summit meeting. U-2 flights ceased. In the United States the incident was seen as reflecting adversely both on the American intelligence services and on the conduct of American diplomacy, points emphasized later in the year by Kennedy and the Democrats in the Presidential election campaign. Powers was returned to the United States in February 1962 in exchange for a high-ranking Soviet spy in American custody.

UDI ►Unilateral Declaration of Independence.

Uganda. Treaties concluded with the local ruler allowed the British East Africa Company to open up the area of Uganda, 1890–94. The British protectorate, established in September 1894, divided Uganda into five regions, four of which were under direct British administration with the help of native chiefs, and the fifth – ►Buganda – ruled by its traditional prince, the Kabaka, under the British crown. A ministerial system was established in 1955, and Uganda became an independent member of the Commonwealth on 9 October 1962, Buganda continuing to enjoy much self-government. When in September 1963 Uganda was declared a republic within the Commonwealth, the ruling Kabaka of Buganda became the country's first President. Dr Milton Obote (1924–), the Prime Minister, wished to establish a one-party state, to which the Kabaka objected. In 1966 Obote carried through a *coup d'état*, depriving Buganda of its privileges and forcing the Kabaka into exile. Dr Obote was himself overthrown on 25 January 1971 when the army commander, Major-General Idi ►Amin, seized power while Obote was at the Singapore meeting of Commonwealth Prime Ministers. Amin's years of office were marked by a rule of terror, culminating in an invasion of the country by dissident Ugandans and Tanzanians in March and April 1979. Amin departed to Libya and a provisional government was established in Kampala on 14 April 1979. In June a much respected lawyer, Godfrey Binaisa, became President and sought to re-impose the rule of law in Kampala as a prelude to the reconstruction necessary to combat famine and economic disaster. A general election in December 1980 was viewed with some suspicion by foreign observers; the results favoured the

Uganda People's Congress (UPC), led by Milton Obote, who was sworn in as President once more on 15 December 1980. His return re-opened old tribal conflicts and aroused strong resentment among the Bugandans. Lawlessness, aggravated by food shortage and corruption, continued to flourish. Obote was overthrown in a military *coup* in July 1985 and fled to Zambia. From six months of virtual anarchy Yoweri Museveni (1945–), the pragmatic socialist leader of the National Resistance Movement, emerged victorious and was sworn in as President on 29 January 1986, subsequently gaining British help in restoring the country's shattered economy. Even so, Uganda continued to be plagued by armed rebellion along the eastern and northern borders for several months. Throughout 1987 a rebel priestess, Alice Lakwena (1959–), led her ill-equipped 'Holy Spirit Battalion' in a fanatical campaign against Museveni in eastern Uganda, eventually crossing into Kenya where she was imprisoned. The Uganda People's Democratic Movement maintained a bitterly cruel civil war until July 1990, when an uneasy truce of exhaustion was accepted. Although political party activity remains banned until 2000, elections were held in 1996; they confirmed President Museveni in office and gave his supporters a majority in the newly created National Assembly.

Ukraine. The second largest country in Europe; capital, Kiev. From about 882 to 1240 the heart of the Ukraine, around 'holy' Kiev and the middle Dnieper river, formed the earliest Russian state. It was invaded successively by Mongols, Tatars, Magyars, Lithuanians and Poles but enjoyed a token independence from 1648 until 1781, when it was formally incorporated in the Russian Empire. A brief spell of independence in 1918 after the ►Russian Revolution was followed by a Polish invasion under ►Pilsudski, until the Ukraine became a constituent republic of the ►Soviet Union in December 1922. Enforced collectivization of naturally rich farmland brought famine to parts of the Ukraine under ►Stalin, though the great dam created at Dnepropetrovsk under the ►Five-Year Plans enabled hydroelectric power to stimulate industry. More extensive industrialization formed part of a recovery programme after devastation in the Second World War. The political authority in Moscow of the Ukrainian-born ►Khrushchev led in 1954 to the transference of the Crimea from the Russian Soviet Republic to the Ukraine. Grievances against Russian domination returned during the Brezhnev era and were intensified in 1986 by Soviet mishandling of the nuclear disaster at ►Chernobyl, eighty miles north of Kiev. But when on 24 August 1991 Ukraine asserted its independence of the Soviet Union, the political lead was taken by Leonid Kravchuk (1934–), the former Communist Party boss, who accepted a reformist government headed in 1992–3 by Leonid Kuchma (1938–) who in June 1994 defeated Kravchuk in a presidential election. A dispute with ►Russia over division of the former Black Sea Fleet was resolved in 1996 but it proved harder to satisfy deputies in the Crimean assembly who rejected autonomy in pursuit of independence. Briefly in 1995 President Kuchma imposed his personal direct rule on the Crimea, though advances were at last made towards autonomy in 1996–7. Constitutional revision in June 1996 gave greater authoritarian power to the President, though elections for a People's Council were promised for March 1998. Although Ukraine was a founder member of the ➤Commonwealth of Independent States, Kuchma stopped short of commitments to full economic cooperation or collective security. The Ukrainians preferred to look towards Europe. With American backing, Ukraine became on 9 July 1997 the first ex-Soviet republic to sign a 'special relationship' treaty with ➤NATO.

Ulbricht, Walther (1893–1973), head of state, German Democratic Republic. Born in Leipzig, a social democrat and trade unionist during the First World War but an active communist from 1919 onwards, sitting as a Reichstag member, 1928–33, before emigrating to the Soviet Union. Returning to Germany in April 1945, Ulbricht became the first organizer of the new communist movement in Berlin and was effective head of the Socialist Unity Party from 1946 until May 1971. From September 1960 until his death Ulbricht was also Chairman of the Council of State in the German Democratic Republic, president in all but name. He was a convinced Stalinist, less accommodating to shifts in Soviet policy under Stalin's successors than any other East European leader. (➤German Democratic Republic.)

Ulster. Traditionally a province comprising the nine most northerly counties in Ireland. Since 1920 six of the nine counties – Antrim, Armagh, Down, Fermanagh, Londonderry and Tyrone – have formed ➤Northern Ireland. The remaining three counties (Cavan, Donegal and Monaghan) continue to form the province of Ulster within the Republic of Ireland. Protestant defence organizations in Northern Ireland have used the word 'Ulster' since 1913, when the first Ulster Volunteer Force was set up. The UVF was revived in 1966, rapidly becoming a para-military body which considered itself at war with the IRA, although limiting its campaigns of terrorism to Ireland. The Orange Order, a hardline Protestant society dating from 1795, organizes triumphant processional marches each July through Catholic areas, to commemorate the victory of King William III (of Orange) over his Catholic uncle, King James II, at the battle of the Boyne in 1690. In 1996 and 1997 these marches led to a furious Catholic nationalist reaction and to rioting and arson across much of the province. In July 1998 a sustained attempt by hardline Orange marchers at Drumcree to discredit attempts at reconciliation was defeated by heavily armed troops, the Royal Ulster Constabulary, and the good sense of Ulster moderates.

Ulster Peace Movement. On 10 August 1976 a stolen vehicle driven by IRA gunmen and pursued by British soldiers crashed into a family of pedestrians in south-west Belfast, killing a girl of eight, a boy of two and a half and a six-weeks-old baby. This tragedy, following on the deaths of many others in ➤Northern Ireland, led to demonstrations in favour of peace and reconciliation, with Roman Catholic and Protestant women joining in prayers and hymn-singing in both Catholic and Protestant areas of Belfast (14 and 28 August). The movement held similar gatherings in Londonderry and other centres of the old province of ►Ulster, as well as in Dublin, Glasgow and English cities. Representatives of the Peace People travelled to the United States, New Zealand, West Germany and other lands speaking in favour of an end to violence within Northern Ireland. Two of the leaders of the Ulster Peace movement, Maire Corrigan and Betty Williams, were subsequently awarded the Nobel Peace Prize for 1976 in recognition of their endeavours.

Unconditional Surrender. A statement issued by Roosevelt, after consultation with Churchill at the ►Casablanca Conference (24 January 1943), insisting on the unconditional surrender of the Axis Powers rather than a peace on negotiated terms. The formula was intended to convince Stalin of his partners' good faith and resolve to continue the war. Nazi propaganda exploited the phrase in order to warn the German people of the greed of their enemies.

Unilateral Declaration of Independence (UDI). On 11 November 1965 the 'Rhodesian Front' Government of Ian ►Smith declared Rhodesia an independent state, an act rejected by the British Government and condemned by members of the United Nations, who saw in this gesture of rebellion a refusal of the white minority to contemplate any constitutional arrangement providing for majority rule by giving the Africans a wider franchise. (►Rhodesia.)

United Arab Emirates. The British Government negotiated treaties with the sultans and sheiks of seven Emirates on the southern shore of the Persian Gulf and the Gulf of Oman between 1820 and 1892, a legacy of even older contacts made by the East India Company. From 1892 until 1971 Britain was responsible for the defence and external policy of these Emirates, the ►'Trucial States': Abu Dhabi, Ajman, Dubai, Fujairah, Ras al-Khaimah, Sharjah and Umm al-Qaiwain. Independence was conceded in 1971. Discussions aimed at establishing a federation of the Trucial States and Bahrain were held in 1968 and July 1971, but came to nothing. The seven Emirates therefore established an independent federation, the UAE, between December 1971 and February 1972. The principal revenue comes from the oil of Abu Dhabi, and the Sultan of Abu Dhabi became first President of the UAE.

United Arab Republic. A political union between Egypt and ►Syria proclaimed on 1 February 1958, with ►Nasser elected as head of state by plebiscite three weeks later. Syria seceded on 29 September 1961 but Egypt retained the title and flag of the UAR until 2 September 1971.

United Nations. Originally the term 'United Nations' was used to describe the allies fighting against the Axis Powers in the Second World War and is employed in a joint pledge not to make a separate peace with the enemy, issued on 1 January 1942. The nature of the international organization which should succeed the discredited ►League of Nations was discussed at a conference of Foreign Ministers in Moscow, October 1943, and worked out in detail at ►Dumbarton Oaks, ►Yalta and ➤San Francisco. The main differences from the League were the stronger executive powers assumed by the ➤Security Council, the extent of specialized agencies (ultimately fifteen) and the requirement that member states should make available armed forces to serve as peace-keepers or to repel an aggressor. The Secretary-Generals have achieved greater influence as arbitrators than their predecessors in the League: Trygve ➤Lie, Dag ➤Hammarskjöld, U ➤Thant, Kurt ➤Waldheim were followed by: Javier Perez de Cuellar (1920–), 1981–91, a Peruvian who helped check the spread of the ➤Falklands Crisis and gained success in ➤Namibia; Boutros Boutros-Ghali (1922–), 1992–6, an Egyptian, much criticized by the US State Department over Bosnia; and in January 1997 Kofi Annan (1938 –), the son of a paramount chief in Ghana, and from 1993 UN Under-Secretary for peacekeeping operations. Unlike the League of Nations (maximum membership of sixty) the UN has every world power among its 185 members. The successes of the UN include the well-being promoted by the specialized agencies, mediation in Palestine (1947), Kashmir (1948), Indonesia (1962), Cyprus (1964), ceasefires in the Middle East (1956, 1967 and 1973) and sponsorship of a convention against bacteriological warfare (1972). Patient diplomacy to end the ➤Gulf War was followed, on 20 July 1987, by Security Council Resolution 598 calling for an immediate ceasefire; but even this firm Resolution could only be enforced after a further eleven months of negotiation. Intervention in the ➤Korean War and in the Congo from 1960 to 1964 was, on both occasions, on a large scale. The UN failed to halt Soviet military intervention in Hungary and Czechoslovakia, has been unable to secure a lasting peace in the ➤Lebanon and has consistently run into difficulties when seeking to impose its Resolutions on the Republic of South Africa or on Rhodesia (➤Zimbabwe). Between 1978 and 1988 three UN delegations travelled to southern Africa on fact-finding visits on ➤Namibia. Not until December 1988 did South Africa agree to implement the UN Resolution of 1976 favouring Namibian independence. The General Assembly has tended to become an arena for forensic propaganda rather than for constructive parliamentary argument, but it has shown itself to be a useful safety-valve. Soviet–American agreement over the Iraq problem in 1990 enabled the UN to sanction military support for resolutions condemning the occupation of Kuwait. (➤Gulf War, Second.) Although member states have not lived up to the ideals of the Charter or to the declaration of Human Rights, the United Nations has survived longer than any previous institution designed to 'save succeeding generations from the scourge of war.'

United Nations Educational, Scientific and Cultural Organization (UNESCO). A specialized agency of the United Nations, with its headquarters in Paris, UNESCO was established in November 1946 to promote education, understanding and cultural contacts between UN members. The Reagan administration withdrew US membership in December 1984 claiming that UNESCO was extravagant and unduly 'politicized'; Mrs Thatcher's Government followed suit a year later. Britain rejoined UNESCO on 1 July 1997.

United Nations Relief and Rehabilitation Administration (UNRRA). This body differed from any of the other specialized agencies of United Nations in having been established during the Second World War (on 9 November 1943) at a time when the term 'United Nations' was in use as a description of the anti-Axis allies. UNRRA was intended to provide help in reconstruction and in rehabilitating refugees once the war was over. Between 1943 and 1949 it spent some £600 million on relief work, three-quarters of the funds coming from the United States. UNRRA relieved starvation in Italy, Greece, Poland, Yugoslavia and Albania, 1945–7, and assisted the European states to reconstruct their industrial and agricultural economy before the coming into force of the ►Marshall Plan. The diversified character of UNRRA activities resulted in their being shared later among specialized agencies, such as the Food and Agriculture Organization, Unicef (the United Nations International Children's Emergency Fund), and the ►World Health Organization, international refugee organizations and smaller voluntary and charitable bodies, such as Oxfam (Oxford Committee for Famine Relief, founded in 1942). UNRRA formally ceased its activities on 31 March 1949.

Uruguay. For long, the smallest and most politically stable of the South American republics. Uruguay was under Portuguese rule in the seventeenth century and then under Spanish rule for a century, eventually becoming a sovereign state in 1828. After a succession of local disturbances, mounting at times to full civil war, the Uruguayan Liberals (Colorados, or 'redshirts') triumphed in 1872 and remained in office until 1958, when the elections were won by Clerical Conservatives (Blancos, or 'whites'), last in power 1863. The Colorados gained a narrow victory in the elections of November 1971, and returned to office, though forced to share power in a coalition. A revolutionary urban guerrilla movement, the Tupamaros, was founded among sugar-workers in northern Uruguay in 1963, spreading to Montevideo in 1967–8 and showing Marxist, and at times more specifically anarchistic, sympathies. By 1973 the general instability led to thirteen years of presidential rule with military support; but it was possible to hold a 'supervised' general election in 1984 and free multi-party elections once more in 1989 and 1994. Each confirmed in power centre-right coalition governments.

Ustaše. A name traditionally used by patriotic rebel bands in ►Croatia, and revived in 1929–30 by the fanatical Croatian nationalist, Ante Pavelić (1889–1959) for his secret terrorist organization, which operated at various times in the 1930s from Hungary, Austria and Italy against the Yugoslav Kingdom. Sometimes the Ustaše collaborated with ►IMRO, notably in the murder of King ►Alexander at Marseilles in 1934. The Ustaše set up an 'Independent Croatian State' in 1941, collaborating closely with the Germans and Italians and becoming notorious for atrocities committed against people of other nationalities in Yugoslavia, some of whom were communists but many of whom were Serbian Orthodox religious believers. Pavelić fled to Spain in 1945 and subsequently to Argentina, where he died. Grim retribution was enforced on Ustaše sympathizers in Yugoslavia, but the movement survived as a Croatian separatist and anti-communist terrorist organization and was responsible for assassinations, bombings and attempted murders in Sweden, West Germany and Australia in the late 1960s and early 1970s. Ustaše insignia reappeared in Croatia in 1990 as a new generation of nationalists invoked their predecessors' dark record so as to intimidate Serbs and the Muslims of ➤Bosnia-Herzegovina.

V

Vatican City-State. An area of about one-sixth of a square mile, under the direct sovereignty of the Pope, and established in Rome by the ►Lateran Treaties of 11 February 1929. The City-State contains the Vatican palaces and parks, the palace of the Lateran and the papal villa at Castel Gandolfo.

Vatican Council (1962–3). The first ecumenical council in 300 years was summoned by Pope Pius IX to the Vatican in 1869, at a time when the papacy was losing its traditional temporal power in Italy and was challenged over faith and morals by new teachings and doctrines. In January 1959 Pope ►John XXIII summoned a second Vatican Council to discuss renewal of the faith and ways of promoting church unity. The Council opened in Rome on 11 October 1962 and was attended by more than 8,000 bishops, including observers from other Christian communions, notably the Orthodox and Anglican churches. The Council's deliberations, lasting a year, were published in sixteen decrees which represented a more tolerant approach to the traditions and structures of other churches, and also encouraged the use of the vernacular, rather than Latin, in the Catholic liturgy.

Venezuela. Federal republic in north-western South America, Spanish until 1821 and then united to Colombia until 1830. A frontier dispute with the UK government over the borders with British Guiana in 1895–6 led to strong American intervention on behalf of the Venezuelans, and the Americans had to give further diplomatic support when a joint British–German–Italian naval blockade was imposed in 1902 to secure the payment of debts due to foreign bondholders. From 1909 to 1935 Venezuela was under the harsh dictatorship of General Juan Gómez: much wealth came into the republic after he authorized the development of oilfields in 1922–3, but little of it reached the people. By 1950 Venezuela was the chief exporter of petroleum in the world. The first free Presidential elections were held in 1947 but the victory of a moderate left-wing anti-communist party was followed by the intervention of army officers and the dictatorship of General Jiménez. Venezuela had to wait until 1959–63 for a democratically elected President (Rómulo Betancourt), who was allowed to complete his term without a military *coup*. Although the influence of the army has remained considerable, there have been a succession of democratically elected governments since Betancourt's Presidency. Christian Democrats were in power from 1968 until the elections of December 1973, which returned the moderate socialist, but strongly anti-Castro, 'Democratic Action Party', led by Carlos Pérez. Urban guerrilla activity, strong in the mid sixties, died down with the legalization of a Communist Party in 1969. An electoral swing to the Christian Democrats in 1978 was followed by a return to Democratic Action in December 1983. Despite two abortive military *coups* in 1992 and a corruption scandal a year later which forced Pérez to retire, the electoral appeal of Democratic Action remained considerable. But a centre-right National Convergence coalition took office in February 1994 and introduced austerity measures ahead of the privatization of state concerns. Good oil prices maintained a high level of prosperity in Venezuela as a whole. Occasional demands for some two-thirds of the territory of neighbouring ►Guyana seemed no more than a fashionable echo of nineteenth-century anti-colonialism.

Venizelos, Eleutherios (1864–1936). Greek statesman. Born in Canea, western Crete, participated in the anti-Turkish movement, 1895–1905, and, as President of the Cretan Assembly, announced the union of the island with Greece (March 1905), a *fait accompli* not officially recognized until 1913. Venizelos settled in Athens in 1909 and became Prime Minister in October 1910: his government reformed the financial and military administration, revised the constitution, and led Greece into the ►Balkan Wars, thus acquiring Macedonia. Twice in 1915 Venizelos tried to bring Greece into the First World War on the side of the Entente but was forced out of office by ►Constantine I. In September 1916 Venizelos set up a rebel government in Crete (later moving to Salonika) and declared war on Germany and Bulgaria. Nine months later he engineered Constantine's abdication and returned to Athens as Prime Minister. Although prominent at the ►Paris Peace Conference, his hopes of securing Anatolia led to war with Turkey and to his own electoral defeat in November 1920. He was in office briefly in January 1924, from May 1928 until October 1932 and for seven weeks early in 1933, but he could not bring stability to the Greek Republic (although he was able to improve Greece's relations with her Balkan neighbours during 1930). His followers, hoping to purge the administration of royalists, attempted a rising in March 1935 and there was a brief civil war before Venizelos fled to France, dying in Paris twelve months later. A son, Sophocles Venizelos (1894–1964), was leader of the right-wing liberals after the liberation of Greece and headed three short-lived governments.

Verdun, Battle of (21 February to 16 December 1916). The most sustained battle of the First World War, in which the French suffered more than 400,000 casualties and the Germans nearly 350,000. The battle arose from a plan of General von Falkenhayn (1861–1922), chief of the German General Staff, who claimed that it would be possible 'to bleed France white' by launching a massive attack on a narrow sector where national sentiment would force the French to 'throw in every man they had'. He chose Verdun, a fortified city on the Meuse, whose fall in 1792 had precipitated panic in Paris. The 300-day battle destroyed French reserves and left the French too weak and shell-shocked for a resolute offensive without help from other allies. But the Germans, too, suffered considerable loss of morale for, although two key forts (Douaumont and Vaux) were captured by the Germans and although in June the French were dependent on a single second-class road for supplies, Verdun itself never fell. French counter-attacks from 23 October onwards recovered the forts and most of the shell-cratered wasteland overrun by the Germans. Verdun was a triumph for French fortitude and the generalship of Charles Mangin (1866–1925), Robert Nivelle (1856–1924) and ►Pétain.

Vereeniging, Treaty of (31 May 1902). Peace settlement ending the ►Boer War. The ►Transvaal and Orange Free State ceased to be Boer republics and accepted British sovereignty, with a promise of eventual self-government (conceded 1907) and a grant of £3 million for restocking and repairing farm lands.

Versailles, Treaty of (28 June 1919). Settlement with Germany, determined at the ►Paris Peace Conference. The main terms were: surrender of all German colonies as ►League of Nations mandates, return of Alsace-Lorraine to France; cession of ►Eupen-Malmédy to Belgium, Memel to ►Lithuania, the Hultschin district to Czechoslovakia, Poznania, parts of East Prussia and Upper Silesia to Poland, and ►Danzig to the League as a free city; plebiscites to be held in northern Schleswig to settle the Danish–German frontier; occupation and special status for the ►Saar under French control; demilitarization and fifteen-year occupation of the ►Rhineland; payment of ►reparations; a ban on the union of Germany and Austria; a clause accepting Germany's guilt in causing the war; provision for the trial of the former Kaiser and other war leaders; limitation of Germany's army to 100,000 men with no conscription, no tanks, no heavy artillery, no poison-gas supplies, no aircraft, no airships and no General Staff; and limitation of the German Navy to vessels under 10,000 tons, with no submarines and no air arm. The Treaty also contained the basic Covenant of the ►League of Nations. Germany signed the Treaty under protest and the US Congress refused to ratify it; but many people in France and Britain complained that the terms were too lenient. There was no trial by the victors of the Kaiser or other war leaders, and General ►Seeckt found ways of circumventing the disarmament clauses. The 'war-guilt' clause was ruthlessly criticized as unjust and inept, particularly by German and American historical specialists. Hitler, in power from 1933 onwards, always refused to be bound by the treaty, the denunciation of which had contributed considerably to Nazi electoral successes.

Verwoerd, Hendrik Frensch (1901–66), South African Prime Minister. Born in Amsterdam, his parents emigrating to South Africa when he was a child; educated at the Universities of Stellenbosch, Hamburg, Leipzig and Berlin, holding a teaching post at Berlin before returning to Stellenbosch as a professor of sociology, 1927–37, resigning his chair in protest at the admission to South Africa of Jewish refugees from Nazi persecution. Verwoerd edited a Nationalist newspaper in Johannesburg until 1948, opposing South African participation in the Second World War. He was elected a Senator in 1948 and appointed Minister of Native Affairs in 1950 with responsibility for enforcing ►apartheid. He became Nationalist Party leader, and thus Prime Minister, on 2 September 1958. An unsuccessful attempt to kill him was made at Johannesburg on 9 April 1960, after the ►Sharpeville shootings. He led South Africa out of the Commonwealth in 1961, when the country became a republic. On 6 September 1966 he was assassinated by a Portuguese East African of Greek origin, whom the South Africans declared mentally deranged.

Vichy France. On the defeat of France in 1940 the National Assembly was convened at the spa town of Vichy, in the unoccupied zone. There, on 10 July 1940, it authorized the Prime Minister, ►Pétain, to assume full powers, pending promulgation of a new constitution. Later in the day Pétain declared himself 'Head of the French State', and for four years France was administered by this interim autocracy, using Vichy as a capital. Vichy France was fundamentally anti-republican. It emphasized the virtues of 'order and authority', substituting 'Work, Family, Fatherland' (*Travail, Famille, Patrie*) for the famous Revolutionary principles, 'Liberty, Equality, Fraternity'. The history of Vichy France falls into four phases: (1) July–December 1940, resigned acceptance of German victory, a period dominated by ►Laval; (2) January 1941 to April 1942, the primacy of ►Darlan and growing collaboration with Hitler; (3) April 1942 to January 1944, the second Laval phase, adroit manoeuvring to avoid deep commitments to Germany, despite German entry into unoccupied France, November 1942; and (4) January–July 1944, dominance of French fascist groups. After the liberation Pétain and his ministers were taken to Germany, to establish an *émigré* Vichy Government at Sigmaringen.

Victor Emmanuel III, King of Italy (1869–1947, reigned 1900–1946). Born in Naples, the son of Umberto I, on whose assassination at Monza (29 July 1900) he came to the throne, Victor Emmanuel – so diminutive that Kaiser William II habitually called him 'the dwarf' – married Princess Elena, daughter of the King of ►Montenegro. Although alarmed by the 'red peril', Victor Emmanuel kept outside politics for the first twenty years of his reign, winning scholarly respect as a numismatist. He was, however, responsible for summoning ►Mussolini to office in 1922. During the fascist era Victor Emmanuel was created Emperor of Ethiopia (1936) and King of Albania (1939) but never visited either royal appendage. When he sensed the need for peace in July 1943 the King dismissed Mussolini, replacing him by ►Badoglio who concluded an armistice within seven weeks. The King, narrowly escaping internment by the Germans, fled to Brindisi on 9 September and a month later declared war on Germany. With the liberation of Rome in 1944 Victor Emmanuel withdrew from public life, hoping anti-fascists would accept his son, Umberto (1904–83), as a national figure. When the future of the monarchy was submitted to popular vote, Victor Emmanuel abdicated (9 May 1946), three weeks before a referendum which rejected 'Umberto II' by 12½ million to 10½ million votes. Victor Emmanuel died in exile in Egypt.

Vienna Awards (1938, 1940). Instances of German–Italian arbitral diplomacy at the height of Axis power. The first Vienna Award (2 November 1938) assigned the ➤Felvidék, formerly Czechoslovak, to Hungary. The second Vienna Award (30 August 1940) retroceded to Hungary rather more than two-thirds of ➤Transylvania, previously Romanian.

Vietnam. Until the Second World War part of ➤Indo-China, becoming a republic under ➤Ho Chi Minh in September 1945. Attempts by the French to recover their influence around Saigon led to warfare between the French armies and Viet-Minh forces from December 1946 until July 1954. The ➤Geneva Agreements of 1954 recognized a partitioned Vietnam: a 'Democratic Republic' in Hanoi; and a state of southern Vietnam, which rejected the former Emperor of Annam, Bao Dai, in favour of a republic, proclaimed on 26 October 1955, with Ngo Dinh ➤Diem as President. Repression, and in particular an anti-Buddhist campaign, discredited President Ngo, whose government was overthrown in November 1963. By then, communist guerrillas (known to the Saigon authorities by the opprobrious term, Viet-Cong) were in occupation of several rural areas and received supplies and advice from Hanoi. Four years of political instability in Saigon benefited the North Vietnamese, whose attempts to win the South by default were repulsed by the massive military intervention of the USA in the ➤Vietnam War. A stable, though despotic, 'Second Republic of Vietnam' was proclaimed by President Nguyen Van Thieu, a South Vietnamese general, in Saigon on 30 October 1967. Attempts to build up a modernized South Vietnamese army with sophisticated weapons supplied by the Americans coincided with peace efforts made by ➤Kissinger in Paris. The ceasefire agreement in Paris (27 January 1973) provided for talks between the Hanoi and Saigon Governments on the political future of Vietnam. These political exchanges made no progress; hostilities between the two Vietnamese armies continued intermittently, and the talks were broken off in April 1974. Eleven months later a meticulously planned North Vietnamese offensive overwhelmed the South Vietnamese army; Saigon fell on 30 April 1975 (and was renamed Ho Chi Minh City). An assembly representing all Vietnam met in Hanoi on 24 June 1976, and eight days later approved unification of the country as the 'Socialist Republic of Vietnam'. Until 1978 the Hanoi authorities astutely played off Peking against Moscow, benefiting from the major feud of international communism. Chinese infiltration into northern Vietnam induced Hanoi to come down firmly on the Soviet side: in June 1978 Vietnam joined ➤Comecon and five months later signed a 'treaty of friendship and cooperation' with the Soviet Union. The Vietnamese increased their influence over ➤Laos and marched into Kampuchea (➤Cambodia) on Christmas Day, 1978. China duly invaded Vietnam on a wide front on 17 February 1979 and inflicted substantial damage before withdrawing on 5–6 March. This renewed warfare aggravated Vietnam's economic difficulties, making Hanoi increasingly dependent on Soviet and Comecon aid. The isolation of Vietnam was intensified by sympathy in Britain, the United States and other western countries for the Vietnamese 'boat people', a Chinese minority expelled from Vietnam by sea, with much loss of life. The original Chinese refugees were joined later in 1979 by professional and commercial families of Vietnamese origin fleeing, for the most part from the South. The stark hardship of the immediate post-war period was eased after 1986 by the Doi Moi reform era of gradual liberalization in the economy. A revised constitution, effective from June 1992, confirmed rigid communist political doctrine but included clauses to perpetuate the free-market reforms of the past six years.

Vietnam War (1965–73). The name generally given to the military involvement of the United States and other powers in the fifteen-year civil war within ➤Vietnam. From the summer of 1961 onwards American policy sought to build up the South Vietnamese as a barrier against the spread of communism in south-east Asia, but by the beginning of 1964 it looked as if this barrier would soon collapse. Provocative movements by US warships off North Vietnam prompted action by communist naval forces and the ➤Tonkin Resolution in the US Congress in August 1964, which provided President Johnson with authority for executive action in Vietnam. Attacks by the Viet-Cong on US bases at Pleiku and Qui Nhon early in February 1965 were followed by heavy bombing of North Vietnam: US marines landed in March 1965, an airborne brigade two months later. By August 1965 the US had an army of 125,000 men on active service in Vietnam: and by the end of 1966 this figure had risen to almost 400,000. Bombing 'missions' over Vietnamese territory averaged 164 a day in the early months of 1966. The weight of the attack checked Viet-Cong and North Vietnamese activity in 1967 but the war aroused greater resentment within the USA than any previous military undertaking in American history. The ➤Tet offensive of February 1968 was militarily a failure for the communists: ultimately, however, it convinced American public opinion of the futility of maintaining large-scale operations in Vietnam. Bombing raids were curtailed from March 1968 onwards; discussions on the possibility of peace talks began on 13 May 1968. President ➤Nixon began to withdraw troops in June 1969, a further revulsion in American feeling taking place at the end of the year with reports of the ➤My Lai massacre. Under Nixon the Americans concentrated on building up Vietnamese units, but US troops were caught in severe fighting again in February and March 1971 and in March and April 1972. Heavy air raids on North Vietnam were made in March 1970 and November 1972. A ceasefire, with the withdrawal of American forces, was signed in Paris on 27 January 1973, the last US combat troops leaving a fortnight later. US advisers remained in South Vietnam until the final communist victory in April 1975.

Vilna Dispute. The city of Vilna (Vilnyus, Wilno), the ancient medieval capital of ➤Lithuania, was seized by Polish irregular troops in October 1920 and formally incorporated in Poland in 1922, being returned to Lithuania by Soviet Russia in October 1939. The dispute over the Polish occupation of the city prevented military or diplomatic collaboration between Poland and Lithuania throughout the inter-war period.

Vimy Ridge. A German defensive position on high ground north-east of Arras, in northern France, taken by the Canadian Corps under General Byng (1862–1935), 9–12 April 1917. The Canadians suffered nearly 10,000 casualties – one in ten of the combatants – but captured one of the key points on the Western Front, subsequently safeguarding both Arras and Amiens during the German offensive of March 1918.

Vo Nguyen Giap, general. ➤Giap.

Volgograd. ➤Stalingrad.

Vorster, Balthazar Johannes (1915–83), South African Prime Minister. Born at Jamestown in Cape Province, educated locally and at Stellenbosch University. He joined an extreme right-wing Afrikaner movement, as leader of its militant wing of *Stormjagers* (stormtroopers), and was interned by the Smuts Government, 1942–3. He became a Nationalist Party member of the South African parliament in 1953 and was appointed Minister of Justice in 1961, assuming responsibility for police and prisons in 1966, and introducing a series of measures for tightening security against 'subversion'. On 13 September 1966 he became Prime Minister in succession to the assassinated Dr ➤Verwoerd. Although Vorster's intensification of repressive measures and his strict maintenance of ➤apartheid led to widespread condemnation of South Africa in other lands, the white South African voters endorsed his policies and enabled him to win a landslide electoral victory on 30 November 1977. Ill health forced him to resign as Prime Minister in September 1978, although he then became President of the Republic. On 4 June 1979, after only eight months in the Presidency, Vorster resigned and retired from public life after criticism of the way in which, as Prime Minister, he had tolerated irregularities in the Department of Information. (For this so-called 'Muldergate Scandal' ➤South Africa.)

Vyshinsky, Andrei Yanuarievich (1883–1954), Soviet Russian politician. Born at Odessa; studied law at Moscow University, supporting the ➤Mensheviks, served in the Red Army, 1918–21, before becoming Professor of Criminal Law and a state prosecutor. He became notorious as the public prosecutor in all the major trials of the ➤Yezhovshchina, but transferred from the legal administration to the foreign service in 1940, assisting ➤Molotov during the war years, attending the United Nations as chief Soviet delegate 1945–9 and again, 1953–4. From March 1949 until March 1953 he was Soviet Foreign Minister, consistently pursuing a negative and coldly impersonal policy.

W

Wafd. Principal inter-war nationalist party in ➤Egypt. The name derives from the Arabic word for a delegation and commemorates the rejection by the British Government of a delegation of Egyptian nationalists sent to urge the establishment of an independent Egypt (1918). The Wafd leader, Nahas Pasha, headed several governments in the late 1920s and early 1930s. In April 1936 the Wafd won a large majority at the general election: Nahas became Prime Minister, concluding an agreement for the retirement of British forces to the Canal Zone; and he also served as Regent for the under-age King ➤Farouk. In 1938 Farouk dismissed Nahas and the Wafd, but they were reinstated in February 1941 on British insistence since the government in London considered the Wafd a surer guarantee against Italian-inspired subversion than the ministers chosen by Farouk. The Wafd remained in power until October 1944, but collaboration with the British discredited the movement as a nationalistic force. Younger officers, such as Nasser and Sadat, considered the Wafd effete and corrupt. When the Wafd again won elections in 1950 the 'Free Officers' encouraged resistance and there was much rioting, especially in the last week of January 1952. Farouk dismissed Nahas and the Wafd yet again but left himself without political supporters, and was deposed by Neguib seven months later. The Wafd, together with other Egyptian parties, was dissolved in January 1953.

Waldheim, Kurt (1918–), UN Secretary-General and Austrian President. Born in Vienna, serving in the German Army in Russia and the Balkans and subsequently in the Austrian foreign service 1945–64, helping to negotiate the ➤Austrian State Treaty in 1955. He was Austrian Foreign Minister 1968–70 and in April 1971 he was the 'People's Party' candidate in the Austrian Presidential election but was narrowly defeated by the socialist candidate and sitting President, Franz Jonas. At the end of 1971 Dr Waldheim was chosen to succeed ➤U Thant as UN Secretary-General. With the Security Council frequently deadlocked, more and more disputes were passed to the Secretary-General for executive action. But regional conflicts and mutual suspicion between the power blocs hampered Dr Waldheim's efforts, especially in the Middle East, while he lacked any practical means of overcoming the procrastinating tactics of the South Africans over ➤Namibia. He secured some success in the Cyprus disputes but his mission to Teheran to secure the release of the American hostages in January 1980 was a failure, his lack of success earning him much unmerited criticism in New York and Washington. He retired to Vienna in January 1982 after ten years as Secretary-General and was succeeded by the former Peruvian foreign minister, Javier Perez de Cuellar. Waldheim was elected Austrian President in 1986, beginning six years of office on 8 July amid controversy over his actions as an intelligence officer in Greece and Yugoslavia, 1942–4. It was alleged he received a decoration from the ➤Ustaše regime in ➤Croatia and must have known of atrocities for which his commanding general was executed as a war criminal. Waldheim sought to refute these allegations. Several governments, however, followed the US lead in banning the President from their countries so long as his wartime record remained suspect.

Wales. The Principality of Wales has been dynastically an adjunct of the English crown since the end of the thirteenth century, and became administratively linked to England by an Act of Henry VIII's reign. The Welsh retained their distinctive nationality, preserving their language and folk culture and, in particular, their bardic festival (Eisteddfod), dating from 1176. Nonconformist religious traditions also safeguarded the Welsh heritage. In 1900 about half the population of the Principality could speak Welsh, but this figure fell sharply from about 1910 onwards. Partial disendowment of the episcopal Church of Wales, after it ceased to be 'by law established' in 1914, made funds available for a Welsh national library, museums and university education. In 1949 the Labour Government acknowledged the distinctive problems of the Principality by establishing a National Council for Wales. A 'Minister for Welsh Affairs' was first appointed by Harold Macmillan in 1957. The desire for autonomy thereafter became more demonstratively expressed: protest bombs exploded at reservoirs serving English needs, and beneath television masts, in 1966 and 1967. On 14 July 1966 the chairman of Plaid Cymru, Gwynfor Evans, won a by-election at Carmarthen, to become the first Welsh nationalist MP. Three Plaid Cymru members were returned in the general election of October 1974. Devolution proposals, including the establishment of an elected assembly in Cardiff, were discussed in parliament at Westminster, 1976–8. They culminated in a bill, introduced in November 1977, and becoming law in July 1978, which made devolution dependent on support from at least 40 per cent of the Welsh electorate. In a referendum, on 1 March 1979, 11·9 per cent of the electorate favoured devolution and 46·9 were against it. The return of a new Labour government led to a second referendum (17 September 1997): 50 per cent of the registered electorate voted, with 50.3 per cent in favour of a Welsh assembly.

Wałęsa, Lech (1943–), Polish trade unionist. Born near Mochowo on the Vistula. After training as an electrical mechanic he worked in the Gdańsk shipyards 1967–76 but was sacked for criticizing the management. He remained in touch with the shipyard workers and in 1979–80 set up an inter-factory strike committee to seek greater civil rights and higher wages to meet the soaring cost of food and essentials. On 31 August 1980 the Gdańsk Agreement between Wałęsa's committee and the government in ➤Poland paved the way for an independent trade union, ➤Solidarity, of which Wałęsa was chairman. Counter-action by General ➤Jaruzelski led to Wałęsa's arrest and internment from December 1981 to November 1982. Upon his release he was able to restrain the more impetuous members of Solidarity while he negotiated with Jaruzelski and his ministers. Wałęsa was awarded the Nobel Peace Prize in October 1983. His wife and son travelled to Oslo to accept it and to read an address by Wałęsa on civil rights. Thereafter he was allowed greater freedom of movement, even visiting Rome. He took a leading role in talks with the Polish government between February and April 1989 and in organizing the publicity campaign of Solidarity for the June 1989 General Election. He later sought support for the Mazowiecki government, addressing Congress in Washington in November 1989. He was elected Poland's President in December 1990 and undertook a State Visit to London four months later. His term of office did not, however, run smoothly. He frequently complained that the left-wing coalition was obstructing economic reform. The anti-socialist Catholicism of Solidarity which brought him to power was no longer politically relevant by November 1995, when Wałęsa was defeated in seeking re-election to the presidency. He retired into private life a month later, critical of much around him.

Wall Street Crash (1929). Climax of the inter-war ➤Depression. From early 1927 until the late summer of 1929 the American economy had experienced an artificial boom, fed by rash speculation in securities which lacked adequate cover. Fear of the probity of certain concerns led to panic selling on the New York Stock Exchange in Wall Street on 24 October 1929, 'Black Thursday', when 13 million shares changed hands on the day, the panic continuing until the end of the month, with heavy selling on 28 October and with the sudden disposal of 16 million shares on 29 October. Banks failed, there were major business disasters and rapidly rising unemployment, reaching an estimated 17 million. The Crash led to a business recession throughout the Americas and, by disrupting the European market, carried the Depression across the Atlantic.

Warsaw Pact (14 May 1955). Technically, the 'Eastern European Mutual Assistance Treaty', concluded by Albania, Bulgaria, Czechoslovakia, German Democratic Republic, Hungary, Poland, Romania and the Soviet Union and signed in Warsaw. The timing of the Pact marked both a Soviet response to West German membership of NATO (October 1954) and to the withdrawal of occupation forces from Austria, agreed in the ➤Austrian State Treaty, which was signed in Vienna the next day. Basically the Warsaw Pact provided for the establishment of a unified military command, with headquarters in Moscow, and obliged signatories to assist each other to meet any armed attack on one or more members of the Pact in Europe. Albania declined to cooperate with the Pact in 1961 and formally withdrew in September 1968. Hungary tried unsuccessfully to secede in 1956 (➤Hungarian National Rising); Romania vainly sought a change in command structure in 1964, the Czechs in 1968. The Soviet Union invited Finland to subscribe to the Pact in September 1955, but the Finns declined, although confirming their intention of remaining neutral and 'non-aligned'. Apart from joint annual manoeuvres, the Warsaw Pact armies (excluding the Czechs and Romanians) only collaborated on one joint action, the armed intervention against Dubček in ►Czechoslovakia in 1968. Member states, meeting in June 1990, recognized that the ending of Cold War confrontation made the Pact obsolete. Eight months later it was agreed to dissolve the Warsaw Pact from 31 March 1991.

Warsaw Rising (1 August to 3 October 1944). In July 1943 the Polish government-in-exile in London secretly ordered General Count Tadeusz Komorowski (1895–1966) to take command of the 'Home Army', a resistance organization in the Warsaw area, and secure the Polish capital in advance of the Red Army. Komorowski (an officer in a crack cavalry regiment before the war and known since 1943 by his code-name 'Bor') gained control of two-thirds of the city during the first four days of August 1944, at a time when Marshal Rokossovsky's Russian army was approaching the eastern bank of the river Vistula after advancing 400 miles in five weeks. 'Bor's' rising surprised the German defenders but they were able to bring up SS reinforcements and isolate the units of the Home Army, which could only keep in contact through sewers. Rokossovsky, observing the normal Soviet plan, halted on the Vistula for regrouping and for supplies. This Russian inactivity left the Home Army short of food and ammunition. British, Polish and South African airmen flew in supplies from bases in Italy, but aircraft losses were heavy and it was difficult to drop the supplies at points known to be in Bor's hands. A Soviet attack in mid September came too late and met heavy resistance. The Polish Home Army was forced to capitulate at the beginning of October after a revolt sustained for nine weeks. The Poles suffered 15,000 casualties, the Germans about 10,000 casualties. By quelling the Warsaw Rising the Germans removed the only powerful anti-communist organization in eastern Europe. The Red Army entered Warsaw on 17 January 1945, fifteen weeks after Bor and the Home Army had gone into captivity.

Washington Conference (21 November 1921 to 6 February 1922). An international conference was organized on the initiative of the US Secretary of State, Charles Evans Hughes (1862–1948), to reduce naval armaments and ease tension in the Far East. Representatives of Belgium, Britain, China, France, Italy, Japan, the Netherlands, Portugal and the USA convened in Washington and agreed on three main treaties: (1) a guarantee of each other's existing Pacific possessions, signed by Britain, France, Japan and the USA; (2) a collective guarantee of China's independence, with a Japanese pledge for the eventual return to China of ►Kiaochow; (3) a naval convention by which the nine states undertook not to build capital ships for ten years; a ratio of 5:25, 5:25, 3:15, 1:75 and 1:75 was established for capital ships between America, Britain, Japan, France and Italy respectively, and the British and Americans agreed not to strengthen the fortifications of any naval bases between, and including, Singapore and Hawaii. The Conference also reaffirmed the ►Open Door policy in China.

Watergate Affair (1973–4). In the summer of 1972 employees of a Republican

Party organization were caught while seeking to remove electronic bugging devices from Democratic Party campaign headquarters in Watergate, an apartment block beside the Potomac in Washington, DC. Members of President Nixon's White House staff hushed up the affair until after his electoral triumph in November; the case of the intruders came before the Washington Federal District Court on 8 January 1973, at a time when the *Washington Post* was already accusing top officials of seeking to 'cover up' the incident, an accusation given great publicity in mid April after ►Nixon declined to allow his personal aides to give testimony, pleading 'executive privilege'. On 30 April 1973 Nixon accepted the resignation of his principal White House advisers H.R. Haldeman and John Ehrlichman, and dismissed a third member of his personal staff, John Dean. A few days later former Attorney-General, John Mitchell, was indicted before a New York Grand Jury. When, in mid July, it was revealed that the President had secretly taped all conversations held in his White House office, many public figures became convinced Nixon was either implicated in illegal activities or so abnormally suspicious that he was not fit in mind for the responsibilities of a Chief Executive. The President was reluctant to hand over the tapes for Senate investigation, only agreeing to surrender them on 23 October 1973 at the order of the Supreme Court and under imminent threat of impeachment by the House of Representatives. For technical reasons the handing over of the tapes was then further delayed. Mounting indignation led to renewal of the process of impeachment in the early summer of 1974. Nixon then admitted he had been involved in the attempt to cover up the original crime at the Watergate and on 9 August 1974 became the first US President to resign, receiving from his successor, President Ford, a pardon. The fallen members of his White House staff, accomplices in his act of deception, were not covered by the pardon and were subsequently imprisoned.

Wavell, Archibald Percival (1883–1950, created viscount 1943, earl 1947), British soldier and Viceroy of India. Born and educated at Winchester, commissioned in the Black Watch, 1901, fought in the Boer War, and served on Allenby's staff in Palestine in the First World War. He was appointed commander-in-chief, Middle East, in July 1939. He successfully defended Egypt in 1940, turning the Italians out of Cyrenaica in the first of the North African campaigns and assisting in the conquest of Ethiopia and Italian East Africa. In 1941 he had to fight in Greece and Crete, Iraq and Syria as well as in North Africa and his resources were overstretched. He took command in India in July 1941, but was unable to stem the Japanese advance in 1942. In June 1943 he became Viceroy, helping both to relieve famine and to maintain order at a time when India was faced with invasion. He relinquished his Viceroyalty in February 1947. Wavell, created a field-marshal in 1943, was a cultured soldier, with a love of books and a clear prose style.

Weimar Republic. The German Federal Republic, 1918–33, is known by the name of the town at which the National Constituent Assembly gathered in February 1919. A constitution providing for a seven-year presidential term, bicameral government, proportional representation, and guaranteeing federal rights was adopted in Weimar on 31 July 1919 and the assembly did not return to Berlin until the spring of 1920. There were two Presidents of the Republic; until 1925 Friedrich Ebert (1871–1925), a democratic socialist; and then Field-Marshal von ➤Hindenburg. The Weimar Republic suffered economic difficulties, caused by the aftermath of a lost war and ➤reparations. Government economies, and the Dawes Plan, helped recovery from the financial collapse of 1922–3 but the Depression of 1929–31 led to a worse economic crisis and to mass unemployment. It destroyed the political balance achieved under ➤Stresemann from 1924 to 1929. The elections of September 1930 won Hitler's ➤Nazi Party 109 seats in place of its previous 12 seats. This trend continued, and the Nazis became the largest single party in July 1932 with 230 seats. Their success sprang from anti-Semitism, exaggeration of a communist menace, centralism as opposed to divisive federalism, denunciation of the unpopular ➤Versailles Treaty and the promise of a vigorous foreign policy. Hitler's hostility to socialism secured for his party the backing of powerful capitalist interests. Despite the verdict of the electorate President Hindenburg sought to keep out of office a party that was clearly hostile to the Weimar constitution. Attempts (notably by ➤Brüning) to administer Germany by delicately balanced coalitions failed, and on 30 January 1933, the President appointed Hitler as Chancellor. Less than two months later (23 March) Hitler carried through an Enabling Act which suspended the Weimar Constitution; and democratic republican Germany made way for the ➤Third Reich.

Weizmann, Chaim (1874–1952), first President of Israel. Born near Pinsk in Russian Poland, studied in Germany and became a distinguished scientist who was appointed reader in biochemistry at Manchester University in 1906 and was naturalized as a British subject four years later, although he was already an inspired advocate of ➤Zionism, convinced of the need for the Jewish people to find a national home in Palestine. He was director of the Admiralty Laboratories, 1916–19, and played a major part in securing the ➤Balfour Declaration of 1917. He was President of the World Zionist Organization and of the Jewish Agency in Palestine, 1921–31 and 1935–46, returning to British service at the outbreak of the Second World War as a scientific adviser to the Ministry of Supply. He was elected President of Israel as soon as the Jewish state received independence and held office until his death on 9 November 1952.

Welensky, Roy (1907–92, knighted 1953), Prime Minister of the Federation of Rhodesia and Nyasaland. Born in Salisbury, Rhodesia, in a Jewish family of Lithuanian origin. He became an engine-driver and trade-union official for the railway-workers' union, as well as being an amateur heavyweight boxing champion. In 1938 he founded and led a Labour Party in Northern Rhodesia (➤Zambia) and was a member of the Northern Rhodesian Legislative Council from 1938 to 1953, supervising manpower problems during the Second World War. He was an early believer in establishing a federation of Rhodesia and ➤Nyasaland, achieved largely through his skilful negotiating gifts in 1953. He was Minister of Transport and Communications in the Federation from 1953 until November 1956 when he became Prime Minister. Constitutional changes in 1959, reducing African representation in parliament, provoked unrest and friction with the Macmillan Government in London which decided (in the Monckton Report of October 1960) that members of the Federation had a right to secede – a decision described by Welensky as the 'death-knell of the Federation'. When the Federation was dissolved in December 1963, Welensky failed to command a following among white Rhodesians, who preferred the Rhodesian Front of Ian ➤Smith. Welensky opposed the ➤Unilateral Declaration of Independence but supported Smith in his struggle against a trade boycott.

West Indies Federation (1958–62). In 1947 proposals were made for linking Barbados, Jamaica, Trinidad and Tobago, the Leeward Islands and the Windward Islands in a federation, which it was vainly hoped would also be joined by British Guiana and British Honduras on the mainland. Long negotiations brought the island colonies together (apart from the Virgin Islands, which separated from the Leeward group) and the Federation was created in January 1958, with its capital in Trinidad. Strong opposition developed within Jamaica (and to a lesser extent in Trinidad) where it was felt that the British Government was trying to force the richer areas of the Caribbean to accept responsibility for the poorer regions and islands. The vigorous Jamaican politician ➤Bustamente turned against the Federation: a referendum in Jamaica voted in favour of secession; and the Federation was dissolved on 31 May 1962. Loose unity was maintained among the smaller Caribbean islands, which constituted the West Indies Associated States. The 'big three' islands achieved independence: Jamaica on 6 August 1962, Trinidad and Tobago on 31 August 1962, Barbados on 30 November 1966.

Western Sahara. ➤Morocco.

Westminster, Statute of (11 December 1931). The basic charter of the modern Commonwealth: the Statute confirmed resolutions of the ➤Imperial Conferences of 1926 and 1930 seeking to clarify the status of dominions, which it defined as 'autonomous communities within the British Empire, equal in status . . . united by a common allegiance to the Crown, and freely associated as members of the British Commonwealth of Nations'.

Weygand, Maxime (1867–1965), French general. Born at Brussels, of uncertain parentage although it is possible he was a son of the Empress Charlotte of Mexico, only daughter of King Leopold I of the Belgians. Weygand entered the French military college of St Cyr in 1886; as a young cavalry officer, he was respected for his brilliant horsemanship. Throughout the First World War he was Chief of Staff to ➤Foch, the collaboration of the two men forming one of the famous partnerships in military history. He served as military adviser to ➤Pilsudski in 1920, commander-in-chief in the Levant, 1923–4, director of France's principal military studies college, 1924–9, Chief of the French General Staff, 1930–35. After four years in retirement he returned as commander-in-chief in the Levant in 1939 but was recalled to take command in northern France on 19 May 1940, when the Germans had already broken the allied defences and taken Amiens. It was on Weygand's advice that ►Pétain sought an armistice a month later, although Weygand remained strongly hostile to Franco-German collaboration under ►Vichy. He was arrested by the Germans in November 1942 and held captive until 1945. In his last years he engaged in historical writing and occasional criticism of de Gaulle, for Weygand distrusted all offers of self-determination to the parts of Africa which he regarded as France's 'natural patrimony'. Although Weygand's prestige and influence were considerable from 1920 to 1940, his achievements never matched the legendary promise of earlier years, perhaps because he remained for too long the officer standing in Foch's shadow.

Whitlam, (Edward) Gough (1916–), Australian Prime Minister. Born in Melbourne and received his high-school education in Canberra before graduating from Sydney University; served in the Royal Australian Air Force, 1941–5, practised as a lawyer in Sydney and entered parliament in Canberra in 1952, becoming leader of the Australian Labour Party early in 1967, with the reputation of being a 'moderate'. Labour won the elections of November 1972, and he became Prime Minister. His premiership was stormy, he ended conscription and Australia's involvement in the Vietnam War (December 1972); a proposed new system of 'honours' substituting the Order of Australia, with three grades, for traditional knighthoods was rejected by four out of the six Australian state governments; an angry exchange in parliament prompted the Speaker to resign (27 February 1975); attempts to secure loans led to a conflict in the party, which forced Whitlam to dismiss his Deputy Prime Minister (2 July 1974) and his Energy Minister (14 October 1975) as well as leading to a long dispute with the Upper House in Canberra. On 11 November 1975 the Governor-General, Sir John Kerr, took the unprecedented step of dismissing the government and appointing the leader of the opposition, Malcolm ►Fraser, as caretaker Prime Minister, pending a general election. Labour lost the election, but Whitlam was re-elected party leader (27 January 1976), although severely criticized by many members for errors of judgement. In the following general election (December 1977) Labour lost so heavily that Whitlam immediately resigned the party leadership.

William II, German Emperor and King of Prussia (1859–1941, reigned 1888–1918). Born in Berlin, the son of Emperor Frederick III (who died after a reign of ninety-nine days) and the eldest daughter of Queen Victoria. He received a strict upbringing, in which he showed strength of character by triumphing over a withered arm and other disabilities. In March 1890 he dismissed Chancellor Bismarck and followed a 'new course', seeking world leadership as opposed to primacy on the Continent, with which Bismarck had been content. William's personal vanities – a pride in 'my navy', a genuine conviction he was the adjutant of Providence – induced him to strike attitudes of arrogance which made foreign contemporaries regard him as a warmonger. He was ill-advised by the Chancellor in whom he long had greatest trust, ►Bülow, and, after the disgrace of his friend ►Eulenburg and an ill-judged attempt to court British friendship in 1908, he was increasingly isolated. He convinced himself of the need for a short, preventive war in 1914, anticipating neither its length nor its scale. From 1916 onwards both he and his Chancellors were overshadowed by the military leadership of ►Hindenburg and ►Ludendorff. On the advice of the officer corps William fled to Holland in November 1918, since it was clear that his enemies would not make peace so long as he remained on the throne. A request by the Paris peacemakers that Holland should hand over the 'ex-Kaiser' for trial was rejected by Queen Wilhelmina and the Dutch Government. William lived for twenty years at Doorn, near Utrecht, dying with German invaders at his gates, having declined (in 1940) offers from Churchill of asylum in England and from Hitler of returning as a private citizen to one of his former estates.

Wilson, (James) Harold (1916–95, knight of the Garter 1976), British Prime Minister. Born in Huddersfield, educated at Wirral Grammar School and Jesus College, Oxford, economics don and wartime civil servant before being elected Labour MP for Ormskirk in 1945, changing his constituency to Huyton in 1950. He was President of the Board of Trade from 1947 to 1951, showing a respect for traditional socialism, marked by his resignation at the imposition of health charges in the 1951 budget and by his later conflict with ►Gaitskell over commitment to principles of common ownership in the Labour programme. Wilson became party leader in February 1963, a month after Gaitskell's death, and won the general election of October 1964 by a small majority which he increased to 99 in April 1966. He succeeded in 'balancing the books' and in raising the personal influence of the Prime Minister in world affairs, and he promoted 'technology' as no previous head of a British Government had done. Critics said he concerned himself excessively with details of administration, and he was faced by hostility from many commentators and most of the Press. Bad timing led to an electoral defeat in June 1970. He returned to Downing Street on 4 March 1974 as head of a minority government with the balance-of-payments situation five times as bad as when he first became Prime Minister ten years before. In these circumstances he depended upon the 'social contract' bargain with the ►trade unions. This new doctrine of industrial relations was sufficiently acceptable to the electorate for him to gain a slender majority in the election of 10 October 1974. The following year showed, however, that he was becoming a tired man and he unexpectedly announced his retirement soon after his sixtieth birthday, handing over the premiership to ►Callaghan on 5 April 1976. He was created a Life Peer, Baron Wilson of Rievaulx, in 1983.

Wilson, (Thomas) Woodrow (1856–1924), twenty-eighth President of the USA.

Born in Staunton, Virginia, his father being a strict and austere Presbyterian minister. He was educated at Princeton and the University of Virginia and Johns Hopkins University, becoming a professor at Princeton, 1890–1902, and president of the University, 1902–10, before being elected Democratic Governor of New Jersey where, in 1911–13, he became a national figure because of his progressive reforms. He won the Presidential election of 1912, his success coming in part from the rift between the Republican President, Taft, and the independent ex-Republican, Theodore ▸Roosevelt. In home affairs Wilson concentrated on anti-trust measures and on reorganizing the federal banking system. Border raids forced him to send a punitive expedition into Mexico (1916). From 1914 to 1917 he observed strict neutrality in the First World War, being prepared to mediate, and winning the 1916 election on the slogan 'He Kept Us Out of War'. Unrestricted submarine attacks and the intrigues revealed in the ▸Zimmermann Telegram forced him to enter the war on 6 April 1917, although insisting that the USA was a co-belligerent 'associated power' rather than an ally of France and Britain. On 8 January 1918 he issued his ▸Fourteen Points as a basis for peace and he attended the Paris Peace Conference in 1919, hoping to realize his internationalist ideals, especially the creation of a League of Nations. Wilson's rapturous reception in Europe blinded him to political realities both among allied statesmen less high-minded than he and also in the US Senate, in which Republicans gained a majority at the mid-term elections. In Paris Wilson reluctantly compromised, trusting that the League would later right wrongs in the treaties. On returning to America he found the Senate would not ratify the Treaty of Versailles, which contained the League Covenant, and that the USA could not therefore be a member of the League. Wilson began a nation-wide campaign to win support for his ideals, but three weeks later he collapsed (26 September 1919) and was an invalid for the last three and a half years of his life.

Wingate, Orde Charles (1903–44), British general. Born at Naini Tal, India, his parents being strict Plymouth Brethren. He was educated at Charterhouse and the Royal Military Academy and was commissioned in the Royal Artillery in 1922. For five years he served in the Sudan and later in Palestine and Transjordan, where he won the admiration of the leaders of the Jewish community, who hoped he would be seconded to found the army of a Jewish state. In 1940–41 he led a guerrilla group, 'Gideon's Force', operating on the Ethiopian–Sudanese frontier with astonishing success, capturing many forts and taking hundreds of Italians prisoner. He then suffered a physical and nervous breakdown. His former com-mander-in-chief, ▸Wavell, had great faith in Wingate's unusual gifts and summoned him to the Burma Front in May 1942, where he worked out plans for penetrating the Japanese lines with long-range guerrillas supplied by air and kept in communi-cation by wireless. These 'Chindits' operated effectively from February to June 1943 harassing Japanese supply routes and causing chaos along the river Irrawaddy. In February 1944 a second wave of Chindits helped stem a projected Japanese invasion of India (►Burma Campaign). During these operations Major-General Wingate's plane crashed in Assam (24 March 1944) and he was killed.

Witte, Sergei (1849–1915), Russian statesman. Born in Tiflis of a Baltic German family, long in Tsarist service, educated at Odessa and became an administrator of provincial railways. From 1892 to 1903 he held ministerial appointments which made him responsible for commerce, industry, labour relations, finance and communications, his most impressive achievement being the construction of the Trans-Siberian and Chinese Eastern Railways, linking Moscow, Peking and Vladivostok. Witte's policy of cautious economic expansion in the Far East was too slow for an influential group of militarists at St Petersburg who secured his dismissal (29 August 1903). Their folly led to the disastrous ►Russo-Japanese War and Tsar Nicholas II recalled Witte to negotiate peace at ►Portsmouth, New Hampshire, in September 1905. Witte became Russia's first Prime Minister on 16 November 1905. He floated a loan for £80 million from Britain and France, but Tsar Nicholas and his court disliked Witte and took the opportunity to dismiss him on 5 May 1906. He spent his last years as a Russian Cassandra, never again offered a government post, critical of the decision to go to war in 1914 and confident that revolution was imminent.

Women, Emancipation of. The greatest revolution in the twentieth-century world has been the changed status of women in society. Educational opportunities denied earlier generations opened the professions to upper- and middle-class women in western Europe and the USA during the inter-war years, while in Russia the Soviet constitution of 1918 promised equality before the law, equal pay and equal opportunity to millions in eastern Europe and Asia. During the early years of the century a struggle for the vote became the most publicized feminist activity in the English-speaking countries and in Scandinavia (►Fawcett, Mrs Henry; ►Pankhurst, Mrs Emmeline; ►Suffragettes). Elsewhere interest centred primarily on property rights, the right to initiate divorce proceedings and problems of childbearing.

Advocacy of birth control first made headway in the Netherlands. Family planning was championed in Britain by Marie Stopes (1880–1958): her widely read book, *Married Love* (1918), was followed by the establishment of a birth-control clinic in north London in 1921 and by a successful series of public meetings a year later. Her American counterpart, the nurse and writer Margaret Sanger (1883–1966), was jailed in 1916 for opening a clinic in Brooklyn, but public feeling in New York had changed by 1923 and she was able to sponsor clinics in many states, as well as in India some years later. The publicizing of artificial means of birth control was officially banned in countries where the power of the Roman Catholic Church remained considerable. By 1930, however, the birth rate was falling in America and in every European country except Portugal, and a woman's right to regulate her pregnancies was sufficiently widely accepted for the summoning of an international conference on birth-control clinics at Zürich that autumn. In 1933

Sweden became the first country to make sex education for girls compulsory. From 1952 onwards a contraceptive pill was available in many parts of Europe and America. It was condemned by the Catholic Church, notably in Pope Paul's encyclical *Humanae Vitae* of July 1968. Many other churches joined Roman Catholics in opposing the spread of abortion, legalized in Britain in April 1968, in the USA after a Supreme Court judgement in 1973 and in France in 1975.

Manpower shortages during the First World War opened up millions of jobs for women in factories and offices. Men reasserted their predominance in industry with the return of peace, but women maintained a hold on the former 'white-collar' jobs; and, except among the Germans and the Irish, domestic service ceased to attract large numbers of working-class girls. Labour-saving devices freed women from long hours of home management while the change in working habits enabled more women to remain employed after marriage. Yet progress in the higher professions was slow. Thus no woman became a High Court Judge in Britain until 1965 and, even with an influx of Labour MPs in 1997, never comprised as much as one-sixth of Commons' members. Frenchwomen, by contrast, comprised more than one-fifth of the legal profession by 1970 and formed a slightly higher proportion of practising doctors: in the same year, 25 per cent of doctors in Britain were women, 22 per cent in West Germany and only 6 per cent in the USA. The least 'emancipated' professions have been the Stock Exchange and the Church. The Anglican Consultative Council, meeting at Limuru in Kenya in 1971, voted narrowly in favour of permitting bishops to ordain women to the priesthood in particular circumstances; but the decision provoked considerable opposition in England. So, too, in 1987–8, did the possibility of women bishops. In the Episcopal Church of the USA, however, women were ordained priests in 1980, and the Revd Barbara Harris was elected suffragan bishop of Massachusetts in September 1988. The General Synod of the Church of England voted in favour of women priests on 11 November 1992. The first women priests were ordained in England at Bristol Cathedral on 22 March 1994. The Roman Catholic and Orthodox Churches remain hostile to the ordination of women. The Swedish Lutherans had ordained women pastors as early as 1960. In America the Methodists had a woman minister (Anna Shaw) in 1880 and Dr Maude Royden became assistant minister of the City Temple, London, in 1917.

Women's emancipation outside Europe and America has been imposed from above. Thus in Turkey the government of ►Atatürk introduced a series of measures, 1925–8, freeing women from Islamic legal and social restraints. This precedent was followed by several Arab republics in the late 1950s and by Shah Reza Pahlavi of Iran in 1963. The Japanese constitution of October 1946, reflecting American influence, accorded women a political and social status which offended conservative matriarchs. Chinese women did not gain economic, social and legal independence until the 'socialist transformation' of 1953–7. Attempts by the Congress Party in India to promote the social emancipation of women ran into difficulties of caste: the practice of male sterilization, subsidized by several Indian state governments in the 1960s, aroused an anti-feminist reaction. Nevertheless the rapid social advancement of Asian women has been remarkable. By 1971 there were women heads of government (Mrs ➤Bandaranaike, Mrs ➤Gandhi, Mrs ➤Meir) in three Asian countries. By contrast, women's emancipation in black Africa was delayed by persistent tribal taboos and, in many areas, by unreformed Muslim beliefs. President Nyerere, however, appointed two women ministers in the Tanzanian Government in 1976, and women also attained cabinet rank in Liberia.

The Second World War actively involved women to a greater extent than its predecessor, notably in the anti-Nazi resistance movements. In Britain unmarried women under the age of thirty were made liable for military service in December 1941. The emancipation struggle after the war was concerned more with equal pay and legal equality than with political rights. In France, equal pay was conceded in 1946, some eighteen months after Frenchwomen were first given the vote, and the comprehensive 'Law of 13 July 1965' guaranteed Frenchwomen legal equality with Frenchmen from February 1966 onwards. On 15 May 1991 Edith Cresson, a Socialist, became France's first woman Prime Minister. In the United Kingdom financial and legal equality came only in 1975, when the Sex Discrimination Act was followed at the end of the year by the establishment of an Equal Opportunities Commission. Similar campaigns to redefine the status of women took place in several other countries, notably in Australia and the USA (where, in 1982, a long campaign for an 'Equal Rights Amendment' to the constitution failed because less than three quarters of the states in the union fulfilled the constitutional requirement of ratifying the amendment within the prescribed time period). Between 1969 and 1974 a vocally active pressure group favouring 'Women's Liberation' from a society which it believed to be male-dominated and 'sexist' achieved much publicity, both sympathetic and hostile, especially in the English-speaking countries. More importantly it achieved much for women's rights.

World Bank. Name commonly given to the 'International Bank for Reconstruction and Development', a specialized agency of the United Nations, proposed at ➤Bretton Woods in 1944 and established in December 1945 to provide loans to the governments of UN members for economic development. An affiliated specialized agency, the International Finance Corporation (IFC), was set up in 1956 in order to provide loans for private enterprise within member states, especially those countries which appear to have less-developed economies. The International Development Association, a soft-loan subsidiary of the World Bank for the poorer countries, was set up in 1960.

World Health Organization (WHO). One of the fourteen specialized agencies of the ➤United Nations, founded on 7 April 1948 to give advice and help develop resources for family health, environmental health, drug monitoring, and international collaboration in controlling diseases. The organization extended earlier forms of international medical cooperation, the Red Cross movement in time of war (recognized 1864), the International Office of Public Health (set up in Paris in 1909, later moving to Switzerland) and the Health Office of the League of Nations (established in 1923 at Geneva). WHO, too, has headquarters in Geneva.

World War, First. The immediate cause was the spread of Balkan nationalism as shown by the assassination at ►Sarajevo and the determination of the Austrians to destroy the Serbian 'hornets' nest'. The conflict could not be localized because Europe was divided by a system of alliances, originally defensive in character, but made dangerous through a lessening of international trust in successive crises over the previous nine years – ►Morocco, ►Bosnia, ►Agadir. Although Britain was not a member of these alliances, naval rivalry and trade competition had alienated her from Germany, and she was bound by treaty obligations to uphold Belgium's integrity. Austria–Hungary declared war on Serbia on 28 July 1914; Russia mobilized along the frontiers of Austria and Austria's ally, Germany, on 29 July; Germany declared war on Russia on 1 August and on Russia's ally, France, on 3 August, invading Belgium on the same day as part of the ►Schlieffen Plan; Britain declared war on Germany on 4 August. Germany and Austria–Hungary were joined by Turkey (November 1914) and by Bulgaria (October 1915). The original 'Allies' were supported by eighteen other states, among them Japan (August 1914), Italy (May 1915) and Romania (July 1916). The United States entered the war against Germany as an 'associated power' in April 1917.

Western Front. After the repulse of the initial German advance to the Marne, both sides constructed defensive positions so that lines of trenches extended from Nieuport on the Belgian coast through Ypres, Arras, Albert, Soissons and Rheims to Verdun. For three and a half years neither side advanced more than a few miles along this line despite new weapons such as poison gas (first used by Germany at Ypres, April 1916) and tanks (first used by Britain on the Somme, September 1916). The German spring offensive of 1918 once more reached the Marne, but by August the allied armies were advancing on all sectors.

Eastern Front. Initial Russian advances to the Carpathians and into East Prussia were followed by long, exhausting defensive operations by the Russians, apart from Brusilov's offensive on the Austrian sector in the summer of 1916. The western allies tried to relieve the Russians by opening up a sea route through the Black Sea, but the attempt to penetrate the Dardanelles and seize Gallipoli failed. The Russian will to resist succumbed to revolution in 1917.

Balkan Front. Serbia repulsed the initial Austrian offensive but was overrun by a combined force of Germans, Austrians and Bulgarians, 1915–16. A multinational expeditionary force based on Salonika broke through the Bulgarian lines and advanced northwards to the Danube in September–October 1918.

Italian Front. Stabilized along the Isonzo river for two and a half years. The Italians were forced back from Caporetto to the Piave river in October 1917, avenging this defeat by a final victory at Vittorio Veneto a year later.

Outside Europe. Campaigns against the Turks in Palestine and Mesopotamia;

protracted campaigns against German colonies in Africa, the Japanese mopping up German possessions in the Far East.

There were small naval actions in the Pacific and south Atlantic against German surface vessels and against the Austro-Hungarian fleet in the Adriatic, but the main Anglo-German naval engagement was off Jutland (1916). German use of submarines caused heavy losses of British merchant ships in the spring of 1917, but these 'U-boats' were countered by revival of convoys and the development of new weapons, such as the depth charge. Aircraft and airships supported military and naval operations and brought total war to cities behind the lines, including towns in Britain.

Fighting ceased with the German armistice of 11 November 1918. The Paris Peace Conference to determine treaties and settle the form of the new Europe opened ten weeks later.

(*See also under individual battles, campaigns etc.*)

World War, Second. Originated in Hitler's hostility to the Versailles frontiers and in the Anglo-French pledge to support Poland, given in April 1939. Germany invaded Poland on 1 September 1939, overrunning the country in four weeks. Britain and France declared war on Germany two days later but avoided major land operations. In April 1940 German troops occupied Denmark and invaded Norway. The invasion of Belgium and Holland on 10 May 1940 opened seven weeks of 'lightning-war' (*Blitzkrieg*) in which penetration by German tank columns ('panzers') and use of air power encompassed the fall of the Netherlands and Belgium by the end of May and of France by 22 June. Failure to secure air superiority over Britain frustrated Hitler's invasion plans. While continuing attacks by submarine on British supply routes and bombing British cities, Germany turned eastwards, invading Yugoslavia and Greece (April 1941) and attacking Russia on a 2,000-mile front on 22 June 1941, in alliance with Finland, Hungary and Romania. British military efforts concentrated on the Italians, who entered the war on Germany's side on 10 June 1940 but who soon suffered defeats in North Africa, East Africa and Albania. Relentless German advances in Russia reached the Volga and the outskirts of Leningrad and Moscow: from November 1942 the Germans were gradually thrown back, the last invaders being expelled from pre-war Russia in August 1944. Japan's desire for a 'Greater Asia' led to surprise attacks on American and British bases, 7 December 1941, Germany and Italy declaring war on the USA three days later. Within four months the Japanese were masters of Burma and south-east Asia, their advances not repulsed until June 1942 with allied naval victories in the Pacific. Allied victories in North Africa (October 1942 to May 1943) marked the turn of the tide for Germany. The allies invaded Sicily from Tunisia, landing in Italy and forcing the Italians to make a separate peace (September 1943) and join the anti-Hitler allies. The German hold on Europe was weakened by partisan guerrilla insurrections. A 'Second Front' was launched against Germany by the Normandy landings of 6 June 1944, Paris being liberated on 25 August.

Despite the German use of flying bombs and rockets against British bases, the western allies advanced to the prewar German frontier (crossed early February 1945) and linked up with the Soviet Red Army on the Elbe, 28 April 1945. Germany formally capitulated at Rheims, 7 May 1945. Meanwhile British and Commonwealth forces mounted a land offensive against the Japanese in Burma, supporting American island-hopping operations towards Japan, which was subjected to heavy air attacks, culminating in the dropping of atomic bombs on Hiroshima and Nagasaki. Japan, uninvaded, surrendered on 14 August 1945.

(*See also under individual campaigns, battles, personalities etc.*)

Wright, Wilbur (1867–1912) and Orville (1871–1948), pioneers of aviation. Born near Millville, Indiana, the sons of a bishop in one of the smaller American sects. They ran a bicycle-shop in Dayton, Ohio, having had only limited elementary schooling, but began to construct gliders which they tested at Kitty Hawk, North Carolina, thus acquiring a natural understanding of the effects of air-currents on wings. In the course of 1903 they used their mechanical knowledge to build a glider which could be powered by a 12-h.p. petrol engine and Orville piloted the aeroplane for a flight of forty yards on 7 December 1903 – the first flight by a powered aircraft. After two more years improving the machine they were able to fly a distance of twenty-four miles. Three years later they brought their aircraft to Europe, pioneering powered flight in France, Britain and Italy. The Wright Aeroplane Company was developed, with US Army backing, in 1909.

Y

Yahya, Agha Mohammad Khan (1917–80), third President of Pakistan. Born at Peshawar, educated at Punjab University, fought in the Middle East and Italy in the Second World War and subsequently participated in operations in ►Kashmir. He was commanding general of the Pakistan Army in 1966 and was appointed by ►Ayub Khan as martial-law administrator in March 1969, in order 'to save the integrity of Pakistan'. At the end of that month he assumed the Presidency. He hoped to resolve political disputes by permitting the first-ever 'one man, one vote' elections in the republic. They were held in West Pakistan on 7 December 1970 but postponed in East Pakistan until 17 January 1971 because of severe floods. Yahya Khan's refusal to accept the East Pakistani verdict in favour of the Awami League led to civil war over ►Bangladesh, a disastrous brief conflict with India, and to the President's precipitate resignation (December 1971). He was detained under house arrest from January 1972 until July 1974.

Yalta. Resort on the Black Sea Coast of the Crimea, the setting for the second wartime summit meeting of Stalin, Churchill and Roosevelt (4–11 February 1945). Roosevelt succeeded in gaining Stalin's agreement to enter the war against Japan and to collaborate in the establishment of the United Nations Organization, the Soviet delegation having raised difficulties at the preliminary discussions at ►Dumbarton Oaks. Churchill secured Russian approval for the eventual creation of a French zone, as well as British, Soviet and American zones, in occupied Germany. Stalin gained acceptance of the ►Curzon Line as the Soviet–Polish frontier and tacit acknowledgement that the Polish state would have the ►Oder–Neisse Line as a western boundary; he agreed to 'free elections' in Poland as soon as possible, and accepted British pleas for the inclusion of members of the exiled Polish and Yugoslav Governments in the new governments established in those countries. A 'Declaration on Liberated Europe' affirmed the three leaders' desire for democratic institutions in the lands formerly under German control. US policy at Yalta was later much criticized by American commentators: it was held that Roosevelt had 'brought Russia into the Far East' and 'handed over eastern Europe to Stalin'. These criticisms ignore the conditions of the time: the Soviet military threat was thought essential to complete Japan's encirclement and end the war speedily; and most of eastern Europe was already occupied by the Red Army. Soviet–American relations were certainly more cordial at Yalta than on any other occasion, not least because Roosevelt's military advisers were suspicious of alleged British monarchist sympathies in Germany and of British neo-imperialism in the Far East.

Yamamoto, Isoruku (1884–1943), Japanese admiral. Born at Nagaoka, educated at colleges in Japan and at Harvard, serving briefly as Japanese naval attaché in Washington. As commander-in-chief of the Japanese Navy he argued that Japan could not win a long conflict with America but might secure good peace terms by rapid successes gained within six months of declaring war. He worked out details of the Pearl Harbor attack early in 1941, though assuming it would follow delivery of an ultimatum at Washington. His initial strategic victories at Pearl Harbor and in the Java Sea sprang from his masterly understanding of naval air power. His further plans were checked at the battle of the ►Coral Sea in May 1942 and by a decisive defeat a month later at ►Midway. On 17 April 1943 US intelligence agents decoded wireless signals giving details of a projected tour of inspection by Yamamoto and on the following day American fighters intercepted his plane over the Solomon Islands. It was shot down with no survivors.

Yamashita, Tomoyuki (1885–1946), Japanese general. Born near Tokyo, served in the Russo-Japanese War, First World War and Sino-Japanese War before being appointed inspector-general of Japanese aircraft in 1940 and sent on a special military mission to Rome and Berlin at the end of the year. As commander of the Japanese Twenty-fifth Army he invaded Malaya, capturing ►Singapore on 15 February 1942. In July 1944 he was appointed commander-in-chief in the Philippines, defending Leyte and Luzon against the Americans. In the fighting around Manila many atrocities were committed. Yamashita continued resistance in the hills of the Philippines until 2 September 1945. Eight weeks later he was put on trial in Manila for war crimes and hanged on 28 February 1946.

Yeltsin, Boris (1931–), Russian radical politician. Born in Sverdlovsk and was a construction engineer in the Urals from 1955 to 1968 when he became a Communist Party worker. He was elected to the Supreme Soviet at the age of forty-five and in 1985 became both Secretary of the Central Committee and First Secretary of the Moscow Party. From 1987 onwards he favoured democratic reform and in February 1990 was the only member of Central Committee to vote against ►Perestroika on the grounds that Gorbachev's proposals were too limited. He was elected Chairman of the Russian Soviet in May 1990, resigned from the Party in June, and in July proposed a programme for achieving a full market economy for the Russian Soviet Republic within 500 days, a measure which was too radical for Gorbachev and for his conservative critics. Yeltsin continued to lead a liberal - radical opposition in Moscow, publicly calling for Gorbachev's resignation in a television broadcast on 19 February 1991. He became Russian President in June 1991, gaining prestige and authority in late August by resisting an attempted *coup* in Moscow by Communist hard-liners. He retained the presidential office when the ►Soviet Union dissolved. His reform programme was hampered by threats of secession from within Russia, by suspicion of his personal ambitions from the Congress of People's Deputies, by low morale in the army and navy, and by rising crime, particularly in Moscow and St Petersburg. In March 1993 he assumed special powers to rule by decree, a measure for which he won backing in a referendum. Five months later there was street fighting in Moscow as he faced an open revolt by the Deputies. Yeltsin's health began to fail; he suffered heart attacks in June and October 1995 but rallied sufficiently to stand in the presidential election at midsummer 1996. Although Yeltsin failed to win outright on the first ballot he made an electoral pact with the third candidate, General Lebed, and accordingly won the second ballot, though with only 54 per cent of votes. His health was so poor that in November 1996 he accepted heart surgery from an eminent American specialist, but by May 1997 he was fit to travel to Paris to sign a treaty of accord between Russia and ➤NATO. His political behaviour remained unpredictable. In March 1998 he dismissed every government minister and forced the Duma into accepting as Prime Minister a young and politically inexperienced banker, Sergei Kiriyenko. At the interment of the remains of ➤Nicholas II in St Petersburg he unexpectedly expressed public contrition over the fate of the imperial family.

Yemen. The south-western corner of Arabia, comprised two states: the Yemen Arab Republic, capital San'a; and the People's Democratic Republic of Yemen, capital Aden. The territory of the Yemen Arab Republic was under Turkish suzerainty, 1517–1918, and there was intermittent fighting in the First World War between the Turkish garrison of 14,000 men and British troops defending neighbouring ➤Aden. The Imam Yahya became King of an independent Yemen in 1918 and ruled until his assassination in February 1948; his sadistic son, Imam Ahmad, ruled from March 1948 until September 1962. Whereas Yahya had kept the Yemen isolated and backward, Ahmad hoped to secure his position by collaboration with ➤Nasser, 1958–61, and by gaining support from the Soviet-bloc countries for anti-British activities along his southern border. The backwardness of the Yemen led General al-Sallal to proclaim the Yemen Arab Republic on 26 September 1962, within ten days of Imam Ahmad's death. Tribal resistance, backed by Saudi Arabia, led to a civil war lasting intermittently from October 1962 until April 1970, the republicans receiving occasional assistance from the Egyptians and Syrians. The People's Democratic Republic of Yemen was set up in November 1967, and was known as 'Southern Yemen' for three years. Discussions began in 1972 for union of the two Yemeni states but were hampered by political instability at San'a. In January 1986 there was considerable bloodshed around Aden during an uprising against the excessive influence of 6,000 Soviet 'advisers' (who were subsequently withdrawn). Unification of the two Yemens was proclaimed in May 1990, but the southern Yemenis seceded in May 1994 and there was a brief civil war until northern troops entered Aden in July. Voting for a multi-party parliament and for a President are promised before October 1999.

Yezhovshchina. Word used in Russia to describe the Stalinist purge, 1936–8, and derived from N.I. Yezhov (1894–1939), head of the Soviet secret police at the time. The purge rid the Bolshevik Party of possible rivals to Stalin's leadership; many of the accused were alleged to have been in treasonable contact with 'a foreign power' (presumably Germany), but no evidence has emerged to substantiate the charge. Among the victims were ten close associates of Lenin, three Marshals of the Soviet Union (including the Chief of the General Staff, Tukachevsky), six Politburo members, and more than half the generals in the Red Army. Many prominent exiled communists living in the Soviet Union were shot, imprisoned or disappeared. Non-Russian minorities (notably the Germans living around Saratov) suffered heavily, although mass arrests normally led to forced labour rather than execution. Hundreds of thousands of Soviet citizens were sent to open up the Arctic lands or to build new industrial centres in Siberia. Yezhov was dismissed as secret-police chief in November 1938 and appointed Minister for Water Transport. He disappeared soon afterwards and the pace of persecution slackened. Many forced labourers were allowed to return home during 1939. Persecution of the German minority was resumed after the outbreak of war in 1941. Possibly as many as 7 million arrests were made by secret police during the Yezhovshchina terror, and some non-Soviet sources consider that 3 million people perished, either through execution or through the grim conditions in forced-labour camps.

Yom Kippur War (1973). A name frequently given to the ►October War because it began with surprise Arab attacks on Israeli forces on the Day of Atonement (Yom Kippur), the holiest day of prayer and fasting in the Jewish calendar which, in 1973, fell on Saturday, 6 October.

Yoshida, Shigeru (1878–1967), Japanese Prime Minister. Born in Yokohama, he graduated in law but served in Japan's diplomatic service from 1906 to 1938, ending his career as ambassador in London. Two months after Japan's surrender in 1945 he became Foreign Minister. Subsequently he headed five governments between May 1946 and December 1954. Yoshida was able to exploit American fears of 'red China', particularly during the Korean War, and he insisted on preserving Japan's political unity rather than experiment with autonomy. When he concluded a defence pact with the USA in March 1954 he had hopes of inducing the Americans to join the Japanese in a 'Marshall Plan for Asia', but ►Eisenhower and ►Dulles were wary of commitments which a Democratic administration might have accepted. Younger conservative politicians forced 'Japan's ►Adenauer' into retirement in December 1954.

Young Plan. A plan for settling German reparations proposed by a committee headed by the American businessman, Owen D. Young (1874–1962) on 7 June 1929, reducing the original figure by some 75 per cent and proposing payments should be made in the form of annuities to an international bank until 1988. Germany accepted the Plan two months later, and a payment was made in May 1930. The world financial crisis prevented payment 1931–2. When Hitler came to power in 1933 he declined to pay further reparations. The Young Plan was thus, in effect, stillborn.

Young Turks. Reform movement in the Ottoman Empire, 1903–9. A rebellion of progressively minded and basically liberal army officers in Salonika (July 1908) was followed by the establishment in Constantinople of a 'Committee of Union and Progress', headed by three officers who had been urging the modernization of Turkey for several years: ►Enver, Mehmed Talaat (1874–1921) and Ahmed Djemal (1872–1922). This Young Turk triumvirate induced Sultan ►Abdul Hamid to restore the constitution of 1876 and a Turkish parliament was convened in December 1908. Thereafter serious splits developed between liberal reformers, most of whom had been in exile, and the Young Turk triumvirate, who rapidly adopted a narrowly nationalistic policy. The influence of the triumvirate increased during the ►Balkan Wars and led to stronger links between Turkey and Germany, Enver and Talaat continuing to dominate Turkish politics until the autumn of 1918.

Ypres, Battles of. The medieval Flemish city of Ypres was the scene of four battles in the First World War: (1) 12 October to 11 November 1914, a German assault on British defensive positions, capturing the Messines ridge; (2) 22 April to 24 May 1915, a second German assault, again failing to break the British line, despite the first use in warfare of poison gas; (3) 7 June to 10 November 1917, a British, Canadian and Australian offensive, opening with the explosion of nineteen mines tunnelled under the German positions around Messines and ending in the mud of ►Passchendaele; (4) 9–29 April 1918 (also known as the battle of the river Lys), an attempt by the Germans to encircle Ypres, primarily by a south-west to north-east advance. There was further fighting on the Ypres salient in September 1918 as part of the general offensive which ended the war. Although war raged in the salient for four years, devastating city and countryside, Ypres never fell. More than half a million British and British Empire troops were killed or seriously wounded in the battles around Ypres.

Yugoslavia. Movements in favour of uniting the Balkan Slavonic peoples in a South Slav State – a 'Yugoslavia' – flourished intermittently in the nineteenth century, the idea becoming practical during the First World War with the imminent destruction of multinational Austria–Hungary. The ►Corfu Pact of July 1917 provided for the establishment of a unitary kingdom of Serbs, Croats and Slovenes under the Karadjordjević dynasty of ►Serbia. This kingdom came into being on 4 December 1918, formally adopting the name 'Yugoslavia' on 3 October 1929 by a decree issued by King ►Alexander. The governments of Prince-Regent Paul (1893–1976) in the late 1930s came increasingly under German and Italian influence until, on 27 March 1941, a *coup* in Belgrade led principally by air-force officers established a government more sympathetic to the British. Ten days later the Germans invaded Yugoslavia, destroying Belgrade by dive-bombing, overrunning the country within a fortnight, and forcing the young king, Peter II (1923–70), into exile. Resistance was maintained by rival guerrilla groups: the ►Chetniks of ►Mihailović; and the partisans of ►Tito. Allied help, originally given to the Chetniks, shifted to Tito's communist partisans because of the collaboration of some Chetnik units with the Germans and Italians. On 29 November 1943 Marshal Tito established a 'government' at liberated ➤Jajce in Bosnia. British attempts to reconcile this government with the royalist ministers exiled in London and Cairo were unsuccessful. Yugoslavia formally became a republic on 29 November 1945, a federation of the socialist republics of ➤Serbia, ➤Croatia, ➤Slovenia, ➤Montenegro, ➤Bosnia-Herzegovina and ➤Macedonia. Marshal Tito – who became President on 14 January 1953, and was elected life-President in May 1974 – sought in home affairs to establish a unique form of socialism, permitting workers' self-government in the 'self-management' of industrial enterprises, together with as much decentralization and 'liberalism' as possible within a one-party system. Experiments were made with four constitutions, 1945–74, some of them extensively amended before being finally replaced, the basic problem remaining the reluctance of the more westernized areas (Croatia and Slovenia) to shape their development to the needs of the poorer south. In foreign affairs Tito survived the condemnation of Stalin and the ➤Cominform in 1948 to establish Yugoslavia as a leader of the unaligned nations and the champion of 'positive neutrality' and 'active coexistence'. The resumption of 'fraternal relations' between Yugoslavia and the Soviet Union under Khrushchev in May 1955 did not prevent the Yugoslavs from criticizing Soviet actions in Hungary in 1956 and later in Czechoslovakia in 1968. Concern for the unity of the multinational Yugoslav state induced the League of Yugoslav Communists to accept, in Tito's lifetime, an arrangement by which the office of Head of State would be vested, on his death, in an eight-man collective Presidency; the post of President would be rotated among the eight men with no one person holding it for more than twelve months. This system ensured a smooth transfer of executive authority during Tito's long final illness and after his death, in May 1980. The collective Presidency was also given the task of choosing, every four years, a Prime Minister for Yugoslavia. In May 1982 the Presidency chose Mrs Milka Planinc (1925–), a Croat, to succeed Veselin Djuranović who had been Prime Minister since February 1977. Milka Planinc failed to reduce inflation or curb foreign debt and was succeeded in 1986 by Branko Mikulić whose anti-inflationary measures were even more disastrous, provoking over a thousand strikes in 1988. Nationalistic demonstrations in Serbia and Montenegro also posed grave problems for Mikulić. When the Yugoslav parliament threw out Mikulić's budget and proposed economic reforms on 30 December 1988 the entire government resigned. Thereafter economic reforms were initiated by individual republics, especially Croatia and Slovenia which turned against communism. These threats of secession precipitated the collapse of the Yugoslav League of Communists Congress in January 1990. Over the following fifteen months persistent unrest led to a complete breakdown in central government (March 1991). The refusal of Serb political leaders to accept the election of the Croat, Stipe Mesić, as Chairman of the federal Presidency on 15 May 1991 was followed on 25 June by Croat and Slovene proclamations of independence. After a week of fighting between Yugoslav troops and Slovene militia, mediators from the European Community secured a truce, the recognition of Mesić, and a return of troops to barracks. Renewed fighting between Serbs and Croats in August and September made prospects of avoiding a protracted civil war look slim. The rival nationalism of the Serb leader, ➤Milošević, and the elected Croat President, ➤Tudjman, ruled out any lasting accord. Croatia, Macedonia and Bosnia-Herzegovina all broke away from the federation, plunging Yugoslavia into an internecine war from the Danube at Vukovar, through western Slavonia and Bosnia, and southwards to Mostar and Dubrovnik. Peace came only with the compromise ➤Dayton Accord of November 1995. A new federation of Serbia and Montenegro, retaining the name 'Yugoslavia', was formed in April 1992.

Z

Zaire. Republic in equatorial Africa. When the ►Belgian Congo was given independence in 1960, a 'Democratic Republic of the Congo' was proclaimed in the capital, Léopoldville (now Kinshasa). The ►Congo problem confounded solution until 1965 when a stable but ruthless regime was established under the Presidency of General ►Mobutu. The 'People's Revolutionary Movement' (as the governing party called itself from 1965 onwards) favoured national unity as opposed to tribalism and 'Africanization' rather than socialism. A serious military insurrection in the east and north of the country was suppressed between July and November 1967. As tokens of Africanization, the fourteenth/fifteenth-century name of the Congo river – Zaire – was revived for both river and republic in October 1971, while three months later a Nationality Law decreed the abolition of all European names, for persons and places. In May 1978 killings and near-anarchy in Shaba Province (►Katanga) emphasized the continued weakness of the central government in the more distant regions. Political discontent with Mobutu's one-party rule provoked repeated crises in government in Kinshasa, Zaire's capital, from 1990 to 1994, when the President set up a transition council to prepare for elections in 1997. Before then, however, rebellion broke out among the Tutsi people of eastern Zaire, who were influenced by events in neighbouring ►Burundi and ►Rwanda. The rebellion was coordinated from late October 1996 by Laurent Kabila (1941–) who, from 1960, had sustained guerrilla activity by his People's Revolutionary Party, whose ideology owed much to ►Guevara, with whom Kabila had fought in Latin America. From capturing Goma on 2 November 1996 Kabila's 'Alliance of Democratic Forces for the Liberation of Zaire-Congo' advanced on Kisangani, which fell early in the new year. There were mass desertions from Mobutu's army until some crack troops offered resistance at the approaches to Kinshasa itself. Attempts at mediation, notably by President ►Mandela, failed to bring about a peaceful transfer of power. Mobutu escaped to Morocco to seek medical treatment in May 1997, when Laurent Kabila became self-appointed President of a 'free, democratic republic', discarding the name Zaire in favour of 'Congo' once more.

Zambia (formerly Northern Rhodesia). A central African republic within the Commonwealth, first came under white rule in 1889 and was administered by the British South Africa Company until 1924, when it became a protectorate for which the Colonial Office in London assumed responsibility. For ten years (1953–63) the territory was federated with Southern Rhodesia and Nyasaland but the dominance of the white Southern Rhodesians stimulated the growth of a specifically

Zambian nationalist movement, led by Dr ►Kaunda, which contributed to the disintegration of the Central African Federation. In January 1964 Northern Rhodesia at last achieved internal self-government, becoming only ten months later the independent republic of Zambia (24 October 1964). Zambia has suffered from the economic problems caused by her former dependence on ►Rhodesia, a problem aggravated by the extraordinary status of Rhodesia after November 1965. The unity of Zambia has been threatened by inter-tribal conflicts, for there are more than seventy tribes within the republic, some of them traditional enemies. The 1964 constitution gave Zambia multi-party parliamentary government but the threat of internal disorder led President Kaunda to abandon this system in December 1972, introducing a revised constitution eight months later which made Zambia a one-party state, with political life determined by Dr Kaunda's 'United National Independence Party' (UNIP). Multi-party democracy was restored in October 1991, with elections in which Kaunda and UNIP were defeated. The new President, Frederick Chiluba, encouraged a free-market economy in place of the strict planning of the Kaunda era, but the abolition of protective subsidies and the impact of the soaring inflation brought hardship to many workers in the 'copper belt' enterprises and in the farms, raising doubts over the continued stability of the republic.

Zeebrugge. A Belgian seaport artificially created in the first years of the century by the construction of a 1½ mile mole that protected the entrance to a ship-canal to Bruges, 8 miles inland. When the Germans occupied Bruges in 1914, they developed its dock resources to accommodate U-boats which entered the North Sea from the canals at Zeebrugge and Ostend. A major combined operation was mounted against both places, aimed at blocking the exits from the canals. Admiral Sir Roger Keyes (1872–1945), aboard HMS *Vindictive*, landed a naval and marine force on Zeebrugge Mole on 23 April 1918, while three block-ships were sunk in the canal entrance. A simultaneous raid on Ostend failed, as two block-ships collided after running aground on a sandbank in the harbour approaches. A second raid on Ostend on 9 May, when *Vindictive* herself was used as a block-ship, was only partially successful. The raids bottled up the larger U-boats and some destroyers caught in the canals, but small submarines were able to pass the block-ships at high tide. The courageous raid – prototype for commando operations in the Second World War – boosted morale at a time when the allied cause was under severe strain. The Victoria Cross was awarded to eight participants in the Zeebrugge raid and to three participants in the Ostend raid. In the 1960s Zeebrugge was redeveloped as a roll-on/roll-off ferry port, with regular services to Dover and Felixstowe. On 7 March 1987 *Herald of Free Enterprise*, a Townsend Thoresen ferry bound for Dover, capsized as it left Zeebrugge with more than 500 passengers and crew aboard. Although it settled on the sea bed in shallow water 188 people perished. A subsequent inquiry revealed that the bow doors were still open when the vessel put to sea.

Zeppelins. Rigid airships invented by Count Ferdinand von Zeppelin (1838–

1917) in 1900. A twelve-hour flight over Switzerland and Bavaria fired German national enthusiasm for the invention in 1908, and in the following year these airships were used for the first passenger-carrying air service, flying 100,000 miles without loss of life, 1909–14. Zeppelins were used by both the German army and navy in the First World War. They bombed Antwerp, Liège and Warsaw in the early months of the war and Paris in March 1915, but they were particularly employed to bring the war to England, making fifty-three raids (twelve on London) and killing 556 civilians. The first raid was on Norfolk (19 January 1915), London being bombed for the first time on 31 May 1915. Improved defences exposed the vulnerability of Zeppelins, four out of eleven airships being lost during a raid on 19/20 October 1917. With the return of peace, Zeppelins were built for commercial service again, maintaining a transatlantic passenger route from 1928 until 6 May 1937 when the most modern of German airships, *Hindenburg*, inexplicably burst into flames while approaching the mooring mast at Lakehurst, New Jersey. Zeppelins cruised off the British coast on the eve of war in 1939, reconnoitring radar defences, but were broken up for scrap metal a few months later.

Zhukov, Georg Konstantinovich (1896–1974), Marshal of the Soviet Union. Born at Strelkovka, near Kaluga, the son of a peasant, and apprenticed to a furrier in Moscow but conscripted into the ranks in 1914. He joined the Red Army in 1918 and fought as a junior officer, subsequently receiving tank training from German specialists at Kazan, 1921–2. Zhukov achieved wide recognition by defeating Japanese infiltrators into Mongolia, May to September 1939, and became the outstanding Red Army leader of the Second World War, helping defend Leningrad (September 1941), holding Moscow against two German offensives and mounting the first Russian counter-offensive (6 December 1941). He planned the decisive counter-attacks which relieved ➤Stalingrad late in 1942. Zhukov was responsible for the tank victory at ➤Kursk, the breakthrough in Byelorussia in 1944 and the final offensive on the Oder (16 April 1945) which led to the fall of Berlin on 2 May. He was commander-in-chief of the Soviet zone of occupation, and Minister of Defence, 1955–7, under Khrushchev. On 26 October 1957 Zhukov was suddenly relieved of his duties and accused of having prevented party development within the armed forces as well as of encouraging a cult of his own personality. He was permitted to live the rest of his life in retirement.

Zia ul-Haq, Mohammed (1924–88), Pakistan soldier and President. Born at Jalandhar, he fought in Burma and Malaya against the Japanese, received staff training in the USA after Pakistan achieved independence and became a full General in 1976. After overthrowing Zulfiqar Ali ➤Bhutto in July 1977 he served as martial law administrator for fifteen months. In September 1978 he became President, remaining in office until August 1988 when he was killed in an unexplained air crash in southern Punjab. Zia was a virtual dictator, retaining martial law until December 1985 and seeking to impose a strict Islamic code of conduct on the country.

Zimbabwe. The African name for the region covered by ▶Rhodesia, associating modern movements of liberation with the African medieval civilization emanating from the ruined city of Zimbabwe between the ninth and fourteenth centuries. The Zimbabwe African People's Union (ZAPU) was founded as a Rhodesian nationalist party by Joshua ▶Nkomo in 1961, banned by the Southern Rhodesian authorities in September 1962, continuing to function in exile from Tanzania. An 'illegal' compromise constitution, which the Rhodesian authorities hoped would acquire international recognition, established a white-dominated 'Zimbabwe Rhodesia' on 1 June 1979, a political improvisation which lasted only until the return of British colonial rule on 12 December 1979. The independent Republic of Zimbabwe was proclaimed on 17–18 April 1980, with Robert ▶Mugabe as the new nation's first President. Constitutional changes introduced in December 1987 strengthened the presidency as a step towards making Zimbabwe a one-party state in 1990. Early experiments in socialist planning were abandoned in 1991, partly under pressure from the World Bank, whose advice Mugabe treated with a shrewd respect which some other African leaders mistakenly lacked.

Zimmermann Telegram (19 January 1917). A coded message from the German Foreign Minister, Arthur Zimmermann (1864–1940), to the German envoy in Mexico was intercepted by British naval intelligence. The telegram suggested a possible German–Mexican alliance so that, if the USA entered the war against Germany, Mexico would march northwards and, at the peace settlement, would recover 'lost territory in New Mexico, Texas and Arizona'. There were further indications in Zimmermann's message that Germany was seeking to induce Japan to change sides in the war and to attack American bases in the Pacific. The Americans were informed and news of the telegram released to the Press in Washington on 2 March. Anti-German feeling was already considerable because of the resumption of unrestricted submarine warfare four weeks previously, and the telegram provoked widespread protests. Additional resentment sprang from the revelation that the Germans had used a privileged wire, put at their disposal by the State Department for transmitting peace proposals. Indignation over Zimmermann's telegram played a considerable part in reconciling Congress to a declaration of war on Germany (6 April 1917). Neither Mexico nor Japan collaborated with Germany.

Zinoviev Letter. On 25 October 1924 extracts were printed in British newspapers from a letter allegedly sent to British communists by Grigory Zinoviev (1883–1936), chairman of the ▶Comintern, urging them to promote revolution through acts of sedition. The letter appeared in the Press four days before the British general election, and seems to have rallied middle-class opinion into voting Conservative. It was therefore believed, among Labour leaders, that the letter was a forgery planted in the Press to ensure the return of a Conservative Government. Copies of the letter had reached both the Foreign Office (who treated it as genuine) and the *Daily Mail*. There is no reason why the letter should not have been authentic

– fomenting revolution was an object of Comintern policy – but many forged documents were, at the time, being circulated by *émigré* organizations. Zinoviev lost his party posts in 1926 when Stalin alleged he was a supporter of ►Trotsky; he was charged with plotting with an enemy power, in August 1936, sentenced to death and shot in the Lubyanka Prison within hours of the verdict.

Zionism. Originally a movement for the return of the Jews to Palestine, a reaction against the anti-Semitism of the late nineteenth century. It was launched by the Hungarian-born journalist Theodor Herzl (1860–1904) who convened a Zionist congress at Basle in 1897 'to secure for the Jewish people a home in Palestine guaranteed by public law'. During the First World War the chemist Chaim ►Weizmann won British support for some aspects of Zionism, prompting the ►Balfour Declaration of 1917. Zionist congresses were held, between the wars, at Carlsbad 1923, Vienna 1925, Basle 1927, Zürich 1929, Basle 1931, Prague 1933, Vienna 1935, Zürich 1937, Geneva 1939. Some assimilated Jews at first opposed Zionism, believing it might prove divisive for the communities in which they had settled, but funds and political support mounted, especially with the Nazi persecutions of the 1930s. After the establishment of Israel in May 1948 Zionism changed character, becoming a sign of support for Israel by Jews and Jewish enterprises outside the Middle East and, since 1968, an agitation in favour of the emigration of Soviet Jews to Israel. Opponents of Israel at United Nations headquarters claimed that Zionism sought to perpetuate Israeli rule over Arabs, especially on the west bank of the Jordan. On 10 November 1975 a resolution condemning Zionism as 'a form of racism and racial domination' was carried at the UN General Assembly by 72 votes to 35, with 32 abstentions.